THE JOURNEY OF A KNIGHTLY FAMILY

The Journey of a Knightly Family

The Hercy/Hersey Family, 1000–1650

ELISABETH MEIER TETLOW

WIPF & STOCK · Eugene, Oregon

THE JOURNEY OF A KNIGHTLY FAMILY
The Hercy/Hersey Family 1000–1650

Copyright © 2024 Elisabeth Meier Tetlow. All rights reserved. Except for brief quotations in critical publications or reviews, no part of this book may be reproduced in any manner without prior written permission from the publisher. Write: Permissions, Wipf and Stock Publishers, 199 W. 8th Ave., Suite 3, Eugene, OR 97401.

Wipf & Stock
An Imprint of Wipf and Stock Publishers
199 W. 8th Ave., Suite 3
Eugene, OR 97401

www.wipfandstock.com

PAPERBACK ISBN: 979-8-3852-2693-1
HARDCOVER ISBN: 979-8-3852-2694-8
EBOOK ISBN: 979-8-3852-2695-5

VERSION NUMBER 11/11/24

For my mother Margaret Hersey Meier
My daughters Tania, Maria, Sonia, and Sarah
And my cousins David, Marilyn, Linda, and Jill

Contents

Illustrations | ix

Acknowledgments | xi

Abbreviations | xii

The Journey of a Knightly Family | 1

Part I   Setting the Stage: Northern France | 5

Part II   England | 54

           Worcestershire | 69

           Warwickshire | 76

           Nottinghamshire | 93

           Berkshire | 241

           The Talbot Earls of Shrewsbury and the Hercys | 264

Conclusion | 280

Appendix I: Neighbors of de Hercé in Maine: de Gorron, d'Ambrières, de Laval | 283

Appendix II: Lords and Neighbors of the de Hercy Family in Warwickshire | 290

Appendix III: Lords and Neighbors of the de Arches Family in Yorkshire | 299

Appendix IV: Other Possible Places of Origin of the de Hériz Family | 314

Appendix V: Neighbors and Lords of the de Hériz Family in Normandy | 321

Appendix VI: Buckinghamshire: Wingrave and Rowsham | 333

Appendix VII: John Hercy the Surveyor | 344

Appendix VIII: Some Notes on the de Hercé Family in France after 1066 | 346

Maps | 352

Genealogies | 358

Illustrations | 361

Bibliography | 371

Index of Persons | 387

Index of Places | 391

Illustrations

1. La Cour-Hercé | 361
2. Mayenne | 362
3. St. Mary the Virgin Church in Pillerton Hersey, Warwickshire | 362
4. Tickhill Castle Gate, Tickhill, Yorkshire | 363
5. St. Helen's Church, Grove, Nottinghamshire | 363
6. Incised Grave Stones of Hugh IV and Elizabeth Leek Hercy, St. Helen's Church, Grove | 364
7. Grove Hall, ca. 1900. | 364
8. Hériz Tomb Effigies, Church of St. Laurence, Gonalston, Nottinghamshire | 365
9. Hériz Arms in Window, Church of St. Laurence, Gonalston | 365
10. Tomb Effigy of William Saundby, St. Martin's Church, Saundby, Nottinghamshire | 366
11. Tomb Effigies of Sir Samson and Elizabeth Hercy Strelley, All Saints Church, Strelley, Nottinghamshire | 366
12. Elizabeth de Hercy de Strelley, All Saints Church, Strelley | 367
13. Will of Sir Thomas de Hercy | 367
14. Crown and Rose | 368
15. West Retford Hall, Trinity Hospital, Retford, Nottinghamshire | 368
16. King Edward VI School, Retford | 369
17. St. Mary's Church, Winkfield, Berkshire | 369
18. Cruchfield Manor, Berkshire | 370

Acknowledgments

I WOULD LIKE TO offer my deepest gratitude to Professor Michael Prestwich for reading the manuscript at various stages and offering innumerable valuable suggestions and to Professors David Carpenter, Simon Payling, and Constance Bouchard for answering my many questions. And I am especially grateful to Thérèse and Lucien Jahyny for taking me to Hercé the first time and to my friend Rachael Kerr for driving me around the many small villages and churches in Nottinghamshire and Berkshire. I also wish to thank the International Medieval Congress in Leeds for making it possible for me to visit Tickhill and Conisbrough.

I am very grateful to the following libraries for their generous help in my research: the Bibliothèque Nationale de France, the Archives Départementales de Mayenne in Laval, The National Archives at Kew, the Bodleian Library of Oxford University, the Special Collections of the University of Nottingham, the Borthwick Institute of the University of York, the Berkshire Record Office, the Special Collections of the University of Reading, Tilton Library of Tulane University, Loyola University Interlibrary Loans, and Butler Library of Columbia University. I am also grateful to the churches and church wardens in Warwickshire, Nottinghamshire, and Berkshire who allowed me to explore and photograph the riches of their artifacts. I want to thank Emma Harlan for designing the maps and genealogy charts and Roland Wiltz for saving me from drowning in the deep waters of computer technology. And my deep thanks to Loyola University of New Orleans for supporting me in my research by giving me the position of scholar in residence.

Abbreviations

Actes Henri II: *Recueil des actes de Henri II: roi d'Angleterre et duc de Normandie.*

Alumni Oxoniensis: *The Members of the University of Oxford 1500–1714.*

AN: *Annales de Normandie.*

BeauchampChart: *The Beauchamp Cartulary Charters 1100–1268.*

BL: British Library, London.

BNF: Bibliothèque Nationale de France, Paris.

BRO: Berkshire Record Office.

BSAN: *Bulletin de la Société des Antiquaires de Normandie.*

BT: Bayeux Tapestry. *La Tapisserie de Bayeux.*

Cart: Cartulary, *Cartulaire*, or *Cartularium*.

CartAbbayette: *Cartulaire de Saint-Michel de l'Abbayette.*

CartBlyth: *The Cartulary of Blyth Priory.*

CartStFrideswide: *Cartulary of St. Frideswide Oxford.*

CartFontaine-Daniel: *Cartulaire de l'abbaye cistercienne de Fontaine-Daniel.*

CartHotel-Dieu: *Cartulaire de l'Hotel-Dieu de La Haye-Pesnel.*

CartLuzerne: *Cartulaire de l'Abbaye de la Luzerne.*

CartOseney: *Cartulary of Oseney Abbey.*

CartRameseia: *Cartularium monasterii de Rameseia.*

CartRievelle: *Cartularium abbathiae de Rievelle.*

CartRonceray: *Cartulaire de l'Abbaye du Ronceray d'Angers.*

CartSt-Leonard's: *Cartulary of St. Leonard's York.*

ABBREVIATIONS

CartTréport: *Cartulaire de l'Abbaye de Saint-Michel du Tréport.*

CartSte-Trinité: *Cartulaire de l'Abbaye de Sainte-Trinité du Mont de Rouen.*

CartStVincent: *Cartulaire de l'Abbaye de Saint-Vincent au Mans.*

CartWhitby: *Cartularium Abbathiae de Whiteby.*

CartWorcester: *Cartulary of Worcester Cathedral Priory.*

CChR: *Calender of the Charter Rolls Preserved in the Public Record Office.*

CCR: *Calendar of the Close Rolls Preserved in the Public Record Office.*

CDF: *Calendar of Documents Preserved in France 918-1206.*

CDS: *Calendar of Documents Relating to Scotland.*

CEC: *The Charters of the Anglo-Norman Earls of Chester, ca. 1071–1237.*

CFR: *Calendar of the Fine Rolls Preserved in the Public Record Office.*

ChronAbingdon: *Historia Ecclesie Abbendonensis. The History of the Church of Abingdon.*

CLR: *Calendar of the Liberate Rolls Preserved in the Public Record Office.*

CPE: Complete Peerage of England.

CPR: *Calendar of the Patent Rolls Preserved in the Public Record Office.*

CRR: *Curia Regis Rolls of the Reigns of Richard I and John.*

CSPD: *Calendar of State Papers, Domestic Series of the Reigns of Edward VI, Mary, Elizabeth 1547–1580.*

CSTP: *A Calendar of the Shrewsbury and Talbot Papers.*

DB: *Domesday Book.*

DGH: *Dictionnaire généalogique, héraldique, historique et chronologique.*

ERW: *Episcopal Registers, Diocese of Worcester.*

EYC: *Early Yorkshire Charters.*

FA: *Inquisitions and Assessments relating to Feudal Aids.*

Glanvill: *The Treatise on the Laws and Customs of the Realm of England.*

HistParl: *The History of Parliament. The House of Commons.*

HKF: *Honours and Knights' Fees.*

HMSO: *His/Her Majesty's Stationary Office.*

HV: Heraldic Visitation.

IPM: *Inquisitionum Post Mortem.*

ABBREVIATIONS

LCNN: *Lists of the Clergy of North Nottinghamshire.*

LPFD: *Letters and Papers, Foreign and Domestic of the Reign of Henry VIII.*

LPL: Lambeth Palace Library.

MA: *Monasticon Anglicanum.*

MC: Magna Carta

MGH: *Monumenta Germaniae Historia*

MRSN: *Magni Rotuli Scaccarii Normanniae sub Regibus Angliae.*

MSAN: *Mémoires de la Société des Antiquaires de Normandie.*

MSHAB: *Mémoires de la Société d'Histoire et de l'Archéologie de Bretagne.*

NMS: *Nottinghamshire Medieval Studies.*

ODNB: *Oxford Dictionary of National Biography.*

OV: Orderic Vitalis. *Ecclesiastical History.*

ParlRolls: *Parliamentary Rolls of Medieval England 1275–1504.*

ParlWrits: *Parliamentary Writs and Writs of Military Summons.*

PR: Pipe Roll.

PRO: Public Record Office.

RADN: *Recueil des actes des ducs de Normandie de 911 a 1066.*

RBA: *The Battle Abbey Roll.*

RBE: *Liber Rubeus de Scaccario. Red Book of the Exchequer.*

RBW: *The Red Book of Worcester.*

RCR: *Rotuli Curiae Regis.*

RDP: *Rotuli de Dominabus et Pueris et Puellis de Donatione Regis.*

Recueil l'Échiquier de Normandie: Recueil de jugements de l'Échiqieur de Normandie.

RHGF: *Recueil des Historiens des Gaules et de la France.*

RL: *Rotuli de Liberate ac de Misis et Praestitis.*

ROF: *Rotuli de oblatis et finibus in turri Londonensi asservati.*

RRAN: *Regesta Regum Anglo-Normannorum.*

RotChart: *Rotuli Chartarum in Turri Londonensi asservati.*

RotClaus: *Rotuli Litterarum Clausarum in Turri Londonensi asservati.*

RotHund: *Rotuli Hundredorum temp. Hen. III and Edw. I.*

ABBREVIATIONS

RotParl: Rolls of Parliament.

RotPat: *Rotuli Litterarum Patentium in Turri Londonensi asservati.*

RotScot: *Rotuli scaccarii regum scotorum.*

RP: *Rotuli Parliamentorum.*

Testa de Nevill: *Liber Feodorum. The Book of Fees.*

TNA: The National Archives, Kew Gardens.

Torigni: *The Chronography of Robert of Torigni.*

VCH: *Victoria History of the Counties of England.*

Wace: *The History of the Norman People. Wace's Roman de Rou.*

WJ: William of Jumièges. *Gesta Normannorum Ducum.*

WM: William of Malmesbury. *Gesta Regum Anglorum.*

WP: William of Poitiers. *Gesta Guillelmi.*

YAJ: *The Yorkshire Archaeological and Topographical Journal.*

YAS: The Yorkshire Archeological Society.

The Journey of a Knightly Family

THE JOURNEY OF A FAMILY through centuries of medieval and reformation history is perilous to capture. Sources are limited and fragmentary and embedded in the legal, political, and religious history of their time. There are no autobiographies or contemporary biographies to shed light on the inner lives of the persons who made up the family. Yet it is possible through analysis of the extant sources and prosopography to create a narrative history of the family with its interconnectedness to other families of the same times and places. Each member of the family is a product of his or her ancestral heritage as well as present individual and community life. There is continuity but also development and change. The history of this family illustrates the development in the understanding and practice of knighthood, the lives of women, and the changing experiences of religion through these six centuries. All of the available published and unpublished archival sources about this family are presented in order to understand how knighthood, women, and religion developed through these centuries by studying the journey of this one knightly family as it was embedded in the history of its times.

THE MEDIEVAL JOURNEY OF A KNIGHTLY FAMILY

In medieval England after 1066, there were many Anglo-French families. But very few of these continued to exist after a few centuries had passed. This is the story of the journey of one medieval knightly family from France to England, from Warwickshire to Nottinghamshire to Berkshire, and from the Catholic Church to the Church of England to Puritanism, over a period of six hundred years. It is preceded by a glimpse into its prehistory, before the advent of written sources, and the poorly documented lives of its members in France before venturing to England in 1066. The name of the family in France was spelled de Hercé, in England de Hercy, and in the sixteenth and seventeenth centuries came to be spelled Hersey, which was used by later generations.[1]

In the Middle Ages, families existed within complex relationships with other families, through intermarriage, as lords and vassals, through geographical proximity, and support of monasteries. The story of the journey of one knightly family from Maine and Normandy to England cannot be told by tracing only the male name-holders of that family. The maternal ancestors of a family are equally important but more difficult to document. When sources are limited for the journey of one family during this period, the stories of the proximate interrelated families shed greater light by providing context of the origins and history of the family in focus. Single families evolved in clusters of interrelated families.

This book will attempt to tell the story of the origins of the de Hercé/Hercy/Hersey family by first focusing on three knightly families, one from each of three principal geographical clusters of knights who followed William the Conqueror to England: the de Hercé family from northwestern Maine, the d'Arques family from Eastern/Upper Normandy, and the de Hériz family from Western/Lower Normandy. The d'Arques and the de Hériz families represent the two earliest known maternal lines of the de Hercy family. The members of each of these three families went to England in 1066 within the context of their relationships: their kinship networks, vassalage networks, and geographical networks. Each family became established with lands and descendants in England. And by 1250, all three of these families had intermarried, creating the great Anglo-French de Hercy family of Nottinghamshire. The book focuses on gathering and presenting all the available primary sources for this history and analyzing them for insights into the evolution of knighthood, the roles of women, and the changes in religion.

The history of each family began within the context of its place of origin. This place had a prehistory going back to the beginning of time, but was poorly documented before the eleventh century. When information is limited about the first origins of a specific individual or family, much can be learned from the geography and history of their place of origin and by study of other persons and families from the same place and time with whose branches the lives of the focal family were intertwined.

  1. Hercé was the place of origin of the family in Maine; Hercy was the most common spelling of the name in England until the sixteenth century, when, especially in the cadet branch in Berkshire, the name was also spelled Hersey; it was also spelled Hearsay, Hearsey, Hersi; there was a significant shift in spelling of French names in England after 1066: de Hercé became de Hercy, d'Arques became de Arches; spelling of names was not standardized until the early twentieth century.

THE JOURNEY OF A KNIGHTLY FAMILY

There are few straight lines in this history. There are zigzags, gaps, crossovers, and probabilities. The clusters of families which left Maine and Normandy did not necessarily remain intact in England. All the lords of each cluster went to England, but not always to the same places in England as their vassals. Some families in England maintained ties with their families in Maine or Normandy; others did not. The three families considered here did not. By 1204, when King John of England lost Normandy, most such ties were severed.

The earliest sources for reconstructing history are archaeological and geographical. There were few written sources in the late tenth and early eleventh centuries. Illiteracy was still pervasive, and, for the most part, only clerics could write. Monasteries recognized early the need to document donations of land, which were written down in monastic charters. These documents show which families supported which monasteries and reveal a significant network of relationships among such families. Kings and magnates began to make written proclamations, each of which was witnessed. Lists of witnesses demonstrate that the persons named were in the same room on a specific date in some sort of relationship to each other. Such lists often named witnesses in order of rank: royals, titled aristocrats, and knights. Women were seldom mentioned but if they were, it was generally after their husbands or at the end of the list, even when they outranked the men named above them. As the late eleventh and twelfth centuries progressed, there was a multifold increase in the numbers of written documents.[2]

The written sources not only mention individuals but reveal the networks of family, intermarriage, vassalage, co-witnessing, support of monasteries, and geographical proximity in which the individuals lived. Especially in the earlier centuries such a perspective creates a rich portrait of the lives of the people then living. The context in which the three families described here were embedded was different for each family. Little is known about the de Hercé family in Maine before 1066, so understanding it is dependent upon the history of the county and of neighboring families. The history of the d'Auffay and d'Arques families is richly documented in Eastern Normandy. The history of the de Hériz family before 1066 is known in general from the history of Western Normandy and is reconstructed from later sources. Thus, the history of Maine and of Normandy is significant for understanding the origins of these three families.

   2. There were a few written sources in northern Francia by kings and bishops in the Carolingian period; Duby, *Rural Economy*, 61; Pichot, *Bas-Maine*, 14–17; most of these earlier writings, especially those kept in monasteries, were destroyed in the Viking invasions.

The extended family in focus in this work is called "knightly." The meaning of knighthood and its evolution will be discussed in greater detail later. Knights were below royals, magnates, and titled aristocrats, although many of these also claimed the distinction of knighthood. Knights were above the peasants. Knights were free persons, well born, who at times shared a sense of nobility with the higher ranks of society. Knights formed the bulk of William's army in the conquest of England in 1066. In this work, "noble," an adjective, will be used as a term of quality of both knights and those above them; "aristocrat," a noun, will be used only of magnates and titled peers. Later in England, knights came to form the highest rank of the gentry, holding offices administering counties and serving in the House of Commons. Thus, in modern terms they came to form the heart of the emerging middle class. There are many sources for the histories of monarchs and magnates, as well as some for the peasants. But there are far fewer for the history of the class in between: first called the knights and later the gentry. The place and role of women in the family will be investigated although the sources are generally few and often even their names are unknown. Finally, the role and evolution of religion will be illustrated through the history of this family. Each generation of the Hercy family will be explored for hints it may provide about the evolution of knighthood, the roles of women, and the changes in religion.[3]

---

3. Most family studies focus on a much shorter period, one or two centuries, and do not deal with Anglo-French families; some examples are Blakely, *Brus Family*; Saul, *Death, Art and Memory*; Young, *Making of the Neville Family*.

PART I

Setting the Stage

Northern France

BEFORE THE ELEVENTH CENTURY

Before the advent of written source documents, generations of the ancestors of the de Hercy family lived in northern France, where they experienced Celtic, Gallic, Roman, Frankish, and Scandinavian invasions. Such affected their identity, language, customs, and religion. In ancient times, the territory of northern France was part of Gaul. In the first century BCE, the Roman emperor Julius Caesar conquered Gaul and called this part *Gallia Celtica*, because he considered its inhabitants to be Celtic tribes. The Romans integrated Gaul into their empire, introduced the Latin language and Roman roads and administrative districts, and ruled the area for five hundred years. But in 486 CE, the Salian Franks under Clovis I won a definitive victory over the Romans at Soissons and established the kingdom of Francia under the Merovingian dynasty. Later, in 751, Pepin the Short became the first king of the Carolingian dynasty, which was named for his father Charles Martel. In 800, Pepin's son, Charlemagne, was crowned Holy Roman Emperor. His mighty empire, which extended from Germany to France, Italy, and Spain, was divided among his grandsons, and later further divided into rival principalities.[1] Northwest France became the kingdom of

---

1. In 496, Clovis became Christian; after his death in 511, his kingdom was divided among his four sons; West Francia was also called Neustria; the Merovingian dynasty ruled it for almost three centuries from 486 to 751; the Carolingian dynasty from 751 to 987.

the West Franks and was called Francia. In the ninth and tenth centuries, it was invaded by Scandinavian Vikings from the north and Celtic Bretons from the west.

Society in Francia was predominantly rural, with agricultural villages, surrounded by forests, but few towns. Carolingian kings gave parcels of land to their followers, which became manors. Lands accrued to manors by gift and by inheritance. A manorial system developed in which the peasants worked the land for their lords. Most manors had a large house, a mill, and a church. Peasants paid for use of the mill and tithes to the church. Peasants worked the demesne and other lands of the lords for wages or for part of their rent. The lord gave them protection, but the peasants in turn owed the lord service, including military service. Manorial lords were also the agents of higher lords and kings, for whom they collected taxes and provided soldiers. This system evolved into feudalism. Society in northern Francia was disrupted in the ninth and tenth centuries by Viking assaults in which churches and monasteries were destroyed. Society stabilized in the eleventh century and prospered. Heretofore unused lands were cultivated and new villages created. Monasteries and churches were rebuilt.[2]

MEDIEVAL NORMANDY

High cliffs along its northern coast, granite in the west, limestone in the east, formed a natural border along the English Channel. Normandy did not have other natural boundaries, but utilized those of the old Roman province. Traversed by great rivers and forests, hills and flat plains, it was a land of potential prosperity.

Vikings raided the northern coast of Francia and sailed up the Seine to attack Paris in the ninth century. In 911 the Scandinavian forces under Rolf/Rollo the Viking[3] were defeated at Chartres. Their leader, the Danish noble, Rolf, made a treaty at Saint-Clair-sur-Epte with the Carolingian king Charles III the Simple of Francia, whereby Rolf did homage to King Charles, converted to Christianity, was baptized by the archbishop of the Franks, took the baptismal name Robert, and thus became Count Robert

---

2. Duby, *Rural Economy*, 5–10, 28–31, 33–34, 39–40, 57, 72–76: some peasants became wealthier than others and expanded their holdings, the holdings of aristocrats were decreased when divided through inheritance; 212–13: from Carolingian times, manors collected rents from peasant tenants.

3. Hrolf—Scandinavian; Rollo—Latin (Roluo), French (Rou); Wace, *Roman*, 1; WJ, 1:ii, 2, and OV, 2:6–9, state that he was Danish; *Torigni*, 2:4–5, 152–53: Danish; WM, vol. 1, no. 127, said he was Norwegian; the Scandinavian sagas called him son of Rognvald, Norwegian jarl of More.

I of Normandy. In return the king gave him the county of Rouen, the land along the Seine valley between the Epte and the sea, which was thenceforth called Normandy, after the invaders from the north.[4] The descendants of Count Robert I would become the counts and dukes initially of eastern Normandy and later of all of Normandy.

Viking migrations continued during the middle years of the tenth century. The Scandinavian influence was strongest on the northern coast, in the Cotentin peninsula in western Normandy and in the Pays de Caux through the Seine valley to Rouen in the east. It may be seen in place names, specifically those beginning with a Scandinavian name but ending in *-ville* and in those ending in *-tot*, which tend to be from the earliest settlements. Some Danish warriors and peasant immigrants settled down in their new territory, warriors on estates and peasants on forest lands previously unoccupied. They married women of Normandy and Brittany. Count Robert I married Papia, daughter of Count Berengar of Bayeux, with whom he had children. The language spoken in families was generally the language of the mother. Each generation became ever more Frankish and Christian, adopting the French language, law, customs, religion, political organization, and mode of warfare. From this mélange of peoples, a new Norman aristocracy emerged.[5]

In the tenth and first half of the eleventh centuries, the land was divided into Eastern or Upper Normandy (*Haute Normandie*) and Western or Lower Normandy (*Basse Normandie*). After King Charles III was deposed in 922, King Radulf of Francia ceded to Count Robert I the diocese of Bayeux in Western Normandy. By 925 Count Robert I of Normandy ruled lands from the rivers Vire in the west to the Eu in the east. In 933, his son, Count Guillaume I Longuespée, was granted the Avranchin and Cotentin up to the border of Brittany.[6] The Norman capital was in the east at Rouen,

---

4. *Simplex* meant "straightforward," not simpleminded; Charles ruled from 898 to 922; *homage de la paix* (a meeting of equals in a neutral place), not *homage vassalique*; OV, 2:8–9; *Torigni*, 2:152–57; *Recueil Charles III*, vol. 1, no. 92; WM, vol. 1, nos. 112, 127, 145, 236; WJ, 1:ii, 11–12, 17–18; Douglas, *William*, 28–29 states that the relationship implied vassalage and continued to do so with later kings of Francia and the Capetian kings of France; Hollister, *Monarchy*, 18; Bates, *Normandy*, 2, 8: the *pagi* of Caux, Talou, and Rouen, and parts of the Vexin and Évrecin.

5. *AN* (1951) 1:373–435; Douglas, *William*, 20, 22; Bates, *Normandy*, 12, 16–18, 21, 36, 266–67; examples Tocqueville=Toki's vil, Yvetot=Yve's toft; R. Allen Brown, *Normans*, 17, 19; Norman coins were found in Scandinavia, Scotland, and southern England through the end of the tenth century, indicating contact and commerce.

6. Flodoard de Reims, *Annals*, 6F, 9C, 21A, 22A, 22C, 23F, 24C; Flodoard included Maine, but there is no other record of the Norman counts taking Maine at this time; *Torigni* 2:4–7, 160–61; Bates, *Normandy*, 9, 265; see maps (upper and lower Normandy) on p. 353 [X-REF]; a tenth-century coin was found at Le Mont-Saint-Michel inscribed

which was also the ecclesiastical capital, ruling over the old dioceses of Avranches, Coutances, Bayeux, Lisieux, Évreux, and Sées. This organization of Normandy dated to the fourth- and fifth-century Romans. The main arteries of commerce through Normandy were Roman roads. The Roman communication system made possible trade between Francia and Britannia, and enabled ecclesiastical reform from Cluny to reach Normandy.

Count Robert I abdicated in 927 and later was buried in Rouen. He was succeeded by his son, Count Guillaume I Longuespée, who secured his borders by marriage alliances. Guillaume "married" by *more danica* Sprota, a Danish-Breton woman, who was mother of his son Richard, and legally married Luitgardis, daughter of the count of Vermandois and Adele Capet. Guillaume married his sister to the count of Poitou, another strategic alliance. He endowed the reestablishment of the mint at Rouen and the reconstruction of the abbeys of Jumièges and Saint-Ouen at Rouen, which had been destroyed by earlier Viking raiders. Guillaume I had no children by his wife and was killed at Picquigny by the count of Flanders in 942. He was succeeded by his son by Sprota, Count Richard I the Fearless.[7]

Since Count Richard I was still a child when his father died, King Louis IV of Francia seized Normandy, but Count Richard won it back in 947. Count Richard I, in 956, made peace with Hugues, Grand Duc des Francs, who made him guardian of his son, the future King Hugues Capet, and gave him his daughter Emma in marriage. After her death without children, he married his concubine, Gunnora, daughter of the former Danish ruler of the Cotentin. Richard and Gunnora had many children, among whom were Count Richard II, who succeeded him, Robert, count of Évreux and archbishop of Rouen, Emma, wife of two English kings, Aethelred II and Knut, Maude, wife of Odo count of Blois, and Hawise, wife of Geoffroy I, duke of Brittany, son of Duke Conan I of Brittany and Ermengarde of Anjou. Thus, he secured the borders of his realm in the east, west, and south, and from about 960 on his reign was a time of peace and stability. In 965 he made peace with the king of Francia and in 966 he refounded the abbey of Le Mont-Saint-Michel with Benedictine monks. From 966 he took the title marquis, showing his superiority over other counts. By coining his own money, he indicated his independence from the kings of Francia. The beginning of the Capetian dynasty in 987 signified the end of the Carolingian dynasty and the change of the name of the kingdom from Francia to

---

Vvileim Dux Bri, presumably referring to Guillaume I Longuespée.

7. Flodoard de Reims, *Annals*, 25A and D; WJ, 1:iii, 11–12; Picquigny was an island in the Somme river in Picardy; *RADN*, nos. 36, 49, 53, 66–67. French names are written in French spelling except for names of those who went to England, which are anglicized.

France. In 990 Count Richard I issued a charter for the Benedictine abbey of La Trinité de Fécamp, for which he rebuilt the church.[8] He died in 996 and was buried at Fécamp. He was succeeded by his eldest son by Gunnora, Richard II, who took the title of duke.

Duke Richard II the Good built castles on his frontiers, staffing them with members of his family as castellans. He made donations to the abbeys of Saint-Wandrille, Fécamp, and Le Mont-Saint-Michel. He also generously donated to religious institutions outside Normandy, as far afield as the monastery of St. Catherine in Sinai. Like his father, he secured his borders through marriage alliances. He married Judith, daughter of Duke Conan I of Brittany and Ermengarde of Anjou. Judith founded the abbey of Bernay. Duke Richard and Judith had two sons who both became dukes of Normandy, Richard III and Robert II, and daughters Adelaise, who married Renaud, count of Burgundy, and Eléanore, who married Baudouin IV, count of Flanders, thus securing the eastern borders. After his wife's death in 1017, Duke Richard II "married" according to Danish custom Papia, by whom he had Mauger, who became archbishop of Rouen, and Guillaume, who became count of Arques-Talou. The reign of Duke Richard II was generally peaceful, in concord with the Capetian kings of France. In England, Duke Richard II supported his brother-in-law, the Anglo-Saxon King Aethelred II, instead of his Scandinavian opponents, thus ending the long-standing Norman alliance with the Scandinavians.[9]

Duke Richard II died on 23 August 1026 and was buried at Fécamp. He was succeeded by his eldest son, Duke Richard III, who died within a year, reputedly of poison.[10] Richard's younger brother, Robert II the Magnificent, became duke from 1027 to 1035. He supported the abbey of Sainte-Trinité in Rouen and gave protection to the two sons of King Aethelred and

---

8. WJ, 1:iv, 18; OV, 2:8–11; *Torigni*, 2:8–9, 162–69, 258–61; Delisle, *Pièces justificatives*, nos. 1, 2; the new dynasty established by Hugues Capet in Francia in 987 lasted until 1792; Richard made his illegitimate sons Geoffroy de Brionne and Guillaume both counts of Eu, Guillaume succeeding his brother, and son Robert count of Avranches; *RADN*, no. 4; 8,584 coins were found at Fécamp dated between 980 and 985 demonstrating Norman coinage, but also extensive trade by coins from Arles, Pavia, and Cologne, and in addition Norman coins have been found in England, Scotland, Denmark, Poland, and Russia; Bates, *Normandy* 25–29, 34, 36.

9. OV, 2:10–11; *Torigni*, 2:8–11, 172–79, 260–61; Delisle, *Pièces justificatives*, nos. 3, 4; most donations to Le Mont-Saint-Michel in late tenth and early eleventh centuries were from Brittany and Maine: see cartularies from Saint-Victeur-au-Mans and l'Abbayette; Bates, *Normandy*, 33, 57, 67.

10. WJ, 2:vi, 2–3; OV, 2:10–11; *Torigni* 2:10–13; Duke Richard III had two illegitimate children: Nicolas, who became a monk of Fécamp and abbot of Saint-Ouen, and contributed fifteen ships and one hundred knights to his nephew Duke William II in 1066, and Alice, who married Ranulf, vicomte of Bayeux and the Bessin.

his aunt Emma, Edward and Alfred, princes of England, who spent most of their youth in Normandy. Duke Robert II had no legitimate children, but by his mistress, Herleve of Falaise, he fathered William, whom he proclaimed his successor as duke. Duke Robert's reign was marked by instability and conflict with supporters of his late brother and with Duke Alain III of Brittany. His uncle, Archbishop Robert of Rouen, count of Évreux, mediated and helped to resolve the conflicts. In 1034–35, after making his counts swear fealty to his illegitimate minor son William, Duke Robert II went on pilgrimage to Jerusalem, but died at Nicaea on his way home.[11] After his death, William became Duke William II. Herleve married Herluin, vicomte de Conteville in Calvados and had two sons, Duke William's half-brothers: Odo, who became bishop of Bayeux, and Robert, who became count of Mortain.

Duke William II was born in Falaise, Calvados, Western Normandy, in 1027/28. William was seven or eight years old in 1035 when his father died. At the time, there were numerous counts in Normandy, most of whom were related to the ducal family, and many of whom guarded the borders.[12] During William's minority, members of the ducal and of the various aristocratic families of Normandy engaged in a struggle for power.

The primary Norman supporter of young Duke William II was his great-uncle Robert, archbishop of Rouen and count of Évreux, son of Count Richard I and Gunnora, and brother of Duke Richard II. Archbishop Robert ended the war between Duke Robert II and Duke Alain III of Brittany, governed Normandy after the departure of Duke Robert, and was the guardian of young Duke William until his death in 1037. The subsequent guardians of the vulnerable young Duke William were Duke Alain III of Brittany, who died suddenly, probably murdered, in 1040, Count Gilbert de Brionne, who was murdered when out riding several months later, Turchetil de Neufmarché, who was also killed, and Osbern, brother of Duchess Gunnora and steward of Duke Robert II, who was killed in a fight in the young duke's bedroom. Walter, brother of William's mother Herleve, slept

---

11. OV, 2:10–11; WJ, 2:vi, 12; *Torigni*, 2:14–15; *RADN*, no. 102; Delisle, *Pièces justificatives*, nos. 10, 12; Herleve was the daughter of Fulbert, who was a tanner or furrier; according to Planché, *Conquerer*, 1:10–11: Robert sent an ambassador to her father, a furrier, asking for her hand, and treated her as his wife; as duke, Robert made her father his chamberlain, and gave her brother Walter a position in his court; Duke Robert also had a daughter by Herleve, Adelise, who married successively the counts of Ponthieu, Lens, and Aumale.

12. OV, 2:10–11, 4:76–79.

in his room and smuggled him out at night to sleep in huts of poor families, thereby saving him from nocturnal assassination attempts.[13]

During Duke William's minority, many of the most powerful aristocratic families of Normandy were fighting with each other, hoping to take power over Normandy. The strongest support for young Duke William after the death of Archbishop Robert came from King Henri I of France, who approved the boy's succession and to whom the young Duke William did homage. King Henri used his right as overlord of Normandy to exercise wardship of William and helped to protect the boy from the Norman aristocracy.[14]

Just as he came of age in 1046, public order broke down again and Duke William II faced rebellion in Western Normandy. The rebels first tried to assassinate the young duke at Valognes in the Cotentin, but he escaped by horse, riding overnight through perilous swampland to Falaise. With the help of King Henri I of France, Duke William was victorious over the rebels at Val-ès-Dunes and gained control of Western Normandy in 1047. In October 1047, there was an ecclesiastical council at Caen, in which Duke William actively participated, which established the Truce of God in Normandy, prohibiting private wars from Wednesdays through Mondays and during Advent, Lent, Easter, and Pentecost, although kings and dukes could still fight. The bishops had the duty of enforcement.[15] This in effect pacified and stabilized Normandy, aiding Duke William in establishing his authority over Eastern and Western Normandy, throughout which he personally traveled and which he united.

During the next decade, Duke William became more aggressive, fighting numerous wars to retain and increase his power in Normandy. In 1050 he drove Guy of Burgundy from the castle at Brionne and then from Normandy. In 1051, Count Hugues IV of Maine died and the citizens of its capital, Le Mans, gave their city to Count Geoffroy of Anjou, who then moved northward, occupying Domfront and Alençon. Duke William

---

13. Archbishop Robert married a different Herleve and by her had three sons, Richard, who succeeded him as count of Évreux, Radolf, sieur de Gacé, who married Basilie Fleitel (after his death, Basilie married Hugues de Gournay), and Guillaume, who married Hawise d'Echauffour, daughter of Giroie, whose first marriage had been to Robert I de Grandmesnil; OV, 2:28–31, 4:76–87; WJ, 2:vii, 1; Douglas, *Norman Achievement*, 232; Douglas, *William*, 40; Walter had a daughter Mathilde who married Raoul II Taisson/Tessson; 17.

14. Delisle, *Pièces justificatives*, no. 17; Douglas, *William*, 38,45.

15. Wace, 3:3509–60, 3641–736, 3801–990; *Torigni*, 2:14–15; Douglas, *William*, 49–52, 54: William fought against Ranulf of the Bessin, Néel de Cotentin, Haimo de Creully; Ralph Tesson changed to his side; Val-ès-Dunes is in Calvados; Bates, *Normandy*, 176, 204–5.

responded, taking both towns, which resulted in the district of the Passais becoming part of Normandy. However, Count Geoffroy of Anjou still controlled Maine and his alliance with King Henri I of France put an end to the alliance between France and Normandy.[16]

In 1051–52, Duke William II married Mathilde, daughter of Count Balduin V of Flanders and niece of the king of France. They had at least four children: Robert Curthose, who became duke of Normandy, William Rufus, who became king of England, Adele, who married the comte de Blois, and Henry Beauclerc, who succeeded his brother as King Henry I of England.[17]

Count Guillaume d'Arques-Talou, Duke William's uncle, deserted him at Domfront and with his brother, Archbishop Mauger of Rouen, started a rebellion in Eastern Normandy. First Count Guillaume gathered followers in the area around his castle stronghold at Arques. He was initially opposed by Richard de Saint-Valéry and Geoffroy of Neufmarché: Richard was the father, and Geoffroy the brother-in-law, of Gulbert d'Auffay, a relative of the d'Arques and de Hercy families. Duke William rushed there with a small force and determined that the castle of Arques could be taken only by siege. Duke William put Walter Giffard in charge of the siege while he went to block supplies from King Henri I of France. The castle of Arques fell in 1053 and Count Guillaume d'Arques-Talou was expelled from Normandy.[18]

In 1053, King Henri I invaded Normandy through the Évrecin. But now Duke William had a strong force of his nobles. In 1054 Duke William defeated the French and rebel forces at Mortemer. The double threats of Norman rebels and the king of France were ended. In Maine, William built a castle at Ambrières, placing a Norman, Robert d'Estouteville, as castellan. The French king confirmed William's possession of these lands taken from the count of Anjou. Normandy was no longer the vassal of France.[19]

---

16. OV, vol. 4, 7:80–93; Douglas, *William*, 58–61; Bates, *Normandy*, 76.

17. Delisle, *Pièces justificatives*, no. 30; William and Mathilde were related as cousins in a prohibited degree and therefore had to have their marriage legitimized by the pope, for which each built a monastery at Caen as penance; Douglas, *William*, 76, 391–95, 419–20: other possible children: Richard, who died young without children, Agathe, betrothed to Harold of Wessex and Alphonse of Leon, and possibly first to Héribert of Maine, Cécile, abbess of Sainte-Trinité, and Constance, married to Alain count of Brittany; Planché, *Conqueror*, I, 82–85.

18. Wace, 3:3400–54, 3515–60; Douglas, *William*, 62–66; Douglas incorrectly states that the wife of Geoffroy de Neufmarché, the sister of Gulbert d'Auffay, was the daughter of Duke Richard III; both Ada and Gulbert were the grandchildren of Papia, daughter of Duke Richard I; Bates, *Normandy*, 77.

19. Wace, 3:4811–940; his nobles included Count Robert of Eu, Walter Giffard, Hugh de Gournay and William de Warenne, all from Eastern Normandy; Bates, *Normandy*, 78; Douglas, *William*, 67–70.

Duke William's policy of aggression increasingly united his Norman vassals under his command.

Before Duke William II, Normandy did not have a system of military feudalism. The dukes and the new aristocratic magnates competed to enhance their own power. Before 1053, Duke William could not bind them to serve him by gifts of land without diminishing his own lands and power. However, after his victories at Arques and Mortemer, he was able to give the lands of his defeated enemies to his faithful nobles, concretizing their loyalty and binding them to military service. Duke William secured his borders with his own family members. He betrothed his son Robert to the sister of Count Héribert II of Maine, thereby establishing a claim to Maine. William made his half-brother, Robert, count of Mortain to secure his border with Brittany.

By this time the personal authority of the duke had increased to include making laws, dispensing justice, levying taxes, collecting customs and tolls, minting money, and commanding military service. The ducal court expanded and included the duke's wife and eldest son, his half-brothers, his counts, and his bishops. Following the example of the Capetian court of France, the ducal court developed the offices of steward/*dapifer*, chamberlain/*camerarius*, butler/*pincerna*, and constable, which were held by the highest aristocrats.[20] This system increased the power and cohesion of the ducal court and was significant in enabling William later to govern England.

Duke William had shown himself to be a brave and valiant warrior and commander. He was also renowned for his wisdom and gentleness. He was tall and strong and an able tactician.[21] He ended the rivalry between Eastern and Western Normandy and forged them into one. Beginning in 1060, Duke William built his capital at Caen, constructing an imposing ducal castle and two abbeys. By 1066 Duke William II had stabilized and consolidated his rule over all of Normandy and held the county of Maine.

Duke William II believed that his cousin, King Edward the Confessor of England, had named him as his successor, the information having been conveyed to him by Harold Godwinson. But when King Edward died on 5 January 1066, Harold himself seized the throne. Duke William held a great council at Lillebonne to decide what to do. The majority of his nobles agreed on invasion and declared their promises to provide knights and ships. This was enthusiastically supported not only by the aristocracy of Normandy but was joined by others from Maine, Brittany, and Flanders. After extensive

---

20. Douglas, *William*, 133–35, 145–46; Bates, *Normandy*, 155.

21. *Anglo-Saxon Chronicle*, 163–64 (1087); *Torigni*, 2:264–65; D. Carpenter, *Struggle*, 71, citing William of Poitiers.

preparation, on 28 September 1066 Duke William set sail with his army from Saint-Valéry-sur-Somme, the caput of the de Saint-Valéry/d'Auffay family, to England. On 14 October 1066 he defeated and killed King Harold at Hastings. On Christmas Day 1066 in London, he was crowned King William I of England. About eight thousand Normans knights then settled in England. King William died in 1087, leaving Normandy to his eldest son, Robert Curthose, and England to his second son, William Rufus.[22]

The economy in eleventh-century Normandy was thriving. Money was minted and exchanged. There were mortgages and installment payments. Commodities traveled on the rivers through tolls and locks to urban trading centers such as Rouen. New towns were founded and older ones expanded. New cathedrals, monasteries, and stone castles were built, after the destruction of the ninth century and the wooden structures of the tenth.[23]

One reason for the success of Normandy was that its dukes, especially William II, had created a coherent and consistent political and organizational structure, with increasing loyalty to themselves, and maintained better defined and secured borders than other counties and the kingdom of France.[24]

NORMAN ARISTOCRACY AND LORDSHIP

Little is known about the aristocracy of Normandy before the Viking invasions. There were rural estates in Carolingian times, centered on the domain of the lord, whose lands were cultivated by free peasants and slaves. In the early eleventh century, the term *nobiles* was rarely used and was not a fixed category. The highest aristocrat in Normandy was the duke and under him, the count (*comte*, *comes*), and under him the viscount (*vicomte*). The duke held all of the duchy of Normandy, the *comte* held a *comté* or county, the *vicomte* held a *vicomté*. In the time of Count Robert I, there were no other counts in Normandy with any significant power. His descendants made their younger and illegitimate sons counts, generally in frontier counties. In the time of Duke William II, many of the counts were still members of the extended ducal family; the viscounts were members of the aristocratic families, who served at the duke's pleasure as his agents, collected taxes, enforced laws, and provided defense for the duke, and the offices became hereditary.

---

22. OV, 4:76–97; *Torigni*, 2:220–21; J. Green, *Aristocracy*, 35: the greatest numbers were from the Pays de Caux and de Bray and Calvados, secondly from the Avranchin-Cotentin.

23. Bates, *Normandy*, 96–98.

24. Hollister, *Monarchy*, 20; Bates, *Normandy*, 57–59.

Counts defended the borders and the castles of the duke. Marriages indicated a sense of social conformity: counts generally married daughters of counts, and *vicomtes* married daughters of *vicomtes*.[25]

In the eleventh century, prominent families, many related to the dukes, gained power, held lands from which they often took their names, defeated their neighbors, built castles, and endowed monasteries. Initially, castles were restricted to the ducal family and the counts, but later others were built along the frontiers. The monasteries of St. Ouen, Fécamp, Jumièges, and Saint-Wandrille were restored and endowed. New monasteries were built or refounded at Rouen, Préaux, Le Bec, and Le Tréport in the 1030s, Saint-Évroul in the 1050s, and Caen in the 1060s. Abbeys symbolized and augmented the power of noble families. Such families also endowed colleges of canons, often in the cathedrals.[26]

Many families gained power through relationships by marriage or descent with the dukes and their duchesses and through ducal gifts of land. Those who fought for the dukes against rebel families were given their lands. Strong families became even more dominant by expanding their estates, as for example, Walter Giffard from Bolebec to Longueville. Families distributed acquired lands to their dependents to cement their allegiance. In addition, some of the aristocracy of Eastern Normandy acquired properties in Western Normandy, as for example Archbishop Robert of Rouen, who held land near Valognes in the Cotentin.[27]

During the early Norman period, the relationship between lords and vassals was more significant than the amount of land held. When a knight died, his lord often took wardship over his minor children and the lands they inherited, and had the right to give his widow and children in marriage, both of which could entail significant income for the lord.[28]

In medieval Normandy and Maine, landholders generally either left their estates to their eldest son (primogeniture) or divided them among their sons (*parage*). Inheritance of landed property was divided among sons by the Giroie, de Grandmesnil, Giffard, and de Vieilles families and by

---

25. Douglas, *William*, 138–42; Bates, *Normandy*, 109.

26. Bates, *Normandy*, 115–16, 274; Robert Fitz Onfroy de Vieilles had churches in the Cotentin; Herluin de Conteville acquired an estate in the Cotentin; Douglas, *William*, 86–88.

27. Roger de Beaumont regained the properties of his uncle Turchetil and of his younger brother Robert; Roger de Beaumont, William de Warenne, and Walter Giffard received the properties of exiled Count Guillaume d'Arques-Talou; Bates, *Normandy*, 100–104.

28. In England, this was limited by Magna Carta, arts. 7–8, giving widows the right to dower, marriage portion, inheritance, and the right not to marry.

Archbishop Robert of Rouen. But by the second half of the eleventh century more and more was given to the eldest son.[29] This made the family structure more linear and often connected it to a specific place. As the use of toponyms increased, more family names were based on the place where they held land. Occasionally, if a wife brought greater land to a marriage, a man might adopt the place of her land as the family toponym. Younger sons who did not inherit were married into other families or sent to a monastery to study for the priesthood, which included learning to read and write. Many younger sons disappeared from written history unless they gained land through special legacy or marriage or held a high position in the church. Daughters could marry into another noble family or enter a convent. However, for both options they generally needed a dowry. Since descendants were preferable to collaterals, when there was no male heir, daughters could be heirs, serving as conduits of their fathers' lands to their husbands.[30]

THE CHURCH IN NORMANDY

The church in Normandy, though founded in the Roman period, had to be reconstituted in the tenth century, following the decline and major destruction by the pagan Vikings. Churches and monasteries were built or rebuilt and dioceses were reestablished under the Christian dukes. By 990 there were finally bishops in all seven of the Norman dioceses and there were five monasteries, four in Eastern Normandy and Le Mont-Saint-Michel on the western frontier. Count Guillaume I Longuespée rebuilt the monastery of Jumièges and brought back its monks from exile. Count Richard I reconstituted Le Mont-Saint-Michel with monks and Fécamp with secular canons, which Duke Richard II replaced later with a community of Benedictine monks in 1001. Bernay was founded in 1010/17 by Duchess Judith. Bishops began building cathedrals in Rouen, Avranches, Coutances, Bayeux, and Lisieux. Ecclesiastical progress was interrupted during the reign of Duke Robert II and the minority of Duke William II when stability and social order broke down. However, by the mid-eleventh century, Duke William II had unified the church in Eastern and Western Normandy, reformed the episcopacy by appointing bishops on the basis of their qualifications, held

29. The custom of primogeniture was Carolingian, that of *parage* was Scandinavian; Bates, *Normandy*, 111, 118–20, 127, 136: when Bishop Jean d'Avranches left property outside of his family, his nephew brought suit in court; J. Green, *Aristocracy*, 336, 340–41: *parage* was prevalent in the Pays de Caux.

30. Daughters of the aristocracy were often married to secure borders; Lemesle, *Société aristocratique*, 120–33; D. Carpenter, *Struggle*, 69: toponyms such as de Beaumont began to appear about 1040; J. Green, *Henry I*, 203.

synods and councils, and founded the two abbeys of Sainte-Étienne and Saint-Trinité at Caen. Monastic foundations were both a matter of honor and a means of consolidating power.[31]

Members of the new Norman aristocracy also founded monasteries. In Eastern Normandy, Sainte-Trinité and Saint-Amand at Rouen were founded by Goscelin, vicomte de Rouen, and his wife Emmeline, ancestors of the vicomte d'Arques, in the time of Duke Robert II. Onfroy de Vieilles refounded Saint-Pierre in 1033–35 and his wife, Aubrée, founded Saint-Léger in 1040, both at Préaux. Lesceline d'Eu, great-aunt of Duke William, founded Saint-Pierre-sur-Dives for nuns, although she transferred it to monks in 1046. Her son, Count Robert d'Eu founded Saint-Michel-du-Tréport in 1036. In Western Normandy, the Giroie and de Grandmesnil families refounded Saint-Évroul in 1050. The monasteries were interconnected by the Cluniac reform and by the practice of the older abbeys, such as Jumièges and Saint-Ouen, of supplying abbots and monks to newer abbeys. Herluin, a knight of Count Gilbert de Brionne, became a monk and founded an independent abbey at Le Bec-Hellouin in 1034. The school of Le Bec Abbey was renowned and produced many scholars, including Lanfranc and St. Anselm, who later both became archbishops of Canterbury in England. Monasteries produced important historians, such as William of Jumièges in the eleventh century and Ordericus Vitalis of Saint-Évroul, who wrote in the early twelfth century. The monasteries also provided a primitive banking system as agents for deposit, credit, and transfer of funds in the new developing money economy.[32]

The bishops of Normandy were often members of the ducal family in the most important dioceses: Rouen, Bayeux, Lisieux, and Avranches; other bishops were from the new aristocratic families allied with the dukes, and served in Coutances, Sées, and Évreux. Church councils were held in Rouen, Caen, and Lisieux, which were attended by Duke William II. Some bishops also held secular offices, which were inherited by their sons. The son of Robert, archbishop of Rouen and count of Évreux, inherited the rank of count. Both the monasteries and the episcopacy helped unify Normandy under the authority of Duke William II.

---

31. OV, 2:10–13, vol. 3; WJ, 2:vii (22); the Cluniac reform of monastic life extended to Jumièges, Saint-Ouen, and Le Mont-Saint-Michel; Power, *Norman Frontier*, 302; Bates, *Normandy*, 213–14, 221.

32. OV, 2:252–55; *Torigni*, 2:12–15, 20–21, 30–31, 182–85, 190–91, 196–99, 206–7, 212–13, 224–29, 264–67; Bates, *Normandy*, 224, Lanfranc was also abbot of St. Étienne, Caen; Douglas, *William*, 114–15; J. Green, *Aristocracy*, 25.

PART I | SETTING THE STAGE

MEDIEVAL MAINE

Maine, the place of origin of the de Hercé/Hercy family, lay south of Normandy and north of Anjou, between these two very powerful states. Maine was more rural and forested than Normandy. There were no natural boundaries, although on the east Brittany had a series of fortresses guarding its border. Traces of settlements dating back to paleolithic times have been found in Maine. Later it was occupied by the Gallic Aulerci Diablintes and Cenomani tribes. The Romans governed it under their empire and later the Carolingian kings ruled it as part of Francia. There were Celtic incursions from Brittany and some raids by Vikings in the Loire valley, mostly in the ninth century, but the effects were much less than the invasions and settlements of the Danes in Normandy. In Carolingian times, Maine was a dukedom, held by members of the royal family of Francia. Later it was a county, administered by counts initially related to the Carolingian dynasty. Its capital was at Le Mans, which was also the seat of the bishops of Maine.

By the year 1000, there was major growth of population and new parishes and towns. Castles were built and there were more knights. In the eleventh century, Maine became a battleground in the power struggle between Normandy and Anjou. Héribert I succeeded as count of Maine on the death of his father in 1015. He fought against Fulk III d'Anjou and the counts of Blois. Count Héribert was captured by Fulk d'Anjou in March 1029 and died in 1032/35. He was succeeded by his son, Hugues IV, a minor, who was until 1036 in ward of his great-uncle, Bishop Gervais of Le Mans. Count Hugues IV fought against Geoffroy Martel of Anjou and married Berthe de Blois; they had one son Héribert II. Hugues IV died in 1051.[33]

During this period the power of the counts of Maine decreased as that of independent lords of castles, such as Mayenne and Laval, increased. In the tenth century castles consisted primarily of a stone donjon or tower with some buildings surrounding it. In the eleventh century more elaborate stone castles were built, often on the borders and guarding major rivers. After 1050, counts had little authority over the castellans.[34]

Count Héribert II succeeded his father. However, the citizens of Le Mans rose up and ceded their town to Geoffroy Martel of Anjou. Martel occupied Maine and exiled the dowager Countess Berthe and Bishop Gervais,

---

33. *CartStVincent* vol. 1, no. 15; he was also in constant conflict with Avesgaud de Bellême, bishop of Le Mans; Pichot, *Bas-Maine*, 61, 84.

34. Barton, *Lordship*, 15, 112, 115, 122, 210; according to Barton, 199, there were: "overlapping circles of lordship in which lords of differing prestige, landed wealth, and authority competed for further power and sought to provide peace and security"; Latouche, *Histoire*, 58; Pichot, *Bas-Maine*, 132–33, 181.

who fled to the court of Normandy. In 1056, Count Héribert II escaped from Le Mans and also fled to the Norman court, where he did homage to Duke William. Duke William betrothed his own daughter to Count Héribert and Héribert's sister, Marguérite, to his son, Robert Curthose. An agreement was written into Count Héribert's will that if Héribert died without children, Duke William would inherit Maine. The young Count Héribert did die without children in 1062. His sister died in 1063. These contracts of betrothal were the basis on which Duke William claimed Maine in 1063.[35] His strongest opponents, King Henri I of France and Count Geoffroy Martel of Anjou, both had died in 1060. Duke William successfully fought against their weaker successors, Count Fulk IV of Anjou and the young King Philippe I of France, as well as against the local castellans, including Geoffrey of Mayenne.

By 1064 Duke William II had secured control over all of Maine. William of Poitiers, writing in the 1060s, described his conquest of Le Mans by laying waste the countryside as more merciful than attacking the city itself. Duke William made his eldest son, Robert Curthose, count of Maine, but did not replace most Manceau castellans. William also ruled Maine through bishops and abbots, and kept troops in Le Mans. This was not disruptive to the lords in northwest Maine. After the conquest of England in 1066, King William I did not give English lands to the nobles of Maine, distrusting them since many of them still had ties to Anjou. In 1069/70, the people of Le Mans again revolted against the Normans and returned to Angevin control. In 1073, King William brought troops from England, attacking and defeating Maine. In 1086, Domesday Book in its great inventory of landholders still did not mention Manceau lords holding lands in England, although they began to acquire lands later under kings William II Rufus and Henry I. The border between Normandy and Maine remained unstable until 1144, when Anjou came to rule Normandy.[36]

Gersende, the sister of Count Hugues IV of Maine and aunt of Count Héribert II, transferred the comital succession to her legitimate son by an Italian father, Hugues, who preferred to remain in Italy. Gersende was regent and also the mistress of Baron Geoffrey of Mayenne, who became very powerful and was the unofficial lord of Maine. After another rebellion of Maine against Normandy in 1090, Geoffrey brought young Hugues to Maine and he became Count Hugues V from 1090 to 1092. Hugues V was not very competent or intelligent. In 1092, he sold Maine to his cousin Elias,

35. Douglas, *William*, 71–73; Bates, *Normans*, 75.

36. WP, 1:38; *Anglo-Saxon Chronicle*, 155 (1073); Bates, *Normans*, 72, 77–78, 80–81; in 1069 William was facing rebellions in England which delayed his response; Power, *Norman Frontier*, 317; Hollister, *Monarchy*, 23, 40–41.

son of Paule, another sister of Hugues IV, for ten thousand *solidorum*. Elias I succeeded as count, ruling from 1092 to 1110, and fought against Robert Curthose. In 1098 and 1099, King William II Rufus had two campaigns against Maine. He recruited some Manceau castellans and rewarded a few with land in England. Later Count Elias and many of the magnates of Maine supported King Henry I at Tinchebrai. Then King Henry I brought many Manceaux to England, where he gave them lands, and also gave lands to some of the Manceau knights who had remained in England after the conquest. After the death of Count Elias I in 1110, his daughter Erembourge succeeded to Maine. Erembourge married Fulk V of Anjou in 1110, becoming countess of both Maine and of Anjou. Thus, in the end the Angevins took Maine by marriage.[37] The son of Fulk V of Anjou and Erembourge of Maine, Count Geoffroy V of Anjou and Maine, became duke of Normandy in 1144, and Geoffroy V's son, Henry, duke of Normandy, Maine, and Anjou, became King Henry II of England. Both Geoffroy and Henry were born in Maine at Le Mans. The Plantagenet kings of England, Henry II, Richard I, and John, were all counts of Maine.

ARISTOCRACY AND LORDSHIP IN MAINE

Maine was not ruled by kings but by counts and later by local castellans. In ninth- and tenth-century Maine, lordship was determined by the model of Carolingian Francia. In Normandy this had changed after the Viking invasion and settlement in the first half of the tenth century, but not in Maine. In Maine the counts, whose authority derived from their Carolingian relationships, lost their power after the demise of the Carolingian dynasty in France in 987 and the rise of the independent castellans under the new Capetian dynasty. To an extent, the Carolingian model, although disconnected from the dynasty itself, still influenced Manceau lordship. However, it was also influenced by geography, events, and relationships. In eleventh-century Maine, the authority of the aristocracy was based on possession of land, military valor, and also on honor and reputation and personal relationships with those above and below them, which involved loyalty and fidelity. Lords

---

37. OV, 2:304–9, 4:190–99, 5:226–33, 302–7, 6:174–79; *CartStVincent*, vol. 1, no. 117 (1093); Hollister, *Monarchy*, 254; Count Elias had been an ally of King Henry I, but after his death, Fulk broke this relationship off, resulting in war with Henry until 1113, when Fulk did homage for Maine; Latouche, *Histoire*,153; Bates, *Normans*, 100–103, 105, 120–21, 146; *solidi* were small coins but larger than pennies and were the basis for the English shilling.

exercised power over those who lived and worked on their lands and resolved disputes among those below them.[38]

The eleventh-century aristocracy of Maine was, in the cases of Mayenne and Laval, appointed by the counts of Anjou and Maine in the early years of the century, thereafter becoming hereditary. In the case of Ambrières, the lord was appointed by Duke William II after he conquered Maine. His brother, Robert de Mortain, appointed a Breton as lord of Gorron, which was adjacent to Hercé. All four cities were castle towns. The authority of the castellans and landed aristocracy after 1050 gradually replaced that of the counts of Maine.

The lord generally had possession of land. A greater lord held power over his vassals who gave him homage and service, and to whom he gave tenure of land. Lesser lords had power over the peasants who worked the lands of which they were lords. The lord administered justice within his lands. A duke was lord over his counts; counts were lords over their barons, and barons over their knights. Bishops were lords of their priests, abbots of their monks and sometimes over lay vassals. The nature of lordship was not, however, monolithic. It was also determined by the honor, reputation, and status of individual lords, as well as their relationships with other lords and with their tenants. These could change as lords died and were succeeded by their sons or other lords. Lordship was also influenced by conflicts and rivalries among lords seeking greater power, prestige, and dominance over others, by external wars, and by relationships between lords and bishops to each other and to a central authority. There were times of peace and stability, and times of conflict and chaos. In general, medieval society accepted the model of lordship and the authority of lords over others, and the subordination of the many to those above them. In the ninth and tenth centuries there were fewer lordships, but these greatly increased in the eleventh.[39] Little is known about the lordship of Hercé before 1066. The 1060s were a time of great conflict between Normandy and Anjou, which engulfed Maine.

THE CHURCH IN MAINE

The lives of all people in medieval France were dominated by the church. In Maine the episcopal see was located in Le Mans from Roman times. The bishop of Le Mans had authority over all of Maine from Merovingian and Carolingian times, and played a significant political role in the eleventh century, often holding more power over the city of Le Mans than the counts

---

38. Barton, *Lordship*, 1–3, 7, 15, 17–19, 104, 110–12.
39. Latouche, *Histoire*, 70–71; Barton, *Lordship*, 2–18; J. Green, *Aristocracy*, 196.

of Maine. Geoffroy Martel of Anjou had Vougrin, monk of Marmoutier in Tours and abbot of Saint-Serge in Angers, installed as bishop of Le Mans. Vougrin rebuilt the cathedral of Le Mans and died in 1064. He was succeeded in 1066/67 by Bishop Arnaud, born in Avranches, but educated in Le Mans, who welcomed Duke William II of Normandy to Le Mans and held office until 1081.[40]

There were far fewer monasteries in Maine than in Normandy and they were established later. In 1000 CE there were the seventh-century Benedictine abbey of Évron and the priory of L'Abbayette, a foundation by the Norman abbey of Le Mont-St-Michel at La Dorée. The small priory of St. Martin was founded at Mayenne in the 1120s. The Cistercian abbey of Clermont, west of Laval, was founded by St. Bernard of Clairvaux in 1152. The abbey of Fontaine-Daniel, southwest of Mayenne, a cell of Clermont, was founded in 1205. In Le Mans, there were the ancient Benedictine abbeys of Saint-Pierre de la Couture and Saint-Vincent du Mans, and the priory of Saint-Victeur au Mans, a cell of Le Mont-Saint-Michel.[41] In the later eleventh and twelfth centuries there were increasing contacts between the church in Maine and that in Normandy.

KNIGHTHOOD IN MAINE AND NORMANDY

Knighthood evolved from the militarization of society in the tenth century, with the development of metalworking to make armor, and the invention of the stirrup and horse shoes. Knights in medieval Normandy and Maine were mounted chevaliers, generally from landed families, although not necessarily from the high nobility; some were rural landowners and others landless mercenaries. Some learned the arts of medieval combat by becoming squires and later knights at the court of their ruler or lord. However, this was not absolutely necessary since every landholder rode horses and had to be able to defend himself. Eleventh-century charters name knights as holders of land, donors to churches and monasteries, and witnesses of deeds. Knights were called *milites*, soldiers or warriors, in Latin documents. In a society where warfare was common, it was deemed an honor to be called a warrior. Knights were not destitute, since each knight had to possess armor, that is, a sword, a lance, a shield, a hauberk or shirt of chain mail, a helmet, a

40. Latouche, *Histoire*, 78–87; Pichot, *Bas-Maine*, 49–50.
41. King William I appointed a Norman abbot to Saint-Pierre in 1075, whose family then donated lands in the Avranchin to the abbey; the great Benedictine abbey of Marmoutier in Tours had priories in Maine; *CartAbbayette*, nos. 1–3; Bates, *Normans*, 47; Power, *Norman Frontier*, 318–19; Pichot, *Bas-Maine*, 50, 54–56, 161.

specially trained warhorse called a destrier, and, generally, also a palfrey or riding horse, and a squire to care for the equipment and horses. Later chain mail was replaced by plate armor which was heavier and more expensive. Only a family of at least some wealth or a wealthy liege lord could provide such equipment. Castle knights were provided with their accoutrements by their lord. Vassals were expected to perform military service for their lords, although in eleventh-century Maine and elsewhere this was generally limited to a certain number of days, often forty, each year. Sometimes knights were permitted to return to their homes at night if their service was close by. The splendor of their regalia reflected the prestige of their lord. Knights were soldiers, *milites*, who fought on horseback with couched lance; *chevaliers* who, theoretically, lived by an unwritten code of chivalry. Knighthood was prestigious, but was not rigidly defined in eleventh-century Normandy or Maine. Knighthood was more a function or profession than a social class. Medieval society was divided into three classes by Adalbero of Laon in the 1020s: those who prayed (*oratores*), those who fought (*bellatores*), and those who worked (*laboratores*), that is, monks, knights, and peasants. The terms *miles* and *nobilis* were often used interchangeably in the eleventh century. Those who fought on horseback with William the Conqueror at Hastings were knights. In the twelfth century, the social status of knight was increasingly elevated, and knighthood became more exclusive and aristocratic. However, artistic portrayals of knights were similar in the eleventh and twelfth centuries. Not only warriors on horseback but their families also began to be considered knightly.[42]

Norman and Manceau knights, from their origins in the late tenth century Normandy and Maine and flowering in England after the conquest,

---

42. Bouchard, *Strong of Body*, 14; Guilhiermoz, *Essai sur l'origine de la noblesse*, 340–41, 370, 392, 450–51, 462–74, 478; Lemesle, *Société aristocratique*, 148–49; R. Brown, *Castles*, 291, 293, 298, 300–301, 303; John de Laval, knight of Maine, retired at age thirty and became a monk; Latouche, *Histoire*, 66–67: knights also had to have spurs and gaiters and bits for their horses, 68; Bates, *Normandy*, 109–11; Duby, *Chivalrous Society*, 76–79, 96, 159–60: *miles* was first used in 971 in the charters of Cluny and its use expanded greatly in the eleventh century, when *nobilis* and *miles* were often used interchangeably, in the eleventh century they was applied to families; Coss, *Knight*, 4–10, 13, 24: according to St. Anselm, a man could not truly be a knight if he lacked any of the equipment; J. Green, *Aristocracy*, 10–11; Crouch, *Image*, 121: in the late tenth century in France, *miles* began to be used of landholders, 122: Richer of Reims contrasted *milites* with *pedites* (foot soldiers) in the 990s, 123: in 1000, in French society, knights were a distinct group, an *ordo*, and were free persons, Richer attributed the fall of the Carolingian dynasty to the marriage of the last heir, Charles of Lorraine, to the daughter of a knight rather than to a royal, 124: *militia* was a quality of manly status even for kings, King Henri I of France was called *miles accerimus*, 129: knights without land could be quite poor and some castle knights did not receive wages.

were initially a warrior class. According to William of Poitiers, Duke William distinguished between *milites mediae nobilitatis* (knights of middle nobility) and *milites gregarii* (common knights). Knights were expected to be brave and loyal. Knights served and fought for their lords and castellans. As the estates of the lords expanded, some of their knights served their lord as a company and were sometimes members of the lord's household. Many of those who were castle knights had originally been peasants, whereas those who held land were often of the *petit noblesse*. By the twelfth century many knights had moved from *milites castri*, that is, knights of the lord's castle, to holding land and fortified manor houses in their own right, and their social status increased accordingly. When they held land, they often adopted toponyms, family names based on place where they or their ancestors first held land. In the twelfth century knights fought in splendid tournaments.[43] The heads of the families de Hercé, d'Auffay, d'Arques, and de Hériz were landholders, knights, and mounted soldiers who fought with Duke William II in the conquest of England.

WOMEN IN KNIGHTLY FAMILIES IN MAINE AND NORMANDY

The image of women in the medieval Francia was in large part dominated by the male hierarchy of the church. Although pictures and frescoes in churches illustrated many biblical stories, lay people had no direct access to the Bible until the sixteenth century. Clerics, using the Latin Vulgate translation, controlled the selection and interpretation of biblical passages. Genesis 2:21–23 was misinterpreted to show that woman was created secondarily out of man and was therefore inferior. Genesis 3:1–19 was misused to show that woman was the source of evil by allegedly succumbing to temptation and leading man into it. First Corinthians 11:3–15, 14:34–35, and 1 Tim 2:11–15 were used to demonstrate the inferior status of women in society and in the church. Modeled on the household codes of the Roman empire, Eph 5:22–24, Col 3:18, and 1 Pet 3:1–6 were used to emphasize the subordination of wives to husbands. Ecclesiastes 7:26–28 declared that

---

43. *MA*, 2:18, no. 9, 267, no. 11, 3:447–48, nos. 2–3, 544–46, no. 1; OV, 2:260–63, 6: 26–28; Bates, *Normandy*, 104; Power, *Norman Frontier*, 263–65; Coss, *Knight*, 7, 10–12, 19–21: household knights could serve the king, a lord, an abbot, or a bishop; there are contemporary accounts of such households; especially vivid are those of Gilbert Crispin, monk of Le Bec and abbot of Westminster, in his *Life of Herluin*, describing the household of Count Gilbert de Brionne, and Orderic Vitalis's description of the household of Hugh d'Avranches; Crouch, *Image*, 291–92: household of earls of Shrewsbury in the early twelfth century; Prestwich, *Armies*, 12, 15–16, 167–68.

it was impossible to find a good woman. Bearing of sons, especially to patriarchal husbands, by Sarah, Rebecca, Rachel, and Leah was lauded and gave some status to the mothers. Jezebel was portrayed as the archetypal bad woman, transgressing both religious and civil law. The judge Deborah, the queen Esther, and the women prophets of the Old Testament were mentioned but their roles were generally qualified as only in exceptional cases or in obedience to men or in the absence of men.[44]

Many medieval theologians utilized Aristotle's understanding of woman as a physically defective man, to whom she was therefore inferior. Thomas Aquinas, citing Aristotle, called women unstable and defective in reason. Tertullian called woman "the devil's gateway." In about 1140, the *Decretum* of Gratian, which became the basis for canon law, upheld the subjection of wives to husbands and sanctioned wife beating in moderation, although it upheld the freedom of widows to remarry. It also based the exclusion of women from all exercise of authority, administration, and teaching as the punishment of Eve. By about 1200, male church authorities had suppressed the history of women deacons, priests, and bishops and were curtailing the episcopal authority of abbesses. On the other hand, some theologians were beginning to challenge some of the misogynistic presuppositions. In the late eleventh and early twelfth centuries, in Angers, Marbod of Rennes taught that women and men were equal in the order of creation and that men would not exist without mothers. At the same time, Peter Abelard taught about the strength of women, who were able to exercise authority. He focused on strong women, contrasting them to weak men: the woman prophet who anointed Jesus, Anna who preached, the women at the cross who proclaimed the resurrection to the cowering men, and noted women deacons.[45] When men wrote that women should not preach or teach, it usually meant that some women were doing just that.

The saints played a large role in the image of woman. Mary was venerated as virgin and mother and put on a pedestal as a font of grace and as the "queen of heaven." Abelard went so far as to say that Eve was restored through Mary before Adam was restored through Christ. Old Testament women saints were honored for their strength and courage, deemed appropriate in cases of national emergency or saving a victim; New Testament women saints for preaching, leadership, and courage. Later medieval women saints were venerated for their abnegation, piety, generosity, great deeds, and miracles of healing. A cult of Mary of Magdala developed, erroneously

44. Trible, *God*, 12–20, 75–115; Schüssler Fiorenza, *In Memory of Her*, 304–7.

45. *Torigni*, 1:96–97; Thomas Aquinas, *Summa Theologica* II-II, Q. 156, a. 1, Resp. ad 1; Gratian, *Decretum* 3.119; Aristotle, *Metaphysics*: women are inferior to men in body, mind, and ethics; Blamires, *Case*, 19–20, 30, 59–60, 72, 136, 177, 196, 202–7.

portraying her as a penitent sinner. Many early medieval women saints were wealthy aristocrats who founded monasteries. By the twelfth century there were strong, independent, well-educated women. Queen Eléanore of Aquitaine, politician and administrator, corresponded with Abbess Hildegard of Bingen, who preached and wrote books and music.[46]

Medieval written documents provide information mostly about the comital and ducal families and those of the highest aristocracy. Such documents were written by men and generally underrepresented women. The voices of women themselves were rarely, if ever, heard. However, families in medieval France were defined in terms of maternal as well as paternal ancestry. Marriages were arranged by the families of both bride and groom, and the ancestry, honor, and status of the family of the bride was of equal importance to that of the groom. Brides often brought property and land to their husbands. But girls had no legal status outside of marriage and were married as young as twelve or thirteen. Once married and having given birth, women had some power within their households, but fathers and husbands continued to have the greater authority over their daughters and wives.[47]

There had been many double monasteries of monks and nuns. But after they were destroyed by Viking invaders, the refounded monasteries were only for men and there were few convents for women. In the eleventh century, husbands made gifts of property to monasteries, often with the consent of their wives. Sometimes husbands and wives both founded monasteries. Vicomte Goscelin founded Sainte-Trinité and his wife, Emmeline, founded Saint-Amand, both at Rouen. At Préaux, Onfroy de Vieilles refounded Saint-Pierre and his wife, Aubrée, founded Saint-Léger. In Caen, Duke William built the abbey of Saint-Étienne and his wife, Mathilda, that of Sainte-Trinité.

Medieval knights were part of the ideal of chivalry, but this did not totally exclude women. Women were commended for their beauty, not only of their bodies but for the interior beauty of their souls and comportment. Women were expected to be courteous and have good manners, kindness, self-control, and be able to restrain their husbands from ill deeds. Women were expected to manage their households and servants, to be hospitable

---

46. Mary of Magdala was misidentified with the prostitute by Pope Gregory the Great in the sixth century; Blamires, 202; Goldy and Livingstone, *Writing*, 131–34: women often were seated on the north side of churches and sometimes the art on that side featured figures of women, 139–46: women made decisions about the furnishing and art of their parish churches; Jewell, *Women in Dark Age*, 124–29; Jewell, *Women in Late Medieval*, 25–28; Blamires, *Case*, 172.

47. Leyser, *Medieval Women*, 107.

to visitors, to support their husbands' enterprises, and to perform religious duties of almsgiving and prayer. Some women of the higher classes were taught to read and write, others to perform on musical instruments.[48]

The sources on women are scant, and the family names of wives of the earliest named men are not known, probably because they were not regarded as important since they were women or because they were not from prestigious families. However, the ancestry of wives was of great importance in medieval society. Therefore the ancestry of the first two wives of the de Hercé family whose family names are known, d'Arques/de Arches and de Hériz, will be discussed in detail.

RELATIONSHIPS AMONG FAMILIES IN MEDIEVAL NORMANDY AND MAINE

In the Middle Ages, families were related through geographical proximity, intermarriage, feudal vassalage, and support of particular monasteries, such as Saint-Évroul, Le Mont-Saint-Michel, Lucerne, Savigny, and Caen in Western Normandy, or Jumièges, Rouen, Tréport, Fécamp, Préaux, and Bec in Eastern Normandy.

The main geographical clusters of families which made the journey to England and settled there who were neighbors and lords of the de Hercé/Hercy family and their wives came from three areas: Northwestern/Bas Maine (de Hercé, de Mayenne), Eastern/Haute Normandie (d'Arques, d'Auffay, de Bolebec, Talbot), and Western/Basse Normandie (de Hériz, d'Avranches, de Saint-Jean, de Lascelles, Peverel). Many of the lords of these places took their vassals with them to England and they settled near their former continental neighbors. Many played a role in the history of the de Hercy family in England.

In addition to geographical proximity and vassalage, families were related by intermarriage and descent. For example, the families d'Avranches, de Bolebec, de Brus, d'Eu, Giffard, de Laval, Peverel, d'Auffay, and de Saint-Valéry were related by marriage or descent, legitimate or illegitimate, to the dukes of Normandy. In Western Normandy, the families d'Avranches, de Beauchamp, de Brus, and Paynel were interrelated. In Eastern Normandy, the families of de Saint-Valéry and d'Auffay were related by descent, as were the de Bolebec, Giffard, and d'Arques families, and the Talbots and de Gournays were related by marriage. Family relationships were documented in property titles, monastic cartularies, and wills. In the twelfth century a

---

48. Women even had a role in tournaments and heraldry; marriage was first defined as a sacrament by the council of Verona in 1184.

few knights, such as Lambert of Flanders, wrote personal histories of their families, showing that men were considered more important than women and elders more than juniors, but that kinship by marriage was as important as kinship by blood.[49]

CLUSTERS OF FAMILIES WHICH JOURNEYED FROM MAINE AND NORMANDY TO ENGLAND IN 1066 NORTHWESTERN/BAS MAINE

Maine was geographically divided by the Mayenne river into northwestern/low or Bas Maine, called Mayenne, and southeastern/high or Haut Maine, called the Sarthe. Northwestern Maine is hilly and in the Middle Ages was heavily forested. There were farms, but the soil was poor and *pannage*, the release of pigs to root for food in the forests, was common. Population was sparse and farming was difficult. The local barons ruled Bas Maine. Haut Maine, surrounding the capital of Le Mans, was more heavily populated, had better agriculture and was more directly ruled by the counts and bishops.[50] In the eleventh and twelfth centuries, all of Maine was a battleground in the power struggle between Normandy and Anjou.

After the decline of the counts of Maine in the first half of the eleventh century, castellans emerged as the most influential authorities in their provinces, but did not exercise central authority. In the eleventh century many small rural lordships came into being. Regional courts were made up of the most important lords, namely de Mayenne and de Laval in Northwestern Maine. Disputes were often resolved on the basis not of legal principles, but on what outcome would lead to social harmony.[51]

There is little information about the de Hercé family of northwestern Maine before the conquest of England. And in England little is known about the family before the reign of the Plantagenet kings, since William the Conqueror did not give land to his Manceau knights. Much is known about it later. But information may be gained about the family in the eleventh and twelfth centuries through what is known about its neighbors and immediate lords in Northwestern Maine.

---

49. Duby, *Chivalrous Society*, 134–36.

50. Pichot, *Bas-Maine*, 30, 35, 40–42, 44–45, 49–51; Bas Maine was inhabited from the Iron Age through the Roman period by the Gallic Aulerci Diablintes tribe with its capital at Jublains, Haut Maine by the Aulerci Cenomani tribe; *pannage* was a right for which a farmer had to pay the lord of the forest; Latouche, *Histoire*, 77.

51. Barton, *Lordship*, 10, 25, 73–74, 216–18.

DE HERCÉ

The ancient Anglo-French family de Hercé, later spelled de Hercy and Hersey in England, originated at Hercé, in the county of Maine, arrondissement Mayenne, canton Gorron. Hercé lies in the northwest of Maine, adjacent to Gorron and between the larger towns of Fougères in Brittany and Ambrières in Maine. Fougères was subject to the duke of Brittany. Hercé, Gorron, and Ambrières were subject to the lords of Mayenne until 1054, when Duke William II conquered Ambrières and then fortified it against Mayenne. Mayenne, Ambrières, and Gorron were castle towns. Geoffrey de Mayenne had eighty knights, to many of whom he gave land. Some of his knights were resident in Mayenne, others were not. From about 1050, some knights used toponyms of the places they held as their family names.[52] It is possible either that de Hercé had been a castle knight of Mayenne and thereby acquired land or that his family held the land and then owed service to Mayenne. When Duke William consolidated his rule over Maine in 1064, the lords of Mayenne, Ambrières, Gorron, and Hercé owed fealty and knight service to Normandy.

Hercé was a small rural lordship, although it had authority over several smaller villages and agricultural settlements. At various times Hercé held Colombières-du-Plessis, Levaré, Brecé, La Tannières, La Haie-Peau-du-Loup, Vaudemusson, Condray, and even Gorron. The area around Hercé had great forests, and rocks of granite, basalt, quartz, and loess. Hercé lies in the Colmont river basin, crossed by winding valleys along the Bailleul creek. There were small villages, farmsteads, forests, and moors. The primary crop was wheat, although by the seventeenth century there are records of crops of rye, oats, and buckwheat, as well as groves of chestnut, hawthorn, hazelnut, elm, and poplar trees. Hercé is a town and now a commune, lying between Levaré on the west, Gorron on the east, and Colombières-du-Plessis on the south.[53]

The first documented ancestor of the de Hercé family was known simply as of Hercé. In his youth, Maine had been ruled indirectly by the counts of Maine and Hercé directly by the lords of Mayenne. In 1054 Duke William built a castle at Ambrières, weakening the power of Mayenne.

---

52. Pichot, *Bas-Maine*, 148–51: de Saint-Berthevin and Robert de Levaré were mentioned among his knights; in 1059 Hamelin de Levaré was probably the first of these knights to use a toponym; Hercé lies directly south of Mortain, the caput of Duke William's half-brother, Robert, count of Mortain.

53. Angot, *Dictionaire historique*, 424–25, 640: Levaré was held by Hamelin de Levaré, who donated the church of Marcilly to Saint-Vincent du Mans; *Cartulaire Manceau*, vol. 2, no. 5 (1063, Hamelin de Lévaré, vassal of Mayenne, donated forest passage right to Marmoutier); Lemesle, *Société*, 87–93; Pichot, *Bas-Maine*, 95.

PART I | SETTING THE STAGE

Eventually Mayenne and all of Maine were conquered by Duke William, but the situation remained unstable. Duke William did not dispossess the nobles of Maine from their lordships. He recruited many Manceau lords and knights to accompany him to England in 1066. De Hercé, along with the lords of Mayenne and Ambrières, fought bravely at Hastings. The Roll of Battle Abbey names de Hercé and de Mayenne; the French sources include the lord of Mayenne and Achard d'Ambrieres. Wace, in his *Roman de Rou*, mentions "all the barons of Maine" (*e del Maine toz les barons*) and "many Manceaux and Angevins" (*mult out Mansels e Angeuins*), and "old Geoffrey from Maine/Mayenne" (*de Meaine il viel Giffrei*). William of Poitiers named "men of Maine" first among the fighters.[54]

After the conquest, King William did not reward the Manceaux knights with lands in England, as he did the Normans, because of their suspected ties to Anjou. De Hercé may have returned to Maine until the reign of William Rufus or Henry I, both of whom did give Manceaux knights land in England. However, he may well have remained in England. He was a knight and many knights without land remained, serving as household knights of the king or of the greater lords who held castles. It was a time of significant building of castles which most magnates desired to possess and needed to staff with knights. The sons and grandsons of household knights could follow their fathers as household knights. A later lord of Hercé in Maine, Guillaume I de Hercé, born about 1150, was a *chevalier banneret*, who went on the Third Crusade with kings Philippe-Auguste of France and Richard I of England in 1190 and fought under King Richard after the French king went home. A knight banneret was one with sufficient wealth, stature, and vassals that he led a company of men in battle. He carried a square banner while other knights carried a pennant. In England, King Richard I gave lands in Warwickshire to Hugh de Hercy, possibly related to Guillaume I or a castle knight descendant of the lord of 1066. In the reign of King John, Malveysin de Hercy acquired lands in Nottinghamshire. But the family also continued at Hercé in Maine. The de Hercé who went to England in 1066 was part of the family at Hercé. Inheritance then was more likely by parage

---

54. Roll of Battle Abbey (RBA), Auchinleck, 2180 (Hercy); roll posted in Battle Abbey (Hercy, Maine); Le Tailleur (Guillaume de Mayenne: probably mistake for Geoffrey); Leland (Hercy, Mounceux, Mouceals, Mauncel, Lovel, Levele, de la Valet); Hollingshed (Hercy, Maine, Levell); Dives (Achard); Falaise (Achard d'Ambrières, Hamon de Laval, possible chronologically, Juhel de Mayenne, Juhel not possible chronologically); Wace, 3:4227-86, 4387-491, 4995-5114, 7660-82, 8449, 8524, 8667; WP, 130-31; J. Green, *Aristocracy*, 25: Wace was a canon of Bayeux cathedral and stressed names from Calvados and Western Normandy.

than primogeniture. Thus, he might or might not have been the eldest son or heir. If he was not an heir, he would have had more reason to remain in England.[55]

For the de Hercé family, although many of their known familial relationships emerged in England after the conquest, some were rooted in earlier history in Maine. De Hercé in Maine had a distant vassal relationship with the counts of Maine but a direct vassal relationship with the lords of Mayenne. The most immediate neighbor was the lord of Gorron, himself also a vassal of Mayenne. Later Gorron was held by Count Robert de Mortain, brother of King William I, who appointed a Breton as its lord and castellan. The authority of the counts of Maine had disappeared in Maine and did not extend to England. But the lords and members of this cluster of families, de Mayenne, d'Ambrières, and de Hercé, followed Duke William to England. Members of the de Gorron family also went, but not until the reign of Henry I. Later in Maine the de Hercé family intermarried with the families de Mayenne and Achard d'Ambrières.

In England the de Hercé family came to hold lands possibly in Worcestershire, and definitely in Warwickshire and Nottinghamshire by the twelfth and early thirteenth centuries. They intermarried with the d'Arques family of Eastern Normandy and the de Hériz family of Western Normandy. Since these families were Norman, King William I had given them English lands soon after the conquest. The d'Arques family settled in Yorkshire, just north of the main settlement of the de Hercé family in Nottinghamshire; the de Hériz family settled in Nottinghamshire and Derbyshire.

THE LORDS OF DE HERCÉ: DE MAYENNE

Mayenne (*Meduana*) became the most powerful lordship in Northwestern Maine. It was the caput of the cluster of lesser lordships, which included Ambrières, Gorron, and Hercé, all of which were related through lordship and vassalage. By 1050 Mayenne had become powerful on its own merit and without the patronage of the count of Maine, as had the other major lordship in Northwestern Maine, Laval. The lords of at least three of these towns went with Duke William II to England and fought at Hastings.

---

55. A brief subsequent history of the de Hercé family in France will be found in Appendix VIII; Hozier, *Armorial*, 151; Courcelles, *Dictionaire*, 289; Prestwich, *Armies*, 13–15, 167–68; Crouch, *Image*, 86–90; Bates, *Normans*, 77–78, 100–103, 105, 120–21, 146; the de Hersi(n) family in Buckinghamshire, discussed in Appendix VI, documented from the reign of King Henry I, is not included here because it was more probably from Hersin in the Artois.

PART I | SETTING THE STAGE

In the beginning of the eleventh century, Fulk III Nerra, count of Anjou, established Hamon de Château-du-Loir in the Sarthe as baron of Mayenne and *fidelis* of both the counts of Maine and of Anjou. The dependency was fluid, as sometimes he served the count of Anjou and other times the count of Maine. His son Geoffroy I de Mayenne was also a *fidelis* of Fulk III of Anjou and held the castle, *castrum*, at Mayenne. His son Gauthier I was succeeded by Geoffrey II as lord of Mayenne.[56]

Geoffrey II de Mayenne initially fought against Duke William II for control of Maine. According to the contemporary historian William of Poitiers, Geoffrey II of Mayenne went to Geoffroy of Anjou "terror-stricken . . . and complained fearfully and wretchedly that once the castle at Ambrières was built by the wealth of the Normans, his land would lie at the mercy of the enemy, to be invaded, ravaged, and laid waste at his will." Duke William won and fortified Ambrières against him. Geoffrey then swore fealty to William as his vassal. The castle at Mayenne was deemed impregnable. "On one side this Castle, which is washed by a swift and rocky river (for it is perched on a high rock jutting out above the river Mayenne) cannot be stormed by either force or cunning. . . . On the other side, stone fortifications and an equally difficult approach protect it." Geoffrey was still angry at Duke William and refused to attend his victory celebration at Le Mans, returning to his castle at Mayenne. William punished him by besieging and setting fire to the castle. Afterward William's knights took "rich booty, thoroughbred horses, knightly arms, and every kind of equipment." William then stationed a garrison in the castle. By 1064, Duke William was undisputed lord of Maine. Geoffrey II de Mayenne was now his vassal and fought alongside him in the conquest of England. Wace called him "old Geoffrey" (*li vieil Giffrei*). But King William did not give him land in England and he returned to Maine. Geoffrey II had three children by his wife, Mathilde: Hamelin, Gauthier II, and Hersende, who married Radulf de Gorron. Geoffrey II later became the lover of Gersendis, the mother of the young, incompetent Count Hugues V of Maine, and exercised considerable power over the county of Maine from 1069. Geoffrey II founded a monastery in honor of St. Nicholas in 1092 at La Chartre-sur-le-Loir.[57]

56. *CartStVincent*, vol. 1, no. 245; Barton, *Lordship*, 78, 123; in 1014, he witnessed the donation of Hugues comte de Maine to Le Mont-Saint-Michel; Geoffrey II was the brother or son of Gauthier I; Pichot, *Bas-Maine*, 54: there is archeological evidence of some sort of castle at Mayenne about nine hundred CE, 133–34, 139.

57. WP, 1:32–33, 40, 2:19; WJ 3:122, 151; Wace, 3:5075–114: called him strongest man in Maine (Wace, 3:8449); Le Tailleur has Guillaume de Mayenne, probably a mistake for Geoffrey; Falaise Roll has Juhel, which was chronologically impossible; RBA, Leland B., and Holingshed mention Manceaux; *Chronique de Normandie*, RHGF, 13:236; Geoffrey II married first Mathilde d'Alluyes, southwest of Chartres, and second

Geoffrey II de Mayenne died in 1098 and was succeeded by his son Gauthier II, who went on the First Crusade with Robert Curthose in 1096–98. Gauthier confirmed a donation of the church at Brecé, arrondissement Mayenne, canton Gorron, a dependency of Hercé, to Marmoutier by Ruallon, son of Geoffroy de Gorron. This indicates the complexity of the relationship between Mayenne, Gorron, and Hercé. Gauthier II supported Curthose, for whom he witnessed a charter for Sainte-Trinité de Caen. Gauthier II married Adeline de Presles and thereby acquired lands in the Avranchin.[58] He died in Italy after 1116. They had sons Hamelin, who succeeded but died about 1119, and Juhel/Judhael I, who succeeded his brother.

Hamelin was lord of Mayenne, Ambrières, Gorron, and Hercé. King Henry I gave Hamelin de Mayenne a manor in Somerset and two in Devon in exchange for the castles of Ambrières and Gorron. This shows that both castles had reverted to the control of the lords of Mayenne. Hamelin donated the church of St. Martin in Mayenne to Marmoutier. Hamelin was succeeded by his brother Juhel I.[59]

Juhel I married Clémence de Ponthieu, daughter of Guillaume I Talvas de Bellême, comte de Ponthieu, and Ela of Burgundy. Juhel I donated to the abbey of Marmoutier in Tours in 1120 to have them found the priory of St. Martin in Mayenne. The foundation also involved donations by his men and the labor of his peasants. A charter reveals how he was dissuaded from an act of violence against a vassal by his wife, aided by Bishop Hildebert of Le Mans and Abbot Guillaume of Marmoutier. This is a rare documented case of a nonroyal woman influencing a man in the twelfth century. A charter dated July 1128 of Bishop Guy of Le Mans called Juhel "prince of Mayenne, . . . acting in the king's stead" when necessary, suggesting that he was the secular power for the whole diocese of Le Mans. It also mentioned his wife, Clémence, and firstborn son, Geoffroy III. The three restored property to Le Mont-Saint-Michel in a charter dated July 1128.[60]

Hildebourge, daughter of Hoel, count of Cornouailles and Hawise de Bretagne; *CartSt-Vincent*, vol. 1, no. 251; Latouche, *Histoire*, 36–38, 147; R. Brown, *Normans*, 35.

58. Guyard de la Fosse, *Preuves*, iii; CDF, no. 423; *Cartulaire Manceau*, vol. 2, no. 7 (1106, gift of Brecé by Rivallon); *RRAN*, vol. 1, no. 121, 323, vol. 2, 956; Power, *Norman Frontier*, 370–71, n. 21.

59. *Testa de Nevill*, 86, 97; *RRAN*, vol. 2, no. 1183 (1118, charter of Henry I to Savigny, Hamelin witness with Thomas de St. John); PR Henry I (1129/30), 41, 108; *Cartulaire Manceau*, vol. 2, no. 1; CDF, no. 792; *CartAbbayette*, no. 9 (1116, Hamelin lord, confirmed charter of Juhel); Loyd, *Origins*, 62–63; Power, *Norman Frontier*, 386.

60. CDF, no. 792; Juhel I witnessed a charter for Radulf de Fougères's donation to the abbey of Savigny on the border of Western Normandy on 7 March 1113; *Cartulaire Manceau*, 2:13, 15–17; Barton, *Lordship*, 130–31, 184–86, 192–94; *CartAbbayette*, no. 10 (1128, gift of Guillaume de Gorron, confirmed by Juhel, Clémence, and son called

PART I | SETTING THE STAGE

In 1123, Juhel I was a witness for charters of King Henry I. By 1130, Juhel I held land in Devonshire and was surety for Empress Mathilde for her alliances with the dukes of Essex and Oxford. In 1135, Juhel I de Mayenne reclaimed the castles of Gorron, Ambrières, and Châteauneuf-sur-Colmont from Geoffroy d'Anjou because he said they were on his land. In 1144, Juhel I transferred the monks of St. Martin to his castle at Mayenne. Also in 1144, Pope Lucius II stated that Juhel de Mayenne and Henri de Fougères held their lands by divine right.[61] That was the year when Count Geoffroy of Anjou took Normandy and Maine became part of the new Angevin duchy.

Juhel I de Mayenne died on 23 November 1161 and was succeeded by his eldest son, Geoffroy III. The following year King Henry II took back the castles of Ambrières and Gorron. Geoffroy III married first Constance de Bretagne, daughter of Duke Conan III of Brittany and Margaret of England, and second, Isabelle de Beaumont, daughter of Waleran IV de Beaumont, comte de Meulan and earl of Worcester. She donated to the abbey of Savigny on the Normandy-Maine border in 1180/83, where she was buried. Geoffroy III and Constance had a daughter, Mathilde, who married André de Vitré of Brittany, and a son Juhel II. Geoffroy III went on the crusader campaign in Egypt in 1163 and died about 1169/70, when his son Juhel II was still an infant. Geoffroy's younger brother Walter married Sybil de Lacy, granddaughter and heir of Geoffrey I Talbot of Swanscombe, Kent.[62] Later the Hercy family intermarried with the Talbots.

Juhel II succeeded his father, Geoffroy III, in 1169/70, although he was a minor until 1183. Juhel II married a niece or relative of the king of England

---

Gaufred, although son Geoffroy III succeeded him and was presumably the eldest); Power, *Norman Frontier*, 475–76, n. 31.

61. *RRAN*, vol. 2, nos. 1391, 1569; vol. 3, nos. 275, 634; *Torigni*, 1:188–89, 232–33; PR 31 Henry I, 120; OV, 6:455 n. 4; *RHGF*, 15:416 (letter of Pope Lucius II); WJ, 2:viii, 38: Empress Mathilda claimed they were part of her inheritance; *Torigni* 1:200; Guyard de la Fosse, *Preuves*, iv; Châteauneuf-sur-Colmont, now Châtillon-sur-Colmont, is eleven km southeast of Gorron, south of Brécé; Power, *Norman Frontier*, 393–94, 477.

62. *Actes Henri II*, vol. 2, no. 628; Guyard de la Fosse, *Preuves*, xvii; Broussillon, *Laval*, 1:120, 165; after the death of Geoffrey, Isabel married Maurice II de Craon and their daughter married Guy de Laval; RBE, 1:35, 58, 70, 79, 96, 131, 186–87, 189, 195–96, 2:644; scutage payments for exemption from military service were made in 1166, 1190–91, 1194/95, 1196/97; *CartFontaine-Daniel*. 6:9, 7:10; *RRAN*, vol. 3, no. 914; Walter III, younger brother of Geoffroy III, married Cecilia, daughter of Payn FitzJohn and Sibil de Lacy; she was the granddaughter and heir of Geoffroy I Talbot; in 1135 Walter de Mayenne held land in Kent, where Geoffrey II Talbot held twenty fees of him; in 1166 Walter was a tenant-in-chief in Kent, holding twenty-nine knights' fees; he also held a fee in Yorkshire, of which Richard Giffard was tenant; he died about 1190; Cecilia died in 1207; they had no children; Power, *Norman Frontier*, 508; Keats-Rohan, *Domesday Descendants*, 577.

(*neptis regis*), Gervaise de Dinan, daughter and heir of Alain de Vitré, great-grandson of Robert de Mortain and Clémence de Fougères, through whom he acquired lands in Brittany. In 1189, Juhel II de Mayenne, Guy V de Laval, and Radulf de Fougères supported Prince Richard against his dying father, King Henry II. Juhel II and Guillaume de Hercé followed kings Richard I of England and Philippe-Auguste of France on crusade in 1190. Juhel regained the castles of Ambrières, Gorron, and Châteauneuf-sur-Colmont, as well as the forest of Fosse-Louvain near Gorron, in 1199 from Arthur, count of Brittany and son of Geoffrey, elder brother of Kings Richard I and John. After King Richard's death, Gorron and Ambrières joined Mayenne in supporting Arthur of Brittany against King John, who was fighting against Arthur for the throne of England. In the end, John could only negotiate oaths, but not full submission, from the knights of Juhel, among them Guillaume de Gorron, who were faithful to Juhel. John did finally capture Ambrières and Gorron, but returned them to Juhel in a peace treaty in exchange for pledges of loyalty. After King John lost Normandy in 1204, Juhel II de Mayenne was one of the two most powerful lords in western France and served the French King Philippe-Auguste. Juhel II and his wife, on 19 May 1205, founded the Cistercian abbey of Fontaine-Daniel, a cell of Clermont, in his forest as a burial place for his family. Juhel II died in battle in April 1220.[63] In the fourteenth century, Péronnelle de Mayenne, the great-granddaughter of Juhel II de Mayenne, married Robin de Hercé. This indicates that the family de Hercé had risen in status in relation to the lords of Mayenne.

There were three strategic castles on the southern border of the Passais: Ambrières, built by Duke William about 1055, Gorron, built by the count of Mortain in 1082, and Châteauneuf-sur-Colmont, built by King Henry I in 1120. The latter two were very close to Hercé. The castles passed back and forth between the lords of Mayenne and the dukes of Normandy, later the kings of England. King Henry I exchanged lands in England and a gold cup with Hamelin de Mayenne for the castle of Ambrières. King Stephen forced Geoffroy of Anjou to return the three castles to Juhel I de Mayenne. After the death of Juhel I de Mayenne, in 1162 King Henry II retook possession and the Angevin rulers collected the taxes. However, after the death of King Richard I, Arthur of Brittany granted them back to Juhel II de Mayenne.

63. In the rebellion against King Henry II in support of Henry the Young King in 1173, Juhel de Mayenne, either the young Juhel II or his uncle Juhel, and Guillaume de Gorron were taken prisoner at Dol; PR 31 Henry II, 216 (1184–85); *CartFontaine-Daniel*. 1:18; d'Anisy, *Extraits*, vol. 1, Fontenay-le-Pesnel, 1, 354; *RotChart* 9; Guyard de la Fosse, *Preuves*, xviii–ix, xxx–xxxi; *Chronicon Savigniacensis Monasterii*, RHGF, 18:351; Power, *Norman Frontier*, 72, 245, 251–52, 399, 402–3, 405, 436–38, 461–62, 508: the lord of Vitré and Hasculf de Subligny were also pledges.

King John took Ambrières and Gorron briefly in 1201, but returned them to Mayenne as a condition of peace negotiations.[64]

The family de Mayenne intermarried with descendants of the dukes of Normandy and with the families de Hercé and de Laval of Maine, de Bellême of the Orne, de Presles of the Avranchin/Cotentin, de Lacy of Calvados, Talbot of the Pays de Caux, whose descendant later intermarried with a de Hercé, de Beaumont of the Eure, and de Vitré of Brittany. They founded the abbey of Fontaine-Daniel in Maine and supported the abbeys of Savigny in the Avranchin and Marmoutier in Tours. They were lords of the de Hercé family in Maine and the commanding officer of de Hercé in the conquest of England. However, they were not given land in England by William and returned to Maine, where a later daughter married Robin de Hercé. In the twelfth century members of the family held land in Worcestershire and in Leicestershire of the Talbots, who were Hercy relatives, and also in Yorkshire, where they may have interacted with the de Arches.

NORMANDY

There were two large clusters of Normans who went to England with William the Conqueror: one from Haute Normandie, Upper or Eastern Normandy, which included the Pays de Caux, Pays de Bray, and Eure, the other from Basse Normandie, Lower or Western Normandy, which included the regions of the Avranchin, Cotentin, Calvados, and Orne.

EASTERN UPPER NORMANDY (HAUTE NORMANDIE)

In Eastern Normandy, the Pays de Caux is a plateau with white cliffs of chalk on the northern coast and small valleys inland. Dieppe lies to the east on the coast, at the mouth of the river Arques and just east of the mouth of the river Scie. Dieppe was a natural deep harbor which attracted Scandinavian invaders, who gave it its name. Further inland the Pays de Bray was fertile agricultural land of clay soil, which was traversed by many rivers and springs. The name derived from the Gaulic word *braco*, meaning marsh or swamp. It lies between the Pays de Caux on the west and north and the Beauvaisis on the east, south of Eu and north of the Vexin. Farther south,

---

64. OV, 6:455, n. 4; *Testa de Nevill*, 1:86, 97; WJ, vol. 2, 8:38 *Torigni* 1:334–35; Stapleton, *MRSN*, 1:9, 23–24, 220–23, 2:353–56, 368; Power, *Norman Frontier*, 72–74, 163; J. Green, *Henry I*, 50.

Rouen lies on the Seine, and was a major center of trade. The region surrounding Rouen, the Roumois, was fertile agricultural land extending to the river Risle. The Eure is south of the Roumois.

Relatives of the de Hercé family from Eastern Normandy were from the d'Auffay, d'Arques, de Bolebec, and Talbot families. In the western Pays de Caux lived the family de Bolebec. To the east, in the arrondissement of Dieppe, which overlaps the Pays de Caux and the Pays de Bray, were the families d'Arques, d'Auffay, de Gournay, and de Neufmarché. The Talbot family originated in the Roumois but moved early to the Pays de Caux.

D'AUFFAY/DE SAINT-VALÉRY

According to Domesday Book and Orderic Vitalis, Osberne d'Arques /de Arches, ancestor of Théophanie de Arches de Hercy, received many of his lands in Yorkshire from his relative Gulbert d'Auffay, son of Richard de Saint-Valéry and Ada d'Heugleville. Auffay lies about fifteen miles south of Arques. The family of Auffay descended from the family of Saint-Valéry. Saint-Valéry-sur-Somme lies on the coast east of Normandy and was the port from which Duke William II sailed off to conquer England. There the cliffs of the Normandy coast disappear into the flat marshes of the bay of the Somme. The town grew up around the Benedictine abbey of Saint-Valéry, built in 615 by the Merovingian King Clothar II. The abbey was destroyed by the Vikings, but rebuilt by Hugues Capet in 981. The "avocat de Saint-Valéry" governed the town under the abbey. The first known avocat de Saint-Valéry married Emma *dite* de Ponthieu. They had a son, Gulbert I de Saint-Valéry, who married Papia, a daughter of Duke Richard I, *filiam Ricardi ducis*.[65]

Gulbert I and Papia had two sons, Bernard and Richard. Bernard I de Saint-Valéry welcomed Duke William II in 1066 and generously provided his large army with hospitality and supplies for two and a half weeks. Duke William prayed every day in the abbey for the weather to change so that

---

65. WJ 1:iv, 18: Duke Richard I had two illegitimate daughters; OV, 3:246–57, 5:34–35 calls him *Ricardi junioris ducis ex filia nomine Papia nepos*; however, a later Richard would be chronologically improbable; Dukes Richard I died in 996, Richard II in 1026, Richard III in 1027; Richard I de St-Valéry, son of Gulbert and Papia, had adult children by 1054; he had been given his wife Ada in marriage by his uncle Duke Richard II, who died in 1026; Keats-Rohan, *Domesday People*, 453–54, posits Richard III, but that does not fit the chronology; Chibnall, in OV, 3:367, has Papia the daughter of Duke Richard II and Richard de St-Valéry as the son of Bernard, but again this is not possible because it would make Papia born in the 1020s with an adult grandson by 1054.

he could leave for England. The weather finally became auspicious, and Duke William embarked with his army and Bernard's son, Walter. Walter de Saint-Valéry fought at Hastings with Duke William in 1066. He was a tenant-in-chief in Middlesex and Suffolk in 1086. He went on the First Crusade and took part in the siege of Nicaea. He married Hodierna de Montlhéry, who had visited Cluny where the abbot gave her a gold chalice. They had a son Bernard II de Saint-Valéry who was also at Nicaea in the First Crusade and may have fought at Hastings. Bernard II married Mathilde, the widow of a count. They had a son, Reginald/Rénaud de Saint-Valéry, who held lands in Oxfordshire and Berkshire, which he lost in 1144 because he supported Henry of Anjou against King Stephen, who granted his lands to John de St. John. Reginald served first Duke Geoffroy of Anjou and then his son, Duke Henry of Normandy and Anjou, the future King Henry II of England. As king, Henry II restored Reginald's lands. In 1151/53 Reginald donated to the Angevin convent of Fontevrauld, where Queen Eléanore of Aquitaine and kings Henry II and Richard I were buried later. In 1163, he and Bishop Rotrou of Évreux affirmed the rights of King Henry II over Normandy. Reginald had three sons: Bernard III, who held Saint-Valéry and land in Oxfordshire and donated to Fontevraud and Berteaucourt Abbeys, Gauthier, archdeacon of Rouen, and Guy, who witnessed charters of King Henry II, and a daughter Béatrice, who married Guérmond de Picquigny of Amiens and was mother of Gérard II de Picquigny.[66]

The second son of Gulbert and Papia was Richard de Saint-Valéry, who had fought for his uncle, Duke Richard II. In gratitude, Duke Richard II arranged Richard's marriage to Ada, widow and heir of Herluin, lord of Heugleville-sur-Scie, arrondissement Dieppe, canton Longueville-sur-Scie. Thereafter he was known as Richard de Heugleville. He built a castle and a

---

66. Wace, 3:6353, 6399-464, 8701-3, Brompton; Le Tailleur; Falaise has Bernard and Renouf; Dives has Gauthier, Bernard, and Renouf; if Renouf refers to Renaud, it is chronologically impossible; OV, 3:252-53, 366-67, 5:34-35, 58-59; Walter may have had a first marriage or affair with Papia, illegitimate daughter of Duke Richard II, making the latter his uncle; *Torigni, RHGF*, 1:240-41, 2:200-201, 10:270, 11:275, 13:238, 23:452; *Actes Henri II* vol. 1, nos. 8, 11, 36-37, 44-45, 395; Reginald made an extensive pilgrimage to the Holy Land, where he witnessed charters in 1159 and 1160; RBE, 1:31, 32, 51, 204-7, 305, 2:586, 638, 645, 696, 698; MA, 4:363, 5:425; *CartOseney*, vol. 4, no. 20b; *RRAN*, vol. 2, no. 797, vol. 3, nos. 17, 53, 57, 71-72, 303-4, 329, 601, 665, 729, 732, 806, 853; PR 31 Henry I, 14, 119; letter of Pope Alexander III to Henri archbishop of Reims dated 29 March 1154 links the Pinkeny and de St. Valéry families; Bernard III had a daughter Maud, wife of William de Braose, who herself administered a castle in Wales and voiced her opposition to King John, who then starved her and her son to death; there is a possible connection between the Hercy family in Buckinghamshire and the Pinkeny family; Keats-Rohan, *Domesday People*, 453-54; Keats-Rohan, *Domesday Descendants*, 698-99.

town nearby at Isneauville, which he called Auffay after its hill covered with beech trees (*alfagium*). Both Heugleville and Auffay lie on the Scie River. Auffay was in the bailliage of Arques. Richard and Ada had three children: Gulbert d'Auffay, Ada, who married Geoffroy de Neufmarché, and Robert de Heugleville. Richard fought for Duke Richard II's grandson, the young Duke William II, against the revolt of Count Guillaume d'Arques-Talou in 1052–54 with his son-in-law Geoffroy de Neufmarché and Geoffroy's brother Hugues de Morimont, who was killed in the battle; both were sons of Turchetil de Neufmarché, one of the guardians of young Duke William.[67]

Gulbert d'Auffay fought bravely at Hastings at the head of his vassals for his *consanguinus* Duke William. King William rewarded him by giving him lands in Yorkshire. Gulbert returned the English lands, stating that he did not want to profit from war and was content with his estates in Normandy. He returned to Normandy and his English lands went to his relative, Osberne d'Arques/de Arches. It is not known exactly how they were related, but it is well documented that they were related. Between 1144 and 1150, Geoffroy duke of Normandy and Anjou addressed an order to Gulbert's cousin, Reginald de St-Valéry "*et ministeriis suis de Archis*," indicating a familial or vassal relationship between de Saint-Valéry and d'Arques. Gulbert married Béatrice, the daughter of Christian de Valenciennes of Flanders and a cousin of Queen Mathilda (*reginae consobrina*). A supporter of St.-Évroul, Gulbert, with the consent of wife, made the parish church of Sainte-Marie in Auffay a college of Augustinian canons, Collégiale de Nôtre-Dame, then gave it to St. Évroul as a Benedictine priory in about 1060, when Robert de Grandmesnil was abbot. They also gave it two assloads of wood daily, two measures of wheat per year, and more from two churches which were prebends of Auffay, and urged their vassals also to give it support. The document dated 1079 confirming the donation was witnessed by Bernard de Neufmarché and Robert de Heugleville. For his gifts, Gulbert was called *generosus in Normannia miles* by Orderic Vitalis, who was a monk of St. Évroul. There is a later inscription in the church of the Collégiale de Nôtre-Dame, Auffay, thanking Gulbert for building it, calling him: "*petit neveu de Guillaume le Conquerant et l'un de ses compagnons a Hastings, fondateur.*" After he returned from England to Normandy, Gulbert dedicated his son, Hugues, to the abbey of Saint-Évroul as a monk. In 1085, King William judged a case between Gulbert and the abbey of Fécamp concerning a wood. In attendance were Abbot Mainier of St. Évroul and Abbot Fulk of Saint-Pierre-sur-Dives. The same year Gulbert donated a tenth of his cheese

---

67. OV, 3:226–27, 252–53 (Richard called the duke "uncle," *avunculo*), 254–55 (Arques); Le Parquier, *Cahiers*, 2:400, 410.

production to Fécamp. Gulbert d'Auffay died on 15 August 1087 and was buried in the monastery church of Nôtre-Dame d'Auffay. After his death, his widow became a nun at the priory of Nôtre-Dame until her death four years later, when she was buried there with her husband. They had three children: Gauthier, who succeeded, Hugues, who became a monk at St.-Évroul, and Béatrice d'Auffay.[68]

Gauthier d'Auffay, son of Gulbert, was lord of Auffay and married Avice. Orderic Vitalis said that Gauthier was handsome but lacking in wisdom. However, he also said that Avice lived in joy with her husband, something which was not always the case in arranged marriages. Avice had three brothers who were knights, Jordan, Guillaume, and Robert, who helped her husband manage the estates. Gauthier and Avice confirmed and added to the gifts of his father to St. Évroul. Avice donated out of her own funds wax and oil for lamps and incense. They had twelve children, of whom eight died in infancy. They had four surviving sons: Richard, who died young, Jordan, who inherited, Gauthier, who was called *consanguinus* of Roger, son of Richard de Clare, Gauthier, and Elias. They were minors at the time of their parents' deaths, and were taken to England where they were held in ward and raised by King Henry I.[69]

Gulbert d'Auffay's sister Ada married Geoffroy de Neufmarché, arrondissement Dieppe, canton Gournay-en-Bray, in the valley of the Epte. Geoffroy's father, Turchetil de Neufmarché, was one of the murdered guardians of the young Duke William II. He had two sons: Geoffroy de Neufmarché, who succeeded, and Hugues de Morimont. In 1053/54, Geoffroy and Hugues fought with Geoffroy's father-in-law, Richard de Heugleville, for Duke William against Count Guillaume d'Arques et Talou. Hugues fought in the battle at the castle beside the church of St. Aubin and was killed near Morimont. Geoffroy and Ada had three sons: Bernard, who fought for three English kings and became lord of Brecknock, Dreux, who left his military career and became a monk of St.-Évroul, and Osbern. All three supported St.-Évroul. In 1081, the abbot of St.-Évroul took Dreux and Roger de Warenne to England to witness a charter confirming the

---

68. Dives; Falaise; OV, 3:244–61, 4:112–13; *RRAN*, 1:207; 3:732; Bates, *Normandy*, 219; Gulbert was the great-nephew of Duke Richard II but second cousin of Duke William II, although if his mother was the aunt instead of cousin of Queen Mathilde, he would have been her grandnephew.

69. OV, 3:250–61, 4:236–37 (Gualterius de Alfagio); RBE, 2:633; the king gave Jordan a manor in Somerset at the time of his marriage; Jordan's son Richard had a son, Jean, who had a daughter Aude, dame d'Auffay, who married Guillaume IV de Tancarville in 1239, at which time the family name ceased at Auffay.

possessions of St.-Évroul by King William, visiting the king and Lanfranc, archbishop of Canterbury.[70]

The family d'Auffay and de Saint-Valéry descended from the ducal house and intermarried with the families de Heugleville and de Neufmarché of arrondissement Dieppe in Eastern Normandy and Picquigny of Picardy, and were related to the family of Arques. The d'Auffay family founded the priory at Auffay and supported the abbeys of St-Évroul in the Orne, Fécamp in the Pays de Caux, and Fontevrauld in Anjou. In England, the de Saint-Valéry and de Neufmarché families held many lands in Yorkshire, as well as lands in Warwickshire, Nottinghamshire, and Worcestershire where they may have interacted with the de Hercy family.

D'ARQUES/DE ARCHES

The de Hercé family of Maine married into the d'Arques family of the vicomté of Arques in Eastern Normandy. In England the name was anglicized to de Arches. The caput of the *vicomté* was at Arques-la-Bataille, arrondissement Dieppe, canton Offranville. Arques lies in a region of forested hills where three rivers, the Arques, Varenne, and Béthune, come together.

The history of Arques is confusing because it was briefly a *comté*, but also for much longer a *vicomté*. In the mid-eleventh century, Arques had both a *comte* and a *vicomte*. Documents from about 1043 show Guillaume comte d'Arques et Talou governing at the same time Godfroy was vicomte d'Arques. The two were not related. Guillaume, the illegitimate son of Duke Richard II, persuaded his young nephew, Duke William II, to make him count of Arques and Talou. The Pays de Talou was a larger district from Roman times and Arques was its capital. By about 1040, Arques had come to overshadow Talou, which gradually faded from notice. Count Guillaume built a great castle at Arques atop a rocky cliff, dominating the town and the river valleys. In 1052, Count Guillaume d'Arques-Talou and his brother Mauger, bishop of Rouen, uncles of the young Duke William, rebelled against him and tried to seize power in Eastern Normandy. They were opposed by Richard de Heugleville of Auffay, his son-in-law Geoffroy de Neufmarché, and Geoffroy's brother Hugues de Morimont. In the end, Duke William and Walter Giffard besieged the castle of Arques, which fell

---

70. Neufmarché was first mentioned in the treaty of St-Clair-sur-Epte; the name means new march, frontier, border; OV, 2:128–31, 3:226–27, 232–33, 246–47, 252–61; *RRAN*, 1:62, 113, 207, 220, 325, 2:1041, 1280; EYC, vol. 8, no.5; *MA*, 3:264, 546; Ward, *Women*, 26–27; Bates, *Normandy*, 57, 77, 177; Keats-Rohan, *Domesday Descendants*, 616–17.

in 1053. Duke William expelled Count Guillaume from Normandy and had Mauger deposed as archbishop by papal decree. Mauger was then exiled from Normandy by the council of Lisieux.[71]

The vicomté d'Arques existed for a much longer period than the *comté*. In 1025 Rainald, vicomte d'Arques, donated his possessions in Arques and Tourville to the abbey of Fécamp, as attested by Duke Richard II, witnessed by Goscelin de Rouen, and confirmed by Duke Robert II. Later, Abbot John granted the lands to Vicomte Goscelin of Rouen, who thereby became also "by the grace of God vicomte d'Arques." Goscelin was the regulator of weights and measures for all of Normandy and an important lord in the courts of Dukes Richard I and Richard II. Goscelin and Emmeline, his wife, were founders of the abbeys of Saint-Amand and Sainte-Trinité at Rouen. Their daughter, Béatrice, married Godfroy, son of Osbern de Bolebec.[72]

Godfroy succeeded his father-in-law as vicomte d'Arques. Godfroy was a donor to the abbey of Sainte-Trinité like his father-in-law. Shortly before their deaths, Godfroy entered the abbey of Sainte-Trinité as a monk and Béatrice entered the abbey of Saint-Amand, which her parents had founded at Rouen. Godfroy and Béatrice were the parents of William, who succeeded as vicomte d'Arques, and Gislebert d'Arques, bishop of Évreux, and possibly also of Osberne d'Arques.[73]

Vicomte William d'Arques, son of Godfroy, rose to prominence as administrator of Arques and benefactor of the abbeys at Rouen. However, William neglected the abbey of Fécamp and the monks complained to William, now King William I. On his way to reprimand Vicomte William, the king was summoned back to England and the punishment never took place. Later Vicomte William witnessed charters for the king and received lands in the south of England. Vicomte William d'Arques married Béatrice Malet, daughter of William Malet and Hesilia Crispin.[74]

---

71. Wace, 3:1855–57, 3400–54, 3515–60; Loyd, *Origins*, 5–6; Arques is from Latin *Arx*, which means citadel; WJ, 2:viii, 37; Deville, *Histoire*, 1, 4, 41–43, 87, 405; WP, 1:24–27.

72. MA, 6:2, 1101; *CartSte-Trinité*, no. 1; Goscelin's charter to Ste-Trinité with Duke William in 1035–50, witnessed by *filii Turchitili* Hugues et Godfroy; OV, 2:11–12; WJ, 2:viii, 37, wrote that Osbern de Bolebec and the sister of Gunnora had Walter Giffard first, then Godfroy; Haskins, *Norman Institutions*, nos. 6 and 10, 258, 260–61; Power, *Norman Frontier*, 219; Douglas, *William*, 93–94.

73. Deville, *Histoire*, 13, 20, 95; the relationship between William and Osberne and the parentage of Osberne are disputed and there is no conclusive evidence, although it is significant that the same first name was held by Osbern de Bolebec and Osberne de Arches, who may have been grandfather and grandson; such naming was common usage at the time.

74. RRAN, 2:933; in 1086 William d'Arques held lands in Kent and elsewhere of

William d'Arques and Osberne d'Arques accompanied Duke William to England, although probably after Hastings. William became lord of Folkstone in Kent and Osberne lord and tenant-in-chief in Yorkshire and Lincolnshire. There is no proof of the exact relationship between William and Osberne, although both were presumably from the family of Arques-la-Bataille. A charter in which Duke William returned some churches to Saint-Wandrille was witnessed by Vicomte Godfroy, and by both William and Osberne d'Arques together. This is perhaps the best evidence for the close relationship between William and Osberne, and places them physically in the same room at the same time with each other and with Godfroy, who would have presumably been the father of both. Once in England, both William and Osberne lost contact with Arques in Normandy after the death of King William I.[75] The descendant of Osberne d'Arques, Théophanie de Arches, married Malveysin de Hercy in Nottinghamshire.

DE BOLEBEC

The history of the complex interrelated families of de Bolebec, Giffard, and d'Arques began in the Pays de Caux. The name Bolebec is a toponym, a name derived from a place. The name Giffard is a sobriquet, a nickname derived from physical characteristics, meaning "fat cheeks." The de Bolebec family were from Bolebec, arrondissement Le Havre, canton Bolebec, on the river Bolebec, probably named for a Scandinavian called Bolli, and "bec" meaning stream. Osbern de Bolebec was the first known lord of Bolebec in the late tenth century. He was the grandfather of the d'Arques family. He married Avelina or Wevia, a sister of Duchess Gunnora, the mistress/wife of Duke Richard I. They had sons Walter Giffard and Godefroy, who through marriage to the daughter of Goscelin, vicomte of Rouen and Arques, became vicomte d'Arques and father of William d'Arques, and probably also of Osberne d'Arques. It was a common practice to name sons after their

---

Odo of Bayeux and Robert Malet, and in 1093 he held Folkestone (of Odo; 3:634–35; *MA*, 4:674; the younger daughter of William d'Arques and his wife Béatrice was Maud d'Arques, who married William de Tancarville, chamberlain of Normandy, and inherited her father's estates in Normandy; their elder daughter, Emma, inherited Folkestone in England, married Nigel de Monville, arr. Rouen, and had a daughter, Mathilde, who married Rualon d'Avranches; their son William d'Avranches inherited Folkestone; *RBE*, 1:192–3; Keats-Rohan, *Domesday People*, 302, 470.

75. Only mentioned in Le Tailleur (erle), and late French sources; Dives and Falaise name both William and Osbern; OV, 3:252–57; *RRAN*, 1:123, 2:1086, 3:634, 635; *MA*, 3:547–48; Hollister, *Monarchy*, 142–43; Power, *Norman Frontier*, 369, 377; Keats-Rohan, *Domesday People*, 314, 470; Green, *Aristocracy*, 377–78, citing Douglas.

grandfathers. Osbern de Bolebec was himself also called Giffard. The names de Bolebec and Giffard were sometimes used interchangeably. Inscriptions, now lost, named Lora, wife of Robert Hampdon, as both "daughter of de Bolebec" and "daughter of Giffard." Osbern de Bolebec had two brothers, as well as other children and the name de Bolebec continued, although henceforth those called de Bolebec were subject to the descendants of his eldest son, Walter Giffard. Hugh de Bolebec fought at Hastings.[76]

The Bolebec family was closely interrelated with the Giffard family and the names were used interchangeably. Both families descended from Osbern de Bolebec and the dukes of Normandy, as did the family d'Arques with which they intermarried.[77] In England they were related to the de Arches family, and interacted with the de Hercy family in Warwickshire, with the de Arches in Yorkshire and the de Hériz in Nottinghamshire.

TALBOT

The Talbot family originated at Sainte-Croix-sur-Buchy, arrondissement Rouen, under the Gournay lords of Gournay-en-Bray. Then from about 1071 they held a *fief-franc* under the Giffards at Cleuville, in the Pays de Caux, arrondissement Le Havre, which became the caput of the Talbots in Normandy. The two earliest documented Talbots, Guillaume and Hugues, lived in the early to mid-eleventh century. Guillaume Talbot was lord of Cleuville. He donated to the abbey of Saint-Michel-du-Tréport with the consent of Robert count of Eu and his wife Béatrice. Guillaume Talbot was reputed to be the son of Robert d'Eu. Hugues was a donor to the abbeys of Sainte-Trinité at Rouen and Saint-Victor-en-Caux, the former donation witnessed by Gulbert d'Eu and Osbern son of Goisfrid d'Eu.[78] Guillaume Talbot had two sons: Richard and Geoffrey.

76. Wace, 3:8535, "old Hugh de Bolebec" at Hastings; Le Tailleur mentions Bolebec at Hastings; WJ, 2:viii, 37; *Torigni*, vol. 8, 35; CPE, 11:683; *RRAN*, vol. 3, no. 874; CDF, no. 702; the daughter of Osbern and his first wife married Tesselin de Vascoeuil, vicomte de Rouen, and had a daughter, Béatrice de Vascoeuil, who married Radulf de Warenne, called *filius episcopi* because his father Hugues was bishop of Coutances, about 1010; Lipscomb, *History*, 229 note: inscriptions on broken glass; Lora was actually the daughter of Richard de Bienfaite and Rohaise Giffard, 347.

77. EYC, vol. 2, no. 788; J. Green, *Aristocracy*, 45.

78. *Fief-franc* was a fief held by one not of noble birth who paid a tax rather than knight service; CartSt-Michel, 5, 13: charters dated 1036 and 1059; Archbishop Hugues of Rouen in 1137 confirmed his donations to Saint-Victor-en-Caux; *CartSte-Trinité*, 451; MA, 49, 105; Loyd, *Origins*, 40, 100.

Richard I Talbot supported Duke William in the conquest of England and fought at Hastings. Richard I held land at Cleuville and, through the abbey of Saint-Ouen in Rouen, exchanged land in Gouy, near Rouen, for land in Ancourteville-Héricourt in the Pays de Caux near Cleuville. In England in 1086 he was a tenant of Walter Giffard in Bedfordshire. Richard married Amicie de Gournay, daughter of Gérard de Gournay. They donated to Valmont Abbey and the priory of Sainte-Foi de Longueville in the Pays de Caux between Auffay and Arques. They had a son Hugues who inherited Cleuville and married Marie de Meulan, daughter of Waleran de Beaumont.[79]

The Talbot family was closely related to the counts of Eu and the de Gournay family of the Pays de Bray. In England they held lands in Worcestershire, Yorkshire, Nottinghamshire, Derbyshire, Buckinghamshire, Bedfordshire, Leicestershire, Devon, Norfolk, Essex, Kent, and Herefordshire. Later a Talbot descendant would marry into the de Hercy family. They were related to the de Hercy and de Hériz families in Nottinghamshire by marriage and the Talbot earls of Shrewsbury in Yorkshire were the primary lords of the de Hercy family in the sixteenth and early seventeenth centuries.

WESTERN LOWER NORMANDY (BASSE NORMANDIE)

There are four regions in Western Normandy: in the west the Avranchin and north of it the Cotentin peninsula; in the east Calvados, and further south, the Orne. Some families which played a prominent role in the history of the de Hercé and de Hériz families had roots in both the Avranchin/Cotentin and Calvados, notably the d'Avranches, Paynel, and de Percy families. Other families, including the Basset family, straddled Calvados and the Orne.

DE HÉRIZ

The second known intermarriage of the de Hercé family in England was between Sir Hugh I de Hercy of Grove, Nottinghamshire, and Elizabeth, the daughter of John de Hériz of Gonalston, Nottinghamshire, and South Wingfield, Derbyshire. The roots of the de Hériz family in Western Normandy are complex and the documentary sources only begin in the twelfth century. The de Hériz were vassals of the vicomtes of Avranches in the Avranchin. They were tenants of the de Saint-Jean family in the Avranchin.

---

79. Brompton; Leland; Holinshed; Duchesne; Falaise; Dives; Keats-Rohan, *Domesday People*, 368.

Robert and Geoffrey de Hériz were documented accompanying Duke William II in the conquest of England and fighting at Hastings. In England, they emerged early with a group from the Avranchin who were tenants and vassals of William Peverel. They settled in the Honour of Peverel in southern Nottinghamshire and south Derbyshire. The sources about the family in Normandy are later, from the mid- to late twelfth century, and derive from several different locations in Western Normandy. Some persons are named de Hériz, suggesting that they are from a place of that name; others are called Le Héricy, which could be a sobriquet, meaning "spiky," which might correlate with the distinctive hedgehogs in the family coat of arms. The origin of the family was most probably in the Avranchin, but possibly also may have had roots in the Cotentin and/or Calvados.[80]

The de Hériz family was documented at La Rochelle in the Avranchin in the mid-twelfth century. Their holding was then called La Rochelle, arrondissement Avranches, canton La Haye-Pesnel. It was later called La Rochelle-le-Héricière, and now La Rochelle-Normande. It was rocky land, surrounded by small rivers and streams, with a church and a small château. It was a third part of a *fief d'haubert*, land held by a knight, at this time by their landlord, William II de Saint-Jean, directly of the duke of Normandy. The twelfth-century church of Sainte-Marie in La Rochelle was dependent on Lucerne Abbey. The stalls in the church came from the abbey. A small castle was built in the eleventh or twelfth century, replacing an earlier smaller fort.[81]

The family de Hériz were tenants at La Rochelle of the family of Saint-Jean-le-Thomas, arrondissement Avranches. Radulf de Saint-Jean fought with Duke William at Hastings and had sons Thomas, Guillaume I, Jean, and Roger. Thomas de Saint-Jean supported King Henry I of England, fighting for him at Tinchebrai in 1106. Roger and Jean de Saint-Jean fought for King Henry I in Maine in 1118. Jean, Roger, and Thomas de Saint Jean were vassals of Le Mont-Saint-Michel.[82]

In 1162 Robert de Hériz was the tenant at La Rochelle of William II de Saint-Jean, who had succeeded on the death of his father, Roger, in 1130.

80. Other possible places of origin will be discussed in Appendix IV; *MA*, 4:111–12; HKF, 1:181; Keats-Rohan, *Domesday People*, 376–77.

81. *Revue de l'Avranchin*, vols. 27–28 (1934) 388: "le sire de Hériz fit construire son château de la Hérisière"; Rochella in *CartLuzerne*, in 1698 the church had three priests; Le Héricher, *Avranchin*, 131–33; Stenton, *First Century*, 15–16.

82. CPE, 11:340; *Chronique de Normandie*, RHGF, 13:257; CDF, nos. 710, 723; OV, 6:94–97, 194–97; *RRAN*, 2:1400–1401, 1407, 1418, 1422: Thomas and his brothers were raised by the monks of Le Mont-Saint-Michel; RBE, 1:65, 72, 124, 126, 204–7, 301, 326, 2:638; Hollister, *Monarchy*, 282; Le Héricher, *Avranchin*, 132–33: case of Le Mont-Saint-Michel against Thomas, resolved by King Henry I; J. Green, *Henry I*, 239.

William II served Kings Henry I, Henry II, and Richard I of England. William II was a founder of Lucerne Abbey and in 1145 it was moved onto his land. William II de Saint-Jean, his wife, and his brother Robert were major donors to Lucerne Abbey in 1162.

Lucerne Abbey, canton La Haye-Pesnel, lies between La Rochelle and La Haye-Pesnel in the Thar valley. The land was hilly, with forests and fields. At first, in 1143, the monastery was only a chapel in the forest of Courbefosse with two monks from Calvados: Tancred, of the Dammartin family, the first prior, and Etienne. On the feast of St. Luke in 1145, it was moved to the Thar valley, to land of William II de Saint-Jean. The abbey was cofounded by Hasculf de Subligny and his brother Richard, bishop of Avranches. Hasculf married Denise, daughter of Gilbert d'Avranches. They had a son who died in 1170 and a daughter Lesceline, who married Fulk I Paynel of La Haye-Pesnel and Drax, Yorkshire. His younger brother, Robert, had a son, Jean de Subligny, who was in the court of King Henry II. The king married Jean's son Hasculf to Isolde, heiress of Dol in Brittany, in an attempt to bind Brittany and Normandy together. Jean de Subligny witnessed the Breton-Norman marriage of Eléanore de Vitré of Brittany and his cousin William Paynel.[83]

Lucerne Abbey of the Most Holy Trinity was staffed by Premonstratensian canons. In 1161, when Blessed Achard was bishop of Avranches, it was moved again to its final site, between the Thar and Tharnet, on land belonging to Hasculf de Subligny at Lucerne d'Outremer. The move was confirmed by King Henry II and witnessed by Richard du Hommet, constable of Normandy, in 1162. At this time, William II de Saint-Jean donated the church of Saint-Jean-le-Thomas and its revenues to Lucerne Abbey. The stone abbey was built before 1171 when Blessed Achard de Saint-Victor, bishop of Avranches, was buried there. William II de Saint-Jean and Hasculph de Subligny are buried side-by-side in the chapel in the left transept of the abbey church. The wide interior world of this small monastery was described as encompassing religion, science, art, agriculture, and diplomacy. Although located in the rural Avranchin, Lucerne Abbey was a major intellectual centre patronized by kings.[84]

---

83. A lord of Subligny was mentioned in two of the 1066 rolls, Le Tailleur and Falaise, and in Wace, 3:8469; a member of the Subligny family accompanied Robert Curthose on the First Crusade; *CEC*, nos. 10, 141, 147; *RRAN*, vol. 3, nos. 332, 810–11; PR 31 Henry I, 1:6; RBE, 1:430; EYC, vol. 6, nos. 21–22; Lesceline de Subligny and Fulk I Paynel had sons Fulk II, William, and John; Broussillon, 153; Le Héricher, *Avranchin*, 68, 136–37; Power, *Norman Frontier*, 234, 240, 518–19; Keats-Rohan, *Domesday Descendants*, 725–26.

84. *CartLuzerne*, 3 (Henry II), 221–28; witnesses to a document of 1161 included Robert de Saint-Jean, Robert de la Rochelle, and Roger Paupère de la Rochelle; *Gallia*

Robert de Hériz, with consent of his sons Roger and André, made generous donations in 1162 to the parish of La Rochelle and to Lucerne Abbey for his own soul and that of his wife Agnes. The same year, the charter of William II de Saint-Jean on the donation to the abbey of the church of La Rochelle states that Roger, Robert's son, held the right of patronage in the church of La Rochelle. Donations of his other son, André de la Rochelle, were also noted in 1162 and confirmed in 1175 by Richard, bishop of Avranches. Both charters were witnessed by Roger de Saint-Jean and Roger de la Rochelle. Both charters were later confirmed in a bull of Pope Urban III in 1186, noting the gifts of Robert de Hériz and his son Roger to Lucerne Abbey. By the late twelfth century, the family de Hériz was also called de la Rochelle, although the name de Hériz was still used at La Rochelle-la-Héricière. Roger de Hériz died in 1213. His heirs were his sons, Robert de la Rochelle and Roger, both of whom were knights. Another son or grandson, Olivier, was a cleric. Thomas de la Rochelle had a daughter with the name de Hériz.[85]

The de Hériz family was well documented at La Rochelle in the twelfth century. The de Hériz family in England was amply documented in the eleventh century under the lordship of William Peverel of Vengeons in the Avranchin, which was about twenty-two miles from La Rochelle. This makes it most probable that the home of the de Hériz family in the eleventh century was in the Avranchin.[86]

LORDS OF THE DE HÉRIZ FAMILY: AVRANCHIN AND COTENTIN

The western part of Western Normandy, between the Vire estuary and the bay of Le Mont-Saint-Michel, consists of the Avranchin in the south and the Cotentin peninsula in the north. It was invaded by Vikings from the mid-ninth century until 933. The Norman lords from the Avranchin/Cotentin who went to England and were interrelated by blood, marriage, or vassalage

---

christiana. Lucerna, vol. 11, cols. 556–57; donors also included nearby lords of Mortain and Sartilly; RBE, 2:638 (1172); *Actes Henri II*, vol. 1, no. 80; Le Héricher, *Avranchin*, 72, 75–79, 82; the de Beauchamp family were also patrons of Lucerne and were buried there from 1300.

85. *CartLuzerne*, 4–8: *Carta de Willelmi de Sancto Johannae*, 1162; 11–14: *carta* of Bishop Richard of Avranches, Saint-Jean, and la Rochelle, 1175; 222–27: *Bulla Urbani III* (Robert de Percy also mentioned as donor); RBE, 1:124, 176; CDF, no. 776; Olivier may have been the son of Roger.

86. The other possible locations of the de Hériz family are discussed in Appendix IV.

were from the de Hériz, d'Avranches, de Beauchamp, de Brus, du Hommet, Paynel, Peverel, and Tesson families. Five of these families, including the d'Avranches, du Hommet, Paynel, and Tesson families and possibly the de Hériz family, also had roots in Calvados.

The Avranchin and the city of Avranches were named for the Gaulic tribe of Abrincatui.[87] Avranches was the site of a Roman town and a Merovingian diocese. The city of Avranches lies near the coast, on a granite hill facing the bay of Le Mont-Saint-Michel. It was the caput of the vicomté of the Avranchin.

The first known *vicomte* of the Avranches, Turstin le Goz, was the son of Ansfrid the Dane. Turstin served the dukes of Normandy and witnessed donation charters for Duke Richard II in 1025 to Fécamp and in 1027 to Bernay Abbeys, and for Duke Robert II in 1030 to Le Mont-Saint-Michel. He also witnessed donations of Guillaume comte de Talou et d'Arques to Jumièges in 1040 and of Vicomte Goscelin of Rouen to Sainte-Trinité de Rouen, both in Eastern Normandy. He rebelled against Duke William II at Falaise and fled into exile.[88]

Turstin was succeeded as vicomte d'Avranches by his elder son Richard le Goz, who was a loyal supporter of Duke William II, for whom he had the duty to defend Normandy against Brittany. Richard le Goz witnessed charters for donations and claims concerning the abbeys of Le Mont-Saint-Michel, Saumur, and Marmoutier. In 1066, Vicomte Richard donated sixty ships to Duke William, accompanied him to England, and fought at Hastings. He witnessed a royal charter for King William in 1069 and one for Odo of Bayeux in 1074.[89] Richard married Emma de Conteville, the sister of Robert de Mortain and Odo of Bayeux and half-sister of Duke William. Richard le Goz and his wife had children: Hugh d'Avranches, who succeeded and went to England, Marguérite, who married Ranulf, vicomte du Bessin et de Bayeux of Calvados, and was the mother of Hugh's successors, Hélisende, who married Count Guillaume II d'Eu, and Judith, who married Richer de Laigle.[90] Richard le Goz died about 1082.

Hugh d'Avranches succeeded and went to England, where he was given many lands and made earl of Chester. In Normandy, he was survived, but

---

87. Pliny the Elder, *Naturalis historia*, iv, 18/107.

88. WJ, 2:vii, 3(6); Delisle, *Pièces*, nos. 6, 7, 9, 16; Douglas, *William*, 140–41.

89. Delisle, *Pièces*, nos. 22, 25; Broussillon, 1:28, 39; Wace, 3:8467 (*d'Aurencein i fu Richarz*); Le Tailleur, Falaise (Richard vicomte d'Avranches), Dives (Hugues); *Extrait de la chronique de Normandie*, RHGF, 8:237; CartSte-Trinité, lxvii, 455; Bayeux Livre Noir, 1:3–4.

90. MA, 2:384; OV, 2:120–21, 260–63; CDF, no. 622; Guillaume d'Eu later married Béatrice de Bully, heir of Tickhill; Douglas, *William*, 93.

not succeeded, by his younger brother, Gilbert, who witnessed charters for earl Ranulf I and for Thomas de Saint-Jean. Gilbert d'Avranches supported the abbey of Saint-Sever. He left a daughter, Denise, who about 1140 married Hasculf de Subligny of La Haye-Pesnel in the Avranchin, cofounder of Lucerne Abbey. Hasculf's brother Richard was bishop of Avranches from 1142 to 1153.[91] This illustrates the close connection between Avranches and Lucerne Abbey.

Wimund/Guitmund d'Avranches was possibly a younger brother of Turstin or Richard le Goz. Wimund was lord of La Haye-Pesnel. He witnessed charters with Turstin in 1027 and 1040. He had a daughter who married William II Paynel, and a son Robert, who married first Hawise de Dol in Brittany, and second Mathilde d'Avenel of the Cotentin. The daughter of Robert and Mathilde, also named Mathilde, married Robert FitzRoy, illegitimate son of King Henry I and Edith Forne.[92]

The d'Avranches family were the overlords of all the families of the Avranchin, including the de Hériz. The d'Avranches family intermarried with the ducal family and the families de Subligny and Paynel of the Avranchin, du Bessin of Calvados, de Laigle of the Orne, and d'Eu of Eastern Normandy. They founded the abbey of Saint-Sever and supported the abbeys of Lucerne, Saint-Sever, Saint-Évroul, and Bec in Normandy, and in England founded St. Werburgh in Chester and supported Abingdon and Whitby Abbeys. In England they interacted with the locus of the de Hercy family in Warwickshire, with the de Arches in Yorkshire and with the de Hériz in Nottinghamshire.

PEVEREL

The Peverel family was of low stature in Normandy, but very quickly rose high in England. William Peverel was reputed to be the illegitimate son of Duke William II by his mistress, Maud Ingelrica, who later married Ranulf Peverel, but this is unsubstantiated. The name Peverel does not refer to a fief or place, but derives from the Latin *piperellus* or *puerullus* meaning "little boy child."[93]

91. CEC, nos. 3, 10, 12 (1121–29), 24–28 (1136–53); RBE, 2:640, 643; Hasculf de Subligny lived from 1092 to 1169; *Torigni*, 1:132–33, 178–79, 2:366–67; HKF, 2:1–293; in 1172, Gilbert d'Avranches held two fees in the *bailliage* of Tinchebray, and Guillaume d'Avranches held one fee of Mortain; Keats-Rohan, *Domesday People*, 258–60.

92. OV, 4:112–13; *Neustria pia*, 398; Bracton, *Notebook*, 2:137, no. 170; MA, 5:378.

93. RRAN, vol. 3, no. 345; MA, 3:294–95; Planché, *Conqueror*, 2:259–73; Dugdale, *Baronage*, 1:436; J. Green, *Aristocracy*, 45, 89; Keats-Rohan, *Domesday People*, 355–56, rejects the hypothesis of his ducal parentage.

William I Peverel and his father or stepfather, Ranulf Peverel, lived in Vengeons near Mortain, arrondissement Avranches, canton Sourdeval, in the Avranchin. Ranulf and his wife had another son, Robert. Robert donated land in Vengeons to the monks of Savigny with permission of Stephen of Mortain and Richard d'Avranches, earl of Chester, which was confirmed in 1106 by King Henry I. William I Peverel also held Turgistorp/Clitourps in the diocese of Coutances in the northern Cotentin. He donated land from Turgistorp to the monastery of Saint-Sauveur-le-Vicomte.[94]

William I and Ranulf Peverel went to England with Duke William in 1066. William I held south Nottinghamshire and parts of southern Derbyshire, which formed the Honour of Peverel. He founded Lenton Priory in Nottinghamshire with others from the Avranchin, including Robert and Geoffrey de Hériz. The Peverel family dominated southern Nottinghamshire and Derbyshire, where they were the immediate lords of the de Hériz family in Nottinghamshire.

DE SAINT-JEAN

The family de Saint-Jean was from Saint-Jean-le-Thomas, arrondissement Avranches, a fief of the abbey of Le Mont-Saint-Michel, of which they were vassals. They held La Rochelle, canton La Haye-Paynel, where the de Hériz family were their tenants. Radulf de Saint-Jean was called one of "St. Michael's men" in a charter of 1053 to Le Mont-Saint-Michel. Radulf fought at Hastings. He had sons Thomas, Guillaume I, Jean, and Roger, all of whom supported King Henry I of England.[95]

Thomas de Saint-Jean fought for King Henry I against his brother Robert Curthose at Tinchebrai in 1106. Roger and Jean de Saint-Jean were garrison commanders of King Henry I against Fulk V of Anjou in Maine in 1118. Thomas, Jean, and Roger de Saint-Jean were still vassals of Le Mont-Saint-Michel in 1123-24, according to a charter witnessed by Robert and Gilbert d'Avranches. Thomas de Saint-Jean built a castle at Saint-Jean with wood from the land of Le Mont-Saint-Michel, for which he eventually paid, agreeing in the presence of King Henry I of England in 1123/24, after he returned from being held prisoner at Gorron in Maine. He had been imprisoned by Angevins and Manceaux for leading a contingent of knights

---

94. Turgistorp was an early Scandinavian settlement; Turgistorp means Turgis' village; Clitourps means small village; Drouet, *Recherches*, 233, 238–39; *Actes Henri II*, 1:329, 331, 455–56; HKF, 1:146ff; Keats-Rohan, *Domesday People*, 494.

95. *Chronique de Normandie*, RHGF, 8:257; RBA, Leland, Holinshed; Wace, 3:8512; CPE, 11:340; CDF, nos. 710, 723–24.

fighting for King Henry I. Thomas died without children and his brother Roger was his heir. Roger de Saint-Jean married Cécile de la Haye of the Cotentin, and they were the parents of William II, Robert, and Muriel.[96]

William II de Saint-Jean succeeded on his father's death in 1130. He was the lord of Robert de Hériz in La Rochelle in 1162. He was a knight of the abbey of Le Mont-Saint-Michel in 1172. William II was a founding donor to Lucerne Abbey, which in 1145 was moved onto his land. He married first Olive de Penthièvre of Brittany, widow of Henri de Fougères and daughter of Stephen, count of Brittany and lord of Richmond in Yorkshire, and married second Godehilde Paynel. William II de Saint-Jean, his wife Olive, and brother Robert were major donors to Lucerne Abbey in 1162. He and Olive were also supporters of Savigny and Fontevraud Abbeys. William II farmed the vicomté of Coutances and served Kings Henry I, Henry II, and Richard I of England.[97]

The de Saint-Jean family were the immediate lords of the de Hériz family in La Rochelle, and were supporters of Lucerne Abbey, and also of Savigny in the Avranchin, Lessay in the Cotentin, and Fontevraud in Anjou. They intermarried with the Paynel and de Beauchamp families of the Avranchin, and the comital family of Brittany. A member of the family fought at Hastings, and family members held lands in Warwickshire, Worcestershire, Buckinghamshire, Oxfordshire, and Sussex. In England the name was spelled St. John and they interacted with the de Hercy family in Warwickshire. But their primary importance here is shedding light on the origin of the de Hériz family in the Avranchin.

---

96. OV, 6:84–85, 194–95; *RRAN*, vol. 2, app. lxi, nos. 1407, 1418, 1422; *RRAN*, vol. 3, nos. 296, 362a, 365a, 632, 644, 651; *Torigni*, 2:368–69; *MRSN*, vol. 1, called the de Saint-Jean family among the most powerful of the Anglo-Norman barons, xcviii, clx; RBE, 1:204–7, 301, 326–27; *MA*, 2:267; PR 31 Henry I, 3, 30, 34, 80, 97; CDF, nos. 710, 713, 723–24; *CartOseney*, vol. 4, no. 19a; Thomas and his brothers were raised by the monks of Le Mont-Saint-Michel; *BeauchampChart*, nos. 5, 176; Muriel married Renaud d'Orval, and their daughter, Mabel, married Adam de Port, but their children took the name de St. John; Hollister, *Monarchy*, 282; J. Green, *Henry I*, 239; Keats-Rohan, *Domesday Descendants*, 690–91.

97. *Torigni*, 2:284–85, 368–69, 392–73; *CartLuzerne*, 4–8, 227–28, 230; *Gallia christiana*. Lucerna, II, IV, X, in *CartLuzerne*, confirmed by bull of Pope Urban III; *Neustria Pia Lucerna*, III-IV, 239–40, V, 243; CDF, nos. 437, 456, 734, 745–46, 776–77, 784, 849–50, 1066, 1085; CEC, no. 303; *RRAN*, vol. 2, no. 1422; *Actes Henri II*, vol. 1, no. 282, vol. 2, 578, 629; RBE, 1:65, 72, 126; *BeauchampChart*, no. 176; Keats-Rohan, *Domesday Descendants*, 691.

1066

In 1066, Duke William II of Normandy planned and prepared his army for the invasion of England. The lords and knights of Maine, including de Hercé, rode north to join his forces in Normandy. The lords and knights of Western Normandy, including Robert and Geoffrey de Hériz, rode eastward, joining the main force. In Eastern Normandy, Gulbert d'Auffay with his vassals, possibly William and Osberne d'Arques, and other lords and knights joined the army of Duke William, and waited at Saint-Valéry-sur-Somme, the ancestral home of Gulbert's family, until the weather became auspicious to venture across the Channel. The force landed at Pevensey on 28 September. On 14 October they fought and won the battle of Hastings against the English. On Christmas Day in Westminster Abbey, Duke William II of Normandy was crowned King William I of England.

PART II

ENGLAND

IN 1066 ENGLAND WAS greatly transformed. The Norman conquest replaced almost all of the Anglo-Saxon lords with Normans. The language of administration and the courts changed from English to Norman-French, enhancing the gap between the two peoples. In 1086, King William commissioned the compilation of Domesday Book, which provides a unique portrait of the country at this time. In 1066 England was predominantly rural. Domesday described the towns and manors, ploughlands, meadows and woods, mills, priests, numbers of villagers, their status as free or male or female slave, in every part of the country. Although there were a few towns, most of the land was held by the king or by lords in rural manors. There were between five and ten thousand lords in England, mostly all male although Domesday mentioned a very few women. Some lords held many manors, others only one. Each manor included one or more villages. Most of the lords, both lay and ecclesiastical, were Norman; the peasants were Anglo-Saxon or of Danish ancestry. There were slaves but slavery soon disappeared. Villeins provided agricultural labor for the lords and some peasants paid rent to farm their lands. The country was divided into counties called shires. These in turn were divided into hundreds, which were called wapentakes in the Danelaw. The land was further divided into hides, called carucates in Danish areas, each of which contained about 120 acres. A hide or carucate was the amount of land a team of eight oxen could plough in a season. It was subdivided into oxgangs or bovates, the area which could be ploughed by one ox. These divisions were the basis for taxation before 1066 and were kept by the Normans after. Land was also the basis for raising an army. The lords had to provide military service of knights, the number of which depended on the amount or value of land they held. The land holdings of a lord were measured in knights' fees. The estates of greatest lords with the most extensive holdings were called honours and held honourial courts. King William kept about 17 percent of the land for himself. However, he was the ultimate owner of all the land; the lords held their land of the king: tenants-in-chief held directly of the king, other tenants held of a higher lord, who himself held of the king. About two hundred tenants-in-chief, the greater barons, held half the land in England. Holding of land was the source of wealth and power. By 1200 society had stabilized and was no longer migratory. Landholders had become established on their lands and with their neighbors.[1]

In the twelfth century the number of official written sources greatly increased. Kings issued writs, letters ordering their subjects to, for example, resolve disputes over land tenure or to convene courts or to order sheriffs to perform their duties. Then the Exchequer issued pipe rolls with the annual audit of accounts. The earliest surviving pipe roll was one of King Henry I in 1130; then later the annual pipe rolls of the reign of Henry II are extant. In 1166 Henry II compiled the *Cartae Baronum*, in which the tenants-in-chief listed the knights holding of them both at that time and previously at the death of Henry I in 1135. By the late twelfth century, Chancery issued charter rolls, addressed to all subjects, conferring rights and properties, with lists of witnesses; patent rolls which made appointments to offices, granted exemptions, and conveyed government decisions with one witness; and close rolls, administrative orders to individuals and institutions with one witness which were folded and sealed. There were also liberate rolls, which recorded payments by the government for fees, pensions, salaries, and palace expenses, and fine rolls, which recorded promises to pay the king for various concessions.[2] Property transfers were recorded in Feet of Fines, written in documents which were cut in three pieces: the first two of which went to the buyer and seller, the third or "foot" was kept and recorded by the court. In the early centuries, monasteries compiled charters, naming those who had donated lands. Many of these documents provided information about knightly families either directly or in witness lists. The Chancery made *inquisitiones post mortem* from 1236 to determine death duties owed to the king. In addition, wills of individuals began to be recorded by the

---

1. Payling, *Political Society*, 2–12, 87–88, 221–27; J. Green, *Aristocracy*, 50, 54, 82: in the north and in coastal areas, King William distributed lands according to his military needs; in addition to military service, kings and lords could demand "feudal incidents," that is, money for the knighting of the eldest son, marriage of the eldest daughter, wardship, payment of relief for inheritance or ransom of the lord; Given-Wilson, *English Nobility*, 8–13; Stenton, *First Century*, 9, 42–45, 57–59.

2. D. Carpenter, *Henry III*, 372–74; D. Carpenter, *Struggle*, 153, 199; Stenton, *First Century*, 137–38.

prerogative courts of the archbishops of Canterbury and York, providing additional information.

KNIGHTHOOD IN ENGLAND

The Normans who came to England were knights whose status was primarily military, but who were identified as holding a certain nobility and who were expected to exhibit courage and loyalty. On his seal, William the Conqueror was portrayed as a knight, wearing armor and riding a horse. Domesday Book cited several hundred knights, some of whom were nameless, but these did not represent all the Norman knights in England. Many of them had very small holdings of land, often under a greater lord. In their first century in England a great number of knights did not hold land, but were members of the households of the king, high magnates, and abbeys. Their military service was often in Normandy, fighting wars and garrisoning Anglo-Norman castles. By 1130 the ceremony of knighting was perceived as a coming-of-age rite denoting adulthood. King Henry I paid the knights in his court higher wages than non-knights holding the same offices. In 1166 King Henry II recognized knights as a special group in society in the Assize of Clarendon. Later the majority of knights came to hold land, denominated in knights' fees, specifying military service and castle-guard for the king or lord. In the rural shires not dominated by magnates, the knights later became the local civil leaders of their counties. By the end of the reign of Henry II, knights staffed the shire and assize courts as well as holding the office of sheriff. By the time of King John, kings began to consult county knights, who were summoned to confer with the king. This eventually led to the creation of Parliament. In the reign of King John, there were about four thousand five hundred knights in England. In the thirteenth century, men began declining knighthood because it was too expensive and because it involved many administrative and judicial duties and responsibilities. King Henry III began requiring that men of certain landholding and income levels become knights, but allowed them to pay a fine for exemption. By the reign of King Edward II, the number of knights was down to about one thousand two hundred fifty. Over time, military service became less important for knights and administrative and legal ability became more significant. Knights came to be needed to serve on assize courts and in county offices. Lineage, especially if Anglo-French, became more important and served to differentiate knights from the rising merchant class.[3]

    3. DB lists about five hundred knights who were far from wealthy; WP, 102; Glanvill, *Treatise*, 11–12, 30–37, 99, 102; Crouch, *Image*, 120–21: knighthood began in the

The meaning of knighthood evolved beyond military service and coming of age. In the mid-eleventh century, the church opposed knights, whom it accused of perpetrating violence. But by the First Crusade in 1097, the church came to regard knights as holy warriors, fighting for God and Christianity in the Holy Land. This was augmented by the foundation of the Knights Templar in 1119, who were both monks and knights. The knight became a defender of the church, of the poor, and the epitome of virtue. All aristocrats were knights, but not all knights were aristocrats. Wace noted that knights of the conquest were rich and poor, rude and courtly. But the ceremony of knighting was perceived to confer and denote nobility. Knights were addressed as "messire," meaning "my lord." Knights who held land and were of knightly ancestry were more highly respected. A mark of special status and prestige was to bear a name which was a toponym from France. The de Hercy family held land by the late twelfth century and were Anglo-French with a toponym in France. A sense of knightly nobility was passed on to the descendants of knights. Knights were often the leaders of their counties, especially if the county was not dominated by a local magnate. Knights were expected to maintain a proper residence and household. Knights were supposed to observe the honor code of conduct of chivalry: to be polite, respectful, and courteous, to do justice and defend the weak, to be intelligent and reasonable, faithful and loyal, generous to and protective of their dependants.[4]

---

lands of the Western Franks, and in the twelfth century was still part of the French cultural world, 130–31, 134, 136–37: there was a ritual of giving of arms or girding with a sword for new knights, 141–43: the Assize of Northampton gave knights quasi-judicial duties; Coss, *Knight*, 15, 20–25, 32, 60–62, 66–70: in 1176, twelve law-worthy knights (*legales milites*) were chosen to serve on the county assize courts, knighthood involved homage to a king or lord, often performance of castle-guard for their lord, in the thirteenth century men were incurring debts to pay for knighthood, the king occasionally helped pay for robes and equipment and mass knighting ceremonies; Crouch, *English Aristocracy*, 3–6, 9 (*foeda militum*), 13, 15–18: King John 1212 and 1213, Henry III issued orders to take knighthood in 1224, 1232, 1236, 1241, lists were drawn up in 1246, sheriffs needed 12 knights for grand assizes, 20; J. Green, *Aristocracy*, 12, 18; Goldberg, *Medieval England*, 115–16: there were even fewer knights in the early fifteenth and sixteenth centuries; Prestwich, *Armies*, 15–16; the Anglo-Saxon *cniht* was more a servant retainer, perhaps deriving from the German *Knecht*, although he could have had a military role; Coss, *Knight*, 10–12; Given-Wilson, *Nobility*, 19; Stenton, *First Century*, 11: called the Assize of Clarendon the foundation of a new legal system, 193, 209.

4. Crouch, *English Aristocracy*, 3–4, 13–15, 19–20, 52–53, 196–204; Crouch, *Image*, 127–29, 132–33: the image of knighthood was changed by the foundation of the Knights Templar in 1119, who combined knightly and monastic virtues, 134, 139, 148–51; Coss, *Knight*, 46–58: in the second half of the twelfth century, the perception of knighthood was changed by tournaments and crusades, making it a source of prestige, promotion, and sometimes wealth, the trappings and ceremony of knighthood

PART II | ENGLAND

In the shires, knights normally lived in manor houses. The manor was the basic unit of land tenure and was often self-sufficient, making its own food, clothes, and buildings, but also sometimes engaged in commerce in market towns. A manor included a manor house, open cultivated fields, pasture, woodlands, fisheries if near water, and one or more villages. The manor house, at first made of timber, later of brick or stone, had a hall where the family dined and entertained guests. Meetings with relatives and neighbors or local court sessions would take place in the hall. Manors generally had servants, at least a laundress and a cook, often many more. Larger manors had stewards, chaplains, and grooms. The village generally consisted of wattle and daub huts and a stone church. There were common lands on which the villagers could graze their animals, cattle, horses, and sheep. The peasants held strips within the open fields which they cultivated for their own food or to sell at market. Crops were wheat, beans, peas, barley, oats, and rye. The woodlands provided material for houses, carriages, carts, furniture, tools, as well as fuel. The knight and his family attended the parish church in the village and generally were given special seating in the front. Some affluent knights had family chapels inside the manor house, as did the later Hercy family. Knights and their families were expected to dress well according to their rank and to entertain guests hospitably in their manor hall.[5] The de Hercy, de Arches, and de Hériz families all were knights who lived in manors.

By the thirteenth century direct military service of knights came to be replaced by payment of money for scutage (exemption) and was abandoned in the fourteenth, when offices were granted for a different type of service. The class of knightly gentry had evolved between the peerage and

---

became more elaborate and expensive, knighthood became more elite as the numbers of knights decreased, 120: tournaments were licensed at only five sites in England, one of which was Blyth, Nottinghamshire, where then Prince Edward fought his first tournament in 1256; for the knights in medieval Nottinghamshire, there is very little evidence about how they came to be knighted; there was no dominant magnate in Nottinghamshire; they could have been knighted by the king or a magnate or possibly even by their own father; when a knight died, his lord often paid the king for wardship over his minor children and the lands they inherited, and had the right to give his widow and/or daughters in marriage, both of which involved significant income for the lord; Given-Wilson, *Nobility*, 2, 18.

5. CCR, Edward II, 1323–27, 33; Goldberg, *Medieval England*, 120–21; Denholm-Young, *Country Gentry*, 35: the manor buildings of Kirby-Knowle, held by the coheir of Roger de Lascelles, consisted of a hall, with a pantry and buttery, kitchen, a chamber, brewhouse, bakehouse, stable, garden, chamber for knights, gatehouse, water mill and windmill; Mertes, *English Noble Household*, 47–48, 139–43, 149; Given-Wilson, *Nobility*, 89: in the late fifteenth century it was estimated the manors of knights employed about sixteen servants, those of esquires about ten.

the peasant class. In some counties, including Nottinghamshire, the landed gentry came to hold greater wealth than the baronage. The gentry were a form of lesser nobility, which included knights and esquires. Gentry held land. Kings came to recognize the importance of the gentry as they had an increasing need of a local elite to administer the shires. The landed gentry administered the county as sheriffs and represented the county in Parliament as knights of the shire. The gentry exercised control over the populace through judicial offices, especially that of commissioner of the peace. The gentry came to have common interests and a collective identity. There were gradations of status within the gentry: knights, esquires, and gentlepersons. The gentry took pride in possession of an ancient name and lineage, in their manors, offices, wives, and children. Knights and some esquires had coats of arms, which further underlined their status. They often chose to be buried depicted in their full armor in tomb effigies. The life expectancy of landed gentry in the late Middle Ages was twenty-five to thirty years.[6]

The men of the de Hercy, d'Auffay, de Arches, and de Hériz families arrived in England as knights. In subsequent centuries their role as knights changed from fighting for their kings on horseback in wars, mostly in Scotland, to serving in county offices involving administrative and legal functions. After this shift occurred they often took respite from the title of knighthood but maintained the status of county leadership and continued to be regarded as part of the knightly class of gentry.

WOMEN IN MEDIEVAL ENGLAND

In the Middle Ages, the documentary sources were predominantly written and controlled by men. Royal and aristocratic women were mentioned often; women of the knightly class rarely. Order in medieval society was determined by hierarchy of gender and marital status as well as by rank. Knights enhanced their status through marriage to women who augmented the family's property holdings and kinship network. Thus women were of great importance, although their role was often personally invisible.

The image of women in the Middle Ages was in part formed by the misogynistic misinterpretation of biblical passages from Genesis and the

6. Coss, *Origins*, 7, 9, 11, 161, 179, 184, 212, 218, 239, 251: the term "gentleman" was recognized by Parliament in 1413; Coss, *Foundations*, 1–2; Saul, *Knights and Esquires*, 158, 257, 259; Keen, *Origins*, 71–76, 82–86, 101–6, 109–15, 120; Crouch, *Image*, 164–71: esquires were variously called *armiger*, one who had the right to bear arms, *scutifer*, *scutiger* or *scutarius*, one who bore a shield, *valletus*, little vassal, and sergeant, from *serviens*; Denholm-Young, *Country Gentry*, 16; Prestwich, *English Politics*, 49, 59–60, 63.

Pauline and post-Pauline letters, which were used to emphasize the alleged divinely instituted inferiority of woman, women as the source of temptation and evil, and the subjugation of wives to their husbands. Much of this was based on the patriarchal household codes of the Roman empire. Passages which portrayed women as leaders were ignored or interpreted away, although Prov 31 was sometimes cited to exalt the ideal wife in many areas, some of which were lauded in medieval England: spinning wool, making clothes, feeding her household, generosity to the poor, making fine clothing, not going out at night, increasing the status of her husband, speaking wisdom, and teaching kindness.[7]

Some theologians taught women to perceive themselves as vile, imbued with all the vices. But there were exceptions. The early twelfth-century English woman Christina of Markyate resisted forced marriage and founded and led a priory of women. She was the spiritual director of the abbot of St. Albans, one of the most powerful monasteries in England. In the first half of the fourteenth century, Nicholas of Bozon, a friar minor in Nottingham, wrote that the myth of the fall of Eve was overcome by finding the sin of Adam greater, noting the power of women which is greater than their physical strength, and the pain of women in forced marriages and with abusive husbands. Christine de Pizan, a French court writer in the late fourteenth and early fifteenth centuries, wrote *Le Livre de la cité des dames*, in which she described women exercising leadership roles in history. It was translated into English in 1521 and Queen Elizabeth I had a personal copy. Her work *Le Livre des trois virtus* treated the three daughters of God: Reason, Rectitude, and Justice, who would guide women in learning virtue. She held that women and men were created equally in the image of God and God would relate to women as companions, never as slaves. She, herself educated in rhetoric and law, believed that women could perform any leadership role if they were given the same education as men. One of the pillars of androcentric religion was the image of God as male, which was immortalized in the sixteenth century by Michelangelo's painting of creation. If God is male, then the male is God. This was used to justify the exclusive power of men in

---

7. The people had no real access to the Bible until the sixteenth century; clerics controlled the selection and interpretation of biblical passages; Gen 2:21–23 was cited to show that woman was created out of a man and was therefore inferior; Gen 3:1–19 was used to show woman was source of evil by succumbing to temptation and leading the man into it; 1 Cor 11:3–15, 14:34–35 (a later addition) and 1 Tim 2:11–15 were used to demonstrate the inferior position of women in society and in the church; Eph 5:22–24, Col 3:18, and 1 Pet 3:1–6 were used to emphasize the subjection of wives to husbands; Schüssler Fiorenza, *In Memory of Her*, 304–7; Prov 31:10–31 also praised the ideal wife with other qualities not so much valued in medieval England, such as buying and planting her own fields and vineyards and making a profit in trade.

the church. In the late fourteenth century, Julian of Norwich wrote of God as mother. But the majority of theologians, including Ambrose and Augustine, John Scotus Erigena, Hugh of St. Victor, and Peter Lombard, wrote of a patriarchal God and church and negatively of biblical and historical women and the roles of women in church and society. Historians, such as William of Malmesbury and Orderic Vitalis, frequently wrote negatively of women, although the latter also wrote at length positively of women as regents and even noted the occurrence of mutual love between spouses, in the case of the son of Gulbert d'Auffay.[8]

Hagiography and art also played a large role in the image of woman. Litanies named men and women saints, although the women, with the exception of Mary, were mentioned after the men. Women saints were venerated for their goodness, generosity, virginity, and miracles; male saints for their high status and heroic deeds. Medieval women read books about the lives of the saints. In the early fifth century, St. Jerome had advocated teaching daughters to read. In visual art women were portrayed as the devil, but also as the virtues. Mary was considered the epitome of virtue, through childbearing, motherhood, compassion, advocacy, and virginity. Later medieval art portrayed Anne teaching Mary to read, Mary reading books at various stages of her life: reading the prophet Isaiah at the annunciation, reading before, during, and after childbirth, on the donkey in flight to Egypt, and while raising Jesus at Nazareth. Many of these images were contained in the books read by women. Mary was a symbol of wisdom and the bearer of the incarnate Word of God. The image of the visitation of Mary with Elizabeth provided a positive basis for women coming together for mutual support. The twelfth-century St. Albans Psalter portrayed the apostle Mary of Magdala proclaiming the resurrection to the eleven fearful men. But God was generally portrayed as a man.[9]

Church courts admitted women as plaintiffs and witnesses; secular courts did not, except in very limited circumstances. Women could found monasteries and make donations to monasteries with the consent of their husbands and male heirs or occasionally out of their own funds. By the twelfth century, the church completely excluded women from their

---

8. OV, 3:250-61; Blamires, *Case*, 19-20, 30-33, 45-47, 55, 59-60, 62, 72, 74, 91, 103, 106, 109, 123, 144, 136, 150: citing Anselm of Canterbury who wrote of Jesus as mother hen, 177-78, 196, 202, 220-29, 236, 243; Johnson, *She Who Is*, 34, 102, 212; Daly, *Church*, 38; Wilkinson, *Women*, 68, 76; Michelangelo, *Creation*, Sistine Chapel, 1512.

9. Bitel and Lifschitz, *Gender and Christianity*, 87-91: note that "virgin" denoted heroic sanctity, not absence of sex, and was used of married women and men; Coss *Lady*, 73-114.

previous sacramental ministry as priests and bishops, from preaching and from serving as judges in church courts. Women still could hold powerful positions as abbesses, who had the jurisdiction of bishops, although this was soon reduced. Women were entrusted with the religious education of their children and servants. Women were sometimes advised to preach to their husbands to reform their lives. Women embroidered altar cloths and vestments, baked the bread which was blessed and distributed after mass, bought pews, and helped maintain and furnish their parish churches. Canon law sanctioned wife beating, although theologians frowned upon beating wives to death. Domestic abuse was common and sometimes litigated in the courts. Under the rule of coverture, the legal personhood and rights of a married women were subsumed under the authority of her husband. Conduct literature, such as "What the Goodwife Taught Her Daughter," was used to socialize behavior, urging girls and women to stay home, dress modestly, be chaste, pious, silent, not imitate women of higher social rank, and obey their fathers and husbands. After the advent of heraldry, both women and men had seals with coats of arms, although women often utilized the arms of their husbands; however, the arms of the husband could be quartered with those of his wife. As long as land tenure was based on feudal military service, landholding by women did not fit the system and women were merely a conduit through whom lands were transferred to their husbands. This changed with the demise of military feudalism. In the thirteenth and fourteenth centuries, women were named in property tax records. Women were generally not soldiers, although they had to defend their manors when their husbands were absent. Nevertheless, women very occasionally donned armor and fought in battle. Women were barred from holding office, and those below the rank of queen rarely did. But one noble woman, Nicolaa de la Haye, held office as sheriff of Lincolnshire and castellan of Lincoln, defending her castle against the French in 1217, which turned the tide and won the war for young King Henry III.[10]

10. Goldberg, *Medieval England*, 3–4, 6; Coss, *Lady*, 26: joint gifts to monasteries were made by the husband from the *maritagium* of the wife, 32–33: Petronilla, countess of Leicester, fought in battle with her husband, 54–55: "Goodwife" derives from about 1350 in the West Midlands, 160; Keen, *Origins*, 149; Goldberg, *Women in England*, 102: "Goodwife" also advocated beating disobedient children with a rod and marrying off daughters as soon as possible; Nicolaa inherited Lincoln, as eldest daughter, on the death of her father and again inherited as *femme sole* on the death of her husband; she was named sheriff by King John in 1216, shortly before his death; some parishes had women's guilds and women held fund raisers for church maintenance; Butler, *Language*, 30–35, 71–74, 86–87: spousal homicide was a crime; Shopkow, *Saint*, 96–99: in the twelfth century wife beating was sanctioned on the basis of the right of abbots to beat monks; in the thirteenth century this was challenged on the basis of wives not being servants.

The status of women in the Middle Ages was regulated by both secular and ecclesiastical laws. The secular law was concerned with legitimacy of inheritance of rank and property; the religious law with marriage and moral behavior. Female adultery was punished more severely than male adultery because it could affect the legitimacy of heirs. Murder of a husband by a wife was considered treason, the same as murder of a lord by his servant; murder of a wife by a husband was a lesser crime if prosecuted at all. Secular common law denied women the right to own or bequeath property, but in practice and under church law women did both. Daughters could inherit and were preferred over collateral male relatives. Women were barred from filing suits in secular courts, although they could file pleadings and be witnesses in church courts. Men needed six witnesses to prove their case in court; women needed thirty-six male witnesses. Yet in manorial court rolls, women appeared about 30 per cent as often as men. Women could not be jurors, but single women and widows could sometimes be pledges. English law navigated between positive and negative images of woman. Bracton presumed the inferiority of women. Church law, beginning with Gratian, became more egalitarian.[11]

The church gradually made marriage more formal, with vows spoken by both bride and groom before a priest. In the later twelfth century, Popes Alexander III and Innocent III advocated a view of marriage as a loving partnership with mutual affection, and the church soon required consent of both partners for valid marriage. This was especially important for brides dealing with arranged marriages. The church prohibited marriages based on consanguinity between cousins up to the seventh degree, but this was reduced to the fourth degree in 1215. Marriages were arranged by the families of the bride and groom together. The groom was generally older than the bride and probably had a greater role in choosing his spouse. The parents of the bride provided a *maritagium*: lands and property which the bride would bring to her husband in the marriage. The wedding vows generally took place at the door of the church, where the groom gave the *dos*, dower, to the bride. This could consist of nominated properties, including money, rents or chattels, or otherwise one-third of the lands held by the groom on

---

11. Bracton, *Notebook*, 2:31 (ca. 1250); women could file an appeal, that is, a private complaint accusing someone of a felony which could result in the incarceration of the accused; Magna Carta stated that no one could be imprisoned on a woman's appeal, but this was not implemented in practice; Coss, *Lady*, 23: an exception was the civil war which was fought over whether the heir of Henry I should be his daughter, the Empress Mathilda, or nephew, Stephen, who won, 29, 32–33, 113; Wilkinson, *Women*, 3, 5–6, 13–26; Williams and Echols, *Between*, 159; Goldberg, *Women*, 35–43; Hanawalt, *Wealth*, 51: in London, girls could inherit at sixteen if they were married, otherwise at twenty-one.

the day of the marriage or in his lifetime. Then the couple proceeded into the church for a nuptial mass to bless their union and afterwards the families held a great feast. During marriage, the husband could alienate lands and the wife could not protest because she was *in potestate viri*. But when the husband was absent, the wife could manage the estate. However, estate management by both sexes often involved reliance on male stewards, clerks, and lawyers. Together a married couple could build a manor house and decide the marriage interests of their children. Couples had many children, but infant mortality was very high. After childbirth feasts were sometimes held to celebrate the churching of the mother. It is difficult to document whether a marriage was happy, but there are sometimes hints of trust or even a working partnership in letters, wills, the choice of the wife as executor, and funerary art. Women who survived childbirth were likely to outlive their husbands. When a husband died before his wife, the widow could manage the family property. Only when she became a widow did she have a legal right to her dower and to control her lands as long as she did not remarry. A widow was a *femme sole*, who could administer her estates, hold patronage of advowsons, plead in court, and make her own decisions. Rich widows were generally forced to remarry, and the bestowal of widows in remarriages was a great source of revenue for kings Henry II, Richard I, and John. This was restricted in Magna Carta and it became possible for widows to pay a fine to the king to be allowed not to remarry and prevented the king from withholding the widow's *maritagium*, dower, and inheritance. When parents died without sons, daughters could inherit. Sometimes the eldest daughter received all or most of the property; other times it was shared equally among sisters, as came to be required by law. The inheritance rights of daughters and even nieces were recognized. Orphaned daughters held in ward could be married off at the age of fourteen; the choice of husband was at the mercy of the man who held them in wardship.[12]

---

12. Wilkinson, *Women*, 3, 82–83; J. Green, *Aristocracy*, 21, 129: 54 out of 189 baronies in England descended through women between 1086 and 1166, 367: parents were not bound to treat all daughters equally; Chibnall, *Anglo-Norman England*, 174–76: *statutem decretum* of Henry I (1130–35), Glanvill (1187–89); Coss, *Lady*, 26, 28: in 1185, the *RDP* recorded the names and lands of widows and minor children, which were also recorded in the pipe rolls and fine rolls of King John; MC 6 forbade disparagement, marriage to one of lower rank, MC, 7–8: right of a widow to *maritagium*, dower, and inheritance, and not to remarry if she gave security that she would not without the consent of the king; Waugh, *Lordship*, 85, 116: late thirteenth century, more difficult procedure for widows; Ward, *Women*, 6, 18, 48, 122–23, 193; Goldberg, *Women in England*, 14–23; Goldberg, *Medieval England*, 124; Jewell, *Women in Medieval England*, 123, 125, 129.

Forms of address were significant in the demonstration of rank. Knights were first called *milites*, the Latin word for soldier for which there was no feminine equivalent. Later in Latin and French they were called *dominus*, *seigneur* or lord, and their wives were called *domina*, *dame* or lady. Social status was manifested in dress. Secular sumptuary laws attempted to regulate what persons, especially women, of different ranks could wear.[13]

Knightly gentry families lived in manor houses on their lands. The men managed the estates and the villeins in the villages who worked the land for them. When husbands were absent, their wives managed the estates. In the 1240s, Robert Grosseteste, bishop of Lincoln, wrote a manual of rules for estate management for a woman friend, advising comprehensive knowledge of the estate, how to manage the servants, and to make sure they had the means to live through the year. In another slightly later work, a knight instructed a widow to teach her children "husbandry and management" and to improve their French. Women managed the manor house and generally had at least one or two servants, who did the laundry and sewing, cooked and fetched water. There were often many more servants, some of whom lived in the manor house. Women embroidered and spun, carded and wove cloth, bore and raised children. Wives of knights could enhance the careers of their husbands through their role of hospitality. Some women hunted with their husbands. Lower class women were midwives and wet-nurses. Most villages had women who brewed and sold ale in an alehouse and baked bread in the common oven. Women also worked with poultry and cattle, made butter and cheese, and sometimes worked in the fields with the men, although they were paid less if at all.[14]

Men preferred women to be uneducated because they were thus easier to control. Fathers would rather not spend money on the education of daughters, but save it for their dowries. Boys and girls were generally educated by their mothers to age five or six. Then boys were often sent to another household, usually of higher rank, or given a tutor at home, and later some attended grammar schools. Girls were taught to memorize prayers and spin and sew. Mothers who read books sometimes taught their sons

---

13. Coss, *Lady*, 36: examples from Wace and others, 51–54: in 1337 only knights and ladies could wear fur, in 1363 dress was regulated by class and sub-class; sumptuary legislation increased after the Black Death and lasted until 1483; Crouch, *Image*, 148–50; Goldberg, *Medieval England*, 4–5, 7–8.

14. Goldberg, *Women, Work*, 85, 99, 101, 139, 141–42, 148; Goldberg, *Women in England*, 3–8; Leyser, *Medieval Women*, 125–26, 147, 151, 226; Coss, *Lady*, 67: women even poached deer from royal forests, 70–71; Jewell, *Women in Medieval England*, 58–59, 74; midwives learned their skills through apprenticeship to other midwives; some women also practiced herbal medicine or general medicine on a very limited basis; Bennett, *Women*, 22–36, 55, 115–18, 120–27.

and daughters to read, often using the psalter as an alphabet primer. Boys were taught more and longer than girls. Girls were taught skills appropriate to women at home, but some did learn to read. Women were excluded from the universities and Inns of Court, where a small number of men were able to study theology and law, which greatly enhanced their status. Study of medicine, theology, and law required mastery of Latin, which was generally not taught to girls. However, many women were literate and some owned books, most of which were in Norman-French. Adele, daughter of King William I, read books, knew philosophy and the liberal arts, and was a patron of poets, as was Mathilda, queen of Henry I. Eleanor of Aquitaine, queen of Henry II, read books and corresponded with kings, queens, and saints. She was depicted in her tomb effigy reading a book. The book used most widely by women was the *Book of Hours*, a simplified and shorter breviary of the hours of the monastic office with prayers to Mary. The hours were to be read or prayed eight times a day. Through the use of such books women could escape the clerical control of their spirituality. Women read *Lives* of the saints, a few of which were written by women. Women read romances, generally written in the Norman French, later in vernacular English. The romances were mostly written by men and upheld their image of women; they were male-centered, and women appeared as spectators who appreciated and rewarded the heroic deeds of men. The *Roman de la Rose* was especially misogynistic and was denounced by Christine de Pizan. By acquiring, reading, and passing on such books, women influenced the increased use of the vernacular. Women read to each other and to other women in their households. Reading was facilitated by the inventions of the fireplace, window glass, and eyeglasses. Sometimes wills revealed bequests of books by or to women, which were expensive. The *Book of the Knight of the Tower*, which appeared in England in the fifteenth century, wrote about the education of women and expected the daughters of knights to be able to read. The number and availability of books greatly increased after the printing press came to England in 1476.[15]

15. Leyser, *Medieval Women*, 139–40, 233–35, 240–42, 244–48; Wilkinson, *Women*, 14; Goldberg, *Medieval England*, 261–69; Coss, *Lady*, 37, 71–72: alphabet psalters and fourteenth-century paintings of St. Anne teaching Mary to read, 170: husbands commissioned books of the hours for their brides as wedding gifts, 173–75; official books were still in Latin; J. Green, *Aristocracy*, 13–15; Jewell, *Women in Late Medieval*, 93, 138–39: the knight said "as for wrytynge it is no force yf a woman can nought of hit, but as for redynge I saye that good and prouffytable is to al wymen"; Given-Wilson, *Nobility*, 2–4; according to Thomas More, in 1533 60 percent of the people could read English; Chase and Kowaleski, *Reading and Writing*, 23; Erler and Kowaleski, *Women and Power*, 149–50, 154, 160, 162, 166: Thomas More advocated teaching Latin to girls, in 1382 Anne of Bohemia (wife of Richard II) brought a vernacular Bible to England;

Women of knightly families were able to enhance their status by monastic foundations and support of abbeys and priories. Most of the convents of Anglo-Saxon times had been destroyed by the Danish invaders. Thus there were few monasteries for women in 1066. Many were founded in the twelfth century, often through the generosity of women donors, including the de Arches family. The abbeys and priories of women were smaller and poorer than those of men and their libraries were inferior. However, nuns had to have been literate. Their daily lives involved singing the divine office eight times each day, which required being able to read the numerous psalms and canticles in Latin. The convents offered women education in theology and sometimes medicine and the sciences, and the chance to exercise power as administrators and teachers. Sometimes women made donations to monasteries with their husbands, but other times made them in their own right. Their status was further enhanced when their donations were confirmed by bishops and archbishops. Their support of new orders may even have had an influence on the direction of monasticism. In addition, women influenced which monasteries their children supported. However, this ceased in the thirteenth century when men and women stopped endowing monasteries. The power of abbesses diminished after the Cluniac and Gregorian reforms with the segregation of women and men in monasteries and ecclesiastical roles, the promotion of negative images of women as temptresses, and the shift of property rights of monasteries from the founding families to the church. The mendicant orders of Dominicans and Franciscans at first welcomed women, but soon restrained them by strict enclosure in convents. Widows remarried or managed their estates instead of founding and joining convents. Women issued charters, both jointly with their husbands or sons and in their own right. As widows and heiresses, women held land and could divide their inheritance by leaving some lands to their daughters, which resulted in less land for their sons. Some women of knightly families had knights and vassals of their own. However, in the fourteenth century the law of entail was developed to limit inheritance of estates to men.[16]

The extant legal documents depict names and dates of birth, marriage, and death, and transfers of property. Some more personal detail occurs in wills and the few extant letters. Literature, such as Chaucer, shows women characters with diverse personalities interacting with other women and with men. It is obvious that individual women in medieval England had

Blamires, *Case*, 6, 36, 45, 47–48, 128, 132, 220.

16. EYC, vol. 1, nos. 535–36, 538, 541, 548–49, 552–53, vol. 3, no. 1331 (by Agnes de Arches), Williams and Echols, *Between*, 216; Jewell, *Women in Medieval England*, 156–59; Jewell, *Women in Late Medieval*, 48–51, 105.

personalities and personal stories. Yet the historian is blocked by lack of sources and cannot legitimately enter into the realm of speculation.

The women of the Hercy, Arches, and Hériz families were part, although not spoken of as often, of the history of their fathers and husbands. There are glimpses of their roles at many points. In later centuries more is known of their actions and roles. They founded monasteries, read books, inherited and managed estates, taught their children, and were active in their parish churches and communities. And there is an absence of court cases against any of these women for divorce, being assaulted by their husbands, assaulting their husbands, or filing litigation against their husbands, which may indicate stable and perhaps happy marriages.

Worcestershire

There are traces of a family called Herce in the county of Worcestershire in the twelfth century. However, little is known of this family and it did not survive in Worcestershire. Because of the proximity of its holdings in Worcestershire to the much better documented de Hercy family in Warwickshire, it is possible that they were related. This section is included because it may show members of the Herce/Hercy family holding land in England in the realm of Henry II and possibly during the reign of Stephen or even Henry I. It also shows the close connections between Worcestershire and Warwickshire in the late twelfth century.

WORCESTERSHIRE BEFORE KING HENRY II

At the time of the conquest, most of the lands in Worcestershire belonged to the church. According to Domesday Book, in 1086, Oswaldlaw Hundred was held by the bishop of Worcester and Urse d'Abetot. Urse d'Abetot was from Saint-Jean d'Abbetot, a small hamlet in the western Pays de Caux, arrondissement Le Havre, adjacent to Tancarville and holding its land of the Tancarville family. The d'Abetot family was undistinguished in Normandy. Three brothers from Abbetot went to England with or soon after Duke William, where they prospered. Robert the Dispenser was the eldest. In 1086 he held seventeen tenancies-in-chief in Lincolnshire, eighteen in Leicestershire, four in Warwickshire, including Fillongley, and one in Worcestershire. He witnessed documents with Roger de Bully, W. de la Rochelle, Hugh de Beauchamp, and for the earl of Warwick. He held the hereditary office of royal dispenser, bursar, an important official in the royal court. Robert married Lesca, but died without children in 1097. His title and most of his lands went to his brother Urse.[1]

1. DB Worcestershire, 2.13, 19, 49, 67, 73, 9.1d; DB, 11:1–2: Hugh de Grandmesnil also had a small holding in Oswaldslaw Hundred; *RRAN*, vol. 1, nos. 220, 285, 315,

PART II | ENGLAND

Urse d'Abetot was tenant-in-chief and sheriff of Worcestershire from about 1069 until his death in 1108. Urse was quite greedy for property and used his power as sheriff, which at that time included control of the shire courts, to acquire more and more land, often in conflict with the church, seizing church lands for himself through less than legal means. Urse was in a long-term power struggle with Wulfstan, the saintly bishop of Worcester, who died in 1095.[2] In 1069 Urse built a motte and bailey castle at Worcester, partly on land belonging to Worcester cathedral. For this Urse was cursed by the bishop because the castle encroached on the monks' cemetery. However, in 1075, with Bishop Wulfstan of Worcester, the abbot of Evesham, and Walter de Lacy, Urse helped put down a rebellion of earls against King William I.

Domesday Book recorded that Urse d'Abetot held fifteen tenancies-in-chief and forty-three other estates in Worcestershire. Urse was appointed royal constable by King William II, and royal marshal by King Henry I. He witnessed charters for King William I and King William II, including one in January 1091 confirming the status of Bath Abbey and also documents concerning Yorkshire. After the death of his brother, Robert the Dispenser, in 1097, Urse acquired the office of dispenser and most of his brother's lands. Urse married Adelise and they had children: Roger and Emmeline.

After Urse died in 1108, his son Roger inherited the estates and the office of sheriff. However, in 1110, after committing a serious crime, reputedly the murder of a member of the royal household, he was exiled and forfeited his lands and office. Osbert d'Abetot, probably Urse's younger brother, then held the office of sheriff until 1114. Urse's daughter Emmeline married Walter de Beauchamp and King Henry I made her husband viscount and sheriff of Worcestershire, giving him the d'Abetot lands. Emmeline d'Abetot thereby became the maternal ancestor of the Beauchamp earls of Warwick.[3]

318–19, 326, 349, 370, 388, vol. 2, 903, 976, vol. 3, nos. 68, 749; *CartWorcester*, vol. 1, nos. 5, 21; *MA*, 2:267, no. 10; Loyd, *Origins*, 1; Round, *Ancient Charters*, 1:2; Keats-Rohan, *Domesday People*, 383.

2. DB Worc, 1.1b–c, 2.3, 17–18, 25–28, 35, 49, 51, 54, 75, 79, 3.2, 5.1, 8.2, 4, 7–8, 9e, 10b, 11, 16–18, 27, 9.1b–c, 1e, 4, 5b–c, 6c, 10.12, 11–1–2, 12.2, 14.2, 15.9, 19.14, 26.1–17, E34; E14: Urse so oppressed the men that they cannot pay the salt; *RRAN*, vol. 3, nos. 68, 964; *MA*, 3:447, 4:149; EYC, vol. 2, nos. 930, 932; *CartWorcester*, nos. 2, 3, 5; Urse also witnessed documents regarding Yorkshire for Kings William II and Henry I. Dugdale, *Baronage*, i, 462; Loyd, *Origins*, 1–2; J. Green, *Aristocracy*, 52, 72, 95–96, 131, 282–83; the name Urse may be a sobriquet, a play on the Latin word for bear, "*ursus*," in French, "*ours*"; characteristically bears are stocky, powerful animals; Keats-Rohan, *Domesday People*, 383, 436, 439, 500, 510, 528.

3. *BeauchampChart*, nos. 1–2, 4–6; *MA*, 2:266, 3:447–48, nos. 1–2, 4:149, no. 3; *RRAN*, vol. 2, App. lxxxi; *RRAN*, vol. 3, no. 68; *CartRameseia*, nos. 157, 159, 164; John d'Abetot witnessed a quitclaim to William de Beauchamp of a field in Church Lench in

Walter de Beauchamp and his brother William Peverel de Beauchamp came to England after the conquest from Beauchamp, arrondissement Avranches, just north of La Haye-Pesnel and La Rochelle. Walter de Beauchamp held Elmley Castle in Worcestershire and witnessed royal charters for King Henry I between 1108 and 1123. In 1114, King Henry I granted Walter de Beauchamp all the lands of Roger of Worcester in and around the town of Worcester. Walter married Emmeline, daughter of Urse d'Abetot and thereby obtained all the fiefs of Urse and his brother, Robert the Dispenser, as well as the hereditary office of dispenser, a member of the royal household. Walter de Beauchamp was sheriff of Worcestershire from 1114 to 1130. Walter and his brother William Peverel I de Beauchamp donated land to the Benedictine priory at Worcester Cathedral. William Peverel I de Beauchamp also held lands in Nottinghamshire. The donation was confirmed by his son of the same name, who succeeded him. The name suggests a relationship with the Peverel family of the Avranchin and south Nottinghamshire, but the exact nature of the connection is not known.[4] Walter de Beauchamp was succeeded in 1131 by his elder son, William I de Beauchamp.

William I de Beauchamp inherited the lands in Worcestershire and the offices of dispenser and royal forester. After the death of King Henry I in 1135, the earl of Worcester, Waleran de Beaumont, and William I de Beauchamp supported the succession of Stephen as king. One of the first battles in the civil war which followed was the defeat and sack of the city of Worcester. King Stephen granted William de Beauchamp the office of sheriff in 1139 and made it hereditary in 1141. William de Beauchamp was sheriff of Worcestershire from 1139 to about 1169 and of Warwickshire in 1157–58. William married Berta, daughter of William II de Braose and Maud de Saint Valéry. They had five sons and a daughter. In 1166, William de Beauchamp had seventeen men holding fees under him, including Stephen de Beauchamp holding two fees. William I de Beauchamp died in 1169/70.[5]

---

return for a loan to repay the Jews, the moneylenders of the time; *RRAN*, vol. 3, nos. 68, 749, 795, 964; *BeauchampChart*, nos. 1–2, 6, 24, 48; *CartWorcester*, vol. 1, nos. 335–37, 339; RBE, 1:299–300; *MA*, 6:2, 1066; *Actes Henri II*, 2:dxciv, 188; Round, *Ancient Charters* 1:1; Keats-Rohan, *Domesday People*, 439; Keats-Rohan, *Domesday Descendants*, 261–62, 314–15.

4. *BeauchampChart*, nos. 1–7; *RRAN*, vol. 2, App. lxxx, 329, vol. 3, nos. 68, 964; *MA*, 2:601, 3:447–48, no. 2, 5:399; PR 31 Henry I, 5, 17, 18, 22, 63, 70, 80–81, 88–89, 96, 99, 102, 121, 126; *Actes Henri II*, 1:iii, 7; *CartWorcester*, vol. 1, nos. 18, 73, 77, 119–20, 338, 551; Round, *Ancient Charters* 1:18; RBE, 1:314, 340, 343; Hollister, *Henry I*, 361; Keats-Rohan, *Domesday Descendants*, 314–15.

5. D'Anisy, *Extraits de chartes*, vol. 1, nos. 23, 85, 143, 149; in 1166 William de

PART II | ENGLAND

In 1166, Stephen de Beauchamp held one knight's fee in Buckinghamshire with William Peverel de Beauchamp, three knights' fees in Wolverton, Worcestershire, and two fees of William de Beauchamp in Worcestershire. Stephen married Isolde de Ferrers, daughter of Robert II de Ferrers, earl of Derby, and Margaret Peverel. They had a son, Stephen II, and a daughter, Mathilde, who married William de Vascoeuil, of the family which had held Pillerton Hersey in Warwickshire.[6]

William I de Beauchamp was succeeded by his eldest son, William II, who held seven fees in Worcestershire where he was sheriff from 1190 to 1195. In 1190–91, William II de Beauchamp was the only lay landholder mentioned in Worcestershire, holding with the bishop of Worcester and the abbots of Evesham, Pershore, and Westminster. He married Amice, and they had William III, who succeeded as a minor in 1197, but died in 1210/11, and Walter III, who succeeded his brother and married Joan Mortimer, daughter of Roger Mortimer and Isabel de Ferrers. Walter III held 207 knights' fees in Worcestershire.[7] They had one son, William IV, who succeeded.

William IV de Beauchamp married Isabel Mauduit, daughter of Alice de Warwick, heir through her grandmother, Margaret de Beaumont, of the earldom of Warwick. She was also the granddaughter of Isabel Basset. William IV de Beauchamp and Isabel had eight children. The eldest was William V de Beauchamp, who succeeded and became sheriff of Worcestershire when his father died in 1268. On the death of his mother's brother in 1267, he became earl of Warwick. His sister, Sarah de Beauchamp, married Richard Talbot, a Hercy relative, son of Gilbert Talbot and grandson of Aline Basset.[8]

Beauchamp held fifteen fees of the church of Worcester, with Elias Giffard and Hugh de Lacy; William also held a fee of Evesham Abbey, two fees of the Honour of Wolverton and two fees of Gervaise Paynel; RBE, 1:188–98, 269–70, 278–79, 287–88, 299–302, 335; RRAN, vol. 2, App. cclvi, 374, no. 1710, vol. 3, nos. 68, 115–16, 795, 964; *BeauchampChart*, no. 8; *CartWorcester*, vol. 1, nos. 37, 73, 77, 212–14, 338; MA, 4:382, 5:175–76; *Annales monastici*, 4:382; Keats-Rohan, *Domesday Descendants*, 315–16, 1056.

6. RRAN, vol. 3, nos. 136, 964, PR 31 Henry I, 11, 38, 47–49, 60, 76, 83, 104; MA, 4:101–2, 5:399; RBE, 1:299–300, 314–15, 403–7, 2:478, 502, 566; Earl Robert had supported King Stephen, who made him an earl; when William Peverel was imprisoned, Earl Robert called himself earl of Nottingham; CCR, Henry 3:126; HKF, 2:48; Keats-Rohan, *Domesday Descendants*, 312–14.

7. RBE, 1:72, 85, 108, 177, 188, 299–300, 2:566–67, 660–61; *Annales de Wigornia*, 101, 389, 400, 418, 428; *BeauchampChart*, Introduction, xxii–xxiii; PR 12 John, 64; RRAN, vol. 3, no. 964.

8. *BeauchampChart*, nos. 24, 30.

WORCESTERSHIRE

ROUS LENCH AND CROWLE

There were five towns in southeastern Worcestershire with the name Lench, meaning "rise" or "little hill": Ab Lench, Atch Lench, Church Lench, Rous Lench, and Sheriffs Lench, all clustered together. Rous Lench and Ab Lench were in Oswaldslaw Hundred, all of which traditionally had belonged to the bishop of Worcester. Rous Lench was also called Bishop's Lench in the eleventh century, Lench Randolph later in the twelfth, and Randolphs Lench in the thirteenth through sixteenth centuries. In 1086, Urse d'Abetot held seven hides in Rous Lench and five hides in Ab Lench of the church of Worcester, and Sheriffs Lench of Odo of Bayeux. He also held two tenancies-in-chief and four other fees in Warwickshire. Bishop Odo of Bayeux, half-brother of King William I, took the land of Sheriffs Lench from the church and gave it to Urse. The abbey of Evesham still held Atch Lench and Church Lench, but after the death of Aethelwig, abbot of Evesham, in 1077, Urse violently seized them. The case was adjudicated in his favour by Bishop Odo of Bayeux. In 1086, the bishop held Blockley and Fladbury; Rous Lench was under Fladbury. Crowle was held by Urse and Roger de Lacy. Nearby Wick was held by St. Peter's Westminster and by Pershore Abbey.

In 1086, Rous Lench was held by the bishop of Worcester and Urse d'Abetot. Then it consisted of five villages, seven smallholders, four slaves, one priest, nine acres of ploughland, six acres of meadow, and a mill. Urse held seven hides in Rous Lench and the bishop two hides. Rous Lench must have been a significant manor, as Robert the Dispenser held five hides of it, and Roger de Lacy, ten hides.[9] A hide was the amount of land which could be worked with one plough, about a hundred acres. After Urse died it was held by Walter de Beauchamp until his death in 1131, and then by his son William I de Beauchamp. Later the two fees of Rous Lench and Crowle came to be held by William Herce and Henry, son of Herce. The *Red Book of Worcester* in 1182 named Randolph de Lench, son of Roger, holding five hides in Rous Lench of William Herce "*antiquitus.*" Randolph held Rous Lench in the reign of King Henry II. Herce may have held it earlier in that reign or in the reign of Stephen or even of Henry I. Walter, then William, de Beauchamp were lords of Rous Lench, and William Herce would have held of them. At some time before or during the reign of Henry II, tenancy of the manor of Rous Lench in Worcestershire was transferred from William

---

9. DB Worc, 2.6 (Wick), 15 (Fladbury), 17 (Ab Lench), 18 (Rous Lench), 38 (Blockley), 76 (Atch Lench),78 (Crowle); 8.2 (Wick), 9.1a (Wick), 10.14 (Atch Lench),16 (Church Lench); 11.2 (Sheriffs Lench), 19.14 (Crowle).

Herce to the Lench family. The father or grandfather of William Herce may have held Rous Lench earlier.[10]

The town of Crowle lay to the northwest, near the city of Worcester. In 1086 it consisted of two parts: the first contained seven villages, three smallholders, five slaves, ploughland for six teams, sixteen acres of meadow, some woodland and forest, a mill, and a salthouse. This part of Crowle belonged to the priory of Worcester; Roger de Lacy was tenant, but was banished in 1096 for rebelling against King William II with Bernard de Neufmarché, and died after 1106, his lands going to his brother Hugh de Lacy, who died in 1115. He was the eldest son of Walter de Lacy and nephew of Ilbert de Lacy of Yorkshire. The second part of Crowle, consisting of three smallholders, two cottages, four slaves, five ploughlands, a woodland, and two salthouses, belonged to Osbern Fitz Richard in 1086, with Urse d'Abetot as its lord.[11]

Henry, son of Herce, sold his lands in Crowle to Emma de Hales, who later gave all of them to St. Wulfstan's Hospital in Worcester. Emma of Hales, also called Emma of Anjou, lived from about 1140 until 1214. She was the illegitimate sister of King Henry II, who gave her the manor of Hales in 1174 on her marriage to David, prince of north Wales. Her gift was confirmed in 1232. The exact date of the sale is not known, but it probably occurred late in the reign of King Henry II or early in the reign of King Richard I, since she returned Hales to Richard in 1193.[12] Henry son of Herce held lands in Crowle before that time.

The *Red Book of Worcester* mentioned a Margery de Pillardinton, of Pillerton, Warwickshire, three times as holding a messuage of the curia of Wick, a few miles south-southwest of the Lenches in Worcestershire. A messuage is a dwelling house with its land and outbuildings. It is possible that William Herce of Rous Lench, Henry Herce of Crowle, and/or Margery

---

10. RBW, 2:145 (*Randolphus filius Rogeri in Rogberlinge v hidas, geldantes de Willelmo Ferce antiquitus*—Herce transcibed Ferce, but considered by most to be Herce); *RRAN*, vol. 2, nos. 1024–25, 1062, 1550, 1710, vol. 3, 68; *CartWorcester*, vol. 1, nos. 73, 77, 551; PR 22 Henry II, 17; *BeauchampChart*, nos. 36-37; *Survey of Worcestershire*, 2:171; *VCH, Worcester* 3:497–500, no. 11, Rous Lench partly under the manor of Fladbury; Dugdale, *Baronage* 1:462; J. Green, *Aristocracy*, 131, 282–83; Keats-Rohan, *Domesday People*, 262, 315–16, 439, 500, 510–11.

11. In 1086, Crowle was in Esch Hundred (DB, 2.78, 19.14), but later became part of Oswaldslaw; the daughter of FitzRichard married Bernard de Neufmarché.

12. OV, 4:24; FW, ii, 25–26; both were against Bishop Wulfstan; the hospital was founded about 1085 by Bishop Wulfstan; the donation was at the latest in 1220; *RotChart*, 44; *RHGF*, 12:535; *CartWorcester*, vol. 1, no. 528; *Testa de Nevill*, 1:146; CChR, 1226–57, 173; RBW, 1:6, 10; *VCH, Worcester*, vol. 3, "Crowle," 329–34, n. 97; Coss, *Knight*, 20; J. Green, *Aristocracy*, 275–76; Keats-Rohan, *Domesday People*, 264–65, 316, 404.

of Pillerton were related to each other and to the de Hercy family who held lands in Pillerton Hersey, Warwickshire, in the reign of King Richard I. There is no record that the Herce family survived in Worcestershire, except for a later mention of one Henry Herce in Blockley, due north of Rous Lench, in about 1280.[13]

There is no definitive proof that the Herces of Worcestershire were related to the de Hercy family of Pillerton in Warwickshire. However, it is probable, and they may have been ancestors or relatives of Sir Hugh de Hercy of Pillerton or of his nephew Malveysin de Hercy. Rous Lench and Pillerton are only about twenty miles apart. If true, it would indicate that the descendants of the Sieur de Hercé of 1066 remained in England and he and his descendants began to hold land in Worcestershire by the early or mid-twelfth century.

---

13. RBW, 1:42–43: in 1299 Margerie de Pillardinton held one messuage *cum curtilagio per servitium xviiid per annum ad iiii terminos* and another *cum croft per servitium iis per annum ad iiii terminos*; Wick was just west of Fladbury; Matthew Chokes was also named here; the thirteenth-century Cartulary of Worcester Cathedral Priory mentions lands and appurtenances in Doddenham formerly of a Walter Heresey: *Cart-Worcester*, vol. 1, nos. 101, 111; *Lay Subsidy Roll*, 75.

Warwickshire

Since the de Hercé family came from Maine, they and their Manceau neighbors and lords were not given lands in England after the conquest. De Hercé and his immediate descendants were probably castle knights, although it is possible, but less likely, that they returned to Maine and came back to England later. In England the spelling of the name was modified to de Hercy. The family was firmly documented holding land in Warwickshire in the reign of King Richard I and possibly earlier in Worcestershire.[1]

THE PILLERTONS AND KINETON, WARWICKSHIRE, 1066–1184

Warwickshire was an important county in central England in the Middle Ages and a major intersection of roads leading from east to west and south to north. Warwickshire was less urban and less populated than neighboring counties and was predominantly agrarian. In Domesday Book, it was not dominated by a single lord, but by multiple bishops and abbeys and lay tenants-in-chief, although most of these held greater lands in other counties. Southern Warwickshire was called the Felden, with open fields, unfree peasants, and significant grain production. The Pillertons lie in southern Warwickshire, between Worcestershire to the west and Buckinghamshire to the east. The Roman road called the Fosse Way, built about 43 CE across England from Exeter through Nottinghamshire to Lincoln, crossed the northern part of both Pillertons. The name Pillerton came from Pilardinton, meaning "town of Pithard" in Anglo-Saxon. There were two Pillertons: Upper (Over) Pillerton, so called because it was about a hundred feet higher

---

1. The related families were Norman and so received lands immediately: Gulbert d'Auffay and Osberne de Arches were documented in Domesday Book as landholders of many fees in Yorkshire; Robert de Hériz was documented in Domesday holding Stapleford, Nottinghamshire; Picot de Lascelles in Yorkshire and Lincolnshire.

in altitude, which was also called Pillerton Priors, and Lower (Nether) Pillerton, which later became Pillerton Hersey. In 1066, King William gave the lands of Pillerton to one of his most loyal and trusted companions in the conquest, Hugh de Grandmesnil, and after his death, to one of the most important men in England, Hugh d'Avranches, both of Western Normandy. The king kept Kineton for himself. Later the manors of Lower Pillerton and Kineton were given to the de Hercy family. In Domesday Book, Over Pillerton and Nether Pillerton were ascribed to Tremelaw Hundred and Kineton to Fexhole Hundred. By 1169 these and two other hundreds were combined into Kineton Hundred with the vill of Kineton at its center. According to Domesday Book in 1086, Kineton, meaning "King's town," was held by King William I and had 111 tenants and five slaves. Lower Pillerton was a vill "of 10 hides and land for 10 ploughs, in lordship three," with twenty-nine tenants, twelve slaves, "a mill worth 5s., a woodland one league square," and a messuage in Warwick, consisting of a dwelling house with its adjacent buildings and land, which rented for 4d.[2] Before the Norman conquest, it belonged to Baldwin, the chamberlain of King Edward the Confessor. This was a good size estate. At some point before 1081, Hugh de Grandmesnil donated Upper Pillerton to the abbey of Saint-Évroul in Normandy. In 1086, St. Évroul was listed as holding "6 hides and 1 virgate" in Pillerton Priors with forty tenants, and the earl of Chester, Hugh d'Avranches, holding "1 hide and 3 virgates," with four tenants and one slave, granting one hide to Saint-Évroul. These were units of tax. A hide was the amount of land that could be worked with one plough. A virgate was a quarter acre. In 1086, Hugh de Grandmesnil held most of the lands in both hundreds. Hugh de Grandmesnil also held four buildings in the city of Warwick, "and the monks of Pillerton had one of him." The bishop of Worcester held nine buildings, Hugh d'Avranches seven, the count of Meulan twelve, Henry de Ferrers two.[3]

Hugh I de Grandmesnil of the Orne in Western Normandy was Duke William's cavalry commander in the Norman invasion of England and fought bravely at Hastings. The de Grandmesnils were of the higher nobility in Normandy, one of the few families called *nobiles* by Orderic Vitalis. They

---

2. The abbreviations "s." and "d." refer to English shillings and pennies, respectively.

3. DB Warwickshire, 1, 3, 4, 11, 13, 16, 18, 23, 27, 35, 45, B6, EG2; 18.3 Pillerton Hersey, Pillerton Priors, 13.1, 18.11, B2, Kineton 1.2, 16.19; OV, 2:14–19, 30–35, 3:234–39; CEC, 1; *VCH*, Warwick, 5:133–37: the earl of Rutland came to hold Pillerton from 1594 at least until 1800 and still has unpublished manuscripts pertaining to it; Pillerton Hersey had about 1,389 acres; Priors about 1,566 acres; the church at Priors burned down in 1666 and was not rebuilt; C. Carpenter, *Locality*, 17–20, 23, 31.

were *fideles* of Duke William II.[4] Hugh I de Grandmesnil was the eldest son of Robert I de Grandmesnil of Grentemesnil in Calvados and Hawise d'Echaffour who had seven children. Hugh de Grandmesnil lived in the Risle valley in the Pays d'Ouche region of Normandy, which overlapped the Orne and the Eure, where his family raised and trained warhorses. Robert I de Grandmesnil was killed in battle on 17 June 1040 and left his estates to his two elder sons, Hugh and Robert II. These sons, with the help of their maternal uncle Guillaume I FitzGiroie, refounded, restored, and endowed the abbey of St. Évroul in the Orne in 1050 where the historian Orderic Vitalis was later a monk. Robert II entered the monastery and became abbot in 1059; their sister married Richard le Goz, vicomte of the Avranchin; their widowed mother Hawise became a nun at Saint-Évroul.[5] By 1086, Hugh had been made viscount and castellan of Leicester, and tenant-in-chief of seventeen manors in Warwickshire, including Pillerton Hersey, Pillerton Priors, and Butlers Marston, six manors in Worcestershire, two in Nottinghamshire, Edwalton and Thrumpton, and others. After the death of King William I, Hugh de Grandmesnil supported Robert Curthose against King William II Rufus, and the status of his family declined as a result. He died in 1094 and was buried in St. Évroul. After his death, Pillerton passed to Hugh d'Avranches of the Avranchin.[6]

---

4. OV, 2:12–43, 74–79, 90–91, 106–7, 174–75, 264–65, 3:226–27, 234–41, 4:124–25, 230–31, 336–39; *Ex Uticensis monasterii necrologio, RHGF*, 23:487; Orderic Vitalis called him *ex magna nobilitate Francorum et Britonum*; Giroie le Goz d'Echauffour was a knight and a vassal of William de Bellême, for whom he fought bravely against Count Héribert I of Maine; Duke Richard II rewarded him with Echauffour, arr. Argentan, in the Risle Valley, and Montreuil, the promised dower estates of his deceased betrothed; he married Gisela de Montfort, daughter of Thurstin de Bastembourg, lord of Montfort-sur-Risle, Eure, arr. Bernay; Giroie and his wife had eleven children, seven sons, whom Guillaume de Jumièges called "a race of knights," (WJ, 2:vii, 11) and four daughters; *RRAN*, vol. 3, no. 774; WJ, 2:vii (23); *MA*, 2:602; Power, *Norman Frontier*, 119–20, 186, 317, 377: Duke William II sent Robert II into exile after a false accusation by Mabel de Bellême in 1061; Brown, *Normans*, 44; J. Green, *Aristocracy*, 8; Bates, *Normandy before 1066*, 170; Keats-Rohan, *Domesday People*, 262–63, 520.

5. Grentemesnil is now L'Oudon, arr. Lisieux, canton Saint-Pierre-sur-Dives; OV, 2:101–11, 150–53, 3:118–19, 158–59, 4:380–81, no. 2; *Torigni*, 2:224–25, 264–65; in the 1050s, he used Neufmarché in the Eure as a base to ward off attacks against Normandy; in 1065 Duke William granted him half of Neufmarché, the other half to Gérold de Roumare, his dapifer/seneschal; Hugh married Adelise de Beaumont-sur-l'Oise and they had ten children; *Ancient Charters*, no. 18; *MA*, 2:602; Loyd, *Origins*, 47; Power, *Norman Frontier*, 339, 379–80, 415, 418: by the reign of Richard I, Neufmarché was held by the king of France.

6. OV, 4:336–37; the son of Hugh de Grandmesnil, Ivo, owed much in fines, and mortgaged his lands to Robert de Beaumont; but Ivo died on crusade and his two sons died in the wreck of the *White Ship* in 1120, marking the end of the family.

Hugh d'Avranches did not fight at Hastings; since his father was still alive, he had no wealth or vassals to contribute to the conquest. However, Hugh went to England in 1067 and was made commander of the castle of Tutbury on the border of Derbyshire. He helped to defeat the rebellion of the northern earls, for which King William gave him Whitby in Yorkshire. Hugh led the fight to pacify Wales, for which King William made him Count Palatine of Chester in 1071. In 1082, he succeeded his father in Normandy as vicomte of the Avranchin. By 1086, Hugh was one of the ten richest men in England and held lands in twenty counties, including Warwickshire, Nottinghamshire, Yorkshire, and Buckinghamshire. After the death of King William I, Hugh supported his son, King William II Rufus, although as vicomte of Avranches, he was a vassal of Rufus's elder brother, Count Robert Curthose. Hugh fought with Rufus against the Scots in 1091 and against the French in the Vexin in 1097. After Rufus's death, Hugh supported Henry Beauclerc, of whom he was a vassal in the Avranchin, when he succeeded his brother in 1101 as King Henry I of England.[7]

The contemporary historian Orderic Vitalis disliked Earl Hugh and called him a glutton, so fat he could hardly walk, generous but profligate with his wealth and debauched in carnal pleasures. He was called brave but cruel in war, gouging out eyes, cutting off hands and feet, and castrating his captives, including his own brother-in-law, William, count of Eu. Earl Hugh was called "the Fat" by the Welsh and *Lupus* (wolf) by the Normans. But he was also a good soldier, with a retinue of hundreds of knights, and he was generous and religious.[8]

Earl Hugh was a great patron of monasteries. With his father, Earl Hugh refounded the abbey of Saint-Sever in Western Normandy, and was a donor to the abbeys of Saint-Évroul in the Orne, where his son Robert became a monk, and Bec in Eastern Normandy. He was cofounder of Whitby Abbey in north Yorkshire with William de Percy. In 1093, he refounded the Benedictine abbey of St. Werburgh at Chester, persuading Abbot Anselm of Bec to come to England and take charge of installing a community of monks from Bec. Anselm became his confessor and later archbishop of Canterbury and a saint. Earl Hugh received confraternity, burial, and

---

7. DB Warkwickshire, 13.1 (Pillerton Priors); *MA*, 1:406, 409; OV, 2:264–65, 4:138–39, 5:296–99; EYC, vol. 8, no. 5; according to the Register of Whitby Abbey, 1:409, Hugh went to England with William de Percy in 1067; *Torigni*, 2:44–45; J. Green, *Aristocracy*, 75, 94, 151–52, 248; Hollister, *Monarchy*, 99, 106, 110; Power, *Norman Frontier*, 370.

8. OV, 2:260–63, 4:40–41, 220–21; *Florence of Worcester*, 1098, 204; EYC, vol. 8, no. 5; Coss, *Knight*, 19.

prayers from Chester Abbey, which he entered as a monk shortly before his death on 27 July 1101, and where he was buried.⁹

King William I's third son, King Henry I, gave Pillerton to Henry de Beaumont, first earl of Warwick. On his death in 1119, it passed to his son, Roger de Beaumont, and on Roger's death in 1153, to his son William de Beaumont, both earls of Warwick. In 1166, Earl William testified that his father had mortgaged fees of Ivo de Harcourt to the earl of Leicester in warrantied exchange; Pillerton was one of the fees. The knight's fee of Pillerton was then held by Robert, son of William, surname unknown. Earl William married Mathilda de Percy, who had Alan de Arches in ward; they did not have children. When Earl William died in 1184, his brother Waleran de Beaumont became earl.¹⁰

PILLERTON HERSEY AND KINETON, 1184–1215

Pillerton Hersey is in southern Warwickshire, where the land consists mostly of rolling fields, with a few small hills. It lies at the confluence of two streams and four roads and was heavily forested. Each Pillerton was about three miles long and one mile wide. The manor house at Pillerton Hersey stands atop a hill, with gardens and trees sloping down the incline.¹¹

In 1130, Ingelran de Vascoeuil of the Eure in Eastern Normandy held land in Warwickshire. During the reign of King Stephen, he supported Anjou. When the Angevin Henry II was king, Gilbert de Vascoeuil held land at Vascoeuil in the Eure, between Rouen and Gournay-en-Bray. Sir Gilbert de Vascoeuil held Pillerton of the earl of Warwick. After the death of King

---

9. OV, 2:260–63, 5:296–99, 6:38–41, 56–61; Charter of Saint-Évroul 1071/81; ChronAbingdon, 2:24–27, 160–61; CartWhiteby, vol. 28, no. xxv, 312, no. ccclxxvi; MA, 1:409; Torigni, 2:24–27, 32–33, 52–53, 232–33, 270–71; EYC, vol. 2, no. 854; Earl Hugh had married Ermentrude, daughter of Hugues comte de Clermont in the Beauvais; they had one son and heir in 1093, Richard, who succeeded in 1101 as a minor in ward of his mother; in 1115, Richard married Mathilde de Blois, daughter of Count Stephen de Blois and Adele, daughter of King William I; both died without issue in the wreck of the White Ship in November 1120; Hugh had three illegitimate children: Otuel, tutor to the children of King Henry I, who also drowned in the White Ship, Robert, monk of Saint Évroul, and Geva, who married Geoffrey Ridel, and whose son married Richard Basset; CEC, nos. 1, 3, 4, 5, 8, 11, 12–13, 22, 25, 27–28; Planché, 2:16–24; Annales Cestrienses, 17 (1101); J. Green, Aristocracy, 253, 413, 418–20, 424–25.

10. RBE, 1:325.

11. The Pillerton Manor house still exists, although the earliest part is no longer there; the extant parts were built in 1680 and in the reign of Queen Victoria; the gardens are extensive and cover the hillside, at the bottom of which are woods; in 1790, the estate was quite large, containing two thousand seven hundred acres.

Henry II in 1189, his son Richard I Coeur de Lion, became king of England and four months later departed on the Third Crusade. On 2 April 1191, in Sicily en route to the Holy Land, King Richard entrusted his mother, Eleanor of Aquitaine, on her journey home to Sir Gilbert de Vascoeuil and another lord, and gave Sir Gilbert charge of his castle of Gisors, on the border between Normandy and France, the traditional place of meeting between the kings of France and England and strategically crucial to King Richard. However, after King Richard was taken prisoner in December 1192 in Austria, Sir Gilbert switched his allegiance to the king of France and betrayed Gisors into his hands. Hugh V de Gournay, also of Eastern Normandy, had held the fee of Pillerton as subtenant under de Vascoeuil. Hugh de Gournay was one of King Richard's commanders on the Third Crusade, fighting with Richard at Acre, but in 1193 he collaborated with King Philippe-Auguste of France during King Richard's imprisonment and surrendered the fiefs he held of Richard in Normandy to the French king. When King Richard was freed, in February 1194, he judged Gilbert de Vascoeuil and Hugh de Gournay traitors and they forfeited their estates, including Pillerton, which escheated to the king. Richard I then gave Lower Pillerton to his knight, Sir Hugh de Hercy. Waleran earl of Warwick complained about the transfer, since Pillerton was his fief, but gave in "to please the King." Subsequently Hugh de Hercy had to pay the earl a palfrey for his confirmation of the grant to himself and his heirs.[12]

King Richard, who had spent most of his early years in the Aquitaine, came to England to raise funds for the Third Crusade and later to repay his ransom to the German emperor. This he did by high taxes and by selling lands which had been forfeited. The knights who accompanied him to the Holy Land were extremely loyal to him. King Richard was a charismatic military hero, a hardworking professional soldier of integrity, who commanded the respect of his troops. When he went on crusade, he left England under able administrators and at peace with the border regions. He left the Angevin empire, extending from Normandy to the Aquitaine, where he had built many castles and made strategic political alliances, strong and secure, but this changed during Richard's imprisonment.

After the death of King Richard I, his successor and younger brother, John, was very different. King John was mentally unstable, paranoid, cruel,

---

12. PR 3 John (1201), N.S. 14, 119, 4 John (1202), N.S. 15, 19, 5 John (1203) N.S. 16, 53, 6 John (1204), N.S. 18, 89, 7 John (1205), N.S. 19, 266; Matthew Paris, *Chronica Majora*, 2:402; *RRAN*, vol 3, nos. 75, 304, 598, 665, 735; *RL*, 34–35; PR 31 Henry I, 86; RBE, 2:637; *Actes Henri II*, 2:744; *VCH*, Warwick, 5:133–34; Dugdale, *Antiquities of Warwickshire*, 1:614; West, *History*, 690; Waleran de Beaumont, earl of Warwick from 1184–1204.

untrustworthy, arrogant, and cowardly. He had betrayed his brother when Richard was in captivity and tried to seize the throne, taking Nottingham and Tickhill castles. John lost the entire Angevin empire in Normandy, Maine, and Anjou in 1204. He also created conflicts with the English border regions of Ireland, Wales, and Scotland. He so alienated the barons and knights of England with his theft of their properties, exorbitant taxes and fees, especially for wardship and marriage, punitive forest laws, perversion of justice, and abuse of power, that they forced him in 1215 to agree to Magna Carta.

SIR HUGH DE HERCY AND MAUD AND NAMELESS DE HERCY

Hugh de Hercy served King Richard I, who named him in a list of prominent pledges after his ransom from captivity in 1194. In 1195, King Richard I gave Hugh possession of the manor of Lower Pillerton. According to a later charter, this was a gift for homage and faithful service. Hugh de Hercy may have been a household knight of the king. Contemporary documents did not explicitly call Hugh de Hercy a knight, *miles* or sir, but the same documents did not apply these titles to Hugh de Gournay and others who were clearly knights. The fact of his service to King Richard and the grant of Pillerton by the king for his service indicate that he was a knight. So does the fact of his later capture in battle and holding for ransom in 1204, since a person of lower status would most likely simply have been killed. At this time, it was not common practice in such documents to specify whether a man was or was not a knight.[13]

Although he had served King Richard, after Richard's death Hugh de Hercy was not deemed an enemy by King John, who in 1201 confirmed his tenancy. However, the subsequent tenure shifts of Pillerton raise questions about the mental state of King John. In 1202, King John, who favored King Richard's enemies, gave Pillerton back to Hugh V de Gournay and gave Kineton, a larger town three miles from Pillerton, to Hugh de Hercy. However, in 1203, after King John failed to save Gournay-en-Bray in Normandy and killed Prince Arthur, Hugh de Gournay changed sides again and betrayed

---

13. PR 6 Richard I, 169; *CRR*, 9 Richard I (1199), 77, 2, John (1200), 254; OV, 6:240; Prestwich, *Armies*, 68: King Richard I did not have a large number of knights, only three hundred for his campaign of 1197 in France; PR 12 John: Duncan de Lascelles lost three and a half knights' fees for refusing to serve, and had to pay sixty marks and one palfrey to regain them; J. Green, *Aristocracy*, 10-12; Coss, *Origins*, 88: in 1204 King John knighted all his household knights; Bouchard, *Strong of Body*, 120; Crouch, *Image*, 125–26.

the castle of Montfort-sur-Risle to the king of France. King John judged him a traitor and seized all his lands. On 16 May 1203, King John gave Pillerton to Osbert de Roveray, stating that Hugh de Gournay had been a feudal tenant of the traitor Gilbert de Vascoeuil. Three days later, on 19 May 1203, King John gave Pillerton and Kineton back to Hugh de Hercy, whom he called *dilecto et fidele nostro*. This indicates some sort of at least temporary positive relationship between Hugh and King John. King John had great difficulty raising knights for his wars in France, and forced his chief tenants to serve. In 1204 Hugh fought for King John in France, was captured, but was ransomed. On 7 March 1205, the king took Kineton back for himself. Then on 13 February 1206, the king pardoned de Gournay and restored his lands. On 20 March 1206, the king gave Pillerton back to Hugh de Gournay, and gave Kineton to Hugh de Hercy, with the provision that if de Hercy should succeed in recovering Pillerton from de Gournay, "either by King's love or a plea" in court, then Kineton would revert back to the king. On 3 April 1206, the fourth day of the Warwickshire Assizes, Hugh de Hercy appeared to argue his plea for the land and appurtenances in Pillerton. Hugh de Gournay did not appear, thereby defaulting. The court ordered the land be seized for the king and that de Gournay be summoned to appear before the king six weeks after Easter. De Gournay then pleaded *replevin* (repossession) against the default and appointed an attorney. On 12 May, the matter was tried in the Warwickshire court. Hugh de Hercy presented written documentation: the charter in which the earl of Warwick granted him Pillerton on the order of King Richard I for homage and service and the confirmation of his right by King John, putting de Hercy in *seisin* (possession) of Pillerton. De Gournay, through his attorney, offered to defend his right "by the body of one of his men." Trial by combat was unnecessary because Hugh de Hercy won his case in court. The name was changed to Pillerton Hercy, which it remains, although now spelled Pillerton Hersey.[14]

The holder of the fee of Pillerton owed knight's service to the king and the earl of Warwick. Thus, Hugh de Hercy had no choice but to fight in the wars of King John. King John conscripted Hugh de Hercy to fight in France in 1204, when the king lost Normandy to the French. Hugh was captured by the French and a large ransom was paid for his release, for which he had to mortgage his lands for three years. His nephew, Malveysin de Hercy, who at this time was the childless Hugh's presumptive heir, contributed the large sum of twenty marks toward the ransom. A mark was equal to two-thirds of a pound. Wars were, in part, financed by holding prisoners for ransom.

14. *CRR*, 1:77, 254, 4:84, 100, 111, 6:170; *RotChart*, 89; *RL*, 5 John, 137; *RotPat*, 1:39, 57; *RLC*, 1:667; CDF, no. 1315 (1204), 459–478; *Lands of the Normans*; Gurnay, Supplement, 757–58.

The higher the rank of the prisoners, the better they were treated and the greater the ransom. After being ransomed, the former prisoners were expected to promise never to fight against their captor again or to retire from fighting altogether. On 5 September 1204, after his return from captivity and perhaps as a reward for his service, King John gave Hugh de Hercy the manor of Garthorpe in Leicestershire, valued at £15, which had passed to the king on the death of Fulk Paynel. The grant further ordered the sheriff of Leicestershire, if this manor were not possible to assign, to give Hugh other land from the escheats in Leicestershire.[15]

The immediate lords of the de Hercy family in Warwickshire were the earls of Warwick. Waleran de Beaumont was earl of Warwick until his death in 1204, when his son, Henry de Neubourg de Beaumont, became the fifth earl. Henry was then a minor and in ward to Thomas Basset, who later had John I de Hercy in ward. As a teenager Henry had married Margaret d'Oilly, who died giving birth to twins. Henry married second Philippa Basset, daughter and coheir of Thomas Basset, who as guardian had probably arranged the marriage. In 1213 and 1214, Earl Henry paid scutage to avoid fighting in King John's wars, although later he did fight for kings John and Henry III. When Earl Henry died in 1229, his widow, Philippa, retained one third of his estate in dower and lived until 1265. Henry's son, Thomas de Beaumont, became the sixth earl. After his death in 1242, his widow, Ela, retained one third of his now much smaller estate and lived until 1298. Thus, by dowry and inheritance the status of the earls of Warwick diminished. Thomas's sister, Margaret, became seventh countess of Warwick until her death in 1253. Since she also had no children, the eighth earl until 1268 was her half cousin. The ninth earl was William de Beauchamp, great-grandson of Waleran. The earldom continued in the Beauchamp family until 1499.

In 1207 King John imposed a high tax of 13 percent of rents and movables and raised the amounts knights had to pay for scutage, not to serve in the army. In addition, local courts were closed and the king took over the administration of justice which he sold at high price.[16] Despite the repayment of his ransom and the high taxes, Hugh de Hercy managed to keep his

---

15. CLR, John, N.S. 21:97; *VCH, Warwick*, 5:135–36; at this time foreign ransoms were sometimes paid by the king, sometimes by a knight, his family, or his feudal tenants; Powicke, *Loss of Normandy*, 244–45; the *terrae normanorum* were lands in England which had belonged to Normans who changed allegiance to the French when King John lost Normandy; such lands escheated to the king; *RL*, 118: King John gave £10 to one of his knights toward payment of his ransom; King John was called John Lackland (*Jean Sans Terre*); Prestwich, *Armies*, 106.

16. D. Carpenter, *Struggle*, 272–73; Coss, *Origins*, 100: extremely great burden of taxes from 1210–14; Waugh, *Lordship*, 152–53: wardship could include other children besides the heir.

holding of Pillerton intact. After his ransom in 1204, but before his death in 1212, Hugh de Hercy remarried and had a son, John, who became his heir. He also had a second son, Luke. His nephew Malveysin was no longer his heir and left to start a new life in Nottinghamshire.

Sir Hugh and Maud acquired and expanded their landholdings in Warwickshire and redeemed them from debt. They defended their rights to their lands in a court of law. Sir Hugh served two kings, Richard and John, exercising his knighthood through military service, although he became exempt after having been ransomed from captivity. Hugh was close to his nephew and one time heir, Malveysin, who so generously contributed to his ransom; if Hugh had died then, Malveysin would have inherited. Nothing is known about his wife Maud and not even the name of his second wife, who gave him children and an heir to Pillerton. One of his wives administered the estate while Hugh was fighting in France and during his captivity. In this period, they, like everyone else, were members of the Catholic church. They had given their advowson income to St. Neots. Their son became a vicar. Thus, they were a committed part of the mainstream faithful.

SIR JOHN I DE HERCY AND ISABELLE DE HERCY

Hugh de Hercy left Pillerton to his minor son John, who was held in ward by Thomas Basset, baron of Headington, Oxfordshire, and sheriff of Oxfordshire from 1202 to 1214, who collected the rents from the estate until John de Hercy reached majority. John was the much younger cousin of Malveysin, who departed for Nottinghamshire. Previously, Hugh had, with permission of his wife Maud and his then heir apparent Malveysin, given the income of the advowson of Pillerton to the priory of St. Neots in Huntingdonshire. Thomas Basset challenged the grant, claiming that Hugh had remarried a second wife, who was the mother of his heir, John, and that, since the original grant of Pillerton to Hugh by King Richard, the estate had thus changed hands. Thomas Basset and the prior of St. Neots finally compromised and agreed to share the revenues. After he came of age, John de Hercy reconveyed the advowson income to Hugh, prior of St. Neots.[17] Thomas Basset raised John de Hercy, who may have maintained contact with his guardian after he reached majority. Thomas Basset was very close to King John and he and his brother Alan were named as counselors of the king in Magna Carta.

17. CDF, 223 (1121–29), 230 (1190–1204); CRR, 6:122, 170–71, 308; MA, 3:463; RRAN, 3:777–8; Testa de Nevill, 508; Dugdale, Antiquities 1:615; VCH, Warwick, 5:135–136, n. 52; Waugh, Lordship, 132.

King John bankrupted his treasury by his wars in France, selling royal lands and privileges and forcing loans on his barons and on monasteries. He lost the wars and alienated his barons. In 1212, King John tried to organize another invasion of France, but his barons rebelled. The king disbanded the army and hired mercenaries. King John had been excommunicated by Pope Innocent III in 1209. This affected all the people, since there could be no masses or burials in parish churches. Some barons refused to serve the king until the ban was finally lifted by Archbishop Stephen Langton of Canterbury in 1213. King John again tried to mount a campaign against Poitou in 1214. He led it himself, taking much money and many mercenaries, but was defeated at Bouvines. His treasury was empty and his own knights refused to fight for him. In 1215, the barons and knights openly rebelled against him. The conflict was resolved by negotiation and resulted in *Magna Carta* in 1215, in which the king surrendered some of the rights of absolute monarchy, although he retained the right to appoint officials. Thenceforth no persons could have their lands taken or be imprisoned except by law and the judgment of their peers. Courts were permanently established at Westminster for common pleas and judges went to the shires four times a year for petty assizes. Fees for inheritance were limited. Taxes were to be approved by an assembly of tenants-in-chief. Twelve knights from each shire were authorized to investigate and prohibit abuses by royal officials in the counties. Four knights in each shire were to sit with the royal judges on the courts of petty assize. Thus, the position of knights in the counties greatly increased.[18] The following year, King John died at Newark-on-Trent in Nottinghamshire and was succeeded by his minor son by Isabelle of Angoulême, Henry III, who reigned from 1216 to 1272.

The tenure of John I de Hercy at Pillerton is documented in a fee list in 1235, which stated that he "held the manor of the Earl of Warwick for one knight's fee." Henry de Beaumont was earl of Warwick until 1229, then Thomas de Beaumont until 1242. In December 1235, a *mandatum*, command, was issued to John Hercy, Robert Marmion, Robert de Gournay, and others concerning tenements of the countess of Warwick. On 20 September 1235, Stephen of Pillerton, Richard his brother, and Mathilda his daughter paid five marks to appeal against John de Hercy, Luke his brother, William priest of Pillerton, and five others in a case of robbery and breach of the king's peace. The sheriff was ordered to take security and the defendants were ordered to appear before the justices at Westminster in fifteen days. Since the outcome was not recorded, it was probably resolved by settlement

---

18. Henry de Neubourg de Beaumont, earl of Warwick paid 204 marks and 42 marks respectively not to serve in King John's wars in 1213 and 1214; D. Carpenter, *Struggle*, 268–69, 289–90.

or arbitration or possibly later by a duel. In March 1236, Richard, son of Stephen, and John de Hercy were cited for fighting a duel. In 1238, King Henry III absolved John de Beauchamp of a debt of ten marks to the Exchequer, a pledge on behalf of John de Hercy. Isabelle de Hercy, wife of John, gave the king two marks for herself and her pledges in August 1249 because she had withdrawn herself from a claim. In June 1250, Isabelle gave the king one mark for taking an assize of novel disseisin, a remedy for the taking possession of land unjustly and without due process, which protected both landlords and tenants. The plaintiff petitioned the king for a writ to the sheriff to appoint a jury of twelve men to investigate and determine a verdict, which was given to the royal judges for judgment, disposition of seisin, and damages. The process limited the ability of lords to dispossess their tenants. It is interesting that Isabelle, John's wife, could file these cases in the courts in her own name and presumably was not a widow at this time. She may have held property in her own right. In 1256 John de Hercy paid a fine for respite from knighthood, although he retook it later. In 1262 a document about land in Pillerton named John de Hercy and his wife Isabelle. Other documentary evidence from a jury trial at the Warwickshire Assizes, dated in 1262, concerning land in Warwickshire, stated that Robert de Stafford, who was mortally ill in London, gave John de Hercy letters patent to put his son and heir in seisin, possession, of his estate fifteen days before his death, which he did. This illustrates that John was a man of trust and respect. In the turbulent period of 1263–65, the majority of knights in Warwickshire opposed King Henry III. In 1272, King Henry III died and his son by Eléanore of Provence became King Edward I, who reigned from 1272 to 1307.[19]

There is no evidence that John I de Hercy exercised his knighthood by military service, and at one point he took respite from knighthood. He may have resisted fighting for King John, as did so many of his contemporaries. He did not increase his estates and incurred debts, although these

---

19. CFR, Henry III, 1234–35, no. 451, 1248–49, no. 378, 1249–50, 33, no. 426; TNA, 60/35; CRR, 25:20 Henry III, nos. 1565, 1780; CCR, Henry III 1234–37, 220, 247, 1237–43 (21 April 1238); Plea Roll Henry III, Tower Records, Roll 33, Warwickshire Assize, (5 June 1262); one of the adversaries in the case, who was trying to dispossess the young heir, said he did it in the name of Prince Edward, the future King Edward I; however, on questioning by the jury, he admitted that was not true and that Prince Edward was not even in England at the time; an appeal was an accusation of felony lodged by private complaint; Dugdale, *Antiquities*, 1:615: called him *dominus* of Pillerton; *VCH*, Warwick, 5:135–36; J. Green, *Aristocracy*, 325; D. Carpenter, *Struggle*, 236–41: the process for novel disseisin was instituted by King Henry II and was based on Roman law and Glanvill, 379; Coss, *Lordship*, 263; Coss, *Origins*, 96: in 1256, seventeen knights in Warwickshire paid fines for respite from knighthood.

were probably repaid. John was a defendant in several court cases. His wife, Isabelle, was quite active as a woman and came to court in her own right as a plaintiff.

SIR JOHN II DE HERCY AND LETTICE DE HERCY

John I de Hercy was succeeded by his son, also named John. Documents suggest that John II de Hercy may not have been doing very well. He owed a debt of £22 secured by his lands and chattels in Warwickshire to Ralph de Hengham in 1274. In 1275, Ralph de Hengham, chief judge of King's Bench, was appointed to take assize, or judge, a "novel disseisin arraigned by John de Hercy and Isabel his wife against John, son of John Hercy, and others, touching a tenement in Pillerton-Hercy." This indicates serious conflict between father and son that resorted to the court for reconciliation. Two other men were appointed to take assize of a novel disseisin arraigned by John, son of Robert de Pillerton, and Richard de Hercy against John de Hercy and others, and a novel disseisin by John, son of Richard de Pillerton, against John de Hercy and others concerning a tenement. There were suits and countersuits. In 1277, a similar case was filed against John de Hercy over common pasture in Pillerton. In 1301, John II de Hercy attested a Stafford charter.[20]

In 1307–8, John de Hercy the Younger was named as patron of the church of Pillerton. On 14 June 1310, John II de Hercy, Lettice his wife, Luke de Hercy, and many others were pardoned on payment of a fine of £20 for entering the close of the late pastor of the church of Pillerton Hersey, breaking his doors and windows and taking away his goods. John II de Hercy was the last Hercy at Pillerton. John II de Hercy and Lettice his wife, who had no male heir, conveyed the manor of Pillerton to Thomas Wandard/Wandek and his wife Alice in 1307, with the provision that John and his wife could continue to live there until their deaths on payment of "6 quarters of wheat and the same of barley." John and Lettice de Hercy had at least one or, more likely, two daughters and it is probable that Alice Wandard was their daughter. Robert Wandard held one knight's fee in Shotteswell, Kineton Hundred. He was on the list of knights for 1200–1214 and 1220–32, but fined for respite from knighthood in 1256. Robert Wandard

---

20. CCR, Edward I, 1272–79, 136, 227; HKF, 2:279; Ralph de Hengham was appointed chief judge of the King's Bench in 1274 and served until 1290; TNA, E 40/8809: Luke de Hercy held a messuage and virgate of land in Goldicote which he enfeoffed to Hugh de Caldewelle rector for the rent of ten marks—no date, but Caldewelle was rector of Wytleye in 1297; CPR, Edward I, 1272–81, 187, 213, 253, 1292–1301, 277.

was coroner of Warwickshire in 1272. Robert's son, William, was sheriff of Warwickshire in 1272-73 and justice of the peace in Nottinghamshire for the Honour of Peverel. William's holding was in litigation and he was not well off. He also fined for respite from knighthood in 1256, although he retook his knighthood in the mid-1280s, but by then held only one half a knight's fee. His son, Thomas, married Alice and thereby acquired Pillerton Hersey through his wife. In 1318, Thomas held a messuage and garden, twenty virgates of demesne land, and fourteen acres of other land in Pillerton. However, in 1317 he was already in debt for £92, secured by his lands in Pillerton which were worth less than the debt. In February 1319, Thomas Wandard sold Shotteswell for £100 and in 1320 he sold most of Pillerton Hersey for forty marks, keeping only one carucate, two virgates, and 8s. 8½ d. in rents. He had a son, John Wandak of Pillerton Hersey, who had multiple debts for which he was sued: for £100 in 1349, £60 in 1350, £50 in 1351, £20 in 1355, and £50 in 1368.[21]

During the reign of Edward II, Sir Robert le Harpour of Chesterton, Warwickshire, married Isabelle, daughter of "John Hercy, lord of Pillerton Hercy." Their great-grandson, John le Harpour, held land in Pillerton, but died without issue in 1352. John II de Hercy was documented still living as lord of Pillerton in 1312 and 1316.[22] John was the last person named de Hercy holding the manor of Pillerton. However, by this time, descendants of his cousin Malveysin de Hercy were well established in Nottinghamshire.[23]

21. CPR, Edward II 21 (1307-13), 232, 241-42; TNA, C 131/1/12 (20 December 1318); Shotteswell was held of the earl of Warwick by Eustace de Mortain in 1224; TNA, C241/128/67, 241/128/149, 241/128/183, 241/129/217, 241/234/89, 241/149,85; VCH, Warwick, 5:133; this Luke de Hercy was probably a brother or son of John II, as Luke the priest had died in 1284; Coss, *Lordship*, 235, 256, 259-63, 299-300, n. 131; Coss, *Origins*, 77: Wandard was an example of a knightly family which survived into the fourteenth century but at reduced means and status, 150: coroner.

22. *Register Diocese Worcester*, 15, 17; RLC, 1:611b, 2:83b; HKF, 1:159, 2:245-47, 5:175; Shotteswell by mid-fourteenth century passed to the Beauchamps; CPR, Edward II, 1307-13, 232, 242; Henry VI, 87, 133; FA, 5:174-75 (1316); he called himself "Lord of Pillerton" in 1312: Dugdale, MSS (Bodleian) 17, fol. 19; IPM, 5:9 Edward II (12 January 1316: one fee in Pillerton-Hersey to John of Pillerton); Collins, *English Baronetage*, vol. 2, no. 73; Dugdale, *Antiquities*, 1:478.

23. TNA, E 40/8339:17 August 1372, document, possibly citation of earlier document, concerning the rents of three parishes at Avene Derset, now Avon Dassett, four miles east of Kineton, certified by the seals of the claimants, John Hercy and two others; *Descriptive Catalogue*, 4:293 (A8339), Warwickshire County Records Office, CR 299/367: 17 August 46 Edward III; after the death in 1421 of John Cokkes of Longebrugge, now Longbridge, just south of the city of Warwick, John Hercy of Longebrugge was enfeoffed by Cokkes's widow and son with his lands and tenements; thus there were Hercys in Warwickshire at least until 1421.

PART II | ENGLAND

The de Hercys of Warwickshire were knights and maintained their manor of Pillerton. Hugh was favored by kings. Hugh exercised his knighthood by military service. He was sufficiently prosperous to pay off the mortgage on his land resulting from his ransom from captivity. The de Hercy men and at least one of their wives appeared in court cases, both as plaintiffs and as defendants. But the grandchildren gradually lost their estates, both by debts and by lack of a male heir, and the family died out in Warwickshire.

ST. MARY'S CHURCH, PILLERTON HERSEY

St. Mary's Church in Pillerton was built in the thirteenth century when the de Hercy family held the advowson. Hugh de Hercy, with the assent of his wife Maud and his nephew and heir apparent Malveysin, had granted its income to the priory of St. Neots in the late twelfth century. The priests at St. Mary's in Pillerton during this period were often younger sons of the de Hercy family. Luke de Hercy was vicar from 1239 until he retired due to old age in 1284. The following year several persons were accused of unlawfully occupying the house of the "aged and incapacitated vicar," Luke de Hercy. Lesoar de Hercy became pastor of the church in 1284. John II de Hercy, lord of Pillerton and patron of the church, put his son, Nicholas de Hercy, in the office in 1289, although Nicholas was still a minor at the time. By December 1292, Nicholas was listed as priest and incumbent and remained there until 1299. John made his last appointment in 1308. In 1309, John II de Hercy conveyed the advowson to the earl of Warwick. Nicholas de Hercy then became rector of St. Cuthbert's in North Meols, Lancashire, from 1308 until his resignation on 2 October 1314.[24] St. Mary's Church still stands, but only the chancel dates from the thirteenth century.

24. *Episcopal Registers*, ccxxvii, 91 (1277, Luke to study theology in Worcester), 152 (1282, John retired for old age), 153 (1282, Hugh given one day to negate transfer of church), 246 (1284, curate given to Luke incapacitated by old age), 335 (1289, John presented his son Nicholas under age), 428 (1292, Nicholas priest); Smith, *Studies in Clergy*, 60; a Lucas de Hercy was listed as rector of St. Laurence Church in nearby Oxhill, Warwickshire, in 1284; John de Hercy at Pillerton in 1282, then Luke in 1284; Walter de Berton served during the minority of Nicholas, who served in his own right by 1292; Dugdale, *Antiquities*, 1:612, 615; Nicholas served at North Meols from May 1300 until he resigned in December 1314; *VCH, Warwick*, 5:134–135; *VCH*, Lancashire, vol. 3, "North Meols."

KINETON

Members of the de Hercy family were documented in Kineton, Warwickshire. Kineton was both a town three miles northeast of Pillerton and also a hundred. Kineton was founded in the Saxon period with several smaller villages around it, including the Pillertons. There are remains of a motte and bailey castle attributed to King John, where he was reputed to have held court leet. The motte was a great earthen mound, the bailey a wooden enclosure. There was a ditch around them and a stockade on top. Kineton lies on the small river Dene. The town, Kineton or Kington, belonged to the king. Before the conquest it consisted of ten hides, but in Domesday was listed with only three, with thirty-eight ploughs and 111 tenants. In 1169, Kineton became a hundred, incorporating four previous hundreds. In the thirteenth century Kineton became a market town.[25]

Hugh de Hercy paid sixty shillings tax in Kineton in 1202 and 1203 for a quarter part of the year, £12 in 1204 and in 1206, £6 for half the year. In 1270 King Henry III "during pleasure" gave Richard de Hercy the whole hundred of Kineton for life, "that he render to the King therefor yearly as much as other keepers and 100s. of increment to the Exchequer." Richard actually paid £24, 117s. a year for Kineton to William de Mortain, sheriff of Warwickshire. By 1279 Kineton had 102 tenants.[26]

Since they are frequently mentioned together in documents, it is probable that John II de Hercy and Richard de Hercy were brothers or cousins. Richard de Hercy and Margery his wife held in Kineton a toft, land on which a house formerly stood, three and a half virgates of land which had been her dowry, one messuage, and two other virgates. Richard de Hercy filed a complaint in 1274, noting that King Henry III had made him keeper of Kineton, but that William de Mortain, former sheriff of Warwickshire, had ejected him therefrom without order of the king. Richard petitioned that he be restored as keeper. John de Hercy of Pillerton and Richard of Kineton were named as co-witnesses to a property transfer document. In 1281, Richard de Hercy sued for novel disseisin of a tenement in Hampnett, Gloucestershire, southwest of Pillerton.[27] It is possible that Richard was the

---

25. Kineton; according to a royal charter in 969, a Saxon noble was given land in Kineton (then spelled Cynton) by King Edgar; in Domesday, Kineton, spelled Quintone in French, was still owned by the king; DB Warwickshire, 1.2.

26. PR 4 John 31 (1202), 5 John 28 (1203), 6 John 1 (1206), 220, 7 John (1205), N.S. 19, 28; *IPM*, 54 Henry III, 34; CFR, *Edward I*, 1272–1307, 19; Dugdale, *Antiquities*, 1:599; *VCH*, Warwick, 5:1–2; PR Henry II, 1166, 67, 1192, 245; CPR, Henry III, vol. 6 (1266–72), 426; TNA, C 143/3/1.

27. Warwickshire County Record Office, L1/15 (thirteenth century); Warwickshire Feet of Fines, 18:19–20; CPR, *Edward I*, 1272–81, 105; CCR, *Edward I*, 1272–79, 322;

grandnephew or the younger grandson of Hugh de Hercy and that Richard was possibly a younger cousin of Malveysin de Hercy.

The de Hercy family of Warwickshire were knights, although later took respite from knighthood. Sir Hugh primarily exercised his knighthood through military service to the kings. His son and grandson were not documented fighting. Hugh received and maintained his lands, redeeming them from mortgage after his captivity and ransom. Gradually the next generations became less prosperous and after the death of his grandson the name died out in Warwickshire. The nephew of Hugh, Malveysin, left Warwickshire, and became a knight and prosperous castellan in Nottinghamshire.

Coss, *Origins*, 192: by 1332 Kineton was held by someone else.

Nottinghamshire

MALVEYSIN DE HERCY: WARWICKSHIRE TO NOTTINGHAMSHIRE

The nephew of Sir Hugh de Hercy of Warwickshire was Malveysin de Hercy. The name Malveysin was a sobriquet, from the Latin *malus vicinus* and French *mauvais voisin*, meaning "bad neighbor." Mauvoisin was the name of a family which lived in Mantes and Rosny in the French Vexin, a region that was constantly fought over between the dukes of Normandy and Anjou and the kings of France in the eleventh and twelfth centuries. Early members of the family were donors to the abbey of Saint-Évroul, indicating a possible relationship with the de Grandmesnil family, who first held Warwickshire. A member of the Mauvoisin family fought at Hastings. Domesday mentions one Malus Vicinus holding the small village of Bradley in Suffolk under Richard Fitz Gilbert de Brionne de Clare of the Eure. The village of Maveysin Ridware in Staffordshire was early associated with the family, who were founders of Blithbury Priory there in the early twelfth century. William Mauvoisin was influential in the court of King Henry II from 1174. In 1210–12 Adam Moveisin held there with Eudes de Dammartin and Thomas de Saint-Valéry. Raoul IV de Mauvoisin married Agnese d'Aulnay, daughter of Gauthier d'Aulnay, seneschal of Dammartin. The Dammartin family also held in Warwickshire and Nottinghamshire, including for a time the manor of Dunham, Nottinghamshire, of which the Hercy manor of Grove was soke, under its jurisdiction. Aubrey de Dammartin married Joan Basset, sister of Thomas Basset of Headington who held John de Hercy of Pillerton, Warwickshire, in ward. It is possible that the de Hercy family of Warwickshire knew or was related to the Mauvoisin family and therefore gave the name to their son.[1]

1. Brompton (Malvoisin), Leland (Mauveysin); RBA 5302 has Mannasyn, which, if the *n*'s are inverted *u*'s and *v*'s, would be Mauvasyn; King Richard I had given the name to one of his catapults; *VCH*, Staffordshire, vol. 3, no. 5; RBE, 1:29, 65, 110, 126, 149,

When Gilbert de Arches of Yorkshire died in 1175, his minor son, Alan, was held in ward by Mathilde de Percy, wife of William de Beaumont, earl of Warwick. William died in 1184 and Mathilda returned to Yorkshire. It is possible that contact occurred between the young Alan de Arches and Malveysin de Hercy that resulted in the latter migrating north after he was replaced as heir of Hugh de Hercy in Warwickshire and then marrying Théophanie de Arches of the Yorkshire de Arches family. Malveysin de Hercy was still in Warwickshire in 1204 when he contributed to the ransom payment for his uncle Hugh. Thus, he was an adult with his own money. By about 1207 he had moved to Nottinghamshire.

Sir Malveysin de Hercy became established in Nottinghamshire by marrying Théophanie, daughter of Gilbert II de Arches, baron of Grove, Nottinghamshire. She and her sister Isabel, who married William Rufus, were coheirs of Grove after the death of their father in 1209, and their husbands, Sir Malveysin de Hercy and William Rufus, acquired Grove through them. Théophanie de Arches was the mother of the de Hercy family of Nottinghamshire, the first woman whose family name is known and thus the history of her family is very important to that of the Hercy family.

YORKSHIRE FROM 1066–1208: D'AUFFAY AND DE ARCHES

In 1086 the greatest landholders in Yorkshire were Robert, count of Mortain, with 234 fees, who also held 7 in Nottinghamshire, and Count Alan of Brittany and Richmond, with 219 fees, and 8 in Nottinghamshire. The second tier were Ilbert de Lacy with 186 fees in Yorkshire and 10 in Nottinghamshire, and William de Percy, with 132 in Yorkshire. In the third tier were Roger de Bully, with 65 in Yorkshire and 114 in Nottinghamshire, Earl Hugh d'Avranches of Chester, with 39 fees in Yorkshire, and Pillerton in Warwickshire, Osberne de Arches, with 38 fees in Yorkshire, and Ralph Paynel, with 23 in Yorkshire. Some of these cross-county holdings illustrate links between Yorkshire and Nottinghamshire. Later, other great landholders in Yorkshire in the reign of Henry I were Hugh II de Laval from Maine,

---

2:477; Raoul/Radulph I and II de Malveysin were donors to St-Évroul; the de Malveysin family lived in the Vexin, disputed territory between Normandy and France, hence were called "bad neighbors," controlled traffic on part of the Seine, and were closely connected to powerful families of Normandy and Bretagne; *Testa de Nevill*, 1:65–66; *Rolls of Arms*, Walford's Rolls, no. 127, p. 193; EYC, 2:119n.: Reginald Dammartin held Dunham before 1218; the Dammartin family held a fee in Yorkshire in 1161–62; "Maison Mauvoisin"; another Raoul de Mauvoisin may have married Eustace de Dammartin; *RL*, 94; RBE, 1:273; Power, *Norman Frontier*, 233, 236, 404, no. 93–94.

who took over the de Lacy lands, and Robert de Brus. The descendant of Osberne de Arches married Malveysin de Hercy. Roger de Bully had held the lands which went to the de Hercy family in Nottinghamshire after they intermarried with the de Arches family. De Bully built Tickhill Castle in Yorkshire where Malveysin de Hercy later became constable. Earl Hugh d'Avranches preceded the de Hercy family at Pillerton in Warwickshire. The de Brus family intermarried with the de Arches family.

D'AUFFAY AND DE NEUFMARCHÉ

Gulbert d'Auffay of Eastern Normandy, son of Richard de Saint-Valéry and second cousin of William the Conqueror, fought at Hastings and was given lands in Yorkshire. He renounced these lands because he did not want to profit from war and returned to Normandy. His lands then went to his younger relative, Osberne de Arches. Gulbert died on 15 August 1087.[2]

Gulbert d'Auffay had nephews, sons of his sister's family de Neufmarché, who also went to England and were given lands in Yorkshire.[3] Ralph de Neufmarché held in Yorkshire and was a donor to Blyth priory in Nottinghamshire. His brother Payn donated lands in Yorkshire to Blyth. Both brothers were tenants of Roger de Bully. Ralph's son, Adam de Neufmarché, donated to Roche Abbey in south Yorkshire. In 1201–12, Ralph and Adam de Neufmarché held of Honour of Tickhill with Gilbert de Arches and Roger de St. Quentin, a relative of Agnes de Arches. On 1224, Adam de Neufmarché and William de Cressy were appointed justices to take assize of *mort d'ancestor* at Nottingham. Adam had a son Henry, who married Frethesant Paynel, daughter of William Paynel, and held lands in Yorkshire.[4]

2. DB Yorkshire, vol. 2, CW 1 (Thorner), 36 (Appleton): Gulbert was the *antecessor* of Osberne de Arches; OV, 3:246–47, 4:112–13.

3. Neufmarché first mentioned in treaty of St-Clair-sur-Epte; means "new march," i.e. frontier, border; OV, 3: 248–51, 4:124–25; Bernard de Neufmarché fought for King William II to pacify Wales and was given lands in Wales; Bernard witnessed the foundation charter for Battle Abbey and a charter to Fécamp for King William I in 1086; he was also a supporter of the church and priory of Auffay; he died between 1121–25 and was succeeded by his daughter, Sybil, who was given in marriage along with her inheritance by King Henry I to Miles of Gloucester; *RRAN*, vol. 1, no. 62, 113, 207, 220, 325, vol. 2, 1041, 1280, vol. 3, 345; EYC, vol. 8, no.5; *MA*, 3:259–64; Ward, *Women*, 26–27.

4. EYC, vol. 8, 140–62, vol. 9, no. 236; OV, 2:128–31; about 1064, Geoffrey, father of Bernard, lost the castle of Neufmarché to the duke and Gérold de Roumare became castellan; during the reign of Henry II, William de Roumare gave land in Lincolnshire to Reginald de Neufmarché; *RRAN*, vol. 1, no. 255, vol. 3, nos. 34, 139, 655; Osberne was a tenant of Hugh de Grandmesnil; *CartBlyth*, 190–91; PR *31* Henry I, 29; *MA*,

PART II | ENGLAND

There were connections either of blood or of vassalage between the d'Auffay/de St. Valéry and de Arches families both in England and in Normandy. In the period 1144–50, Duke Geoffroy Plantagenet of Normandy and Anjou wrote to Reginald de Saint-Valéry "*et ministris suis de Archis*," ordering them to restore the forest tithe to Saint-Amand in Rouen. In the same period, Duke Geoffroy wrote to Robert de Neufmarché and Robert Vernon as his justices to restore the tithes of ducal rents from Arques and the vicomté of Arques and Dieppe, to the abbey of St. Wandrille.[5] In 1086 and in the mid-twelfth century the relationship was documented between the d'Auffay/de Saint-Valéry/de Neufmarché family and the d'Arques family.

DE ARCHES/D'ARQUES

In England, the Norman name d'Arques was anglicized to de Arches. Osberne de Arches of Eastern Normandy went to England during the reign of King William I, but was probably too young to have fought at Hastings. Before 1086, King William had given both Gulbert d'Auffay and Osberne de Arches lands in Yorkshire, settling his strong and reliable Norman knights around the important city of York. Osberne de Arches was both lord and tenant-in-chief, holding thirty-eight manors in Yorkshire as tenant-in-chief, principally in the fee of Percy in the West Riding, in the hundreds of Ainsty (Thorp Arch), Barkston, Burghshire, and Craven. Some of his lands were held under the king, and others under or with the archbishop of York, the count de Mortain, Ilbert de Lacy, William de Percy, and Ralph Paynel. Domesday Book recorded the lands of Osberne de Arches in Thorner and Appleton and other fees as previously held by Gulbert d'Auffay. There was a court case over whether Gulbert, the antecessor of Osberne, had held all of Appleton, Thorner, and other lands in Yorkshire without dispute, which he did, or whether they infringed on the lands of Ilbert de Lacy. Domesday attributed Thorner to Ilbert de Lacy and Appleton to Osberne de Arches. The majority of Osberne's holdings were in Ainsty Hundred, around and on the west side of the city of York. His caput was at Thorp Arch, on the river Wharfe in Ainsty, where he built his manor hall. In 1086 Thorp Arch had a church, a priest, and the site for a mill. The medieval village of Thorp

---

5:502, 505; *Testa de Nevill*, 1:248; RBE, 1:181, 188, 296–97; CPE, 9:543–44; Bates and Curry, *England*, 54, n. 10; Loyd, *Origins*, 72; Keats-Rohan, *Domesday People* 314–15: Osbern de Neufmarché was a Domesday tenant of Hugh de Grandmesnil; Keats-Rohan, *Domesday Descendants*, 615–16.

5. *RRAN*, vol. 3, nos. 732, 779–80; Ellis, "Biographical Notes," 243, holds that Osberne was the son of Godfroy d'Arques.

Arch consisted of farms and dwelling houses facing a central green, with common fields on the outskirts along the river. The manor house stood on the west side of the village near the river, but no longer exists. In the city of York, Osberne held two houses of Brun the priest, twelve lodging houses, and two houses of the bishop of Coutances. In addition, Osberne was also tenant-in-chief of Redbourne, Scawby, and Sturton in Lincolnshire.[6]

Osberne de Arches was high sheriff of Yorkshire in 1100. The sheriff, from the old English "shire reeve," was the representative of the king in the shire, the chief administrator of the shire and of justice in the shire, and collector of revenues for the king. Sheriffs were then generally appointed by the king. Osberne was a generous benefactor of St. Mary's Abbey in York during the reign of King William I. King William II confirmed the donations of his father and of Count Alan of Richmond, Osberne de Arches, Ilbert de Lacy, and others to St. Mary's York. Osberne had donated lands in Appleton, Poppleton, and Hessay, and two houses in York. These gifts were later confirmed by King Henry II with additional donations by Ralph Paynel, Robert de Brus, and others. Osberne's steward, Fulk Fitz Reinfrid, was the son of the monk behind the founding of Whitby Abbey on the coast of north Yorkshire. Osberne may have given land to Fulk. Fulk donated to Whitby and his son, Robert, confirmed the donation and married Alice, the granddaughter of Osberne.[7]

6. Le Tailleur mentioned "le erle d'Arques," presumably referring to William; Dives and Falaise mentioned both Guillaume and Osberne d'Arques, Dives also named Gulbert d'Auffay; DB, Yorkshire 1:25, C 16, vol. 2, CW 1, 24, 26–29, 32–33, 35–36, 38, 40–41, SW Ba 4, 8, 13, SW An 4, 5–15, SW Bu 1, 2, 6–7, 10, 18; other DB holders in Craven were William de Percy and Gilbert Tesson; Thorner was land of Ilbert de Lacy in Skyrack Hundred in the West Riding (9W12, SW Sk8); DB, Yorkshire vol. 2, CW 1: *Gulbtus antecessor ej*; 36: "*Gulbt antecessor suus*"; Domesday also mentions an Osbern who was lord of West Retford, Weston, Sibthorpe, Odestorp, Old Clipstone and Beckingham in Nottinghamshire in 1066, all but Sibthorpe were fees of Roger de Bully in 1086, Sibthorpe of Count Alan; four of these became Arches and/or Hercy lands later; Domesday notes Osberne as lord of Colsterworth, Easton, Skillington, Little Carlton, North Reston, and Wickenby in Lincolnshire in 1086; Bogg, *Lower Warfeland*, 3: lands formerly belonging to his antecessor Gulbert included Stiveton, Hornington, Oxeton-Colton, and Thorp; Fleming, *Domesday*, 208, 266, 270, 272–74; Keats-Rohan and Thornton, *Domesday Names*, 104; Ellis, "Biographical Notes," 140: two surveys of the lands of Ilbert de Lacy were done before 1085, the first stating that the whole of Thorner was within the boundaries of his castle, the second that it was not; Appleton was near Bolton Percy, held by William de Percy, but mentioned with Osberne de Arches's nearby holdings of Appleton and Steeton, 214; YAJ, 5 (1879), 298–99; Thorp Arch was near Toulston and Newton Kyme, also held by Osberne.

7. *RRAN*, vol. 2, nos. 795–96; EYC, vol. 1, nos. 350–52, 354, 527, 529–31, vol. 5, 19, 266, 269, 300–301, 353; J. Green, *Aristocracy*, 402, states that the list "reads like a roll call of the Normans in the north in the late eleventh century"; *MA*, 3:547–48; witnesses included Robert and Adam de Brus and Roger, son of Picot de Lascelles; Lindsay

Osberne de Arches was one of the great tenants-in-chief in Domesday Yorkshire, holding numerous lands of the king and of other magnates. He was the father of William I, Agnes, Robert I, Peter I, and Gilbert I de Arches. He generously provided for his children by *parage* and also gave lands to the church and possibly to one or more of his vassals. As a result, his descendants did not have the same high status since status was based on quantity of land held. Osberne de Arches died by 1115 in Thorp Arch, Yorkshire, and was succeeded by his eldest son and heir William I de Arches there and in many other fees. William was born in Newton Kyme, Yorkshire, and lived from about 1095 until about 1154, when he died in Thorp Arch. William I held seven fees in Yorkshire and also held land in Lincolnshire. His gifts to St. Peter's York were confirmed by King Henry I. He was a donor to Nostell Priory and the diocese of York along with Hugh II de Laval of Maine. Sir William I married Juetta I. Together they donated land to Elias de Hou, a vassal knight, who was also called a *cognatus*. They had daughters Mathilda and Juetta II. William I and Juetta I de Arches and their descendants were founders of and generous donors to monasteries for women in Yorkshire. They founded the priory of Nun Monkton during the reign of King Stephen, granting the churches of Thorp Arch, Hammerton, Askham, and Kirkby, and six carucates of land in Nun Monkton to the nuns and to their daughter Mathilda, who became its prioress. The foundation enhanced the prestige of William and Juetta as well as did the status of their daughter as prioress. Juetta I was buried in Guisborough, an Augustinian priory in north Yorkshire, founded by Robert I de Brus and supported by the de Brus family. Their daughter Juetta II married Adam II de Brus, grandson of Robert I de Brus. William I died about 1154.[8]

The heir of William I and Juetta I de Arches was Juetta II, who was born about 1138 in Thorp Arch. She married first Roger de Flamville, who held one and a half fees in 1166, and died in 1169. Juetta II married second, in about 1170, Adam II de Brus, lord of Skelton, Yorkshire, son and heir of Adam I de Brus, grandson of Robert I de Brus and Agnes Paynel, daughter

---

Survey (1115–18), 77–81; Coss, *Lady*, 7: the sheriff was in many ways equivalent to the *vicomte* in France; Keats-Rohan, *Domesday People*, 314.

8. *MA*, 3:558; EYC, vol. 1, nos. 534–35; vol. 3, nos. 1466–67, vol. 7, nos. 9–10, 12, p. 272, vol. 11, 28; *RRAN*, vol. 2, no. 1889; *Pedes finium*, 34; *Charters of the Honour*, nos. 11, 42–45, 77, 222, 256, 318, 359, 379–80, 390, 400; Juetta I died in 1152, buried Guisborough; Helto, son of William de Arches, held three carucates of land in the Honour of Skipton in 1166; this mysterious Helto did not succeed William de Arches; thus he was either not a legitimate son or died young or perhaps had become a cleric; a person named Helto witnessed charters for the abbey of St. Ouen in Rouen, which had been founded by Goscelin d'Arques; RBE, 1:424, 432; Keats-Rohan, *Domesday Descendants*, 287–88.

of Fulk Paynel. Juetta II issued many charters in her own right and donated to Nostell and Nun Monkton priories. Juetta II and Adam had a son Peter and a daughter Isabel. Juetta granted land to her daughter, which may have helped enable her marriage to Henry de Percy, but diminished the inheritance of Peter.[9]

Agnes, daughter of Osberne and sister of William, was born about 1100 in York. She married first Herbert de St. Quentin, second Robert de Fauconberg, and third William Foliot. St. Quentin was an old Norman family from the Avranchin, whose ancestor Hugh fought at Hastings and held land in Domesday. Agnes appears to have been a dominant wife to St. Quentin; she was called *Sire Agnetum suam viraginem* (Sir Agnes his virago). Agnes donated land in her own right to Nunkeeling Priory between 1144 and 1154. Her donation was confirmed by the archbishop of York and later by Pope Alexander III, which enhanced the importance of her donation. The daughter of Agnes, Alice de St. Quentin, married Robert Fitz Fulk, son of her grandfather's steward, and had sons Robert II and William. After the death of her husband, Alice and her son Robert endowed the Cistercian priory of Nun Appleton.[10]

Robert de Arches, second son of Osberne, inherited his fees of Redbourne, Scawby, and Sturton in north Lincolnshire. At some point Robert or his son Sir William or grandson Sir Robert acquired fees in Wrawby, where they built Archesmanor, and Bigby, both in north Lincolnshire. In 1166, the wife of Robert de Arches held two fees in Nottinghamshire, which were perhaps her dower lands. Robert had a son, Gilbert. About 1200, Sir Gilbert de Arches held the land and the advowson of Wrawby, witnessed by his sons Robert and Gilbert. Later Robert, now a knight, enfeoffed his son John in Wrawby. In 1212, Robert de Arches held a half fee in Bigby, which he continued to hold in 1242–43, 1275 and 1282.[11]

9. Adam II was nephew of Robert, lord of Annandale and ancestor of the kings of Scotland; William and Juetta I de Arches granted land in fee to Elias de Hou, knight and their relative by marriage; Juetta granted land to Adam of Hammerton, son of Elias, her knight, half of which Adam/Alan donated to Fountains Abbey; eight carucates in Hammerton and Kirkby; EYC, vol. 1, nos. 529–31, 534, 536–38, 548–49, 552–53; *Charters of the Honour*, nos. 183, 389; MA, 4:192–194; Blakely, *Brus Family*, 45: Juetta's son, Hugh, by her first marriage, died young and without children; Keats-Rohan, *Domesday Descendants*, 287, 463, 521.

10. EYC, vol. 1, nos. 456, 541, 543–45, vol. 3, 1331, 1333, 1135–38, vol. 11, no. 96; MA, 4:186; TNA, MD335/7/16, 426, no. 556; Alice, her second husband, Eustace de Merc, and her heirs donated land to the priory of Nun Appleton about 1163; Keats-Rohan, *Domesday Descendants*, 696.

11. RBE, 1:343, 2:590, 598; PR 31 Henry I, 83; *Manuscripts of the Duke*, 4:65, 66; HKF, 2:194, 4:65–66; Sir Gilbert de Arches held Archesmanor in Wrawby about 1200 and was named patron of the church there in 1234; this Gilbert had sons Robert

PART II | ENGLAND

In the early twelfth century Gilbert de Arches, son of Osberne and brother of William I, Agnes, Robert, and Peter I, was enfeoffed in Yorkshire by Alan I de Percy. Gilbert I de Arches witnessed charters of Alan de Percy between 1125 and 1135 and for William II de Percy between 1142 and 1154 with William I de Arches, and for the archbishop of York in 1154-60. In July 1141, Gilbert witnessed the grant of Worcestershire to William de Beauchamp for the Empress, with Milo, Geoffrey, Walter, and Stephen de Beauchamp. Gilbert also witnessed a charter to the Cistercian Fountains Abbey in 1154-56. Fountains had been founded in 1132 by a group of disaffected monks of St. Mary's York who sought a more simple and devout life and moved to a wooded valley in north Yorkshire. Gilbert de Arches, with Peter and Peter's son, witnessed a charter of Thurstin de Arches giving land in Arncliffe to Fountains Abbey. William II Percy confirmed gifts by himself and by Gilbert de Arches to Sallay Abbey in Craven. In 1166, Gilbert de Arches held three quarters of a new fee of William II de Percy, from whom he had formerly held two old fees. He held in Yorkshire: Rainton, Kearby, Kettlewell, Arncliff, Linton, Treshfield, Addingham, and houses in Tadcaster, York, and Stamford Bridge, in service of one and three quarters knights' fees, as well as land in Somerby, Lincolnshire. Gilbert had sons Alan, Robert, and Gilbert. Alan, who succeeded, was a minor in ward of Mathilda de Percy, countess of Warwick, daughter and coheir of William II de Percy. Gilbert died by 1175.[12]

Countess Mathilda restored Gilbert's lands to Alan when he came of age. In the 1180s he had received back five bovates in Rainton worth 5s. for a payment of two marks. In 1211, Alan filed a writ in a case asking that a

---

and Gilbert; all three were witnesses with Peter de Arches and Walter de Percy about 1200; in 1256 there was a dispute in the court between Gilbert de Arches, querent, and Adam Paynel, deforciant, concerning fishing rights in the river Ancholme; Sir Robert enfeoffed his son John in the toll of Wrawby church in 1300; RL, John ,55; *Lay Subsidy Rolls*, Edward I, 66; CPR, Edward III, 1358-61, 36; Isabel, daughter of Sir Robert, inherited Bigby which passed to her husband, Sir John Skipwith, by 1300; in 1319, he acknowledged holding lands in Bigby by the right of his wife; in 1338, Thomas de Arches held in Summerby and Gilbert in Bigby, both of the constable of Chester; Massingberd, *History*, 54-55: "Sir John de Thorpe de Skipwith married Isabel, daughter of Robert de Arches as appeareth by divers deeds yet extant both of Gilbert and Robert and she brought the Manor of Wrawby the ancient seat of the Arches. Her grandfather was Sir Gilbert de Arches, knight"; 40 Henry III, case 130, file 39 (27 October 1256); Adam Paynel had founded the hospital at Wrawby in the late twelfth century, which was administered by the abbot of Selby.

12. EYC, vol. 2, nos. 908-9, 970, 1202, vol. 3, 1825, vol. 11, nos. 5-7, 10, 12, 14, 16-17, 20-21, 27, 88, 128-29, 208, 268; RBE, 1:424-26; MA, 5:512; RRAN, 3:68, 634-35; TNA, MD, 335/7/18, 19; *Charters of the Honour*, nos. 145-46, 343; Turner, *Bingley*, 87-88; Ellis, "Biographical Notes," 245, suggests Gilbert was younger son and probable ancestor of Nottinghamshire Arches; Keats-Rohan, *Domesday Descendants*, 287.

duel be waged. He witnessed documents for Fountains Abbey. Alan had two sons, Thomas and Osbert, and two daughters, Joan and Christiana. When he died in 1218, William de Briwere was given custody of his lands and heir. King John had given Briwere the Peverel lands in Nottinghamshire and the Briweres intermarried with the de Hériz family. By 1227 Thomas de Arches held Rainton and donated land to Fountains Abbey and St. Leonard's Hospital. The same year William III de Percy sued Thomas de Arches over land in Rainton and Bennington. Thomas responded that the land had been transferred to his father, Alan, by Countess Mathilda of Warwick and was originally the land of his grandfather, Gilbert. In 1235 Thomas gave twenty-one bovates in Rainton to St. Leonard's York and also much land to Fountains. Thomas also held land in Normanton, Nottinghamshire. In 1245 Thomas released his claim to sixteen acres in Normanton to the prior of Lenton for one hundred shillings. He married Sarah, but died without children before 1252. Osbert succeeded and confirmed his brother's gifts to Fountains. Osbert held lands in Aston, Kearby, and Kettlewell, Yorkshire, and in Normanton, Nottinghamshire. Osbert was high sheriff of Yorkshire.[13]

In 1130, Peter I de Arches, youngest son of Osberne, gave account of twenty marks of silver to Blyth Priory in Nottinghamshire. He witnessed a charter for Henry de Lacy and leased one knight's fee to William de Beaumont. In the mid-twelfth century he held fees in Kettlewell and Arnford, Yorkshire, both Percy fees. Peter I married Emma and they had sons Peter II and Herbert I. Peter II inherited Kettlewell and was a donor to Bolton Priory. He was in a grand assize case against Walter de Fauconberg over a caracute of land in Kettlewell. He hired a substitute for a duel with Peter de Fauconberg, his cousin through the marriage of Agnes de Arches to Robert de Fauconberg. Peter II was succeeded at Kettlewell by his son William II de Arches, who was a major donor to Fountains Abbey.[14]

---

13. *RCR*, 2:241; *CRR*, vol. 6, 157, 321, vol. 8, no. 87, p. 19; *RotClaus*, 1:367b; *Yorkshire Fines*, 1218–31, 134, 1232–46, 35, 1272–1300, 77; *EYC*, vol. 3, no. 1586, vol. 5, 326, vol. 7, no. 66, 63, 74, vol. 11, 96, 128, 133, 136, 144, 147–48, 276, pp. 146–151; *MA*, 3:486, 531, 534, 536, 548; Thoroton, *Nottinghamshire*, vol. 1, "Normanton"; *CChR*, Henry III, 1226–57, 471; *CFR*, Henry III, 1252–53, 37, no. 838, 1255–56, 40, no. 1085, 1256–57, 41, no. 846; *FA*, 6:12; *BridlingtonCharter*, 12–14, 20, 53: Osbert donated to the church in Aston and to Bridlington Priory; in 1253 and 1256, he paid for respite from knighthood; in 1257 he paid a half mark in gold for a charter of warren; he married Maud, and they had a daughter, also named Maud, who died without children.

14. *PR 31 Henry I*, 22; *EYC*, vol. 3, nos. 1501, 1587, vol. 11, nos. 96, 128–30, 133, 136–49, 241; *CRR*, 6:281, 297; *Pedes finium*, 14 (1202, William de Arches held of countess of Warwick); *Lost Cartulary of Bolton Priory*, 248, 258; *FA*, 4:108, 115: Henry de Fauconberg held Cokeney, Nottinghamshire, in 1316; Keats-Rohan, *Domesday Descendants*, 287–88.

PART II | ENGLAND

Peter I's other son, Herbert I de Arches of Shadwell, a de Lacy fee, held Conistone and other fees in the Honour of Skipton. In 1166, Henry de Lacy held sixty fees of the old Honour of Pontefract, of which Guy de Laval held twenty. Herbert de Arches held his two fees directly of Henry de Lacy. Simon de Lascelles, whose family would become Hercy relatives by marriages, held fees of both. Herbert I de Arches paid ten marks for fines in 1176. Herbert I confirmed a testamentary gift of his mother, Emma, to the Cistercian monks of Kirkstall Abbey in west Yorkshire during the reign of Henry II. Herbert I de Arches married Ingenolda and they had sons Herbert II and William, and a daughter Ingeleis. Herbert I witnessed grants to Fountains Abbey in 1165-70, one by Thurstin de Arches, another with Gilbert de Arches and Roger de Lacy, and another with Peter de Arches and Gilbert de Arches. Herbert and William witnessed a grant to the monks of Pontefract. Herbert II died in 1179. William married and had sons named William, who witnessed grants to Fountains, Herbert III, Roger, and Peter, and died in 1236.[15]

The co-witnessing by Peter, Gilbert, and Herbert and other members of the family, as well as their support of the same monasteries, indicate the close relationship among all the branches of the de Arches family. The descendants of Gilbert, Alan, and Peter de Arches had land interests in northern Nottinghamshire, as did the wife of Robert de Arches of Lincolnshire.[16]

Gerbert de Arches held the lands in Nottinghamshire that descended to the de Hercy family. The name Gerbert could have been a mistranscription of either Herbert or Gilbert, but was also itself a name, albeit rare. Gerbert had a son named Gilbert. Herbert II or Gilbert de Arches, son of

15. RBE, 1:145-46, 421-24, 2:598-99; CRR, 6:324, 330; EYC, vol. 2, no. 1040, vol. 3, nos. 1508 (1166, old fees: Simon de Lascelles under Guy de Laval, under Henry de Lacy forty fees, including Simon de Lascelles, Eudo de Longvilliers and Ilbert Paynel, Herbert de Arches, Jelebert Paynel), no. 1586, 1612, 1634, 1638, 1778, 1782; EYC, vol. 11, nos. 128-29, 208, 247; MA, 3:490; Ingenolda suggests a Germanic name, and Ingeleis a Danish name; Keats-Rohan, *Domesday Descendants*, 287.

16. There were other branches of the de Arches family in Yorkshire; Henry de Arches witnessed a quitclaim in Yorkshire between 1190 and 1200; Alice de Arches married Robert du Hommet, holding one knight's fee 1193-1208; in 1086, Newsam was held by Ilbert de Lacy; in 1155, Henry de Lacy gave it to the Templars; when the Knights Templar were disbanded in England in 1308 by King Edward II, the last preceptor of Temple Newsam in Yorkshire was Geoffrey de Arches; thereafter the knights were sent to abbeys to do penance; Geoffrey de Arches was one of the few preceptors in Yorkshire arrested, because he had a French name, and was therefore suspected to be a foreign agent; RBE, 1:343; EYC, vol. 2, no. 786, vol. 3, no. 1276; vol. 11, nos. 128-30, 138-40; Wheater, *Temple Newsam*, 96; Lord, *Knights Templar*, 114; Thurstin de Arches held land in Arncliffe, of which he made several donations to Fountains Abbey; his donation of land in Arncliffe was witnessed by Peter de Arches of Kettlewell and Herbert and Gilbert de Arches.

Osberne, or Gilbert his son might possibly have been this Gerbert. Gerbert died after 1176 and by 1179 or 1181. Herbert II de Arches of Yorkshire died in 1179. Gilbert de Arches of Yorkshire died in 1175, but he had a son named Gilbert and his grandson held lands in Bassetlaw Hundred, Nottinghamshire, where Grove is located. However, his son Gilbert was still a minor in 1175. The wife of Robert de Arches of Lincolnshire held two fees in Nottinghamshire in 1166. Robert and his wife could have been the parents of Gerbert. The son of Robert de Arches of Wrawby, Lincolnshire, was named Gilbert, who had a son named Gilbert. The immediate ancestry of Gerbert is uncertain, but he was definitely a descendant of Osberne de Arches and a member of the de Arches family of Yorkshire and Lincolnshire.

In Nottinghamshire, Gerbert de Arches paid ten pounds, Robert de Hériz five, Adam de Mortain thirty marks, William de Saundby four marks, and Sampson de Strelley ten marks for forest amercements, punishments by fine, in 1176. In 1179, Gerbert's wife Hawise, paid five marks for a judgment concerning her dowry, and an additional twenty shillings for her dower in 1181, when the lands were in the king's hands. Gerbert had probably died by or in 1179. Gilbert I de Arches of Nottinghamshire, son of Gerbert de Arches, paid fifty marks and two palfreys for the inheritance of his father in 1182. Thus, the family was fairly well off. His mother, Hawise, in 1185 accounted for ten marks paid for possession of her dowry and for freedom not to remarry except by command of the king. The monastery of Welbec held Gledethorp/Oldethorp in fee farm for 5s. of Gerbert de Arches and his heirs. Gilbert I de Arches donated his land in Gledethorp and his body to the church and canons of Welbec with the consent of his son, Gilbert II. Gilbert I also donated the church of Weston Hercy, so called because it became a fee of the de Hercy family, to the monastery of Blyth, which gift was confirmed by his son Gilbert II. Peter I de Arches had been a donor to Blyth in 1130. Blyth had been founded in 1088 by Roger de Bully of Tickhill. The lands in Nottinghamshire were held of the Honour of Tickhill. In 1185, Gilbert I summoned a sergeant to warrant the land. His son, Gilbert II de Arches, inherited the barony of Grove and the manor of Weston in Nottinghamshire. He supported John against King Richard in 1194 and lost his lands, but they were restored by Richard in 1195. In 1203 Gilbert de Arches was amerced along with Yvo de Hériz. The same year and the following year scutage was paid to avoid military service by Gilbert de Arches, Eustace de Mortain, Ralph and Adam de Neufmarché, Robert de St. Quentin, Yvo de Hériz, Gervase de Wiverton, Hugh de Saundby, Eustace de Fauconberg, and John de Bully, all of the Honour of Tickhill. In 1205 Gilbert de Arches, Ralph de Neufmarché, Robert de St. Quentin, and Hugh de Saundby paid fines to the Honour of Peverel in southern Nottinghamshire. Gilbert again paid scutage in 1208 with Yvo de Hériz. These documents indicate a relationship between the de Arches, de Hériz, and de Saundby families even before the marriage of Théophanie de Arches and Malveysin de Hercy. Gilbert II de Arches died in 1209 leaving two daughters, Théophanie and Isabelle. Théophanie de Arches had already married Malveysin de Hercy; Isabelle had married William Rufus, who had paid twenty marks to the king for permission to marry. The daughters with their husbands were coheirs of their father. In 1209, both husbands paid fifty marks and two palfreys for their fees in Grove.[17]

Gilbert de Arches, son of Osberne, and his descendants were vassals of William II de Percy. After the death of Gilbert de Arches in 1175, his minor son, Alan, was held in ward in Warwickshire by Mathilda, daughter of William II de Percy and wife of William de Beaumont, earl of Warwick. William of Warwick died in 1184 and Mathilda returned to Yorkshire where she died in 1204 and was buried in Fountains Abbey. The de Arches family had been strong supporters of Fountains Abbey. Her nephew, Sir Henry de Percy, married Isabel de Brus, daughter of Juetta II de Arches. It is possible that contact occurred between the young Alan de Arches and the de Hercy family in Warwickshire that resulted in Malveysin migrating north after he was replaced as the heir of Hugh de Hercy. Malveysin de Hercy was still in Warwickshire in 1204 when he contributed to the ransom payment for his uncle Hugh. By about 1207 he had moved to Nottinghamshire where he married Théophanie de Arches. After the death of her father in 1209, he inherited Grove in Nottinghamshire.

Osberne de Arches held lands in Yorkshire as tenant-in-chief with William de Percy of Western Normandy and Hugh II de Laval of Maine, and later the family held under de Lacy, de Mortain, and Paynel, all of Western Normandy. The de Arches family was related to the ducal family of d'Auffay/de Saint-Valéry of Eastern Normandy. They intermarried with the de Hercy, de Brus, and Paynel families. Some of these families still had

17. PR 6 Richard I: also named among the king's foes were Eustace de Mortain, Robert de St. Quentin, and Sampson de Strelley; PR 4 John (1203, Yvo de Hériz, Gervase de Wiverton, Richard de Stapleford, Eustace de Mortain, Ralph de Neufmarché, Simon Basset, and Sampson de Strelley also applied for the Honour of Peverel), 5 John (Fourth Scutage, Fines of the Honour of Peverel of Tickhill of the Fifth Scutage), 8 John, 9 John (Seventh Scutage, with Ivo de Hériz), 11 John (Malveysin de Hercy); RBE, 1:182, 424–26; *CartSt-Leonard's*, 2:840–41; EYC, vol. 8, 162; *CartBlyth*, xlvi, nos. 219–20, 226; Thoroton, *Nottinghamshire*, vol. 3, "Grove," "Welbeck," "Gledthorp," "Weston"; Round, "Barons and Knights," 58; Yeatman, *Feudal History*, 1:119, 124, 127–28, 131, 137, 154–57, 160, 166, 173, 175: citing PR 22 Henry II, 25 Henry II, 26 Henry II, 27 Henry II, 28 Henry II, 31 Henry II; Chadwick, *King John*, 164; *Early Charters*, no. 252: in about 1200, a Gilbert de Arches in London witnessed gift to St. Paul's; Keats-Rohan, *Domesday Descendants*, 287.

lands in Normandy and functioned on both sides of the Channel, but the de Arches did not. The de Arches family generously supported the monasteries of St. Mary's York, Fountains, Whitby, Nostell, Kirkstall, and Pontefract in Yorkshire, and Blyth and Welbec in Nottinghamshire. They were founding benefactors of the convents of Nun Monkton, Nun Keeling, and Nun Appleton. The de Arches family began as major landholders in Yorkshire but, by dividing the inheritance among their descendants, lost their great importance, although they remained prominent knights and landholders in Yorkshire, Nottinghamshire, and Lincolnshire.

NORTHERN NOTTINGHAMSHIRE AFTER 1086: DE BULLY TO THE COUNTESS D'EU

After the Norman conquest, the northern parts of England were less stable than the south of England. Much of northeast England had been colonized by Danes. Borders were undefined. There were frequent incursions by the Scots. There were rebellions against the Normans by English earls from 1067 to 1072 in which the city of York was sacked. King William I came to Nottingham and built a defensive castle, but also laid waste much of Yorkshire. Norman rule was finally established and lordships were organized, although there were fewer Normans in the north. King William divided Nottinghamshire between two prominent lords, both of whom had been his companions at Hastings, giving much of the land in northern Nottinghamshire and southwest Yorkshire to Baron Roger de Bully, forming the Honour of Tickhill, and giving southern Nottinghamshire and parts of southern Derbyshire to William Peverel, forming the Honour of Peverel. An honour encompassed the lands a tenant-in-chief held of the king and included numerous manors and fees and an honourial court.[18]

The status of Malveysin de Hercy was greatly enhanced by his being chosen by the descendant of Roger de Bully to be constable of the Bully castle of Tickhill. Roger de Bully came from Busli, now Bully-en-Bray, arrondissement Dieppe, northeast of Rouen in Eastern Normandy. He was the first lord of Busli, a fief created in the eleventh century, possibly by the count of Eu. Sometime before 1066, he sold the tithe of Bully to the Abbaye de la Sainte-Trinité at Rouen for seventy-two pounds of silver pennies and a horse. He accompanied Duke William in the conquest of England and fought with him in subsequent campaigns. By 1086, King William I had granted Roger de Bully tenancy-in-chief of 114 manors in Nottinghamshire,

---

18. J. Green, *Aristocracy*, 100–109: York was the only significant city in the north and there were few monasteries.

including Grove, the caput of the de Hercy family, and sixty-five in south Yorkshire, which together became the Honour of Tickhill, and others in Lincolnshire and other counties. His seat in Nottinghamshire was at Blyth and in Yorkshire close by at Tickhill. His estates in Nottinghamshire were subject to the Honour of Tickhill in Yorkshire.[19]

Roger de Bully built a motte and bailey castle at Tickhill, a wooden tower on a mound with stables and kitchen within a wall and a water moat. This motte is the highest known early Norman motte in England. The extant gatehouse dates from 1070–80. Tickhill was the caput of his barony, a town of thirty-one burgesses and three mills, which had been a wealthy and important Saxon site. In 1088, Baron Roger founded a Benedictine priory at Blyth, over the border in Nottinghamshire, endowing the building and the food and clothing of the monks with numerous lands in England, except for an annual payment of forty shillings to Sainte-Trinité in Rouen, of which it was a cell. The donation was witnessed by his brother and tenant Ernald de Bully, by Radulf de Neufmarché, Robert the Dispenser, and others. It was confirmed by Kings Henry I and Henry II. The brother Payn and sister of Radulf de Neufmarché and her husband William of Whatton were also donors to Blyth, as were their descendants William, Adam, and Ranulf de Neufmarché. The endowment of de Bully included the whole town of Blyth with its customs, "ploughing, carrying, mowing, reaping, harvesting, paying merchet, and making the millpond," plus toll and passage from Retford to Thornewad and from Frodestan to the River Idle with "market and fair in Blyth and all his privileges there, namely, sake and soke, toll and team, infangenthief, iron and pit, and gallows." Merchet meant money paid to the lord to give permission for a villein woman to marry. Sake and soke meant the right to hold court and summon people to attend it. Toll meant the right to exact tolls on rivers or roads, team the right to control market sales of cattle. Infangenthief was the right to hang a thief caught in the act; the last three were punishments which could be imposed on criminals. Retford, on the River Idle, was the market town adjacent to the de Hercy manor of Grove, Nottinghamshire, and the Hercy family later came to hold West Retford.[20]

19. *RADN*, no. 200; *RRAN*, vol. 1, no. 315, vol. 2, nos. 588, 598, 1138, 1319; Countess Judith de Lens, niece of King William I, held Hallam, Sheffield, and Ecclesfield in Yorkshire, and other manors in Nottinghamshire, which Roger de Bully held of her; Loyd, *Origins*, 21.

20. DB tenant-in-chief; *RRAN*, vol. 3, nos. 109, 178; *CartBlyth*, xxi, xxxiii–iv, nos. 133, 134, 135, 190–91, 325, 326, 364; Thoroton, *Nottinghamshire*, 3:174, plus ninety townships and many other towns, 425; 60 3/4 knights' fees; J. Green, *Aristocracy*, 89–90, 336, 415–16; Keats-Rohan, *Domesday People*, 192, 401–2.

Baron Roger I de Bully died in January 1099; his son and heir, Roger II, was a minor in ward. The Honour of Tickhill escheated to King William II, who assigned it to Robert de Bellême who held Roger II de Bully in wardship. However, Bellême lost his estates in 1102 for supporting Curthose against Henry I and Tickhill was restored to Roger II de Bully, who died soon thereafter without children.[21] Tickhill then belonged to King Henry I who added walls and fortifications.

Baron Roger I de Bully had a daughter, Béatrice, who inherited; in this case a daughter was given preference over a brother. Béatrice married William I, count of Eu, tenant-in-chief in nine counties in 1086. The counts of Eu descended from Guillaume de Normandie, illegitimate son of Duke Richard I. After the revolt of 1095, Count William I d'Eu was blinded and castrated for treason and his widow inherited his title and lands in England. They had a son, Henry, who succeeded as Count Henry I of Eu and supported the abbey of Saint-Michel du Tréport. At the end of his life, Count Henry became a monk at Fécamp. Henry had a son John, who succeeded as count and who married Alice d'Albini. Tickhill was held by the crown until it was granted back to Count Henry of Eu by King Stephen. John supported King Stephen who acknowledged his right to Tickhill, but John lost it to the empress when captured in the battle of Lincoln. John and Alice had a son Henry, who succeeded as Count Henry II of Eu. Tickhill continued to be held by the king. King Henry II expanded the castle with a new stone keep, curtain wall, and stone bridge, building a unique eleven-sided stone tower on top of the motte in 1179. Queen Eleanor of Aquitaine endowed there a chapel royal of St. Nicholas with four priests.[22]

Count Henry II d'Eu married Maud de Warenne, sister of William de Warenne, a powerful supporter of King John and lord in Yorkshire. Their daughter and heir was Alice/Alix. Alice d'Eu was a minor in 1186 when she succeeded her father as countess of Eu and lady of Hastings. King Richard I took Eu back from the French king and fortified it at great expense. King Richard gave Countess Alice in marriage to Ralph I de Lusignan, son of Hugh IX de Lusignan of Poitou. When he became king, John invested much in Tickhill, building a barbican, kitchen, granary, stables, a new curtain

---

21. OV, 5:224–27; J. Green, *Aristocracy*, 113, 277, 281.

22. *RotPat*, 116; OV, 4:284–85, 5:224–27; *RHGF*, 23:441–42; *RRAN*, vol. 3, no. 178; King Stephen gave Tickhill to Count Henry I of Eu, but later to Earl Ranulf of Chester; *RCR*, 2:162; John and Alice supported Le Tréport and the Cistercian abbey of Robert's Bridge in Sussex; Tickhill was confiscated by Henry II and it was held until King John gave it to Alice; R. Brown, *Castles*, 119; Keats-Rohan, *Domesday People*, 477–78 (sister); Chibnall article (sister or daughter); Loyd, *Origins*, 21 (sister); J. Green, *Aristocracy*, 90 (daughter), 259, 309, 312.

wall, and did additional work on the moat. In 1201, Ralph de Lusignan rebelled against King John, but supported him in 1214 and as a result lost his Norman lands to King Philippe-Auguste of France. As part of his treaty with the Lusignans, King John gave Tickhill to Alice in 1214 which she then held in her own right. However, Robert de Vipont/Vieuxpont had been in possession of Tickhill and refused to leave until forced out. After Ralph died in 1219, Alice became administrator of Eu for her minor son after paying the French king fifteen thousand silver marks for her French lands and the right not to remarry. Countess Alice retained nothing in demesne, that is for her own use, at Tickhill where she had thirty-nine fees, of which twenty-three paid for the castle guard, and five and three quarter fees had no service, but scutage and relief when needed. She donated the prize oxen and cows from Blyth fair to the monks of Blyth Priory. She hired Malveysin de Hercy as constable of her castle at Tickhill.[23]

Baron Roger I de Bully had subinfeuded his brother Ernald in several manors, which descended to Ernald's son, Jordan, who had four sons: Richard, Thomas, Hugh, and Robert. Jordan became a monk of Blyth Priory before his death in 1147. He was succeeded by his eldest son, Richard de Bully, cofounder of the Cistercian abbey of Roche in Yorkshire. He married Emma and had sons John, William, and Robert. The lands of Ernald descended through Richard's son John to John's daughter and heir, Idonea, who confirmed her father's gifts to Blyth.[24]

In 1213, Idonea de Bully married Robert de Vipont, whom King John had appointed sheriff of Nottinghamshire from 1203 to 1208. Vipont was a bad sheriff but a highly favored supporter of King John. In 1214 King John

---

23. *RHGF*, 23:441–43, 452; *MA*, 5:505 (*carta* for Roche, witnessed by Malveysin de Hercy, Baldwin de Hercy, William Cressy knights and others); *Torigni*, 1:282–83, 300–301; *MGH*, 23:842, 947; CPR, Henry III, 1216–25, 95; *MRSN*, 2:ccxxx–vi; *Excerpta e Rotulis*, 1:168, 357, 371; their children were Ralph II, who married first Jeanne of Burgundy, second, Yolande de Dreux, and third, Philippa de Dammartin, and Mathilde who married Earl Humphrey IV de Bohun, constable of England; Alice was the niece of William de Warenne, whom she called "uncle"; he called her *nepta* and *cognata*; the Warenne family was from Varenne, near Arques, in Eastern Normandy; after King John lost the support of his barons and knights, all he could rely on were sheriffs and the castellans of his castles, 304–5: after John's death, the hated castellans and sheriffs were dismissed; this was before Malveysin de Hercy was appointed; Power, *Norman Frontier*, 56–57, 212, 239, 276–77, 424–26, 454, 457, 497.

24. PR 31 Henry I, 7, 22; *CartBlyth*, nos. 325, 327–31; RBE, 1:109, 138–39, 181–82; Rufford Charters, 1:431; EYC, vol. 3, nos. 1509–11, 1527, 1528–32, 1629, 1786, 1798; Richard supported Kirkstead in Lincolnshire; John de Bully was first witness of a grant to the monks of Kirkstead Abbey in 1208; William de Bully witnessed charters for Henry and Robert de Lacy in Yorkshire between 1177 and 1188; EYC, vol. 8, no. 5; Keats-Rohan, *Domesday Descendants*, 358.

had given Tickhill to Alice, countess of Eu, but Vipont refused to leave. On 29 September 1217, King Henry III ordered Vipont to turn over the castle to Countess Alice and her son Guérin. In 1219 there was a legal battle between Idonea, through whom her husband claimed Tickhill, and Alice, over possession of Tickhill. Alice was the descendant of the daughter of the original holder, Idonea of the son of his brother and his male heirs. But Alice won although her succession was through a female heir. In the settlement, King Henry III forced Vipont to return Tickhill to Alice who retained the honour and castle of Tickhill.[25]

Alice countess of Eu employed Malveysin de Hercy as the constable of her castle at Tickhill at least in 1219–22. He was her first constable after she regained possession of Tickhill. At this time, she was still in litigation with Vipont and the situation was stressful. Under King John, Tickhill had become the chief defense for north Nottinghamshire. The constable or castellan was in charge of the knights and garrison of the castle and its adjacent lands; he had the duty to keep the peace, execute writs, convene courts and manage juries. Tickhill had a garrison of about twenty-six knights. Constables had under them dispensers in charge of supplies and marshals in charge of horses. For a knight to be a constable was an indication of his high social status.

Alice held Tickhill in her own right. She granted a mill at Turnewod and other properties, witnessed by Earl William de Warenne, her uncle, and by Malveysin de Hercy her seneschal. She gave some lands from the Honour of Tickhill to Roche Abbey in 1219 for prayers for her late husband, witnessed by William de Warenne and by her constable, Malveysin de Hercy, and Baldwin, his brother, of Cateby, Yorkshire. At about the same time, Malveysin and Baldwin de Hercy witnessed a quitclaim and a confirmation for Earl William de Warenne concerning lands in Yorkshire. Sir Baldwin de Hercy was constable of Conisbrough Castle, caput of the de Warenne family in Yorkshire and a major castle. The first Earl William de Warenne had built a motte and bailey castle at Conisbrough about 1070. Between 1180 and 1190 a great stone cylindrical tower was built, and also a hall, kitchens, and a chapel, making it the primary residence of the earls of Warenne in Yorkshire. These documents illustrate the connection of the de Hercy brothers to the countess of Eu and her uncle Warenne and of their

---

25. CFR, Henry III 1220–21, 5, no. 158; CPR, Henry II, 1216–25, 95; RBE, 2:803; Vipont was replaced by Philip Marc, sheriff from 1208–17, who was so bad that there was a clause in Magna Carta stripping him and his many relatives of their lands; Thoroton, *Nottinghamshire*, 3:425; D. Carpenter, *Minority*, 89, 261, 275, 397: the case was finally closed in 1222 by giving Vipont £100 and 6 ½ fees.

ongoing connection with Yorkshire. At this time the Hercy brothers were constables of two of the ten castles in Yorkshire.[26]

Sir Malveysin de Hercy held two fees of the Honour of Tickhill and land in Dadesley, adjacent to Tickhill, in Yorkshire. In 1232, he granted these to Alice, countess of Eu, in exchange for release from the military service he owed to the castle of Tickhill to hold by scutage from the two fees. This meant that she would have to fulfill his obligation of knight's service, not personally, but pay one of her other knights to do it. The transaction was confirmed by King Henry III. In 1232, Sir Malveysin also held Osberton, Nottinghamshire, of the countess by his service as her dispenser or steward.[27] This indicates that they remained on good terms and Malveysin in her employ.

Countess Alice supported Blyth Priory and Roche Abbey. She had four children: Ralph II, Guérin, Mathilde, and Jeanne. In 1244 she gave up her English possessions to keep those in France. Countess Alice d'Eu died in Poitou in May 1246. In 1254 King Henry III gave Tickhill to his son, Prince Edward.

The only certain intermarriages of the main line of the de Bully family were to the count of Eu of Eastern Normandy and Lusignan of Poitou. In England they held extensive lands in Nottinghamshire and south Yorkshire.

26. DB Nottinghamshire, 9.22, 24, 30; *CartBlyth*, no. 332; EYC, vol. 3, no. 1413, vol. 8, nos. 89 (1202–10, Baldwin witnessed for same), 92, 94 (1202–25, Malveysin and Baldwin constable witnessed for Earl William de Warenne), 123, 126 (1230, Sir Baldwin, constable of Conisbrough, first witness, gifts to Lewes), 129 (1230, Sir Malveysin and Sir Baldwin constable witnessed gift to Lewes Priory); Bassetlaw was also spelled Bersetlowe; the word "constable" derives from the Latin *comes stabuli*, count of the stable, in charge of the king's horses and arms; the title existed in the Roman empire and was brought to England by the Normans; the Lord High Constable of England was in charge of the military and was second in importance to the king; TNA, BCM/D/5/97/1: Turnewod is probably Turmworth in Dorset, Friebec is Firbeck in South Yorkshire; Nottinghamshire Archives DD/FJ/1205/14: in 1300 Baldwin de Hercy witnessed two deeds of title, one in Cateby; BCM/D/5/97/1; DD/FJ/1/205/16: on 13 May 1328, a grant was registered in the name of Custance, daughter of Baldwin Hercy of Cateby; in 1284–85, Jocelyn de Hercy donated land in Acastre Seleby, Ainsty, Yorkshire, to the prioress of Appleton; much of Ainsty formerly belonged to the de Arches family;West Yorkshire Archives, SpSt /4/11/113/3 (thirteenth century); Tickhill was the second most important town in south Yorkshire after Doncaster; it sent two members to Parliament until 1295, but then declined; West Yorkshire Archives KM/8; Morehouse, *History*, 100; J. Green, *Aristocracy*, 209–10; D. Carpenter, *Minority*, xix, 20: some castellans became rich through ransoms and extortion; Ward, *Women*, 2.

27. *Lands of the Normans*; White, *Nottinghamshire*, cites the *Testa de Nevill* and states that the countess of Eu (Augi) was the chief representative of the Bush (Busli) family at that time, but she lost her lands in 1245; in 1245 Alice had to pay £60 15s. for her 60 ¾ knights' fees in the Honour of Tickhill into the collection for the marriage of the eldest daughter of King Henry III.

They supported the abbeys of Ste-Trinité de Rouen and Le Tréport in Eastern Normandy, founded Blyth Priory in Nottinghamshire and Roche Abbey in south Yorkshire, and supported Kirkstead Abbey in Lincolnshire. Countess Alice d'Eu was a very important woman and she chose Malveysin de Hercy as her constable and seneschal.

SIR MALVEYSIN DE HERCY AND THÉOPHANIE DE ARCHES DE HERCY AT GROVE

Sir Malveysin de Hercy was the nephew and original heir apparent of his uncle, Sir Hugh de Hercy of Pillerton Hersey in Warwickshire. When Hugh had a son, Malveysin was no longer his heir and he moved north to northern Nottinghamshire and southern Yorkshire, where he acquired land in Grove by marriage to Théophanie de Arches and became constable of Tickhill Castle in Yorkshire. Malveysin and his wife were both Anglo-French. At this time, such persons were proud of their heritage and sought to preserve their French heritage or *normanitas*. Many who no longer held lands in Normandy or Maine still married wives from other Anglo-French families in England.[28]

Nottinghamshire was different from many other counties because, although under the umbrellas of the Honours of Tickhill and Peverel, it was not dominated by one powerful aristocratic family, but by a group of influential knightly families, which included the de Hercy, de Arches, and de Hériz families. Tickhill was about twelve miles from Retford to which Grove was adjacent. Retford was a market town and proximity to a market town was a great advantage to manors which produced a surplus of crops which could be sold there for cash. When the de Bully estates in Nottinghamshire escheated to the king, they were divided into five great manors. The manor of Dunham included the lesser manors of Grove, Headon, Normanton, Little Gringley, Ordsall, Ragnall, East Markham, and others, which were sokes of Dunham and subject to its manor court.[29]

---

28. Malveysin de Hercé was mentioned as constable of Tickhill in 1221; PR 14 Henry III, N.S. iv, 89, 276, mentions Mauvesin de Hersy in Nottinghamshire, Derbyshire, and Yorkshire in 1230; *RL*, 94; Thoroton, *Nottinghamshire*, 3:235, "Grove"; J. Green, *Aristocracy*, 209–10; D. Carpenter, *Struggle*, 7; Anglo-French is used here to denote both Normans and Manceaux who settled in England after 1066.

29. Retford was earlier spelled Reddeforde, for a ford over the River Idle colored red by red clay; some suggest the name was "Strete-Ford," derived from the Latin *strada*, because it was close to the major Roman road from Southampton to York, and many Roman coins (dating from Domitian to Constantine) and artifacts have been found there; the earliest reference to Retford was a battle in 617 between the usurper king

PART II | ENGLAND

The manor of Grove lay in the Bassetlaw Hundred in northern Nottinghamshire, which bordered Yorkshire. Grove was situated on a hill, where the Roman army had maintained a camp. In the seventeenth century, when enclosures were ploughed up, coins from the Roman emperors Nerva, Trajan, Hadrian, and Constantine, and intaglios, urns, and a discus were found there. Evidence has also been found of an extensive double trench opening to the southeast where there are traces of a foundation on a mound surrounded by a moat, perhaps an early motte and bailey castle. Although the builders of what has been called a castle are unknown, it came to be called "Castle Hill Wood."[30]

In 1086, Grove consisted of a manor with ten households, six villagers, three smallholders, one freeman, and one priest. It had three ploughlands, with one and a half plough teams for the lord, and two and a half for his tenants. There were eight acres of meadow, a woodland, and a church. Robert the Dispenser was lord under Roger de Bully, who was tenant-in-chief. Later Grove came to include fifteen hundred acres, in old enclosure except for one hundred acres. Roughly two hundred acres were woodland, primarily with oak and ash trees; the rest was used for grazing and crops. From the hilltop, it was possible to see Sherwood Forest to the west, Yorkshire to the north, and Lincoln Minster to the east. The manor house was situated on top of the hill, overlooking a terraced garden, parklands, and majestic old oak trees. Although there were remains of a stone tower, the earliest recently extant part of the later manor house was built in the reign of King Henry VII. Made of brick, it had stone copings, gabled ends, and mullioned windows. The emblem of King Henry VII, the crown and the rose, was found in a stone wall in the house. The dining room was originally upstairs with an imposing staircase lined with tapestries. Additions were made to the house in the reigns of Henry VIII and Queen Anne, a distant relation of the de Hercy family. Grove Manor had a small gothic church, named for St. Helen, and a rectory, which were located about two hundred yards from the house. Domesday mentioned the existence of the church before 1086, which signifies that Grove was of some importance. Few villages had an actual church before the conquest; priests were sent out from minsters in

---

of Northumberland and the king of East Anglia; Retford is mentioned in Domesday and was incorporated during the reign of Richard I; Piercy, *History of Retford*, 5–6; the earliest extant records of the manor court of Dunham date from 1652; CPR, 1 Henry III, 1216–25, 39: in 1217, King Henry III granted the manor of Dunham to the count of Boulogne, Reginald de Dammartin; the Norman knightly class replaced the Anglo-Saxon thegns.

30. Piercy, *History*, 12–14, 220–23: suggests it was Roman, since no medieval artifacts were found there; Lawson, *Black's Guide*, 264; *VCH*, Nottingham, 1:294–96.

the towns. The church consists of a nave and chancel and a small tower with two bells. In 1226, the church had two rectors under two patrons: Malveysin de Hercy and William Rufus. From about 1200, incised slabs were used to demonstrate the importance of a family. In Grove church, there are two large incised alabaster slabs, originally on the floor of the chancel, now in the tower chamber, six feet six inches long and three feet three inches wide, with the figures of Hugh IV Hercy in armor, with a shield, a hat on his head, and a greyhound at his feet, and his wife, Elizabeth Leek Hercy, with a headdress and saltiere. These are inscribed "Hugh Hercy, who died 6 December 1455," and his wife Elizabeth. Although the extant church was rebuilt in the nineteen century, these incised floor stones are still visible and intact.[31]

Sir Malveysin de Hercy married Théophanie, daughter of Gilbert de Arches, baron of Grove. She and her sister Isabel, who married William Rufus, were born at Grove in 1177 and 1179 respectively, and were coheirs of the barony of Grove, then a large estate with a wood, pastures, and fields. In 1209, Malveysin de Hercy and Théophanie his wife, and William Rufus and Isabel his wife, paid fifty marks and two palfreys for the two knights' fees with appurtenances inherited from Gilbert de Arches. In 1211–12, Malveysin de Hercy held two knights' fees in Grove of the Honour of Tickhill; William Rufus held one. This indicates that Grove was assigned two or maybe three knights' fees, not the usual one fee per manor. The manor of Grove was held by the Hercy family for fourteen generations over more than four and a half centuries, from 1209 until 1570 by male descendants, and through the marriage of Barbara Hercy to George Neville by their descendants until 1686.[32]

The identity of William Rufus is difficult to establish. Rufus was a sobriquet, meaning "red." In 1201 William Rufus paid twenty marks and a palfrey for seven bovates of land in Rampton, inherited by his eldest

31. DB Nottinghamshire, 9.22; Thoroton, *Nottinghamshire*, 3:264; Piercy, *History*, 219-20; Jacks, *Great Houses*, 57-58; Burke, *Visitation*, 2:205, Lawson, *Black's Guide*, 265; University of Nottingham, Manuscripts and Special Collections, "Eyre and Harcourt-Vernon"; LCNN, 82-83; Coss, *Lady*, 48; before 1066, most manors were served by itinerant priests from minsters, local churches were built by Norman lords between 1086 and 1150, thus it is significant that Grove already had a church in 1086; Grove Manor was used to house Polish troops during World War II, was severely damaged, and torn down in 1952.

32. RBE, 2:592-94 (1211-12, Malveysin of Grove of Honour of Tickhill, with John de Bully, Adam and Ranulf de Neufmarché, William de Markham); Round, "Barons and Knights," 57-58 states that Gerbert de Arches held two fees in Grove in 1203 and that Grove under the de Hercy family was not a barony, but a tenancy of Tickhill, as indicated by scutage payments; Thoroton, *Nottinghamshire*, vol. 3, "Grove"; Burke, *Commoners*, 543, 1099; PR 14 Henry III, N.S. iv, 89, 276; Powicke, *Military Obligation*, 68-76, 80; Prestwich, *English Politics*, 103.

PART II | ENGLAND

brother's children who were in wardship. In March 1237, William Rufus of Grove was named as patron of the church in Grove in the appointment of a rector. Thus, he lived at least until that date. William Rufus of Grove and Isabel de Arches had a daughter Eyncina, who inherited their share of Grove and married Eustace de Mortain. The de Hercy family later bought Isabel's half of Grove from her descendant William, son of Eustace de Mortain, although there was continuing litigation over it as late as 1331.[33]

Malveysin de Hercy was the primary patron of the church of St. Helen in Grove, which existed before the Norman conquest. The patron had the right to appoint the rector. The benefice was forty shillings a year. In 1226 the parish had two halves with two priests because there were initially two patrons. Under Malveysin, Ger. [sic] de Hercy resigned as rector in 1226 and was replaced by G. de Ordsall. Rufus appointed William Malovel rector in 1233, who may have been his relative. In May 1227, the archbishop of York consolidated the halves and gave the advowson to Sir Malveysin de Hercy, with the obligation that he pay twenty-eight shillings per year. Rufus did, however, make one appointment later. Sir Malveysin was also patron of the churches in Ordsall and West Retford.[34]

---

33. EYC, vol. 4, p. 84: Count Alan of Brittany who died in 10-89 was called Rufus; EYC, vol. 5, nos. 179, 264, 267, vol. 8, no. 110; HKF, 3:87-88; the successor of King William I was called King William II Rufus; there were many called Rufus; sometimes called "le Ros" or "the Rufus," meaning someone with red hair; there was a William Rufus who was named as witness to a charter of Henry II between 1176 and 1186 confirming gifts made by Robert de Brus; a Harcoit Rufus held Cleasby of Richmond in North Yorkshire and his son Robert also held a Richmond fee; a Wido Rufus was rector of Conisbrough in South Yorkshire where Baldwin de Hercy was constable; William Rufus of Grove was most probably the grandson of Pavia Malovel and son of Richard Malovel, which then should have been his surname; the tax lists of 1284-85 mentioned a William Rufus who held in Gringley in the name of his wife Eustachie; in 1302-3, William Rufus held in Gringley of the Honour of Peverel and in Muscham of the archbishop of York; FA, 4:93, 95, 99, 115, 138; RBE, 1:122; Robert de Mortain, ca. 1096-ca. 1176, husband of Emma, father of Adam de Mortain, Basford, Nottinghamshire, ca. 1125-ca. 1210, who was father of Eustace I de Mortain; Thoroton, *Nottinghamshire*, 3:242; Robert de Moretonio was a donor to Lenton Priory; confirmed by his grandsons Adam and Eustace, Strickland, *Anglo-Norman Warfare*, 85, 112, connects William Rufus to the Norman family of Ralf Rufus, household knight of Henry I, benefactor of St. Évroul and grandson of Giroie; Keats-Rohan, *Domesday Descendants*, 600.

34. CRR, 8: 400, no. 1908 (1229), 14:94, no. 471 (1230): Malveysin, Theophania, William Rufus, and Isabelle sued the archbishop of York in the grand assizes for the advowson of St. Swithin in East Retford, claiming that it had belonged to the family of Theophania and Isabelle; Piercy, *History*, 104: an early stained glass window in the church of St. Swithin contained the arms of Hercy, 186; HKF, 1:158-61; LCNN, 82-83: from March 1308 one rector was presented by both patrons, from 1331, Hercy was the sole patron of Grove.

Before 1216, Malveysin de Hercy and William Rufus bought ten and eight acres respectively in Eaton. Sir Malveysin de Hercy and Sir William Rufus paid four marks for two fees in Ordsall and Weston. Ordsall was a de Bully fee of four manors, one carucate and three acres of meadow, soke of Dunham and dependent upon Grove. Sir Malveysin's interests in Ordsall and West Retford were noted in 1246. The de Hercy family were patrons of the church of Ordsall until 1565. Laurence de Hercy was rector from 1322 to 1364. Weston had been held by Gerbert de Arches and by Gilbert his son in 1182. Gilbert gave the church of Weston to Blyth Priory, which was confirmed by his son Gilbert II. The de Hercy family held in Weston, part of which came to be called Weston Hercy and was separated by a brook from Weston Normanville, held by the family of Normanville, which was later called Normanton. Malveysin held land in Old Lindley, Yorkshire, which he let for eight marks of silver and 40d., reserving to himself all the oak trees. In 1249, Malveysin and Théophanie de Hercy also held the fee of Nettleworth, Nottinghamshire, which was under the Honour of Tickhill.[35]

On the death of King John in 1216 and the invasion of Louis of France there was much chaos and lawlessness in Nottinghamshire. But the reign of King Henry III that followed was a time of peace and prosperity in the region. In June 1230, King Henry III summoned men from each shire to appear with arms when called to defend king and country. Sir Malveysin was already a knight. The prior of Lenton and William de Cressy were called from Nottinghamshire; the archbishop of York, Malveysin de Hercy, the seneschal of Count "Albem" and three others were called from Yorkshire. Also in 1230, the king appointed Adam de Neufmarché, William de Cressy, and Malveysin de Hercy justices of assize in Nottinghamhire.[36] In 1234 there was famine in Nottinghamshire.

Malveysin de Hercy was called *dominus* as constable of Tickhill Castle. As such he was in charge of the knights of the castle, and he was also justice of assize, both of which offices were held by knights. He may have been knighted by Countess Alice of Eu when she made him her constable or by

---

35. *RotHund*, 2:300: Thomas de Wirington held thirty acres in Eaton, called Kingsmoor, of King John of which his son and heir sold eighteen acres to Malveysin and William, keeping the rest for his own son; EYC, vol. 8, no. 162; Thoroton, *Nottinghamshire*, vol. 2, "Nettleworth," vol. 3, "Ordsall," "Osberton," and "Weston," 183: Weston Hercy and Weston Normanville, noted in 16 Edward IV; *IPM*, 23 Henry III, File 8, 157: Geoffrey de Bakepus and Emicina (Eyncina) his wife held a half knight's fee of Malveysin and Theophanie de Hercy; Thomas Cox, *Magna Britannia*, 183; White, *Worksop*; LCNN, 147.

36. William de Cressy, Adam de Neufmarché, and two others were appointed justices to take assize of *mort d'ancestor* in Nottingham on 23 August 1224; *Rolls of Arms*, Glover's Roll, no. 121, p. 138.

her uncle Earl William de Warenne. In England, it is possible to distinguish two tiers of knights, those of the aristocracy and service knights. Aristocratic knights who owned castles were dubbed by the king or a magnate in elaborate ceremonies. Service knights, who owned manors, did not always undergo such ceremonies. They were generally members of knightly families, of which the heads were knights over many generations. Laws were passed in the thirteenth century requiring men who held a minimum of land in knights' fees to become knights. In 1224, King Henry III ordered all men who held knights' fees to become knights. The king or a lay lord could conduct the ceremony of knighting. This may have sometimes occurred without dubbing, especially in a county such as Nottinghamshire without a dominant magnate lord, or by a less formal girding with a sword. In the thirteenth century, documents called such men "knight" and "sir." They formed a class which dominated the offices of the shire, being appointed sheriffs, elected as knights of the shire, as well as serving as justices of the assize and peace, and performing other local duties.[37]

Sir Malveysin and Théophanie de Hercy had at least two sons, and probably three. The eldest, Robert, in 1255 donated his right in the advowson of Weston to the prior and convent of Blyth for perpetual works and prayers for himself and his heirs. But Robert died young and unmarried. The possible third son, Malveysin II, paid half a mark for a writ of false judgment in 1271.[38] The second son, Sir Hugh I de Hercy inherited Grove and married Elizabeth de Hériz.

Sir Malveysin greatly increased his stature and that of his family by marriage, becoming lord of Grove, and acquiring lands and advowsons in Eaton, Ordsall, and West Retford. He was appointed to one of the highest positions in north Nottinghamshire and south Yorkshire as constable of Tickhill Castle. He exercised his knighthood in a military fashion, commanding the knights of Tickhill, but not personally fighting in wars, although he was on call to do so, and served as judge of assize, indicating that knighthood was already expanding to include judicial functions. His role in religion was to appoint rectors of the churches of Grove, Ordsall, and West Retford. Théophanie de Arches de Hercy was an heiress, wife, mother, and administrator. She provided the land inherited from her father as his eldest daughter, two-thirds of Grove Manor and land in Weston, and membership

37. CartBlyth, xlvi, nos. 219–20, 223–24–26; B 101 (1233, *dominus Maueseinis de Hersun constabularius de Tikehull*), B 105; CCR, Henry III (1230) 400; D. Carpenter, *Henry III*, 170, 353, 521, 620, 678–79; J. Green, *Aristocracy*, 10–12; Bouchard, *Strong of Body*, 120; Crouch, *Image*, 136–37.

38. CFR, Henry III, 1270–71, 55, no. 193: in Yorkshire, so this Malveysin could possibly have been the son of Baldwin de Hercy.

in the prestigious Anglo-Norman de Arches kinship network. While Sir Malveysin was away with his administrative duties at Tickhill Castle and his judicial responsibilities, she was in charge of managing Grove and the other manors in Nottinghamshire.

THE DE HÉRIZ FAMILY IN NOTTINGHAMSHIRE SOUTHERN NOTTINGHAMSHIRE AFTER THE CONQUEST: PEVEREL

William I Peverel of Vengeons in the county of Mortain in the Avranchin went to England with Duke William in 1066. The knight de Hériz fought under Peverel at Hastings. By 1086, William I Peverel was rewarded and made tenant-in-chief of King William in England.[39] William I Peverel was given the castle of Nottingham by King William in 1068 to defend against the rebellion of the English earls in the north. The same year he was made sheriff of Nottinghamshire. William I Peverel was tenant-in-chief in Nottinghamshire and Derbyshire. He held 162 manors in south Nottinghamshire and Derbyshire, as well as sixty-nine houses: forty-eight houses of merchants, thirteen of knights, and eight of serfs, and three churches in the city of Nottingham. All of these holdings together formed the Honour of Peverel. William also held manors in Buckinghamshire, Oxfordshire, and Yorkshire. William I Peverel founded Lenton Priory, a cell of Cluny, in Nottinghamshire between 1102 and 1108. The foundation charter of Lenton Priory lists Robert I de Hériz and Geoffrey de Hériz as founding donors. William I Peverel also donated land in the East Riding of Yorkshire to the monastery of St. Mary in York.[40]

39. RBA: Pevrell; Leland: Peverelle; Holingshed: Peurell; Duchesne: Peverell; Dives: Guillaume Pevrel, Renouf Pevrel; Falaise: Guillaume Pevrel, Renouf Pevrel; only the very late sources gave the two first names William I Peverel may have been the illegitimate son of King William I by Maud Ingelrica, who later married Radulf I Peverel; Radulf I and Ingelrica were the parents of Radulf II; Ranulf II was Domesday tenant-in-chief, holding thirty-seven manors in Essex, including Hatfield-Peverel, and twenty-five in East Anglia and had a son William; PR 31 Henry I, 6–7, 9, 68; donations by William to Hatfield-Peverel between 1100 and 1122; *MA*, 3:294–97, 5:111–17 (*carta* Lenton), 120, 125; *RRAN*, vol. 2, App. cvi, vol. 3, 345; there is a spurious tradition that the priory at Hatfield Peverel was founded by Ingelrica to atone for her sins, but William did offer it for his parents; J. Green, *Aristocracy*, 89; Keats-Rohan, *Domesday People*, 355–56, 494.

40. DB Nottinghamshire, B9,18, 10.1–66; DB Buckinghamshire, 16; *Recueil Cluny* 5:162, no. 3813; CPE, vol. 4, App.1, 761, p.70; Lenton Charter, 345; *MA*, 3:549; *RRAN*, vol. 2, nos. 502, 503–4, 509, 538, 559, 570, 723, 743–44, 807–8, 870, 920–21, 981, 1241, 1282; EYC, vol. 1, nos. 452, 453; RBE, 1:161, 2:619, 622; *Torigni*, 1:116–17; J. Green,

PART II | ENGLAND

William I Peverel married Adeline. They had a son William II and a daughter Adelise. After William I Peverel died on 28 January 1114, his son William II inherited. William II Peverel of Nottingham was a companion of King Henry I at Rouen and St. Évroul in 1113. In 1121–22, William II Peverel, together with Ranulf the chancellor, Ranulf earl of Chester, Walter Giffard, Peverel de Beauchamp, and others witnessed a grant of donation by King Henry I. William II supported Lenton Priory and Colchester St. John. William II confirmed the earlier donations to Lenton, witnessed by Robert de Hériz and Adam de Mortain.[41] William II married first Oddona, by whom he had Henry, who predeceased his father, and Margaret, who married Earl Robert II Ferrers of Derby; he married second Avice of Lancaster. William II was a military commander for King Stephen. He was taken prisoner with Stephen at Lincoln by the Empress Mathilda in 1141, who granted his lands to William Paynel. They were restored in 1143, but in 1153 he was charged with poisoning the earl of Chester. 1154 King Henry II confiscated the Honour of Peverel because William II had supported King Stephen and poisoned the earl. The king regranted the lands to Earl Ranulf of Chester, but he died from the poison. William II Peverel took sanctuary in Lenton Priory, where he ended his life as a monk.[42] Later King John granted the Peverel lands to the Briwere family, who intermarried with the de Hériz family.

The Peverel family was allegedly related by illegitimate descent to King William I and came from Vengeons in the Avranchin. They held great lands in Nottinghamshire and Derbyshire, and also held in Yorkshire, Buckinghamshire, and Oxfordshire. They supported the abbeys of Savigny in the Avranchin and Saint-Sauveur-le-Vicomte and Montebourg in the Cotentin. They founded Lenton Priory in Nottinghamshire in conjunction with their vassals from the Avranchin, including the de Hériz family, and supported St. Mary's York and Bridlington Priory in Yorkshire. The family lost its lands and influence in Nottinghamshire at the beginning of the reign of King Henry II.

Aristocracy, 89.

41. PR 31 Henry I, 6, 7; EYC, vol. 3, no. 1427; vol. 5, 108–17; *RRAN*, vol. 3, no. 441; Thoroton, *Nottinghamshire*, 2:17–18.

42. *MA*, 5:111–13, 6:1, 361–62; RBE, 1:344, 2:767; *RRAN*, vol. 3, nos. 46, 75, 117, 204, 271, 441–42, 634–35, 739, 831, 944; PR 31 Henry I, 6, 7, 68; CPE, IV, 761–65, 767–68; *BridlingtonCharter*, 365; J. Green, *Aristocracy*, 315, 323; Keats-Rohan, *Domesday Descendants*, 1069.

NOTTINGHAMSHIRE

DE HÉRIZ OF THE HONOUR OF PEVEREL

The de Hériz family most probably came from La Rochelle-Normande in the Avranchin near the seat of the Peverel family in Vengeons. One or more members of the de Hériz family came to England with Duke William in 1066, probably as part of the Avranchin contingent led by Count Robert de Mortain in the group under William Peverel. Robert I de Hériz was a tenant of William Peverel in England. The descendant of the de Hériz family, Elizabeth de Hériz, was the second known wife in the Hercy family.[43]

In 1086, Robert I de Hériz held Stapleford, Nottinghamshire, of William I de Peverel: four manors, two caracutes of land and six bovates taxable land for three ploughs, six villagers with six ploughs, two slaves, a priest, a church, and fifty-eight acres of meadow. The north window of the church at Stapleford contained the arms, three hedgehogs *or* (gold), of the de Hériz family, quartered with those of Willoughby. Beside Stapleford, Robert de Hériz held four bovates in Sibthorpe in Nottinghamshire, and Bolsover, which included Oxcroft, and eleven households, one priest, and four acres of meadow in South Wingfield in Derbyshire, all under William I Peverel. Robert held as well three carucates, nine villagers, two ploughs, one acre of meadow, and one league of woodland in Tibshelf on the Nottinghamshire-Derbyshire border of King William with the manor in the custody of William Peverel. Robert I de Hériz served as sheriff of Nottinghamshire and Derbyshire from 1110 to 1114 and died in 1128. His son or brother Geoffrey de Hériz held Stapleford early in the reign of King Henry I; his son Ivo I succeeded elsewhere.[44]

When William I Peverel founded Lenton Priory in Nottinghamshire between 1102 and 1108 many of his co-donors were his knights and vassals from the Avranchin. Among them were Robert I de Hériz, who donated two-thirds of his tithes in Ashbourne and Oxcroft in Derbyshire, and Geoffrey de Hériz, who with his mother's consent, donated two-thirds of the tithes from his fees in Stapleford to Lenton. Other donors from the Avranchin included Count Robert de Mortain and his heirs, who donated an annual monetary stipend of ten shillings, and Herbert, knight of William Peverel. The original charter was confirmed by King Henry I and later by

---

43. Auchinleck, Leland, Dives, Falaise; Robert de Mortain fought alongside his brother, Duke William; Wace, 3:8635–38; *MA*, 4:222; Keats-Rohan, *Domesday People*, 376–77.

44. DB Nottinghamshire, 10:2 (Sibthorpe), 16 (Stapleford), Derbyshire 1:36 (Tibshelf, King,William Peverel, Robert), 7:1 (Bolsover), 13 (South Wingfield, William Peverel, Count Alan, Robert); *RRAN*, vol. 2, nos. 704–5, 870, 1355; HKF, 1:154, 156, 181, 211; Thoroton, *Nottinghamshire*, vol. 2,"Stapleford"; Green, *Aristocracy*, 221, 249.

King Stephen.[45] The foundation documents of Lenton Priory show lords and vassals from the Avranchin continuing to work together in England after the conquest.

Geoffrey de Hériz had a son Robert, who died in 1177 without children, as did his daughters Agnes and Mabilia. His daughter Avicia inherited *in capite*, in chief, married Richard de Cazmera, and had a daughter who married Philip de Strelley, for which he paid ten marks and a palfrey. But they had no children. Geoffrey's remaining daughter Alicia married Geoffrey Eccleston, who paid ten pounds for the lands of Avicia. They had five sons. The eldest, Geoffrey II, inherited Stapleford and took the name Hériz of his mother, probably because it was more prestigious than Eccleston. Geoffrey II and his sons Richard and Hugh supported Newstede Priory. Geoffrey II died in 1249 and Richard succeeded. Richard held in Stapleford and Thrumpton and died in 1267. He was succeeded by his son or brother Hugh whose service at Stapleford was assigned to Queen Mother Eleanor in 1283. Hugh died in 1297. Stapleford remained in the de Hériz family at least into the reign of King Edward III.[46]

Ivo I de Hériz, son of Robert I, was sheriff of Nottinghamshire and Derbyshire from 1127 to 1129, and possibly longer. Ivo followed William I Peverel, who was sheriff from 1114 to 1125, and was succeeded by William II Peverel, sheriff from 1129 to 1153. This indicated that de Hériz had become almost as important as their lords Peverel in south Nottinghamshire. Ivo I, who held South Wingfield, married Emma de Bilborough and Gonalston, daughter and heir of Herbert, knight of William Peverel, another of the founding donors to Lenton Priory. Bilborough was a town in the Honour of Peverel where Petronilla, wife of Stephen de Fauconberg, relative of the de Arches family of Yorkshire, also held. The family of Strelley held land in Bilborough and later came to hold the whole manor. Herbert had donated two-thirds of his tithes in Gonalston and one mark per year to Lenton Priory. Emma, his daughter, inherited the manors of Gonalston in Nottinghamshire and Kelmarsh in Northamptonshire. Thus, she brought considerable property to her husband. Ivo acquired Gonalston, which lies between Lowdham and Thurgarton, through his wife. In 1086, Gonalston

---

45. *MA*, 5:111-13; HKF, 1:154; Thoroton, *Nottinghamshire*, 2:210-05; Yeatman, *Some Observations*, 51, 57; the Avenel family was reputed to have been seneschals to Robert count of Mortain, although the references are to the reign of King John; Power, *Norman Frontier*, 52, 60; Keats-Rohan, *Domesday Descendants*, 513, calls Geoffrey probably the son of Robert.

46. CFR, Henry III, 8, no. 197; HKF, 1:181-82; FA, 4:94, 99, 117; CPR, Edward I, 1281-92, 87 (1283); *MA*, 5:108, 111; *IPM*, 1:33, 3:266, 436, 7:139; *RotHund*, 2:313b-14; Thoroton, *Nottinghamshire*, 2:191.

consisted of seven villages, three ploughlands, ten acres of meadow, two mills, and three furlongs held of William Peverel, and ten and a half households, five acres of meadow, and sixteen acres of woodland held of the king. Ivo held land in Oxcroft, Tibshelf, Welbec, and Widmerpole in 1130, and also held Willoughby, Nottinghamshire, a de Bully fee of the Honour of Tickhill, consisting of three villagers, fifteen smallholders, two freemen, ploughland, and thirteen acres of meadow, which he bought for five destriers, war horses, of which he delivered two to the Exchequer in Winchester and three in Normandy. This indicates that he was sufficiently well off to own five destriers and mobile enough to deliver them in Normandy. Ivo also held land in Pillerton, Warwickshire, under Hugh de Grandmesnil, which would later be held by Hugh de Hercy. Ivo held the advowson of the church of Gonalston. He continued the tithing commitments of his father to Lenton. Ivo and Emma built a hospital at Gonalston, where they made a chantry, which came under the Augustinian canons of nearby Thurgarton Priory. Ivo and Emma had four sons: William I, who succeeded, Robert II, Philip, and Richard.[47]

In 1140, William I de Hériz was a witness to the second foundation charter for Thurgarton. About 1155, he swore to King Henry II with the sheriff of Nottinghamshire and Sampson de Strelley to tell the truth concerning the customs and liberties of the archbishop of York in Nottinghamshire. This shows he was known to the king and given an important commission. Before 1157 he was a witness to a gift to St. Peter's York. William I de Hériz married Adelina of Whatton, Nottinghamshire, and through her came to hold four fees in Whatton, Aslacton, and elsewhere, as well as his inherited lands. Adelina donated two tenants and land in Aslacton to Lenton Priory. Her mother, Beatrice de Whatton, had donated two bovates in Newthorpe to Lenton with permission of Adelina and William de Hériz. This shows that both families were involved with Lenton Priory and with each other. Adelina also donated the church of Whatton to Welbec in about 1174, which was confirmed by Adam de Neufmarché. In the thirteenth century much of Aslacton and Whatton came to the family of Neufmarché (then also called Newmarch), who held there into the early fifteenth century

---

47. DB Nottinghamshire, 10.3, 14.6, 30, 49 (Gonalston); PR 31 Henry I, 6; *CRR*, 6:279; *RCR* 2:95; CPR, Henry III, 1266–72, 541; *MA*, 6:125, 359; TNA, MD335/7/20: in about 1150, John de Hériz witnessed a donation to Sallay Abbey in Yorkshire, a Percy foundation, with William de Mortain and Robert de Percy; Bilborough associated with Kyme, Fauconberg, and from 1316 Strelley; Rose and Illingworth, *Domo Capitulari*, 79–80: lawsuits between families of Kyme and de Hériz over inheritance of Emma and her sister Ivicia; HKF, 1:154–55, 182; Thoroton, *Nottinghamshire*, vol. 1, "Widmerpole," vol. 2, "Bilborough," vol. 3, "Gonalston," "Thurgarton"; Ward, *Women*, 99; Keats-Rohan, *Domesday Descendants*, 513.

and supported Welbec. The Whatton family were also supporters of Blyth Priory. The arms of de Hériz were quartered with those of Whatton. In 1166, William de Hériz held two knights' fees in Nottinghamshire and four in Lincolnshire. In 1169 he paid to Tickhill into the fund for the marriage of the king's daughter. With permission of his wife and his brother Robert, he donated land and a mill in Widmerpole and half a mill in Gonalston to Lenton Priory. Later the families of Cromwell and Leek also held in Widmerpole. In 1170 William granted some land in Thrybergh, Yorkshire, to a tenant, witnessed by Robert and Philip de Hériz. In 1171–72, he held land worth £4 of William Peverel in Nottinghamshire. He lost these lands to the king in 1171 over a debt of £5, 3s., 6d. In 1173, the sheriff accounted for the lands at £31, 10s., of which £13, 1s., 8d. was paid out for plough-oxen, horses, sheep, cows, pigs, and fifteen beehives, and for scutage of his knights. At Easter 1173, William regained his lands by paying a fine of one hundred marks, which he paid off by 1177. In 1176 he was involved in a case with Jolan de Neville over land. He died in 1179 and his lands escheated to the king since they did not have children. His widow paid one hundred marks so she would not have to marry again.[48]

Robert II de Hériz, second son of Ivo I, succeeded his brother William I in 1181 when he paid the large sum of £100 relief for his brother's lands. In 1175 Robert had been fined for trespassing in the forest. In 1186 Robert confirmed a grant of lands in Willoughby to the Knights Hospitallers of Jerusalem. In about 1190 he confirmed a grant and grant of service in Willoughby. In 1195, Robert de Cromwell owed five marks to Robert de Hériz for rights in Widmerpole. Robert II married Agnes Alcher, coheir of her father, Gilbert Alcher, tenant of Henry de Ferrers in Sudbury, Derbyshire. Robert II and Agnes had a son, Ivo II de Hériz, who succeeded to lands in the Honour of Peverel and Wiverton, Nottinghamshire. He also held land of de Lacy in Derbyshire and Kelmarsh in Northamptonshire. Robert and his son Ivo were donors of twenty acres of land for the soul of William, Robert's brother, to the Augustinian priory of Felley, a cell of Worksop. Ivo II was in a dispute with the bishop of Rouen over the church of Gonalston, which King John, as count of Mortain, had given to the canons of Rouen.

48. RBE, 1:50, 161, 342, 380, 383; EYC, vol. 9, nos. 79, 108; CPR, Henry III, 1266–72. 541; CChR, Edward III, 1327–41, 27; *Thurgarton Cartulary*, nos. 1,4; VCH, Berkshire, 4:507: in 1189 a William de Hériz was tenant of Ralph Basset in Kingston, Berkshire; *Reports Manuscripts Lord Middleton*, 7–8; Cox, *Magna Brittania*, 104; EYC, 5:156; HKF, 1:155–56,182–83; Thoroton, *Nottinghamshire*, 1:77–79, 162, 210, 260–61, 268, 2:237–39; Morris, *Medieval English Sheriff*, 82; the church of Whatton contains two early fourteenth-century tomb effigies which may have the quartered arms of de Hériz, and also the tomb of Archbishop Thomas Cranmer; Keats-Rohan, *Domesday Descendants*, 514.

Ivo was successful in his suit and got back the advowson. Ivo II held four fees of the Honour of Peverel in Nottinghamshire between 1199 and 1212, with Eustace de Mortain, Simon Basset, Gervaise (de Hériz) of Wiverton, and Richard de Stapleford, who had married Robert's daughter Avicia. Ivo II received certain rights and privileges which King John had granted to his father. Ancher de Freschenville of Cusworth, Yorkshire, witnessed a charter for John count of Mortain in 1197 and in 1200 received £50 yearly for his stipend as an official of King John. In 1218, Ivo II de Hériz was ordered to deliver Ralph, son and heir of this Ancher, to another in wardship. In 1215, Ivo paid a fine to the king for certain lands of Ralph Basset. The same year, he sided with the northern barons against the king in the Magna Carta crisis and forfeited his lands. But they were restored by King Henry III. Ivo II held South Wingfield, Gonalston, Willoughby, Widmerpole, Wiverton, and Tibshelf. In 1199, Ivo II had married Hawise de Briwere whose family had been given the Peverel lands by King John; they had sons John and William. Ivo II died in 1225.[49]

Sir John I de Hériz, son of Ivo II, succeeded to four knights' fees of his father, including Gonalston, South Wingfield, and Widmerpole. He took respite of knighthood in 1227. One of his tenants in Widmerpole was John de Leek. In 1235–36, John de Hériz sold his two and a quarter fees in South Wingfield to his brother William de Hériz of Wiverton. In 1235, John made gifts of pasturage of fifty cattle in Gonalston and pannage of fifty swine in the woods, or sixty in a year fertile with acorns, to nearby Thurgarton Priory. In 1241, John was one of two lords of Willoughby. He donated land in Tibshelf to Felley Priory, witnessed by William and Ivo de Hériz and Roger de Somerville. John married Sarah and they had a daughter Elizabeth and sons Henry and John II. John I died in 1241. Their children were in wardship and

---

49. RBE, 1:122, 161, 180, 342, 2:533, 583–85 (1211–12, Ivo, four old fees in Nottinghamshire and Derbyshire: Oxcroft ½, Gonalston ½, Widmerpole 1, Tibshelf, Ogstone, Hustone/Ufton, Thurne-Hudone/Over Haddon 1, with Eustace de Mortain, Walter de Strelley, Robert de Stapleford, Gervais de Wiverton, Hugh de Beauchamp new fee), 593–94 (1211–12, Willoughby of Honour of Tickhill, Malveisin de Grove 2); PR 7 Richard I, 16, 8 Richard I, 266; in 1086, Alchere was Domesday lord of Aston, Sudbury, and three other small lordships in Derbyshire; in Normandy in 1162, a Robert de Hériz, who was married to Agnes, donated to Lucerne Abbey in the Avranchin; they may or may not be the same person, but the chronology makes it improbable: if William was born in 1149, then Robert after 1150, so still a minor in 1162; RBE, 2:554, 623, 792–93 (temp John, William de Rochelle); University of Nottingham, Special Collections, Doc. MiD1162 (ca. 1190); PR 10 Richard I, 8; *Thurgarton Cartulary*, nos. 470–71; *Reports Manuscripts Lord Middleton*, 32–33, witnessed by Samson de Strelley, 270–71; HKF, 1:156–57, 3:418–19; Thoroton, *Nottinghamshire*, 1:68–69, 78, 2:272–74, 3:49–50; the widow, Sarah, of John II remarried Jocelin de Neville with the manor of Gonalston as her dowry, though it returned to her son John II.

Sarah held Gonalston in right of dower. The daughter of John and Sarah, Elizabeth de Hériz, married Sir Hugh I de Hercy of Grove. Her brother, Henry de Hériz, was lord of Widmerpole, where he took assignment of feudal service from his tenant at Willoughby between 1250 and 1260. He died in 1273, holding in Widmerpole, Willoughby, Wingfield, and Tibshelf. He was succeeded by his brother Sir John II, who likewise held his lands of the Honour of Peverel. In about 1280, John released his manor of Willoughby to Richard of Willoughby for life, witnessed by Nicholas de Whatton and Richard de Stapleford. In 1283, the knights' service of John II in Tibshelf, Gonalston, and Widmerpole was transferred to Eleanor, mother of the king. In 1302-3, John II de Hériz was documented holding Gonalston and Widmerpole. The church of St. Laurence in Gonalston is so isolated that it cannot be approached by road, only by single dirt lane. It contains the thirteenth-century tomb effigies of two knights, probably Sir John I and John II, since Henry went to Widmerpole, thus the father and brother of Elizabeth de Hériz de Hercy, and a lady. The lady was the wife of John I or John II, thus Sarah or Mathilda de Hériz, but more likely Sarah since her tomb is beside that of John I. She is depicted under a canopy with leaves wearing a veil with a barbette, a circlet around her head, and fillet, a band under her chin, with some of her curly hair visible, and a cloak, holding an *unguentarium*, a vessel for oil. The elaborate headdress indicates her status. The arms of de Hériz are on the shield of one of the knights. The arms of de Heriz are also found in a north window of the church, three hedgehogs with fleurs de lis. The other effigy of a knight is headless, probably Henry or John II. John II married Mathilda de Lowdham and had a daughter, Sarah, who married Sir Robert de Pierrepont of Holme-Pierrepont. John II was the last of the name de Hériz. The de Hériz manors of Gonalston, Widmerpole, and Tibshelf came to the Pierrepont family. Their descendants married members of the Babington, Clifton, Cavendish, and Talbot families, neighbors and relatives of the de Hercy family. Members of the Pierrepont, Talbot, and Cavendish families are buried in the church of Holme, where the arms of Hériz, Talbot, Stanley, and Neville are quartered. Members of the Talbot, Stanley, and Neville families later married into the Hercy family. In June 1317 the king ordered Robert de Pierrepont, Hugh II de Hercy, and another to furnish and lead two thousand foot soldiers for the war in Scotland. John II de Hériz died in 1329.[50]

50. RBE, 2:539-40, 791, *Testa de Nevill*, 529, 531; Wingfield Manor was held by Cromwell in 1428, although it was contested by Sir Henry Pierrepoint, descendent of the de Hériz family, who lost his suit in 1431; in 1455 it went to the Talbot earls of Shrewsbury, who held the property for the next two hundred years; Mary queen of Scots was held prisoner there; Yeatman, *Feudal History*, 3:177; *Thurgarton Cartulary*,

Sir William de Hériz, younger brother of John I, lived during the reign of Henry III. William was commissioned as judge of the court of assize in Nottinghamshire in 1230. He married Mathilda Basset, daughter of Sir Ralph Basset of Drayton-Basset in Staffordshire and Joan de Somery. The Basset family also held in Wiverton, Colston-Basset, and Thrumpton in Nottinghamshire. In 1086 Thrumpton was held by Roger de Bully, William Peverel, and Hugh de Grandmesnil. The Peverel part of it, consisting of three messuages, twenty-one bovates, and twenty acres of meadow, came to be held by de Hériz of Stapleford and later by John I de Hériz; Reginald Basset held the advowson. The de Bully part was later held by the Basset family and the de Grandmesnil part came to be held by the Leek family, with which the de Hercy family later married. The manor of Wiverton went to the daughter of William and Mathilda de Hériz.[51]

The de Hériz family came to England in 1066. In Normandy, they had been vassals or tenants of the d'Avranches and de Saint-Jean families and were close neighbors of the Paynel, de Beauchamp, Peverel, and de Mortain families. In England, they were vassals or tenants of the Peverel family and held lands in the Honour of Peverel in Nottinghamshire and Derbyshire by 1086. They gained many lands through marriage. They intermarried with the de Hercy, de Strelley, de Bilborough, de Gonalston, de Whatton, de Briwere, Basset, and de Pierrepoint families in Nottinghamshire. They were knights, but may not have actually fought. They early held the high office of

---

nos. 472–75; University of Nottingham, Doc MiD1153 (ca. 1280) and MiD1183 (1250–60); PR 26 Henry III 1241–42, 95, 186, 43 Henry III 1259, 375, 386; PR 7 Edward I, 15 Edward I, 30 Edward I; *IPM*, 27 Edward I; EYC, vol. 9, no. 108; TNA, MD335/7/20; HKF, 1:156–58; FA, 4:95, 102, 123; Lawrence, *Military Effigies*; there was a case of trespass in 1274 filed by Hériz v. Wynne in county court in Leicestershire, TNA, CP, 40/5; Palmer, *County Courts*, 244; Thoroton, *Nottinghamshire*, 1:69, 175–80; Simon Payling, "Inheritance," *NMS*, 30 (1986) 69–96: the Hériz manors were taken by fine from the common law heir Robert Pierrepont, but much later his descendent, Sir Henry Pierrepont reacquired Gonalston and Widmerpole; 19 Henry 6; arms on tombs and in windows of St. Edmond's church of Holme-Pierrepont with quartering of Pierrepont, Hériz, Talbot, and Neville; Coss, *Lady*, 77–78, 83; *Southwell and Nottingham*, "Gonalston St. Laurence," Monuments: the chancel walls are Norman, as are the stoup and bowl of the older font and the piscina.

51. DB, 10:58, 60: Wiverton: manor one and three-quarter b. (bovates) taxable, land for half of a plough, three villagers, meadow, six acres; soke three and a half b. taxable, land for one plough, seven freemen, one smallholder with three ploughs and two oxen, meadow eight acres; 11:29, 32, 27:2; CPR, Henry III, 1258–66, 610; PR 27 Edward I; *Thurgarton Cartulary*, cliii–v, 220–22, 226, 257, 297, 1020, 1026, 1048; *MA*, 5:284; Thoroton, *Nottinghamshire*, 1:30–31, 97, 161–65, 194–97; the daughter of William and Mathilde married Sir Jordan le Brett; their daughter to the Caltofts, whose daughter Alice married Sir William Chaworth; she was the last Basset heir of Drayton-Basset and Colston-Basset; Wiverton then remained in the Chaworth family.

sheriff. They served as judge of assize, a knightly office. They were founding supporters of Lenton Priory and supported other monasteries. Their women held the roles of wife, mother, and heir. The de Hériz family died out in the male line in 1329.

SIR HUGH I DE HERCY AND ELIZABETH DE HÉRIZ DE HERCY

Sir Hugh I de Hercy of Grove made an excellent marriage to Elizabeth de Hériz, daughter of Sir John I de Hériz of Gonalston in Nottinghamshire and South Wingfield in Derbyshire, which were held by the de Hériz family from the reign of William the Conqueror. King John gave all the lands of their lord Peverel to the Briwere family, but Ivo II de Hériz married Hawise de Briwere so they kept their estates. South Wingfield and Gonalston were substantial manors. Elizabeth de Hériz would have had a comfortable life in her increasingly wealthy family at South Wingfield and Gonalston. When her father died in 1241, Elizabeth was still a minor in wardship.[52]

This was a time of unrest and famine, when the English rebelled against the many foreigners in the government of King Henry III and restricted his ability to rule. The role of Parliament increased and came to control taxation. In 1254, two knights were elected by the county courts to represent each county in Parliament. It was a period of major conflict between the king and his son, the king and the barons, rebellion of the barons, and civil war. There was severe famine in 1257. In 1258–59, it was decreed that sheriffs were to be local county knights, serve only one year, and be paid a salary. In 1261, the nephew of Thomas Basset, guardian of Hugh's cousin John I de Hercy in Warwickshire, Philip Basset, was appointed justiciar of England by King Henry III.

Sir Hugh and Elizabeth de Hercy had at least one child in their marriage, Hugh II. Sir Hugh I de Hercy was killed in the service of Prince Edward. This probably occurred in 1267 or earlier since when a vacancy occurred in St. Michael's Church in West Retford in 1267, in the half which was under the patronage of the Hercys, the new priest was chosen by the archbishop of York. This indicates that Hugh was either dead or away on service to the prince. On 1 May 1268, Prince Edward established guardians for Hugh's heir and a chaplain to celebrate the anniversary of Hugh's death forever. The last provision is unusual and may indicate that Hugh died

---

52. RBE, 1:180, 2:583–84; Nottinghamshire Archives, DD/SR/102/90 ca. 1275); South Wingfield Manor grew in importance over the years until it was enlarged by Sir Ralph Cromwell in 1441 and later by the Talbot earls of Shrewsbury.

bravely for the future king who remembered him with gratitude. This document was recorded in another document in 1272, which said that Hugh died in Wales. The problem is that there were no military campaigns in Wales in 1267–68. There had been skirmishes on the Welsh marshes where Prince Edward pursued Simon de Montfort late in the Second Barons War, which ended in 1265. Knights often had judicial duties, but these were generally within the knight's shire. Prince Edward had recruited knights in Nottinghamshire for his service in October 1265. Hugh could have been one of these knights or a household knight, sent on a mission to Wales. His brother-in-law, Henry de Hériz, had a mandate whereby he owed a horse, a sack, and a halter to the king whenever he went on expedition into Wales. Hugh might also have been a judge, as judges at this time were knights and itinerant. Although after the battle of Evesham in 1265, there had been provisions for widows of rebels, it is uncertain whether this would have occurred for the widow of a faithful knight in 1268.[53] Elizabeth would have been in charge of the Hercy estates during the absence of her husband in Wales. However, the terms of wardship for the son made no mention of a widow, so it is possible that Elizabeth had died by 1268. Society was becoming more mobile and knights fulfilled roles which took them beyond their own estates and even counties.

In his short life, Sir Hugh I de Hercy exercised his knighthood working for Prince Edward, probably either in military or judicial service, in Wales. Sir Hugh I inherited the lands of his father: Grove and other fees in Nottinghamshire. He had a prestigious marriage, but it did not increase his land since his wife's brother inherited her family's holdings. Elizabeth managed the estate of her absent husband and brought the de Hercy family into the de Hériz kinship network. The family was presumably religious and Prince Edward arranged for annual masses to be said for Hugh.

SIR HUGH II DE HERCY AND ELIZABETH DE SAUNDBY DE HERCY

The son of Hugh I de Hercy and Elizabeth de Hériz was Hugh II Hercy, who was still a minor at the time of his father's death. On 1 May 1268, Prince Edward appointed guardians for the young heir and his estates, giving them

---

53. Coss, *Knight*, 32–45, 124; Prestwich, *Edward I*, 54–55, 59–60: affairs in Wales were a major concern for Prince Edward in 1267; LCNN, 158: Sir Robert Mortain appointed the rector of the other half in 1268; the two halves were combined by 1307; Waugh, *Lordship*, 201: the king could give a widow custody of dower lands during the minority of her children.

the right to marry the heir at a time and to a person of their choice, and to hold the revenues of the lands and of the marriage, and out of the assets to establish a priest to celebrate the anniversary of the late Sir Hugh *in perpetua*. The original guardians were Sir Walter de Lowdham, whose daughter Mathilda was married to John II de Hériz, brother of Elizabeth, and who was steward of the barony of Pontefract, and Simon de Headon, sheriff of Nottinghamshire in 1258–59 and 1267. Headon was adjacent to Grove. These guardians died and the lieutenants of Prince Edward appointed new guardians on 16 October 1272, Oliver de Sutton, dean of Lincoln, and Sir Robert de Sutton, of Warsop and Worksop in Nottinghamshire, with the same duties and conditions. The appointments were confirmed and sealed by King Edward I on 7 November 1275 at the request of Oliver de Sutton. The choice of such guardians indicates the status and prestige of the de Hercy and de Hériz families. Since Hugh was still a minor in wardship, the new rector of the church of Ordsall was appointed by the crown, "in the King's gift by reason of his custody of the land and heir of Hugh de Hercy, tenant-in-chief," on 27 December 1276. In 1280, the king appointed two men to judge a complaint about the church of Weston by the prior of Blyth against Robert de Mortain, Richard de Weston, and Sutton, now bishop of Lincoln, guardian of the land and heirs of Hugh de Hercy. In the following document, the same parties made a complaint against John II de Hériz concerning a tenement in Weston.[54]

King Henry III died in 1272. His son became King Edward I, although he was then on crusade and did not return to England until 1274. He was tall and stately, courageous in battle. He recouped the authority of the monarch, which had been diminished in the latter days of his father. He appreciated the reforms of the later part of his father's reign and in 1278 appointed good men as sheriffs of the counties. He reformed the practice of law in England, increased efficiency and speed of judgment, promulgated many statutes and corrected abuses. The political situations in Gascony, France, and Scotland involved him in wars and the necessity to raise money to supply and pay for

---

54. *RotHund*, 2:308; CPR, Edward I, 1272–81, 110, 187; both were recorded on 7 November 1275, but the original decrees are dated 1 May 1268 and 16 October 1272; Edward was still called "prince," and became king on 20 November 1272; Oliver de Sutton became bishop of Lincoln in 1280; the three lieutenants of Prince Edward in October 1272, regents of King Edward after 20 November 1272, were Walter Giffard, archbishop of York, chancellor from 1265–66, Roger de Mortemer, earl of March, greatly involved in Welsh campaigns, and Robert Burnell, bishop of Bath, chancellor from 1274–92; *Register of William Wickwane*, 67–68; LCNN, 147; Piercy, 186: the Hercys held Ordsall and its advowson from the mid-thirteenth century; presentation to the church of Ordsall directed to the archbishop of York; Burke, *Commoners*, 1099; Waugh, *Lordship*, 134–35: Edward had his agents administer royal wardships until 1273.

them. He was successful in Scotland, but illness and national debt made it impossible to retain the benefits of his success.[55]

Sir Hugh de Hercy, knight, was named as witness to a grant of various feudal estates by Sir John Grey, sheriff of Buckinghamshire and justiciar of Chester, for which the first witness was Sir Philip Basset, chief justiciar of England. There was a dispute between Sir Hugh de Hercy and the abbot of Rufford over lands leased by the abbey, which were part of Sir Hugh's fee in Morton. Hugh made an agreement that the abbot owed no suit of court or any other service for the land held by the abbot and monastery of Hugh and his heirs. The problem is that the first of the above documents is dated in January 1275 and the second in the mid to late thirteenth century, probably after the death of Hugh I de Hercy but while Hugh II was still a minor. The agreement with Rufford Abbey may refer back to Hugh I or be dated later. Also in 1275, the rights of Hugh de Hercy and the co-holder of Grove, Robert de Mortain, to gallows and infangenthief were tested and approved, while similar claims by their neighbors were denied.[56]

Hugh II de Hercy married Elizabeth de Saundby. It is probable that the marriage was arranged by the guardians of both under the terms of wardship. Elizabeth de Saundby held in her own right the "moyety [half] of the town of Saundby by two parts of the service of one knight's fee, and held in Saundby, Misterton, Holbek, Woodhouse, and Burton, one fee and the eighth part of a fee, and paid for ward of the castle x s. xv d. and for the meat of the watchmen 9d. and for the common fine 10s. and to the sheriffs aid 9d." Thus she was a wealthy woman, owning land and obligations herself and bringing wealth to her husband. In 1165, Robert de Saundby had held two knights' fees of Tickhill. In 1196 and 1202, Hugh de Saundby held in Saundby, Markham, and elsewhere. In 1201–12, Hugh de Saundby held of Tickhill with Radulf and Adam de Neufmarché, Gilbert de Arches, and John de Bully. In 1211–12, Robert de Saundby held of Tickhill with Malveysin de Grove, William Rufus, Ranulf de Neufmarché, Robert de St. Quentin, and Richard de Willoughby. In 1272, Alice, Joane, and Sarah de Saundby, probably sisters of Elizabeth, complained of their own diminished inheritance and sued Hugh de Hercy over one messuage, thirty-two acres of

---

55. Prestwich, *Edward I*, 267–70, 296, 469, 559–67.

56. CCR, Edward I, 1272–79, 227 (1275): Hugh was witness to grant by Sir John Grey; *Rufford Charters*, 2:533, no. 982; Nottinghamshire Archives, DD/SR/102/90 (ca. 1275); Rufford Abbey was in Lincolnshire, given by Gilbert de Gant on his deathbed in 1148 to the Cistercian abbey of Rievaulx; on 8 September 1285 King Edward I knighted forty-four men at Winchester and extended scutage; *RotHund*, 2:26, 302; *VCH*, Nottingham, 2:273: under Henry III summary justice was administered in local courts where the lord had the rights of gallows, pillory, tumbril, and infangenthief.

land, and six acres of meadow in Saundby. Still in ward, he was represented by the bishop of Lincoln and won the case. The terms of Hugh de Hercy's wardship were coupled with the grant of the lands and heirs of Robert de Saundby, knight of Tickhill, to the dean of Lincoln as guardian. In 1289, Alice, Joane, and Sarah de Saundby again complained concerning the messuage, thirty-two acres of land, and six of meadow in Saundby, but did not prosecute when Hugh de Hercy called the bishop of Lincoln to warrant his right. In the church of Saundby there is a floor inscription to William de Saundby who died in 1318 and a tomb effigy of him or a later fourteenth-century William de Saundby.[57] Later Elizabeth Leek de Hercy would establish a chantry in this church for her husband, Hugh IV de Hercy.

In 1290, Robert de Bakere of Retford brought suit against Hugh II de Hercy of Grove for the right to fish in the River Idle between Ordsall and Sutton. The jury found for the plaintiff. Debts were recorded in Chancery against Sir Hugh on 23 February 1293 for £40 owed to John Sampson, citizen and merchant of York, and on 22 April 1296 stating that Hugh de Hercy owed 40s. on another debt with the lands and chattels he held in Lincolnshire as surety. Indebtedness was then common among the upper classes, incurred to express social status and sometimes for the expenses of knighthood. In 1299, a jury found that Robert de Mortain held a fee in Grove, doing homage and fealty to Hugh de Hercy, and paying 10s. yearly to Tickhill as ward fee. Robert de Mortain left his rights to his son Eustace, who was then about thirty. In 1302–3, Hugh de Hercy held two fees in Grove, and Eustace de Mortain held one of him. Hugh II de Hercy also held two fees in Weston of the Honour of Tickhill. In about 1307, Sir Hugh de Hercy, Sir Robert de Saundby, and others witnessed the quitclaim deed of a widow donating her lands to Mattersey Priory.[58]

Sir Hugh II was named as patron of the church at Grove, appointing rectors in 1302, 1306, 1307, 1308, 1309, and 1315. In 1302 Hugh appointed the rector of one half, Eustace de Mortain the rector of the other half in 1303. By 1308 the two halves were consolidated and both patrons presented one rector. On 18 September 1308, Sir Hugh and Eustace de Mortain together appointed and were present for the induction of John de Hercy,

57. CPR, Edward I, 1272–81, 110; EYC, vol. 2, nos. 727–28; RBE, 1:182, 2:592–93; HKF, 4:108: in 1316, Saundby was held by Robert de Saundby and the king; Thoroton, *Nottinghamshire*, 3:312–14; *Southwell and Nottingham*, Saundby St. Martin's, Monuments; the effigy is legless and missing lower arms and hands.

58. Suthall, modern Sutton, northwest of Retford; a main writ was filed against him in the county court of Wells, Lincolnshire, in 1292, CP, 52; Palmer, *County Courts*, 273n.; TNA, C241/23/53 23 February 1293; CCR, Edward I, 1288–96, 541; IPM, Edward I, file 87, 27 June 1299; HKF, 4:94, 97; FA, 4:94, 97; Thoroton, *Nottinghamshire*, vol. 3, "Mattersey," "Ordeshall," "Grove"; VCH, Nottingham, 2:274; Coss, *Knight*, 51.

cleric, as rector. In October 1309, John Corbridge was appointed but given license to study for three years. Hugh appointed another rector to Grove in 1315. The church of St. Michael in West Retford was similarly divided between the Hercys and the Mortains, but consolidated in 1301. Sir Hugh was patron and chose rectors in 1307 and appointed his son, Thomas de Hercy, in January 1316 with license to study, which was extended for six years. Thomas was ordained and continued as rector until 1326. As patron of Ordsall, Hugh appointed the rectors in 1301 and 1314. In November 1322, he appointed his son Laurence, a cleric in holy orders, who remained in that position until 1364.[59]

As Sir Hugh acquired more lands, his feudal obligations of knight service also increased. By the fourteenth century, many of the original Anglo-French families in Nottinghamshire had died out for lack of a male heir, but the de Hercy family and a few others remained.

During the reigns of Kings Edward I and Edward II, there were many wars, primarily against Scotland. In 1296, King Edward I invaded Scotland, deposed the king and took the Stone of Scone to London. In 1297, the Scots revolted, led by William Wallace and Andrew de Moray. There was a general muster of men by county on 24 May, which, for Nottinghamshire, included Hugh de Hercy, John de Hériz, Robert de Saundby, Robert de Strelley, Thomas de Neufmarché, Henry de Fauconberg, Ralph and Robert Basset, William de Cressy, and Richard Bingham. Sir Hugh was called by the king to muster at Nottingham on 7 July, to come in person to perform military service, bringing horses and arms. The English marched from Berwick to the river Forth, just outside Stirling. The Scots under Wallace were on the other side. On 11 September the English attempted to cross the wooden bridge. When about two thousand, mostly infantry, had crossed, the Scots attacked, killed most and cut off escape. The English were demoralized and retreated. After their victory at Stirling Bridge, the Scots attacked Northumberland. The English king realized the serious threat the Scots posed and issued more calls to muster troops. On 16 September 1297, Sir Hugh was summoned to appear with horses and arms at a military council in London before Prince Edward on 6 October. On 24 September, he was discharged from this order and told to proceed to Scotland to serve under John de

---

59. *Register of William Greenfield*, 4:39; *Register of Archbishop of York* 7, f. 229, 237, 244, 255, 8, f. 191,194, 203, 301, 5A, f. 137, 138, 194, 197, 9B, f. 400, 406, 412, 421, 729; LCNN, 82–84, 147, 158–59; 16 September 1308; a tomb in Ordsall parish inscribed "*ici gist ___ de Hercy*" may have been that of Laurence de Hercy; *History of Ordsall Parish*; a church document for the parish of North Meols in Lancashire, named Nicholas de Hercy as rector from 13 May 1300 to 20 December 1314; one Thomas de Corbridge was archbishop of York from 1300–1304; Piercy, *History*, 186, 216, 226.

PART II | ENGLAND

Warenne. On 8 January 1298, Hugh was again summoned, with Richard de Bingham, Gervase de Clifton, and Roger de Mortain, to be ready to perform military service with horses and arms against the Scots when the king returned to England, and on 25 May to muster at York. The order was not a feudal obligation, but relied on loyalty to the king. Sir Hugh fought for the king, not under a magnate. On 16 June he received letters of protection from the king and advanced with him. On 27 June it was recorded that Sir Hugh came with a horse worth ten pounds, and a squire or groom (*valletus*), William de Mortain, with a palfrey, a riding or packhorse (*runcinum*), worth six marks. These were not expensive horses, but the lord of a county manor would have had little use for a valuable destrier or war horse. At this point, Hugh was called *dominus* and was a knight; Mortain was his subordinate as a *valletus*, which meant "little vassal." A valet was the servant of the knight, but could be an armiger. Thus, although originally descendants of the coheirs of Grove and social equals, by this time a Mortain had become subservient in rank to a Hercy. In 1299 Robert de Mortain swore fealty to Hugh de Hercy. William may also have been a younger son. There were about three thousand cavalry and the army was commanded by the king himself. They first had to march through Northumberland where the Scots had plundered and scorched the earth. Again the army ran out of supplies. They met the Scots under William Wallace at Falkirk on 22 July. On the way into battle, the king and bishop stopped to hear mass. The battle was hard fought. The English had to break open the Scottish schiltrons, compact pike formations. Both sides suffered many casualties, but in the end King Edward I defeated the Scots at Falkirk. He continued on into Fife, taking St. Andrew's. However, low on supplies and with matters to attend at home, Edward led the army back to Carlisle in September. In this campaign there were almost 800 household knights of the king and 564 other knights.[60]

Sir Hugh acquired lands in Barkeston Hundred, Yorkshire, worth £40 or more. In 1300 he was summoned to perform military service in the Yorkshire contingent against the Scots and to muster at Carlisle on 24 June. This was a feudal obligation, for which he would be paid 2s. per day for a maximum of forty days. About nine thousand arrived to serve at Carlisle, including 522 household knights and 850 paid cavalry. The king organized

---

60. ParlWrits, 1:286–87, 300–301, 309–10, 331, 356, 665; Gough, *Scotland*, 21, 43, 69, 212; Phillips, *Edward II*, 82–84, 89–90; C. Brown, *Nottinghamshire Worthies*, 27–28: he called those arrayed in 1297 "the flower of Nottinghamshire gentry"; Coss, *Lady*, 56: general government inquiry about land ownership for military service; Prestwich, *Edward I*, 476–82; Coss, *Knight*, 101; Prestwich, *Armies and Warfare*, 77–78; Coss, *Origins*, 226–28; Keen, *Origins*, 75; Crouch, *Image*, 170: by the mid-fourteenth century, the word armiger was preferred for an esquire and valetus came to denote a yeoman; Mertes, *English Noble Household*, 26–29.

ships to bring supplies to the army. In July the English under King Edward I and Prince Edward successfully besieged a small castle at Caerlaverock. The army was divided into four units; each unit had fifteen to twenty bannerets who commanded retinues of knights and esquires. A herald vividly described the campaign:

> In our Lord's year thirteen hundred on St. John's Day at Carlisle Edward held great court,
> and ordered that all the men in little while should prepare to march on Scotland, 'gainst his
> foemen of the north. Ready were they to the hour, and the good king led them forth.
> Not in coats and surcoats rode they, on their chargers dearly bought,
> but well armoured and securely, wary of surprise assault.
> There were richly broidered trappings of or [gold] silk or satin made,
> many a lovely lance-head pennon, many a banner proudly displayed.
> Far was heard the horses neighing; far-flung o'er the hills and vales were the sumpter beasts
> and wagons bearing stores and tens in bales.
> Through fair days, by easy journeys, moved the host in squadrons four...
> Mighty was Caerlaverock castle...
> There the host, at the king's bidding, was reformed in squadrons three,...
> there the banners you could see bravely spread;
> and many a warrior trying out his horses's pace;
> there stout men-at-arms three thousand;
> and aglow was all that place with gold, silver and rich colors...
> Where the Marshal set quarters, houses on all sides appeared
> not by carpenters and masons builded, but of cloth upreared;
> many were their forms and colors, and by many a taut cord held;
> many a peg in the earth was driven; many a tree for huts was felled;
> and to strew within the lodgings leaves and herbs and flowers were culled.
> Timely came the ships with stores and engines;
> then the foot-men bold forward with discharging arrows, bolts and stones against the hold.[61]

---

61. "Siege of Caerlaverock" (with permission of The Harleian Society).

There were several skirmishes but no great battles, and with money to pay the troops running out and winter approaching, King Edward made a truce until the following Pentecost.[62]

On 12 March 1301, the king issued a general muster by counties. Hugh de Hercy was summoned to perform military service, again listed under the county of Yorkshire, with Thomas de Lascelles, Adam de Brus, and Walter de Fauconberg, and ordered to muster at Berwick on 24 June. The army was divided into two: one part under King Edward marching from Berwick, the other under Prince Edward, from Carlisle. There were about one thousand paid cavalry and more than eight thousand infantry. Hercy and the first group marched north under King Edward I, taking Edinburgh and Glasgow with minimal resistance by 24 September. The other group under the prince took Turnberry and then both groups came together to winter at Linlithgow. They had achieved very little. The skirmishes of 1300 and 1301 led to a truce in 1302, which ultimately strengthened the claim of Robert Bruce to the kingship of Scotland. About this time, Robert of Gloucester wrote a history of England in English verse, indicating that baronial and knightly families were by then able to speak English. King Edward had argued that the French wanted to destroy the English language in order to motivate the people for war.[63]

Sir Hugh II de Hercy was knight of the shire in 1305, an important position. Two knights of the shire were elected to represent the shire or county in a single parliament. Knights of the shire were paid 4s. per day for their expenses. Knights of the shire were supposed to be elected by the full county court, but in practice were sometimes picked by magnates or sheriffs, who in turn were often influenced by the king. The House of Commons had emerged in the late thirteenth century. Its members were knights of the shires and burgesses elected by the towns (boroughs). The members represented the people to the king, having a say in the granting of taxes. Knights of shires such as Nottinghamshire, which did not have a resident magnate lord to control their votes, were much more independent. The Parliament of February 1305 was important, because no parliaments had been held for three years. Beginning 28 February 1305 at Westminster, 487 petitions were

---

62. "Roll of Arms of the Princes, Barons and Knights who attended King Edward I to the siege of Caerlaverock castle in 1300," British Library. Cotton Caligula A VXIII f. 23, V30; also fighting were Robert Willoughby, John de St. John, Pojn/Pain Paynel, John de Cromwell, Basset the Elder and the Younger; Prestwich. *Edward I*, 484–90; Coss, *Knight*, 101; Coss, *Origins*, 242: knights listed were bannerets and nobles with retinues.

63. ParlWrits, 1:665; Prestwich, *Edward I*, 493–95; feudal military service was abolished in 1352; D. Carpenter, *Struggle*, 9–10: by 1350 most of the upper classes could speak English.

heard, concerning England, Scotland, Ireland, Gascony, and Aquitaine. But no taxes were requested or granted.[64]

In 1307 King Edward I died and was succeeded by his son, King Edward II. The new king continued fighting wars against the Scots in 1311, 1314, 1316, and 1317 which depleted the economy. In 1308, Edward II certified the arms of Hugh II de Hercy as *"de goules, od le chef de argent, e un lable de azure,"* that is, red with a bar of silver and a label of blue. On 25 June 1310, King Edward II ordered the archbishop of York to lend him provisions of wheat, oats, malt, bean, pease [*sic*], forty beeves (beef cattle) and one hundred sheep by the gule (first) of August for his coming campaign against Scotland. The order listed the men in each county to whom individual letters stating substantially the same instructions were addressed. Most of the men listed were abbots and priors, but the list for Nottinghamshire named Hugh II de Hercy, Richard de Bingham, and Robert de Strelley. Sheriffs of each county were dispatched to facilitate the collection. The king promised to repay the loan in money on the following Candlemas (11 February 1311).[65]

Sir Hugh II de Hercy was knight of the shire again in 1311. Parliament met in London beginning on 16 August 1311. A group called the Lords Ordainers confronted King Edward II with forty-one Ordinances which limited the powers of the king especially in appointment of officers and embarking upon wars, for which consent of Parliament would be necessary. The payment of revenues was changed from directly to the king to the Exchequer. There were also reforms of existing criminal and civil laws. The king did his best to prevent passage, but on 27 September he capitulated and the Ordinances were published in St. Paul's churchyard by the bishops, and on 5 October signed by the king with the great seal. On 8 October, two days before the end of Parliament, writs were issued to reconvene Parliament on 10 October and copies of the Ordinances were sent to the sheriffs to proclaim to the people of the shires. Sir Hugh was again member of Parliament in 1316, a time of famine. The Ordinances shifted much power of government from the king to Parliament. However, the king evaded them and they were annulled by Parliament in 1322.[66]

---

64. *Memoranda de Parliamento*, 1305; *RotParl*, 1:281–86; ParlWrits, 1:655; *Annals of Nottinghamshire*, 1:183, 187, 194; Ormrod, *Reign*, 145, 153, 157; Prestwich, *English Politics*, 139–41: King John had summoned knights from each shire, but Parliament did not then exist; two knights from the shire were called under King Henry III by 1254; D. Carpenter, *Henry III*, 580; Prestwich, *Edward I*, 456, 463, 467.

65. CCR, Edward II, 1307–13, 262, with the abbots or priors of Blyth, Worksop, Rufford, Welbec, Thurgarton, Lenton, and Richard de Bingham and Robert de Strelley.

66. RotParl, 1:281–86; *Annals of Nottinghamshire*, 1:183, 187, 194; Ormrod, *Reign*,

PART II | ENGLAND

King Edward II had left the north to deal with the crisis of the Ordinances and the loss of his beloved Piers Gaveston. Robert Bruce had become king of the Scots in 1306. In 1313, he demanded that the English surrender Stirling Castle to which he laid siege in 1314. Sir Hugh II de Hercy was commissioner of array in Nottinghamshire and Derbyshire from 1314 through 1317 with his father-in-law Robert de Saundby. A commissioner of array was appointed to call up soldiers for the king. An abbot or bishop administered the oath of office; the abbot of Welbec for Nottinghamshire. The commissioner had to swear not to take money for food or drink or anything else and not to spare able bodied men. In 1314 King Edward II attempted to muster a huge army of two thousand five hundred cavalry and twenty-five thousand infantry, not all of whom came. The king left London on 3 March, arrived at Tickhill on 28 March and at Roxburgh in 25 May. Sir Hugh mustered his men to Berwick, where they became part of the great army of the king. The Scots had about six thousand men. The English had many more cavalry and archers with longbows. The Scots had primarily axes, swords, and pikes, with a few archers. The English had enormous supplies. The two armies faced off near the Bannock Burn, a stream in a marsh just south of Stirling. The English were led by King Edward, and commanded by the earls of Gloucester and Hereford; the Scots by King Robert Bruce. The battle lasted two days, 23 and 24 June, which was very unusual since medieval battles normally lasted only a few hours. On the first day, Robert Bruce personally killed Henry de Bohun, nephew of the English commander. Then the Scots killed and took prisoner other English lords. The second day, the Scottish schiltrons, phalanxes of pikemen, pressed the English back. The English cavalry was hemmed in by the stream. The English soon were defeated and retreated. They took the king to safety, arriving in Berwick on 27 June. It has been estimated that only a third of the English troops survived, although some were captured and ransomed, and their horses, equipment and supplies were taken by the Scots. On 12 August 1314, King Edward II personally issued an order to the masters and brothers of the hospital of St. John in Brackele to care for William, son of Thomas the charetter, carter, of Grove, a servant of Sir Hugh, giving him maintenance, "food, clothing and other necessities" for life, since "the Scotch rebels having inhumanly cut off his hand whilst engaged in the King's service," which rendered him unable to earn his living. Knights were paid two shillings per day, infantry two pence, if the king actually paid their wages. In 1314, Earl John de Warenne granted the manor of Stanley in Yorkshire to Sir Hugh de Hercy as a reward for his service in Scotland. Sir Hugh then granted it to his daughter Maud

---

145, 153, 157: Phillips, *Edward II*, 173–80.

and her husband, William de Midgeley. It was noted then that the arms of Sir Hugh were gules on chef d'argent with three points azure.[67]

In September 1314, Sir Hugh and his sons Thomas, Laurence, and William, with William and Eustace de Mortain, John priest of Grove, as well as a number of their men from Grove, were accused by John de Corbridge, rector of Grove, of cutting down his trees, breaking his houses, driving off three of his horses worth ten marks, and assaulting his men, all of which were under the king's protection. On 8 April 1315, Hugh de Hercy replaced Corbridge as rector with John de Scarborough, who at the time was only an acolyte. John de Corbridge had been appointed by Hugh de Hercy and served from 1309-15, but was absent most of the time. Corbridge himself, who may have been a relative of Thomas de Corbridge, who was archbishop of York from 1300-1304, was in trouble for debt in 1313 for which he was almost excommunicated. In the complaint, Corbridge claimed ownership of houses, trees, and horses, suggesting wealth beyond the benefice of Grove. On 18 September 1314, a commission of *oyer et terminer* was convened to hear and determine the case against the Hercys. John de Doncaster was head of the commission, but a subsequent order on 6 October included Hugh de Cressy and Laurence de Chaworth, and another on 9 March 1315 included Richard de Willoughby as members of the commission, all of whom were Hercy associates. This was a time of famine and social disorder, so the situation may have been more complicated than the extant sources reveal. In 1315, the price of wheat at Tickhill was five times the normal price. Attacks such as this sometimes occurred as tactical manoevres in the context of lawsuits, in this case perhaps the suits against Corbridge for debt. There is no evidence of the verdict and the case was probably resolved by arbitration. But the case shows that the parish of Grove was not always peaceful, that there were many men on the estate, and that the Hercys and Mortains still worked together, at least in doing mischief if that was what had happened.[68]

Sir Hugh was appointed to a commission to perambulate royal forests on 8 August 1316, for which a writ on 29 July ordered that his expenses for attending the council on this matter be submitted by 8 August. Kings and parliaments appointed knights to perambulate, walk around, survey,

---

67. *CCR, Edward II, 1313-18*, 116, 192; TNA, SC 8/43/2125 (c.1315); *Roll of Arms Edward*, 69; ParlWrits, 2:392 (7 July 1324); *Antiquarian Repository*, vol. 5 (1784) 125-26; Phillips, *Edward II*, 223-35; Prestwich, *Armies*, 84, 87-88, 123-25; Coss, *Origins*, 166-67.

68. CPR, Edward II, 1313-17, 232, 241, 312; *Southwell and Nottingham*, "Grove St. Helen"; Goldberg, *Medieval England*, 157; LCNN, 83-84: the John priest of Grove may have been John Hercy; Coss, *Knight*, 113.

and fix the boundaries of the forests against encroachment by neighboring landholders. Under the laws of William the Conqueror, all forests belonged to the king. In 1215, Magna Carta had limited these rights, but they were still disputed. Forest law was further reformed in the Ordinances of 1311 which this perambulation sought to implement. Sherwood Forest was the largest royal forest in Nottinghamshire at the time.[69]

On 26 March 1316, Sir Hugh was appointed commissioner of array to raise men for war against the Scots and to bring them to Newcastle in midsummer. Then on 5 August, Sir Hugh and Robert de Saundby were ordered to muster foot soldiers for duty in Scotland. The original order said the towns were to pay for the arms and expenses of these men for sixty days of service. Indentures would be given for such payments for a credit on the tax of a sixteenth on movable goods. On 27 June 1317, King Edward II wrote to Sir Robert de Pierrepont and Sir Hugh de Hercy to furnish two thousand footmen, spademen, and miners from Nottinghamshire and Derbyshire, with Sir Robert and Sir Hugh to lead them in the war against Scotland. On August 1, Hugh de Hercy and Robert de Strelley were ordered to array two thousand foot soldiers, two hundred of them slingers, who would receive the king's wages for their service, and lead them to Newcastle to muster on 15 September. On 20 August of that year, King Edward II wrote to Sir Robert de Pierrepont from York, to come with horse and arms for the war in Scotland. In September, King Robert Bruce laid siege to Berwick, which fell to the Scots in June 1318.[70]

The years of war were complicated by civil unrest between the barons and the king and famine, which depressed the people and made supply of military campaigns difficult. Prosperity and population growth ended with a great famine from 1315 to 1317 in northern Europe. Climate change from warm to cold and rainy caused flooding, crop failures, food price increases, and many deaths by starvation. The people ate their livestock and seed grain, wild roots, and bark. Many lost their land, some abandoned children they could not feed and there were stories of cannibalism. Mills were unused for lack of grain and repairs not kept up. The famine affected all levels of society. There was another famine in 1321. Ten to fifteen percent of the

---

69. ParlWrits, 2:xciv, 167; Young, *Royal Forests*; Grant, *Royal Forests*.

70. CPR, Edward II, 1313–17, 460; ParlWrits, 2:198, 392: names bishops and abbots to administer oath; ParlRolls, Parliament of January 1316, TNA, SC 9/20 Sureties, 408, will of Robert Morton, 1424; FA, 4:1316: Nottinghamshire, Wapentake Bersetlowe; Thoroton, *Nottinghamshire*, vol. 1, "Holme-Pierrepont," vol. 3, "Weston"; Holme-Pierrepont was part of escheated estate of Roger de Bully; Phillips, *Edward II*, 268, 297–307, 329; C. Brown, *Lives*, 39; Prestwich, *Armies*, 78–81.

population died of hunger. The food supply in England did not fully recover until 1325 and the people were weak and vulnerable to disease.

Sir Hugh appointed his son Thomas de Hercy rector of the church in West Retford in February 1315, where he served until March 1325. In February 1317, the rector of the church at Grove, John de Scarborough, borrowed £16 from Thomas de Hercy, rector of West Retford, pledging his lands, chattels, and ecclesiastical goods in Nottinghamshire. Thomas de Hercy delegated to Thomas de Grove, clerk, the collection of the £16 owed to him by the rector of Grove. On 15 November 1333, John acknowledged a debt of £16 that he owed to Thomas de Hercy, now priest of Wyntringham, Yorkshire. On 2 July 1334, Thomas de Hercy, priest of Wyntringham, acknowledged that he owed £16 to a different priest, pledging his lands, chattels, and ecclesiastical goods in Lincolnshire. Sir Hugh also appointed his son Laurence de Hercy rector of Ordsall in 1322, where he served through 1364, the longest term of any rector. He was a cleric in holy orders, which in that time many appointees to advowsons were not. Thus, two of Sir Hugh's younger sons were placed in promising positions in the church.[71]

The other younger son, William, held land in Hayton. On 8 March 1325, the king issued a pardon to John, son of Henry le Cartwright of Wadworth, near Doncaster, indicted for the death of Roger de Emeldon and for outlawry, with William de Aune, constable of Tickhill Castle, and William de Hercy named as sureties (mainpernors) that the accused would go into the king's service. In 1334, William de Hercy leased his lands in Hayton to Thomas de Calverley, consisting of eight and a half acres and one rood of land, for a term of twenty years for a rent of 7s. 3½ d. in silver.[72]

Sir Hugh II de Hercy's eldest son, Sir Robert Hercy, did not inherit Grove, but bought the fees still held by his cousin, Eustace III de Mortain, descendant and heir of Robert's great-aunt Isabel de Arches, wife of Sir William Rufus and sister of his great-grandmother Théophanie de Arches de Hercy. Sir William Rufus and Isabel had a daughter, Eyncina, who married

---

71. *History of Ordsall Parish*; *Register of William Greenfield*, 5:273; *Register of Archbishop of York*, 5A, 112, 115, 11, f. 256; Thomas de Hercy was rector of the church of West Retford from 7 February 1315 until 7 March 1325 and of Wyntringham, Yorkshire, on 15 November 1333; CCR, Edward III, 1333–37, 182, 319; Piercy, *History*,186, 216; there was also a John de Hercy, priest of Grove, who may also have been his son.

72. *Gascon Rolls*, C61/37:139.1; de Aune was later accused of oppressing the people, stealing supplies from farms, and was in conflict with the Mowbrays; *Calverley Charters* 6:198, no. 268; Hayton was northeast of Retford, near Welham; Thomas de Calverlay was a younger son of the de Calverley family in Calverley, Yorkshire, members of which were sheriffs of Yorkshire and Rutlandshire; Walter de Calverley died in 1466, leaving lands in Clareborough, Hayton, and Welham, Nottinghamshire.

PART II | ENGLAND

Eustace II de Mortain and had sons, William and Robert. The Mortain interest in Grove descended from them to Eustace III de Mortain.

Mortain lay in the Avranchin. Count of Mortain was the title of Robert, half-brother of William the Conqueror, and also of the future King John during the reign of his brother King Richard I. The counts of Mortain were lords of the Peverels in Normandy and held lands in Nottinghamshire. It is not known whether the Mortain family of Grove descended from the counts de Mortain. In England the name Mortain was anglicized to Morteyn, Moretonie, Moreton, and Morton. There are several towns in Nottinghamshire bearing such names. Robert de Morteyn, son of Warner, was present at the founding of Lenton Priory. His father was further specified as Warner of Toton, which in Domesday was held by Warner de Codnor. It is possible that Warner or his son married a Mortain and hence took her name. It is also possible that they were connected to Stephen count of Mortain, whose wife was Mathilde, daughter of Eustace count of Boulogne. Eustace was a common name in the Mortain family of Nottinghamshire. Robert de Mortain held Wollaton, Nottinghamshire, during the reign of King Henry I. Robert had a son Adam I, who was fined thirty marks for forest trespass. In 1179, Adam and two others inspected work done at Nottingham and Clipston. Adam I had sons Adam II and Eustace who confirmed the donations of their father Adam and grandfather Robert to Lenton Priory. From 1186 to 1194, southern Nottinghamshire was under control of John Lackland, count of Mortain, later King John. Eustace I de Mortain was his knight. In 1194, Eustace was fined twenty marks for supporting John against King Richard I. In 1197 and 1201 Eustace paid scutage to avoid military service overseas under both Kings Richard I and John. In 1198 Eustace held twenty-six fees with Richard Basset, Stephen de Beauchamp, William Briwere, and Fulk Paynel. In 1202 Eustace de Mortain held lands in Wingfield, Derbyshire, along with the de Hériz family. In 1212 he held fees in Wollaton and Cossal, Nottinghamshire, and also lands in Bedfordshire. He sided with the barons against King John in 1215, was arrested, and lost his lands. But he regained them when he did homage to the next king, Henry III. He lost them again in 1218 for not paying his ransom. In 1221 he was coroner of Nottinghamshire, but died soon after. He had married Hillaria Salvain and they had a son Eustace II, who succeeded and married Eyncina, daughter of William Rufus and Isabel de Arches. Eyncina was the niece of Malveysin and Théophanie de Hercy. Eustace II held the fees in 1223 and 1237; those holding fees assessed at two marks of the Honour of Peverel included Eustace, who also held Cossal and Wollaton, John, Geoffrey, and William de Hériz, Richard (Hériz) de Wiverton, Robert de Strelley, and Milo de Beauchamp. Eustace II was succeeded by his son William, who took respite of knighthood in 1242. In 1249, there was a lawsuit over lands against William. In 1252, William sued the Peverels over eight knights' fees on behalf of his son, Adam de Mortain. In 1252 William was a commissioner appointed to investigate excesses and injuries in Nottinghamshire. In 1263, he was given license to hunt with his own dogs in the forests of Staffordshire. Adam succeeded, but died without issue in 1283. In 1284–85, the abbey of Neubo in Lincolnshire held of the heirs of Eustace of Mortain in the Hundred of Bingham, Nottinghamshire. Adam was succeeded by his nephew, Roger de Mortain, who in 1284–85 and 1302–3 held Cossal and Wollaton of the Honour of Peverel. Roger de Mortain held estates of the Peverels and of Hugh de Hériz in Stapleford. In 1299 a jury found that he held in Grove by doing homage and fealty to Hugh II de Hercy and paying an annual ward fee of 10s. to Tickhill, and confirmed the inheritance of his son Eustace III. In the tax lists of 1302–3, Hugh de Hercy held Grove, and Eustace III de Mortain held a part of Grove of Hugh. In 1309, Eustace held three parts of a knight's fee in Grove, and four parts in Weston, then in the king's hands. In 1311, Wollaton was held by William de Mortain. In the tax lists of 1316, Hugh II de Hercy, Eustace de Mortain, and Laurence de Chaworth held Grove and Headon.[73] At some point between 1316 and 1322, Sir Robert de Hercy bought the fees in Grove from his cousin Eustace III de Mortain. Sir Robert probably had died by 1322.

The life of Sir Hugh II de Hercy was firmly based in his manors of Grove, Ordsall, and West Retford. Marriage to Elizabeth de Saundby brought the Hercy family lands in Saundby and elsewhere. Hugh also acquired lands in Yorkshire and Lincolnshire. He was a plaintiff and defendant in lawsuits. He incurred debts but repaid them. In his role as knight, he traveled even beyond these neighboring counties, fighting under Kings Edward I and Edward II in Scotland. He did both feudal and voluntary knightly service. He was appointed commissioner of array and served twice as knight of the shire in Parliament. He appointed rectors of the churches of Grove, Ordsall, and West Retford, two of whom were his own sons. Hugh and his sons allegedly had conflict with Rufford Abbey and with the parish priest of Grove,

73. Although in Normandy, Mortain lies almost directly north of Hercé in Maine and they were linked by road; CDF, 562, 564–66; PR 22 Henry II 94, PR 6 Richard I, m.6, 9 Richard I, , m. 10d; ROF, 168, 179; RBE, 2:484, 583–85 (1211–12, Honour of Peverel, Ivo de Hériz, with Eustace de Mortain, Walter de Strelley, Richard de Stapleford, Gervais de Wiverton); HKF, 1:158–61; *Rolls of Arms*, "Glover's Roll, no. 215, p. 158; FA, 4:92, 94, 97, 107, 111–12, 114–15, 126, 137–38; in 1428, it was stated again that Eustace formerly held Grove of Hugh de Hercy; the Chaworth family was from Sourches in Maine, near LeMans; Loyd, *Origins*, 27; Yeatman, *Feudal History*, 390–91, 419, 446–47; Thoroton, *Nottinghamshire*, 2:208–10; Ellis, "Origin of the Morteynes," 117–19; J. Green, *Aristocracy*, 278, Keats-Rohan, *Domesday Descendants*, 600.

but remained faithful Catholics. Elizabeth was an heiress, wife, and mother. She helped defend Hugh in lawsuits brought against them by her sisters. She managed the estates when Hugh was away, as when he was fighting in Scotland or attending Parliament. Sir Hugh and Elizabeth raised five sons to adulthood, two of whom became rectors.

SIR HUGH III DE HERCY AND ALICE DE HERCY

On 27 October 1322, Sir Robert's younger brother, Sir Hugh III Hercy, received the estate of Grove held in chief of the Honour of Tickhill from their father, Sir Hugh II, to whom he would pay £40 a year during his life, and for which privilege he paid the king 20s. In 1322, Hugh was named as surety in a case in Yorkshire. In 1323 a transfer of tenants of fiefs in Lindley and Quermby in Yorkshire held by Thomas de Lacy of Hugh de Hercy was recorded, showing that Sir Hugh held properties in Yorkshire. Sir Hugh III de Hercy was summoned to the Great Council at Westminster in 1324. In 1324 there were only twenty-two resident knights in Nottinghamshire and forty-five knightly families.[74]

King Edward II was deposed for incompetence in January 1327 by the queen and both houses of Parliament, a phenomenon rare in medieval Europe. He was succeeded by his fourteen-year-old son by Isabelle of France, who became King Edward III. Sheriffs read the proclamation of the change in monarchs in public places throughout the kingdom. Edward III reigned from 1327 to 1377. From 1337 to 1340, his wars in France required very high taxation in England which was a burden on his subjects. In his reign, the House of Commons, consisting of knights and burgesses, was firmly established in Parliament. Commons had power because it had the authority to pass or reject the king's requests for taxes. In 1361 the king established commissions of the peace in the shires, consisting of royal judges and provincial gentry. By 1362 the language of the lawcourts was for the most part changed from Norman French to English.[75]

On 25 May 1327, Sir Hugh III de Hercy was witness to the enrollment of a document for release of debt. On 17 February 1328, Sir Hugh was witness to a document concerning the transfer of some rents from tenants of

---

74. CPR, Edward II, 1321–24, 210; CFR, Edward II, 1319–1327, 155; TNA, C 143/160/16; YAJ, 8(1884) 519–21; Wapentake of Agbrigg, AA.132, 147b, K.116; Prestwich, *English Politics*, 62–63; Crouch, *Image*, 145–46; Payling, *Political Society*, 63–64; Coss, *Origins*, 213.

75. Ormrod, *Edward III*, 371, 478; Edward III was a warrior, called *invictus pardus* (unconquered leopard) by Richard II; Given-Wilson, *Nobility*, 9.

Grove to a widow for her life by Henry de Clyf, master clerk of the Chancery and keeper of the great seal of King Edward III. On 4 August 1328, Sir Hugh acknowledged a debt of twenty marks for which he had pledged his lands and chattels in Nottinghamshire, but which was then cancelled on repayment. On 28 August 1328, William, son of Eustace III de Mortain, relinquished his rights to a tenancy in the manor of Grove called "Le Bourehalle" to Master Henry de Clyf. Sir Hugh de Hercy and Sir Laurence de Chaworth were witnesses to the transaction. On 20 February 1330, Henry de Clyf assigned various rents from tenants of Grove. Sir Hugh was again witness. On 22 October 1331, William de Mortain personally appeared in Chancery in London and acknowledged his release of his right in the manor of Grove to Hugh de Hercy, knight; the release was officially enrolled and Henry de Clyf was a witness to the document. On 6 November 1331, a debt of Sir Hugh for £200 to Master Henry de Clyf was cancelled after repayment. Sir Hugh claimed to have in Grove the rights of infangenthief, gallows, and free-warren; the last was the right to keep birds and animals which only he had the right to kill. These minor franchises gave him additional income, status, and jurisdiction over the peasants.[76]

On 15 September 1330, a man convicted of trespass by a jury of twelve and imprisoned appealed to the king, complaining of malfeasance by the jury, asking for a new trial before a jury of twenty-four knights of the original jurors, among them Hugh de Hercy, knight, and for release from prison to prepare for the trial. The king granted his request and ordered the sheriff of Nottingham to release him pending trial. On 15 September 1330, Sir Hugh was named surety (mainpernor) in Chancery for the large jury trial. On 14 April 1331 Hugh de Hercy won a suit for the manor of Marton for which he paid one hundred marks in silver and the defendants did fealty to him in court.[77]

During the reign of King Edward III, Sir Hugh III Hercy may have been a member of the March 1337 Parliament in York, but the rolls for this short Parliament no longer exist. At this time knights of the shire were elected by local authorities on the basis of good character and sufficient property to serve in a specific parliament. The king asked this Parliament for high taxes to pay for his wars in Scotland and France. The campaign against the Scots cost £25,000 per season. On 15 September 1337, Hugh was appointed with two others to explain the king's need to collect subsidies for

---

76. CCR, Edward III, 1327–30, 363, 403, 412; Thoroton, *Nottinghamshire*, 3:434, "Harworth"; Coss, *Origins*, 160.

77. *Gascon Rolls*, C61/37:139.1 (8 March 1325); CCR, Edward III, 1327–30, 404; CFR, Edward II, 1319–27, 155; TNA, CP, 25/1/185/27, n. 74.

the defense of the realm. The focus for war was then shifting from Scotland to France.⁷⁸

On 3 October 1337, King Edward III and his council addressed an order to Sir Hugh de Hercy, Sir Thomas de Longvilliers, and one other to supercede his previous order to collect £600, which represented the assessment on Nottinghamshire for the king's "affairs," because the council at Westminster had granted the king "a tenth and fifteenth for three years" from the whole realm. On 6 July 1338, Sir Hugh was appointed commissioner of array for Nottinghamshire to raise troops to defend England against the French and to keep the peace at home and "to hear and determine trespasses." The king of France had taken Gascony from the English, which began the Hundred Years War. But the English did not fight at this time. In 1339, Sir Hugh was again appointed commissioner of array for Nottinghamshire and Derbyshire to raise ten men at arms and twenty archers for war against Scotland and to proceed to Newcastle. With the help of the French, who sent supplies and men, the Scots held back the English army from engaging. In October of that year Sir Hugh was commissioned to array men in Nottinghamshire to keep the peace and to hear and determine crimes.⁷⁹

The vicar of Lanum complained to the king that he had not received his stipend. The king ordered his treasurer and the barons of the Exchequer to investigate. Then on 10 March 1341 the king appointed Sir Hugh de Hercy, Sir Thomas de Longvilliers, and a priest to hold an inquisition, investigating the discrepancies in payment of 60s. a year to the vicar of Lanum, and the most recent payment from which "the vicar never took any rent or profit by himself or another in recompense for the said sum, and that he never released the said 60s. yearly or part thereof." On this basis, on 18 May 1341 the king ordered the archbishop of York to pay the vicar his arrears. The same year, Sir Hugh appointed the rector of the whole church of Grove and witnessed a quitclaim for William de Wentworth with Sir Thomas Longvilliers. On 22 November 1342, a debt of twenty marks for which Hugh III had pledged his lands and chattels in Nottinghamshire was cancelled on repayment. In 1342, a court case assigned two parts of the manor and advowsons of Ordsall and Grove to Hugh, on his decease going to his son John and John's heirs by his wife, and a third part of the manor and advowson of West Retford, to John de Hercy, his wife Joane and their heirs. Also in 1342, John and Joan de Hercy sued his parents, Hugh and

78. CFR, Edward II, 1337–47, 43; CPR, Edward III, 1334–38, 371.

79. CPR, Edward III, 1334–38, 135; 1338–40, 135, Edward III, 1338–40, 135, 363; ParlRolls, vol. 2, 1327–77, Edward III (1339) 110; CCR, Edward III 1337–39, 186; Payling, *Political Society*,109.

Alice, over the manor of Weston and some rent and won, gaining Weston and the rent for themselves and their heirs.[80]

Sir Hugh III de Hercy was high sheriff of Nottinghamshire and Derbyshire in 1341–42 and 1346. Sheriffs were generally appointed by the king through the Exchequer. The sheriff had financial and judicial duties. He was the agent responsible for collecting taxes owed from the county to the king and had to render an account every year to the Exchequer. At this time the sheriff also handled thousands of writs each year, royal writs, summonses, orders for distraint and attachment, which he had to register on his rolls, copy, send the copies to the bailiff, and send back the originals with reply to the issuers. The sheriff was responsible for convening, presiding over, and executing judgments of the county courts. When the office of sheriff was twinned for two counties, as it was for Nottinghamshire and Derbyshire, the sheriff was responsible for these duties in both counties. The sheriffs were not paid, but many enjoyed collecting excess taxes, fees, and bribes. However, the sheriff took an oath of good conduct and could be held liable for inefficiency or injustice. The sheriff generally had a staff of six or seven, with an undersheriff, clerks, a keeper and returner of writs, receivers of money, and bailiffs, as well as servants to care for horses and buildings. The office of sheriff was the highest office in the county or shire; knight of the shire was the second most important. On 15 January and 19 November 1341 and again in 1343, Sir Hugh was ordered to submit his accounts for the previous year as sheriff to the Exchequer, which he did. On 4 May 1342, the king ordered the judges of Nottinghamshire not to punish Hugh de Hercy, former sheriff of the county, who, having indicted and imprisoned a man named John for numerous felonies and trespasses, allegedly failed to deliver the prisoner to them on a certain day. But since Hugh on the order of the king had delivered the man to the king's officers instead on the appointed day, he was acquitted. On 11 January 1346, the king commissioned Hugh Hercy, sheriff, and others to raise money for the knighting of the Black Prince.[81]

---

80. CCR, Edward III, 1341–43, 78, 264, 678; CPR, Edward III, 1340–43, 208, 272; *Register of Archbishop of York* 5A, f. 112, 9B, f. 453; TNA, CP, 25/1/185/30, numbers 224 and 225; Meaby, *Nottinghamshire*, 278–280; Burke, *Commoners*, 1099; LCNN, 84; Piercy, *History*, 216; later Humphrey Hercy married Joan Stanhope, a descendant of the Longvilliers family.

81. CFR, Edward III, 1337–47, 201, 251, 349, 351, 491; CPR, Edward III,1361–64, 293; CCR, Edward III, 1341–43, 526–27; *RP*, 2:189; Thoroton, *Nottinghamshire*, vol. 3, "Grove"; Palmer, *County Courts*, 28–32, 37, 41–52; Ormrod, *Reign*, 155, 157–58; when a sheriff took too much in excess taxes, he was reported to royal judges or parliament; Prestwich, *English Politics*, 51–54; Young, *Making of the Neville Family*, 18; Russell, "Politics and Society," 265.

PART II | ENGLAND

In 1343, Hugh was escheator of Nottinghamshire and Derbyshire, for which he was ordered to render accounts to the Exchequer. Escheator was a county office held for one year, with responsibility for properties which escheated to the king and certification of them to the Exchequer. On 13 January 1344, the king ordered Sir Hugh, as escheator of Nottinghamshire, to deliver certain inherited properties to Joan de Grey, widow of Ralph Basset of Drayton, as her dowry. In 1347, the sheriff of Nottingham and two others were appointed "in the room of Hugh de Hercy."[82] This indicates that Sir Hugh had an office in the city of Nottingham.

In 1346, Sir Hugh III de Hercy held the lands in Grove and Weston which had formerly been held by Eustace de Mortain. Yet Hugh de Hercy and John de Mortain continued in litigation over ownership of parts of Grove. John de Mortain, son of Eustace, had pursued a writ *de forma donationis*, a transfer of title by gift without payment, against Hugh and his wife Alice for half of the estate of Grove. Sir Hugh argued that the will of the late Maud, aunt of John, barred others from actions against them concerning any right to Grove. Hugh de Hercy and John de Hakthorn of Retford acknowledged a debt of two hundred marks to their adversaries, who in turn had acknowledge a debt of two hundred marks to Hugh de Hercy and John de Hakthorn of Retford, pending litigation. On 23 November 1348, the documents of the case were enrolled at Westminster, setting out hearing dates, court costs, and attorney's fees depending on the outcome, type of trial (*nisi prius*; before one judge and a jury), renouncement of excuse for nonappearance (*essoin*), and an order to the sheriff to summon twelve men for a jury (*venire facias*). The four parties appeared in Chancery court at London on 25 November. Since no judgment was recorded, the parties probably settled the case at this point. In 1350, Hugh de Hercy transferred fees he held in Stanley, Wakefield, and Ossett in West Yorkshire. In May 1364, Hugh appointed a new rector to replace his brother Laurence at Ordsall, and in 1368 a new rector of West Retford. On 26 April 1366, Hugh de Hercy, his wife, Alice, and the vicar of Kirklington, in litigation against the co-rectors of Treswell, signed a covenant in court affirming their rights to the manors of Grove and Weston and the advowsons of Grove, Ordsall, and West Retford for life, which after their deaths would descend to Thomas, son of John de Hercy, and his wife Elizabeth, and to their male heirs to hold as chief lords forever. On 13 October 1366 and 6 October 1369, a case was heard over the manor of Marton near Bawtry, naming Hugh de Hercy

82. CFR, Edward III, 1337–47, 351, 491, 493; CCR, Edward III, 1343–46, 211; Brown; YAJ, 8 (1884) 9; Ralph Basset had been knighted by King Edward I in 1306, later made seneschal of Gascony, steward of Aquitaine, constable of Dover Castle and knight banneret of King Edward II.

as an alleged deforciant, one who took property from its rightful owner. Hugh claimed that the manor after the death of Joan should revert to him from her dower, but later acknowledged it belonged to Robert de Morton. In 1371, the will of Thomas de Chaworth showed that he held the manor of Osberton of Hugh de Hercy for 30s. per year.[83]

In the first half of the fourteenth century, county knights received a great number of county offices and commissions, confirming their status and prestige. They were appointed by the king for specific services, but came to regard their role as partners in the government of the realm. The House of Commons was fully established in Parliament and through it county gentry could represent themselves and their counties to the king. In the Middle Ages, kings did not keep standing armies. During the years 1346 to 1348, the king had drafted local arrays for wars in France and imposed large assessments for provisions. Both actions greatly angered the House of Commons. Then the Black Death decimated England and the continent in 1348–49, killing at least 40 percent of the population. Although brought to England through the port cities in the south, the plague traveled north and was documented in York in May 1349. The poor were more affected than the aristocracy and gentry because of the squalid conditions in which they lived. In rural areas there was great infestation by rats in barns, granaries, and the wattle and mud-daub huts in which peasants lived. The number of knights and esquires decreased, peasants left their lands, and villages were depopulated. Land values declined. In Nottinghamshire, 65 out of 126 parish benefices were empty because their clergy had died. The result of the Black Death was an acute shortage of labor. Wool production decreased and with it foreign trade. Taxes were not lowered even though there were no active wars, except for the Black Prince's campaign against France. Estates of lords who died without children escheated to the king. The plague recurred in England in 1361, 1369, 1375–1376 and 1379, further aggravating the problems. By 1400 the population of England was about three million, half that of the six million in 1300. Peasants who left the land went to the cities looking for paid work. The position of women shifted since they could leave the land, marry later, have fewer children, and get jobs. In the towns

83. FA, 4:111, 114–15, 126, 137–38; CCR, Edward III, 1342–49, 600–601; West Yorkshire Archives, SpSt /4/11/113/3 (thirteenth century): at some time during the thirteenth century, one Gyot de Hercy held land in West Yorkshire, between Wakefield and Stanley; TNA, CP, 25/1/185/34, nos. 403, 424; Joan was married to Gerard de Sekington of Warwickshire and left the land to Anna la Dispensor to revert to Robert de Morton; the basis for Hercy's claim on her dower is unexplained; Robert de Musters was the pastor of Kirklington, then spelled Kirtelyngton; the defendants were the two pastors of the two halves of the church of Treswell; Thoroton, *Nottinghamshire*, vol. 3, "Harworth"; LCNN, 147, 159; J. Green, *Aristocracy*, 247, n. 106.

women became weavers, fullers, dyers, seamstresses, leather workers, and millers, generally working in crafts which did not require capital. In the countryside, women who remained were active in formerly male roles of harvesting, winnowing, and reaping. They sheared sheep, milked cows and sheep, made butter and cheese. Landholders shifted from farming their own lands with the labor of their peasants to renting out their lands to free tenants and from growing crops to raising sheep. There were no wars with France between 1360 and 1369. In this period Parliament met only six times and taxation more or less ceased. Commissions of the peace no longer required royal judges, although the requirement was reinstated in 1368 for felonies. The House of Commons standardized weights and measures, an important advance for commerce. After Queen Philippa died in 1369, King Edward III, old, feeble, and possibly demented, retired from governing. The "Good Parliament" took place in 1376, the longest and most productive Parliament to date. Commons rejected requests for taxes and used the tool of impeachment against royal officials. Some of its accomplishments were soon reversed. But it is remarkable that knights and burgesses of medieval England were capable of standing up to monarchy and magnates.[84]

Sir Hugh III de Hercy continued as lord of Grove and his other estates. His brother had purchased the holdings of the de Mortain family in Grove and Weston. Although he was several times appointed commissioner of array, Sir Hugh exercised his knighthood more in political than military roles. He was twice high sheriff of Nottinghamshire and Derbyshire. He was commissioned by the king to explain and collect taxes. He was appointed escheator of Nottinghamshire and a juror. He was plaintiff and defendant in law cases. He incurred and repaid debts. He appointed rectors of Grove, Ordsall, and West Retford. Although she was joined with Hugh in lawsuits, little is known about his wife, Alice, not even her family name. Alice would have managed all the Hercy estates while her husband was sheriff, commissioner of array, and performing other county offices.

SIR JOHN DE HERCY AND JOAN DE HERCY

Sir Hugh III and Alice de Hercy had two sons. Their elder son, Sir Malveysin, sold a parcel of forty-three acres of his father's land in Netherhaigh, Lindley,

84. VCH, Nottingham, 2:57, 274; Ormrod, *Reign*, 20–22, 32, 35–37, 148, 166–7; Coss, *Origins*, 179–80, 186–87; Kelly, *Great Mortality*, 60: price of wheat in 1313 was 5s. per quarter, 40s. in 1315; 71, 86: possibly 50 percent of population of England died; 224; Goldberg, *Medieval England*, 165; Goldberg, *Women, Work*, 7, 12, 139–41, 148; Given-Wilson, *Nobility*, 119–20: in 1377 knights of the shire petitioned the king in Parliament over the failure of peasants to remain on the land and work their estates.

Yorkshire, for a sum to be paid over three years. But he died without children. The younger son, Sir John Hercy, did not actually inherit Grove since his father lived at least until 1369 and had designated John's son, Thomas, as his successor. During his father's lifetime, John, already a knight, held some fees in Weston and Grove. But father and son did not get along, as shown by their lawsuit over the manor of Weston and Hugh's decision to disinherit John in favor of his grandson.[85]

Sir John Hercy married Joan and they had three or four sons and two daughters. Both daughters had important marriages. Their elder daughter, Elizabeth, married Sir Sampson de Strelley. Lands held by William Peverel in 1086 had descended to the Strelleys. The Strelley family is documented at Strelley from the reign of Henry I. Walter de Strelley had a son, Sampson, who supported Prince John against King Richard I. He lost his lands but they were restored when John became king. He died in 1207 and his son, Walter II, married Cecily, the daughter and heir of Robert de Somerville. Their son Sir Robert I succeeded to Bilborough, but lost his lands for rebelling against King Henry III. He died in 1302. His son Sir Robert II married Constance and had a son, Sir Sampson, who married Elizabeth de Hercy. Sir Sampson de Strelley was knight of the shire for Nottinghamshire, serving in the Parliaments of 1368, 1379–80, 1382, and 1383. He built All Saints Church at Strelley in 1356, perhaps in gratitude for surviving the plague. There he and his wife, Elizabeth de Hercy, are buried in the middle of the chancel in an alabaster tomb, with the effigies of both sculpted on top and fourteen angels with shields around the base. He is depicted in full armor with sword and dagger. His head rests on the family crest; his feet rest on a lion. His right hand crosses over to hold her right hand. His hand is on top and dominant. Clasped hands were rare in sculpted tomb effigies; the deceased were more commonly depicted with their hands folded in prayer. The effigies probably indicate that their presumably arranged marriage had become a marriage of love. Two other effigies with clasped hands of this time, John of Gaunt and his first wife Blanche of Lancaster in St. Paul's, which was destroyed, and King Richard II with his wife Anne of Bohemia in Westminster Abbey, were both marriages of love. Elizabeth de Hercy was portrayed with her hair trussed at the sides, covered by a jeweled net, and a coronet. She wore a necklace and pendant. Her feet rest on two dogs. Sir Sampson died in 1390; Elizabeth in about 1405. Their son Nicholas de Strelley married Elizabeth Pierrepont, a descendant of John II de Hériz, whose sister had married Hugh I de Hercy. Nicholas was knight of the shire in 1394 and died

85. TNA, CP, 25/1/185/34, no. 403; CPR, Edward III, 1361–64, 12; a John Hercy held in Mertone, Wiltshire, which had previously been held by William de Mertone in 1336; TNA, C 241/151/12 (1/7/1359), CP, 25/1/185/30, no. 225.

in 1430. Nicholas and Elizabeth were also buried in the church of Strelley, as were their sons John, who died in 1421, and Sir Robert III, who had fought as a lancer at Agincourt where he was knighted. Sir Robert was knight of the shire in 1460–61. Robert III married first Agnes Stanhope and second Jane Harcourt. He died in 1438. His descendants married members of the Markham, Mering, Stanhope, and Whalley families, all Hercy relatives.[86]

The other daughter of Sir John and Joan Hercy, Maud, married Alexander Mering. The Merings were an old family from Mering, Nottinghamshire. In 1156–62, Alan de Mering donated land, with the assent of his father Hervé, from Marton in Yorkshire to Fountains Abbey, witnessed by Gilbert de Arches, whose family also supported Fountains. His brother Gilbert donated land in Mering to Lenton Priory. His great-grandson, Sir Thomas Mering, had several sons, of whom the youngest was Alexander. Alexander I Mering married Maud Hercy and they had two sons. Alexander II Mering was dean of York Cathedral. Sir William Mering, was sheriff of Nottinghamshire and Derbyshire in 1432–33 and 1438–39. He was knight of the shire for Nottinghamshire in the Parliaments of 1421, 1425, and 1442, and justice of the peace. He led a retinue at Agincourt and was favored by Kings Henry IV and Henry V with a grant of two tons of wine. He married Elizabeth Neville and had daughters, Elizabeth, who married John Strelley, and Margery, who married Thomas Basset, and sons Sir William and Alexander. In the sixteenth century, their great-great-grandson John Mering married Katherine, sister of Sir John Hercy.[87]

An older son of Sir John and Joan Hercy, Sir Laurence Hercy, married Elizabeth, but died without sons. A younger son, William Hercy, held an estate at Welham (also spelled Wellum and Wellom), two miles northeast of Retford, and lived there and in London during the lives of his grandfather, Sir Hugh III de Hercy, and father, Sir John de Hercy. William married the widow of William Saundby. Records from August 1355 document that

---

86. PR 6–7 Richard I, 10 Richard I, 7 John, 9 John; *RegWelbec*, 165; Thoroton, *Nottinghamshire*, vol. 2, "Strelley"; Edge, "Monuments in Strelley Church"; Burke, *Commoners*, 1099; Fellows, *Arms*; Saul, *English Church Monuments*, 104, 119, 228: Saracen crest probably from early participation in tournaments, 302–5; the Somerville family were possibly distant relatives of the de Hériz family; Coss, *Lady*, 86, 94–104; the hands of Richard II and Anne of Bohemia were broken off several centuries ago; there are alabaster slabs in Strelley church to Sir Nicholas and his young son John (1421) and his older son, Sir Robert (1438), as well as full tomb effigies of Sir Robert's son John (1501) and his wife Sanchia; there is a brass of Sir Robert IV, who died in 1487, and his wife Isabel Kemp, sister of Cardinal John Kemp, archbishop of Canterbury (1450–52) and chancellor of England (1450–54).

87. EYC, vol. 11, nos. 20, 21, 146, 249; HistParl, House of Commons 1439–1509, 585; Piercy, *History*, 249–50 (1156–75); Payling, *Political Society*, 241.

William owned a building in London. In 1355, butchers of London purchased a shop that lay between the wall of the Preaching Friars and the building of William Hercy. But William seemed to have been a spendthrift. In a case recorded on 3 November 1354, William de Hercy of Welham acknowledged a debt to Thomas Aylmer in London of £100, pledging his lands and chattels in Nottinghamshire against it. The sheriff of London issued a writ of *scire facias* (a writ based on a matter of record requiring the party against whom it was issued to show cause why the other party should not prevail or that the record should be vacated) on 5 April 1355 for William to appear before him, but he did not. However, the sheriff of Nottinghamshire replied that he received the writ too late to execute it before the return date. In January 1357, a writ was again issued and sent to the sheriff of Nottinghamshire with requests for information on properties that William owned in London, namely two buildings and part of a third worth 53s., 4d., and other buildings worth 20s. John de Hercy of Weston and Grove and William de Hercy of Welham owed a debt of fifty marks to brewers and merchants in London, which had not been paid. The mayor of London, with endorsement by the court of common pleas, sent a writ to the sheriff of Nottinghamshire on 3 February 1357. The king issued another writ on 15 February 1358 to the sheriff of London concerning the debt and a claim against one of the properties. According to Chancery records, on 18 April 1358, £60 was still owed on the debt. William de Hercy also borrowed a hundred marks from John Vykers of Retford, recorded on 6 July 1357. In 1359, Sir John de Hercy owed one thousand marks, a very large sum, to Richard de Stanhope, burgess of Newcastle, which was recorded in Chancery in July 1359. At that time John called himself the heir of his father. On 7 May 1361, Sir John de Hercy received a pardon from King Edward III for his "outlawries" in failing to appear in court to answer Sir Thomas de Furnival and Robert Turald who had sued him for an account of his receivership for both men, since he had since surrendered at the Fleet Prison.[88]

Perhaps because of the irresponsible history and bad debts of Sir John and his son, William, in April 1366, Sir Hugh III de Hercy and Alice, his wife, made a plea of covenant regarding the manors of Grove and Weston and the advowsons of Grove, Ordsall, and West Retford, that, after their deaths, these would go to "Thomas, son of John de Hercy, knight (*militis*),

---

88. CCR, Edward III, 1354–60, 92, 225, 416; TNA, C 241/135/6, original debt 3 February 1354; C131/10/9, 10 January 1357 (writ of *scire facias*); C131/181/2, 18 April 1358; C241/151/12, 25 August 1370 (original debt 1 July 1359); *Calendar of Letter-Books, City of London*, G, 43; Welham meant "hamlet of the well" or "famous spring"; CPR, Edward III, 1361–64, 12; *Register of the Freemen of York*, vol. 1, lists a William de Retford Hercy among the free tradespersons in 1352; Piercy, *History*, 245.

and Elizabeth, his wife, and the male heirs of their bodies," but "in default of such heirs remainder to the right heirs of Hugh." The identity of "Elizabeth" is uncertain, whether she was the wife of John or Thomas. John was married to Joan, unless he had a later marriage to an Elizabeth. Thomas was married to Catherine, unless he had an earlier marriage to an Elizabeth.[89]

England in 1400 was still predominantly rural, consisting mainly of manors and villages, with some market towns, such as Retford, and a few cities. The number of gentry in Nottinghamshire was small and most knew each other well and frequently intermarried.

Sir John de Hercy was called a knight but did not exercise his knighthood either by military service or by holding offices. They were presumably Catholic but he did not appoint rectors. Little is known of his wife Joan, not even her family name. But they aided their two daughters in making prestigious marriages.

SIR THOMAS DE HERCY AND CATHERINE COMBERWORTH CONSTABLE HERCY

Sir Thomas de Hercy, eldest surviving son of Sir John, succeeded to Grove, Weston, and West Retford sometime after 1369 from his grandfather Sir Hugh III de Hercy. It was a time of some turmoil. King Edward III died in 1377. His eldest son by Philippa of Hainault, Edward the Black Prince, had predeceased him. The ten-year-old son of the Black Prince by Joan of Kent became King Richard II, who reigned from 1377 to 1399, but did not have children. King Richard II was a minor until 1384; his uncle John of Gaunt ruled as regent. Poll taxes were levied in 1377, 1379, and 1380–81 to pay for wars in France, causing the people to rebel, attack the wealthy, loot, and burn manors. The rebel leaders were beheaded or hung, drawn, and quartered.[90]

Sir Thomas de Hercy had been knighted by 1382 when he was appointed tax collector. In March 1384, Sir Thomas Hercy was listed among the witnesses with William de Saundby of a royal document concerning the transfer of prebends, with "lands, fisheries, rents, reversions" in Yorkshire and Nottinghamshire by Sir Robert de Morton, including fees of Tickhill,

---

89. TNA, CP, 25/1/185/34, nos. 403, 424; *IPM*, 44 Edward III, File 215, no. 15: will of Thomas de Chaworth, who died 5 December 1371; the deceased older son, Laurence, was married to an Elizabeth; Burke, *Commoners*, 1099, follows this succession; Thoroton, *Nottinghamshire*, vol. 2, 262, posits John to Thomas to William to Thomas, which is unlikely.

90. John of Gaunt, a younger son of King Edward III, was duke of Lancaster through his marriage to Blanche of Lancaster, who died of the plague in 1369.

Great Morton, Little Morton, and Blyth. At Nottingham in July 1384 he arraigned Roger Kirke of Weston on a charge of novel disseisin, but the case did not go to trial. Sir Thomas was commissioner of array in Nottinghamshire in October 1384 and June 1386. In July 1386, King Richard II changed his order of 1 June and told Thomas de Hercy, John de Leek, William de Neville, and five others to exercise their commission to array men at arms without waiting for Robert de Morton, whom the king now excused "as he was too aged to travail without great hurt."[91] However, the threatened French-Burgundian invasion was aborted.

John of Gaunt, duke of Lancaster, held the Honour of Tickhill from 1362. Grove and most of north Nottinghamshire were under Tickhill and, therefore, vassals of the dukes of Lancaster. In 1386, Sir Thomas served under John of Gaunt in the latter's unsuccessful attempt to seize the throne of Castile, which he claimed through his second wife, Constance of Castile. It was the time of the papal schism, when Portugal and Gaunt supported Pope Urban and Castile Pope Clement. Urban granted the indulgences of crusaders, plenary remission of sins without performance of penance, to all who aided the campaign of Gaunt in a bull read by sheriffs in every county. Sir Thomas enlisted voluntarily. Knights who joined Gaunt's force hoped for money or office or suspension from legal actions against them during service or forgiveness of sins or simply adventure. However, war was no longer an easy path to riches from booty or increase in status and had become a financial burden for gentry knights. Among Gaunt's retainers from Nottinghamshire were Sir Robert Clifton, Sir John Lowdham, Sir Edmund Pierrepont, Sir Thomas Rempston, and Sir Thomas Hercy. Gaunt received twenty thousand marks from Parliament and a loan of twenty thousand marks from the king, barely enough to pay his army of about sixteen-hundred men-at-arms and two thousand archers for six months. A fleet from Portugal came to help transport the army from Plymouth on July 7. They stopped en route to aid the English garrison at Brest against the duke of Brittany and did not reach Galicia until July 25. Several towns surrendered, but Orense was taken with some fighting after siege. Since it was too late in the year to begin a campaign against Castile, they spent the winter at Orense. Initially Gaunt had paid the townspeople for food supplies, but his money ran out, leading to conflict when food was taken by force. Gaunt could not pay his soldiers, although for a time he may have drawn upon his

---

91. CCR, Richard II, 1381–85, 440, Richard II, 1385–89, 171; CFR, Richard II, 1377–1383, 337; TNA, CP, 25/1/185/34, no. 403; CPR, Richard II, 1385–89, 176; 1391–96, 232; other parties included John de Markham; John de Leek was also a commissioner of array in 1386 and 1392, Nicholas de Strelley in 1392; HistParl, House of Commons, 1386–1421, 3:347–48.

personal funds to do so. The army suffered from lack of food and disease which caused many deaths, including that of Sir Gilbert Talbot. With barely half of his army remaining, Gaunt negotiated with the king of Portugal, who supplied a much larger army in the spring. They attacked Leon but after some fighting and hampered by lack of supplies, gave up. Gaunt capitulated in May 1387, agreeing to withdraw in exchange for a large sum of money, most of which was never paid. The king of Castile granted safe-conduct to the English soldiers to cross into the English territory of Gascony. Although a few remained with Gaunt during negotiations which lasted until 1388, it is more likely that Sir Thomas Hercy returned with the army in 1387. He witnessed a document in Nottinghamshire in February 1388.[92]

Many of the knights of John of Gaunt were rewarded with political office. Sir Thomas de Hercy was named knight of the shire, serving in the Parliament of 1391, in which King Richard II petitioned for an end to restrictions on his rights as king. The king also asked for a half subsidy of taxes for future needs although it was then a time of peace. Sir Thomas was paid £15, 4s. for thirty-eight days service in Parliament. Sir Thomas was again commissioner of array in 1392, but due to disagreements between the king and Parliament, no war took place. Sir Thomas held the estates of his late tenant and relative Thomas Lascelles in wardship until his daughter came of age in September 1391. His great-grandson would later hold the children of Richard Lascelles in ward. Sir Thomas de Hercy gave £100 as security for his neighbor, Sir Hugh Hussey, who had been bound over to Chancery court, to keep the peace. In July 1392, Sir Thomas de Hercy and Sir William de Neville, knights, with William de Saundby and Robert Cressy, were witnesses to the execution of a quitclaim with warranty involving the manor of Skegby, with its lands, rents, services, servitudes, courts, mill, easements, and advowsons of churches. In July 1392, William Aune gave one hundred marks as a recognizance to Thomas de Hercy and acknowledged receipt of one hundred marks borrowed from Sir Thomas on pledge of his lands and chattels in Nottinghamshire. Sir Thomas was appointed commissioner of *oyer et terminer* in November 1392. In May 1394, Thomas Hercy and eleven others won a land tenure case over messuages and other properties in Allerton and Sowerby in Yorkshire. They received a quitclaim from the deforciants for payment of one hundred marks of silver. In the mid-1390s, Sir Thomas brought charges in Chancery court equity side against William

---

92. S. Walker, *Lancastrian Affinity*, 64, 67, 76–77, 267, 273, 276–77, 279, 282; other retainers of Gaunt included Sir William Beauchamp, Sir Ralph Paynel, Sir Thomas Percy, and several Nevilles and Talbots; Goodman, *John of Gaunt*, 115–31; Armitage-Smith, *John of Gaunt*, 304–5, 309–12; YAJ 8 (1895), 79: Thomas was witness to a document in February 1388 in Laxton, Nottinghamshire.

Denman and others of forcible entry on the manors of Grove and Ordsall, occupation of the manor of Ordsall, destruction of a mill at Ordsall, taking large quantities of food, causing *horribles damages*, riding to Grove with intent to murder Sir Thomas, and other crimes.[93] Much later, a descendent of Thomas would marry a descendant of William Denman.

Sir Thomas de Hercy was named in 1377 as patron of the churches of West Retford and Ordsall, and served as such until his death. He appointed rectors of St. Helen's church in Grove in 1399, of St. Michael's church in West Retford in 1378, 1401, 1408, 1419, 1421, and 1422, and of All Hallows Church in Ordsall in 1379, 1410, 1415, 1416, 1417, 1418, and 1424.[94]

In 1392 a chest full of gold and silver was discovered by a woman who gave it to her priest brother to hide in his cellar. It was the prerogative of the king to decide the disposition of treasure trove. King Richard II appointed a commission of *oyer et terminer*, including Thomas Hercy, knight, John Markham, two others and the sheriff of Nottingham, to investigate. However, the commissioners were accused of having "meddled" in the affair. In June, the king ordered the treasurer and barons of the Exchequer to hear and determine the matter. They decided, by writ of *supersedeas omnino*, an order to stay all proceedings at law, not to proceed against Sir Thomas, because he never received his commission and thus did not "meddle." Sir Thomas swore an oath to this effect in Chancery at Westminster.[95]

In April 1396, King Richard II appointed Sir Thomas to a commission investigating obstructions in the River Idle, which flowed through Retford. The burgesses and tenants of East Retford filed a bill of indictment with the archbishop of York, who was chancellor of England, complaining that Sir Thomas de Hercy, lord of West Retford, had arbitrarily and exorbitantly doubled the fees for pasturing their animals in West Retford, diverted the course of the river, which affected the king's mills, had his men, armed with bows, fish in the common waters of East Retford, while taking the fish and nets of the burgesses away, breaking their houses, and threatening their "life and limb." Such cases were most often resolved by negotiation between the parties and then, as here, no judgment is found in court records. In February 1397, Sir Thomas, nobleman, and his wife Catherine, noblewoman, of

---

93. CCR, Richard II, 1389-92, 168, 560, 666; TNA, C 1/1/11; C 1/7/302 (1391-1396), (the later possible dates, 1426-32, are after the death of Sir Thomas in 1425); CP, 25/1/279/147, no. 8, 10 May 1394; HistParl, House of Commons, 1386-1421, 347-49; there is a tomb effigy of William Saundby, who died in 1418, in the church of St. Martin of Tours in Saundby.

94. *Register of the Archbishop of York*, Reg. 12, f. 75, 16, f. 72, 80; LCNN, 84, 147, 159; Piercy, *History*, 186, 216-27.

95. CPR, Richard II, 1391-96, 232; CCR, Richard II, 1392-96, 74, 269, 484.

PART II | ENGLAND

the diocese of York received a papal indult for remission of their sins at the hour of their deaths. If this was the same Sir Thomas Hercy, it indicates an earlier marriage to another woman named Catherine since the marriage to Catherine Comberworth Constable occurred after the death of her first husband in 1404. On 7 April 1402, an inquest was conducted in Durham concerning Thomas Hercy and others regarding the manor of Croxdale and land in Quarrington, both in county Durham.[96]

From 1397 King Richard II dissolved Parliament and ruled as an autocrat. In 1398 he exiled Henry of Bolingbroke for ten years. On the death of John of Gaunt, son of King Edward III and uncle of King Richard II, in February 1399, Gaunt's son and heir, Henry of Bolingbroke, succeeded as duke of Lancaster. But King Richard increased the term of his exile to life, revoked his previous Letters Patent, confiscated Henry's inheritance, seized Gaunt's lands, and denied Henry his title of duke of Lancaster. In July 1399 Henry returned to England from exile in France to claim his rightful inheritance when Richard was in Ireland. When Henry of Bolingbroke landed on English soil at Ravenspurn in Yorkshire on 4 July 1399, he was met by Sir Thomas de Hercy and his men and other faithful friends, who then marched with him to London, which Henry entered in triumph on 2 September, welcomed by the people. When Richard returned from Ireland, Henry imprisoned him in the Tower. On 29 September Richard II agreed to abdicate. The instrument of abdication was drawn up by justice Sir John Markham of Nottinghamshire, who was also one of the commissioners appointed to receive the crown. The next day the king read his abdication before Parliament, after which the archbishops of Canterbury and York led Henry of Bolingbroke duke of Lancaster to the throne, where he was crowned King Henry IV. King Henry expressed his gratitude to Sir Thomas Hercy and two other men of Nottinghamshire: "*en notre campaignye apres*

96. TNA, C 1/1/11; *Lateran Regesta* 45: 1396-97, *De Plenaria Remissione*: "Thomas Hersy, knight, nobleman, and Catherine his wife, noble woman, of the" diocese of York; TNA, DL 28/27/3, 42/151; CPL, 5:39; Durham Records, Cursitor's Records, vol. 2, fol. 140, 14 (7 April 1402); CPR, Richard II,1396-99, 586; *Calendar of Plea*, 2:61; CCR, Henry IV, 1399-1402, 115: there were two cases at about this time involving Thomas Hercy of London, possibly the younger son of Sir Thomas of Grove, although he was a cutler, a craftsperson who made knives and swords; on 7 March 1394, a writ of *supersedeas omnino* was issued to the sheriff of London by *mainprise* of Thomas Hercy and others as sureties in a case; on 6 February 1399, the same writ was issued to the sheriffs of London by *mainprise* of Thomas Hersey [*sic*], cutler, two goldsmiths, and an armorer, all of London; there was also a Richard Hercy, draper, in London who was owed 50s. by a pastor from Norfolk, recorded 3 July 1399; Richard Hercy, draper, occupied a shop in London; a Richard Hercy was also documented in London in 1419 as a brewer; a Richard Hercy was on a panel of jurors at the London Assizes in 1427; Cantor, *Changing English Countryside*, 15, 18; Payling, *Political Society*, 186-94.

notre darrain arrivaille en Engleterre et a notre parlement a Londres" (in our company from our arrival for combat in England and to our parliament in London). Sir Thomas and his men were part of the king's bodyguard during this crucial period. In November 1399, King Henry gave Sir Thomas an annuity of twenty marks from the Honour of Pontefract and £40 as wages of war for his service. Such an annuity was a substantial increase in income for a county knight.[97]

Sir Thomas Hercy made a prestigious marriage to the wealthy Catherine Comberworth Constable, daughter and heir of Sir Robert Comberworth of Somerby, Lincolnshire, who held several commissions under King Richard II, and Sybil Ergum of Yorkshire. Their son and Catherine's brother, Sir Thomas Comberworth, was sheriff of Lincolnshire in 1415 and 1431, knight of the shire in 1420, 1421, and 1424, and justice of the peace in 1414, with responsibility to hold four court sessions each year.[98]

Catherine was the widow of Sir Marmaduke Constable of Flamborough in eastern Yorkshire, who had died in the summer of 1404. The Constables of Flamborough were descended from the constables of Chester. The name "constable" was originally a job title, denoting a military commander or guardian of a castle. Sir Marmaduke's father, Sir Robert, had been sheriff of Yorkshire in 1385–86 and 1394–95; he died in 1400. Sir Marmaduke Constable held lands in Flamborough, Marton, and Buketon in Yorkshire. The Hercy children had half-siblings from this marriage: Sir Robert, Thomas, Sir John, Sir William, James, and Agnes/Anne Constable, although they did not reside with the family and were heirs to the Constable estates. In 1432, Catherine Constable Hercy was left a book of romances beginning with *Decem Preceptes Alembes* in the will of her first husband's sister,

---

97. CPR, Henry IV, 1401–5, 487 (8 September 1403, array), 518 (12 November 1404, peace); TNA, DL 42/15, pt. 1 fol. 70–71; there were thirty-seven men from England; the other men from Nottinghamshire were Sir Hugh "Husy" and Richard Stanhope; DL 42/15, pt/1, fol.70, DL 28/27/6; TNA, E 101/41/1 (muster rolls); *Medieval Soldier Database*; HistParl, House of Commons, 3:348; in 1400 some of Richard's supporters attempted to assassinate Henry IV and his sons; after the supporters were executed, Richard himself was put to death, probably by starvation; Given-Wilson, *Henry IV*, 81; Payling, *Political Society*, 124–25, 135; Given-Wilson, *Nobility*, 155–56.

98. Robert Comberworth: CPR, Richard II, 1377–81, 299; 1381–85, 245, 509, 589, 1385–89, 385; 1388–92, 209; 1391–96, 85, 110, 515; 1396–99, 11, 54, 128, 234, 310, 370; Henry IV, 1401–5, 199, 289, 347; Ergum is now Eryholme, Yorkshire; Thomas Comberworth: CPR, Henry V, 1413–16, 455 (peace); CPR, Henry VI, 1422–29, 248, 366, 481, 553, 555; 1429–36, 275, 425, 611; 9 Henry VI, 1429–36, 126 (peace), 273 (*walliis et fossatis*, with Robert Willoughby Ralph Cromwell, knights), 303 (arrest); 1436–41, 17, 147, 249, 327, 461, 557; Sir Thomas Comberworth held properties in Claxby and Normanby, Lincolnshire; the family name was sometimes written Comberford; Goldberg, *Medieval England*, 250.

Joanna Constable Hilton, indicating that both women could read and that they read romances. Joanna also left another romance *de Sept Sages* to her niece. Romances were generally written in French, but the first included at least a beginning in Latin. It would be extraordinary if these women could read Latin, which was generally not taught to women. Catherine's son, Sir Robert Constable, was sheriff of Yorkshire in 1428-29. He died in 1441; his will named his uncle Thomas Comberworth to supervise the executor. His son and heir was Sir Robert II Constable. Catherine Constable Hercy was Robert II's grandmother and godmother. Sir Robert II inherited his father's Constable estates and was potential heir to his uncle's Comberworth estates through his grandmother. He was supervisor and beneficiary of the will of his great-uncle Thomas Comberworth, and later an executor of the will of his grandmother Catherine Hercy. He was knight of the shire for Lincolnshire in 1459. In the Wars of the Roses, he served Lancaster until 1461, then York. He held many positions under King Edward IV. Sir Robert was sheriff of Lincolnshire in 1466-67 and sheriff of Yorkshire in 1461-65, 1478-79, and 1480-81. He was knight of the shire for Yorkshire in 1478. Sir Robert II married Agnes, daughter of the king's serjeant Philip Wentworth. He gave his daughter Ela three vills as *maritagium* in a rare extant contract of marriage. In his will Sir Robert II named his wife Agnes, his son, and one other as his executors.[99] The three families of the Comberworths, Constables, and Hercys were continually in close contact with each other and with the de Lascelles family.

99. CCR, Henry IV 1402-5, 488, 1405-9, 97-98, 417 (Robert Comberworth and John Gateford granted Hodsock to Hugh Cressy); Robert Fitz William le Constable was the illegitimate son of the constable of Chester; his son Robert had a son William, who married the daughter of Maud de Percy; their son Robert had a son Sir William who married Alicia, daughter of Lucy de Brus; their son, Sir Robert, had Sir Marmaduke, who had a son Robert, father of Marmaduke (1379-1404), husband of Catherine Comberworth; their son, Sir Robert Constable, lived from 1385 to 1441; his son, Sir Robert II, lived 1424-1488; *Testamenta Eboracensia* 2:23-25, 2:80-81: executors widow Agnes, son and heir Robert, and Thomas Pickering, "Sir Thomas Comberworth, my uncle to supervise"; Robert and John Constable and Hugh IV Hercy, all sons of Catherine Constable Hercy, were left properties in Lincolnshire; there was Comberworth in Lincolnshire and a Lower Comberworth in Yorkshire, which was connected with Ralph Lascelles; William le Constable of Flamborough quitclaimed his share of Sneaton to Richard de Percy; William le Constable and his son and heir Simon le Constable of Burton Constable held in Legsby, Yorkshire, in the late thirteenth century; this Simon was also married to a Catherine Comberworth and died in 1294; they had a son Robert, who married Avice de Lascelles in 29 Edward I; Avice was daughter and coheir of Roger de Lascelles; DDCC/135/5/ 20, 28; Sir William Fauconberg was a witness; CPR, Richard II, 1381-85, 200; CCR, Richard II, 1392-96, 74, 269, 484; *London Assizes*, Roll EE, no. 234, 1427; HistParl, "Constable, Sir Robert"; Wilkinson, *Women*, 69

In December 1399, King Henry IV appointed Sir Thomas de Hercy commissioner of array. Sir Thomas Hercy served as a captain in the first campaign of King Henry IV in Scotland in 1400. In June the king ordered his retainers to muster at York. They had to wait for supplies and were hampered by bad weather. The army crossed into Scotland in mid-August. The king forbade them to pillage the Scottish counties of Berwickshire and Lothian, which had made no attempt to resist. The army reached Leith without fighting but was short on supplies. On 29 August the army returned to England. In September 1402, King Henry IV appointed Sir Thomas de Hercy, his nephew Sir Nicholas Strelley, Sir Richard Stanhope, Ralph Cromwell, Robert Morton, and others commissioners of array. The Scots invaded as far south as Newcastle. In September 1402, the English under Henry Percy defeated them at Homildon Hill. In September 1403, the king appointed as commissioners of array Thomas Hercy, Nicholas Strelley, and Richard Stanhope knights, with John Gateford and Hugh Cressy. In February 1402, Sir Thomas Hercy had been appointed with Ralph Neufmarché, Roger Leek, and others to arrest a vagabond monk and return him to the abbot of Welbec. In April 1402, he was commissioned with others to hold an inquest at Durham. On 24 October 1403, the king issued a writ from Westminster against two men who failed to appear in court to answer for a debt of £40 owed to Sir Thomas Hercy. This indicates that Sir Thomas had sufficient assets to extend credit to others. In 1404, King Henry IV appointed his loyal knights, including Sir Thomas Hercy, to county offices in Nottinghamshire. On 12 November 1404, Thomas de Hercy was appointed commissioner of the peace with Sir John Markham, Sir John de Leek, Sir Richard Stanhope, John Wastenes, John Gateford, William Saundby, and William Babington. Sir Thomas was reappointed to the office through 1407. In the Lancastrian period, the majority of acting commissioners of the peace were men of prominent knightly gentry families, many of whom were trained in law.[100]

Hugh Cressy was knight of the shire the year before Sir Thomas. Both were commissioners of array in 1399 and 1403. Sir Hugh was sheriff in 1403. In 1408, Hugh Cressy gave an interest in his manor of Owlcotes (Oldcoates) to Sir Thomas Hercy. Also in 1408, the Albertini Bank of Florence obtained royal license for a letter of exchange to pay Sir Thomas four marks. On 6 November 1408, Philip de Albertis of Florence paid four marks to Thomas Hercy. Although the amount was small, this indicates that Sir Thomas was to some extent involved in business. The Albertini Bank had been John of

100. CCR, Henry IV, 1399–1402, 98 (*supersedeas omnino* for Hugh Cressy, John Gateford and sheriff Robert Morton); CPR, Henry IV, 1401–5, 68, 287, 336, 518; *Military Genealogy Medieval Record*, Thomas Hercy (1400); *Deputy Keeper of Public Records*, Durham, 45:269; Payling, *Political Society*, 169, 173–76.

Gaunt and King Henry IV's personal bank at least since 1393. On 13 October 1408, Sir Thomas and others made a plea of covenant involving the manors of Skipwith in Yorkshire and Bekeby (Bigby) in Lincolnshire. The deforciants, George and Elizabeth Monboucher, were obligated to pay them a rose each year on the Nativity of John the Baptist and perform feudal service for the manors, which if they died without heirs, would revert to Sir Thomas and his coplaintiffs. In East Retford in 1409, Sir Thomas and seven others, including Sir Richard Stanhope, Sir John and Simon Leek, George Monboucher, and William Saundby, were named arbitrators of a property dispute over division of the inheritance of Hugh Cressy of Hodsock between Sir John Markham and his brother-in-law, which could not be resolved in the courts. Others who helped secure the agreement included Thomas Rempston and Robert Strelley. Arbitration was very important at this time. The process involved the heads of most of the leading gentry families of north Nottinghamshire. Judge Sir John Markham died in 1409 and was buried in the chancel of St. John the Baptist Church in East Markham. In June, 1409, Sir Thomas Hercy *miles* was named as a beneficiary to the will of Sir George Monboucher of Gamelston, Nottinghamshire. In 1410, Sir Thomas Hercy and Elizabeth Monboucher appeared with his grandnephew Sir Robert Strelley and Sir Henry Pierrepont in the Nottingham assizes in a case involving the Monboucher estates. In August 1411 King Henry IV ordered all holders of royal annuities to muster in London on 23 September for possible military action against France. In 1410–11, there were riots in Nottinghamshire over land possession. At the request of Parliament, the king appointed a commission of *oyer et terminer*, and Sir Thomas Chaworth, Sir John Leek, and Sir Richard Stanhope were sent to the Tower for their participation in the riots, although they were soon released. In 1412, the estate income of Sir Thomas de Hercy was valued at £40 for tax assessment. The tax rate was 6s. 8d. per £20 assessed. Records for 1412 indicate that the taxable wealth of landed knights was greater than that of the aristocracy, especially in Nottinghamshire. Because of failure of male heirs, by 1412 only sixteen of the fourteenth-century knightly families in Nottinghamshire still survived extinction, but four of these families had abandoned knighthood before 1400. Among the ten knights listed in 1412 were Sir Thomas Hercy, his nephew Sir Nicholas Strelley, Sir John Leek, and Sir Edmund Pierrepont. Esquires included his brother-in-law Alexander Mering, William Saundby, and Hugh Cressy. The knights and lesser gentry controlled more than 54 percent of the wealth in the county of Nottinghamshire.[101]

101. CCR, Henry IV, 1405–9, 226, 236, 307, 417, 483, 502; TNA, CP, 25/1/290/61, no. 129; TNA, E179/159/48; RBE, 1:312: Hugh de Cressy held one old fee of the Honour of Giffard in Buckinghamshire with Hugh de Bolebec and Richard Talbot; HKF, 3:314,

King Henry IV ruled from 1399 to 1413. He was strong, intelligent, well-educated, courteous, a man of courage and dignity. He was religious and participated in two crusades. He was married to Mary de Bohun, from one of the greatest Anglo-Norman families. King Henry IV died in March 1413 and his eldest son became King Henry V, ruling from 1413 to 1422. Henry V began an excellent king, having served an apprenticeship in war and administration during the reign of his father. He was a reformer, undoing corruption and trying to rebuild the economy. But he was also a warrior, determined to win back England's empire in France. He was revered as a hero for his early victory at Agincourt on 25 October 1415. Yet his day of greatest glory was diminished when he ordered the killing of all prisoners; similar massacres of prisoners later occurred at Caen and Rougemont. By 1420, he had control of Normandy, Brittany, Maine, Champagne, and the Aquitaine. Under the treaty of Troyes on 21 May 1420, he became regent of France, entitled to succeed the mentally ill French king, Charles VI. On 2 June, the treaty was sealed by his marriage to Catherine de Valois, youngest daughter of Charles VI. This was the greatest extent of English conquest in France.[102]

King Henry V confirmed the annuities granted by his father to Sir Thomas Hercy and others, although in 1415 the annuities were reduced by half. Henry V continued to patronize the knights of his father and grandfather. Under Henry V, Sir Thomas Hercy served as sheriff of Nottinghamshire and Derbyshire from 29 September 1414 to 1 December 1415, when he was succeeded by Simon Leek. Since, as sheriff, he had to administer the county, Sir Thomas was unable to fight at Agincourt, although his grandnephew Sir Robert Strelley and nephew Sir William Mering, did. That year Sir Thomas and others brought a case against John Longespee of Dunham at the special assizes for novel disseisin of Oldcotes Manor. On 8 August 1416, Sir Thomas and another were appointed to inventory and evaluate

---

317, 321; *Proceedings and Ordinances*, 2:148; Sir John Cressy of Hodsock had given Owlcotes to Hugh, son of William Cressy of Wadington, who gave it to Sir Thomas Hercy; Sir Hugh Cressy of Hodsock, son of Sir John, died in 1408; Hugh Cressy of Owlcotes was steward of the prior of Blyth and lived until 1421; ODNB, 36:691–92: John Markham was married to Elizabeth, sister of Hugh Cressy of Hodsock; Thoroton, *Nottinghamshire*, vol. 3, "Styrap and Oulcotes," 262, 420–24; Given-Wilson, *Henry IV*, 74, 341–42, 426, 471–75, 479–81; Matusiak, *Henry V*, 49, 72, 88; HistParlOnline, 1386–1421, "Cressy, Hugh of Oldcoates"; Payling, *Political Society*, 4–5: magnates controlled 17.5 percent, 17, 73–75, 125, 191–92, 204, 221–226, App. 1; Cressy is a former commune in the Pays de Caux, arr. Dieppe, canton Bellencombre; Loyd, *Origins*, 35: Cressy eight km south of Longueville, caput of the Giffards, and in 1204–8, Cressy held of Warenne; Keats-Rohan, *Domesday Descendants*, 415–16: in 1242, Hugh de Cressy held two fees in Buckinghamshire.

102. Matusiak, *Henry V*, 116.

PART II | ENGLAND

and put into the king's hands all lands of the late Thomas Annesley. In 1416 Sir Thomas rendered the account of the annuity of Adam Bell, which had been granted by Henry IV in April 1406, but forfeited when Bell changed his allegiance to the Scots. The following year this account was rendered by Sir Simon Leek. There were continuing battles in France after the victory at Agincourt in 1415 until the Treaty of Troyes in 1420. From 1415 to 1421, there was a shortage of knights qualified for high office in England because of the wars in France. In 1421 Parliament limited the appointment of sheriffs and escheators to one-year terms. Sir Thomas served as commissioner of the peace in 1404-7, and from 1414 until 1425; in 1416 with Ralph Cromwell, in 1417 with Richard Stanhope, in 1420 and 1422 with Simon de Leek, Nicholas Strelley, and Richard Stanhope. As such he gained legal knowledge and court practice. Many of the meetings of the commissions of the peace were then held in East Retford. Sir Thomas was commissioner of array in April 1418, with Richard Stanhope, Nicholas Strelley, and Simon de Leek. Sir Thomas Hercy was one of four heads of knightly families in Nottinghamshire to hold all three high offices, sheriff, knight of the shire, and commissioner of the peace, during the Lancastrian period. In 1412 there were only twelve knights in Nottinghamshire. By the 1430s there were only two hundred knights left in England.[103]

In France on 1 September 1422, King Henry V died of dysentery on his way into battle. His ambition to conquer France ended up bankrupting the English economy. His hard-won territories in France were lost during the reign of his son. King Henry V was succeeded by his nine-month-old son by Catherine de Valois, who reigned as King Henry VI from 1422 to 1461. During his minority, power was held by the Regency Council, composed of the late king's two brothers and Beaufort uncles, with Henry Percy, Ralph Neville, Richard and Walter de Beauchamp, Ralph Cromwell, and others.

Sir Thomas Hercy died in 1425. Affluent landholders made wills which are of interest for many reasons. They indicate the wealth of the testator,

---

103. CFR, Henry V, 1413-22, 384, 528; TNA, JUST 1/694/2; CPR, Henry V, 1416-22, 81, 199, 457; TNA, E 101/48/14 (muster rolls); there was an Adam Bell who was a legendary archer connected in ballads with Robin Hood; Child, *English and Scottish Ballads*, vol. 5 (1860) 126-27; one nineteenth-century writer posited the death of Robin Hood in 1347, although his legend connected him to the time of King Richard I; Simon Leek was the father of Sir Thomas Hercy's daughter-in-law; the text is *par pestilences diverses dedeinz le Roiaume, comme par les guerres dehors*; in 1417, one William Hersy, archer, served under Sir Thomas Carew in a naval expedition to clear the Channel of hostile ships in preparation for the king crossing to make war in Normandy; they defeated the French fleet from Honfleur; *Military Genealogy Medieval Record*, William Hersy (1417); HistParl, 3:347; Payling, *Political Society*, 111, 113, 138-40, 181-83; Coss, *Knight*, 134.

some of the lands they held, at least some of the family members, the relatives or close friends the testator chose for executors, and the religious disposition of the testator, which became very important during the sixteenth century. The will of Sir Thomas Hercy was dated the Wednesday before the feast of the Purification in February 1425 and probated 29 May 1425. Sir Thomas left his soul to God, Mary, and all the saints and his body to be buried in the parish church at Grove, donating eight pounds of candles to be burned around his coffin on the day of his funeral. He left to Hugh, his son and heir, his best iron-fitted carriage and four best carriage horses, and his best cart with eight of his best oxen, with *phalleris* (metal ornaments or trappings worn on horse's head and breast) and complete *apparatu* (equipment). To his son Thomas he left the manor of Eaton in which William Babington and others were enfeoffed by himself and Hugh Cressy, and all his lands and tenements in Thrumpton in the tenure of Nicholas Boucher. To Isabel his daughter, he left "*c libras*" (£100), which would have been for her *maritagium*. To his female servant Magote (Margaret) Yerde, a cottage in Grove and three acres of arable land for her life for the symbolic rent of one red rose per year, and after her death the same to her son William Chambers. In addition, he left this William a messuage and bovate in Grove for his lifetime for the service of one apple per year. After their deaths these would revert to the Hercy heirs. He also left a bequest of a hundred shillings to his other servants, to be distributed according to their merit and rank. This shows that he had many servants and that he was generous and kind to them. He left his best bed to Hugh, his second-best bed to Thomas, and his third best bed to Isabel. If his widow remained in the house, he presumably had four beds. This indicates that he was well off and that the manor house at this time was quite large. He left Hugh three tablecloths, towels and napkins, two silver salt shakers, twelve silver spoons, brass pots and platters, twelve pewter vessels, basins, and the contents of the bakehouse. He also left twenty shillings to the friars and a remainder of his goods to be distributed to the poor for the salvation of his soul. He appointed his wife Catherine and three nearby parish rectors as his executors. The probate court left the work of executor to Catherine. The will did not mention succession of lands, except for a special bequest to the younger son, since the widow's and heir's portions were determined by law. After the death of Sir Thomas, his widow, Catherine Hercy, became patron of the church of Grove, appointing rectors in 1429, 1431, and 1435. She was documented holding land in Newsum herself and land in Flamborough and Nafferton, Yorkshire, with her son, Robert Constable, in 1428. She died in 1434. Sir Thomas and Catherine Hercy had at least two sons, Hugh IV and Thomas, and a daughter Isabel. Sir Thomas gave his younger son, Thomas, the manor of Eaton and land in Thrumpton. Sir Thomas was succeeded at Grove by his elder son Hugh IV Hercy.[104]

Sir Thomas and Catherine de Hercy held many estates in Nottinghamshire and Yorkshire. Thomas was sufficiently affluent that he lent money to others. In the early part of his life, Sir Thomas exercised his knighthood by military service. He fought under John of Gaunt in Spain as a volunteer and accompanied his son, Henry of Bolingbroke, from his arrival in England to his ascension to the throne as King Henry IV. For this Sir Thomas received a lifetime annuity. He also fought for King Henry IV in Scotland. In the latter part of his life, Sir Thomas exercised his knighthood by holding county offices. He was appointed tax collector, commissioner of array, commissioner of the peace, commissioner of *oyer et terminer*, attestor of elections, and arbitrator of property disputes. He was one of four knights to hold all three high offices of justice of the peace, knight of the shire in Parliament, and high sheriff of Nottinghamshire and Derbyshire. His lifetime marked a transition in the functions of knighthood, from military service to positions in law and administration. He had done substantial military service but it was by choice, not as a feudal obligation, and the greater part of his life was spent in judicial and political positions. The religious views of Sir Thomas were strong and Catholic. He appointed rectors of the churches of Grove, Ordsall, and West Retford. His testamentary bequest to the friars may indicate that he tended in a more liberal direction. He also generously provided for servants and the poor. Sir Thomas named his wife Catherine as his executor with the help of three nearby parish priests who left the work to her. Thus, he showed trust and mutuality in their relationship. Catherine had been the widow of another knight with whom she had six children. She had inherited some lands, although most went to her children. After her marriage to Thomas de Hercy, she managed his estates when he went off to war, served in Parliament, or had judicial duties. She was literate in Norman French and possibly knew some Latin. Catherine appointed rectors of Grove church. The fact that Catherine exercised patronage in her own right indicates that she held high status in north Nottinghamshire. After the death of Thomas, she continued to manage the Hercy estates and advowsons.

---

104. Archbishop of York, *Sede Vacante* Register, 5A, f. 410 (full will); *Testamentum Domini Thomae Hercy Militis*, in *Testamenta Eboracensia*, 1:409 (abstract); the note states that Hugh was later knighted, but there is no other evidence of this; FA, 4:138, 265, 267; beds were also important as the places of births and deaths; *VCH*, Nottingham, 2:267: tenure by a rose was not uncommon; Jewell, *Women in Medieval England*, 130; Piercy, 186, 226; Payling, "Hugh Hercy," in HistParlOnline 1422–1524.

NOTTINGHAMSHIRE

HUGH IV HERCY AND ELIZABETH TALBOT LEEK HERCY

When his father died in 1425 the young Hugh IV Hercy was still a minor. His mother appointed rectors of Grove church in 1429, 1431, and 1435 and the chapter of York at West Retford in 1426. Hugh was made squire to King Henry VI, then a very young child, an honor accorded the sons of the most favored families of England. Hercy neighbors and friends Hugh Cressy and John Gateford served with him. The Regency Council had decreed that all noble boys in royal wardship be educated with the young king, who was receiving an excellent education at court. Each child was given his own schoolmaster and was taught languages, literature, history, military skills, and chivalry. Some royal squires were paid an annuity of £10.[105]

By 1428, Hugh Hercy, Hugh Cressy, and John Gateford were somewhat wild young adults. According to a complaint filed by the prior of Blyth before Humphrey duke of Gloucester and the Council, that on 27 March 1428, four hundred armed men, led by Hugh Cressy the Younger of Grove [sic], allegedly had damaged his houses and ejected his tenants. This is confusing because Hugh Cressy was not from Grove, but from Oldcoates, and Hugh Hercy was from Grove but not named. In any case, Hugh Cressy was the leader of the attack. The Cressy family, originally from Cressy in the Pays de Caux in Eastern Normandy, had for generations been donors of land to Blyth. More recently there had been disputes over the ownership of some of these lands. Hugh's father, also Hugh Cressy, had been knight of the shire in 1390 and 1397 and held various commissions in Nottinghamshire between 1396 and 1421. Young Hugh was presumably pursuing part of what he believed to be his inheritance with the aid of his friends. The charges were repeated on 20 April before the Nottinghamshire justices of the peace, Sir Richard Stanhope and Sir Henry Pierrepont. Hugh Hercy was not mentioned in these first two petitions. On 16 June, an arrest warrant was issued for Hugh Cressy the Younger, Hugh Hercy, and John Gateford,

---

105. CCR, Henry VI, 1422–29, 410: Hugh Hercy, John Gateford, and Hugh Cressy the Younger were listed together as esquires of the king; this Hugh Cressy was probably the son of Hugh Cressy of Owlcotes; FA, 4:126, 136–38; the Privy Council decreed that "all noble boys in royal wardship" be brought up with Henry at court, and each was to have a master furnished by the court; in 1426 King Henry was knighted and then knighted some of his playmates; in 1427, under his first teacher, Henry mastered Latin, memorized the divine office, which was important to him all his life, and studied the church fathers; in 1428, Richard de Beauchamp, earl of Warwick, was appointed his teacher; under him the young king learned languages and letters, manners and discipline, riding, sword-fighting, and other military arts; *Proceedings and Ordinances*, 3:170 (June 1425); Wolffe, *Henry VI*, 36, 45–46; Payling, *Political Society*, 54.

esquires to the king, to appear before the royal council. The matter was referred to arbitration. On 28 July, these three and other defendants and the prior of Blyth and his tenants were ordered to pay recognizance bonds of five hundred marks each until the case could be resolved by six arbitrators, including commissioners of the peace Sir Richard Stanhope and Sir Henry Pierrepont, who acted for Hugh Hercy. If the case could not be resolved by the arbitrators, it would be submitted to the chancellor, John Kemp, archbishop of York, and Ralph Cromwell. The outcome of the case is not known from court documents, so it was presumably resolved in arbitration. No penalty against Hugh IV Hercy is recorded.[106]

Land records of 1428 show that Hugh IV Hercy held Grove and Weston in the right of his great-grandfather, Hugh III Hercy, and that he also held the lands which had belonged to Eustace Mortain. The tax assessment for Grove remained the same in 1412 and 1436 at £40. Hugh's brother, Thomas, held rights in the nearby manor of Eaton and in Thrumpton. His mother held her dower rights until her death in 1434. These partitions of the Hercy properties weakened the position of Hugh IV. Hugh was an attestor of parliamentary elections in Nottinghamshire in 1423 as a minor with his father, and as an adult in 1429 and 1433. On 8 September 1428, with his mother and Constable half-brothers, he confirmed the estate of his uncle Sir Thomas Comberworth in the manor of Scremby, Lincolnshire, and his own minor interest through an entail dating back to 1400.[107]

The child Henry VI was crowned king of England in 1429. The same year, Jeanne d'Arc led the French to victory over the English at Orleans and the dauphin was crowned Charles VII, king of France, at Reims. Jeanne was captured in 1430 and executed by the English in May 1431. The young Henry VI was in Rouen at the time of Jeanne's trial and was then crowned king of France in Paris in a meaningless rite. It is possible that Hugh Hercy

---

106. *CartBlyth*, 88 (by 1224, Henry), 89, 136–42, 499; TNA, SC, 8/84/4181 (March 1427); KB, 9/223/2/74; KB, 27/671, *rex rot*. 4, 672, *fines rot*.; JUST 1/1524 *rot*. 16; CCR, Henry VI, 1422–29, 409–10 (28 July 1428); CPR, Henry V, 1413–16, 314, 1422–29, 466; Thoroton, *Nottinghamshire*, vol. 3, "Adelocum," states that one third of Eaton was held by Hugh Hercy in the reign of Henry VI; Payling, "Law and Arbitration," 149, 156–57, 159n: thirty-eight of the defendants, including Cressy, paid a fine of one mark in 1429; Hugh Cressy was the nephew of Sir Hugh Cressy of Hodstock who died in 1408 without children; the Cressys were originally from Cressy, arr. Dieppe, canton Bellencombre, in Eastern Normandy and lived in Nottinghamshire from the reign of King Henry II; Payling, *Political Society*, 24; HistParlOnline, 1386–1421, "Cressy, Hugh of Oldcoates"; Keats-Rohan, *Domesday Descendants*, 416.

107. FA, 4:137; Payling, *Political Society*, 7–8, 223, 227; HistParlOnline, "Hercy, Hugh," "Comberworth, Sir Thomas"; Given-Wilson, *Nobility*, 71.

was in his retinue.[108] Hugh IV Hercy had inherited Grove and other estates from his father. On 18 May 1436 he married Elizabeth Leek, daughter and coheir of Simon Leek of Cotham, Nottinghamshire, and his wife Joan Talbot. This was a prestigious and advantageous marriage. The marriages of the four daughters and heirs of Simon Leek resulted in uniting the leadership of Nottinghamshire in the Hercy, Markham, and Willoughby families. The Leeks were a knightly family from West Leek in Nottinghamshire, documented from the time of King Stephen, when the earl of Nottingham gave the town to Alan de Leek in 1141. In 1200-1201, William de Leek was co-sheriff of Nottinghamshire. Sir Simon Leek was knight of the shire for Nottinghamshire in 1362, 1364-66, 1368, 1372-73, 1375-77, and 1381-82. He married Margaret de Vaux, daughter and heiress of Sir John de Vaux of Cotham, who held lands in Nottinghamshire, Leicestershire, and Lincolnshire. They married "without banns," and had to get a papal dispensation because they were related "in fourth degree of kindred on both sides." The document, dated June 1351, granted the dispensation after they performed a "salutary penance," and declared their children legitimate. This dispensation was important, since without it, their descendants, including Elizabeth Leek Hercy, would have been considered illegitimate, and could not have inherited. Sir Simon and Margaret Leek had two sons, Sir John and William. Both were personal esquires of King Henry IV who were granted annuities of ten marks for their service. Sir John Leek was knight of the shire for Nottinghamshire in 1386, 1388, 1390, 1404, and 1416. William was knight of the shire in 1399 and escheator in 1403. Sir John was sheriff of Nottinghamshire and Derbyshire in 1382-83, 1386-87, 1392-93, and 1399-1400. In 1400, Sir John had to raise two hundred men to serve with the king against Scotland. Sir John was one of four men sent to the Tower in 1411 for participating in the riots, but was later pardoned. According to the tax records of 1412, Sir John's lands in Nottinghamshire were valued at £60. Sir John married Isabel, daughter and heiress of Thomas Towers. Sir John and Isabel Leek had two sons and a daughter, Margaret. She married Sir Thomas Rempston, of Rempston, Nottinghamshire, a close companion of Henry of Bolingbroke from 1389, who accompanied Henry from France to Ravenspurn, and thus would have known Sir Thomas de Hercy, and who later became constable of the Tower, admiral of the royal fleet, steward of the royal household and Privy Counsellor, using his influence with the king

108. In 1429, one John Hersy, archer, served under Sir Thomas Kingston in the garrison at Falaise, Normandy; Payling, *Political Society*, 7-8, Table 1-3; the base was one knight's fee, which remained at £40; in Bassetlaw there were more knights holding knights' fees than magnates; *Military Genealogy Medieval Record*, John de Hercy (1429).

to benefit the Leek family until his death in 1406. In 1395, Sir John and his son Simon acquired Sibthorp, an old de Hériz fee, in which Hugh de Bingham held land. Simon Leek and his father were arbitrators with Sir Thomas Hercy in an inheritance case in 1409. The same year Sir John and Simon Leek were named with others in the will of Sir John Markham, judge of common pleas and one of the commissioners who transferred the crown from Richard II to Henry IV, to hold his estates until his minor heir came of age. Simon was named in the will of Sir Thomas Chaworth in 1423 for the same purpose. All of these facts indicate that both Sir John and Simon Leek were important and trusted members of their community. Simon Leek inherited Cotham after his father's death in 1413. He was sheriff of Nottinghamshire and Derbyshire in 1415–16, following Sir Thomas Hercy, and knight of the shire in 1404. He was escheator of Nottinghamshire in 1413–14, justice of the peace from 1420–1429 and attested elections in county court in 1423 with Sir Thomas and Hugh de Hercy. In 1428, Simon held in Cotham, Stoke, and Saundby. Simon Leek married Joan Talbot, daughter of Sir John Talbot of Swannington, Leicestershire, and they had four daughters. Mary, the eldest, married Sir Giles d'Aubeney, but died, and their daughter Joane inherited Cotham and married Sir Robert Markham, nephew of Sir John II Markham; the second daughter, Margaret, married justice Sir John II Markham; the third, Elizabeth, married Hugh IV Hercy; the fourth, Anne, married Richard Willoughby. Simon Leek died in 1434, the last of the male line of the Leeks of Cotham, and his estates went through his daughters to the Hercy, Markham, and Willoughby families.[109]

109. Leek was also spelled Leyk, Leke, Lech, and now Leake; EYC, vol. 3, no. 1269; William de Leek witnessed a charter in Yorkshire between 1171 and 1181; *Calendar of Entries*, vol. 3, 1342–1362, 456; the de Vaux were rewarded for their service to Henry VII and Henry VIII and raised to the peerage by Henry VIII; however, the Vaux remained Catholic and in the 1580s at great personal risk they housed Jesuit priests John Gerrard and Robert Southwell; Stone, *Crisis of the Aristocracy*, 177, 192, 614, 730–32; Thoroton, *Nottinghamshire*, vol. 1, "Cotham, Sibthorpe"; CCR, Edward III, 1364–68, 169, 273 (12 May 1366, paid £6, 8s for sixteen days), 480 (21 May 1368, served with Sir Sampson Strelley, paid £10, 16s for twenty-seven days); 1374–77, 428 (10 July 1376, paid £32 for eighty days); 21 February 1327, Edward III restored lands forfeited to Edward II, including John de Leek, keeper of castle and Honour of Tutbury; CCR, Richard II, 1377–81, 105 (5 December 1377, paid £24, 16s. for sixty-two days), 502 (sheriff); 1381–85, 106 (Sir Simon de Leek for Nottinghamshire and Sir Robert de Leek for Lincolnshire, February, each paid £35, 4s. for eighty-eight days; October, £10 for twenty-five days); 1385–89, 171 (array), 494 (4 June 1388, Sir John de Leek, £44, 8s for 111 days); 1389–92, 178 (1390, paid £20, 16s for fifty-two days); FA, 4:131,137; Thoroton, *Nottinghamshire*, vol. 3, "East Retford"; Sir John Markham was king's sergeant under Richard II, judge of common pleas from 1396 to 1408, drew up the document of deposition of Richard II and was one of commissioners to receive his crown, and died in 1409; his son, Sir John II Markham, son of Elizabeth Cressy, was justice of King's

Joan Talbot, wife of Simon Leek and mother of Elizabeth Leek Hercy, was the daughter and coheir of Sir John Talbot of Swannington in Leicestershire, southeast of Nottingham. Like the Hercys, the Talbots were an ancient family from France, descended from Guillaume or Hugues Talbot of Cleuville in the Pays de Caux. The son of Guillaume or Hugues, Richard I Talbot, inherited Cleuville and fought with William the Conqueror at Hastings. Richard II Talbot married Amicie de Gournay, the daughter of Gérard and sister of Hugh IV de Gournay, in 1086. Richard IV Talbot married Aline Basset, daughter of Alan Basset of Wycombe, Buckinghamshire. Their grandson, Richard V, married Sarah de Beauchamp, daughter of William de Beauchamp of Elmley, Worcestershire. Their grandson, Richard, married Elizabeth Comyn. Their grandson Richard married Ankaret Le Strange. Their second son, John Talbot, fought for King Henry VI in France and Spain and was created comte de Clermont-en-Beauvaisis in 1434 and earl of Shrewsbury in 1442. He married Mathilda Neville, baroness de Furnival, and was killed in battle in France in 1453. Through his wife, he acquired the manor of Worksop in Nottinghamshire, which became part of his estates of Sheffield in Yorkshire and north Derbyshire. His son, John, was buried in Worksop Priory. John's son George died at Wingfield Manor in Derbyshire in 1538. The Hercy family served George and the succeeding Talbot earls of Shrewsbury. In 1086, Geoffrey Talbot held Liston, Essex, under Hugh de Gournay. He or his son was reputed to hold land in Swannington, Leicestershire. He married Agnes, daughter of Hugh de Lacy or of Helto, dapifer of Odo of Bayeux. Their son, Geoffrey II, was called a *cognatus* of Gilbert de Lacy, and held twenty knights' fees in chief at the death of King Henry I, but forfeited these to Payn FitzJohn, husband of Sibil de Lacy, daughter and heir of Hugh de Lacy of Weobley, because he fought against King Stephen. The daughter of Payn and Sibil, Cecilia, married Walter de Mayenne, who then came to hold the twenty knights' fees of Geoffrey II Talbot. During the chaos at the end of the reign of King Edward II, Sir John I Talbot of Swannington attacked and destroyed Whitwick Castle which was being fortified

Bench from 1444–61, and chief justice from 1461–69; after the death of her husband, since she had no children, Anne became a nun; Given-Wilson, *Henry IV*: Thomas Rempston: 62–63, 75, 117, 127, 180–81, 202, 396, 414–15, 418–19, 424–25, 428, n. 17; Payling, *Political Society*, 9, 15, 40, 44–45, 50, 56, 64, 68–69, 83–85, 100–101, 112, 122–23, 129–30, 125, 139, 160, 191, 204, 223, 235; Payling, HistParlOnline, "Hercy, Hugh," n. 2, posits a first marriage existing in or before 1425 based on a grant to "Hugh" and his wife Catherine in the manor and advowson of Sturton-le-Steeple; however, in March 1425 Thomas was still alive and his wife was Catherine, Hugh was still a minor and Catherine was his mother; Hugh's attestation of elections in 1423 does not show he was a major because he did it with his father and future father-in-law; Sturton was held by the Lascelles family, relatives of the Hercys; J. Green, *Aristocracy*, 164.

by Sir Henry de Beaumont, a *consanguinus* of the king. In the process, Sir John ejected Sir Henry and his wife and took "40 horses, 40 mares, 120 colts and 40 cows," fish, and timber. On 26 January 1331, Sir Henry filed a complaint against Sir John. Sir John, who was very tall, died about 1365 and was buried in Whitwick church, with a mailed effigy seven feet in length. Sir John Talbot and his son of the same name were knights of the shire for Leicestershire, serving in the Parliaments of 1361, 1362, 1368, 1369, and 1373. Sir John II Talbot of Swannington, was plaintiff in a lawsuit over rents in 1379. The executor of Sir John II filed suit in 1406 over a debt owed Talbot by James Belers. The executor, a man of eighty, was to collect a debt of £200 owed to the estate by James Belers, whose son came with a band of armed men, dragged him away half-naked from his sick bed to the Belers's estate and kept him imprisoned and maltreated for twelve days until he promised not to collect the debt. However, he petitioned Parliament which agreed to hear the case and issued writs summoning James and John Belers to appear or forfeit £100 each. King Henry IV ordered the Belers to appear before him and Parliament. Sir John II Talbot was the grandfather of Joan Talbot Leek.[110]

Hugh IV Hercy was knight of the shire for Nottinghamshire, serving in Parliament in March 1432. Statutory law restricted this office to "notable Knyghtes"and "notables squires . . . as be able to be Knyghtes," that is, who held property worth at least £40 and were resident in the shire for which they were elected. King Henry V further defined the ability to become a knight as being entitled to bear arms by ancestral right or by grant from an appropriate person. Hugh IV Hercy was an armiger, an esquire who bore a coat of arms and had the right to wear armor. Armiger was a title of honor, distinguishing the holder from the lower classes, and denoting persons who were members of knightly families. At this time, many families, including the Hercys, took respite from knighthood because of the expenses involved. In 1335, there were twenty-two resident knights in Nottinghamshire; by 1412, there were twelve, ten in 1434, and only five in 1450. Sixteen knightly

110. *CartTréport*, 1:1, 3:8, 9:321, 46:75; Florence of Worcester, 259–61; *MA*, 49, 105; OV, 6:192–93; *Gesta Stephani Regis*, 35; RBE, 1:20, 312, 2:496, 632; *RRAN*, vol. 3, nos. 46, 634–35; CPR, Edward II, 1317–21, 571; *IPM*, 5:123, 130 (14 Edward III); TNA, CP, 25/1/126/68, no. 5; TNA, SC 8/23/1107 A and B (1406); the executor of the will of John Talbot filed a petition in Parliament in March 1406, so he died sometime before that date; CPR, Henry IV, 1405–1408, 255; Joan Talbot in most sources is called the daughter of Sir John Talbot, but in a pardon in 1417, noted by Payling, "Hercy, Hugh," n. 4, her father was named Alan Talbot; an earlier Alan Talbot served as knight of the shire for Leicestershire in the Parliaments of September 1332 and 1333; C 67/37/, m.; VCH, Leicester, 1:261–62; William, *Fortified Manor Homes*, 8; Keats-Rohan, *Domesday People*, 126, 231, 368; Keats-Rohan, *Domesday Descendants*, 577, 1122–23.

families in Nottinghamshire survived through the Lancastrian period, the Hercys among them. The Hercys resumed knighthood in the sixteenth century. In 1434, the knights included Hugh Hercy's cousins William Mering and Robert Strelley, his brother-in-law Robert Markham, and Hugh Willoughby. The armigers included Hugh Hercy, Ralph and John Leek, Thomas and James Stanhope, Thomas Mering, Richard Strelley, William Lascelles, and William and Peter Cressy, all from formerly knightly families.[111]

In 1428, Hugh IV Hercy and his half-brothers Robert and John Constable, with their widowed mother Catherine, confirmed the estate of their uncle, her brother, Thomas Comberworth in the manor of Scremby, Lincolnshire. In 1432, Hugh and his half-brother John Constable were mainpernors for Thomas Comberworth over the custody of his manor in Lincolnshire. An official list of commissioners to take the oath in 1434 named both Hugh Hercy and his brother Thomas Hercy, along with his brother-in-law Sir Robert Markham, his cousins Sir Robert Strelley and Sir William Mering, and Sir Hugh Willoughby, knights, and William Lascelles and John and Ralph Leek. The estate income for Grove in 1436 was £40, according to tax records. In 1436, knights and gentry controlled 77 percent of the wealth in Nottinghamshire; lay barons 23 percent. In February 1441, Hugh de Hercy was on a grand jury in Nottingham. In May, he pursued an *inspeximus*, confirmation, of the royal grant of 1254 giving his family free warren in their demesne and elsewhere. In March 1444, he conveyed interest in Weston to his brothers-in-law John II Markham and Richard Willoughby, and Richard Bingham. In May 1445, he conveyed interests in Grove and Eaton to Bingham, Willoughby, and William Babington. This probably had to do with the marriage of his son, Hugh V, to Bingham's granddaughter Marjorie, and may have been her *maritagium*. In 1451 the income of Grove was only £20. Hugh Hercy was documented as patron of the church of Ordsall in 1441 and of the church of West Retford in 1452. In 1455 Hugh was one of the plaintiffs with Ralph Cromwell and Richard Bingham in a suit over lands in Lanum, Rampton, and South Leverton which was settled by fine. During the reign of Henry VI, Hugh leased lands in Headon.[112]

111. HistParlOnline, 1422–61, "Hercy, Hugh"; in the reign of Henry III, Osbert de Arches paid the king in gold for respite from knighthood on 16 May 1253 and 14 September 1256; Fuller, *History*, 577, 12 Henry VI (1434); Keen, *Origins*, 82; Coss, *Origins*, 218, 223; Payling, *Political Society*, 44–45, 50, 63–64, 66, 68–69, 73–77, 112; in 1325 there were forty-five knightly families; by 1400, thirteen had failed in the male line, as would another eighteen in the fifteenth century and eight in the sixteenth.

112. TNA, C 219/13/2, E 179/159/84, 179/240/266; Nottinghamshire Archives, 157 DD/P/8/3; Thoroton, *Nottinghamshire*, vol. 3, "Laneham", "Adelocum, Eaton," "Crumwell"; C. Brown, YAJ, 8 (1884) 7; this probably refers to Malveysin de Hercy in the early

PART II | ENGLAND

In 1437, at the age of sixteen, King Henry VI declared himself no longer a minor and tried to rule. He was mentally unstable, suffering his first documented episode in 1440 and had a complete mental collapse in 1453. In April 1445, he married Margaret of Anjou, niece of King Charles VII of France, a strong and ambitious woman who soon ruled the king. Under the queen, the court became corrupt, wasted vast resources, and abused royal patronage. She soon incurred the people's hatred. She desired to hold onto France by fruitless wars which the English economy could ill afford and hoped one day to be queen of France. In 1447, the English mercenary General Surienne, governor of Le Mans, disobeyed orders to surrender it to Charles VII. He defended it but was defeated by the French. Afterward, shunned by the English command for his disobedience, he took Fougères in Brittany, breaking the truce with France. Then the French under Charles VII took most of Normandy. The English sued for peace, agreeing to leave Rouen if the French would let them keep the towns along the coast. The English commander John Talbot, earl of Shrewsbury, and others were taken hostage by the French at Rouen in 1449. In 1450 there was a rebellion in England by knights, gentlemen, local officials, merchants, sailors, and farmers over the appointment of corrupt local officials, the perversion of justice, rigged parliamentary elections, loss of England's lands in France, and failure to control piracy off the southern coast of England. On the positive side, Henry VI did value education and endowed Eton and King's College at Cambridge for poor scholars. He was also a great patron of music. In general, however, his reign was a disaster for England and the house of Lancaster, precipitating the Wars of the Roses.[113]

King Edward III had five sons. The eldest, Edward the Black Prince, died. His son became King Richard II but had no children. King Edward

---

thirteenth century, but could possibly refer to the man of the same name in the mid-fourteenth century; statute dated 1445–46; LCNN, 148, 160; Payling, *Political Society*, 2, 75, 112, 140; in the same years Clifton paid £193 and £100, Strelley £100 and £100; in 1454, a man sued over land in Netherhaigh, Yorkshire, showing a document in which a de Hercy had sold it to the man's ancestors. HistParlOnline, "Hercy, Hugh."

113. It is speculated that the mental illness of Charles VI passed through his daughter Catherine de Valois to her son Henry VI; Catherine's brother became King Charles VII of France whose wife was the sister of the father of Margaret of Anjou; "Cade's rebellion," named for John Cade, gentleman from Kent; the rebellion was put down by the king's forces, but after they had taken London and forced the king to flee; *Military Genealogy Medieval Record*, John de Hercy (1442, 1447); in 1442, a John de Hercy, archer, served under Surienne; in 1446, one John de Hersy, archer, served under Sir Matthew Gough, cocaptain of the English forces in France, in his personal retinue, doing *retrait et logis* at Alençon; Surienne (Soriano) was a mercenary from Aragon; Talbot was released, promising never to take arms against the French king, which he did not do personally, but he continued as commanding general of the English forces.

had created dukedoms for his other four sons. His second son, Lionel, was duke of Clarence, his third, John of Gaunt, duke of Lancaster, his fourth, Edmund, duke of York, and his fifth, Thomas, duke of Gloucester. Duke Edmund of York had a grandson Richard, who married Anne Mortimer, heir to Duke Lionel, second son of Edward III. During the reign of Henry VI, the popularity of their son, Duke Richard of York, greatly increased through his integrity and competence as a military leader. His claim to the throne was better than that of Henry VI because his mother was heir to the second son of King Edward III, whereas the Lancastrian Henrys descended from the third son, John of Gaunt, duke of Lancaster.

In 1452, John Talbot, earl of Shrewsbury, was instrumental in helping Henry VI against York and in February 1453 he retook the Bordelais in France. However, since the English failed to send reinforcements, the earl was killed in battle, and France retook Bordeaux in July. In 1453, the queen introduced military conscription by sending commissioners of array to the sheriffs to order villages to provide soldiers at their own expense. This was customary in France but very unpopular in England. It was done many times during the reign and contributed to the downfall of the house of Lancaster. In August 1453, Henry VI had a complete mental breakdown and, after eight years of marriage, his queen bore a son, whose legitimacy was somewhat in question. The queen made an attempt to be appointed regent for the ailing king and had her infant son knighted and formally designated prince of Wales. But on 27 March 1454 the House of Lords named Richard of York regent. York made some progress reducing corruption and reforming the government, but on Christmas Day 1454, Henry VI recovered his health and York lost his position. From that time on, Henry VI was introspective and pious, having lost interest in governing. The queen was in effect ruler of England.[114] In May 1455, the first War of the Roses, between Lancaster and York, began with the battle of St. Albans.

Hugh IV Hercy died on 6 December 1455. He and his wife Elizabeth were buried in St. Helen's Church at Grove. In the floor of the chancel there is an alabaster slab, six and a half feet long and three and a quarter feet wide, incised with the figures of Hugh as a knight in armor, on his head a tall hat with a feather, with a greyhound at his feet looking up, and his lady by his side. Dogs were a symbol of fidelity. The large hat indicates that he was an apprentice at law. In the fifteenth century apprentices at law were gentry law professionals who were able to practice many legal functions, called *apprenticius in lege peritus*. They learned law from observing cases in courts,

---

114. The queen authorized levies of twenty thousand archers; a feud between the Nevilles and the Percys in the north in July 1453 drove the Nevilles to give crucial support to York.

PART II | ENGLAND

instruction by judges and reading year books and treatises. They gave legal advice, made pleadings in the county courts and were justices of the peace. Hugh had the advantage that his father was sheriff, knight of the shire, and justice of the peace, and his brother-in-law, Sir John II Markham, was chief justice of King's Bench where the father of his son-in-law, Sir Richard Bingham, was also justice. Most law apprentices were depicted in long robes with wide sleeves. Hugh Hercy was different; he was portrayed in armor because of his rank as armiger of knightly ancestry. Elizabeth wore a cone-shaped headdress set sideways. Above Hugh's head are the arms of Hercy; above hers, the arms of Hercy and Leek. The inscription on the stone reads:

> Hic jacet Hugo Hercy qui obiit VI Decembriis anno dom mcccclv et
> Elizabeth uxor ejus quae obiit anno dom mccccl__. Animae proprietur Deus
> Here lies Hugh Hercy who died 6 December [in the] year of [the] lord 1455 and
> Elizabeth his wife who died [in the] year of [the] lord 14__. Souls belong to God.

The suggested date of Elizabeth's death as 1450 is incorrect; one or more letters are worn off the line where there is a large crack at the point where the date was written. She was Hugh's heir and lived at least until 1467. After the 1882 reconstruction of Grove church, the slabs were moved to the floor of the tower. The quartered arms of Hercy and Leek were also in the west window of St. Swithun's Church in East Retford.[115]

The will of Hugh IV Hercy was dated 21 August 1455 and probated 9 April 1456. The will shows that at this time the manor house of the Hercy family was substantial enough to contain a chapel and that it had a bake-house and malt-kiln. Hugh left to the rector of Grove church his best horse and array in conformity with his station, in the name of his prince/principal, six pounds of burning candles for his funeral, 6s. 8d. for ten masses at the high altar, and 3s. 4d. for art or architectural work for the church. To

---

115. Saul, *English Church Monuments*, 269, 279–84; Greenhill, *Incised Effigial Slabs*, 1:255, 2:8; Musson and Ormrod, *Evolution*, 30, 55–57, 141–43; Brand, *Origins*, 110–14; Pollock and Maitland, *History*, 1:194–95; Baker, *Introduction*, 159, 162, 176, 179, 197: judges knew and intended that their decisions became precedents and therefore wrote them down in year books for the apprentices; Palmer, *County Courts*, 89–91: pleading was the most important activity of legal professionals, 112: local legal professionals made the county courts into respectable legal institutions; Piercy, *History*, 104, 225; Thoroton, *Nottinghamshire*, vol. 3, "East Retford"; the window in St. Swithun's Church no longer exists, although fragments of the glass are embedded in a replacement window; Coss, *Lady*, 38.

his son Hugh, he left a bed, large silver salt shakers, an urn covered with silver and gold, another urn in silver, twelve shell-shaped silver spoons, a tablecloth with hand-burnished cloth of warke, the chalice, missal, portuse (portable breviary) for the rite of York, corporals and altar cloths for the chapel within the manor, two copper pots, pewter vessels, a large pan, a kettle from the kitchen, and other goods. He made a small bequest of twelve sheep to Elizabeth Cressy, who was probably his daughter or godchild. His close friend Hugh Cressy had married an Elizabeth. The residuum he left to his wife Elizabeth, whom he named with Richard Willoughby, a priest, and one other man as his executors. It is unclear exactly when Elizabeth died. Elizabeth Hercy was listed as patron of the church of West Retford, succeeding her husband, where she appointed Thomas Coke rector on 25 May 1461. She made another patronage appointment of a priest, Hugh Smith, on 31 August 1464 and of her son Thomas Hercy to St. Martin's Church in Saundby in 1464, although he died the following year. In documents dated August 1464 Elizabeth was called "widow of Hugh Hercy" and in February 1467, "late the wife of Hugh Hercy late of Grove," but was still living at that time.[116] Hugh IV and Elizabeth had sons Hugh V and Thomas, a cleric who died in 1465. Gervase Hercy was mentioned among the patrons of the church of Saundby as a feoffee of Elizabeth Hercy and among those who set up the chantry, but his exact relationship to Hugh IV and Elizabeth is not known. He could have been their younger son or the son of Thomas Hercy, brother of Hugh IV. His name disappeared after the chantry was set up in 1467 and he may have died soon thereafter.

On 11 November 1465, lord chief justice Sir John II Markham, Elizabeth Leek Hercy, widow of Hugh Hercy, Richard Willoughby, Gervase Hercy, and Geoffrey Staunton received licence to purchase lands to found a chantry of one chaplain in the Church of St. Martin of Saundby. On 4 February 1467 in Westminster, King Edward IV granted licence to Sir

---

116. *Testamenta Eboracensia*, 2:200–201; CPR, Edward IV, 1461–67, 543–44; *Lenton Estate Accounts*, 19:163 (31 August 1464); Elizabeth Cressy was probably the widow of Hugh Cressy the Younger and possibly the daughter of Hugh IV de Hercy; TNA, 25(1)186/38/16; HistParl 1386–1421 "Cressy, Hugh of Oldcoates, Notts"; and "Hercy, Hugh"; Sir Hugh Cressy of Hodsock had a sister and coheir Elizabeth who married John I Markham; the brother-in-law of Hugh Hercy, Sir John II Markham, was the son of Elizabeth Cressy; Hugh Cressy the Younger of Oldcoates was the son of Elizabeth who died in 1411; the sheep were termed *matriae*, which may mean sheep who had lambs and lactated; LCNN, 84: after the death of Hugh, his feoffees Richard Willoughby and Hugh Cressy appointed to Grove in 1464, with Richard Bingham in 1467, and Sir Richard Bingham and William Babington in 1472, 160, 163: after the death of Thomas Hercy, Gervase Hercy, Richard Willoughby, and other feoffees of Elizabeth appointed a priest to Saundby in 1466 and 1467, and possibly Elizabeth herself in 1479, although it is unlikely she lived that long and it may have referred to her chantry.

John II Markham, knight and chief justice of the King's Bench, who was the husband of Elizabeth Leek Hercy's sister, Margaret Leek Markham, to found a perpetual chantry with one priest to celebrate daily "divine services" at the altar of St. Mary the Virgin in the Church of St. Martin in Saundby, Nottinghamshire, for the welfare of the king and queen and their heirs, for John Markham, Elizabeth Hercy, Richard Willoughby, Gervase Hercy, and Geoffrey Staunton, Elizabeth's heirs and executors, for their souls after their deaths, for the king's late father Richard of York, for the late Hugh Hercy, Simon de Leek and Joan his wife (Elizabeth's parents), the late William Saundby, and for the ancestors and benefactors of Hugh and Elizabeth. The chantry would be called the "chantry of Elizabeth, late the wife of Hugh Hercy, esq." The priest was to be paid a hundred shillings per year for sustenance and works of piety through alienation in *mortmain* by the donors of certain lands and possessions. Mortmain, literally "dead hand," meant property held perpetually by the church or a religious order which did not escheat to the king on the death of the property holder since the institution did not die. The foundation of this chantry may indicate a loving marriage between Elizabeth and Hugh Hercy. Chantries were a popular religious practice in this period; people left money in their wills to found chantry chapels in which priests would say masses in perpetuity for the soul of the departed and his or her family. Some of these foundations were very large and comprised whole colleges of priests serving collegiate churches which could house several chantry endowments. Many parish churches were converted into such colleges and beautified accordingly. Sir John II Markham had been appointed to the court of King's Bench by Henry VI and lord chief justice by King Edward IV in 1461, after the previous chief justice ran away with Henry VI. Sir John Markham later ruled against the crown in a case of treason against Sir Thomas Cook who had allegedly plotted with Queen Margaret, because the evidence of the prosecution was obtained under torture. For this reason, he was removed from office in 1468. He died in 1481.[117]

117. CPR, Edward IV, 1461–67, 543–44; Thoroton, *Nottinghamshire*, vol. 3, "Saundby," 264; they chose Saundby for the chantry rather than St. Helen's or the manor chapel at Grove; chantries were abolished by King Edward VI and their assets confiscated; Gunn, *Henry VII's New Men*, 60; *Lenton Priory Estate Accounts*, 31 August 1464, 163; *Visitation of Nottingham*, 14; C. Brown, *Nottinghamshire*, "East Markham"; according to Dugdale, cited by Burke, 204, Cook was the former mayor of London and very rich; the king wanted to fund the grants to his wife's relatives, the Wydvilles, from a source other than his own pocket; Cook had been Queen Margaret's wardrober and had profited from his position; but the charge against him of high treason was contrived; Markham had him acquitted of high treason, a capital offense, and convicted of a lesser offense, for which he was fined £800 to the queen and £8000 to the king; while he was

Hugh IV Hercy was not a knight but was an armiger. As a youth he had been a squire of the king. Hugh was, though, a knight of the shire, serving in Parliament. When his father died, he had left part of the estate to Hugh's younger brother. His mother lived another nine years, holding her dower rights over the estate. After her death, her inherited lands went to her Constable sons. This weakened Hugh's position in land. Yet he made a prestigious marriage to a daughter and coheir of the Leek family which solidified his relationship with the Markham and Willoughby families, both prominent in law. Elizabeth was a strong woman who acted in her own after Hugh's death, setting up a family chantry with her brother-in-law, Chief Justice Markham. Hugh attested elections, served on a grand jury, and became an apprentice at law, which entitled him to a basic practice of law. His life represents the final transition of knighthood from military service to service in county offices, many of which involved law. Yet his knightly background was still important as his tomb depicted him wearing armor, but also a hat denoting the legal profession. In religion, Hugh appointed rectors of Grove, Ordsall, and West Retford, had a chapel in the manor house, and made donations to the church for masses in his will; his widow, Elizabeth, appointed rectors of West Retford and Saundby, including her own son, and founded a chantry in the church of Saundby with her brother-in-law, the lord chief justice. Hugh IV and Elizabeth seem to have had a good marriage and he chose her as executor, although with her brother-in-law and a priest.

HUGH V HERCY AND MARJORIE BINGHAM HERCY

Hugh IV Hercy, who died in 1455, had sons Thomas, a cleric who died in 1465, and Hugh V, who succeeded to Grove, and possibly Gervase. Their mother, Elizabeth Leek Hercy, seemed to have been in charge of Grove at least until about 1467 and would have retained her dower.

The life of Hugh V Hercy coincided with the Wars of the Roses. Beginning in the year 1455, England was torn apart by wars, in which the houses of Lancaster and York fought each other over the throne until 1485. The duke of Lancaster held the Honour of Tickhill, of which the Hercys, Talbots, Willoughbys, Merings, Babingtons, Chaworths, Rempstons, and Cliftons were tenants. Therefore, the Hercy family and most of their relatives, friends, and neighbors in north Nottinghamshire had to support the house of Lancaster. In 1456–57, the queen moved the court to the midlands, where she had sixteen sheriffs in her pay, thus corrupting the government of

---

in prison, the queen's father stole all the plate and furniture from his houses; Payling, *Political Society*, 186–87.

the shires. In 1457 and 1459 she issued more commissions of array. In 1459, John II Talbot, second earl of Shrewsbury, who was also a tenant of Lancaster, fought in the army of Henry VI against the much smaller army of York. He was killed in the battle of Northampton on 10 July 1460. His son, John III Talbot, third earl of Shrewsbury, fought at St. Albans on 17 February 1461. The queen led an army south from Scotland, plundering the northern shires. York led his army north through Nottinghamshire and fought a skirmish at Worksop. Sir Henry Lovelace betrayed York and warned the queen of an ambush. A descendant of the Lovelace family would later intermarry with the Hercy family in Berkshire. The queen won this round and there were many more arrays and arrests of dissidents. On 27 February 1461, York took London, where he was proclaimed King Edward IV by the people. The Yorkist victory at the battle of Towton, Yorkshire, on 29 March 1461, broke the power of Lancaster in the north. Sir Gervase Clifton fought for Lancaster; Sir Robert Markham and the Stanleys for York.[118]

Under Henry VI, England had become bankrupt and lost its remaining territories in France. In 1461, Henry VI was deposed and replaced by King Edward IV. York had a superior claim to the throne over Lancaster because of the marriage of Richard of York and Anne Mortimer, great-granddaughter of Lionel duke of Clarence. Richard of York, Edward's father, had been killed in the war by the Lancastrians. King Edward IV accepted the submission of the northern nobles and granted commissions of the peace in the north to arrest rebels who did not submit. He restored law and order by replacing corrupt sheriffs and judges. He kept strict oversight of the exchequer and restricted array to defense of the realm and to periods no longer than forty days. He was tolerant to his magnates and to heretics. He was an excellent king until his marriage in 1464 to Elizabeth Wydville, who forced the appointment of her family members to the Council, the waste of huge amounts of money, and high taxation, all of which led to popular disenchantment with Edward IV.

Meanwhile, Henry VI was still a fugitive in hiding. He was finally found and arrested in 1465 on the Lancashire-Yorkshire border by John Tempest, with his nephew Thomas Talbot, and placed in the Tower. But opposition to Edward IV grew, especially in the north. In June 1469 King Edward led an army to Nottingham to recruit, but failed. Finally in 1470,

118. FA, 4:106–9, shows many of the towns and manors in Bassetlaw Hundred in 1316 were under the king and the duke of Lancaster, including Grove, Ordsall, and West Retford; some families, such as the Merings, were split; the Markhams, Pierreponts, and Stanhopes became Yorkists; Wood, *History*, 116–17; Piercy, *History*, 218; Payling, *Political Society*, 120, 124; there were two Wars of the Roses: first Lancaster against York from 1455–71; second York against Tudor, from 1483–1485.

an army, including the earl of Shrewsbury and lord Stanley, defeated Edward IV and rescued Henry VI from the Tower, reinstating him as king in 1471. The nobles who supported Lancaster were given back their estates. But Shrewsbury and Stanley were not given seats on the Council and therefore became disillusioned with Lancaster. The Council then put two spies in each of their households, seeking evidence of disloyalty. Edward IV led his army south from York through Doncaster to Nottingham, which would have taken it through Retford. On 4 May 1471, the Lancastrian prince of Wales was killed in the battle of Tewkesbury, leaving no heir. York retook the throne, Henry VI was killed and the queen was exiled, to die in poverty in France. In general, Edward IV punished the magnates who had opposed him, but not the gentry. Thus ended the first War of the Roses.

Hugh V Hercy of Grove married Marjorie, daughter of Thomas Bingham, son of Sir Richard Bingham of Car Colston, who was commissioner of the peace in Nottinghamshire from 1430, escheator in 1431–1432, and justice of the court of King's Bench from 1445 to 1470. The Bingham family descended from Ralph Bugge, a wealthy merchant of Nottingham, who bought up properties. Ralph died in 1248, leaving two sons. King Henry III gave Ralph II, the elder, Bingham, from which his descendants took their name. The younger son, Richard, was given Willoughby, from which he and his descendants took their name. Both families prospered. Ralph II had a son, Sir Richard Bingham, who succeeded his father and had sons William, Richard, and Thomas. William succeeded, but his son Richard died in debt in 1387 and Bingham escheated to the king who gave it to the Rempston family. Bingham was eventually sold to Sir Thomas Stanhope, whose granddaughter married the son of Hugh V Hercy. The younger son of Sir Richard Bingham, Thomas, held Car Colston. He had two sons: Ralph Bingham, the elder, was coroner of Nottinghamshire from about 1418 until 1437. His younger brother, John Bingham, served in the Parliaments of 1416 and 1420. John's son, Sir Richard became justice of King's Bench in 1445. Marjorie Bingham Hercy was the daughter of his son, Thomas.[119]

Hugh V Hercy was something of an enigma. Unlike his father and grandfather, Hugh did not hold office in Nottinghamshire. The Hercys had supported Lancaster, but during much of the adult life of Hugh V the Yorkist Edward IV was king. However, Hugh should have at least been patron

---

119. In 1086, Bingham belonged to Roger de Bully, and later to William Paynel; a cadet line survived at Car Colston; Sir Richard Bingham was a trained lawyer who, like Sir John Markham, rose to high judicial office; he was also an arbiter with other leading men of Nottinghamshire; CPR, Henry III, 1258–66, 536; CPR, Henry VI, 1441–46, 343; Thoroton, *Nottinghamshire*, 1:272; Piercy, *History*, 216; Payling, *Political Society*, 42, 140, 177–79, 199.

of the advowson of Grove, but the rectors of the church of Grove were appointed by the feoffees of his late father, Richard Willoughby and Hugh Cressy in 1464; Richard Bingham, Richard Willoughby, and Hugh Cressy in 1467. This may have been because his mother was still alive. But in 1472 Sir Richard Bingham and William Babington, feoffees of Hugh Hercy, made the appointment to Grove church. It is possible, though less likely, that his mother was even then still living. But this does raise a question about the competence of Hugh V. He should also have been patron of Ordsall, but in 1483 his son, Humphrey, appointed Ralph Stanhope rector of Ordsall.[120] Perhaps the last appointment in September 1483 was delegated if Hugh V was ailing, since it was a year and a half before his death, or because Humphrey had married a Stanhope. But Hugh V Hercy remains a mystery, as does his wife.

King Edward IV died in 1483 and his minor son briefly became Edward V. However, Edward IV's cousin, Richard, duke of Gloucester, seized both his sons, ages twelve and ten, held them in the Tower, and allegedly put them to death. He then proclaimed himself King Richard III and reigned from 1483 to 1485. Richard III was killed in the battle of Bosworth on 22 August 1485 by the forces of Henry Tudor, who then became King Henry VII. This was the second War of the Roses.

Young George Talbot, fourth earl of Shrewsbury, was pardoned after fighting for Richard III, as was Sir Marmaduke Constable. Sir Robert Markham had also fought for Richard III, but turned against him and ended up fighting for Henry VII. The Stanleys and Digbys fought for Henry VII, as did Sir Gilbert Talbot of Shropshire, who was knighted and given lands of attainted Yorkists. The Hercys supported Henry VII, as demonstrated by the sculpted rose and crown prominently displayed in their manor house.

Hugh V and Marjorie Hercy had a son, Humphrey, and a daughter Isabella, who married Thomas Denman. Hugh V Hercy died in 1485, the year that marked the end of the Angevin/Plantagenet dynasty, which had begun with King Henry II in 1154. A stone in the floor of the church at Grove was inscribed to the memory probably of Hugh V Hercy, stating:

"Outstretch'd together are exprest, He and my Lady fair,
With hands uplifted on the breast, In attitude of prayer."[121]

Hugh V Hercy was the only Hercy heir who did not hold office. His land holdings were diminished after the deaths of his grandparents. He did not take knighthood. He did not appoint rectors to the advowsons. There

---

120. LCNN, 84, 148.

121. This undated inscription was for Hugh V Hercy or perhaps his son Humphrey, since it is in English, and thus presumably later than the Latin inscription of Hugh IV Hercy in Grove church dated 1455; Piercy, *History*, 225.

are questions about his compentence. But he did have a prestigious marriage, probably arranged by his parents, although there is no documentary evidence about the role of his wife.

HUMPHREY I HERCY AND JOAN STANHOPE HERCY AND ALICE KNIGHT HERCY

Humphrey I Hercy succeeded at the beginning of a new era, free from war. The first Tudor king, Henry VII, who reigned from 1485 to 1509, was connected to the house of Lancaster through his grandmother, Queen Catherine of Valois, the widow of Henry V and mother of Henry VI; she married second a Welsh commoner, named Owen Tudor (Tewdwr). Their two sons were Edmund, earl of Richmond, and Jasper, earl of Pembroke, who both supported the house of Lancaster. Henry VII was the son of Edmund Tudor and Margaret Beaufort, a Lancastrian descendant of John of Gaunt by his mistress/third wife, Katherine Swynford. In January 1486, Henry married Elizabeth of York, thus uniting the red and white roses of Lancaster and York. King Henry VII rewarded the support and service of the Hercys and other families with a sculptured rose and crown, his own emblem. In the manor house at Grove, the sculpture was embedded in the wall over a large gothic window above the principal staircase.[122]

Henry VII curbed the power of the high aristocracy, who maintained private regional armies, through laws, such as the Statute of Liveries in 1504, restricting the practice of livery, that is, oaths of loyalty to magnates and the wearing of their badge or uniform. The king enhanced the power of the gentry and their offices, which were dependent on the crown, especially the office of the commissioners of the peace, who came to hold great authority in the counties. This also increased the power of the crown and lessened that of the magnates. Henry VII valued education and patronized renaissance art and humanism. He appointed humanist scholars to tutor his sons and to teach at Oxford, where, in the 1490s, Thomas Wolsey and Thomas More were educated. In 1499, Erasmus visited Oxford and was impressed by the level of humanistic learning there. That same summer, the twenty-one-year-old Thomas More took Erasmus to meet the eight-year-old Prince Henry, who, as King Henry VIII, wrote about the meeting twenty-five years later. After the turn of the new century, most of the humanist scholars moved to London, where Erasmus and others frequented the home of Thomas More. The humanists hoped to reform the medieval world through knowledge and education. Renaissance humanism would

122. Piercy, *History*, 219.

soon play a role in the Protestant reformation. The most educated men in England at this time were the lawyers. The courts were the venue where the rights of the people were upheld. Henry VII valued and defended the common law. In 1497, King Henry VII, with the merchants of Bristol, sponsored the voyage of Cabot to North America, which marked the beginning of the British empire.

Humphrey I Hercy married Joan Stanhope, granddaughter of Sir John Stanhope of Rampton, later of Shelford, in Nottinghamshire. The Stanhope family was descended from the ancient de Colville family of Yorkshire and the Longvilliers family of Stanhope, Durham. The Longvilliers family were from Longvillers, Calvados, arrondissement Caen, and were tenants of Henry de Lacy in Pontefract in 1166. In the mid-thirteenth century, Walter de Stanhope married his cousin Margaret de Longvilliers. Their son, Richard de Stanhope in turn married his cousin once removed Ellota de Longvilliers. They had a son, Sir Richard de Stanhope, who fought against the Scots at Berwick in 1334 and 1335. Sir Richard resided in Newcastle-upon-Tyne, of which he was mayor in 1364. His son, Sir John Stanhope, married the heiress Elizabeth Malovel of Rampton and Tuxbury in northeast Nottinghamshire, whose great-grandfather was Sir Thomas de Longvilliers. The Malovel family is documented at Rampton from the reign of Henry II and was related to the Rufus family, formerly of Grove. Sir John Stanhope was MP for Newcastle in 1359 and mayor in 1366. Their son, Sir Richard Stanhope of Rampton, was made knight of the Bath at the coronation of Henry IV in 1399 and was MP for Nottinghamshire from 1402 to 1407. Before 1399, Sir Richard had married Johanna de Staveley of Lancashire, whose father, Sir Ralph Staveley, was Bolingbroke's steward and fought with Henry V at Agincourt. The Staveley family were thanes in Yorkshire before the Norman conquest. Their son, Sir Richard II Stanhope, was MP for Nottinghamshire in 1421, and married Elizabeth, daughter of Sir John II Markham and Margaret Leek. Their daughter, Agnes, married Sir Robert Strelley. Their son, Sir John Stanhope, served in the royal household of Henry VI and was sheriff of Nottinghamshire and Derbyshire in 1455–56 and 1462–64. Sir John married Elizabeth Talbot, daughter of Sir Thomas Talbot and Alice Tempest. There are incised floor slabs in All Saints Church, Rampton, commemorating Sir Richard Stanhope and his wife Johanna who died in 1436 and 1410 respectively, and Elizabeth Talbot Stanhope, who died in September 1455. Sir John and Elizabeth had a son, Sir Thomas Stanhope, who had two sons, Sir Edward and John. John Stanhope was knight of the shire in 1493 and was the father of Joan Stanhope, first wife of Humphrey I Hercy. The Stanhope family initially supported Lancaster since their estates were held of the Honour of Tickhill, which belonged to Lancaster.

In the end they changed their allegiance to York. The Stanhope family was well connected with the Hercy family through marriages with members of the Leek, Markham, Strelley, and Talbot families before the marriage of Humphrey I Hercy and Joan Stanhope. In the fifteenth century, members of the Stanhope family served as sheriffs, as knights of the shire in Parliament, and as commissioners of the peace in Nottinghamshire.[123]

On 22 December 1480, Humphrey I Hercy and others received the manor of Bevercotes and other Nottinghamshire properties from Alexander Bevercotes. On 18 December 1482, Humphrey Hercy, esquire, John Stanhope, and others had been witnesses to a marriage settlement of the manor of Cressy Hall by Gervase Clyfton. On 22 July 1485, Humphrey Hercy received property from the Rev. Robert Dawson in Bevercotes and Eaton. In September 1488, he signed a quitclaim to John Dawson for these properties. On 10 March 1490, Humphrey's wife, Joan Stanhope Hercy, died at Grove at the age of fifty-one. In June 1495 Robert Nevill, Humphrey Hercy and others received lands in Ragnall, Dunham, Wympton, and Swansterne, and the same lands with some in Laneham (Lanum) in June 1503. On 13 February 1496, Humphrey Hercy was escheator of Nottinghamshire. Humphrey Hercy was named as patron of the churches and appointed William Malovel rector of Grove in 1487, Cuthbert Darwen in 1501 and Robert Neville in 1506. He appointed the rector of the church of West Retford in 1494, Ralph Stanhope to the church of Ordsall in 1483 and another there in 1506, and the rector of Saundby in 1500. Ralph Stanhope, MA Oxford, was the first rector of Ordsall documented to have a university degree; he served there through March 1486, when he went to a more prestigious parish in Norfolk.

---

123. Elizabeth Staveley, daughter of another Sir Ralph Staveley, a knight of Henry VI, married Sir Thomas Ashton, lord of Ashton-under-Lyne in Lancashire; Sir Richard Stanhope's second marriage in 1411 was to Maud, sister of Ralph Lord Cromwell, treasurer of England from 1433–43 and owner of Shelford after 1453; through this connection, Sir Richard Stanhope served Thomas, duke of Clarence, brother of King Henry V; Sir Richard's tax assessment in 1412 was £60 and in 1436, the year of his death, it was £107; Cromwell had owned Shelford from 1453; Richard Illingworth, his retainer, bought it in 1463; he and John Stanhope served together on an arbitration panel in 1459; in the sixteenth century, the Stanhopes were elevated to the peerage; in the 1590s there was a serious feud between the earls of Shrewsbury and the Stanhope family; in 1593, Sir John Stanhope, later created the first Lord Stanhope, was attacked in Fleet Street by Talbot's men; Lady Anne Stanhope of Shelford "releved the poor dealy"; Stone, *Crisis*, 47, 192–9, 224–25, 439; Payling, *Political Society*, 47–49, 81–83, 104, 145, 201, 223, 227, 240, 244; Marcombe, *English Small Town*, 70; C. Brown, *Nottinghamshire*, "Rampton"; L. Jacks, *Great Houses*, "Rampton"; *Southwell and Nottingham*, "Rampton All Saints," archaeology.

Robert Neville, rector of Grove, held degrees of BA, MA, and BDiv from Cambridge.[124]

In 1498–99 Humphey held a messuage in Moregate. On 31 August 1498, Sirs Henry Willoughby, Gervase Clifton, John Digby, and Edward Stanhope granted land in Hemsell, which they had by gift of Sir John Strelley, great-grandson of Elizabeth Hercy Strelley, to Humphrey Hercy and others. After Strelley's death in 1501, the manor, land and mill of Hemsell were enfeoffed to Humphrey Hercy and others to the use of Sanchia, Sir John's widow. In January 1499, Humphrey I Hercy, with the bishop of Durham, Sir Henry Willoughby, Sir John Babington, Sir Gervase Clyfton, Sir Edward Stanhope, Sir William Mering, Robert Neville, and others received a gift from Sir John III Markham of all his property in Nottinghamshire for the use of himself and his heirs, which was probably a legal device to avoid wardship of his heirs. At some point between 1490 and 1498. Humphrey Hercy married Alice, daughter of Thomas Knight. In 1498–99, Sir Thomas Knight and his wife Elizabeth appointed four yeomen to receive seisin from John Vavasour, justice of King's Bench, of their lands in Nottinghamshire, including West Retford, Cotham, Gringley, and Welham, and in Derbyshire, to hold for their lives, with remainder to Humphrey Hercy, esquire, Robert Neville, gentleman, and others. Two years later, Thomas Knight filed a similar document addressed to Sir Robert Sheffield, Sir John Hotham, the king's attorney, Robert Constable, sergeant-at-law, Humphrey Hercy, Robert Neville, and others concerning the messuages and lands in Yorkshire of his deceased mother. In 1508, Joan Ormond held Osberton of Humphrey Hercy by fealty only.[125]

Nottinghamshire was not under the authority of a regional magnate. It was governed by the leading gentry families, the Markhams, Hercys, Willoughbys, Cliftons, and later the Stanhopes and Nevilles. Sheriffs were members of the senior gentry of the county. Theoretically sheriffs had to

---

124. Nottingham Manuscripts Collections: deed of gift, Nottingham MSS NeD959 (22 December 1480); deed of gift, NeD961 (1485); quitclaim NeD963 (13 September 1488); ER Yorkshire Archives, DDBR 7/1, 18 December 1482; Gervase Clifton, the son of Sir Gervase Clifton, was an important naval officer for King Henry VI in 1459–60, shortly before his defeat by York; Sir Edward Stanhope was in debt to Henry VII for £600; the king took his lands at Willoughby, farming them out to pay the debt; but only £200 had been paid when Sir Edward died in 1511; Piercy, *History*, 186, 216, 226; LCNN, 84, 148, 160, 163.

125. *Ancient Deeds*, C.4101–230, vol. 6, C.4194; *IPM*, Henry VII 1498–99, nos. 235, 392 (15 January 23 Henry VII, writ 1 November); *IPM*, Henry VIII, 423, 10 May 1501; Nottinghamshire Archives DD/P/CD/51; Lancashire Record Office DDTO K 19/19 (14 January 1499); DDTO O 3/50 (1498),10/14 (1500–1501); *History of Parliament 1439–1501*, 518–19; John and Sanchia are buried in All Saints Church in Strelley with full alabaster tomb effigies, including twins lost in infancy.

have certain wealth to perform their duties since they were not paid a salary. Some expenses were reimbursed by the Exchequer; sheriffs also were allowed to take a percentage of the taxes and fines they collected. Sheriffs had to administer writs, manage the judicial system in their county and oversee elections. Under Henry VII, sheriffs were supervised by the royal council. Humphrey Hercy was high sheriff of Nottinghamshire and Derbyshire in 1500–1501. As sheriff, he was named in Chancery Court pleadings in 1501 about a jurisdictional problem in a case about a debt. The following year, the same case was expanded to include allegations of outlawry and breach of promise. On 20 July 1502 he was seised of Weston which he gave to his son Humphrey II and his wife Elizabeth. In January 1504 he was commissioned as tax collector for Nottinghamshire with Sir Henry Willoughby, Sir Gervase Clifton, Robert Neville, and others for a special tax imposed by Parliament to pay for the marriage of Princess Margaret and the investiture of Henry as crown prince. In January 1504 he was named on the Parliamentary Rolls for Nottinghamshire with Sir Henry Willoughby, Sir William Pierrepont, Sir Gervase Clifton, Roland Digby, Robert Neville, and others. On 14 April 1505, he was enfeoffed with part of the manor of North Leverton, Nottinghamhire.[126]

In 1509, King Henry VII died and was succeeded by his son, Henry VIII, who would rule England until 1547. In his first year as king, Henry married Catherine of Aragon, daughter of King Ferdinand and Queen Isabella of Spain, descendant of Edward III through John of Gaunt and widow of his deceased elder brother, Arthur. She was intelligent, well-educated in classical literature, civil and canon law, fluent in Latin, Spanish, and French. King Henry's first years were a time of good harvests and prosperous trade.

On 18 May 1509 Humphrey I Hercy, esquire, of Grove and Rampton, sheriff of Nottinghamshire and Derbyshire, was listed on the pardon rolls of Henry VIII. Pardon in this context generally referred to debt. On 18 July, he was appointed to a commission of *oyer et terminer*. Sir Thomas Knight died in 1509 and in his will dated 22 September 1509, he left bequests to his widow, "Elizabeth, to Humphrey Hercy and Alice his wife, my daughter." Humphrey Hercy the elder was principal executor. In 1510, the king's attorney was arbitrator between the executor of Elizabeth Knight's will and the executors of Thomas Knight's will, including Humphrey Hercy the elder and Robert Neville. Sir John III Markham had granted all his property

---

126. Parliament of 1504, Commissions on Collectors of Taxes: the tax for Nottinghamshire was £556, 13s, 2d; TNA, C 1/237/55 (1500–1501); C 1/257/27 (1502–3); Sean Cunningham, *Henry VII* (London: Routledge, 2007), 169–72; ParlRolls, County of Nottingham, Sirs Marmaduke and John Constable and John Hotham were appointed for the East Riding of the county of York; *IPM*, Henry VII, App. 1, no. 1023; *IPM*, 2:75.

in Nottinghamshire to the bishop of Durham, Humphrey Hercy, Robert Neville, and others. On 20 June and 17 July 1511, Humphrey I Hercy, Simon Digby, Robert Neville, Robert Basset, John IV Markham, and Richard Lascelles were appointed commissioners of array for Nottinghamshire. At that time, the young King Henry VIII had joined an alliance with Spain and the Holy Roman Empire seeking to gain territory in France, but it is unlikely that Humphrey actually fought. Humphrey I Hercy, was appointed commissioner of the peace for Nottinghamshire on 22 February and 14 July 1511, although he could not have served the entire second term. In the first term he served with George, earl of Shrewsbury, Sir Henry Willoughby, Sir William Mering, Simon Digby, Richard Stanhope, and others.[127]

Humphrey I Hercy died on 9 November 1511. His will was dated 11 June of that year. In the preamble he left his "soule to God Almyghty, to Hys blessed mother our Lady Sanct Mary, and to all the gloriouse company of hevyn," and his body to be buried in the choir or chancel of the church of Grove. He did not mention a widow, so possibly both of his wives were deceased. To his daughter Katherine, he gave many goods, and if that were not sufficient, she should have the living from his lands for her life. He appointed his son Humphrey, age thirty-six, his executor, asking him to pay any debts owed and 40d. for church tithes forgotten, and to bury him in a manner at his discretion for the praise and honor of God and the good of his soul. Witnesses were Master Robert Neville, rector of Grove, and Sir Thomas Elton, parish priest, indicating that Grove church was prosperous enough to have both a rector and a curate. At the time of his death, Humphrey I held lands, messuages, and tenements in Grove, Eaton, Weston, Ordsall, Misterton, Babworth, West Retford, Gringley, Lanum, Thrumpton, Welham, Nettleworth, Saundby, Sutton, and East Retford. Most of his lands were held of the king through the Honour of Tickhill and the duchy of Lancaster; Lanum, Gringley and Thrumpton were held of the manor of Dunham; Welham of Westminster Abbey. Grove, Eaton, and Weston were described as containing 1,640 acres, forty-five messuages, and four water mills. Grove was worth £24, 10s. West Retford, Ordsall, and Eaton were worth £36, 5s. 4d. Saundby had 380 acres, ten messuages, and the advowson. Saundby, Misterton, and Babworth were worth £18, 2s. Among his feoffees were members of the Bingham, Markham, Willoughby, and Cressy

---

127. LPFD, 2:204: Roger Lascelles of Yorkshire was also mentioned, 433, 445; LPFD, 1:1542: commissions of the peace 1511–14: 22 February 1511, 14 July 1511; Lancashire Record Office, DDTO K 22/20 (1510–11); will 22 September 1509, probate 15 December 1509; Elizabeth Knight held a life interest in these lands with remainder to her son; *RotParl*, Index, pt. 1, 386:6, 538b; HistParl, 1439–1501, "Thomas Knight," 519; Gunn, 57.

families. Humphrey also held lands in Lincolnshire. His son Humphrey II succeeded. His daughter Katherine was probably unmarried and needed the bequest for her *maritagium*. He had another daughter Margery who was already married to John Anne of Frikeley, Yorkshire, but died without children, and a younger son, Stephen, who did not inherit.[128]

At this time, the church in England was little different from that of the Middle Ages, and was interwoven with every aspect of society, culture, politics, and economics. During Humphrey's lifetime, two-thirds of the parish churches in England underwent major building and renovation projects. Most who wrote wills left bequests for their parish churches and money for masses and prayers. The people were proud of their churches and endowed them with beautiful art, statues, crosses, vestments, altar clothes, banners, and bells. Feasts and holy days marked the calendar and the seasons. Universal and local saints provided visible and tangible recourse for people's problems. Confession facilitated reconciliation of town or village differences and prevented feuds. Parishes sponsored processions, festivals, fairs, plays, and games. Vocations to the priesthood were at an all-time high. Theology students at Cambridge were still taught scholasticism, although Renaissance humanism was on the horizon. University-educated priests were still a minority and tended to serve in wealthy benefices. Under the patronage of Margaret Beaufort, mother of Henry VII, Bishop John Fisher established two new colleges at Cambridge. He became chancellor of Cambridge from 1504 to 1535, established professorships in theology, Greek, and Hebrew, and enabled preaching in the vernacular. Erasmus lectured briefly at Cambridge in 1506, but did not join the faculty until 1511. Thomas Cranmer, from the lesser gentry in southeast Nottinghamshire, was a student at Cambridge from 1503 to 1513. Humphrey I Hercy had appointed Robert Neville, BA, MA, BDiv Cambridge, rector of Grove in 1506, where he served until 1513. This indicates some degree of openness to the new ways of thinking in theology. Humphrey II Hercy appointed Neville rector of Ordsall where he served from 1513 to 1550, spanning the transition from Catholic to the evangelical branch of the Church of England.[129]

Humphrey I Hercy and Joan Stanhope had two sons, Humphrey II and Stephen, and daughters Katherine and Margery. The elder son, Humphrey II, inherited Grove and the younger, Stephen, left Grove and went

---

128. *Testamenta Eboracensia*, 5:25; *IPM*, 2:74-77 (14 October 1512); church tithes required payment of one tenth of farm produce annually; TNA, C 142/29/76 (Nottinghamshire), 142/29/139 (Lincolnshire), E 150/732/4 (Nottinghamshire), 150/548/5 (Lincolnshire); Tonge, *Heraldic Visitation*, 10.

129. Marshall, *Reformation*, 1, 4-6; Wilson, *Lion's Court*, 88-89; Wilson, *England in Age of Thomas More*, 80.

to Charlton, perhaps spelled Carlton, in Nottinghamshire or Berkshire. Stephen's son founded the cadet branch of the Hercy family, which came to reside in Berkshire.

Humphrey I Hercy, esquire, greatly expanded the holdings of land, partly through his marriages and partly by purchase. Although he was not a knight but an armiger, he served in offices dominated by knights such as tax collector and escheator and held commissions of array, of *oyer et terminer*, and of the peace. He was high sheriff of Nottinghamshire and Derbyshire. He restored the fortunes of the family through acquisition of land and holding of high offices, which had become the exercise of his ancestral knightly role. Although commissioner of array, it is unlikely that he personally did military service. Joan Stanhope Hercy secured entry of the Hercys into the Stanhope kinship network. Alice Knight Hercy inherited from her father. Little is known about either woman and Humphrey did not appoint Alice executor. However, they would have managed the estates while Humphrey performed his many offices. In religion, Humphrey may have been somewhat lax in practice since he left money in his will to pay for church tithes forgotten. He showed interest in a more intellectual and liberal understanding of Christianity by appointing university-educated rectors Stanhope from Oxford and Neville from Cambridge. This marked the very beginning of the transition from strict Catholic toward the evangelical position which would dominate the post-Reformation church. Humphrey I Hercy himself was still Catholic and requested a Catholic funeral.

HUMPHREY II HERCY AND ELIZABETH DIGBY HERCY

When his father was alive, Humphrey II Hercy lived as a gentleman in London, at least in the early years of the century. It was then common for sons of the gentry to spend time in London while their fathers were alive to manage the estates. While in London, he borrowed and repaid money. In May 1508, young Humphrey II Hercy, provided a "demi-launce," eight archers and two billmen, infantry who used a pole-arm weapon, in the retinue of Sir Thomas Lovell "for the warres." Humphrey was probably himself the demilancer, but there is no indication that he actually served in war. Lovell was constable of Nottingham Castle, chancellor of the Exchequer, and high steward of Oxford and Cambridge. After his father's death Humphrey II succeeded to Grove and became active in Nottinghamshire politics. In 1512 he was co-sheriff of Nottinghamshire and Derbyshire.[130]

130. CCR, Henry VII, 1500–1509, 3: recognizances to king for debt of three men

Humphrey II Hercy of Grove married Elizabeth Digby, daughter of Sir John Digby, knight, of Eye Kettleby in Leicestershire. The Digby family held lands from the time of Henry III in the counties of Lincoln, Leicester, Warwick, and Rutland. During the reign of Henry VI, Everard Digby was sheriff and knight of the shire for Rutlandshire. He and his three brothers died fighting for Henry VI at Towton in 1440. His seven sons fought for Henry VII against Richard III at Bosworth. Sir John Digby, Elizabeth's father, was knighted by the king for his valor in that battle. He was appointed knight-marechal of the royal household. He also served Henry VIII and fought for him at Calais in 1513. He was sheriff of Warwickshire and Leicestershire in 1515, and of Rutlandshire in 1491, 1517, and 1523. He died in 1533. His son, Simon, Elizabeth's brother, was sheriff of Rutlandshire in 1548 and 1555. On the side of her mother, Catherine Griffin, Elizabeth was a descendant of Scottish royalty, through the Griffins, Latimers, Hastings, and Huntingdon earls of Northumberland.[131]

The Hercys of Grove were lords of West Retford and Weston. In January 1513, one Thomas Young of Retford, a cousin of Nicholas Denman and George Eyre, left to Mr. Hercy his green crossbow with its rack, "to be good master to his wife, iff enny man wolde doo hir wrong." The other property of Thomas consisted of two other crossbows with racks, a longbow, and a book, indicating that this yeoman could read. Possession of three crossbows may indicate that he was an archer. He also left quantities of malt and rye to the poor of Retford and Rampton. He named his wife, Jane, executor, with Mr. Hercy, Richard Lascelles, and another man as supervisors. This documents a relationship between Humphrey Hercy and Richard Lascelles in 1513. On 20 January 1513, Humphrey II Hercy, Richard and John Basset, Thomas Willoughby, and others received the manor of Colwick from two men for seven years. After the deaths of these men, Hercy and the Bassets remained in possession. In January 1513, Humphrey appointed a new rector for Grove church.[132]

By 1500, the manorial system had long since changed from feudal service, such as military service and farm labor, to tenancy rents paid to the lord of the manor, who in turn hired farm labor for his personal lands. The plagues of the fourteenth and fifteenth centuries had caused the population, labor market, and cultivation of and market for crops to decrease. The

---

for £20; Humphrey II's son John did the same; *Manuscripts of Duke of Rutland*, 4:559–61; West Yorkshire Archives, GB 205 LC00950/4/DZ/191: already in 1510, Humphrey II had received lands from William Neville.

131. Collins, *Peerage*, 8:239–41; in 1485 Simon Digby was made lieutenant of Sherwood and other forests of Nottinghamshire.

132. *Testamenta Eboracensia*, 5:36; LCNN, 85, 148.

raising of sheep, which required less labor and produced wool, England's greatest export, increased, as did the demand for English wool abroad, although export duties made it more economical to manufacture cloth at home and export that. Former crop lands were enclosed to pasture sheep. The Hercy family raised sheep, at least by the early sixteenth century. Some time between 1504 and 1515, Humphrey Hercy sued the widow of John Cost of Nottingham for payment for the wool he had sold her late husband. However, the crown and Parliament soon became concerned about the loss of arable land and made laws in 1515 prohibiting further conversion of arable land to pasture and in 1534 Thomas Cromwell proposed a bill limiting the number of sheep a man could raise.[133]

Henry VIII made war on France in June 1513, which did not go well and sparked an invasion by Scotland. The king had left Queen Catherine as regent and she managed the Scottish situation better than the king did the French. On 27 August 1513, Queen Catherine appointed Humphrey II Hercy, Sir William Mering, John Willoughby, Anthony Babington, and the prior of Lenton as commissioners to seize the property of Scots living in Nottinghamshire. Sir Marmaduke Constable and Sir Edward Stanley fought under the duke of Norfolk in the defeat of the Scots at Flodden Field in September 1513. The wars of 1513 exhausted the treasury left by Henry VII. After a stillbirth, a miscarriage, and two children who died soon after birth, in February 1516, Queen Catherine gave birth to a healthy daughter, Mary. She made sure that her daughter received a thorough education, which was both humanistic and Catholic. She also gave gifts to the universities of Cambridge in 1521 and Oxford in 1524.

Humphrey II Hercy and two others were co-sheriffs of Nottinghamshire and Derbyshire in 1512-1513 and 1513-1514. Hercy and one of the others were sheriffs for both years; the third changed. This is significant because the office of sheriff had theoretically been restricted to one year. Humphrey Hercy received commissions of the peace from November 1511 to March 1512, and October 1512 through October 1515, in which terms the office was also held by Sir Henry and John Willoughby, Sir William Pierrepont, Nicholas de Strelley, Thomas Mering, Simon Digby, Anthony Babington, and Robert Neville; Richard Stanhope and Sir William Mering served only two terms in 1514. All of these families were more or less related. In June 1514, Humphrey II Hercy, Thomas and John Babington, and

---

133. LPFD, 3:294; TNA, C 1/324/68; there were also plagues in 1413, 1438-39, and 1420; the movement from crops to grassland enclosed for sheep occurred from 1440 to 1520; L. Cantor, *Changing English Countryside*, 29; Given-Wilson, *Nobility*, 19.

John Willoughby were appointed commissioners of gaol (jail) delivery for the court at Nottingham Castle.[134]

In 1516, Humphrey II Hercy and Robert Neville were involved in recovery of lands in East Drayton. On 26 July 1516, Humphrey Hercy bought lands in Eaton and Morton for £40. The following year, Humphrey Hercy made claims on lands in Eaton, Welham, and Gringley.[135]

Humphrey II Hercy was co-sheriff of Nottinghamshire and Derbyshire in 1517–1518 with Sir William Pierrepont, and again in 1519–1520. There were three sheriffs, but Hercy was the only one listed for both terms. In 1517, Humphrey II de Hercy, Robert de Strelley, and one other were empowered by commission to raise in Nottinghamshire two thousand soldiers, with two hundred slingers, and march them to Newcastle, presumably against the Scots. On 27 May 1519, recognizances, obligations made before a court, made by Humphrey Hercy on 7 March 1514 were cancelled. On 29 September 1519, Roland Revell transferred manors, other estates and advowsons, and his office of bailiff of the Honour of Peverel to the prior of Lenton, Humphrey Hercy, Nicholas Strelley, and others, seisin to be given according to his will. Michael Stanhope sued servants of Humphrey Hercy and others for alleged assault and corruption of a jury. Humphrey's servants were tried in the court of Star Chamber. In 1518, Sir Thomas More was appointed by Cardinal Wolsey to work in the court of Star Chamber to make it a national court of fairness and justice, a venue for appeals from the often corrupt local courts.[136]

In June 1520, King Henry VIII staged a spectacular meeting with the king of France at the "Field of Cloth of Gold." Cardinal Wolsey began planning this diplomatic summit with France in 1519, theoretically to preserve the previously negotiated peace treaty. Humphrey II Hercy was honored to accompany King Henry and Queen Catherine to France as a county

---

134. LPFD, 1:1100, 1542: commissions of the peace, 12 November 1511, 29 October 1512, 15 February 1514, 5 July 1514, 18 October 1514, gaol delivery 23 June 1514.

135. Northamptonhire Record Office, F(M) Charter/1977 (26 July 1516); in East Drayton they claimed one and a half messuages, "two tofts, 80 acres of land, seventeen of meadow, 12 of pasture and 60 more"; Thoroton, *Nottinghamshire*, vol. 3, "East Drayton," 516, "Wellome," and "Adelocum, Eaton."

136. LPFD, 2:1187, 3:174; *List of Noblemen*, March 1520; TNA, E 150/737/7, STAC 2/28/42; *Hall's Chronicle* (1548); C. Brown, *About Nottinghamshire*, cites ParlWrits, 2:193; gives the first name as Hugh; unless there was a collateral in Nottinghamshire of that name with sufficient stature to be named, it is probably simply a mistake for Humphrey; Wilson, *Lion's Court*, 111; Sir Marmaduke Constable was probably a descendent of his namesake, perhaps through Catherine Comberworth Hercy, wife of Sir Thomas Hercy; Sir Edward Stanley may have been a relative of Humphrey Hercy's future daughter-in-law.

representative for Nottinghamshire, with Sir William Pierrepont, Sir William Mering, Sir Henry Willoughby, Rowland Digby, and four others, in their entourage. Also attending were the earl of Shrewsbury and Sirs Robert, John and Marmaduke Constable, Hercy relatives, representing Yorkshire, and Sir Thomas Lovell. The delegations from Nottinghamshire and Yorkshire made their way to Canterbury to join the assembled notables and then went with them to Dover where they embarked for Calais. For two and a half weeks from 7 to 24 June, the kings of England and France met in a field south of Calais filled with palaces and chapels, pavilions and halls, made of wood and canvas and covered with cloth of gold. The hundreds of participants were housed in tents. The two Renaissance kings tried to outdo each other in spectacle. There were feasts, dancing, music, masses with magnificent choirs, jousts, wrestling matches, and other games. The participants were sumptuously dressed in silk, velvet, and cloth of gold. The event cost a fortune but had no lasting political effect. No treaty was made and in 1522 Henry VIII broke the previous treaty with France, including the engagement of his daughter Mary to the dauphin of France, and made an alliance with Emperor Charles V, who was supported by Queen Catherine.[137]

The Lascelles family of Gateford and Sturton-le-Steeple, Nottinghamshire, were friends and cousins of the Hercy family through their mutual Constable and Comberworth ancestors. Avice de Lascelles of Kirby Knowle, Yorkshire, born about 1268, married Sir Robert Constable, son and heir of Sir Simon Constable of Halsham and Catherine Comberworth. Sir Ralph de Lascelles of Escrick, Yorkshire, born about 1270, married Maud Constable, daughter of Sir William Constable of Flamborough. They had sons Walter and Richard. The great-grandson of Richard Lascelles of Escrick was Raffe Lascelles who held Sturton in Nottinghamshire. He was the father of Richard Lascelles, friend, colleague, and cousin of Humphrey II Hercy. The manor of Gateford by Worksop descended from John de Gateford, an associate of Hugh IV de Hercy, to his daughter Elizabeth, and her husband Thomas Knight. Humphrey I Hercy married Alice, the daughter of Sir Thomas Knight, of whose will he was beneficiary and executor.[138]

---

137. Henry VIII, LPFD, 3:224, 238–46; the local castles in Guisnes and Ardres were too small and in too poor condition to use for the summit; Henry VIII spent more than £13,000; men competed using political influence and bribes to secure places in the entourage; Wilson, *Lion's Court*, 184–88.

138. Dugdale, *Visitation of Yorkshire*, 302; Jones, *History*, 284; MS, Ashmole 831: Sir Ralph, son of Sir John, son of Sir Richard of Escrick; Flower, *Visitations of County of Nottingham*, 57; Hugh IV de Hercy and John de Gateford were fellow squires of King Henry VI and both were arrested together in the dispute with Blyth in 1428.

Richard Lascelles and his wife died by 1520, Humphrey II and Elizabeth Hercy took into their household and raised the three young Lascelles children: George, John, and Mary. After Humphrey's death, his son John Hercy took over responsibility for raising the children. The boys were educated in Latin and possibly Greek; John spoke court French. George was the eldest and on his majority was able to undertake the management of his family estates of Sturton and Gateford to which he succeeded. George Lascelles married Dorothea Paynell of Boothbay Pagnell, Lincolnshire; they had five sons and four daughters. He was commissioner of *oyer et terminer* in 1538, commissioner of the peace from 1547, commissioner of relief in 1550, and MP for Nottinghamshire in 1553. John attended Oxford for two years and then studied law at Furnivall's Inn in London.[139] The Lascelles brothers worked with John Hercy for Thomas Cromwell. John Hercy found a position for John Lascelles serving Cromwell and later in the royal court and a placement of Mary Lascelles with the noble Norfolk/Howard family.

Humphrey II and Elizabeth Hercy had a full household. They had nine children of their own and were raising the three Lascelles children. Humphrey II Hercy died on 14 September 1520, leaving a son and heir John, and eight daughters. His will was dated 6 September and probated 13 October. He left each of his daughters her child's portion, and if she married according to the advice and counsel of his wife and son John, two hundred marks. He left to his "son" Thomas and his heirs £6, 13s., 4d. yearly out of his purchased lands, to be administered by his son and overall heir, John, and his executors. This Thomas may have been illegitimate because he is not mentioned elsewhere, or else he died soon after his father, or was a cleric. Among the executors were Sir Thomas Elton, rector of Grove, and Thomas Denman. The abbot of Rufford and prior of Worksop were to supervise. At the time of his death, Humphrey II Hercy held lands in Grove, West Retford, Saundby, Eaton, Ordsall, Weston, Nettleworth, Treswell, East Retford, Babworth, and Welham which were held of the king in the Honour of

---

139. Wilson, *Queen and Heretic*, 50–51; Wilson, *Tudor Tapestry*, 90–91, 94; one branch of the Lascelles family settled in Scotland; Alan de Lascelles, son of Alan de Lascelles and Juliane de Somerville, donated property to St. Andrew's Priory, witnessed by his uncles Duncan, Henry, and Richard de Lascelles and by William Giffard; *St. Andrew's Priory*, 260, 274–75; Duncan de Lascelles married Christiana de Windsor and inherited her father's lands in 1206/07; they donated to St. Andrew's and had a daughter, Christiana, who married William de Briwere in 1211; PR 13 John; Henry de Lascelles also donated to St. Andrew's, as did his son, Richard; William de Lascelles witnessed Richard's donation and those of Malcolm, son of Duncan, count of Fife; Roger de Lascelles married Beatrice and had a son Theobald, who married Ada, daughter of Patrick earl of Dunbar and Ada of Scotland; in 1296, Sir Ralph and William de Lascelles swore allegiance to King Edward I of England; CDS, vol. 2, 34, 172, 539.

PART II | ENGLAND

Tickhill; Lanum and Scroby were held of the archbishop of York; Drayton, Thrumpton, and Gringley of the manor of Dunham. Gateford and Worksop were held of the earl of Shrewsbury. Among his tenants were Robert Bingham and Thomas Denman. He also held lands in Lincolnshire.[140] All the daughters did marry and succeeded to Hercy lands but son John died childless.

It was written of Grove that the "Barony and Manor long remained in the possession of 'That grate and Aunciente Familie of Hercye,' who added land to land, and field to field, until it culminated in the days of The Worshippfull Maister Humphrey Hercye of Grove, Armiger, who was owner of many fat acres, and was blessed with eight blooming and unmarried daughters, but whose only Son, Sir John Hercy, had no issue, and was the last of his name. Now, Maister Humphrey, from his much land and his many daughters, was a man of exceeding great repute with the young bucks and bloods of the County, who went up to Grove on Sundays, and Week-a-days, and helped him to hunt his foxes, and to shoot his game; and they drank of his sack and his claret, and they married his daughters and multiplied exceedingly, so that all North Notts. was filled with their progeny."[141]

Humphrey II Hercy esquire lived as a gentleman in London while his father was alive. He was called to military service under the earl of Nottingham, but not on the basis of feudal tenure and he probably did not actually serve. When he succeeded to Grove, he raised sheep and greatly increased the Hercy landholdings. He was chosen to attend the Field of the Cloth of Gold in Normandy, during which time his wife Elizabeth managed the estates. He was co-sheriff of Nottinghamshire four times and was a commissioner of the peace and of gaol delivery, creating more times when he was away and Elizabeth had to manage the estates. He accepted the three Lascelles children into his household as wards. The life of Humphrey II Hercy completed the transition from feudal lordship to gentry and county office. The marriage of Humphrey II and Elizabeth Digby expanded their kinship network. Little is known of Elizabeth except that she had nine surviving children and at many times managed the estates. In religion Humphrey promoted Robert Neville of Cambridge to Ordsall, indicating his agreement with new evangelical trend. Humphrey's brother, Stephen, who had not inherited land in Nottinghamshire, moved south and founded the cadet Hercy line in Berkshire.

140. *Testamenta Eboracensia*, 5:25; loan made 26 May 1515; *IPM*, 2:108–15; TNA, C 142/35/2 (Notts), 142/35/23 (Lincoln), E 150/737/7 (Notts), 150/554/13 (Lincoln); BCR, CLP, 1504.

141. Quotation in Wilmshurst, *History of Manor of West Retford*.

NOTTINGHAMSHIRE

SIR JOHN HERCY AND
ELIZABETH STANLEY HERCY

John Hercy, son of Humphrey II Hercy, inherited Grove and all the other estates. John Hercy was born by about 1499. As a young gentleman, he lived in London during the lifetime of his father, where he was creditor of a loan for a hundred marks. About this time, John Hercy, bailiff of the liberty of the abbot of Westminster, held £13, 14s., 2d., in goods and chattels of his manor and soke in Oswaldbeck, Nottinghamshire, according to an inquest. John Hercy probably worked for the abbot of Westminster in London before the death of his father.[142] He seems to have lived there responsibly and was well off.

John Hercy had a long and interesting life, living under three kings, Henry VII, Henry VIII, and Edward VI, and two queens, Mary I and Elizabeth I. By 1520, the honeymoon of approval for Henry VIII, who had squandered the assets of his father, was over. Harvests failed; prices inflated. Exports had changed from raw wool, which was rural, to cloth, which involved manufacturing and was urban; and so people migrated to the cities. Cardinal Wolsey, chancellor from 1515 to 1529, held much of the power in the realm. In the first decade of Henry's reign, the king had been content to let others make the decisions of government, with the exception of his disastrous war in France. In 1520, Henry ordered Wolsey to arrange the useless extravagance of the Field of Cloth of Gold to impress the French king. In 1522–23, the king initiated more failed military incursions into France. He wanted to make a major invasion, but the people, restless because of poor harvests, increased taxes, and forced loans, resisted. Parliament was summoned and passed a tax bill. But commissioners, including John Hercy, were only able to collect about a quarter of the tax. In 1525, the king had Wolsey impose a tax called the "Amicable Grant," a forced loan to the crown, this time without the authority of Parliament. Both the planned invasion and the tax incensed the people and in the end were cancelled. The royal treasury was in dire straits and in 1526 King Henry debased the coinage. In the summer of 1527, the harvest again failed and the people were starving. Yet Henry VIII himself and Cardinal Wolsey lived in ostentatious splendor. Wolsey, with papal permission, closed several small monasteries and used the proceeds to build colleges in honor of himself at Oxford and Ipswich, and the closures angered the people. King Henry and Wolsey built many large luxurious palaces in and around London, including Whitehall and Hampton Court. The government's waste and misuse of money led to

---

142. *Calendar of Nottinghamshire*, 1486–1558, 39–40; TNA, Certificates of Statute Merchant, C241/281/110.

widespread resentment aimed at the king and his chancellor. It was treason to criticize the king, but Wolsey, whose role as head of the church in England and thus the representative of a foreign system of authority, was increasingly criticized. In addition, since 1518 the tracts of Luther had been smuggled into England, and were being read at Cambridge and Oxford. In 1520, King Henry and Wolsey burned such books and also the heretics who promoted them. When Tyndale's English New Testament was published in 1526, it greatly expanded reformist thinking. In 1527, Henry VIII decided to divorce his wife and marry Anne Boleyn. He ordered Wolsey to procure an annulment from Rome. Wolsey tried everything he could think of for the next two years, but failed, in great part because of the political situation of the pope and the opposition of the emperor. Then King Henry turned his frustration against Wolsey. First, he blamed the "Amicable Grant," which the people hated, on Wolsey. In October 1529, the king deprived Wolsey of the great seal and the chancellorship, appointing Sir Thomas More in his stead. The court of King's Bench convicted Wolsey of *praemunire*, support of foreign, that is papal, jurisdiction in England; all his assets were seized and he was exiled to York. A year later, Wolsey was arrested at York and, after a two-week rest with the earl of Shrewsbury at Sheffield, died of a stomach disorder on his way to the Tower.

From 1521, John Hercy, as patron of the advowsons, appointed the rectors of St. Helen's Church in Grove and St. Michael's in West Retford. In about 1521 John Hercy married Elizabeth Stanley, daughter and coheir of Sir John Stanley of Pipe, Staffordshire. The Stanleys were an old family, whose ancestor, Robert de Stanley, was sheriff of Staffordshire under King Henry I from 1123 to 1128. Sir Thomas Stanley was sheriff of Warwickshire, Leicestershire, and Staffordshire. His son, Sir John Stanley, was sheriff of Staffordshire in 1450, 1459, 1465, and 1469. Elizabeth was the granddaughter of his son, Sir Humphrey Stanley of Pipe Ridware, who was knighted by Henry VII at Bosworth, made esquire of the body of the king, and knight banneret at Stoke. He served several times as sheriff of Staffordshire and knight of the shire. Pipe Ridware was a village which was part of the parish of Maveysin Ridware in Staffordshire, connected to the Malvoisin family and maybe thereby also to the ancestor of the Nottinghamshire Hercys, Malveysin de Hercy. Sir Humphrey Stanley died in 1505 and was buried with a brass in the chapel of St. Nicholas in Westminster Abbey. His son, John Stanley, died in 1514, leaving two minor daughters. Elizabeth Stanley and her sister Isabel were coheirs to their father's estates in Staffordshire, Warwickshire, and Derbyshire, including the manor of Pipe, which was under the bishop of Coventry, and the manor of Stotfold, both in Staffordshire, and the manor of Clyfton of the Honour of Tutbury in the duchy of Lancaster. Elizabeth married John Hercy and Isabel married Walter Moyles. John and Elizabeth Hercy, with Walter and Isabel Moyles, had to sue in Chancery Court to settle the estate and for seisin, addressing their pleading to Cardinal Wolsey for detention of the deeds to Clyfton, Pipe, Stotfold, and other properties. In January 1521, liveries for the Stanley estates in Staffordshire, Warwickshire, and Derbyshire were granted to John and Elizabeth Hercy and Walter and Isabel Moyles. Receipt of liveries to "John Hercy for the heirs of John Stanley" was recorded in December 1521. In 1522, after the postmortem inquisitions for Sir Humphrey Hercy and Sir Thomas Stanley and the decree of Chancery, the trustee granted and confirmed to Elizabeth Lady Hercy the half of Clyfton, Pipe, Aston, and other estates; the other half to Isabel and Walter. The properties were large so John Hercy had a steward, John Hyll, to manage them. The manor of Stotford and the other properties in Staffordshire were not finally settled on Elizabeth and Isabel and their husbands until 1526.[143] In 1526, John Hercy sold half of the buildings and lands in Drayton Bassett and Dosthill, part of the Stanley estates in Warwickshire. In 1527, John Hercy, armiger, and Elizabeth Hercy were defendants in two lawsuits concerning some of the estates she had inherited from her parents. At Easter they granted the lands to the bishop of Coventry, who paid them £20. In November, the Hercys remitted lands, which included their half of the manor of Stotfold, their half of thirteen messuages, three burgages, dwelling houses in a borough town, eighteen tofts, one watermill, six hundred acres of land, one hundred acres of meadow, three hundred acres of pasture, and 30s. of rent for £240 sterling, a large sum at the time. In 1528, they granted their interest in a lease of the "pasture called Newhay" to Bishop Blythe of Coventry. Also in 1528, John and Elizabeth Hercy conveyed the estate of Gentylshawe, Staffordshire, to the same bishop. In 1533–1538, they were still in litigation over the manors of Pipe, Clyfton, three other manors, and various other properties. John and Elizabeth Hercy eventually sold their half of Pipe, Clyfton, and Aston to Christopher Heveningham, grandson of Isabel, in 1565.[144] The sale of the

---

143. TNA, C 4/110/206, C1/518/13–16, C1/527/42, C 1/528/17, C 1/1060/68–70; LPFD, 3:426, 1546; Staffordshire Record Office, D948/4/1/1, D948/1/1/2/1; LCNN, 85,160, D(W)1734/J/1580b; *Early Chancery Proceedings*, vol. 8, File 1060, nos. 68–70; the Stanley line had died out at Elford in 1506; during the Wars of the Roses, another branch of the Stanley family first lukewarmly supported Henry VI of Lancaster, then actively supported Edward IV of York when he won the crown, but later switched sides again and supported Henry VI in his brief return to the throne in 1470–71; the intervention of William Stanley and John Stanley at the battle of Bosworth in August 1485 was decisive in the victory of Henry VII.

144. Staffordshire Record Office, D948/4/1/1/2/1: Pipe-Wolverston Estate and Family Papers, Stanley Family Property in Drayton Bassett Area; Records of the

PART II | ENGLAND

Staffordshire and other properties indicates that John Hercy was attached to Nottinghamshire, preferring to live and work there than in more affluent manors elsewhere.

With new lands and wealth, John Hercy rapidly rose to high office in Nottinghamshire. John Hercy was listed on the sheriff rolls of King Henry VIII as co-sheriff in Nottinghamshire and Derbyshire from 1527 to 1534 and from 1537 to 1545, which was an extraordinarily long tenure for the office of sheriff. Three men were named each year; John Hercy was the only one listed for all these years. In 1531, 1532, 1539, 1541, 1542, and 1543, Hercy was listed first. In 1543, he was the one chosen by the king. In 1527 John Hersey [sic] served with Anthony Babington, in 1530 with Sir William Pierrepont, in 1537 with Sir Nicholas Strelley, in 1538 with Sir John IV Markham and Sir William Basset, in 1539 with Sir William Basset and Michael Stanhope, all of whom were related to the Hercy family. They were among the last sheriffs to administer the county. In 1547, King Henry VIII appointed lords lieutenant, who were given the functions formerly held by sheriffs. This was approved by Parliament in 1550. In 1526 and 1527, John Hercy was escheator of Nottinghamshire and Derbyshire; he was listed as escheator in inquests by the Exchequer in 1527, 1529, and 1538. In 1534, he was reimbursed for his expenses as a receiver of abandoned property.[145]

On 30 August 1523, Parliament reluctantly granted a new tax to the king for his futile war in France. In August 1524, John Hersey [sic], Sir John IV Markham, Sir Richard Basset, Sir William Mering, Nicholas Strelley, Richard Stanhope, and others were appointed commissioners to assess and collect subsidies for the previous four years. Collection of the "subsidy" tax

---

Paget Family, Staffordshire Record Office, Title Deed, D(W)1734/3/1580b; TNA, C 1/890/10-13, C 1.1059/53-54, 1/1071/48, C 3/162/31; SHC, 77-78, xi, 268; LPFD III, Pt. 2, 1546; S. Shaw, *History*, 2:292 (arbitration between Hercys and Moyles v. heirs of Humphrey Stanley); Christopher left Pipe to his son Walter, who was sheriff from 1609-1610, knighted in 1619, and died at Pipe in 1636; in 1648, Pipe was sequestrated from Christopher's great-grandson, Walter, because he was a Catholic; however, his wife, and later he also, continued to live there until his death in 1691.

145. LPFD, Henry VIII, Sheriff Rolls, 4:2708 (1529-30), 3029 (1530-31), 5:668 (1532-33), 12:405 (1537-38), 1538-39, vol. 13, Pt. 2, 406, 14:223 (1539-40), 17:640 (1542-43), 18:244 (1543-44); the dates 1533-34, 1544-45, and 1549-50 are from Derbyshire sources; HistParlOnline, 1509-1558, "John Hercy"; in 1537, he was appointed with Sir Nicholas Strelley and Roger Lascelles was co-sheriff for Yorkshire; in 1538, he was appointed with Sir John IV Markham and Sir William Basset, in 1539 with Basset and Michael Stanhope; accounts of the Order of St. John of Jerusalem, May-August 1534; Exchequer, Escheator's IPM, file 742, no. 3; House of Commons: 1509-1558, Appendices, Constituencies, 4:346; TNA, *Annual Report of the Deputy Keeper of the Public Record* 100, 102, 146-48: in 1512-13 and 1520, his father Humphrey II had been an object of an escheator's inquest.

was an influential, but greatly disliked, role in the county. On 23 November 1524, the abbots of Rufford and Welbec, John Hercy, Sir Richard Basset, and others were given a commission by King Henry VIII to survey and report the condition of Nottingham Castle and its weaponry, the manor of Clipston, the parks of Nottingham and Clipston and their deer, and the forests of Sherwood and Thornewood. On 20 February 1531, the abbot of Welbec, John Hercy and others were again commissioned to survey the parks of Nottingham and Clipston and forests of Sherwood and Thornewood as to the number and condition of the deer, and to report this to the lord chancellor, Sir Thomas More. However, they did not receive this commission until 30 April. The commissioners met on 2 May at Nottingham, but Nicholas Strelley, lieutenant of Sherwood, said he needed three more weeks. They gave him fifteen days and met again on 18 May, but Strelley had done nothing to gather the deer for inspection because he said it was the wrong season. This was reported to the earl of Rutland and the situation resolved. The report of the abbot of Welbec, John Hercy, and others, dated 12 January 1532, listed 691 fallow deer, of which 151 were of antler, and 114 red deer, of which 60 were of antler; the report of 15 January listed at Clipston 310 red deer, 70 of antler, 100 fallow deer, 26 of antler, and a total of 1,131 fallow deer and 1,340 red deer. The report was delivered to the Exchequer on 16 November.[146]

Much of the actual administration of the counties in Tudor times was performed by justices of the peace. They were charged with applying and enforcing the law, which required knowledge of the law. They were responsible for collecting taxes, relief for the poor, support for babies born out of wedlock, maintenance of roads and bridges, hearing complaints, punishing crimes, mostly thefts and assaults, and resolving disputes involving labor, family, and neighbors. They settled disputes by arbitration or by recognizances imposed on both parties, requiring keeping of the peace and appearing in court or payment of a set fine. The justices worked from home and rode around the county, individually or with another justice, and met at quarter sessions for major cases and policy decisions, such as taxes, roads, and poor relief. The job was difficult and demanding, requiring dedication to duty and public service, as well as compliance with royal policies either through agreement or fear.[147]

The commissions for justices of the peace reveal the changing political power at the top of the government, as well as deaths and dismissals among

---

146. LPFD, 4:392, 5:58; *Manuscripts of Duke of Rutland*, 24–25; Thoroton Society, 25:39–40; Stapleton, *King's Clipstone*, 1524, 1531–32.

147. LPFD, 5:704; Wall, *Power and Protest*, 99–109.

the members. In February 1526, John Hercy was commissioned justice of the peace for Nottinghamshire under Cardinal Wolsey of York and George earl of Shrewsbury, with Sir Henry and Sir John Willoughby, Sir William Mering, Richard Stanhope, Anthony Babington, Nicholas Strelley, and Robert Neville; in March 1531 under Sir Thomas More, chancellor, and George earl of Shrewsbury, with Sir William Mering, Sir John IV Markham, Sir John Willoughby, and Anthony Babington. Sir Thomas More charged justices of the peace with loyalty to the Catholic church and discovery of Protestant heretics, but resigned as chancellor in May 1532 in dispute with the king over papal authority. Sir John Hercy [sic] was again appointed justice of the peace in 1532 under Sir Thomas Audeley, keeper of the great seal, George earl of Shrewsbury and Sir Francis Lord Talbot, with Sir William Mering, Sir John IV Markham, Sir John Willoughby, Sir Anthony and John Babington; in April 1537 under the same, although Sir Thomas Audeley was named as chancellor, with Sir William Mering, Sir John Markham, Sir John Willoughby, Sir Nicholas Strelley, Michael Stanhope, Gervase Clifton, John Constable, John Babington, and Robert Neville; in July 1538 under the same with the addition of Thomas Lord Cromwell, Privy Seal, with Sir John Markham, Sir John Willoughby, Michael Stanhope, Gervase Clifton, John Constable, John Babington, Robert Neville, and Anthony Nevill; and in July 1539, under and with the same.[148] Almost all of the fellow office-holders were related to the Hercy family. In 1331–32 and 1343 he was both sheriff and justice of the peace at the same time.

In 1526, Edmund Eyre sued the Hercys over messuages and lands in East Retford, West Retford, Ordsall, Welham, Mansfield in Sherwood, Blyth, South Leverton, and other properties. Between 1529 and 1532, Edmund Eyre again sued John Hercy in chancery court over messuages and land in East Retford, West Retford, Ordsall, Welham, Mansfield in Sherwood, Blyth, and South Leverton. The property in Ordsall included a manor and mills as well as the advowson. No judgment is extant and presumably this was settled in arbitration. In October 1531, John Hercy purchased the advowson of the church at Babworth and one acre of land from the priory of Newstead for £15. Later Sir John was sued over distresses, that is, the right of a landlord to seize tenants' chattels for back rents without judicial process, in Treswell, as "Lord of Treswell over a presentation to the church of Treswell, and contempt of the county court and the court in Tickhill." Other undated documents from the reign of Henry VIII record that George Wastnes of Headon brought suit against Roland Digby and servants of John

---

148. LPFD, 4:906, 5:77, 704, 13:565 (1538); MacCulloch, *Thomas Cromwell*, 394, 473–74.

Hercy for trespass and killing of deer in Headon Manor which was adjacent to Grove. George Wastnes of Headon had made a park for deer out of a common waste wood claimed by Grove, but which was not enclosed. The people of Ordsall brought an action against John Hercy for enclosing part of Scrathey Moor, which they claimed was common land. Both cases were filed in the court of Star Chamber. In June 1533, Robert Neville confirmed a grant of land in Dunham and Ragnall to John Hercy.[149] These cases illustrate some of the many properties then held by John Hercy and disputes which were mostly resolved through arbitration.

Thomas Cromwell, son of a brewer in Putney, then a ferry crossing outside London, spent his youth on the continent, where he fought with the French army, served bankers in Italy, and worked for Protestant merchants in the commercial hub of Antwerp, learning the languages and making valuable contacts. After he returned to England, he became a lawyer at Gray's Inn, served briefly as a member of Parliament, married a woman of the gentry, worked for Cardinal Wolsey from 1524 to 1529, became his right hand man, and, as such, personally inventoried, dissolved, and confiscated the assets of twenty-nine small monasteries to fund Wolsey's new colleges. Cromwell survived Wolsey's fall and gained entrance to the royal court through his legal skills and support for the king's divorce. From 1530 to 1540, Cromwell advanced in the king's inner circle to the most powerful man in England. Through his travels on the continent and knowledge of languages, Cromwell was influenced by Renaissance humanism and Protestant reform. He was in favor of education and the English Bible. He reformed the universities, established new professorships in Hebrew and Greek, had the Bible taught in the original languages, with two public lectures daily in Latin and Greek at Oxford and Cambridge.[150]

In the 1520s, Protestant ideas were censored and books burned. But after its publication in 1526, Tyndale's English translation of the New Testament, replete with glosses giving evangelical interpretations to controversial passages, was widely read and influenced individuals to question tradition. In 1530 evangelicals were still a small minority of individuals in the Church of England, some of whom, however, held high positions of power in the court. At this time traditional Catholic parish life in England was virtually unchanged from the Middle Ages. As King Henry pursued his

---

149. TNA, C 1/498/34, C1/629/32 (1529–32); C1/807/57–60 (1533–38); C1/890/10–13 (1533–38); C1/1024/30–33(1538–44); half of Treswell was held of the Tickhill fee; TNA, STAC 2/23/52 and 2/28/117; Piercy, *Historyi*, 186, 226; Manning, *Hunters and Poachers*, 153; in 1316, Babworth, between West Retford and Worksop, was held by Robert de Saundby and the earl of Lancaster.

150. Wilson, *Lion's Court*, 263–67, 309.

divorce, religious changes were introduced gradually and with the approval of Parliament. In 1532, the Act in Restraint of Annates terminated financial payments from England to Rome. In 1533, the king had Thomas Cromwell move the Act in Restraint of Appeals through Parliament, severing the jurisdictional connection between England and Rome and effectively cutting off any possible appeal of the divorce by Queen Catherine. The same year, Henry VIII had Thomas Cranmer, who was heavily influenced by Lutheran doctrine, appointed archbishop of Canterbury, and then had Cranmer grant a him divorce from his wife Catherine. In September 1533, Anne Boleyn gave birth to a daughter, Elizabeth. The divorce campaign had motivated both scholars and politicians to invest their energies in finding a means in the Bible, theology, or canon law for the king to get his way, looking beyond the traditional positions, and thereby to obtain royal favor for themselves. Henry VIII was provisionally excommunicated by Pope Clement VII.

Thomas Cromwell and Anne Boleyn brought many Protestants into the king's service and court. The king may not have agreed with them, but he needed their talents. In the spring of 1534, the English church was formally split from Rome when Parliament passed the Act of Supremacy, declaring the king supreme head of the Church of England. Henry VIII, however, considered himself a faithful Catholic until his death. Papal supremacy was not a central tenet of the church until the Counter-Reformation. Parliament passed the Act of Succession, which declared the validity of the king's new marriage. Also in 1534, Parliament passed an act redefining treason, expanding it to include not just acts, but any words to deprive the king of any of his titles or accuse him of heresy. Sir Thomas More was convicted and executed in July 1535 under this act for refusing to take an oath acknowledging the supremacy of the king over the church. The title "Head of the Church" gave the king even greater power, making him almost a god in the eyes and fears of the people. Loyalty and obedience to the king were so important that neighbor reported neighbor for disloyal talk.[151]

Thomas Cromwell had men in his service in many parts of England. He needed accurate information and people who could carry out his orders in the shires. Only the most qualified and useful were accepted. Service to Cromwell gave his men increased status and power in the shires. In Nottinghamshire, Cromwell's men were Sir John IV Markham, Sir Anthony and John Babington, John Mering, John Hercy, and George and John Lascelles. Sir John IV Markham was one of the most important men in Nottinghamshire at the time. He was the grandson of Sir John II Markham,

---

151. *Testamenta Eboracensia*, 5:25; in England, from 1536, all graduates of Cambridge University had to renounce the papacy to receive their degrees; Marshall, *Reformation*, 55–56; Wilson, *England*, 80.

chief justice of England, who had helped Elizabeth Leek Hercy set up the chantry for her husband. Sir John IV had served in the court of the young King Henry VIII but returned to Nottinghamshire in the mid-1520s. There he was sheriff in 1526, 1532, 1534, 1538, and 1545, knight of the shire in 1529, 1536, 1539, 1542, 1545, 1547, 1558, and 1559 and justice of the peace from 1521 until his death. He served at the coronation of Anne Boleyn and was a close friend of Archbishop Cranmer. He was a convinced Protestant who held theological discussions with dissident monks. He fought in all the king's wars, played an important part in defeating the Pilgrimage of Grace at Lincoln and was a commissioner in the trials of the rebels. Under Edward VI he was appointed lieutenant of the Tower from 1549 to 1551 but was dismissed from that position for being too lenient with Somerset and Michael Stanhope. His first marriage was to Anne Neville and his third to Anne Strelley, widow of Richard Stanhope. He was a relative of the Hercys through the marriages of the daughters of Simon Leek, Margaret to an earlier Sir John Markham and Elizabeth to Hugh IV Hercy. Markham's son John married Catherine, daughter of Anthony Babington. The Babingtons were also relatives by marriage of the Hercys. Sir Anthony Babington of the Inner Temple was sheriff in 1533–34, member of Parliament in 1529 and 1536, justice of the peace from 1511–1536 and steward to the prior of the Knights Hospitaller of St. John. Sir Anthony died in 1536, his will showing that he was Protestant. His son, John, had also studied at the Inner Temple and had served Cardinal Wolsey. He served Cromwell during and after the Pilgrimage of Grace, on juries, and held commissions of the peace, *oyer et terminer*, and musters. He married Sanchia Stanhope, his son George married Anne Constable, his daughter Katherine married Sir John Markham, and his daughter Elizabeth married Sir George Pierrepont, all Hercy relatives. John Mering had studied at Lincoln's Inn and may also have served Wolsey. He represented Cromwell in estate matters and the Pilgrimage of Grace. The Merings were even closer relatives of the Hercys. The sister of Sir Thomas de Hercy had married Alexander Mering and John Hercy's sister Catherine married John Mering. William Mering, son of John Mering and Catherine Hercy, was sheriff of Nottinghamshire in 1560–61. The Lascelles brothers were important messengers to and from Cromwell and Nottinghamshire. George was now an influential Nottinghamshire landholder who gave evidence against Thomas Darcy and Robert Aske, leaders of the Pilgrimage of Grace. John studied at Oxford and Furnival's Inn where he was likely exposed to radical Protestant ideas. With the help of John Hercy, he secured a position in the service of Cromwell, who, in 1539, appointed him to the outer chamber; and he attended the king's table. They had been wards and were cousins of the Hercy family. All these men were important landed gentry, most with legal training, who held multiple offices, were interrelated, and were Protestant.¹⁵²

In 1534 King Henry began a great and expensive enterprise of building new palaces and renovating existing ones. Since the king was ever short of money, Cromwell focused his attention on the wealth of the church. On 4 August 1534, John Hersey [sic] and seven others were reimbursed expenses of £283, 17s., 1d., for their work in London between 15 May and 4 August on the *bonis spolii* left at Eagle, where Anthony Babington was steward, and found at Temple Bruer in Lincolnshire, of £1292, 1s., 11 3/4d. in cattle, corn, and money, owed to the crown by the order of Hospitallers of St. John of Jerusalem under the principle of treasure trove. Both Eagle and Temple Bruer had belonged to the Knights Templar before their dissolution in 1312, when they were taken over by the order of the Knights Hospitallers of St. John of Jerusalem. Subsidy taxes were levied in peacetime in 1535 and 1536, both years of bad harvests and high food prices.¹⁵³

In January 1535, Henry VIII made Cromwell vicegerent and vicar general for spiritualities, a sort of lay cardinal over the church in England. Cromwell had a number of contacts among the gentry of Nottinghamshire, Derbyshire, and Yorkshire, perhaps through his mother's family, the Meverells, and was related to the Babingtons, Bassets, and Leeks, all of whom were related to the Hercys. On 30 January, John Hercy, with Sir John IV Markham, Sir Anthony and John Babington, John Basset, John Constable, Robert and Anthony Neville, and others were appointed to a commission *pro decimis spiritualium*, tenths of spiritualities, to inventory church properties in Nottinghamshire according to unpublished instructions. The commissioners went into monasteries, but also parish churches and cathedrals, looking at account records and assets. This first step, in 1535, was to order a complete inventory of church property in England. The first targets were the monasteries and convents, many of which were very wealthy and run by international religious orders, and thus thought to threaten the king's supremacy over the English church. The result of the work of the commissioners was the *Valor Ecclesiasticus* of 1535. An example from this document: Robert Neville, the rector of the parish of Ordsall, had an annual income from tithes of mills, corn, hay, wool, lambs, pigs, geese, eggs, chickens,

---

152. HistParlOnline: "Sir John Markham," "Sir Anthony Babington"; LPFD, vol. 11, 609, vol. 12, vol. 1, 1015, 1104, 1199, 1227, vol. 2, 321, vol. 13, vol. 1, 609, 787, 887, 1054, 1519, vol. 2, 726, 1884, vol. 14, vol. 1, 652, 905, vol. 2, App. 2, vol. 5, vol. 1, 295; Wilson, *Tudor Tapestry*, 89–91, 94, 99–100; Robertson, "Thomas Cromwell's Servants," 315, 330–33, 379, 442, 514, 525.

153. LPFD, 7:1675; *bonis spolii* were things violently or unlawfully taken from another.

hemp, and flax, in the amount of £20, 8s., 8d., from which was subtracted payment of 17s. to the archbishop of York for synods and procurations, leaving £19, a good living.[154]

In March 1534, May 1535, and April 1539, the king granted mortmain licenses to Thomas Cranmer, archbishop of Canterbury, Sir John IV Markham, John Hercy, John and William Mering, Nicholas Denman, and others to alienate church prebend lands in the parishes and chantries of Norwell and to exchange them for others. *Mortmain* denoted properties held by religious houses and churches, which could never be alienated, that is, unless the king decided to do so.[155]

The next step in raising money for the king, in February 1536, was to have Parliament order the suppression of small monasteries, those with fewer than twelve members and less than £200 annual income, then about two hundred houses. The dissolution of the small and later the great monasteries involved the transfer of so much wealth, a quarter of the landed wealth in England, that it was a great temptation for the aristocracy and gentry to participate in and benefit from it by working for Cromwell. Those who held office as justices of the peace had no choice. The leader in north Nottinghamshire was Sir John IV Markham, who, as early as 1534, reported to Cromwell those who were disloyal to him or to Anne Boleyn, against the supremacy or pro-Catholic. On 8 October 1536, John Babington wrote to Cromwell that he and his cousin Hercy were ready to be enrolled in his retinue and to do the king's service although it was best to keep it quiet for the time. Soon thereafter, they and John Lascelles were all working for Cromwell.[156]

Parliament endorsed distribution of the Coverdale English translation of the Bible and iconoclasm, that is, removal of paintings and statues, and even candles and wax, from churches and shrines. The people were outraged by the second, as their parish churches were stripped of paintings and statues, crucifixes and chalices, and nearby shrines and pilgrimage

---

154. LPFD, 8:50, 10:137–44; Wilson, *Tudor Tapestry*, 98: John Markham and John Babington were on the commission; Wilson, *England*, 145; MacCulloch, *Thomas Cromwell*, 17, 38, 274–75, 306–7, 585 nn. 11–13; Cromwell may have been distantly related to the barons Cromwell of Nottinghamshire and Derbyshire, of whom the last of the male line died out in 1455, although there may have been cadet or illegitimate lines; the six volumes of the *Valor Ecclesiasticus* were compiled in nine months; about this time, the universities were forbidden to teach canon law, which greatly inhibited the function of ecclesiastical courts.

155. LPFD, 7:294 (May, 1534); 14:420, 905.

156. LPFD Henry VIII, Patent Rolls, Westminster, 30 January 1535, April 1539; Westminster, 25 May 1535; no. 609: 10 October 1536; History of Ordsall Parish; MacCulloch, *Thomas Cromwell*, 321.

sites torn down, smaller monasteries dissolved, and monks made homeless. The people were proud of their churches, to the building and furnishing of which they and their ancestors had contributed money and labor, and which dominated their villages and towns. The social structure of their lives, feast days and saints days with their communal festivals and rituals centered around the church, was shattered. The people were now forbidden to celebrate festivals, especially during harvest since it would take time away from their labor, but the king and court continued to celebrate the same feasts with great pomp. In July, to gain support from the German Lutheran princes, Henry VIII had Cranmer publish the Ten Articles of Faith, defining the beliefs of the English church. The king issued orders to parish priests to preach against the papacy. The combination of such measures led to a Catholic rebellion in 1536–37, first in Lincolnshire, and then in the north, centered in Yorkshire, called the Pilgrimage of Grace, whose demands were restoration of the suppressed monasteries and punishment of the dissolution surveyors. The Pilgrimage raised forty thousand men in arms, though few in Nottinghamshire. The king was furious and ordered the aged earl of Shrewsbury into action against the rebels in Lincolnshire. Sir John IV Markham, John Hercy, John Babington, and George Lascelles organized the defense of Nottinghamshire, acting for the king under the command of the earl of Shrewsbury. However, both uprisings were resolved without actual combat, through trickery by the king's agents. Afterwards the king ordered mass executions, which included six abbots and priors. There was no resistance during the later dissolutions. One reason that the king got away with such larceny in the dissolutions was that he had Parliament pass laws which, along with the common law, protected the property rights of lay and religious interests. The properties of abbots, priors, monks, and nuns were exchanged for pensions for life, administered by the court of augmentation, a court set up for this purpose, although those accused of treason received no pensions. The servants of the monasteries were turned out with no pensions. Through the use of parliamentary approval and of distribution of monastic property to the aristocracy and gentry, the king made them accomplices in his program, thus preventing their opposition. The dissolution of the monasteries also destroyed the system of alms for the poor, leaving them destitute.[157]

157. *Visitations of the North*, Dalton in 1558, 133: Hercy relative Sir Robert Constable of Flamborough fought in the Pilgrimage; Marshall and Ryrie, *Beginnings*, 88; Jones, *English Reformation*, 70, 72–73; Marshall, *Reformation*, 52–53; MacCulloch, *Thomas Cromwell*, 325: one of the grievances was the Statute of Uses, limiting how a person could devise land holdings in a will; if Norfolk and Shrewsbury had not supported the king, the Pilgrimage of Grace, which greatly outnumbered the king's forces, probably

In January 1536, Queen Catherine died of cancer, Henry VIII suffered a head injury and aggravated a previous leg injury falling from his horse in a tilting accident, and Anne Boleyn gave birth to a premature, dead and possibly deformed male child. In May 1536, the king executed Anne Boleyn for treason on grounds of adultery and married Jane Seymour.

The king at first introduced changes gradually. In 1536, priests had been ordered to preach against statues, relics, and pilgrimages; but in 1538, orders were sent to remove or destroy them. Commissioners of the peace, including John Hercy, were charged by Thomas Cromwell in Star Chamber in 1538 with dealing with dissent from royal policies, mostly in religion, discovering and reporting recusants, rumors of sedition, vagabonds, and illegal pubs and games. Cromwell sent letters to the justices of the peace, advising them of changes in policy, and they wrote back to him with questions and reports on their enforcement efforts. In 1538 John Hercy, Sir John Markham, George Lascelles, and John Babington were appointed to a commission of *oyer et terminer* to investigate treason and felonies primarily among dissident clergy in Nottinghamshire. The same year, it was ordered that an English Bible be placed in every parish; since compliance was slow, fines were added in 1541. However, for the most part, these Bibles collected dust, unread by the people. There was still a gap between literate aristocrats and gentry, many of whom had their own books, and the illiterate lower classes. The literate were influenced by humanism and many were less sympathetic to traditional religion. Up through the late 1520s, all printed books had been Catholic; soon thereafter the majority of books were evangelical.

In the 1530s, lords of the manors had private pews and chapels, and influenced the theological direction of their areas through their appointment of parish priests. The Hercy family had a private chapel in the manor house at Grove and appointed rectors to the churches of Grove, West Retford, Ordsall, and elsewhere. By the mid-1530s, many university-educated priests in the Church of England were evangelical Protestants, especially those who had graduated from Cambridge. The majority of the people were against the changes, but slowly accepted the inevitable.

During the dissolution of the monasteries of Nottinghamshire, most of the monks meekly surrendered their monasteries and lands to the crown. Lenton Priory did not. The commission at Lenton which oversaw the proceedings consisted of justices of the peace Sir John IV Markham, John Hercy, and John Babington. According to the *Valor Ecclesiasticus*, Lenton had an income of £387, 10s. 10 ½ d. The monks of Lenton provided food, lodging, and money to the poor. The prior, Nicholas Heath, excused

---

would have been successful.

his failure promptly to pay £100 to Cromwell because he needed funds to help the poor. In February 1538, the prior and several monks were imprisoned and in March indicted and convicted of high treason. The alleged basis for the treason of Heath was that he spoke treasonous words, namely that the king was past grace, would never amend in this life, and would have a shameful death. He was also charged with having sold some plate of the monastery to a London goldsmith in 1536 to relieve priory debts, after which the goldsmith who had bought it had to refund the £18, 9s. 4d. to Cromwell's private purse. Another monk, Ralph Swenson, allegedly also spoke treasonous words about the king. The commissioners wrote to Thomas Cromwell from Lenton Priory on 27 March 1538 stating that they had fulfilled the king's commission and Cromwell's instructions and asked for further instructions by George Lascelles who carried the letter. George Lascelles promptly returned with the decision: the sentence was given that the monks were to be hung, drawn, and quartered. On 16 April the four commissioners addressed a letter to Cromwell, informing him that they had carried out their commission of *oyer determiner* [sic] and that the prior of Lenton and the monk Ralph Swenson had been executed. Another man had been indicted for treason, but was reprieved. The justices adjourned the court for evidence and to learn Cromwell's pleasure. Lenton Priory was attainted to the crown. The accounts for the city of Nottingham noted that the judges were given two gallons of wine, costing 16d., after the executions.[158]

On 29 April 1538, Sir John IV Markham, John Hercy, and two others held court at Nottingham Castle, examining four men from Derbyshire. The earl of Shrewsbury accused the priest Nicholas Harrison of saying about the monks of Lenton that "if the Lords of England were as they have been, as they be now but boys and fools, the King would not have pulled down so many abbeys as he hath done." On 30 April 1538, Sir John Markham, John Hercy, and two others were ordered to interrogate him. They wrote a kindly report that "the priest is aged and his wit and memory simple." However, they held him in custody until learning Cromwell's pleasure. In May, John Lascelles returned with Cromwell's response to Markham's report. During the next two weeks, on several occasions, George and John Lascelles visited with John Hercy and discussed the religious situation. Two topics were

---

158. LPFD, vol. 13, 225, 294, vol. 10, 514; vol. 14, pt. 2, 321; *VCH*, Nottingham, 2:93, 98–100; H. Green, *Lenton Priory*, cites Abbot Gasquet, *Henry VIII and the English Monasteries* 2:190, that Heath, William Gylham monk, four laborers, and a priest were convicted of treason and sentenced to be "drawn and hanged"; Wilson, *Tudor Tapestry*, 104–5; Wilson, *England*, 189; there is a story that the rood screen and possibly also the pulpit from Lenton Priory church were boxed up for years until the danger passed and then put in All Saints Church, Strelley.

mentioned: the absolute power of Cromwell and the advancement of the Protestant cause.[159]

On 23 May 1538, John Lascelles took a letter from Sir John Hercy [sic] to Cromwell stating that Sir Edward Eland had taught seditious songs to young people criticizing Cromwell and others and sent him a copy of one such song. Sir Edward had confessed in general on examination, but denied that he had taught the song sent. Sir John Hercy also wrote of the "poor men of Cottam, sorely vexed by Anthony Nevyll, who, besides his own matter, threatens them with consilement [sic] with a lunatic priest put to them by the Archbishop of York's officers." The men had "showed themselves loyal" at the time of the Pilgrimage of Grace. In the end, John Hercy asked the lord chancellor to "take the Lady at Doncaster away and send some good preachers into the country." Doncaster was about twenty miles north of Retford in Yorkshire. The Lady of Doncaster was a statue at a Catholic pilgrimage site, which marked the end of the Pilgrimage of Grace protest against the Reformation. At this time, all the shrines and pilgrimage sites were condemned and destroyed. The last prior of the Carmelites in Doncaster had supported the Pilgrimage and was executed in 1538. The request for "good preachers" denoted educated clergy and may have implied those trained by the Protestant dons at Cambridge. Many of the clergy were still uneducated and thus could only perform the rites by rote, but not expound the meaning of Scripture passages in sermons. In the diocese of York in 1535 fewer than twelve secular clerics were capable of preaching. The Dominican and Franciscan friars, however, were better educated and specialized in preaching. They were knowledgeable about the Bible, schooled in humanism, and made the transition to evangelical preaching after the dissolution of their friaries. The archbishop of York was Anglo-Catholic.[160]

On 9 July 1538, Thomas Cromwell, Privy Seal, again commissioned as justices of the peace for Nottinghamshire John Hercy and other Nottingham gentry in his favor, including Sir John IV Markham, Sir John Willoughby, Michael Stanhope, John Constable, John Babington, Robert and Anthony Neville.[161]

John Hercy was also involved in the dissolution of Worksop Priory. He wrote to Cromwell on 13 October 1538 that "the prior and convent of

---

159. LPFD, 13:320, 387–88; the lord steward may have referred to the earl of Shrewsbury or to Cromwell, who was high steward but more often called Privy Seal; Wilson, *Tudor Tapestry*, 105–106.

160. LPFD, 13:287–88; Whiting, *Blind Devotion*, 167; John Hercy was generally called Sir John from 1538 although he was officially knighted by King Edward VI in 1547.

161. LPFD, 13:565.

Worksop are so covetous, they sell flocks of sheep, rye, corn, woods &c, and all our priors follow the example." He also noted that no one could blame them because they foresaw their demise the following month. On 15 November the prior and the canons signed surrender papers and most were given pensions on 25 March 1539. In 1541, Henry VIII gave the land of the priory to the earl of Shrewsbury in exchange for the manor of Farnham Royal in Buckinghamshire.[162]

Sir John Hercy [sic] wrote from Grove to Thomas Cromwell on 31 October 1538:

> As I understand by my cousin, John Lascelles, your benevolence towards me, I should be glad to obtain the stewardship of Tyckell (Tickhill) and Cunysboro (Conisbrough), which Sir Arthur Darcy has, by joint patent with Sir Harry Wyat, late deceased, which would enable me to serve the King better. I would give you 200 mks., although I am charged 1,000 mks. for the marriage of my sisters, which weighs so on me that I cannot give at all times such as I would. I hope to have 100 or 200 men ready at the King's commands. I rejoice that you are justice of the forests from Trent northward. In Sherwood you ought to have many men if it be well looked on, and I trust your sessions will reform many things, especially waste of woods. . . . Rye is wondrous dear. Leather is risen a third. Your warrant and fee stag have made me and my friends merry. I beg you will remember your servant Lascelles to have the preferment of Beyvall Abbey for the setting forward of a faithful brother, and you shall command me, having no children, to help him. Grove, 31 October.

John Hercy and John and George Lascelles were in the service of Cromwell; John Hercy and George Lascelles hoped to receive some of the lands of Lord Darcy after his execution for treason. John Hercy's request for Tickhill and Conisbrough is interesting for his ancestor Malveysin de Hercy had been castellan of Tickhill and Malveysin's brother Baldwin de Hercy castellan of Conisbrough, perhaps indicting a memory of earlier family history. They did not receive these lands at this time, but in 1540, George Lascelles was given Darcy's fees at Sturton. At about this time, Cromwell had John Lascelles appointed attendant in the outer chamber, where he waited on the king at table. Cromwell secured appointments of his loyal men to the royal court to give himself more influence there.[163]

162. LPFD, 16:718–19 (Pensions to Monks); VCH, Nottingham, vol. 2, "Priory of Worksop"; at the time of its dissolution, there were sixteen monks at Worksop, all of whom were given pensions.

163. LPFD, *Henry VIII*, vol. 8, pt.2, 726 (31 Oct 1538); Wilson, *Tudor Tapestry*, 108;

In 1536 and 1538, Sir John Hercy and two others recovered by *quaere impedit*, an action by which the patron of an advowson could get restoration of rights to the advowson from whomever disturbed them, the west part of the advowson of Treswell from the archbishop of York. In April 1539, the king again granted *mortmain* license to Thomas Cranmer, archbishop of Canterbury, Sir John IV Markham, Sir John Hercy [*sic*], Nicholas Denman, who married John's sister Anne, and others to exchange various church lands and prebends in Norwell, Nottinghamshire. In 1544, John Hercy was again granted licence to alienate lands in Gringley, East Retford, and Welham. The Hercys profited from the dissolution, though not as much as some. In the 1540s, they were able to build a new brick manor house at Grove. Brick was then cheaper than stone and earlier fortified stone manor houses were no longer needed or in fashion. Many Hercy in-laws, friends, and neighbors profited greatly from the dissolution of the monasteries. In October 1537, King Henry VIII granted Rufford Abbey, the lordship of East Retford, and Worksop Priory in 1541 to George Talbot, fourth earl of Shrewsbury, which altered the balance of landed power in north Nottinghamshire. Also in October 1537, the king granted all the lands within the borough of East Retford, which had formerly belonged to the abbey of Rufford, to Sir John Markham. In 1539, the king granted the lands of the abbey of Welbec which lay in East Retford to Richard Whalley and, in November 1539, all the properties of the priory of Mattersey in East Retford to Anthony Neville, Mary his wife, and their male heirs. George Lascelles received Sturton Manor with all its lands in 1540 after testifying against Sir Thomas Darcy, who had supported the Pilgrimage of Grace and was executed for treason. By 1545, Lascelles held over four thousand acres with the manors of Sturton, Gateford, Everton, and Haworth, as well as rents from Worksop, Welham, Babworth, Ordsall, Eaton, West Markham, Blyth, and elsewhere, and was one of the wealthiest men in Nottinghamshire. The rents of the priory of Radford, near Worksop, were granted to Francis Talbot, fifth earl of Shrewsbury, in November 1542. Sir Michael Stanhope received Shelford priory, rectory, and manor, Lenton priory, and in 1548, chantry properties in Retford.[164] Most of these men were relatives or would be future relatives of the Hercy family.

Wilson, *Queen*, 51; Thomas Darcy was executed for his role in the Pilgrimage of Grace, Arthur Darcy was his son—either Hercy was mistaken in the name or assumed the son would not inherit; MacCulloch, *Thomas Cromwell*, 478: Cromwell appointed his men and fellow evangelicals to shore up his own position in the Council; in the thirteenth century, Malveysin de Hercy had been constable of Tickhill and his brother Baldwin de Hercy constable of Conisbrough.

164. LPFD, 14:420; TNA, C1/807/57-60, C1/1024/30-33; *IPM*, (1546), 317-18;

PART II | ENGLAND

The month before the Parliament of 1539 was a time of fear of possible invasions by the emperor and by the French. Commercial ships were detained in harbors along the Channel. Musters were ordered across England. On 24 March 1539, John Hercy, Gervase Clifton, John Babington, Anthony Neville, and Charles Morton were named commissioners of array for Bassetlaw Hundred. Grove had to provide twenty-six men, among them "John Hercy with harness(equipment) for six men and John Stanley with harness for a gunner." The order shows that Grove had at least twenty-six men and that a Stanley relative was in residence there. The totals were 107 with harness, 270 archers, and 480 billmen. The certificate of musters was signed by Gervase Clifton, John Hercy, John Babington, and Anthony Neville. On the same date, George Lascelles was called to provide harness for three men for Sturton.[165] The attacks did not happen and attention was refocused on the Parliament.

The 1539 Parliament was the first Parliament to be held since 1536. Cromwell attempted to get as many of his people elected to this Parliament as possible, including his son, Gregory. John Hercy was knight of the shire for Nottinghamshire and served in this Parliament. In April, Parliament passed the Act for the Dissolution of the Greater Monasteries, which affirmed the "voluntary" nature of dissolution of religious houses up to that time and in the future, whether actually voluntary or by suppression or forfeiture, mandating the transfer of their assets to the king and the court of augmentation. The Act continued the policies of Cromwell and by 1540, all the monasteries in England, which previously had numbered over a thousand, were closed, and there were tens of thousands of homeless monks and nuns. Monastic buildings were destroyed; their stones and lead roofs were sold and used to construct manor houses and palaces. Monks, priests, and bishops who resisted the suppression were executed on charges of treason

---

CPR, Edward VI, 1547–1548, 170, 250, 391, 393–94; Thoroton, *Nottinghamshire*, vol. 3, "Truswell" and "Mattersey"; the Rufford Abbey lands included land in Kirton/Kyrketon held by Humphrey Hercy; *Visitations of the North*, Dalton's visitation of Yorkshire in 1558, 132–33: Elizabeth, daughter of Thomas Darcy, married Sir Marmaduke Constable, whose son Robert, was pardoned by Queen Mary in 1553, was a spy for Queen Elizabeth, knighted at Berwick in 1570 and had a grandson Sir William who signed the death warrant for King Charles I; Jacks, *Great Houses*; Cantor, 82; Doubleday, "Notts Villages: Kirton," in *Nottinghamshire Guardian* (1948); HistParl 1509–1558," George Lascelles"; Wilson, *Tudor Tapestry*, 108; Wilson, *England*, 143–44; not all commissioners of the dissolution chose to benefit: Sir Anthony Fitzherbert, before his death in May 1538, ordered his sons never to accept, buy, or use property or goods which had belonged to the church; Burgess, *Pastor of Pilgrims*, 6–7; on 10 August 1545, George Lascelles sold some lands in Sturton and Fenton to Anthony Thorny for £68; Jones, *English Reformation*, 43–44.

165. LPFD, 14:286–87.

for refusing to recognize the supremacy of the king over the church. Henry VIII filled his treasury by expropriating monastic property, selling the chattels, and leasing the lands. The man who carried out the dissolution of the monasteries, thereby himself becoming the richest and most hated man in England, was Thomas Cromwell. In July 1538, the king ennobled him as Baron Cromwell of Wimbledon and granted him the manor, castle, and lordship of Okeham in Rutlandshire. And in April 1540, the king made him earl of Essex.[166]

However, in June 1539, this Parliament passed the Act of Six Articles, a reactionary move by Henry VIII against evangelical teaching and incendiary preaching. The king personally intervened in Parliament to get it passed. The king wanted to show himself as more orthodox to the continent, as an equal of the Catholic kings of Europe, and also to stabilize and unify the Church of England in a tradition with which he personally was more comfortable. The Six Articles redefined the faith of the English church, requiring assent to transubstantiation, auricular confession, clerical celibacy, vows of chastity, and private masses. It opened a breach between the king and Cromwell and also with Cranmer, who hurriedly sent his wife back to Germany, and led to an exodus of radical evangelicals from England. Nevertheless, King Henry VIII was excommunicated by Pope Paul III in November 1539.

Cromwell had stated his hope that some of the monies from the dissolution of the monasteries would be used for education, expressing his long-standing intention that the dissolution provide a financial basis for Protestantism through education. Unfortunately, all the money went to the king who had other plans. In April 1540, Cromwell, newly made earl of Essex, negotiated the king's marriage to Anne of Cleves, whom the king hated as soon as he saw her. The marriage took place, but was never consummated. Cromwell prepared documents for Parliament to modify the Six Articles as to both doctrine and liturgy. But in June Cromwell was arrested for heresy and on 28 July executed for high treason without trial under an act of attainder. The king married Catherine Howard. Between 1532 and 1540, more than three hundred people were executed for treason. The summer of 1540 was a time of excessive heat, drought, disease, and mass arrests, although many prisoners were released in the fall.[167]

---

166. Wilson, *Lion's Court*, 393–94, 406, 411, 417–21, 448; before the second bill, Cromwell had received bribes from superiors of the great monasteries not to close their establishments; Wilson, *England*, 229–30; HistParlOnline, "Hercy, John"; *Suppression of Religious Houses Act* 1539; MacCulloch, *Thomas Cromwell*, 486, 496–97, 500, 517–18, 538.

167. Marcombe, *English Small Town*, 228–29; Wilson, *Lion's Court*, 445–47, 452,

PART II | ENGLAND

By 1538, John Hercy had obtained for Mary Lascelles a position in the household of Lord William Howard, brother of Cromwell's chief opponent, Thomas Howard, duke of Norfolk. Then she entered the service of the dowager Duchess of Norfolk, where she was an attendant of Catherine Howard. In 1539, Cromwell appointed his loyal associate, John Lascelles, to the outer chamber of the king's household. Catherine Howard became lady-in-waiting to Anne of Cleves and caught the king's eye. On the day of Cromwell's execution, 28 July 1540, Henry VIII married Catherine Howard. On 15 September, John Lascelles returned to court and discussed the situation of Protestants. He urged his more zealous colleagues to be quiet for a while and let God deal with those who opposed Scripture and the king. However, upset at his patron Cromwell's fall from power and execution, and also with the anti-Protestant leaning of the duke of Norfolk and the Howard family, in June 1541, when the king and court were up north on a long progress, John Lascelles questioned his sister about Catherine Howard's premarital affairs with Henry Mannox and Francis Dereham. He compiled a dossier and gave it to Archbishop Cranmer in October 1541, who informed the king on 2 November of the two premarital affairs. The king ordered both John Lascelles and his sister Mary interrogated, then all the other members of the Howard household except Mary. The Lascelles did not deviate from their story under questioning. After the interrogation and torture of witnesses and the accused, the crime of post-marriage adultery with Thomas Culpepper was also confirmed. In December 1541 the male lovers confessed under torture and were executed for treason. Queen Catherine also confessed and on 13 February 1542, was beheaded for high treason.[168]

The fall of Cromwell did not seem to affect the status of John Hercy or of other Cromwell adherents in Nottinghamshire. The commissions for gaol delivery for Nottinghamshire dated 21 December 1540 named John Hercy, John IV Markham, Nicholas Strelley, John Constable, Anthony Neville, and others. On 14 January 1546, Sir John Hersey [sic] was again made commissioner of *oyer et terminer* to hear and determine cases. He continued to serve as justice of the peace through 1547, one of the people in charge of law enforcement in the county. In the summer of 1542, King Henry VIII decided to make war against France with a preemptive strike against Scotland. In September 1542, the countess of Rutland complained because the men of Nottinghamshire had ridden into battle with the men of the earl of Shrewsbury instead of under the earl of Rutland. In October,

---

455; Hutchinson, *Thomas Cromwell*, 201–8, 221–63; Wilson, *England*, 74–75, 148.

168. LPFD, 16:101, 636; Wilson, *Queen*, 64–66; *Tudor Tapestry*, 100, 122, 124–25, 132–37: John Lascelles was also upset with the persecution of an admired preacher, Dr. Edward Crome, 257; Wilson, *Lion's Court*, 459–60, 468–69, 486, 489.

John Chaworth wrote to her that Shrewsbury and Rutland were supposed to fight together, so most of the men from Nottinghamshire went with Shrewsbury, since Rutland was far distant. Therefore she should send letters to the seven Nottinghamshire "captains who go under the King," including John Hercy of Grove, John Mering, and John Babington, when they came north and tell them to follow Rutland. The men were still at home, but would set forth the next day, after the decision of the king's council at York. The October campaign ended with only a brief raid against a few villages. The Scots under James V retaliated, but their raid was stopped by the outnumbered English at Solway Moss. The second conflict brought William Parr to the king's notice, who ordered him to court with his sister Catherine in December. The king married Catherine Parr in July 1543. Her role was primarily that of nurse to the ill and aged king, although she actively promoted the evangelical position in the court until the king became angry. Even at this time, the king was personally still Catholic in practice. In 1545, John Hersey [sic] was named commissioner of sewers. Then such sewers were responsible for removing obstructions in rivers, generally caused by weirs or mills.[169]

In 1543, Bishop Gardiner and the Anglo-Catholic faction began serious persecution of evangelicals under the Six Articles. They were further armed by the King's Book, a very catholic formulary by Henry VIII, and the Act for the Achievement of True Religion, which restricted access to the Bible. The king's marriage to Catherine Parr gave the evangelicals some hope. In Lincolnshire, Anne Askew, whose father was knighted by the king at the battle of Thérouanne, accompanied the king at the Field of the Cloth of Gold, served in his court, and was well-educated in languages and Scripture. Forced into marriage with an uneducated Catholic at a young age, Anne left her husband and later filed for divorce, the first woman to do so. She moved to London where she wrote poetry and preached to any and all. She made contact with John Lascelles, a man of similar education and belief from the neighboring county, who served in the court but was also a leader of evangelicals outside. Anne read the Bible to illiterate poor folk and had intellectual debates with learned theologians. Heretofore upper-class persons were not tried and condemned for heresy. But in June 1545 Anne was arrested and tried for heresy under the Six Articles before a quest court by

---

169. LPFD, 14:286–87, 16:175 (December 1540), 17:447, 812, 1334, 1430, 1432, 1437, 1440, 20:312, 314, 324; *Manuscripts of Duke of Rutland*, 30; 14 January 1545: for "Hants, Wilts, Soms, Dor., Devon, Cormc, and the city of Oxford"; 12 February 1545, Sir John Markham for "Ntht, Wane, Leic., Rutl., Notts, Derb, Linc, cities of Coventry and Lincoln and towns of Leicester and Nottingham"; Thoroton, *Nottinghamshire*, vol. 3, "Little Greeneley."

a jury of twelve men who acquitted her. But in 1546, Thomas Wriothesley, chancellor, had her followed, compiled a dossier based on evidence from his spies, and in March had Anne arrested again. She was again examined before a quest court, but she outwitted her examiners by her intelligent theological discourse. Then she was further examined by the lord mayor of London and held in his prison. He forced her to sign a confession of her beliefs to which she agreed only with the addition of her own definition. She was released after surety was posted. Since she had lost her divorce case and been ordered to return to her husband, she went back to Lincolnshire but to the home of her brother. The most prestigious preacher of the group, Dr. Crome, was arrested. He was supported by John Lascelles. Under threat of death by fire, Crome recanted and named fellow evangelicals. John Lascelles was arrested in April and appealed to the king, who did not respond. He was interrogated by the Council, refused to answer without the king's command and protection, and on 17 May he was sent to the Tower. On 19 June, Anne, captured in Lincolnshire, was brought before the council and then sent to Newgate Prison. Then she was subjected to a formal trial at the Guildhall where she openly stated her beliefs, was convicted and sentenced to death by fire. She was sent to the Tower where she was questioned by Richard Rich but refused to implicate anyone. The chancellor ordered the lieutenant of the Tower, Knyvett, to rack her. He did so gently for awhile, but then refused to continue since it was contrary to law to rack a woman or a gentleperson. He left and Wriostheley and Rich racked her themselves very hard, pulling all her joints apart. She was never again able to stand or walk after this. The intensity of the attempt to break Anne and John was to obtain their recantation as a powerful weapon to dissuade their followers. It may also have been part of the plot to bring down Queen Catherine Parr by implicating some of her ladies if they had given names. But neither goal was successful. In July John Lascelles was tried at the Guildhall, refused to recant, affirmed his evangelical beliefs, and was sentenced to death. In Newgate Prison, he prayed, wrote, and remained defiant. He was able to correspond with Anne, also then in Newgate. On 16 July, John Lascelles, Anne Askew, and two others were taken to Smithfield, a number of their sympathizers walking alongside them. They were burned at the stake and thereafter regarded as martyrs by many. This was the apex of anti-Protestant persecution and the last execution of heretics under Henry VIII. Three weeks later, two powerful evangelical members of the Privy Council returned to England and the persecutions ceased. Neither Anne's brothers nor John's brother George nor John Hercy had come to their defense, which would probably have been risky and futile for them to attempt.[170] The execution of John Lascelles did not seem to adversely affect John Hercy or the Lascelles family because the pendulum had swung back to the Protestant side. George Lascelles remained in Nottinghamshire, prospered, and named his eighth and youngest child Hercye Lascelles.

In January 1547, King Henry VIII died and was mourned with a solemn Latin requiem mass and prayers for the dead. At that time, royal England was still Catholic in practice, with Latin liturgy, altars, stained glass, and feast days, despite being legally separated from Rome. Henry VIII had been sufficiently powerful that he could control the Catholic and evangelical factions in his court, although during his final illness the evangelicals gained more power.

Henry VIII was succeeded by his nine-year-old son by Jane Seymour, who ruled as King Edward VI from 1547 to 1553. On 28 January 1547, Edward issued a general pardon for offenses committed before that date, although those desiring pardon had to sue in writing under the great seal within a year. John Hercy did so on 16 June. On 22 February 1547, two days after his coronation, King Edward knighted John Hercy. In the earlier correspondence with Cromwell, some of the letters had called him "Sir" John Hercy. Landed gentry could lose or decline the status of knighthood if the value of their estates was below £40 or if they found the honor too expensive to maintain. John Hercy greatly increased his estates through his marriage to Elizabeth Stanley and later acquisitions. The estate of Grove alone included more than one thousand five hundred acres and five manors, and was valued at £175. In 1490 there were 375 knights in England; between 1537 and 1558, 374 new knights were created, making approximately 750 knights in the country.[171]

At first, young King Edward VI had little power; the kingdom was governed by the lord protector, his uncle Edward Seymour, a Protestant whose aim was to make England a Protestant state, but who was tolerant

---

170. LPFD, 5:577, 15:790, 848, 873; Burgess, *Pastor*, 395; Wilson, *Queen*, 13, 84, 88–91, 105, 110–20,128–131, 145, 155–160, 163–71, 176–7: one John Grove was arrested in York for having attended the execution of Lascelles, and was still held in December, but not executed because he recanted; Wilson, *Tudor Tapestry*, 181, 186, 199–202, 206, 228–29, 231–38, 253, 267–70; Wilson, *Lion's Court*, 492; Foxe, *Acts and Monuments*, 550–52.

171. LPFD, *Henry VIII*, vol. 20, 14 January 1545; Stone, *Crisis*, 71, 74, 755; Queen Elizabeth created 878 new knights; James I sold knighthoods, creating 1,161 new knights between March 1603 and December 1604; James I and Charles I created 3,281 between 1603 and 1641; *IPM*, Nottinghamshire, 317–18: in 1546, John Hercy held fees in Grove, Eaton, Ordsall, and elsewhere under the lordship of the king and the earl of Shrewsbury.

PART II | ENGLAND

and refused to burn heretics. Edward VI, himself, educated by evangelicals, strongly supported the reform. As he grew older, he grew more radical and intolerant, to the point of burning heretics. In August 1547 he sent commissioners out all over the country with articles of inquiry about the religious positions of bishops, clergy, chantry priests, and laity. The country was divided into six circuits. For the northern circuit, which included the dioceses of York, Durham, Carlisle, and Chester, he appointed two men: the dean of Westminster William Benson and Sir John Hercy. Hercy was present at the visitation at York Minster, but absent at the one in Doncaster. In August at York, John Hercy's appointee to Treswell, Henry Nicolson, was approved, as was Robert Rothwood at Grove; in September Nicholas Pettinger at West Retford and in October Robert Lilly MA at Babworth were approved, all Hercy appointees. In November 1547, Parliament repealed the Act of Six Articles and Henry VIII's treason and heresy laws. Worship was henceforth to be conducted only in English, veneration of images and relics was forbidden, as were vigils and processions and the use of ashes and candles. Images, statues, and paintings, previously just banned, were now destroyed. With the Treasury again empty and money needed for wars, the Chantries Act ordered dissolution of all chantries, hospitals, fraternities, guilds, and other entities which performed or financed prayers for the dead. The government first took inventory of chantry properties, then seized them. Some chantries provided clergy for parishes and some of the commissioners tried to take this into account. Sir John Hercy held commissions for chantries from 1546 to 1548. Presumably he would have been involved in the dissolution of the chantry set up by his great-grandmother, Elizabeth Leek Hercy, for his great-grandfather, Hugh IV Hercy, in 1467 at Saundby. However, this was a parish church and some remnant of the chantry still existed in 1589. Chantry commissioners were also supposed to report on the age and education of parish clergy: the chantry priest of Saundby was deemed "meanley lerned." The commissioners were also to report endowments for candles and lamps and obits for commemorating the dead. The latter funds went primarily to the poor. Treswell had obits of 7d. of which 6d. went to the poor and 1d. to the priest. In 1549, Sir John Hersey [sic], Sir Gervase Clifton, and Sir Anthony Neville, commissioners for the survey of colleges, chapels, and hospitals, certified that Plumtree Hospital in Nottingham was not caring for any poor persons and existed for the benefit of one priest. Thereafter it fell into ruin and was demolished.[172]

---

172. W. Shaw, *Knights of England*, 2:59-60 (Coronation of Edward VI, Knights Bachelor, 22 February 1547); *Royal Visitation of 1559*, xv, 57-60; *VCH*, Nottingham, vol. 2, 61-64; Thoroton, *Nottinghamshire*, vol. 3, "Saundby."

Sir John Hercy served as sheriff of Nottinghamshire and Derbyshire again in 1549-50. Anthony Neville filed a complaint against John Hercy in the court of Star Chamber, alleging that he broke hedges in South Leverton. Hedges were important because they were used for enclosure of pastures and as boundary markers. Since 1515 it had been illegal to enclose crop land for pasture and many people did break down hedges. In 1548, Nicholas Denman, esquire, Charles Denman, and others of East Retford granted property to John Hercy. On 10 April 1549, Sir John Hercy and others were granted rents from Edyall, Staffordshire. Hercy was appointed to the commission for relief with Sir Michael Stanhope, Sir John Markham, Sir Nicholas Strelley, George Lascelles, Richard Whalley, John Babington, John Mering, and others on 15 December 1550 to serve in 1551. Such collections were very unpopular. The sheriffs were ordered to distrain and if necessary, arrest and imprison those who resisted.[173]

Archbishop Cranmer shaped the future Church of England, publishing the *Book of Common Prayer* in 1549. Parliament then banned Catholic worship altogether and required all worship to be according to the *Book of Common Prayer*; all Latin books of rites were ordered to be destroyed. That summer, people revolted against the changes in local parishes, with about seven thousand men under arms in Cornwall and Devon, as well as rioting in London and violent rebellion in Yorkshire. Seymour had tried to walk a middle way, but ended displeasing both sides. John Dudley, earl of Warwick, a more radical Protestant and a Calvinist, whose chaplain was the misogynist Scot John Knox, seized power as president of the Council and governed during the rest of Edward's reign. Seymour was arrested and later executed. In 1550, stone altars were banned and removed from churches, replaced by wooden tables, vestments other than the surplice were forbidden, as was anointing with oil. Walls decorated with frescoes were covered with whitewash; stained glass windows were removed or boarded over. In 1552, Cranmer issued a revised *Book of Common Prayer*, influenced by the Swiss reformers Bucer, Calvin, and Zwingli, and the parliamentary Act of Uniformity required its use in all churches.

Sir Michael Stanhope of Shelford was the first cousin of John Hercy's grandmother, Elizabeth Stanhope Hercy, and his daughter married John Hercy's nephew, John Hotham, son of Mary Hercy Hotham. He fought against the Pilgrimage of Grace, was made justice of the peace, profited from dissolution of Shelford and Lenton priories, was MP for Nottinghamshire in 1545 and 1547, keeper of the royal parks in Nottinghamshire and

173. Fine Roll, 1 Edward VI, 328: nomination as sheriff, chosen by king, 16 December 1550; 4 Edward VI, 357, 7 Edward VI, 415; CPR, Edward VI, 1548-49, 156 (16 June 1547); TNA, STAC 2/23/52, 3/10/2; Piercy, *History*, 216; Wilkinson, *Notes*.

two other shires, and first gentleman of the Privy Chamber. In 1548, he received chantry property in Retford. He was deputy to his brother-in-law, the husband of his sister Anne, Edward Seymour, duke of Somerset, lord protector and guardian of the young king. Sir Michael enjoyed great power and access to the king. But when Seymour fell from power, they were both sent to the Tower. Sir Michael Stanhope was beheaded on 26 February 1552. His widow, Anne, was allowed to keep Shelford during her lifetime. An inscription in Shelford church states that she brought up her "children in virtue and learning," kept a "worshipfull house, releved the poor dealy ... spent the most tyme of her latter dayes in prayer" and in church.[174]

With his treasury empty, King Edward VI had Dudley persuade Parliament to pass an act against objects of superstition, which led to the inventory, confiscation, and destruction of religious objects from local parish churches. The changes were radical, ruthless, and irreversible. The tangible heart of parish-centered English religious, social, and cultural life was now destroyed, as were the bonds of continuity with history and ancestral generations. In September 1552, Sir John Hercy and Anthony Neville were on a commission to inventory the church of Mansfield, where they found a partially gilt chalice, a copper pyx, four vestments, four copes, three bells, two candlesticks, two copper sensors, and a handbell, with one church bell missing for which the town owed the value. With Sir Gervase Clifton, Sir John also inventoried the church at Worksop, where there were two bells, a silver chalice, two corporases (corporals) with cases, a tawny satin vestment from Bruges, another vestment of green worsted, a green cope, three altar cloths, and two handbells. Four parishioners, one of whom was George Lascelles, signed the report at the bottom. John Hercy's inventory of the church of Carlton-in-Lindrick found three vestments, two copes, a silver chalice and paten, three great bells, and a copper cross. To avoid confiscation, the people in some places sold their parish assets and used the money for roads, bridges, canals, and church repairs. In 1553, Sir John Hercy, Sir Gervase Clifton, and Anthony Babington were appointed commissioners to deal with church goods in Nottinghamshire. The king's commissioners came and confiscated the plate, vestments, reliquaries, art, and anything else of value. There was little overt opposition by clergy or laity at this point. Wagonloads of such spoils were on the roads en route to London when King Edward VI died.[175]

174. Marcombe, *English Small Town*, 229; Anne Stanhope died in 1587.

175. *Manuscripts of Duke of Rutland*, 57–58 (inventories of Worksop and Carlton in Lindrick); another example is Anthony Blake, rector of nearby Doncaster, under Henry VIII, who married under Edward VI, was ousted under Mary but given the small parish of Whiston, reinstated under Elizabeth, and kept Doncaster and Whiston and his

Some towns and individuals were able to use some of the proceeds from the sale of chantries to endow grammar schools. Since Sir John Hercy was a chantry commissioner for Nottinghamshire, he had leverage with the archbishop of York, who was also a champion of public education. Sir John Hercy was the predominant benefactor of the foundation of the "Free Grammar School of King Edward VI" in East Retford, established by letters patent on 9 December 1551. The endowment for the school consisted of former chantry lands, and Sir John Hercy continued as its foremost "patron and provider." In 1553 he made grants of property in Retford, including the burgages in Chapelgate, near the parish church, where the school was then located. On 2 October 1554, Sir John granted land in Gringley to the "bailiffs and burgesses" of Retford, and in 1562 he remitted a debt of £70 owed by the town on condition that the corporation contribute £10 *per annum* for four years to the school. In his will, made in 1570, Sir John continued his benevolence. The schoolmaster received a legacy of 3s. 4d. and the usher 2s. 6d. A new piece of land was provided to give them annual pay raises of 5s. and 3s. respectively. Out of another £16 owed to him by the town Hercy directed £14 be used to provide scholarships for three poor students "which shall come out of the school ... and be apt to go to the University of Cambridge," the scholars being selected by George Neville, esquire, the bailiffs, the schoolmaster, and the vicar. Finally, he directed "to every scholar that shall be in the school of Retford at the time of my death, praying for me before, 4d." By using the word "before," he kept his will properly Protestant. The school had four forms and taught reading and writing, English grammar, Latin, Greek, and Hebrew. The school day lasted from 6 a.m. to 6 p.m., with time out for breakfast, dinner, and tea.[176]

Edward VI died and radical Protestants put fifteen-year-old Lady Jane Grey on the throne for nine days. There were armed uprisings of the people, who were upset by the religious and dynastic changes, inflation, and the near bankruptcy of the country. Mary, daughter of Henry VIII's first wife, Catherine of Aragon, then was proclaimed queen, while church bells rang and *Te Deums* were sung in every church. The earl of Shrewsbury was a member of the opposition to Dudley and after King Edward's death, declared his support for Mary and served her during her reign. Dudley and his followers were arrested, tried, convicted, and executed for treason. In November 1553, Jane Grey and her husband, who was Dudley's son, and

---

wife; Jones, *English Reformation*, 65.

176. Marcombe, *English Small Town*, 176, 197, 205, 211; Piercy, *History*, 22; King Edward VI may have contributed the Tuxford chantry to the endowment; White, *History, Gazetteer*, 315–16; *VCH*, Nottingham, vol. 2, 241; Grounds, *History of King Edward VI*, 43–44.

Archbishop Cranmer were tried and pleaded guilty to treason. Lady Jane and her husband were executed in February 1554. In March 1554, Cranmer was taken to Oxford where he was tried and convicted of heresy. He was burned at the stake on 21 March 1556.

Queen Mary I reigned from 1553 to 1558. In the beginning, she was admired for her mercy and goodness, compassion and generosity to the poor, integrity and loyalty, piety and fidelity to her faith. She ruled with the consent of Parliament and went out of her way to give full and fair trials to those accused of treason. She generously subsidized restoration of Catholic worship in parishes and endowed two colleges at Oxford. But she was innocent of politics and out of touch with the religious conflicts among the people. For six years, the previous government had been forcing on them radical Protestantism. Initially Mary simply affirmed her own faith and invited her people to return to it of their own free will. Many did gladly, put back altars and crucifixes, and many churches returned to Catholic worship. There was little resistance, although a few Protestants did rebel openly. Preaching was suspended and those who defied this were arrested. Most of those tried and executed for heresy were from the southeast of England where Protestants were strongest. In the end, the Marian attempt at restoration had little success, in large part because the monasteries, convents, and shrines could not be returned to the church under English law and the monks and nuns, as well as many priests and bishops, had married, converted, or left the country. Clergy ordained by Protestant bishops were not recognized.[177]

In 1550, Sir John Hercy appointed John Robinson rector of Grove but he was removed in 1554 under Queen Mary for being married. Hercy replaced him with William Pierrepont, LLD Cambridge, who was also married and resigned in 1558. Sir John appointed the evangelical William Denman, MA, BD Cambridge, son of his sister, Anne Hercy Denman, rector of Ordsall, where he served until 1557 when he was suspended by Queen Mary I for having a wife, but was reinstated in 1559 under Queen Elizabeth I, serving until his death in 1587. Sir John also was patron of the churches of West Retford, where he appointed rectors in 1521, 1535, and 1559. As patron of the church of Babworth, Sir John named the rector on 19 August 1557.[178]

Sir John Hercy was knight of the shire for Nottinghamshire in the first Parliament of Queen Mary I in October 1553. This Parliament repealed

177. Jones, *English Reformation*, 82, 103; Whiting, *Blind Devotion*, 165, 265.

178. Parish records of Ordsall, West Retford, and Grove; Northamptonshire Archives, F(M) Charter/1981; Marcombe, *English Small Town*, 179–81; LCNN, 85, 148, 160.

nine statutes on religion from Edward VI, including the Acts of Uniformity of 1549 and 1552, restored Catholic worship and clerical celibacy, but left the queen as head of the church. There was some Protestant opposition. Sir John Hercy was one of a group of Protestants in Parliament who claimed to "stand for the true religion." He was not reappointed to Parliament in 1554. At the beginning of Mary's reign, Sir John Hercy had his solicitor draw up a partition of his estates among his sisters, in case he died childless, so that his wealth would not escheat to the crown. In 1553, he granted thirteen acres of land in Gamston to his own use for life and that of his heirs, with remainder on failure of heirs to George Markham, son of his sister Alice.[179]

On 18 December 1553, Parliament passed an Act for the Punishment of Heresies, which gave bishops the power to try and convict persons of heresy and the state power to execute them by burning. Queen Mary supported the Act and refused to grant clemency to convicted heretics. The Act was implemented by sheriffs and justices of the peace to varied degrees, from enthusiasm in a few places to noncooperation in others, and the queen dismissed some of the noncompliant from office. Capital punishment, including burning at the stake, was accepted practice in England, but Queen Mary greatly increased executions by burning. Most Protestants, however, survived, either by conforming or going into exile.

A delegation from Parliament went to ask Queen Mary to marry an Englishman, which she declined. In November 1553, Mary agreed to marry King Philip II of Spain, son of the Holy Roman emperor. In December, Parliament put restrictions on Philip, limiting his power in England and excluding him from the succession. Spain was the enemy of England. Many people found the queen's decision unpatriotic and remembered that her mother was the daughter of the rulers of Castile and Aragon, now united in Spain. Henceforth, many came to regard her Catholicism as adherence to a hated and feared foreign power. Spain was wealthy from its monopoly over the trade with the Americas. And at this time the Inquisition was burning heretics in Spain. In England people demonstrated against the marriage. In January 1554, an armed rebellion broke out against the marriage and there was an attempt, which failed, to put Mary's younger sister Elizabeth on the throne. But the marriage took place in July 1554. Philip had brought with him a very large entourage of Spaniards, whose presence provoked violent riots in London. Philip negotiated with the pope for the reconciliation of England with the Roman church. Parliament repealed the Act of Supremacy on 30 November, and England was again part of the catholic church. But it was no longer possible to replicate the church as it had been before; too

---

179. HistParl, 2:345–46.

much had been destroyed. The papal legate, Cardinal Pole, was in charge. A humanist of the 1520s, Pole had been in exile and out of touch with the religious situation in England for decades. He held a synod of the English church in 1555, which mandated numerous excellent reforms: priests were to be resident in their parishes, bishops were to hold regular visitations, seminaries were to be established, and an English translation of the Bible was authorized. Pole, as chancellor of Oxford and Cambridge universities, established new colleges and appointed good heads to the old ones. Queen Mary and Pole appointed thirteen new bishops, all theologians rather than lawyers.

On 26 January 1555, Sir John Hercy was among those appointed commissioners of sewers in the counties of Lincoln, Northampton, Cambridge, Huntingdon, Nottingham, and the Isle of Ely. This was the last office he held during Queen Mary's reign; he had already been dismissed as justice of the peace. His nephew, William Denman, son of Anne Hercy Denman, was removed by Queen Mary as rector of Ordsall from 1556 to 1559. Lady Frideswide Strelley was one of Queen Mary's ladies-in-waiting and a friend and relative of the Hercys.[180]

Queen Mary I ordered the earl of Shrewsbury to raise four hundred horse in Yorkshire for border service. The earl replied on 1 December 1557, informing her that it would be difficult to procure horses locally because an unknown disease had killed many, already weakened by horse racing and by pulling carts and carriages. He suggested that one hundred of the horses be raised in Nottinghamshire instead, which had heretofore only been charged with raising infantry. He urged her to commission the sheriff of Nottinghamshire, Sir John Markham, Sir Nicholas Strelley, Sir John Hersey [sic], Sir George Pierrepont, and two others to raise such troops on her behalf.[181]

Sir John and his wife were sued in 1556 as deforciants of half of the manor of Aston in Staffordshire. The case was settled and the plaintiff granted a remnant to Sir John and his wife and heirs, and the reversion of the whole of the moiety. In 1558, named as deforciants of another property, Sir John and his wife settled the case by returning the properties to the plaintiffs in exchange for £100. Among the plaintiffs in that case was Bryan Lascelles, eldest son and heir of George Lascelles; also involved were Humphrey Wolfreston and his wife Katherine Stanley, who held the property for the education of their son, Hersey Wolfreston, nephew of Sir John and Elizabeth Stanley Hercy.[182]

180. CPR, Philip and Mary, 1554–55, 110; Piercy, 205, 216.
181. CSPD, 6:462: Addenda, Mary, vol. 8, Sheffield, 1 December 1557.
182. Erdeswicke, *Survey of Staffordshire*, 225: *Final Accords, Staffordshire*. Temp.

The Marian restoration was limited for many reasons. It accepted the Bible in the vernacular, based its doctrine on the 1543 King's Book of Henry VIII, but did not encourage revival of shrines, pilgrimages, or miracle cults, thus maintaining continuity with the two preceding decades of reform. The nobility and gentry who had bought monastic property had a vested interest in retaining England's independence of papal authority. The finances of the English church were still weak. Sources of revenue such as tenths and tithes were not restored until 1556. A new pope, Paul IV, was a personal enemy of Pole, whom he wanted to recall to Rome and try for heresy. Queen Mary protected Pole, taking a stand against the Pope. Henry VIII had closed over a thousand monasteries; Mary was only able to reopen seven. Only about one hundred of the fifteen hundred former monks returned. She restored the abbey of Sion, returning to it properties in Middlesex which included the "Hersey close." Although the people willingly restored Catholic worship in their parishes, no great sums were invested to refurnish them, since the presumptive heir to the throne was a Protestant. Similarly, people did not bequeath much money for masses for the dead, chantries, or guilds.[183] There was a serious influenza epidemic in 1557–58. The famine and unemployment caused by enclosure of croplands and three years of bad harvests were blamed on the queen. The final blow came in January 1558, when Philip's army lost Calais, the last English territory in France. The people began calling for Mary's sister Elizabeth to be made queen. Mary died childless on 17 November. The requiem masses for Queen Mary I and for Philip's father, Charles V, were the last ever celebrated in Westminster Abbey.

The three decades between 1530 and 1560 were a time of turbulent change for all levels of society in England, both socially and religiously. The late fifteenth and early sixteenth centuries had been a time of massive building of churches; the later sixteenth century saw almost none. In the 1530s and into the 1540s, wills indicated that most people remained traditional Catholics. In the early decades of the century, some clergy were trained at university, but many had only minimal instruction in rites before they were ordained priests. Gradually the education of clergy improved and included biblical languages and humanistic and classical studies. Yet their economic status diminished, as stipends for masses and burials were taken away. Under Edward VI they were expected to, and did, perform rites in English, often without altars or vestments. Plain pulpits were placed in the churches, ornate medieval pulpits removed, and preaching was made mandatory. After six years, they had to return to Latin and altars under Mary I. The

---

Philip and Mary, 225–26, Temp Eliz. 238, 332–33, 336.

183. CPR, Philip and Mary, 1555–57, 291.

plate, vestments, church books, and even candles had been taken away and the parishes were expected to replace them. The clergy did not have the funds, so they tried to tax their people, who were also short of funds and refused. Priests who had married under Edward VI had to abandon their wives or their positions under Mary I. Clergy ordained under the new rites of Edward VI, whereby they were given a Bible instead of a chalice and paten, were removed from parishes. Ordinations declined and benefices were too small to support married clergy. With inflation, the clergy needed more money, but the people could not, or would not, pay their church tithes and rents on lands held of the parishes. With the ban on prayers for the dead under Edward VI, bequests to churches diminished and finally disappeared. The people also did not pay for upkeep of the churches, causing many to fall into ruin. With the Bible available for all in English, the gentry and even women and the lower classes now read it. This increased their disdain for the clergy, except in the role of biblical preaching, and led them into the evangelical movement. Householders were responsible for the religious education of their dependents, which was increasingly evangelical. The gentry, as sheriffs, royal commissioners, and justices of the peace, were charged with the implementation and enforcement of each wave of changes. But despite the magnitude and inconsistency of the changes, there was little violent resistance, with a few exceptions such as the Pilgrimage of Grace. Clergy performed the required rites and the people attended church. Two factors were the loyalty of English people to their monarchs, with obedience to the crown held as a religious duty, and secondly, nationalism and xenophobia toward Spain and Rome. As time went on, fewer people remembered the old Catholic rites and traditions.

Queen Elizabeth I ruled from 1558 to 1603. She was well-educated, taught by Cambridge evangelical humanists, and was fluent in Greek, Latin, French, Italian, Spanish, and Welsh. Elizabeth inherited a country heavily in debt, which at first she handled by personal economies, selling crown lands and avoiding war. Elizabeth rejected Catholicism, but steered a middle course, avoiding the radical evangelicals, Puritans, and Presbyterians. In April 1559, Parliament restored her supremacy over the church, gave her the right to appoint ecclesiastical commissions, and passed the Act of Uniformity of 1559, mandating worship according to the *Book of Common Prayer*. The 1559 *Book of Common Prayer* revised the 1552 version, making it less Calvinist in the words for administration of Communion and calling the sovereign the governor, rather than head of the church. In that Parliament, Commons was mostly Protestant, whereas the majority of the House of Lords was still Catholic.

Queen Elizabeth herself loved ritual and ceremony. Her coronation was the last with full Latin ritual, although she was presented with an English Bible. She herself kept crucifixes, candles, and vestments, hated sermons, disliked married clergy, and supported choral church music, including the composers Thomas Tallis and William Byrd. All of these things were denounced by the more radical Protestants. In 1566 there was a controversy over wearing of the surplice at services, which she supported and enforced. Ministers who refused to conform were suppressed and formed a clandestine secret congregation in London, which was eliminated when discovered a year later. Queen Elizabeth required minimal conformity, more organizational than theological, leaving the details to be worked out in local communities. But she insisted on order, and after decades of political and religious chaos, the people agreed. As her reign progressed, people attended church and became familiar with the *Book of Common Prayer*. Over the decades, memories of Catholic liturgy and traditions faded and were lost, and myths of a satanic foreign Catholicism replaced historical truth. Under Elizabeth I, there was one national state church.

As to other institutions in England, in the 1560s the Inns of Court were still mostly Catholic, although many outwardly conformed. But they were tolerant and protective of their own, so change came slowly and mostly by attrition. Thomas Roper, who was Catholic, was not expelled until 1579. By that time, almost all the other Catholics had died.

There was more conflict in the universities. Administrators and professors changed as monarchs changed. Catholics under Henry VIII returned under Mary I; Protestants under Edward VI returned under Elizabeth. The theology professors at Cambridge were increasingly Calvinist, many trained under Calvin in Geneva. Oxford, although under the direction of the Calvinist Knollys from 1564 to 1592, was more tolerant of Catholics. However, in 1569, all faculty had to take the Oath of Supremacy and subscribe to the *Book of Common Prayer*. In 1571, ministers in parishes were examined and forced to do the same. Many did so outwardly, with inward reservation. In the 1570s and 1580s, an increasing majority of bishops and ministers had grown up Protestant and had no memory of Catholic life or practices. The new ministers and schoolmasters graduating from Cambridge were evangelical Anglicans. However, the most radical group, the Puritans, was deemed a threat to social order because they elevated individual conscience over obedience to church and crown. Despite this, in 1584, a Puritan college, Emmanuel, was chartered at Cambridge and produced most of the major Puritan thinkers thereafter.

English society had changed profoundly. Social utility and personal wealth became the moral pillars of society. Feudal relationships had been replaced by monetary relationships. Chivalry was eclipsed. Financial gain was often the motive for religious "conversion," as was also avoidance of social isolation. Magnates ceased to have military retinues and instead had paid bailiffs and lawyers. Over the years, London replaced the countryside as the locus of political and economic activity. As a result, the old aristocracy went into debt to finance new houses and an expensive lifestyle in London, causing a number to sell or lose their country estates. New wealthy classes emerged among lawyers and merchants, many of whom, including the Stanhopes and Stanleys, were raised to the peerage by Queen Elizabeth I and the Stuart monarchs.[184]

Others, including the Hercys and the earls of Shrewsbury, preferred their country manors to the excitement of London. Under Queen Elizabeth, Sir John Hercy served as justice of the peace in 1558–1559 and 1564. There was plague in Retford in 1558, which killed eighty-two people, and again in 1564, killing sixty-six. In the summer of 1563 soldiers returning from France had brought the plague to London and its environs, killing three thousand people each week, twenty thousand altogether. In February 1559, Sir John Hercy wrote the earl of Rutland asking to be excused from muster because of old age and sickness. In 1564, the Privy Council ordered the bishops to report on the gentry and especially the justices of the peace as to their loyalty to the queen and to Protestantism. Only about half of the justices of the peace in England were approved. In Yorkshire, thirty-eight justices of the peace were approved, eighteen rejected, the rest were deemed neutral. The archbishop of York certified that Sir John Hercy adhered to the religious policy of the queen and he was approved. The focus of duty for justices later shifted from service to the crown and their fellow citizens to enforcement of new religious laws against blasphemy, swearing, breaking the sabbath, not attending church, and drunkenness.[185]

Queen Elizabeth disliked, and later persecuted, both Catholics and Puritans, although she included both in government positions in the first decade of her reign. Soon most of the Catholic bishops resigned and were

---

184. Stone, *Crisis*, 11–12, 16, 191–93, 212, 734–35; Whiting, *Blind Devotion*, 167, 175.

185. Jones, *English Reformation*, 164–65; penalties for not attending church began with the Act of Uniformity in 1549, whereby it was punished by a fine of 12d.; *Calendar of Depositions Commissions*, 21 James I (1622–23), concerning earlier transfers of the property; CPR, Elizabeth I, 1563–66, 25; Wall, *Power and Protest*, 49; *VCH*, Yorkshire, North Riding, vol. 1, "Kirkdale"; the property had formerly belonged to the abbey of Rievaulx; Queen Elizabeth I granted the grange of Sonley Cote in Welburn, Yorkshire, to John Hercy and John Howard, who sold it; the grant was dated in a later document as 20 Elizabeth I (1578) and did not say "Sir John," so it is possible that this was a different John Hercy; *Manuscripts of Duke of Rutland*, 71.

replaced by Marian exiles who had experienced religious life in continental Protestant cities such as Geneva and Zurich, and who wanted more reform in England, which the queen would not permit. In 1569, the Catholic earls in the north rebelled, with six thousand men under arms. Sir John Hercy held a commission of musters to defend Queen Elizabeth at the time of the northern rebellion, although he had declined such a commission in 1559 on grounds of age. This rebellion, the supposed threat of Mary Queen of Scots, and the formal excommunication of Queen Elizabeth in 1570, with its implications on the continent, resulted in a significant reduction of her tolerance for Catholics. In 1571, Bryan and Hercy Lascelles were arrested for aiding Mary Queen of Scots. In the early 1570s, the majority of bishops were inclined to Puritanism and filed bills in Parliament to modify the government on a presbyterian model, such as those in Scotland and Geneva. Their moves were blocked by the queen in May 1572, who removed Parliament's jurisdiction over religion. In 1577, Archbishop Grindal of Canterbury defied the queen when ordered to suppress Puritan preaching and prophesying, resulting in his suspension from office. Two years later the Puritans in Parliament made it impossible for Queen Elizabeth to marry the French royal Duc d'Anjou et d'Alençon, ending what was perhaps her last real chance to marry, and in March 1581 passed a strict Recusancy Act against Catholics.[186] In 1583, Archbishop Whitgift removed Puritans from office and made all the clergy subscribe to the *Book of Common Prayer*. Puritan groups continued to be active in religion, but no longer in politics. By the end of the 1580s, the strongest Puritan political supporters, including Leicester and Walsingham, had died. In 1587, the threat of the succession of a Catholic queen, Mary Queen of Scots, was eliminated by her execution. War with Spain in 1587–88 made "Protestant" synonymous with "patriot." At some point in the 1580s, Protestants became the majority in England.

Sir John Hercy died in 1570, his will, dated January 1570. At the time, wills were scrutinized for expression of Catholic ideas, such as prayers for the dead. Sir John's will directed "to every scholar that shall be in the school of Retford at the time of my death, praying for me before, 4d.," adding the word "before," which made the will acceptably Protestant, although the underlying intent was seemingly Catholic. He also made a bequest "to the preachers for making of three sermons at the day of my burial and two days after one hours long." Wills were a concrete indicator of religious change. In Nottinghamshire and Yorkshire in 1530, 89 percent of wills had a Catholic wording, in 1550 only 37 percent; under Mary I, it went back to 76 percent,

---

186. Papal bull *Regnans in excelsis* excommunicated Elizabeth; *Calendar State Papers Scotland*, 4:14.

but in 1570 was down to 24 percent. The wrong phrases in a will could jeopardize its validity and the inheritance of the beneficiaries. Sir John's will named powerful men, including the earls of Shrewsbury and Rutland, Sir Gervase Clifton, and others to quiet any disputes among his eight sisters, and named the archbishop of York to oversee any disputes between his widow and his sisters. This suggests that there may have been some dissension between Elizabeth Hercy and the sisters over the property distribution. John left his wife the plate, the goods in her rooms, two hundred marks in gold and a horse, instead of the usual widow's portion of one third of the whole estate.[187] Sir John Hercy died without children and the bulk of his estates had already been divided and transferred to his eight sisters.

Sir John Hercy lived as a gentleman in London during his father's lifetime, worked for the abbot of Westminster and granted loans. As lord of Grove, he inherited great estates and expanded them by purchase and by marriage to Elizabeth Stanley, who inherited estates in Staffordshire and elsewhere from her father.

Sir John and Elizabeth were litigants in many lawsuits over these estates. They lived in a time of great change under three kings and two queens. By his lifetime, the exercise of knighthood consisted of holding county offices. John Hercy was born an armiger, but from 1538 was called "Sir John," and he was officially knighted by King Edward VI in 1547. Knights were still called by array for military service, but it was not a feudal obligation. John Hercy was called and called others, but there is no evidence he actually fought. He was co-sheriff of Nottinghamshire and Derbyshire for fifteen years. He served as knight of the shire in Parliament. John was named commissioner of the peace for many years and was escheator for Nottinghamshire and held commissions to survey Nottingham Castle and the deer in several parks, gaol delivery, *oyer et terminer*, and special commissions including the *Valor Ecclesiasticus*, the dissolution of the monasteries and chantries. He served as trial judge and executioner in the dissolution of Lenton Priory. John Hercy and his relatives supported the reformation and had gravitated to the evangelical position within the Church of England. John Hercy's appointments of rectors to Grove, Ordsall, West Retford, and Babworth show that he preferred the evangelical graduates of Cambridge. Most were married and removed from office during the reign of Queen Mary. John Hercy supported public education and founded the Free School of King Edward VI in Retford. His estates were perhaps the greatest in the history of the Hercy family. However, since he had no children and partly

---

187. Will of Sir John Hercy of Grove; Wills in Yorkshire Registry, vol. 19, f.482, p. 521 (19 June 1571); *IPM*, 25/9/70, f.13, p. 264; CPR, Elizabeth I, 1569–72, 136; Hist-Parl, 1509–58, 346.

because of the frequent change of monarchs and policies, he divided them among his sisters during his lifetime. The lives of John and Elizabeth were those of county gentry, preferring Grove and Nottinghamshire to London or to their greater estates in Staffordshire, which they sold. Yet John Hercy played a national role in the events of his time and his knighthood embodied honor for his civil accomplishments. Little is known about Elizabeth Stanley Hercy except her involvement in litigation over her inherited estates. She would have managed the Hercy estates when John was serving in Parliament, as sheriff and in his many other responsibilities. John Hercy and his family supported and actively worked for the Reformation, aligning themselves with Thomas Cromwell, King Edward VI, and the evangelical graduates of Cambridge. He publicly supported the Protestant cause in the first Parliament of Queen Mary. His will was Protestant. His ward and cousin, John Lascelles, was burned at the stake as a martyr for the radical evangelical cause.

THE SISTERS OF SIR JOHN HERCY

The death of Sir John was the end of the male line of the Hercy family at Grove, but not of the Hercy bloodline, which continued through the Neville family at Grove until the late seventeenth century and through his other sisters elsewhere. Sir John had given Grove, the advowson of Ordsall and rights in Nettleworth, Weston, Willoughby, Carlton, Warsop, and Morton, to his fifth sister, Barbara, born in 1522.[188]

BARBARA HERCY NEVILLE

Barbara Hercy had married George Neville of Ragnall in 1539. There were Nevilles with William the Conqueror in 1066 and the known genealogy of George Neville goes back to Jollan de Neville in Rolleston, Nottinghamshire, during the twelfth century and at Ragnall from the mid-fifteenth century. This was a minor branch of the great Neville family which was elevated to the peerage in the fifteenth century. Barbara and George Neville were administrators of Sir John Hercy's will in 1572. They had children John, George Jr., who died without children, Mary, and others. The will of George Neville, who died in 1582, left Grove to their son John, who married Gertrude Whalley. In 1586, John transferred Nevilles Manor to his

---

188. Will of John Hercy; *Nottinghamshire Household Inventories*, Thoroton Society Record Series 22 (1963) 146; Whiting, *Blind Devotion*, 263.

son Hercy Neville and John and Hercy Neville together transferred deeds of feoffment of three messuages; these properties were in East Stoke. John Neville died in 1588 and Hercy Neville, grandson of Barbara and George, inherited Grove. His uncle, Francis Neville, BA Cambridge, MA Oxford, was appointed rector of the parish church of St. Helen at Grove by George and Barbara Neville in 1579 and served there until 1611. He also served as chaplain to the archbishop of York in 1580. John Neville appointed him rector of Ordsall in 1588-89. In his will, dated 1606, proved 1611, Francis asked to be buried in Grove church.[189]

On 25 September 1592, Hercy Neville was present at the meeting of the commissioners for recusancy in Nottinghamshire. In a letter to the Privy Council, Sir Thomas Stanhope and others noted their receipt of the Council's orders to "commit to safekeeping the principal recusants of the shire" but could not do so because of their insufficient numbers. Therefore, they had added Richard Whalley's name to their list of commissioners, "as Hercy Neville will testify."[190]

Hercy Neville had first married Bridget Savell in August 1594. They had five children: Gilbert, the eldest, inherited Grove. In 1611, Gilbert appointed Gervase Neville, MA, BD Oxford, rector of Grove where he served until 1642. Edward Neville, son of Gilbert, succeeded and inherited Grove, and his son, Sir Edward Neville, inherited Grove after him. In 1685, Sir Edward Neville, knight and baronet, was appointed deputy recorder to the royal commission for the reincorporation of East Retford. The town clerk was Charles Neville. When Sir Edward Neville died without children in 1686, Grove was sold by his widow. Sir Edward's sister Mary married William Lovelace, whose great-aunt was the wife of John Hercy of Cruchfield, Berkshire. The daughter of Hercy Neville, Mary, married first John Babington, descendent of the Stanhope, Constable, and Markham families. His ancestors Sir Anthony Babington and John Babington had been aids to

---

189. RBA lists a Neuyle (106) and a Neyuyle (243); the first is most probably an eleventh-century French spelling of Neville, the second possibly also; the Neville family was one of the most powerful in England, but it had many branches; Nottinghamshire Archives, DD/SR/102/15: Jollan de Neville confirmed a donation to Rufford Abbey in 1191–1206; Francis Neville: LPL, F1/Bf, 92v (11 February 1580); Thoroton, *Nottinghamshire*, vol. 3, "Darleton, Derlington, Ragnall"; Nottinghamshire University Dept. of Manuscripts and Special Collections, Sm 103 (1586); Sm 156 (will of George Neville), 157–64 (Neville's Manor in East Stoke); Young, *Making of Neville Family*, x–xii, 7–17; Francis also held the parishes of Bawlbroughe and Litchfield; Katharine Neville was buried in the church of Grove in 1683; LCNN, 85, 148; Robert Neville, BA, MA, BD Cambridge, was rector of Grove from 1506–12 and of Ordsall from 1512–50.

190. Sir Thomas Stanhope was commissioner of the peace in Derbyshire in 1594, as was Sir John Stanhope in 1604; LPL, MS, 3199.

Thomas Cromwell with John Hercy in the dissolution of the monasteries. John and Mary Babington had two daughters, Elizabeth and Barbara, who were coheirs to Rampton.[191]

After John Babington's death, Mary Neville Babington married Anthony Eyre. The Eyres were another old Nottinghamshire family. When Gervase Eyre died fighting for the king in the civil war in 1626, his estate went to his son, Anthony Eyre, who married Anne, daughter of John Markham, and they had seven children. A year after her death in 1608, he married Mary Neville Babington, daughter of Hercy Neville of Grove, and had nine more children. Anthony Eyre's eldest son by his first marriage, Gervase II Eyre, married Mary's daughter by her first marriage, Elizabeth Babington, coheir of Rampton. Gervase II Eyre bought his wife's sister Barbara's share of Rampton. His son, Anthony Eyre, who married Lucy Digby, received an MA from Oxford in 1663 and was MP for Nottinghamshire from 1661 to 1671. The eldest son of Anthony and Lucy, Gervase Eyre, matriculated at Oxford at the age of fourteen and three years later entered the bar of the Inner Temple. He was deputy lieutenant for Nottinghamshire from 1692, high sheriff of Nottinghamshire in 1696–1697 and MP for Nottinghamshire from 1698–1701. He died in 1704. In 1762, his grandson, Anthony Eyre, bought the manor and estate of Grove back into the family. He renovated Grove Hall, and made it his principal residence. He was MP from 1774 to 1784. He also owned the nearby estates of Treswell, Rampton, and Headon. His son Charles was rector of Grove and Headon, and Charles's son John was rector of Babworth and archdeacon of Nottinghamshire from 1810 until his death in 1817.[192]

The Neville family prospered at Grove and was Protestant, although perhaps not too evangelical since they appointed Oxford as well as Cambridge graduates as rectors. They served in Parliament and in the legal profession.

ANNE HERCY DENMAN

Anne Hercy, second daughter of Humphrey II and Elizabeth Hercy, and sister of Sir John, married Nicholas Denman and received the manor and church of West Retford. The Denmans were an old Nottinghamshire family, knighted by King Edward I, which had lived first in Yorkshire, then in north

---

191. Nottinghamshire Parish and Probate Records, Archdeaconry Court, 1577–1700, 17 August 1594, Hercy Neville married the widow Ruth Jessop of Hayton at Grove; Thoroton, *Nottinghamshire*, vol. 3, "Rampton"; LCNN, 85.

192. Piercy, *History*, 227–31.

Nottinghamshire at least from 1390. The name derived from "Dane-man"; the Danes had invaded and settled in northeast England from the late eighth century. William Denman, armiger, of Retford, married Joane Bolynbroke, whose father had endowed chantries in St. Swithin's church in East Retford. Their son, John Denman, married Jane Fauconberg. Their son, Thomas Denman, married Isabel, daughter of Hugh V Hercy of Grove. They had two sons, Thomas and John; John was the father of Nicholas, esquire, of East Retford. The will of their elder son, Thomas Denman of West Retford, dated 12 August 1546, and proved 15 May 1552, left most of his property, including his lands in West Retford, to his grandnephew William, son of Nicholas, and to Anne Hercy Denman, wife of Nicholas, a red mantle, which suggests that Nicholas had predeceased him. In addition, he left "to my Lady Hercy, a gold ring," indicating Elizabeth Hercy, wife of Sir John. He requested burial in the church of Ordsall. He also left money to churches, to the maintenance of bridges and highways, to the poor and to his servant £3, 6s., a mattress, sheets, and covers. The elder son of Nicholas and Anne, William Denman, BA (1548), MA (1551) St. John's College, Cambridge, was rector beginning on 2 June 1550 of the parish at Ordsall, which had long been under the patronage of the Hercys of Grove. Either because of his beliefs or his marriage, he was suspended for three years, from 1556 to 1559, by Queen Mary I, but was reinstated by Queen Elizabeth I in August 1559 and served there until 1587. There was a Latin poem inscribed on his gravestone in the church:

> *Filius Armigeri mihi mater militi haeres,*
> *Nomine sum Denman, arte magister eram.*
> *Pastorem Ordsalie Mariae regnante remotum*
> *Restituit princeps Elizabetha gregi.*
> *Continuo & feci caperet Retfordia fructus*
> *Progredier si qui Religione student.*
> *Pauperibus struxisse domos Ordsalia novit,*
> *Mole sub hac tandem mortuus ecce cubo.*
> *Mortuus! Ah fallor, vitam traduco beatus,*
> *Terra cadaver habet, spiritus astra colit.*[193]

> I was a squire's son, my mother was heiress of a knight,
> My name is Denman, I was Master of Arts,
> Rector of Ordsall in Mary's reign removed,
> Restored by Queen Elizabeth to my flock;
> I continued to work that Retford reap the fruits of my labors,
> If any are zealous to make progress in Religion.
> I built houses for the poor of Ordsall.

193. Piercy, *History*, 215.

Beneath this pile, I now am lying dead.
Ah! No, not dead, from life I am brought to blessed,
Earth holds my corpse, in heaven my spirit dwells.

His mother was Anne Hercy, coheir of her brother, Sir John Hercy. In an Indenture of Feoffement on 3 October 1553, Sir John Hercy had conveyed the manor and advowson of West Retford and other properties to Nicholas's use for life in tail general, remainder to the use of his sister Anne for life, and remainder to her son William Denman for life in tail general. William Denman presented his younger brother, Francis Denman, as rector of the church of West Retford from 26 September 1578 to 21 January 1595, when he retired to West Retford Hall. After William's death in 1588, the manor and estates in West Retford went to Francis Denman, esquire, of West Retford. Francis resigned from the parish in 1595 and resided in the manor until his death in 1599. Both William and Francis were evangelical Church of England ministers. Their nephew, John, married the sister of Walter Travers, a Marian exile in Geneva, a radical Puritan who preached at the Temple where he debated Richard Hooker of the Church of England and master of the Temple.[194]

Francis Denman and his wife Anne Blount had two daughters and coheirs: Barbara Denman married Edward Darrel. Her sister, Anne Denman, first married William Darrel, half-brother of Edward. The Darrels were an old family of Sussex. Sir Thomas Darrel also held property in Lincoln, which he left to his eldest son Edward. William died soon after the marriage in 1610 and Anne's half of the properties in West Retford passed to Barbara and Edward. Edward Darrel appointed the rector of St. Michael's Church in West Retford in 1600. Edward died in 1627 and was buried in St. Oswald's Chapel in St. Michael's Church. In 1642, Barbara Denman Darrel appointed the Rev. William Darrel, who served until his death in 1659. Their son Edward II in 1663 bequeathed West Retford Hall to become Trinity Hospital, endowing it with all his estates in West Retford and Ordsall.[195]

194. Wilmshurst, *History of Manor of West Retford*; will of Thomas Denman: apparently Nicholas had predeceased him, since he left bequests to Nicholas's widow and son William; Thomas was buried in the "Lady Quire" in the church of Ordsall; F. Hercy Denman, esq., was mayor of East Retford; John Denman was buried in 1517 in St. Michael's church in West Retford; his mother was Anne Hercy; Ordsall Parish Records; Thoroton, *Nottinghamshire*, vol. 3, "Rectors of Ordsall," list of Denmans buried there; the Temple consisted of the Inns of Court, Inner and Middle Temples; LCNN, 148; the grave and inscription of William Denman were covered over when the Victorian renovators of the church placed a large organ on top of them.

195. Piercy, *History*, 196–98; Wilmshurst; Barbara died on 22 March 1654 and was buried in St. Michael's, West Retford; LCNN, 160: rectors of St. Michael's were appointed: Francis Denman by William Denman in 1578, by Francis Denman in 1595,

PART II | ENGLAND

William Darrel had resided in London. After his death, Anne Denman Darrel, his young widow, worked as governess for and then married a rich widower, Thomas Aylesbury, MA Oxford, in London on 3 October 1611. King Charles I made Thomas a baronet and Master of Requests in 1627 and Master of the Mint in 1635. On 10 July 1634, at Westminster, their eldest daughter, Frances Aylesbury, married Edward Hyde. As a royalist, Sir Thomas fled to Antwerp in 1649 and died in Breda in 1657. Lady Anne Aylesbury died in 1661 and was buried in Westminster Abbey in the Hyde family vault. Edward Hyde had been at Oxford with Prince Charles and also studied law at the Middle Temple. He was MP in the Short and Long Parliaments of 1640 and tried to mediate between the king and the Commons. King Charles I knighted him in 1643 and made him Privy Counsellor and chancellor of the Exchequer. When the king was in prison, Sir Edward Hyde got the crown prince safely out of England. After the king's death, the Hydes had to go into exile, where Sir Edward served the new king, Charles II, in Paris, Flanders, and Holland. After the restoration of the monarchy, King Charles II made Sir Edward Hyde his chancellor, and baron, viscount, and earl of Clarendon. He was also chancellor of Oxford University. At the request of the king, he wrote *The History of the Great Rebellion* and donated the profits to build Clarendon Hall to house the university press at Oxford.[196]

Earl Edward Hyde died in 1674 in Rouen and was buried with his family in the north ambulatory of Westminster Abbey. Edward Hyde and Frances Aylesbury Hyde had six children, among whom Henry succeeded as earl of Clarendon, and Laurence became earl of Rochester. Their daughter Anne Hyde, who lived from 1637 until 1671, was maid of honor to Princess Mary Stuart in Breda during their exile. On a visit to Paris in 1656, she was noticed by Prince James, duke of York. They were engaged in 1659 and married secretly and then officially on 3 September 1660 in London after the Restoration. Thus, Lady Anne Hyde, duchess of York, became the first wife of the last Stuart king of England, James II. She was reputed to be

---

by Edward Darrel in 1600, William Darrel by Barbara Darrel in 1642, and by Thomas Darrell in 1660; thereafter by the corporation of East Retford.

196. *Marriage, Baptismal, and Burial Registers*, 153: Lady Aylesbury was buried in the east end of the Chapel of Kings near King Henry VII in Westminster in 1661; her granddaughter, Anne Hyde, wrote sadly of the death of her aunt Barbara at the age of twenty-four; the youngest daughter, Barbara Aylesbury, was lady-in-waiting to Mary, Princess of Orange, daughter of King Charles I, in The Hague, had died in 1652; after the deaths of her siblings, Lady Frances became sole heir of her father; Earl Edward Hyde lost his chancellorship in 1667, when impeached by his enemies and made prisoner on the Isle of Wight; he was allowed to escape to France, where he died in Rouen in 1674 at the age of sixty-seven; Lady Anne had predeceased him in 1671.

very intelligent, directing political and economic affairs, and was a patron of art and literature. She died in 1671 and was buried in the Lady Chapel of Westminster Abbey, next to Mary Queen of Scots. The couple had eight children, but only two daughters survived to adulthood: Queen Mary II, born in 1662, and Queen Anne, born in 1665. King James II and Anne were Catholic converts and Parliament mandated that their daughters be raised Protestant. Queen Mary II became the wife of William of Orange with whom she co-ruled as "William and Mary" from 1689 until her death in 1694. They had no surviving children. William ruled alone until his own death in 1702, at which time he was succeeded by his wife's sister Anne. Queen Anne reigned from 1702 to 1714. She had eighteen pregnancies, but all miscarried, were stillborn, or died under the age of two, except one son, William, who lived to age eleven. Queens Mary II and Anne were buried in the Lady Chapel in Westminister Abbey with King Charles II. Anne's children were also buried in the Lady Chapel between Mary Queen of Scots and Lady Margaret Douglas Stuart. Queen Anne was the last monarch of the Stuart dynasty.

The Denmans of West Retford had two sons who were evangelical Church of England ministers: William, MA Cambridge, of Ordsall, and Francis of West Retford. Both were married and William had to leave office under Queen Mary. A nephew married a radical Puritan. A descendant of Francis, Anne Hyde, married King James II and became Catholic. Their daughters, Queens Mary II and Anne, were raised Protestant.

ALICE HERCY HATFIELD MARKHAM

The third daughter of Sir Humphrey and Elizabeth Hercy, Alice Hercy, first married Henry Hatfield of Willoughby, and married second Robert Markham. Laurence Hatfield of Willoughby had married a daughter of William Marshal of Carleton. In 1455 they conveyed some of their lands to Justice Richard Bingham, John Stanhope, and others. Their daughter, Agnes Hatfield, was the mother of Archbishop Thomas Cranmer. Their eldest son, Stephen, was the father of Henry Hatfield, who was the surveyor of Cranmer's lands. Henry held lands in Willoughby, Carleton on Trent, Norwell, and Newark of John Hercy by indentures dated 1528. Hatfield later enfeoffed Sir John IV Markham, John Hercy, John and William Mering, and Nicholas Denman in these lands. Henry died on 27 June 1534. Inquisition postmortem was held in November 1541 before John Leek, escheator of Nottinghamshire. After Hatfield's death, Alice married Robert Markham, sergeant-at-arms. They had a son, George, who died without heirs. The daughters of Alice Hercy by Henry Hatfield were Elizabeth, age six at the time of his death, who later married Thomas Whalley, and Barbara, then age two, who later married William Whalley.[197]

The Whalleys were descendants of Thomas Whalley of Sibthorpe, who married Elizabeth Leek and died in 1483. Their grandson, Thomas Whalley, was an important servant of Thomas Cromwell. The Whalleys acquired Welbec Abbey and many other church lands from Henry VIII after the dissolution of the monasteries. The son of Thomas and Elizabeth Leek Whalley married Elizabeth Strelley. Their son Richard had twenty-five children by three wives. He was imprisoned in the Tower, having served Seymour, lord protector of Edward VI, and died in 1583 at age eighty-four. One of his daughters married John Neville of Grove. Richard's son by his first wife, Thomas, married Elizabeth Hatfield and his son by his second wife, William, married Barbara Hatfield, the daughters of Alice Hercy Hatfield. The son of Elizabeth and Thomas, Richard, was sheriff and knight of the shire. Two of his brothers held degrees in divinity from Cambridge. Richard also had three wives. His second wife was Frances Cromwell, aunt of Oliver Cromwell. Their son, Edward Whalley, was a major general in Cromwell's army and for a time in 1647 jailer of the king, whom he treated with courtesy and respect, for which he was thanked by the king. However, he was one of the commissioners who signed the death sentence of Charles I in 1649, and thereby became a regicide. His son-in-law, William Goffe, was also a signatory. After the civil war they were attainted; both men emigrated to Massachusetts, where they were pursued by arrest warrants from England. Francis Lascelles was also on the commission, but refused to sign the execution warrant.[198]

The Hatfields were connected to the family of Archbishop Cranmer. Their daughters married Whalleys who had sons who were Cambridge-educated evangelical Church of England ministers. They were connected by marriage to Oliver Cromwell, whom they supported in the civil war.

ELLEN HERCY MACKWORTH

Ellen Hercy, the seventh daughter of Sir Humphrey and Elizabeth Hercy, married Francis Mackworth, esquire, of Normanton, Nottinghamshire, and

---

197. *IPM*, 2:266–69; Thoroton, *Nottinghamshire*, vol. 3, "Willoughby"; Pollard, *Thomas Cranmer*, 5; the son of Alice Hercy and Robert Markham, George Markham, inherited Eaton from his mother.

198. Thoroton, *Nottinghamshire*, vol. 1, "Screveton," vol. 3, "Willoughby"; Clay, *Familiae Minorum Gentium*.

Wingfield, Rutlandshire, son of George I Mackworth, who was sheriff of Rutlandshire under Kings Henry VII and Henry VIII. Francis was sheriff of Rutlandshire in 1539, 1544, and 1555, the last time under Queen Mary. Francis died in 1557. Ellen Hercy had acquired Ordsall with its manor and mills on the River Idle from her brother Sir John. The son of Ellen and Francis, George II Mackworth, was sheriff of Rutlandshire in 1564, 1572, and 1580. He transferred Ordsall to George Neville, who sold it. The mills and fishing rights in the River Idle belonging to George Mackworth and formerly to Sir John Hercy were contested in 1592. George II's son, Sir Thomas Mackworth of Normanton, was created baronet on 4 June 1619 by King James I and was sheriff of Rutlandshire in 1599 and 1609. His son Thomas was sheriff in 1627 and Thomas's son Henry was sheriff in 1666.[199]

KATHERINE HERCY MERING

The eldest sister of Sir John, Katherine Hercy, married John Mering, and their eldest son, Sir William Mering, inherited Weston. The Mering family was documented at Mering from the reign of Henry II. Alexander I de Mering married Maud, daughter of Sir John and Joan de Hercy of Grove. They had a son, Sir William, who was sheriff of Nottinghamshire and Derbyshire in 1432–33 and 1438–39 and knight of the shire for Nottinghamshire in 1421, 1425, and 1442. He fought at Agincourt and was favored by Henry IV and Henry V with a grant of two tons of wine. He married Elizabeth, daughter of Thomas Neville of Rollesham. They had daughters Elizabeth, who married John Strelley, and Margaret, who married Thomas Basset. Their sons were Sir William and Alexander II, who became dean of York. Sir William Mering succeeded and married Elizabeth, daughter of Robert Markham. Their grandson John married Katherine, sister of Sir John Hercy, and they had a son, Sir William, who inherited Mering. The Merings intermarried with the Hercys, Markhams, Strelleys, Bassets, and Nevilles.[200]

MARY HERCY HOTHAM

The eighth sister of Sir John, Mary Hercy, married Sir Francis Hotham of Storesby. The Hotham family were an old Yorkshire family at Hotham in the East Riding. John Hotham was chancellor of England under Kings Edward

199. TNA, E 134, 34 Elizabeth, 12 February 1592; Burke, *Baronetcies*, 332.

200. Gilbertide Meringes, 30 Henry II, benefactor of Lenton Priory; Alexander I married second Elinor, daughter of Sir Hugh Cressy; HistParl, 1439–1509, 585; Thoroton, *Nottinghamshire*, vol. 1, "Mering"; *Visitation of Nottingham*.

II and III. He was bishop of Ely from 1316 to 1337 and patron of Welbec Abbey in Nottinghamshire, where there was a chantry for Bishop Hotham and his family. In 1313, King Edward II appointed John Hotham custodian of the finances of Lenton Priory. Sir John Hotham was sheriff of Yorkshire and married Lora Constable. They were the grandparents of Sir Francis Hotham, who married Mary Hercy. Sir Francis and Mary had a son, John, who lived from about 1540 to 1609. Sir John Hercy had given his lands and advowson in Saundby to this nephew, John I Hotham, who married Juliana Stanhope, daughter of Sir Michael Stanhope. He was high sheriff of Yorkshire in 1584–85 and MP in 1584 and 1586. John and Juliana had a son, Sir John II Hotham, who lived from 1589 to 1645, was created baronet in 1622, was MP five times between 1625 and 1640, sheriff of Yorkshire in 1634, and governor of Hull. He supported the Parliamentarians in the Civil War. His son, John III, who was MP in the Long and Short Parliaments of 1640, seized Hull, denied King Charles I access to its arsenal, and fought for Cromwell, but, according to captured correspondence, offered to change sides in exchange for £20,000 and a barony. He and his father were arrested, tried, and beheaded by the Parliamentarians in 1645. His son, Sir John Hotham IV, was MP from 1660 to 1685 and in 1689.[201]

Thus, the Hercy family name died out in Nottinghamshire, although some descendants were given Hercy as a forename. The descendants intermarried with other influential families of Nottinghamshire and elsewhere. Perhaps because of the division of the Hercy properties by Sir John among his sisters, they and their descendants rose in stature through good marriages. They continued to hold major offices in Nottinghamshire and some in other nearby counties. They were actors in the events of the time and in the civil war. Some were knighted or raised to the peerage. Some of their descendants emerged on the national stage, even becoming queens of England. The Hercy family of Nottinghamshire remained within the Church of England. However, the choice of rectors appointed by its members in the sixteenth century indicates that they supported the evangelical position.

---

201. Thoroton, *Nottinghamshire*, vol. 1, "Mering"; the ancestor in the time of William was Sir John de Trehouse, who changed his name to Hotham after receiving Hotham Manor; Thoroton, vol. 3, "Saundby"; the other two daughters of Sir Humphrey and Elizabeth Hercy were: the fourth daughter, Jane Hercy, who married Edward Bussye of Hether in Lincolnshire, and the sixth, Ursula Hercy, who married Humphrey Littlebury of Highmore, Lincolnshire.

Berkshire

THE JOURNEY OF THE HERCY family continued from Nottinghamshire to Berkshire and there from the Church of England to Puritanism. The cadet branch of the family which settled in Berkshire lost the status of distinguished Anglo-French knightly and major office-holding family it had had in Nottinghamshire. They began with little in Berkshire but in a very few generations rose to become major landholders, gentry, and prominent lawyers. In Berkshire the name was spelled both Hercy and Hersey.

CHARLTON/CARLTON

Stephen Hercy, younger brother of Humphrey II Hercy of Grove and ancestor of the Hercys in Berkshire, moved from Grove to Charlton. According to the traditional Hercy pedigree of Burke, this Charlton was located in Nottinghamshire.[1] However, there was no Charlton in Nottinghamshire. The manor of Chilwell came to be associated with the Charlton family, but not until the mid-seventeenth century. Charlton could also be spelled Carlton, since spelling was not standardized at this time There are three Carltons in Nottinghamshire: Carlton-in-Lindrick, Carlton-on-Trent, and Carlton, adjacent to the city of Nottingham. Carlton-in-Lindrick is three miles north of Worksop, and thus close to Retford and Grove. Carlton-on-Trent lies near Weston and the border with Lincolnshire. Carlton by Nottingham is near Colwick, Holme Pierrepont, Bingham, Aslockton and Whatton. The historical links between the Hercy family of Grove and the three Nottinghamshire Carltons are strongest for the last.

---

1. Burke, *Commoners*, 4:1099; HV, Berkshire (1623), 97, calls Stephen son of Thomas, but this is not possible; HV, Oxfordshire (1634), 298, calls Stephen son of Humphrey Hercy (knight); Humphrey was his father, but not a knight; Cherry, *Antiquarum*, considered him the son of Hugh V Hercy and Margery Bingham, but this is chronologically unlikely.

PART II | ENGLAND

Carlton was a small town northeast of, now part of, the city of Nottingham in south Nottinghamshire. On 20 January 1513, the manor of Colwick, which was nearby and may have included Carlton, was transferred to Humphrey II Hercy, elder brother of Stephen, to his heirs and assigns, and to others, including Richard and John Basset and Thomas Willoughby. In a will dated 29 September 1519, Roland Revell left his estates in Basford, Adbolton, Radcliffe, and other towns around Carlton to Humphrey II Hercy and others, including the prior of Lenton and Nicholas Strelley. In February 1539, Henry VIII granted Shelford, Carleton, and other manors to the Stanhope family. Humphrey I Hercy was married to Joan Stanhope.[2] Stephen Hercy may have spent time as a tenant of his brother in this Carlton and then gone south to Berkshire.

However, there was also Charlton Hundred in Berkshire. Parishes began to keep records of births, marriages, and deaths in the later sixteenth and early seventeenth centuries. The Charlton parish records for Shinfield and Swallowfield, both just south of Reading, which began in the early seventeenth century, noted Hersey baptisms: Margaret, daughter of Richard (12 April 1607) in Shinfield, and Colleberie (26 September 1614) and Rudolph (21 January 1616), daughter and son of John Hersey, in Swallowfield. The little girl (*puella*), Colleberie or Collisbury Hersey, an unusual name, died young and was buried in St. Mary's, Winkfield, on 8 February 1617, indicating the migration of members of the family to Winkfield, east of Reading.[3]

Stephen Hercy possibly acquired some form of land tenure in Charlton. Stephen had three sons, John, Thomas, and Nicholas. He would have left his property rights in Charlton or elsewhere to his eldest son John. The earliest mention of a Hersey/Hercy in Berkshire is that of John Hersey in East Hendred in 1491, who was probably a child at that time. The second son, Thomas, married Agnes, had a son John, and died in East Hendred, Berkshire. The third son was Nicholas, who also had a son John, who moved to the south of England. This John Hercy had a son William, who married Elizabeth Baker of Kent. They had sons John and Nicholas II. Nicholas II first married Isabel Baker of Kent and they had a son, John Hercy of Oxford,

---

2. FA, IV, 125–29; Thoroton, *Nottinghamshire*, 1:287–92, "Shelford," 3:8–14, "Stoke Bardolph and Carlton"; the others included Richard Bassett and his son John and Thomas Willoughby; the Leek family also had holdings there at the time; attainted to king Henry VIII 28 May, later granted to Lady Anne Stanhope, grant to Michael Stanhope 5 February 31 Henry VIII; "Nether Colwick"; a document dated 1561 included Carlton land in Colwick.

3. *VCH*, Berkshire, 3:237; RBE, 2:799; Collisbury and Rudolph were probably the children of John III Hersey; in the thirteenth century, Shinfield and Swallowfield had belonged to the de St. John family.

who lived from 1604 to 1634. Nicholas II Hercy married second his cousin, Elizabeth Hercy, daughter of John Hercy of Sonning, Berkshire. They resided in Sonning and had many children.[4]

The Hercy/Hersey families of Berkshire had a tradition of naming their eldest sons John. Thus, there are overlapping John Hercys, including several John the elder-John the younger father-son sequences. There were John Hercys or John Herseys in Shinfield, Swallowfield, East Hendred, Sonning, Winkfield, and Cruchfield, Berkshire, and in Fillongley, Warwickshire.

Some John Hercys were not identified with a specific place. There were at least two John Hercys of Lincoln's Inn and John Hercy the royal surveyor. John Hercy in 1602, was paid £97 for legal work, preparing evidence for queen's counsel. On 6 May 1603, a John Hercy wrote to the dean and chapter concerning the lease of the Chichester lands in Oxfordshire and Buckinghamshire. These two probably refer to the elder John Hercy of Lincoln's Inn, later solicitor of the earl of Shrewsbury. John Hercy the surveyor was steward of the manor of Knowle in Warwickshire and may be related to John Hercy of Fillongley in Warwickshire. Both places are in northwest Warwickshire.[5]

THOMAS HERSEY OF EAST HENDRED, BERKSHIRE

East Hendred parish, west-northwest of Reading, contained five manors: the manor of Arches, which belonged to the de Arches family, another which belonged to New College, and three others which belonged to various abbeys. By the thirteenth century the town had become prosperous through the fulling of cloth. The manor of Arches in East Hendred was acquired by William de Arches through the marriage of his parents, Amice de Turberville and William de Arches. Arches Manor came by marriage into the Eyston family in 1443. The will of John Eyston, dated 3 November 1491, named John Hersey as his godson. This may indicate that a connection

---

4. John is attested in Burke, HV, Berkshire 1623 and Cherry; Thomas is attested as son of Stephen in Burke, HV, Oxfordshire 1634, and Cherry, but as son of John in HV, Berkshire; Nicholas is attested as son of Stephen in HV, Berkshire 1665; *London Marriage Licences*, 670.

5. TNA, E 403/2723, fol. 31v; see 403/2726, fol. 43v on three John Hercys; Hoyle, *Estates*, n. 69; TNA, Cap/1/4/9/24 (6 May 1603); a John Hersey married Dorothea Lee or Lear on 16 December 1617 at Winkfield, where she was buried on 31 May 1639; John Hersey the surveyor is discussed in Appendix VII of this volume; *Calendar State Papers, Interregnum*, 11:554: on 12 April 1658, a John Hercy was granted a passport to France by Lord Protector Oliver Cromwell and the Council; Cromwell died that year and soon after the monarchy was restored.

remained between the Arches and Hersey families. Young John could have been the young son of Stephen, recently arrived in Berkshire. The parish church of St. Augustine of Canterbury in East Hendred has extant records of Hersey baptisms from 1554. Records before that time either were not kept or did not survive. There is a baptismal record for John Hersey at St. Augustine's on 29 September 1554. There is another for the baptism of Robert Hersey on 8 January 1556. Edmond Hersey was baptized on 3 October 1557 and another John Hersey on 11 April 1561. Many children in this period died in infancy. These children may have been the grandchildren of John or Thomas Hersey, but not sons of Thomas, since their baptismal dates are later than his death in 1550.[6]

Thomas Hersey and his wife, Agnes, lived in East Hendred, Berkshire. When Thomas died in 1550, the inventory of his possessions made mention of Jane, Alice, and John Hersey. The will of his widow, Agnes, was made on 23 September 1559 and proved on 31 May 1561. She made bequests to her son, John, who was executor, and her daughters Jane and Alice. Although Elizabeth I was now queen, the preamble to Agnes's will was still Catholic, "beseeching our lady with all the holy company of heaven to praye for me." One of the witnesses to her will was Peter Barlowe, who had been appointed rector of the church of East Hendred in 1556 by Queen Mary I, but who remained there until his death in 1569. Agnes also made a bequest to the "mother" church of Salisbury where the bishop resided.[7]

---

6. In the thirteenth century the manor of Arches came by marriage into the de Arches family, from the Yorkshire branch of which all the Hercys are descended; the male line of the de Arches family only lasted a few generations in Berkshire, but the manor retained their name; they were unlikely to have descended from the de Arches of Folkstone, who only had daughters who took the names of their husbands; William de Arches had a son, John, who succeeded in 1375 and was justice of the peace in 1401; his son was Ralph/Rawlin de Arches, escheator of Berkshire, whose daughter Maud married a Stowe in 1422; their daughter married an Eyston in 1443, which family still held the manor in the nineteenth century; in the late fifteenth century, an Eyston married a Hyde; Arches Manor was the residence of the Eyston family, but is now called Hendred House; it has a chapel founded by papal license about 1265 which housed a chantry, dissolved under Edward VI; *IPM*, Edward I, ii, 309; CCR, 1318-23, 616, 1337-39, 277, 1343-46, 328; CPR, Henry III, 1232-47, 200, Henry IV, 1399-1401, 556, 1405-8, 372; CFR, Henry III, 1242, 26, no. 235; Berkshire 22 Henry II, no. 1, 52 Henry III, no. 10, 6 Edward I, no. 3, 2 Edward II, no. 14, 49 Edward III, nos. 4-5, 20 Henry VI, no. 2; *Visitation Berkshire*, 26; FA, 1:66; Eyston Deeds; *VCH, Berkshire*, vol. 4, "Catmore," 9-11, "East Hendred," 294-302; Abbey Manor belonged to Reading Abbey, Framptons to Saint-Etienne, Caen, Kings to Noyon in Normandy, then to Sheen Priory in Surrey; BRO, BMD Records for East Hendred, T/R 10.

7. Inventory of Thomas Hersey 1550, D/A1/193/162 on MF96045, Will and inventory of Agnes Hersey 1561, D/A1/76/073 on MF524, BRO; Barlowe was curate from 1550-1556 under James Brookes, DD, who was rector from 1546-1556, when Queen

The will of their son John Hersey, husbandman of East Hendred, was made on 1 April 1574 and proven in the Court of the Archdeacon. He made bequests to his brothers, Robert and Donald, and to his sisters, now married, Jane Philpott and Alice Smith, and to Donald's daughter Elizabeth. The will mentioned his deceased mother Agnes Hersey, but made no mention of his own wife. He left wages and liveries owed by his master, Adam Funnimore (Fynmore), a knight and military pensioner of Windsor Castle, who had owned property in East Hendred, to his siblings, and various dishes and platters of pewter to his sisters. To Alice he also left two coffers and a chest, a folding table, a brass pot, and two brass pans; to Jane, a pair of sheets, a brass pot, and some grain. He left his clothes to his son, John. To his brother Robert, he left twelve bushels of barley, to Donald three bushels, and one to Donald's daughter. He also made bequests to John Hersey the younger, who might have been his grandson, and to his cousin John Hersey.[8]

A second John Hersey, husbandman of East Hendred, perhaps the cousin of the first, made a will on 7 August 1584 which has many lacunae. It mentions his brother, Thomas Hersey, and his wife, Jane, whom he appointed executrix. It also mentioned Joane, possibly his mother or daughter. He made a bequest of barley to the Rev. Walter Herbert, BA 1572, MA 1578, Jesus College Oxford, who was also a witness. Herbert was rector of the church in East Hendred from 1571 until 1606. Margery Hersey died intestate in 1590; her possessions went to her daughter Joane and Joane's husband, Henry Raynald. She may have been the daughter of Okeham who married John Hersey.[9]

Mary I appointed Barlowe to replace him.

8. Will and inventory of John Hersey 1574, D/A1/76/162 on MF524, BRO; *Wills, Court of Archdeacon 1508-1652*, Berkshire Wills, East Hendred, John Hercy Sr. 1574, F404; name spelled Furinmore, Finnemore, Fynmore; patent in 1576 as Poor Knight (military pensioner) of Windsor Castle; will (1604): held property in East Hendred; Thomas Fynmore was noted in East Hendred records in 1459 and 1582.

9. Will and inventory of John Hersey 1584, D/A1/77/001 on MF524, BRO, *Wills, Court of Archdeacon 1508-1652*, Berkshire Wills, East Hendred, John Hercy Jr. 1584, G445; probated 20 September 1584; Administration of Margery Hersey 1591, D/A1/194/062, BRO; *Four Visitations of Berkshire*, 56:107); 1:97, 223 (1623,1665-66); *Visitations of Oxford*, 298 (1634); according to Burke, *Commoners*, 4:679-81, John Hercy married Margery daughter of Okeham; Okeham was a manor in Rutlandshire. Henry VIII created Thomas Cromwell, son of a tradesman, baron of Okeham in 1538 for his role in the dissolution of the monasteries; Cromwell was executed for treason in 1540, but had transferred Okeham to his children, Gregory and Elizabeth, with remainder to their son Henry, to avoid attainder; however, there was a family named Ockham in Sonning, which is probably more likely; the daughter of Okeham is also attested by HV, Berkshire 1623 and Cherry.

The Herseys of East Hendred were husbandmen, farmers, although their fortunes were beginning to increase. The family were members of the Church of England, although Agnes, the wife of Thomas, was more of a Catholic in spirit.

JOHN I HERSEY AND ANNE PAYN HERSEY OF SONNING, BERKSHIRE

Sonning is four miles northeast of Reading. From 1086 until 1224 it was part of Charlton Hundred, then became Sonning Hundred. Sonning Manor belonged to the bishops of Salisbury until 1574, when it was sold to Queen Elizabeth I. King James I gave it first to his son Henry in 1610, then to his son Charles in 1616. John I Hersey, son of John Hersey and grandson of Thomas Hersey of East Hendred, acquired land in Sonning through his marriage to the daughter, Anne, of John Payn of Sonning. In the time of King Henry II, "Payn the reeve" held lands in Sonning. There is a monumental slab in the south aisle of St. Andrew's Church in Sonning dedicated to the later Payn family. In 1560, there was a lawsuit to set aside a will between Jane Payn, daughter and heir, and her husband against Margery Payn, widow, and John Hersey and his wife, Anne Payn. Sometime before 1603, there was another lawsuit between Jane, daughter of John Payn, and her husband against Margery Payn, widow, and John and Anne Hersey over land in Sonning and a messuage called "The Falcon" in the parish of Saint Sepulchre-without-Newgate in London, located near the Old Bailey and Smithfield. There was a Falcon Inn in Falcon Court in this neighborhood at the time. John and Anne Payn Hersey had at least two children: John and Elizabeth. On 4 May 1603, there was a conveyance of land in Fillongley, Warwickshire, to John Hercy esquire of Sonning and his son and heir John, witnessed by Theodore Sadler. The grantees were either John Hersey of East Hendred and Sonning or his son John Hercy of Sonning and Winkfield. Both had sons named John. A deed signed 11 June 1604 specified conditions of payment for transfer of the estate. The parish of St. Andrew in Sonning had well-educated vicars, including William Whitlock, MA, Christ Church, Oxford (1593–99) and Robert Wright, DD, Trinity College, Cambridge (1600–22), who was chaplain to Queen Elizabeth I and King James I, and thus not a Puritan despite his Cambridge degree.[10]

10. *VCH, Berkshire*, 3:210–25, "Sonning with Earley"; the daughter of Payn is attested by Burke, HV, Oxfordshire 1634, HV, Berkshire 1665 and Cherry; TNA, C 2Eliz/C20/50 (lawsuit against John Hersey concerning cottage and land in Ruscombe, just northeast of Sonning), C 2 Eliz/S2/51, C 2/JasI/C19/87; East Sussex Record Office,

The Hercy/Hersey family became landholders in Sonning and London through marriage. The wife Anne Payn was of a prominent landholding family. Both husband and wife were parties to lawsuits. They were members of the Church of England where their vicars were educated at both Oxford and Cambridge.

JOHN II HERCY AND ANNE HARGRAVE HERCY AND JANE SADLER HERCY OF WINKFIELD, BERKSHIRE

John Hersey of East Hendred and Sonning and Anne Payn had a son, John II Hercy, who inherited the lands in Sonning and acquired Fillongley in Warwickshire. John married Anne Hargrave and they acquired land in Winkfield. They had a son, John III, who studied at Lincoln's Inn and acquired Cruchfield. Anne died in 1612, and was buried in Winkfield. After the death of Anne in 1612, the next year John Hercy married Jane, daughter of Theodore Sadler, gentleman, of Fillongley, Warwickshire. They did not have children. Theodore and Jane Sadler were descended from Henry Sadler of Warwickshire, as was Sir Ralph Sadler, secretary and chief aide to Thomas Cromwell, later privy counselor, co-secretary of state and ambassador to Scotland. Another relative, John Sadler, of nearby Stratford-on-Avon, was a close friend of William Shakespeare.[11]

Winkfield is a large parish southeast of Reading, encompassing Winkfield, Cranbourne (the birthplace of Anne Hyde), Ascot, Bracknell, and Braywood. It lies close to Cruchfield, a few miles east southeast. In the sixteenth century, it consisted of forest, meadows, and fields. The parish church of St. Mary the Virgin underwent a major renovation in 1592. The new roof is supported by four tapering oak columns and semicircular arches. One of the columns contains the Tudor crown and rose, the date 1592, and the queen's initials E. R. Cuthbert Winder was vicar of Sonning

---

ABE/74.1/12–13; inscription in floor of north aisle of St. Andrew's Church, Sonning: "Here Lyeth ye Body of WILLIAM PAYN senior of Eye in the Parish of Sonning in ye County of Oxon Gent who Departed this life the 4 day of may 1714 in the 60th year of his Age"; Cherry, *Antiquarum*; HV, Berkshire (1623), 97; T/R 127 BRO; BMD records, Sonning and Winkfield; Shakespeare Centre, DR 18/10/46/10: John Hercy of Sonning and his son and heir John (4 May 1603), probably indicates that John the son was an adult at this time; DR 18/10/46/11: deed of transfer by Lord Edward Neville and son Sir Henry to John Hercy and others (11 June 1604);the estate had originally been granted by Edward Neville, Lord Abergavenny and Sir Henry Neville, his son, possible relatives of George Neville, husband of Barbara Hercy, in Nottinghamshire.

11. TNA, DL 41/15/3; Hoyle, *estates*, 239; the marriage between John Hearsie of Fillongley and Jane Sadler took place on 8 June 1613 in Packington Magna, Warwickshire; Theodore Sadler died in 1619, Ralph Sadler in 1587, John Sadler in 1583.

from 1574 until he was appointed vicar of Winkfield in 1578, probably by John Payn. The parish birth, marriage, and death records of Winkfield mention Hercys from 1612. The parish also had educated clergy: John Gattes, MA (1550–54), and Samuel Winder, MA, son of Cuthbert (1612–36), who may have been appointed by John Hercy. There is a large twentieth-century memorial cross in the churchyard dedicated to Sir Francis Hugh George Hercy, CBE, who restored it and added a memorial plaque in St. Helen's Church of Grove, Nottinghamshire. This demonstrates the continued conscious connection of the families of Nottinghamshire and Berkshire into the twentieth century.[12]

John II Hercy esquire of Winkfield held lands in Sonning and Fillongley and was the son of John Hersey of East Hendred and Sonning. Records of the church in Winkfield document of the burial of his wife, Anne Hersey, on 28 April 1612, and of his grandchild, Collisbury, on 8 February 1617, who had been baptized in the church of Swallowfield in Charlton Hundred in 1614. The church of Winkfield belonged to the dean and chapter of Salisbury Cathedral. The Hercy family held the lease on the very large rectory in Winkfield in the seventeenth and eighteenth centuries. They may have lived in the rectory and/or leased property in Winkfield, while their son, John III, held nearby Cruchfield.[13]

John II and Anne Hercy had at least three children: John III, Elizabeth, and Margery. According to the London marriage license issued 7 April 1613, Nicholas II Hersey married Elizabeth Hersey, daughter of John Hercy of Winkfield, at the church of St. Martin Orgar in London. Church records of St. Andrew's Church in Sonning show that Nicholas and Elizabeth resided in Sonning, where the children of this marriage were baptized: Jane (1613), Elizabeth (1614), William (1616), Anthony (1618), and Abigail (1619). Abigail and another daughter died in infancy. Court documents from July 1617 called him Nicholas Hersey of Sonning. The will of John Hercy the elder in 1615 left £500 and a house in Brinckfield, Warwickshire, to Nicholas and Elizabeth according to the covenant dated 1 October 1612, but his lands in Sonning to his son John's son John "with remainder to Henry his brother."[14]

---

12. *VCH, Berkshire*, 3:210–25, "Sonning," 85–91,"Winkfield"; at the beginning of the eighteenth century Winkfield was divided into parts, some of which were held by the Nevilles; the parish was next to the old palace of the bishops of Salisbury.

13. CPR, Edward II, 1307–13, 55; *VCH, Berkshire*, vol. 3, "Winkfield," 85–91; BRO, BMD Records; Shakespeare Centre, Fillongley, DR 18/1/291: sum of £1500 (13 July 1617); Wiltshire and Swindon History Centre; CC/Chapter /163/1–22; Feet of Fines Berkshire, Easter 14 George II, 110: William Hercy held land in Winkfield worth £60.

14. DR 18/10/46/14: the probate release first names his brother as Henry, not Richard (20 June 1617).

The manor of Haywards in Sonning was formerly within the Hundred of Charlton. Two farms in Haywards, Colemans More (sixty acres) and Vyalls (forty acres), were held by John Hercy of Cruchfield by 1609. After the death of John Hercy of Sonning and Winkfield in 1615, there was a long ongoing lawsuit between John Hercy of Cruchfield, his heir, and Nicholas II Hersey, over the farms in Haywards and the lands in Fillongley. Nicholas claimed that the elder John Hercy had persuaded him to "take likinge of" and marry his daughter Elizabeth with promises of the lands when he was "in speeches of marrying with another woman with whom hee should have had a good portion." The will of John II Hercy of Winkfield noted the covenant made on 1 October 1612 with Nicholas Hercy of South Ockendon, Essex, just east of London, who married his daughter, Elizabeth, promising to give them £500 initially, another £500 for investment in land, £30 per year, and £100 to each of their first five children on reaching age twenty-one, unless Elizabeth died first and without children.[15] These were large sums and indicate the family was well-off.

The will of John II Hercy of Sonning, and Winkfield was made on 26 December 1615 and proved on 20 June 1617. Besides the £500 to Nicholas, John Hercy left his plate, jewels, and money to the children of his son John, or if John had no children, to the children of his daughter Margery Wotton. He left £500 to Margery and to her children after her death. If these legacies could not be satisfied out of his estate, he directed that they be paid out of the "rents and proffitts of all those my lands tenements and heredaments in the parish of St. Andrew near by old Burnt Bridge London called the Plough or Plough Court" which yielded £82 annually. The Plough Court was a short alley off Lombard Street in the financial district of London which was the birthplace of Alexander Pope in 1688. The two closest churches were St. Andrew Undershaft and St. Andrew Holborn. Several bridges in London were burned in fires, especially those of 1212 and 1381. If this is the correct location of the properties, he was a wealthy man. He also owned an annuity of £10 per year from property in Kent. His personal estate contained "plate 2 called 'Nuttes' with barres of silver gilt, Apostle spones, and beakers, and a ring with a diamond." He left twenty nobles and £4 each year of debt owed him to his son John's son John. He left all his other lands except those in Warwickshire and some cottages in Sonning to his son John, then to John's son John, and if he had no heirs, then to John's second son, Richard. The

---

15. TNA, C 3/276/51; *VCH, Berkshire* 3:210–25, "Sonning"; BRO, BMD Records, "Sonning"; Shakespeare Center: DR 18/10/46/14–15; Chester, *Allegations for Marriage Licences*, 2:20; *London Marriage Licences*, 670; there may have been four more sons: Daniel, Jethro, Charles, and Zidrack; the place was variously called Brinckfield, Brickfield, Bromefield; there is a Brickfield close to Fillongley.

rents from the cottages in Sonning he left for their upkeep and for annual Christmas gifts to the poor. The Warwickshire lands he left to his current wife, Jane, if she was denied her widow's right to the manor and other estates in Sonning, and then to any male heirs of Jane, and if none, then to his son John for life, then to John's son Richard. His father-in-law, Theodore Sadler of Fillongley, held £150 which was to be given to Jane, and if she had no children by him, this would go to the daughters of his son John. He authorized his son-in-law, Thomas Wotton, husband of Margery, to change the patent for selling wines in Andover, for which he was paid five marks yearly by Richard Pope, ancestor of Alexander Pope, and another, into the names of Francis and Henry Wotton for their education. He named his wife Jane and son John as his executors, with his "loving friends" Theodore Sadler and Thomas Wotton as administrators. He made mention of a cousin "William Okam," who could have been of the family of Okeham. The will was written on 26 December 1615. On 14 June 1615, John Hercy of Lincoln's Inn had released the lands of Rawlins and others to his father. On 26 December 1615, John Hercy released the lands of Rawlins and Bromefield in Warwickshire to John, son of John Hercy of Winkfield, his father. On 23 July 1617, the personal estate of John Hercy of Fillongley was released with inventory and list of debts.[16]

The Hercy family in Sonning and Winkfield had become firmly established as gentry, as esquires with expanded landed wealth in Berkshire, Warwickshire, and London. They showed genuine concern for their daughters and granddaughters in their wills. They were members of the mainline Church of England.

JOHN III HERCY AND URSULA LOVELACE HERCY OF CRUCHFIELD, BERKSHIRE

The Hundred of Bray in Berkshire lies on the Thames, within Windsor Forest, between London and Reading. Cruchfield was originally a royal vaccary or dairy farm of Bray at least from 1220, but later became an independent manor. The name Cruchfield derives from "Cross Field," the cross probably a boundary marker. Cruchfield was never itself a parish, nor did it have a church. It lies within the parish of Bray, and on the border of the parish of Winkfield. There are three churches closeby: Winkfield is two miles from

---

16. DR 18/10/46/15–16: releases by John Hercy of Lincoln's Inn to John Hercy of Winkfield (15 has error calling him son of Henry Hercy of Winkfield); DR 18/10/46/13: release of estate of late John Hercy of Fillongley, husband of Jane Sadler; (23 July 1617); DR 18/10/46/14: will of John Hercy, £500 to Nicholas .

Cruchfield Manor and there was a road. Warfield was also two miles away and Bray four and a half, but there were only dirt tracks to both. Thus, it is logical that births, marriages, and deaths for Cruchfield were performed and registered at Winkfield. There are records of John III Hercy and his descendants at Cruchfield from 1608 until 1891.[17]

The litigation with Nicholas continued after the death of John II Hercy of Sonning and Winkfield, now complicated by the interests of his widow. In 1616, there was a suit in Chancery, equity side, between John Hercy of Lincoln's Inn and Nicholas Hercy of Sonning against Theodore Sadler and Jane, widow of John Hercy, over the lands in Sonning and Fillongley. Nicholas had claimed that John Hercy the elder had settled them on his daughter, Elizabeth Hercy, and used this to persuade Nicholas to marry Elizabeth. On 3 and 7 July 1617, articles were signed with sums due between John Hercy of Lincoln's Inn and Nicholas Hercy of Sonning on one side, and Theodore Sadler of Fillongley and Jane, widow of John Hercy, on the other. On 13 July 1617, John Hercy of Lincoln's Inn, esquire, sent a bond to Theodore Sadler of Fillongley, in the penal sum of £1500 "to keep covenants in an indenture of even date." Two years later, on 13 June 1619, a deed was signed concerning the settlement of lands among Nicholas and Elizabeth Hercy of Sonning, Theodore Sadler and Jane Sadler Hercy, and John Hercy of Lincoln's Inn, giving Jane use of the lands for life. There was a final concord in September between Theodore Sadler and John and Elizabeth Hercy for the Fillongley lands at £100. On 19 October 1626, there was a grant by William Dugdale, the historian, of a cottage and nine acres to the widow, Jane Hercy, witnessed by Theodore Sadler. On 21 October 1626, John III Hercy of Lincoln's Inn, executor of his father, John II Hercy, sent a receipt for money owed.[18]

17. VCH, *Berkshire* vol. 3, "Bray"; 100–107; Cherry, *Antiquarum*.

18. Fillongley; Shakespeare Centre Library and Archive, DR 18/1/291: bond of £1500; DR 18/10/46/17–18: articles between John Hercy of Lincoln's Inn and Nicholas Hercy of Sonning with Theodore Sadler and Jane, widow of John Hercy, concerning estate and debts (3 July 1617); DR 18/10/46/19 (13 June 1619); DR 18/10/46/21–22: final catalogue of contents (Michaelmas 1619); DR 18/10/46/28: Dugdale to Jane, 19 October 1626; Hercy v. Hercy, C 3/276/51; *London Marriage Licences*, 670; (1828), vol. 2, 20; Shakespeare Centre, DR 18/10/46/14–16, 29–31, 33–45, 47–48; on 28 January 1657, Jane Hercy of Fillongley granted lands to her "son" John at Fillongley, on 3 February, John Hercy signed a "deed to make a tenant for sale" to William Sadler of London on 24 November 1658, John Hercy made a grant settling the jointure of Jane Hercy, on the same day, Jane signed a release of four properties in Fillongley, two days later, John Hercy signed a lease to Jane, his daughter, and her trustees, three days after that, John Hercy signed a marriage settlement and deed of jointure with his wife Katherine, with John Hercy, gentleman, as trustee, at Fillongley, on 21 March 1662, John Hercy leased land and sold a house in Fillongley, the final concord was filed at Easter 1663,

PART II | ENGLAND

John III Hercy, esquire, of Winkfield and Cruchfield, son of John II Hercy of Sonning and Winkfield, lived from 1579 to 1648. He was seised of Cruchfield in 1608. He matriculated at Christ Church, Oxford, in February 1598, received his BA on 7 July 1600, entered Lincoln's Inn and became a barrister in 1607. John Hercy was paid £97 for legal work in 1602, preparing evidence for queen's counsel. On 6 May 1603, he wrote to the dean and chapter concerning lease of the Chichester lands in Oxfordshire and Buckinghamshire. This was most probably the John Hercy who was the solicitor of Gilbert earl of Shrewsbury. John III Hercy married Ursula Lovelace, daughter of Richard and Anne Ward Lovelace and sister of Sir Richard Lovelace, who was sheriff of Berkshire in 1610–11 and of Oxfordshire in 1626–27, member of parliament for Berkshire for many years, and was made lord of Hurley by King Charles I in 1627, indicating that he was not a Puritan. His son, Francis Lovelace, had a son William, who married Mary Neville, sister of Sir Edward Neville, baronet of Grove and descendant of the Hercy family of Nottinghamshire. This demonstrated continued contact between the Hercys of Nottinghamshire and of Berkshire. In 1652, their son, John Lovelace, and others bought the manor of Winkfield. Another John Lovelace was governor of the colonies of New York and New Jersey from 1708 until his death in 1709.[19]

John and Ursula Hercy had three sons, John, Richard, and Rudolph, and three daughters, Anne, Margaret, and Elizabeth. In 1609, John Hercy settled on his wife Ursula and son John the two farms which he held in the manor of Haywards in Sonning, Berkshire, which later became the subject of litigation. In 1622, he was involved in a property case concerning the chantry and chantry house of East Hendred and the manor of Arches. In 1623, John Hercy and John Blacknall were in possession of these chantry lands, which John Hercy settled on himself and his sons in 1625. In October 1626, John Hercy of Lincoln's Inn received money owed to the estate of his father by Sir Henry Stonor, head of the recusant Stonor family of Blount's Court, Oxfordshire. The sum was paid by Sir Henry's widow, since he had died the previous year. Blount's Court is four miles from Reading

---

in November 1666, there was a "deed to declare the uses of a recovery" between John Hercy and the Sadlers; *VCH, Berkshire*, vol. 3, "Winkfield"; 85–91.

19. Attested by Burke, HV, Berkshire 1623 (as the son of Anne Hargrave), HV, Oxfordshire 1634, Cherry, *Antiquarum*; Ursula Lovelace is attested by Burke, HV, Berkshire 1623 and 1665, HV, Oxfordshire 1634 and Cherry; Kerry, *History and Antiquities*, 9–11, 18, 173; *Alumni Oxoniensis*, 697; Royal Berkshire History, "Richard Lovelace" and "John Lovelace"; *VCH, Berkshire*, 3:85–91; Edward and Mary were great-grandchildren of Hercy Neville, who was the grandson of Barbara Hercy Neville.

and adjacent to Sonning Common. Ursula Lovelace Hercy died in 1634; John III Hercy died in 1648.[20]

The will of John III Hercy of Cruchfield, son of John II Hercy of Winkfield, was probated on 24 April 1648. He left his estate to his daughters, Anne Hercy and Elizabeth Hercy, with "relict Susan renouncing." The use of the Hercy surname for the two daughters suggests that they were not married at this time; Margaret was married in 1637 and was not mentioned. He had probably given her a marriage portion at the time of her marriage. "Relict" literally means "woman left behind" and was often used for a widow. The identity of Susan is unclear. She might have been a daughter who was married and widowed, but had enough property of her own. The will mentioned the daughters of his sisters, Elizabeth and Margery, who had predeceased him.[21]

The son of John and Ursula Hercy, John IV Hercy, esquire, of Cruchfield, was born in 1607. In the family tradition, he studied law at Lincoln's Inn. According to the marriage license issued 7 August 1633, he married Mary, daughter of the Honorable Edward Aungier, esquire, of Cambridge and Gray's Inn, the younger son of Lord Aungier of All Hallows Barking. Their children were baptized at Winkfield: John (1634, died 1635), John (1635, died 1643), Mary (1638, died 1644), Thomas (1640, died 1667), and Elizabeth (1645, died 1648). Other children were Susan (died 1648), Lovelace (ca. 1650), Mary (1657, died 1668), and Edward and John (died 1661). Mary Aungier Hersey died on 29 April 1665 and was buried at Winkfield. Her executor was John Aungier.[22]

Thus, by the early seventeenth century the Hercys of Berkshire had gained wealth and gentility, had come to hold the important manor of Cruchfield, and had risen to prominence in the legal profession. They were members of the Church of England.

20. *Alumni Oxoniensis*, 697; *VCH*, Berkshire 3:92, 101, 218; TNA, SP 46/88/fo115; C 276/51; Cherry, *Antiquarum*, vol. 1; on 1 May 1611, King James I granted Wi(n)ckfield and adjoining lands to Henry Lovelace; Exchange Dep. East, 21 James I, no. 6; *VCH, Berkshire*, 4:294–302, "East Hendred" and 9–11, "Catmore"; Kerry, *History*, 10, 109–111; receipt to the Stonor family of Blount's Court, Oxfordshire, for debt of Sir Henry Stonor; State Papers Domestic: SP 46/88/fo 115.

21. Shakespeare Centre, DR 18/10/46/14–16; *Abstracts Probate Acts Canterbury*, 342; *Notes and Queries*, 2:441.

22. Chester, *Allegations for Marriage Licences*, 2:213; *London Marriage Licences*, vol. 2, 213; BRO: BMD Records, Winkfield; PCC Abstracts, 342, 65 Essex, anno 1648; HV, Berkshire 1665 made Thomas the heir at age twenty-three on 30 March 1665, which may have been his mother's death; Thomas died within two years and was succeeded by Lovelace.

PART II | ENGLAND

READING, BERKSHIRE: ST. GILES CHURCH

Reading is adjacent to Sonning on the northeast and to Charlton Hundred, including Shinfield and Swallowfield, on the south. Reading is about eight miles west of Cruchfield. The parish of St. Giles lies in the southern part of the city of Reading, next to Charlton Hundred. St. Giles was founded in the twelfth century and given to Reading Abbey in 1191 by Pope Clement III. After the dissolution of Reading Abbey in 1539, St. Giles was under the patronage of the crown. Many of the rectors of St. Giles were graduates of Oxford. William Burton, MA New College Oxford, who served from 1591, had ministered in Norwich and written about Calvinism and Puritanism. He was followed by John Dennison, MA, DD Balliol, Oxford, rector of St. Giles from 1612 to 1614, and of nearby St. Mary's from 1614 to 1629, who was domestic chaplain to George duke of Buckingham and chaplain to King James I, indicating that he was not a Puritan. Samuel Radcliffe, MA, BD Oxford, was rector from 1614 to 1617. Hugh Dicus, MA, BD Brasenose College, Oxford, was rector from 1617 to 1648. The fact that he was able to serve during the time of Archbishop Laud in the reign of Charles I shows that he was not a Puritan. Both Radcliffe and Dicus were sequestered by Parliament in 1646 and 1647 respectively, which indicates that they were high-church Anglicans and royalists.

Reading was part of the diocese of Salisbury. The bishops of Salisbury, with one exception, were Oxford graduates. Henry Cotton, MA, DD Magdalene, was bishop from 1598 to 1615. Robert Abbot, MA, BD, DD Balliol, was Regius Professor of Divinity, chaplain to James I, and bishop from 1615 to his death in 1618. The exception was Martin Fotherby, MA, BD, DD Trinity College, Cambridge, a Puritan stronghold at the time, who was bishop from 1618 to 1620. He did not, however, make any appointments at St. Giles. John Davenport, bishop from 1621 to 1641, under Archbishop Laud and King Charles I, was not a Puritan. Under King James I, many Church of England parishes were tolerant of Puritans who were conforming members. This changed when Charles I succeeded his father in 1627. During the civil war, a royal garrison was stationed in St. Giles, and the tower of the church was damaged in 1643. Two of its rectors were sequestered in 1646 and 1647 for being high-church and royalist. St. Giles was not a Puritan parish.

NATHANIEL HERSEY AND ANNE KENTON HERSEY

Nathaniel Hersey was a cooper in Reading and listed as a warden in the London Ward in 1600. He was married to Anne Kenton, born in Reading in

1576. They had two sons, William, who was baptized at St. Giles on 22 August 1596 and Thomas, baptized there on 20 January 1599. Nathaniel and Anne, and their sons William and Thomas, were named in the will of her father, Robert Kenton, baker of Reading, probated 18 June 1611. Nathaniel was a leader of the London Guard in Reading in 1600. He was listed as a juror in October 1623 for testing weights and measures. In March 1624, he was on a list of recognizances for £10. On 2 September 1625, he was a witness in a defamation case heard by the mayor. In March 1625 he was paid 15s. 6d. for work and carriage at Terton. In May 1626 he was included in a list of persons who were "unlicensed, forbidden and bounde not to keep Alehouse." He was appointed skavinger, cleaner of markets and streets, in 1624, 1625, and 1626, for which in 1624 he was paid £11, in 1625, £12, and in 1626, £14. This was a position for which men competed, since it provided a good income and also entitled them to anything found of value. Probably he did not do the work himself, but hired laborers. On 24 December 1628, he was one of five complainants about garbage left "at the grates by the Hallowe Brooke." On 25 February 1629, he was on the list of recognizances for the observation of Lent for £10. Nathaniel was buried in St. Giles parish on 27 December 1629 and his will was probated in the court of the archdeacon on 6 April 1630. In his will, made 3 November 1629, he commended his soul to God and his body to be buried at St. Giles. He left all his shop tools to his son William, and his clothes, with the exception of his best hat and cloak, to his son Thomas. The rest of his goods he left to his wife, Anne, whom he appointed sole executor, with his friend Thomas Hatton of Reading paid twelve pence to be overseer. His widow had a servant in 1632 named Mary Hunt. Anne Hersey died and was buried in St. Giles on 13 May 1635.[23]

Nathaniel Hersey was a cooper and a recognized member of the community as warden, juror, and leader of the London Guard. The Hersey family were members of St. Giles Church in Reading which was high-church Anglican.

---

23. BRO, parish register of St. Giles, Reading; a John Hersey was baptized in St. Giles Church, Reading, in 1569, who could have been the father of Nathaniel; Guilding, *Reading Records*, 1:460, 2:135, 205, 221–23, 248, 268–69, 284, 298, 321–22, 443, 454; 3:107: in 1632, Mary Hunt had been an apprentice for eight years and a servant for five and was chosen to cast lots for St. Giles Parish on Good Friday; BRO, D/A1/79/043a&b on MF526: will of Nathaniel Hersey.

PART II | ENGLAND

WILLIAM HERSEY AND MARGARET GARVES HERSEY AND ELIZABETH CROADE HERSEY

From the Reformation up to this point all the Hercy/Hersey family were members of the Church of England. William was baptized and married in St. Giles Church, as were the children of his first marriage, who, in turn, had their children baptized in the church. But something happened after the death of William's first wife. He married again, a woman who was probably already a Puritan, and after this marriage he became a Puritan. He left Berkshire and moved for a brief time to East Anglia. In 1635, they joined a group of fellow Puritans who left England and sailed to the Massachusetts Bay Colony. There William Hersey became the progenitor of all the Herseys in the colony and the later United States.

William Hersey married Margaret Garves (or Graves) at St. Giles on 1 January 1616. They had three children, all baptized at St. Giles: Gregory (19 November 1616), Nathaniel (13 January 1618), and Cecily (7 January 1619, died 7 December 1619). In 1622 William was sworn in as a guard of the London Ward of Reading and a juror. In February 1622, William signed a recognizance for £10 owed to the king for testifying. In March 1623 he was licensed as a victualler with John Molyns for which he paid £10. On 13 October 1623, as warden of London Ward, William was present officially at the Lawday. On 8 March 1624, William stated that Philip Hodges the tailor had been lodging at his house since midsummer, for which he paid him a groat each week. The context was a complaint by the freemen tailors' guild that strangers were working as tailors in Reading. After the death of his first wife in 1631, William married Elizabeth Croade (born about 1610) of East Anglia. They had six children, the first two born in England in 1632 and 1634, the others in the Massachusetts Bay Colony. William Hersey was appointed as a juror in Reading on 6 May 1633, which term lasted until the Wednesday after St. Bartholemew's Day, 24 August. Thus, it is unlikely that he and his family moved to Norfolk much before 1634 or 1635. The emigration from England was in 1635. At some point between 1631 and 1635 William became a Puritan.[24]

William's brother Thomas Hersey married Anne Hill in April 1618 and had eight children, baptized at St. Giles between 1618 and 1633, two of whom died in infancy. In 1630, a complaint was heard before the mayor that a stranger with many children was at Thomas Hersey's house. Thomas

---

24. BRO, parish register of St. Giles, Reading; Guilding, *Reading Records*, 2:103, 114, 118, 141, 178, 3:172; William's mother died in Reading in May 1635; it has been suggested, without proof, that Elizabeth was from Thrandeston, Suffolk, near the Norfolk border.

died in 1653. The parish records include Hersey grandchildren and their descendants at least until 1738, indicating that Thomas's branch of the family remained in the Church of England.[25]

In 1641, after Archbishop Laud was arrested, the Long Parliament, controlled by Puritans, required that every adult over eighteen swear the protestation oath to maintain and defend, with their lives, power, and estates, "the true reformed Protestant Religion, Expressed in the Doctrines of the Church of England, against all Popery and Popish Innovations." Gregory, eldest son of William, Thomas, and his son William, took the oath at St. Giles, which indicates that they were neither high-church Laudians nor radical Puritans. Gregory Hersey was named a juror in 1645, 1647, and 1648. He was an assistant alderman and named temporary assistant in counsel to the court on 6 January 1646. Gregory married Prudence and had two daughters baptized at St. Giles, Elizabeth (1641) and Marie (1644). He then moved to Sonning where more children were born and baptized: Prudence (1650), John and Constance (1651, probably twins), Robert (1654), Thomas (1656), and Gregory (1659). Constance and John were buried in November and December 1657, possibly dying of the plague.[26]

William Hersey was a successful yeoman in Reading, with a large and stable family and community responsibilities. In a time of religious tension, his second wife, Elizabeth Croade Hersey, appears to have had a major influence on William, causing him to leave his city of Reading and the Anglican church. Together they would found a new family in a new world with a new Puritan religion.

THE PURITAN MOVEMENT

The word "puritan" was first used in a pejorative sense, as an insult connoting hypocrisy and pharisaic self-righteousness. The Puritans called themselves "the godly." The term first appeared early in the reign of Elizabeth I. Puritans saw the reformation under Edward VI as a mere first step with a long way to go. This was directly opposed to the Elizabethan settlement which sought to end further reformation. Puritans were known for their focus on predestination, strict observance of the sabbath, condemnation of others who did not live as they did, and for their iconoclasm. They preferred

---

25. Guilding, *Reading Records*, 3:15, 89, 425, which notes that his son, Thomas, at age twelve was apprenticed to a baker; BRO, parish register of St. Giles, Reading.

26. BRO, parish register of St. Giles, Reading; *Protestation Returns* (1641); Guilding, *Reading Records*, 4:169, 232, 274; Shrewsbury, *History of Bubonic Plague*, 443: suggests plague or possibly influenza were rampant that year.

the 1560 Geneva Bible, with its Calvinist annotations, and followed it literally. Most remained within the Church of England for a time. Trouble arose when they attempted to dominate their parish communities and make them into an eschatological utopian ideal. Puritan ministers denied communion to those not deemed among the "godly." Much of their agenda concerned public mores and manners, criticizing the words and acts of their neighbors. Drunkenness and sexual relations outside marriage were regarded as major sins which they believed they had the duty to denounce and punish. They attempted to suppress all recreation and pleasure-giving activities on the sabbath, such as fairs, theater, sports, music, and dance. Puritans clashed with the established church over wearing of vestments, ritual, music, and art in church. When the bishop of London in 1566 ordered the wearing of vestments and suspended ministers who refused, a secret separatist Puritan group was formed, though it was discovered and disbanded in 1567. That year Philip II of Spain went after the Calvinists in the Netherlands, executing more than a thousand for heresy. In England in 1571, an attempt was made to suppress Puritanism through examination of ministers by an ecclesiastical commission and requiring them to subscribe to the *Book of Common Prayer*. In the 1580s, groups of Puritan ministers gathered and condemned other ministers whom they deemed "ungodly." In 1584, the Puritan Emmanuel College was chartered at Cambridge to train Puritan ministers. There were many educated Puritans in the House of Commons, the universities, and even in the queen's council. But by 1590, those Puritans with political power had died. Puritans turned inward toward pietism and evangelism, although they also published "complaints" against members of the established church. All the works of Jean Calvin had been translated and published in England by 1600. Yet at that time Puritans were still a small minority, despised by many. Shakespeare called a Puritan a "dog" and an "ass."[27] Puritans took the Bible literally and supported a Presbyterian form of church order and government which was a continuing threat to the monarchy. In some areas, such as East Anglia, where the ministers and leading lay people were all Puritan, the parish or town itself became Puritan.

    King James I spent his first thirty-six years in Scotland. In 1560, the Scots Parliament had declared the land Protestant. In 1581, the general assembly of the Scottish kirk abolished bishops. By 1584, James took charge and reinstated bishops. All his life he believed strongly in the divine right of monarchy as supported by a church ruled by bishops and that his own position as king would be threatened if bishops were abolished. In 1590, he married Anna of Denmark, a convert to Catholicism, but appointed Protestant

---

27. *Twelfth Night* (1601), Act II, sc. iii.

tutors for his sons to counteract her influence. In Scotland he contained Catholic lords on one side and Presbyterians on the other, and maintained a middle way which kept the peace. When he became king of England after Elizabeth's death, because of his Protestant upbringing in Scotland, English Puritans thought they could get him to change the liturgy and church order, which he refused to do. King James I called a Puritan "a protestant strayed out of his wits."[28] In 1604 he ordered a new translation of the Bible, enlisting the best scholars of Greek and Hebrew in the universities. He was tolerant of Catholics until the Gunpowder Plot of 1605. Then in 1606 he required an oath of allegiance which was aimed mainly at Catholics. He began the "plantation" of Ulster with Protestant Scottish and English settlers in 1609, giving them 40 percent of the land, with 20 percent more for their schools and churches, leaving only 40 percent for the Catholic Irish who already lived there. He also attempted, but failed, to get the Catholic Irish of the south of Ireland to join the Church of England. In 1618 he issued a *Declaration of Sports* against the Puritans, affirming the right to recreation on the sabbath. Yet he planned a Catholic marriage for his son, Henry, who died in 1612, and did marry his son Charles to the Catholic Henriette Marie, sister of King Louis XIII of France, in 1624. But in 1613, he married his daughter, Elizabeth, to the Protestant elector palatine Friedrich V, who became king of Bohemia. King James was drawn into the Thirty Years War by the deposition of his son-in-law as king of Bohemia by Spain and Austria. But for the most part James maintained peace through negotiation. By 1624, the crown was bankrupt and there was a great national depression. James I died in March 1625. His funeral was the last lavish state funeral until that of Oliver Cromwell in 1658.

James I was succeeded by his son Charles I. King Charles lacked his father's political skills for maintaining balance and keeping peace in the country and in the church. He appointed Buckingham chancellor of Cambridge in 1626, who tried to purge the university of Calvinist theology. Whereas James had appointed many Calvinist bishops, Charles replaced them with high-church anti-Calvinists. He appointed William Laud bishop of London in 1628 and archbishop of Canterbury in 1633. The king had Archbishop Laud advise him as to the merits of the clergy; Laud labeled each one orthodox or Puritan. King Charles exalted the position of clergy and bishops, and appointed both as justices of the peace. He opposed Sabbatarianism and reissued the *Book of Sports* in 1633. King Charles I desired ecclesial and liturgical uniformity, and tried to bring them about by force. He reintroduced altars, mandated their placement at the east end of churches,

28. Porter, *Puritanism*, 7.

and reintroduced communion rails. The implementation of the changes was enforced on the parish level, but at different speeds in different counties; in London it happened in 1635. Puritans and others resisted the changes. Even the moderate Puritans who were comfortable within the Church of England were radicalized and pushed out. Those Puritans who could not find a place in the Carolingian church, chose to emigrate to the Massachusetts Bay Colony or the Netherlands. The Elizabethan settlement was abolished by Charles and Laud in the name of high-church uniformity, which led to the radicalization and separation of the Puritans, and ultimately to civil war.[29]

The power and authority of bishops and kings were very much intertwined at the time; their adversaries sought to shift authority and power to church congregations and to Parliament. In the short term, the latter won, but at the price of civil war. Archbishop Laud was deposed in 1640, taken to the Tower, and beheaded for treason in 1645, as was King Charles I in 1649. Civil war ensued and the parliamentarians were victorious. After the Cromwellian interregnum, the Stuart monarchy was restored in 1660 with King Charles II. His chancellor was Earl Edward Hyde. King Charles died and was succeeded by his brother, King James II, who was Catholic. King James II was deposed in 1688 in favor of his daughter Queen Mary and her husband, William of Orange, who were Protestant. Queens Mary and Anne were distantly related to the Hercy family.

PURITAN MIGRATION TO THE MASSACHUSETTS BAY COLONY

The situation for the Puritans in England was especially difficult in the decade between 1630 to 1640. King Charles I ruled without Parliament. He tried to be an absolute monarch, but had a problem raising revenues without Parliament, which had the exclusive authority to tax. In 1634 the king circumvented the problem by raising "ship money" from the coastal shires; in 1635, he made this a national levy, which infuriated the people. There were also failed harvests, inflated food prices, food riots, anti-enclosure riots, economic depression, unemployment, and disease during the 1630s.[30]

---

29. Charles I ordered a prayer book, very similar to the English *Book of Common Prayer*, to be used in Scotland in 1637; the people rebelled and abolished bishops and reestablished Presbyterianism; Charles could not abide abolition of bishops because he believed it threatened the monarchy itself; in August 1638, his commander issued a call to muster on Castle Hill in Nottingham and the civil war began, dragging on for years, with King Charles ultimately losing; Marshall, *Reformation*, 198–211.

30. Fischer, *Albion's Seed*, 16.

On the religious front, King Charles I himself was a high-church Anglican; his queen, Henriette Marie of France, was openly Catholic. There were many counter-Reformation Catholics in the royal court. William Laud, archbishop of Canterbury from 1633 to 1640, with the king's support, tried to establish high-church uniformity within the English church by removing Puritan bishops, ministers, theologians, and preachers.

During the decade 1630 to 1640, 639 shiploads of eighty thousand Puritans left England for exile; twenty-one thousand of them went to the Massachusetts Bay Colony on two hundred ships. The primary reason people emigrated to Massachusetts was religious: to build a "Bible Commonwealth," focusing on the spiritual welfare of their children and families. The purpose of the majority was to live and raise their children in a Puritan environment, free from the "sinfulness" of the old world. Unlike other English colonies, the Massachusetts Bay Colony only accepted colonists of good character; those few who did not behave were sent back England or to other colonies. These Puritans were an extraordinary group: "a people of substance, character, and deep personal piety." Very few of the emigrants were of the nobility, and only 11 percent were gentry. The majority were middle- and lower-class, yeomen, artisans, craftspersons, and merchants. Most came from towns; few were farmers. The people were literate and Bible readers; their literacy rate was two-thirds, twice that of England at the time. There were 129 ministers and lawyers trained at Cambridge University at Emmanuel, Trinity, and Magdalene Colleges. The religious and civil leaders of the new towns were generally ministers and their wives. Most embarked as families, mature adults with children, and paid for their passage, often by indenture, which cost £50–80 for a family of six. At the time yeomen could earn £40–£60 annually; husbandmen £20, with £3 to £4 left after expenses. They were godly in their living and homogeneous in their faith, which included the principle of serving and helping their neighbors.[31]

The Puritan colonists came from many counties of England, but mostly from the southeast. The majority were from East Anglia, which included the counties of Norfolk, Suffolk, Essex, and Sussex. At this time the people of East Anglia were skilled workers and therefore more independent than the lower classes elsewhere. They also had the most advanced agricultural techniques in England. East Anglia was the most urban and least feudal region in England, a thriving center of textile manufacture and export. However, the trade in textiles was disrupted by wars with France and Spain between 1625 and 1630, causing unemployment and poverty. There was also hunger

31. Fischer, *Albion's Seed*, 16–18, 20, 25–28, 30–31, 39, 42; very few came as servants, which were discouraged; fewer than 5 percent were unskilled laborers and servants; Puritans generally had a negative attitude toward the underclasses.

caused by crop failures in 1629. East Anglia had a long-standing tradition of rebellion against the aristocracy and the established church. During the reign of Queen Mary I, the greatest number of Protestants burned at stake for heresy, 225 out of 273, were from East Anglia. Under Queen Elizabeth I, the majority of Puritans and Puritan ministers were in East Anglia. The center of opposition to King Charles I was in East Anglia.[32]

The greater part of the Puritan community with which William Hersey and his family migrated in 1635 were from Hingham, Norfolk, and gave the name Hingham to their town in the Massachusetts Bay Colony. Some emigrants also came from the counties of Warwickshire, Nottinghamshire, and Berkshire, where Herseys had lived for centuries. Many town names in Massachusetts reflect the colonists' place of origin in England: such as Reading (Berkshire), Boston (Lincolnshire), Plymouth (Devon), and Hingham (Norfolk).

Hingham, Norfolk, was the main town of the deanery. Its church of St. Andrew was ancient and well-endowed, and had previously had a college of chantry priests. In January 1605, a radical Puritan, Robert Peck, MA Magdalene College, Cambridge, became rector. In response to the Laudian changes, he pulled down the communion rails and set the altar a foot lower than the church. For this he was prosecuted by Bishop Wren and had to leave the country. He took most of his congregation with him. The "great migration" from Hingham was a major catastrophic event for the town. Those who left, "sold their possessions for half their value." Those who stayed petitioned Parliament for aid after losing all the upper middle-class citizens. After the bishop had been deposed, Peck returned to England in 1646 and remained rector until his death in 1656.[33]

Peter Hobart was born in Hingham, Norfolk in 1604. His Puritan family dedicated him to the ministry. He was a diligent student and attended Magdalene College, Cambridge, where took his BA in 1625 and MA in 1629. He was a teacher and preacher in Norfolk. His parents and siblings emigrated to Massachusetts in 1633. Peter, his wife and four children joined the main Hingham migration, arriving on 8 June 1635. Offered several positions, he chose to follow his father to the village founded at Bare Cove,

---

32. Fischer, *Albion's Seed*, 31–38, 42–43, 46–47; in 1630, Norwich was the second largest city in England and East Anglia was the most urban and densely populated part of England for centuries; it was the center of trade with the Low Countries and many Flemish weavers settled there and increased the quality of East Anglian textiles, while maintaining contacts with the Calvinist Protestantism at home; East Anglia had been a center of Lollardy in the fifteenth century, was the center of rebellion against Charles I and of parliamentarians in the civil war.

33. Mather, *Magnalia Christi*, 286, 497–501, 587.

which he renamed Hingham. He established the church there and was its pastor until his death in 1679. His flock back in Haverhill, Norfolk, wrote asking him to return to them, but he did not receive the letters. Throughout his life he loved learning and valued education for his many children. He preached well-prepared sermons and delighted in listening to the sermons of others. He deplored profanity and drunkenness, vanity and pride. Most adults in the first generation became church members. This involved standing before the elders and being examined on fidelity to Calvinist doctrines, such as original sin and predestination, living a godly life, and demonstrating a personal conversion experience. There were more women members than men.[34]

This was the world into which William Hersey and his wife Elizabeth with their two small children decided to venture. They boarded the ship which reached Massachusetts in June 1635. They were part of the congregation from Hingham, Norfolk, and settled in Hingham, Massachusetts, with Peter Hobart. William Hersey became a leader in this community. He quickly paid off his indenture, became a freeman in 1638 and a selectman of Hingham. He and Elizabeth had four more children. They and their six children became the ancestors of all the Herseys in North America.[35]

Relatives of the Nottinghamshire Hercys also emigrated. John I Denman of Retford, Nottinghamshire, was born in 1591 and was probably the grandson of Nicholas Denman and Anne Hercy. John I Denman married Judith Stoughton, daughter of the Rev. Thomas Stoughton, son of Henry de Stoughton of Stoughton Hall in Surrey. Their son John II was born in January 1621 and daughter Mary in December 1621. John I Denman died, Judith remarried, had another son, and was widowed again. In September 1634, she and the three children boarded the ship *Dorset* and sailed from Gravesend, arriving in Boston in 1635. They settled in Salem. She had two brothers who had arrived in 1633. One was a merchant and went to Connecticut. The other, Israel Stoughton, returned to England, where he died in 1642. He bequeathed three hundred acres of land in Dorchester to Harvard College. His son, William Stoughton, was lieutenant governor of Massachusetts and donated the funds to build Stoughton Hall at Harvard. His portrait is in Memorial Hall at Harvard. John II Denman's son John III Denman, went to Long Island, where he purchased land from the Native Americans.

---

34. Mather, *Magnalia Christi*, 497–501; Fischer, *Albion's Seed*, 21.

35. Lincoln, *History of Hingham*; F. C. Hersey, *Record Hersey Family*; S. Hersey, *Hersey Family*; Loring, *Descendants of William Hersey*.

The Talbot Earls of Shrewsbury and the Hercys

THE TALBOT AND HERCY families were connected by marriage and by blood, and also as neighbors and lords and employers. In the early fifteenth century, Sir Hugh IV Hercy had married Elizabeth Leek, daughter of Sir Simon Leek and Joane Talbot. His grandson, Humphrey I Hercy, married Joan Stanhope, granddaughter of Elizabeth Talbot and Sir John Stanhope. The second wife of George Talbot, sixth earl of Shrewsbury, was Elizabeth Hardwick, whose mother was another Elizabeth Leek.[1]

The Talbot family was originally from Cleuville in Eastern Normandy. Richard Talbot, son of Guillaume or Hugues Talbot, fought with William the Conqueror and the knights of Hercé, Arques and Hériz at Hastings. The Talbots were closely related to the Gournay family; William Talbot married the sister of Hugh de Gournay. The Gournays played a major role in the Hercy fief of Pillerton in Warwickshire. In 1166 Richard Talbot held three fees of Giffard in Buckinghamshire. His grandson married Aline Basset, and their grandson married Sarah de Beauchamp of Worcestershire, sister of the earl of Warwick. Their son, Gilbert, was chamberlain to King Edward III, who created him Baron Talbot in 1332. Their great-grandson, Richard Talbot, married Baroness Ankaret LeStrange. Their son, John Lord Talbot, was created earl of Shrewsbury on 20 May 1442. He married first Mathilde Neville and second Margaret Beauchamp.[2]

THE NOTTINGHAMSHIRE HERCYS AND THE TALBOT EARLS OF SHREWSBURY

Only about twenty-five miles from Grove were the town and manor of Sheffield, which belonged to the earls of Shrewsbury. Queen Elizabeth I chose

---

1. *Visitations of North*, 13–14; *Notes and Queries* 2:283.

2. RBE, 1:284, 312; *Testa de Nevill* 1:261; CFR, Henry III, 1223–24, 8, no. 421; CPE, 13:1, 616.

George Talbot, sixth earl of Shrewsbury, to imprison her cousin and rival for the throne, Mary Queen of Scots, from 26 January 1568 until 11 August 1586. Much of this time Mary was held at Sheffield. This placed a severe strain on the earl's finances and caused the breakup of his marriage to Bess of Hardwick.

Documents from the reign of Henry VIII connect the two families. The same documents noted the appointments of George, fourth earl of Shrewsbury, and Humphrey I Hercy as commissioners of the peace for Nottinghamshire in February and July 1511, November 1511, March and October 1512, February, July, and October 1514. In February 1526, March 1532, April 1537, and July 1538, Earl George of Shrewsbury and John Hercy were together appointed commissioners of the peace for Nottinghamshire on the same dates and in the same documents.[3]

Earl George of Shrewsbury had fought for the king against the Catholic Pilgrimage of Grace in 1536. On 6 October 1537, Henry VIII granted him the manor and lordship of East Retford. When the earl made his will in 1537, he used the traditional Catholic terminology and made bequests for a thousand masses, plus three daily for twenty years, 40s. each to three charterhouses, £1 each to several friaries in Nottinghamshire and Derbyshire, as well as vestments to Worksop Priory. He died in 1538, and by the time his will was probated in 1539, all of these houses and monasteries had been dissolved. He was succeeded by his son Francis, about whom King Henry VIII wrote: "of great power, young and lusty, and little wit and no experience."[4]

Sir John Hercy wrote a letter to the earl of Shrewsbury, who was privy counselor, sending him a gift of fat swans from Grove. The swan was the personal badge of King Henry IV and of Edward, prince of Wales, son of King Henry VI. Gifts of swans had been used by the Lancastrian Queen Margaret to strengthen the position of her son. Sir John's letter informed the earl of the presence of large numbers of gypsies, whom he called Egyptians, in the area of Scarsdale, who refused to serve in the wars. He asked for orders from the Privy Council as to what he should do. There were many homeless people in England at the time. The gypsies, who first appeared in England in the reign of Henry VII and were outlawed in 1531, were less tolerated than other vagabonds because they were foreign in appearance and language. The letter which was not dated may have been addressed to George Talbot, fourth earl of Shrewsbury, who was lord steward and Privy

3. LPFD IV, 905, V, 77,704, XIII, Pt.1, 565.

4. Scarisbrick, *Reformation*, 8–9; another example, Robert Burgoyne, was auditor of the court of augmentation, which handled the spoils from the dissolution, but in his will, dated October 1545, left bequests for thousands of masses and set up a chantry, a few weeks before the first Act for Dissolution of Chantries; LPFD XIII, Pt. 2, 280.

Counsellor from 1512 until his death in 1538, or Francis Talbot, fifth earl of Shrewsbury from 1538 to 1560 and Privy Counsellor under Edward VI, Mary, and briefly under Elizabeth, although he dissented from the Act of Supremacy of 1558-59 and the new prayer book, or George Talbot, sixth earl of Shrewsbury, who served as Privy Counsellor under Queen Elizabeth I from 1560. The letter was signed Sir John Hercy, which would favor a date after he was knighted in 1547. By this time, Sir John had a well-established relationship with the earl and was sufficiently affluent to send such a gift. In 1557, Earl Francis was ordered by Queen Mary to muster four hundred men for border service, and suggested they should be raised in Nottinghamshire by commission of Sir John Markham, Sir Gervase Clifton, Sir Nicholas Strelley, Sir John Hersey [sic], and Sir George Pierrepont.[5]

George Talbot was the sixth earl of Shrewsbury from 1560-1590. Earl George was earl marshal of England from 1572-1590 and lord lieutenant of Nottinghamshire from 1588-1590, among other offices. He was one of the greatest landholders in England, with rental income of £5000-6000 in 1559. He has also been called the "most active entrepreneur in England." He had coal mines, lead works, ironworks, steelworks, glassworks, smelters, and furnaces. He invested in the colonies and owned a ship, the *Bark Talbot*, from 1574, which sailed to Newfoundland for cod, participated in a military expedition in the Azores, and sailed with Drake against the Armada in 1585. Two of his sons matriculated at Oxford in 1579.[6]

One of the wealthiest peers in England, Earl George had first married Gertrude Manners, daughter of the earl of Rutland. They had four sons and four daughters. After her death in 1566, he married Elizabeth (Bess) Hardwick, a very rich widow who already had six children by her second husband, Sir William Cavendish. Bess solidified the marriage by marrying her son Henry Cavendish to the earl's daughter Grace Talbot, and her daughter Mary Cavendish to her husband's son and successor Gilbert Talbot. In 1568, Earl George was appointed by Queen Elizabeth as guardian and jailer of Mary Queen of Scots, a role he fulfilled from then until 1586. He grew to care for and respect Mary, but the expenses, not reimbursed by the crown, almost bankrupted him and destroyed his marriage to Bess. The

---

5. CSTP, vol. 2, P, fol. 3; Talbot Papers, MS.3206, folio 3; LPL, LY, 222; CSPD, Elizabeth: Addenda Mary, vol. 8, December 1557; Wilson, *England* , 160-61; other papers in this group were dated in 1516, but it is very unlikely that John Hercy wrote the letter before inheriting Grove in 1520, and probably for many years after that: there was no lake in Grove where swans could have lived, although perhaps they lived in the River Idle which was closeby in Retford.

6. Stone, *Crisis*, 341, 343, 347, 351-52, 363, 375, 760; unfortunately, he used much of his woodlands to fire his furnaces; his ship captured a prize ship in the Azores and a pirate ship in the Channel.

accusations of Catholic plots to make Mary queen sidelined him politically. A memo by the powerful Cecil, Lord Burghley, on 18 October 1571, named the sons of George Lascelles, Bryan and Hercye Lascelles, Hercy relatives, as involved in a plot to aid Mary Queen of Scots, provide her with money, free her from imprisonment, facilitate a Catholic marriage, aid her allies in Scotland, and other treasonable acts. The earl of Shrewsbury wrote back on 20 October, admitted that his wife had knowledge of Hercye Lascelles's dealings with Queen Mary, but that it was with his permission in order to gain intelligence, and stated that he had increased security around the queen. On 22 October Countess Bess wrote to Burghley describing her dealings with Hercye Lascelles, trying to use him to gain knowledge of Mary's plots, and confirming her husband's declaration that he had fired the Lascelles brothers from his service at Easter after the northern rebellion. Bess and the earl were anxious to exculpate themselves from any knowledge of Mary's intent to marry without Queen Elizabeth's permission, which would have been high treason. Bryan Lascelles admitted that he had brought greetings and a ring from the duke of Norfolk to Queen Mary and was imprisoned. He defended himself by citing his service against the northern earls in 1569. Bryan Lascelles was rehabilitated, married Isabel, daughter of Lord Chief Justice Montague, inherited Sturton and Gateford, and became commissioner for recusants in 1592, commissioner of musters in 1596, justice of the peace, sheriff of Nottinghamshire in 1584–86 and 1599–1600, and MP in 1589. He was knighted by King James in 1603 and died at Gateford in 1613. Hercye Lascelles also survived, married Anne of Normanton, and was named holding parts of Fledborough, Woodcotes, and Normanton in 1612.[7]

However, in 1574, Bess, countess of Shrewsbury, with the help of Mary Queen of Scots' mother-in-law, Lady Margaret Douglas Stuart, countess of Lennox and granddaughter of King Henry VII, married her daughter Elizabeth Cavendish to Margaret's son, Charles Stuart, earl of Lennox and brother of Mary's husband, Henry Stuart, Lord Darnley, without the queen's permission. Lady Margaret went to the Tower twice for her involvement in weddings of her royal sons without permission of the monarch, first for the

---

7. *Calendar of State Papers Scotland* 4:14, no. 21: Burghley Memo (18 October 1571), 25: Shrewsbury to Burghley (20 October), 26: countess of Shrewsbury to Burghley (22 October), Queen Elizabeth to Shrewsbury (22 October); HistParlOnline, (1558–1603), "Brian Lassells"; CSTP, 1:100, MS, 702, fol. 141, vol. 2, H, 59; M, 237 (called Sir in 1586), M, 536,557; Lovell, *Bess of Hardwick*, 194–230; Thoroton, *Nottinghamshire*, vol. 3, "Fledborough"; his brother George Lascelles was commended by the queen in 1587 for losing an arm in the battle of Zutphen against the Spanish in the Netherlands in 1586, where he fought in the company of Sir William Stanley; the English and their Flemish allies lost to the Spanish, but later regained ground; in 1587, however, William Stanley, who was Catholic, surrendered it to the Spanish.

marriage of Henry to Mary, and again for the marriage of Charles. Charles and Elizabeth Stuart had a daughter, Arbella Stuart, born in 1575. Charles died in 1576; Elizabeth in 1582. Lady Margaret died in 1578 and was buried in Westminister Abbey with her son Charles with a grand funeral paid for by Queen Elizabeth. Arbella, now an orphan, but eminently eligible for the throne, was left with her grandmother Bess as her virtual prisoner at Hardwick Hall until she was twenty-seven, when Queen Elizabeth I, who felt threatened by Arbella's existence, died.[8]

Despite her efforts to avoid war, Queen Elizabeth was drawn into war with Spain after Philip II, planning a crusade against England to depose Elizabeth and crown Mary Queen of Scots, seized English ships in Spanish ports. She built up a navy and attacked Spanish treasure ships. The threat of foreign Catholic invasion was real. But the Puritans Walsingham and Leicester used it to frame Mary Queen of Scots. Anthony Babington, a Catholic and a former page of the earl of Shrewsbury at Sheffield, where Mary was a prisoner, became involved in an elaborate plot to aid Mary Queen of Scots. He was the son of Henry Babington and Frances Markham, grandnephew of John Babington, colleague and relative of John Hercy. His wife was the granddaughter of Thomas Darcy, beheaded for his role in the Pilgrimage of Grace. Anthony Babington was arrested, confessed, was attainted, and executed.[9] Mary Queen of Scots was arrested, taken to Fotheringay, tried by Parliament and executed on 8 February 1587. Although Elizabeth had treated Mary abominably during her lifetime and had her killed, afterward she had her cousin buried with full royal honors. Catholic Europe was enraged. In 1588, Spain sent its entire fleet to attack England, but the armada was defeated by the English navy under Drake, aided by the *Bark Talbot*.

THE BERKSHIRE HERCYS AND THE TALBOT EARLS OF SHREWSBURY

After his father's death in 1590, Gilbert Talbot became the seventh earl of Shrewsbury. Gilbert was still a wealthy man, with his father's industrial revenues and an annual rental income of £10,800. A document from 1591 named John Hercy as the earl's solicitor and Hercy congratulated Gilbert on becoming earl.[10]

8. Lovell, *Bess of Hardwick*, 240–78, 446; Gristwood, *Arbella*, 11–33, 202.

9. Anthony Babington was hung briefly, castrated, and disembowelled; ODNB, 3:76–79.

10. LPL, Talbot Papers, MS.3203; Gilbert Talbot, esq., commissioner of the peace in Derbyshire in 1579, and earl in 1594 and 1604; both father and son enjoyed sumptuous

The period of the late 1580s through the mid-1590s was a time of wars, taxes, increasing population, and crime. There were bad harvests in 1585–87 and from 1594 to 1600, resulting in higher food costs, hunger, and starvation. The 1590s were also a time of anxiety in England, as Queen Elizabeth I declined in health and refused to name her successor. After the elimination of Mary Queen of Scots by execution in 1587, the two principal candidates were Mary's son, King James VI of Scotland, and her niece, the young Lady Arbella Stuart. As long as Elizabeth was alive, Lady Arbella was considered a threat to her throne and to her right to decide her successor. Therefore, Elizabeth kept Arbella under house arrest with Bess Hardwick of Shrewsbury. In the end, Elizabeth did not name her successor and died on 24 March 1603. Her councillors were ready, sending her ring to James VI of Scotland, whom they proclaimed King James I of England. He reigned from 1603 to 1625. James had his mother, Mary Queen of Scots, reburied in splendor in Westminster Abbey opposite Queen Elizabeth, her executioner. Initially King James treated Lady Arbella well and she became the highest-ranking woman in the court of his wife, Queen Anna. However, he would not allow her to marry, lest she produce a son of royal lineage who could dispossess his own son.

During the reign of James I, Gilbert earl of Shrewsbury served the king as Privy Counsellor, but was given a position which required his residence in Sheffield. John Hercy, of the Berkshire cadet branch of the Hercy family, served Earl Gilbert in London, at the royal court, at Sheffield and elsewhere as his attorney. John Hercy studied at Oxford and Lincoln's Inn whence he became a barrister. Some of the correspondence between John Hercy and Earl Gilbert and with Gilbert's wife, Countess Mary Cavendish Talbot, daughter of Bess of Hardwick, has been preserved. Frequently the letters were delivered through the Lady Arbella Stuart, who added messages herself. Lady Arbella had been released from house arrest in Hardwick after the death of Queen Elizabeth I in 1603. Asked to be chief mourner at Queen

---

country living at a time when other magnates were moving to London; Queen Elizabeth had abolished the practice of country magnates having liveried retainers, which functioned as private armies; however, in 1570, Earl George bought two hundred small arms from Hamburg for his retainers; Gilbert Talbot, in the 1570s, asked his father to buy Wilton so that he might have one thousand retainers; in 1593, Earl Gilbert sent four to five hundred men to destroy the Stanhopes' fishweir on the Trent at Shelford; in 1598, Earl Gilbert sent 120 retainers against a man who sent sixty; wealthy knights wore Gilbert's livery because of his influence at court and at Westminster; the Stanhopes, who were Protestants, used their county offices against Earl Gilbert, who was religiously conservative; the conflict between the two caused disorder in the parliamentary election of 1593 and in the county government; Wall, *Power and Protest*, 55; Earl Gilbert incurred many debts and sold off some of his estates; Stone, *Crisis*, 205, 211–12, 215, 219, 257, 264, 539–40, 557–58, 681, 760.

Elizabeth's funeral, since she was her closest relative, Arbella declined. Lady Arbella did, however, attend the coronation of King James I and served in his court as attendant to Queen Anna. Arbella traveled with the court, but in London she stayed at Shrewsbury House in Chelsea and in Earl Gilbert's rooms on Broad Street. In 1608 Arbella purchased a house of her own in Blackfriars.[11]

John Hercy wrote to the earl on 31 August 1603 that he was having difficulty finding lodgings in London because of the plague. He also noted that the queen would acquire Pontefract Park as part of her jointure and the rumor that Lady Margaret Lennox Stuart might marry the Lord Admiral, earl of Nottingham. On 13 September, he wrote the earl that he had received his letter of the 6th on the 11th at Lady Arbella's chambers. Hercy wrote that he had been spending all his time riding through Essex, Suffolk, and other places, looking for William Cavendish, earl of Devonshire, and his officers, about the purchase of the Clipston Manor and parks, concerning which they were at an impasse, and lands in the duchy of Lancaster, regarding which they were discussing security for the sale. As he was writing, he received word from Devonshire to proceed on the transfer of Clipston. He further wrote that the French and Spanish ambassadors were waiting at Oxford for audiences with the king and described the "grumbling" of the French ambassador at the house the king had given him, the ambassador saying that he had given the king one twenty times better when he was but the poor king of Scotland. Of course, such insults reached the ears of the king. In a postscript John Hercy described the "violent plague" in London and its suburbs, which he said had killed three thousand people in two weeks. He noted his inability to get housing within ten miles of London as a result, except at inns, which were too dangerous because of infection. Therefore, he instructed the earl to write to him through Lady Arbella.[12] Since he was unable to find lodgings near London where he was working for Earl Gilbert, it is possible that John Hercy stayed at Broad Street with Lady Arbella at this time.

---

11. *Alumni Oxonienses*, 2:697; TNA, SP 46/88/fo115 (21 October 1626); Chester, *Allegations for Marriage Licences*, 2:213 (7 August 1633); possibly the same John Hercy who pleaded a case concerning a lease in Oxfordshire on 6 May 1603: TNA, Cap/I/4/9/26; his son, John Hercy, later also studied law at Lincoln's Inn, but "John Hercy the Younger" in the Talbot correspondence probably refers to the father—see CSTP, 2:410; Gristwood, *Arbella*, 192, 199–210, 248, 252–56.

12. LPL, Talbot Papers, MS.3203, fol. 110; CSTP, 1:138, MS, 706, fol. 76, 158, MS, 708, 39; vol. 2, M, fols. 257, 389 (earl's solicitor); Lodge, *Illustrations*, 3:174–75; Nichols, *Progresses*, 1:261–62; Gristwood, 214, cites the death toll from the plague in London during the fourth week of July as 1,396, and 1,922 the following week.

On 8 October 1603, John Hercy wrote to the countess of Shrewsbury from Winchester that the Clipston matter had passed the king the previous day but Sir Edward Blount was intervening. He enclosed a letter from Lady Arbella Stuart. He wrote again from Winchester on 12 October 1603 to the earl and countess, forwarding letters from the Lady Arbella and the lord of Worcester, stating that he had not seen Lord Cecil because he was so busy attending the king, and that the term would not be at Reading, as he had previously heard. The next day he wrote a letter to the earl's steward at Sheffield, asking him to remind the countess to send money to pay certain bills. On 27 October Lady Arbella wrote of letters delivered by Mr. Hercy. On 4 November she wrote of a letter of the queen which she received through Mr. Hercy. On 6 December John Hercy wrote to the earl from Wilton that the king had signed the earl's warrant as justice in eyre, that he had asked Lord Cecil to postpone ruling on the rights to certain walks in Sherwood Forest, at present belonging to Sir Griffin Markham, but claimed by the earl of Rutland, and that Sir Aston, who was representing the FitzHerberts for restoration of their property, would desist since he learned that the earl was against it. Sir Griffin Markham was the son of Thomas Markham, who served in the household of Princess Elizabeth during Mary's reign, was MP and gentleman pensioner of Queen Elizabeth. He was sued by Rutland over fees and profits taken from Sherwood Forest during his minority. Sir Griffin was the grandson of Sir John Markham, but despite the strong evangelical adherence of the Markham family, was Catholic. He was a neighbor and friend of Earl Gilbert and Mary Talbot. Sir Griffin and a Protestant named George Brooke were accused of a plot to kidnap King James and force him to promise greater religious tolerance. There was a second plot, by Lord Cobham, Lord Grey, Sir Walter Raleigh, and two Catholic priests, to assassinate King James and make Arbella queen. The conspirators were arrested. On 18 December 1603, Arbella sent a letter to the earl by a messenger of Mr. Hercy. On 19 December, John Hercy wrote to the earl from Hampton Court that the patent for the justiceship in eyre was under the great seal. He mentioned that Lords Cobham and Grey and Sir Griffin Markham had been sent back to the Tower, but that it was unconfirmed whether Sir Walter Raleigh was there. On Christmas Eve 1603, John Hercy wrote to the earl from Hampton Court about the possibility of the earl obtaining the lieutenancies of Derbyshire and Nottinghamshire, and other offices and lands. He included the sentences of the plotters and forwarded letters from Lady Arbella Stuart. The two priests and Brooke were hung, drawn, and quartered. Lords Cobham and Grey, Sir Walter Raleigh, and Markham were convicted of high treason and sentenced to death, but reprieved on the scaffold. In the end, the death sentences were commuted: Markham to exile and Cobham, Grey, and Raleigh to imprisonment in the Tower, where Lord Grey died years later. Lord Cobham was the godson of Bess of Hardwick, dowager countess of Shrewsbury. Thus, the plot was potentially dangerous to the Shrewsburys and to Lady Arbella.[13]

In early November 1603, Lady Arbella Stuart wrote to her aunt, Mary countess of Shrewsbury, that she had received her letter from Mr. Hercy and sent an answer by him, noting that her eyes were swollen. On 8 December, she wrote a long letter to her uncle, Earl Gilbert, describing the corruption of the court and news of the foreign ambassadors. She mentioned that she had delivered his two patents, signed and sealed, to Mr. Hercy and gave advice about thank you and New Year's gifts, suggesting delay on some, which he could then blame on Mr. Hercy or her. On 18 December, she wrote to the earl from Hampton Court, as to "Mr. Hercie's letter, I keep it till I see him which will be very shortly as he lately told me." She wrote about Christmas festivities at Sheffield, the "ridiculous" and "wicked" life of the court, and other news of the court, including the commutation of the death sentences. She thanked the earl for his gift of venison and planned to share it with the court. She noted receiving another letter from the earl to which she sent an answer "by a messenger of Mr. Hercies." On 22 December, she wrote to Countess Mary concerning her request to help an old servant, which she could not do immediately, and since "Mr. Hercy having left this packet of letters with me to be sent by the first sure messenger I could hear of," she was sending this inconclusive reply. In a postscript she added that Mr. Hercy had sent a packet by post which included letters from her to the earl and his wife, saying that if she had known they would be sent by post, she would have written more reservedly, and asked them to let her know if they received them. At the time, letters sent by post were frequently opened and read by royal spies.[14]

On 6 January 1604, John Hercy wrote the earl about negotiations for the purchases of lands, including the manors of Hartington in Derbyshire and Clipston in Nottinghamshire. On 16 January 1604, "at 5 in the morning," he wrote to the earl from Broad Street, London, a house owned by Earl Gilbert in which the earl allowed Lady Arbella to reside, sending patents for the earl's offices of justice in eyre and steward of Sherwood, Clipston,

---

13. CSTP, 1:705, fol. 12, vol. 2, M, fol. 158, 164; there had been a feud in 1592 between John Markham and Sir Thomas Stanhope: 1:701, fol. 67, 707, fol. 134; LPL, Talbot Papers, MS.3203, fol. 158, 164; Sheffield Archives, BFM/2/171; LPL, Sheffield Papers, MS, 708, fol. 39, 137; Lefuse, *Life of Arabella Stuart*, 123,134, 138–39, 142–43; Gristwood, *Arbella*, 211–22, 326.

14. LPL, Sheffield Papers, MS, 708, fol. 51; Inderwick, *Side-Lights*, 85–90; Gristwood, *Arbella*, 215.

Boskwood, and Newark. He noted that letters he sent through Lady Arbella and Sir Richard Gargrave had not been delivered and wondered if the latter was dead or had forgotten him. On 4 February, John Hercy witnessed the sale of property in Sussex to Sir Charles Cavendish. On 12 February 1604, Thomas Coke, a Talbot retainer, wrote to the countess from Broad Street that he was proceeding with the purchase of Hartington and had met with Hercy who was "buying books" of land grants. He also mentioned that he had burned the earl's directions to him in the presence of Lady Arbella, "who is increasing in favor with the King." In fact, at this time Lady Arbella was the highest-ranking member of the queen's court. She was able to secure a barony for William Cavendish, and other favors for Sir Charles Cavendish and Earl Gilbert's son-in-law Henry Grey, earl of Kent.[15]

There is a record of legal expenses paid by John Hercy the elder, dated 24 June 1604. On 18 October 1604, Lady Arbella wrote to the earl, thanking him for his gift of red deer pies, which she received from Mr. Hercy. She wrote that he could not depend on her favor at court. She replied cryptically to letters from the earl and countess delivered to her by Mr. Hercy, asking them to trust her promise, which did not depend only on her will, noting that her "estate being so uncertain and subject to injuries." The next day, John Hercy wrote to the earl from London, giving advice on the performance of a covenant and valuation of land for the next term of court.[16]

On 20 February 1605, John Hercy wrote the earl concerning debts which the earl owed the crown, including a post fine levied on Sheffield Manor and its subsidies, an accounting demanded of monies delivered for the maintenance of the late Mary Queen of Scots, and money owed for purchase of land. On 11 April, Edmund Lascelles wrote to the earl from the court at Greenwich about the birth of Princess Mary, that the countess was sick but had been reconciled with Lady Arbella, and thanked the earl for his gift of £40 in gold. On 30 April, he wrote again, saying that William Cavendish was in London seeking his barony, but was unlikely to get it because he was too sparing in his gratuities. On 12 June, John Hercy and his son, John Hercy the younger, together were witnesses for deeds of transfer by Edward Somerset, earl of Worcester, of numerous manors. On 22 June, John Hercy wrote to Henry Butler, Earl Gilbert's steward at Sheffield, that he had "sued out" fines for the earl, but had not sent them for fear the hot weather would spoil the seals. Other letters from London in October 1606 reported that the

15. LPL, Talbot Papers, MS.3203, fol. 79, 182; CSTP, 1:166, MS, 708, fol. 137, vol. 2, M, fol. 79, 110, 131, 147, 182; Sheffield Papers, MS, 708, fol. 76; Sheffield Archives, BFM/2/17; Inderwick, *Side Lights*, 85–90, 93: Sloan MSS 4161.

16. LPL, Sheffield Papers, MS, 702, fol. 93; Sheffield Archives, BFM/2/181; Lefuse, *Life and Times*, 173–74.

plague was so bad that fifty-six died in a week, the king had left for a month, and there was discussion of moving Parliament. On 22 October 1606 the earl wrote from Sheffield to John Hercy at Salisbury Court to check on the status of a lease in Chylmelyes in the Peak District which he had previously tried to obtain, but now his enemy, "who seeketh to cross me in everything he can," was trying to get it. He instructed Hercy to resort to the chancellor of the duchy of Lancaster and the attorney of that court, and even ask Lord Salisbury, Privy Seal, to stay the action until he could get to London.[17]

On 1 February 1607, John Hercy wrote the earl that a commission was expected for repair of the castle in High Peak and that Sir George Lascelles was being prosecuted for misconduct in office. On 16 October 1607, John Hercy wrote the countess about payments due on purchases of land and chantries, and recommended other properties for purchase. The same day, he wrote to the earl from Salisbury Court discussing the disputes over Clipston and with Bess Hardwick, the probability that the citizens of London would lend the king £120,000 on security of the London customs, and the increase of the plague in London. On 31 October, John Hercy wrote the earl about a case in Star Chamber, for which the lord treasurer would not be present because of health, hoping that his daughter, Lady Arundel, might be able to gain the other lords' favor in the case. He mentioned another case concerning offices in the High Peak and asked instructions about a case in Chancery court against the earl's stepmother, the dowager Countess Bess of Shrewsbury, the patent for Clipston, the indictment against Thomas Markham and his brother, and the lease of a vaccary, dairy, with a long postscript of court news. On 27 November he wrote the earl that a proceeding on a debt was still not settled and that the Markham brothers had been cleared of the indictment for entering Clipston Park. On 30 November, the earl wrote to John Hercy directing him to receive money from the Exchequer for the conduct of the soldiers raised in Derbyshire. On 26 December, John Hercy wrote to the countess about the assignment of the vaccary to the earl and mentioned a letter from the earl of Salisbury about "Mr. Talbott's busyness."[18]

17. Sheffield Archives, BFM/2/183; LPL, MS.3202, fol. 7, 13, 124; CSTP, 1:94, MS, 702, fols. 59, 95, fol. 71; vol. 2, K fols.103, 231, 247, L, fols. 13, 183; East Sussex Record Office, AMS4952/2; Lodge, *Illustrations* 3:246; Edmund Lascelles was a younger son of the Lascelles of Gateford who worked closely with the earl of Shrewsbury and was appointed groom of the Privy Chamber, but fled England in 1607 because of his debts; 3:275–77: Lascelles wrote to the earl about a suspicious preacher at Oxford and that he received £40 in gold from the earl but was not sure what to do with it or whether it was his wages (11 April 1605); 297–99: on 6 August he wrote that he was traveling to the Low Countries until late September.

18. LPL, Sheffield Papers, MS, 702, fol. 17, 91, 124; CSTP, 1:91, MS, 702, fol. 17, vol.

On 10 January 1608, John Hercy wrote to the earl about the affairs of the earl in London, including an arrangement with Lord Salisbury for the assignment of a lease, that the lords of the Council had not yet replied to the earl's letter, some duchy business, and that a license was signed for Mr. Talbot for three months. He noted that he had not received the "coat and contact" money for Derbyshire to support new soldiers before they were on the royal payroll, and described how the Thames was frozen over. He wrote on 1 February that he was attending the chancellor of the duchy of Lancaster for a commission to repair High Peak Castle. He again wrote that he had not yet received the coat and conduct money from the Exchequer, which was "in great want," waiting for the loan from the City of London to materialize.[19]

On 4 February 1608, John Hercy witnessed the transfer of property to Sir Charles Cavendish, which formerly belonged to Derleigh Abbey in Derbyshire but had later been given to Thomas Babington and John Hyde. The sale was executed in Fleet Street, London. On 16 February, John Hercy wrote the earl concerning "coheirs of the late Mr. Talbot," and a court dispute between Lord William Cavendish and his brother Henry Cavendish. On 17 February John Hercy wrote that he had received the earl's letter by his daughter, Lady Arundel, that the lord chancellor had been informed of the death of the dowager Countess, Bess Hardwick, by Lord Cavendish, that he was one of her overseers, had sought the chancellor's favor in the matter, and that he had engaged a Mr. Hacker to protect the earl's interests in his late mother's estate. He noted that Lord Arundel was at Arundel House and Lord Pembroke was with the king at Newmarket. The following day he wrote the earl about legal business: several court cases, the case against the sheriff of Nottinghamshire for entering Clipston Park, a commission on the survey of woods, and the will of his stepmother Bess, the dowager Countess. On 23 February he wrote to the earl about a suit before the chancellor of the duchy of Lancaster, concerning the court of High Peak, that a commission had been appointed to view the state of the castle of High Peak, and that Sir John Bennett had promised him a copy of the will.[20]

2, L, 124, M, 460, 462; Talbot Papers, MS.3203, fol. 460, 462; CSTP, 1:91 MS, 702, fol. 17, 96, fol.81; vol. 2, L, fol. 124; Sheffield Archives, BFM/2/204; Lodge, *Illustrations*, 3:125.

19. LPL, Talbot Papers, MS.3203, fol. 491; CSTP, vol. 2, N, 491; Sheffield Archives, BFM/2/208.

20. Nottinghamshire Archives, 157 DD/P/85/11; LPL, Sheffield Papers, MS, 708, fol.225; CSTP, 1:95, MS, 702, fol. 71, 172, MS, 708, fol. 225, vol. 2, M, 491; Sheffield Archives, BFM/2/212; Lodge, *Illustrations*, 3:128; Dr. John Bennett, commissary of the Prerogative Court of Canterbury.

On Sunday April 10, John Hercy wrote the earl about the wedding of the younger William Cavendish to a gentlewoman of thirteen years and his attempts to find out the terms of the prenuptial agreements regarding lands, thinking that he overheard £500 as annual maintenance. The wedding was attended by Lord and Lady William Cavendish and Lady Arbella, but not by Henry Cavendish. The following day he wrote to the countess that he had sent the earl the commission to survey the king's woods, and was enclosing a letter from the garter king-at-arms concerning the funeral of the dowager countess and requesting further instructions.[21]

On 20 May 1608, John Hercy was witness to a deed to the use of fine and recovery of numerous properties, recognizing the earl and countess as legal holders of the properties without possibility of suit, but allowing two gentlemen from London, servants of the earl, use of the properties. On 15 October 1608, John Hercy was witness to the transfer of a fifty-year lease of a number of mills to Sir Charles Cavendish for £650.[22]

On 10 November, John Hercy wrote the earl about legal matters, including his opinion that the Clipston Park case was not going well, that the judge was "more than tart," that the earl would probably not succeed in having another dispute tried before a church court, and that the coming Parliament might not be held. The same day he wrote the earl with a list of sheriffs appointed, which included Henry Cavendish for Derbyshire. Five days later, he elaborated on the Clipston case, that the earl's barrister had spoken well, but the opposition counsel for Rutland was given a week to prepare their case. He also hoped for money from the countess to pay bills and a subsidy. On 25 November he wrote the earl from Westminster enclosing a copy of the fine acknowledged by Henry Cavendish before the Lord Chief Justice Coke, who expressed pleasure at this reconciliation between Henry and his brother Lord Cavendish. However, Coke offended the king by his opinions in a dispute with attorneys in the king's presence, by saying that the king was defended by his laws. The king responded, saying that he was not defended by his laws but by God. Only an intervention by the lord treasurer on bended knee defused the situation. The issue was the divine right of the king who considered himself above the common law.[23]

21. LPL, Talbot Papers, MS.3203, fol. 519; CSTP, 1:99, MS, 702, fol. 129, vol. 2, M, 519; LPL Sheffield Papers, MS, 708, fol.129; Lefuse, *Life*, 207–8; Lodge, *Illustrations*, 3:233–35.

22. Nottinghamshire Archives, 157 DD/P/42/58; DD/P/17/130; witness to original lease by Queen Elizabeth on 14 November 1601.

23. LPL, Talbot Papers, MS.3203, fol. 544, 547, 553; CSTP, vol. 2, M, 544, 547, 553; Lodge, *Illustrations*, 3:247–250; Hercy's letter was one of four written accounts of the incident; McIlwain, *High Court of Parliament*, 78.

In the same letter John Hercy wrote the earl on 25 November, he noted that the chancellor of the Exchequer had just spoken to him, asking him to bring in the surveys of the woods. The date of Parliament was still uncertain. On 30 November, Mr. Hercy and Anthony Neville were witnesses to an assignment for a fee by a gentleman in London of tithes of corn and hay from four oxgangs in the parish of Orston, Nottinghamshire, to the earl's steward, Henry Butler of Sheffield, yeoman.[24]

On 9 January 1609, John Hercy wrote to the earl that the king had charged the auditor to follow up on a capital case against Browne, gave news of a case concerning the Padley lands which the earl had bought, a report on the survey of royal forests, and news of Henry and Lord William Cavendish. On 17 January, John Hercy wrote to the earl's steward about payment of subsidies and moneys owed to the crown by the earl's father since 1588, and his own need for money to carry on the earl's legal affairs. On 16 February he wrote the earl concerning a case in the Court of Wards between the earl and the coheirs of the late Mr. Talbot. He also mentioned the case between Sir Charles or Lord William and Henry Cavendish, which was set before judges, then postponed for further depositions. On 19 March, John Hercy witnessed the decision of the earl in a dispute between Henry Cavendish and his brother Sir Charles Cavendish over title to lands.[25]

In another letter which is undated, John Hercy wrote the countess about the purchase of property in Blyth or Bawtry, and recommended the manor of Lenton, which adjoined some of her own property. He also wrote that three of the earl's Derbyshire tenants were in London with a petition to the earl concerning their boundaries. Finally, he discussed the possibility of a marriage between his own daughter and a young man named Gilbert, mentioning that he had spoken to Mr. Eyre about him. The son and heir of Hercy Neville of Grove was named Gilbert; however, he did in fact marry someone else.[26]

In August 1609, Lady Arbella went to Sheffield to recover from smallpox and began liquidating her assets. On 2 February 1610, she was secretly betrothed to William Seymour, who like herself was descended from King Henry VII. They were privately married at Greenwich on 22 June. They were soon arrested for the crime of marriage of royals without permission of the crown. Both Earl Gilbert and Mary Talbot tried to get the king to be lenient. However, William was sentenced to the Tower for life; Arbella was

24. Lodge, *Illustrations*, 3:247–50; Nottinghamshire Archives, 1576 DD/P/CD/47 (30 November 1608).

25. Sheffield Archives, BFM/2/219; LPL, Talbot Papers, MS.3203, fol. 566; CSTP, 1:97, MS702, fol. 93, vol. 2, M, 566; Nottinghamshire Archives, 157 DD/P/48/5.

26. Sheffield Archives, BFM/2/287.

to be imprisoned at Durham. On the journey there, during a lengthy halt at Barnet, Arbella was able to meet with Mary Talbot, who helped her collect £2,800 and plan an escape. The attempt failed and Arbella was captured at sea, although William escaped from the Tower and succeeded in getting to France. Mary Talbot was arrested even before Arbella was caught. Both were imprisoned and interrogated in the Tower. Mary Talbot was tried in 1612, fined £20,000, for which the crown took Worksop, and imprisoned in the Tower from June 1611 until 1623.[27]

After the conviction of Mary Talbot, things did not go well for the Talbots of Shrewsbury, either politically or financially, or for those who worked for them. Countess Mary supported Arbella's expenses in the Tower, since prisoners had to pay for their own food, maintenance, and servants, writing to Earl Gilbert for more money when hers ran out. On 28 June 1611 Sir Charles Cavendish wrote from Whitehall that the king appointed six of the earl's servants, including Mr. Hercy, and one woman, "to repair to him at all convenient time, and . . . Mistress Anne to attend her continually there." It was signed by the lord treasurer, the Lord Privy Seal, the lord chamberlain, and the Lords Worcester, Fenton, and Knowles. The "her" was Mary Cavendish Talbot, who had been held in the Tower since early June for aiding Lady Arbella Stuart in her unsuccessful attempt to flee from England. On 16 February 1611, Sir Charles Cavendish wrote to the earl's steward to send £40 to pay the wages of the earl's servants who had not been paid and "have noe clothes nor any mony." Edmund Lascelles wrote to the earl from exile in Utrecht giving account of his miserable situation and asking aid for his wife and children.[28]

On 19 August 1613, John Hercy was witness to the sale of lands by the earl and countess of Shrewsbury to Sir Charles Cavendish. Lady Arbella Stuart died in the Tower on 25 September 1615 of illness associated with her hunger strike. She was buried in the Lady Chapel of Westminster Abbey, between her grandmother Margaret Douglas Stuart and her aunt Mary Queen of Scots. Gilbert Talbot, seventh earl of Shrewsbury died on 8 May 1616 at Broad Street. He left three daughters, no male heirs, and an estate in debt for £17,000. His will left most of his property to pay his debts, with gold cups to the king and queen, Prince Charles, his daughters, their husbands, and his grandsons; his executors were Sir William Cavendish and another. The earldom went to his younger brother Edward, who lived less than a year,

---

27. Gristwood, *Arbella*, 257, 268, 277, 290, 294, 298, 310–11, 314, 319, 324, 333, 356; one William Markham and others were also imprisoned in the conspiracy.

28. Lodge, *Illustrations*, 3:393–94 (23 June 1611); Letter of Sir Charles Cavendish to Henry Butler (16 February 1611), LPL, MS, film 801, fol. 90; CSTP, vol. 2, O, 153; Gristwood, *Arbella*, 315, 325.

and then to their cousin George, a Catholic priest. Gilbert's widow, Countess Mary Talbot, had paid a high price for her support of Lady Arbella. She was imprisoned in the Tower until 1623, except for a brief leave in 1615 to nurse her dying husband. She was freed from the Tower in 1623 and lived until 1632. As a Catholic, she was active in protecting the struggling church. A bishop visited the Shrewsbury house at Grafton in 1625 and the Jesuits rented a Shrewsbury house in London for their novitiate.[29]

The correspondence between John Hercy and the earl of Shrewsbury, his association with Lady Arbella Stuart, the highest-ranking woman in England, and with the court of King James I, as well as his royal appointment to serve Mary Talbot in the Tower, are ample evidence of the prominent activity of John Hercy in the history of England at this time.

---

29. Nottinghamshire Archives, 157 DD/P/50/70; their daughter Mary married William Herbert, earl of Pembroke in 1604; daughter Elizabeth married Henry Grey, earl of Kent; daughter Alethea married Thomas Howard, earl of Arundel and Surrey; the Arundel family also protected priests; Stone, *Crisis*, 730; LPL, Talbot Papers, MS.3203, fol. 183; *Marriage, Baptismal, and Burial Registers*, 112; Gristwood, *Arbella*, 305, 343, 346–54; Arbella Stuart was commemorated in a floor plaque, between the tombs of Mary Queen of Scots and her mother Margaret Douglas Lennox, with Anne Hyde and the children of Kings Charles I, James II, and Queen Anne.

Conclusion

THE JOURNEY OF THE EXTENDED de Hercé/Hercy/Hersey family described here has been long, over six hundred years. Unlike the more common histories of royalty and aristocracy, the sources for this middle-class family have often been scarce and at some points have left gaps. Most Anglo-French knightly families died out after a few centuries. Yet it has been possible to follow this family from its earliest traces through these six centuries as they journeyed from France to England and from the Catholic church to the Church of England to Puritanism.

In the eleventh century, a knight from Hercé, a small rural site in northwest Maine, a region torn by conflict between Normandy and Anjou, rode north to join with Duke William II of Normandy to invade and conquer England. Because he was from Maine and William did not trust the loyalty of his Manceau knights, he was not immediately given land in England. He and his descendants disappear from documented view except for traces of holdings in Worcestershire before or during the reign of King Henry II. There is solid and continuous evidence of the family from the reign of King Richard I, who gave them land in Warwickshire. The intervening years are partially filled in by the history of the first two known families of Hercy wives, de Arches and de Hériz. In Warwickshire, Sir Hugh de Hercy later served King John, for whom he fought in France, where he was captured and ransomed. When he had a son, his nephew and former, but no longer, heir, Malveysin de Hercy, went to Nottinghamshire where he married into the prosperous Eastern Norman knightly family of Arches, thereby acquiring the estate of Grove, and he became castellan of Tickhill, a very important castle in Yorkshire. The status and prosperity of the family in Nottinghamshire was founded on a woman and her inheritance. Their son married into another prominent knightly family, the de Hériz, from Western Normandy. Their descendants enlarged their estates in Nottinghamshire. Many had excellent marriages into other important knightly families in Nottinghamshire. The Hercys held every high office in the county, including those of sheriff, knight of the shire in Parliament, escheator, commissioners of the peace, array, gaol delivery, and *oyer et terminer*. In the fifteenth century some became involved in the legal profession. They administered the county of Nottingham and were greatly respected by other knightly and gentry families. The Hercys were closely linked with the other prominent knightly families of Nottinghamshire as relatives, as neighbors, and as colleagues in county offices. They supported education and the Reformation but remained in the Church of England. However, their appointments of rectors in the sixteenth century indicates that they preferred the evangelical position within the Church of England. By the late sixteenth and seventeenth centuries, north Nottinghamshire had become a center of Puritanism.[1] After the Hercy male line died out in Nottinghamshire, a cadet line emerged and thrived in Berkshire, producing highly respected gentry and members of the legal profession. Most of the Berkshire Hercys remained in the Church of England until William Hersey of Reading became a Puritan.

The Hercys were generally peaceful law-abiding middle-class citizens. For the most part they chose to live and work on their county estates over pursuing military careers and seeking wealth. The court cases of the archbishopric of York and the Honour of Tickhill are abundantly documented in the litigious society of the late Middle Ages, showing countless cases of divorce and separation from bed and board, adultery, murder and wife killing, domestic violence, failure to support wives, punishment of wives for disobeying their husbands, assault, mismanagement of estates, and bankruptcy. However, in no extant case of these courts was the Hercy family charged with any of these common crimes.[2] There is no evidence of divorce among the Hercys. A few of the men remarried after the deaths of their wives but none of the wives remarried after they became widows. There is no evidence of extramarital affairs, although there were two unidentified Hercy relatives or progeny in Nottinghamshire. The Hercy family adhered together and there is no evidence of intrafamilial rivalries. The loyalty of the Hercys to the kings and queens of England was never questioned and in one case, that of Sir Thomas de Hercy and King Henry IV, it was especially commended. The Hercys served the state in many varied roles, especially in the high county offices of sheriff, knight of the shire, escheator, and commissioner of the peace in Nottinghamshire. John Hercy of Berkshire worked for the earl of Shrewsbury and with Lady Arbella Stuart, the highest-ranking

1. Wilson, *Tudor Tapestry*, 239.
2. Butler, *Language of Abuse*; they were charged before a commission of *oyer et terminer* in one ambiguous charge of group assault in 1314 by a priest who may have himself been to blame.

woman in England in the reign of James I. Two of their descendants became queens of England. A member of the Berkshire branch of the family, William Hersey, became a Puritan and founded the Hersey family in North America, where it continues to grow and flourish.

Appendix I

Neighbors of de Hercé in Maine: de Gorron, d'Ambrières, de Laval

DE GORRON

Gorron, adjacent to Hercé, was held under the lords of Mayenne, but later came under the dukes of Normandy. The lords of Gorron are not known until King William I gave Gorron to his brother, Count Robert de Mortain, who built the church and castle there in 1082. When Robert de Mortain held Gorron, he put one of his men, Geoffroy, youngest son of Rivallon I de Dol in Brittany, in charge in the late eleventh century; Geoffroy's family took the toponym de Gorron. Between 1099 and 1116, Gauthier II de Mayenne consented to the donation of the church of Brecé, a hamlet of Hercé, to Marmoutier by Rivallon II de Gorron, son of Geoffroy de Gorron. This indicates that Hercé was at this time subordinate to Gorron. Rivallon II de Gorron et Saint-Berthevin-de-la-Tannière married Hersende, daughter of Geoffrey II of Mayenne, sister of Hamelin and Juhel I de Mayenne. Rivallon and Hersende de Gorron had three sons. The eldest son was Guillaume de Gorron et de la Tannière, knight of Maine and vassal of Juhel II de Mayenne.[1]

---

1. WP, 1:45; *Cartulaire Manceau de Marmoutier*, vol. 2, no. 7; Guyard de la Fosse, *Preuves* iii; Robert's daughter, Denise de Mortain, married Guy II de Laval and another daughter Agnèse married André de Vitré, thereby securing the border regions of Maine and Brittany for Normandy; Power, *Norman Frontier*, 502–3: Guillaume also held some property at Lévaré, a town associated with the de Hercé family, as was Saint-Berthevin-la-Tannière, arr. Mayenne, canton Gorron; Pichot, *Bas-Maine*, 82–83, 85, 96, 114, 143–45, 157–58, 165, 196–99, 206–7, 210–11: a castle was built for Gorron at Saint-Berthevin-la-Tannière in 1128, whose family was very close to that of Gorron and held many lands in the tenth century, giving a church to Le Mont-St-Michel in 997; there was a church at Gorron before 1082; Gorron at times held the parishes of Saint-Berthevin-la-Tannière, Levaré, La Dorée, Ernée, and others.

APPENDIX I

During the dukedom of Robert Curthose, Gorron came again under the lordship of Mayenne. But in 1120, King Henry I of England bought the castles of Ambrières and Gorron from young Hamelin de Mayenne. In 1128, Guillaume de Gorron donated a tenth of the revenues from his forest to the Norman abbey of Le Mont-Saint-Michel. The donation was confirmed by Radulf de Gorron about 1190. On the death of King Henry I in 1135, Geoffroy d'Anjou and his wife, the Empress Mathilde, granted Ambrières, Gorron, and Colmont to Juhel I de Mayenne. After the death of Juhel I in 1161, the castle was retaken from Juhel II de Mayenne by King Henry II of England. In the rebellion in support of Henry the Young King in 1173, Juhel II de Mayenne and Guillaume de Gorron were taken prisoner at Dol. Later Gorron joined Mayenne in supporting Arthur of Brittany against King John. Guillaume de Gorron fought against John and in the summer of 1199 was taken prisoner with two other vassals of Juhel II de Mayenne, but remained faithful to Juhel. King John took the castles back briefly, but returned them to Juhel II de Mayenne.[2] By 1400, the castle at Gorron was destroyed and the town lived from tanning and making shoes.

Henri and Geoffrey de Gorron were recruited by King Henry I to serve in England as monks of St. Albans in Hertfordshire, then the greatest church in England. Geoffroy de Gorron was made abbot of St. Albans in 1119 where he served until his death in 1146. He was a renowned scholar and producer of books. His nephew, Robert de Gorron, son of Guillaume, was abbot from 1151 to 1166. Abbot Geoffrey built a hall for his brother-in-law Hugh at Westwick, whose successors Ivo and Geoffrey spelled their surname Gorham. Geoffrey de Gorron/Gorham held one fee of St. Albans in 1166 at Westwick, and had a son Radulf. His later successor, Henry de Gorham, held in 1210.[3]

---

2. Torigni, 2:86–87; *CartAbbayette*, no. 10; Guillaume de Gorron, before departing on the Second Crusade about 1149, made a donation to the abbey of Noyers in the Touraine, then in the territory of Geoffroy d'Anjou; in 1163, Gilon/Gilles de Gorron, his wife Osanne, and his children Guillaume, Henri and Marie, guaranteed to the abbey of Savigny the tithe of wheat from all their lands; Angot, *Dictionaire historique*, 421; Mathilde, daughter of King Henry I, was called empress because she was the widow of the former Holy Roman emperor; Power, *Norman Frontier*, 72, 162, 399, n. 65, 436, 475–76, n. 31.

3. RBE, 1:359–60 (1166, St.Albans), 2:508 (1210–12, St. Albans); *RRAN*, vol. 2, no. 1203 (1119, Henry I confirmation of Abbot Geoffrey to St. Albans, witness Hugh de Laval); *Gesta Abbatum Monasterii Sancti Albani*, 1:73, 95–96, 108, 110, 131–32, 168–69, 183, 489, 505; Galfridus de Gorham, son Radulf; *Early Charters of St. Paul, London*, no. 154; *CartAbbayette*, no. 21; VCH, Hertford, 2:393–94; Madden, *Collectanea*, vol. 6 (1840) 284–89, vol. 8 (1843) 81–116; Geoffrey's spiritual director was the notable woman Christina of Markyate; Power, *Norman Frontier*, 502–3; ODNB, 22:995; Keats-Rohan, "Le role des Bretons," 189; Keats-Rohan, *Domesday Descendants*, 482.

APPENDIX I

The lords of Gorron descended from the family of Dol in Brittany and were given Gorron by Count Robert de Mortain in 1082. They intermarried with the family de Mayenne in Maine and supported the abbeys of Le Mont-Saint-Michel and Savigny in Normandy. In England they served the abbey of St. Albans. Gorron was the closest town to Hercé. Nothing is documented about the previous lords of Gorron before 1082, but it is possible that an earlier one accompanied de Hercé, de Mayenne, and "all the barons of Maine" and fought with Duke William in the conquest of England. William did not give the Manceau knights land in England. In England there are no recorded interactions with the de Hercy family, although possibly such might have occurred in Wingrave, Buckinghamshire, if the Hersin family there was part of the de Hercy family.[4]

D'AMBRIÈRES

Ambrières lies north of Mayenne in the arrondissement of Mayenne, canton de Gorron, in the border district of the Passais, which King Henri I of France conceded to Duke William II in 1054. Duke William built a castle at Ambrières about 1054 and stationed a garrison there. The Norman Robert d'Estuteville defended Ambrières for Duke William against Geoffrey II de Mayenne and Geoffroy d'Anjou. Duke William made him castellan of Ambrières in 1056, a position he held for many years until he was replaced by another Norman, Achard.[5] The administration of justice in Ambrières was still under the lords of Mayenne until 1162. King Henry I bought the castle of Ambrières from the lord of Mayenne. The castle later went back and forth between the dukes of Anjou, the lords of Mayenne, and the Angevin kings of England.

The Achard family was originally from the Poitou, but in the tenth century migrated to Perthuis-Achard in the Passais forest, gradually expanding their lands to Domfront, which is in the Orne region of Normandy on the border of Maine. In 1020 Achard le Riche was castellan of Domfront. Achard witnessed the foundation charter for the abbey of Lonlay in 1026 for the count of Bellême. His son Achard fought for Duke William at Mayenne and Ambrières in 1063 and then was made castellan of the strategic castle of Ambrières. Achard d'Ambrières married Dunelme de Pont-Audemer, sister of the powerful Roger de Beaumont of Eastern Normandy. In 1066, the three lords of the Passais-Normande, Achard d'Ambrières, Henri de Domfront and Matthieu de la Ferté-Macé, brought eighty men to the

---

4. See Appendix VI.
5. Wace, 3:4490–91, 4995–5046; WJ, 2:vii, 8(18).

APPENDIX I

conquest of England and fought bravely for Duke William. According to Domesday Book, the Norman Achard was given lands in Worcestershire and Buckinghamshire.[6] His son, Robert Fitz Achard, was a vassal of Henri Beauclerc, later King Henry I, when he was count of the Cotentin, helped him to take Domfront and expel the Talvas-Bellême clan, and was made constable of Domfront in 1091/2, serving there until 1102. King Henry I gave Robert Achard lands in Berkshire. Robert's son William held three knights' fees in Berkshire from 1160.[7] Robert's grandsons were Yves Achard, who in 1160 supported the abbey of Savigny, and Blessed Achard of Saint-Victor, who became bishop of Avranches in 1161. Bishop Achard was a patron of Lucerne Abbey in the Avranchin for which he was said to have laid the foundation stone. He died 29 March 1172 and was buried in Lucerne Abbey, which was supported by the de Hériz family. Yves's son, Robert II d'Achard, went on the third crusade with King Richard I in 1190, as did the lords of Mayenne and Hercé.[8]

The Achard family remained active in Maine. Robert II's grandson Robert III went on crusade with King Louis IX in 1249. His fourth great-grandsons, Jean and Macé, fought in the Hundred Years War against the English in the fifteenth century. Macé fought with Jeanne d'Arc, who was executed in 1431. Macé held fees in Saint-Manvieu in Calvados, arrondissement Caen, associated with the de Hériz family, and in La Haye in the Cotentin, arrondissement Coutances. His grandson, Léonard, baptised in 1535, married Olive de Hercé, daughter of Guillaume II de Hercé.[9]

6. Saint-Allais, *Nobiliaire universel de France*, 20:26-29; *RRAN*, vol. 2, nos. 833, 1134; DB Buckinghamshire, 17.22, Worcestershire, 23.11-12; RBE, 1:307-8, 2:513, 639; *perthuis* means "opening, clearing"; Keats-Rohan, *Domesday Descendants*, 132.

7. In 1092, the inhabitants of Domfront invited Count Henri to be their lord because of the cruelty of their current Lord Robert de Bellême; *MRSN*, 2:493, 462, 644; RBE, 1:23, 45, 50, 73, 92, 107, 127, 307-8, 2:513, 696; Keats-Rohan, *Domesday Descendants*, 132.

8. E. de Magny, *Nobiliaire de Normandie*, 202; C. de Magny, *Premier registre*, 1-2; *CartStVincent*, vol. 1, no. 307 (1080-1100, Peter son of Achard); Torigni, 1:230-31; *MRSN*, lxxvii, lxxix; list included Richard de Lucy, chief justiciar of England; a justiciar was a royal judge, but in the reign of Henry II became an important national official; under Henry I it was used for ad hoc and shire judges; Achard was abbot of St. Victor in Paris and bishop of Sées in 1157; in 1172, a list of the knights of the ballio of the Passais named Achard d'Ambrières, Gervaise Paynel, Mathieu de la Ferté (husband of Gundreda, daughter of Fulk Paynel), Henri de Domfront, and others; Chibnall, 121-23.

9. CChR, Henry III-Edward I, 1257-1300, 424; CChR, Edward I-II, 1300-1326, 50, 168-71, 177, 179, 252, 360; CPR, Edward III, 1340-1343, 433; *MA*, 7:528; *IPM*, Henry IV, 1405, no. 1055; in Holy Cross Church in Sparsholt, Oxfordshire, there is a wooden tomb effigy of Robert IV d'Achard, who lived from 1280 to 1353 and rebuilt the church, and was also a benefactor of the Knights Templar; Bretel d'Ambrières was a supporter of Marmoutier and a knight of King Henry I, who gave him land in Devon; he was

APPENDIX I

The earlier family at Ambrières before the time when Duke William came to hold it is unknown. After 1056, it was governed by Normans from the families of d'Estuteville and Achard. Achard went to England with Duke William in 1066. The Achard family supported the abbeys of Lonlay and Savigny in Normandy. One family member was buried in Lucerne Abbey and others came to hold fees in the Avranchin, Cotentin, and Calvados, in places associated with the de Hériz family. In the sixteenth century they intermarried with the de Hercé family of Maine. In England they lived in Worcestershire and Buckinghamshire where they may have interacted with the de Hercy and/or de Hersin families.

DE LAVAL

The second most powerful family in northwestern Maine after de Mayenne was that of Laval. Laval was not part of the vassalage network of the above cluster of families, but its lords were important both in the affairs of northwestern Maine and in the settlement of Yorkshire with the de Arches family. There were significant intermarriages and political and military alliances between the families de Mayenne and de Laval.

About 1020, Count Héribert I of Maine conveyed the territory of Laval on the Mayenne River to Guy de Dénéré to build a castle. Guy then changed his name to Guy I de Laval. He was a donor to the abbey of Marmoutier in Tours and went on pilgrimage to Jerusalem. He married first Berthe de Tosny and they were parents of Jean, who died young as a monk of Marmoutier, and Hamon, who succeeded, and three daughters, all of whom were mentioned in donation charters of Marmoutier. Guy I married second Rotrude, daughter of Hamon de Mayenne and Hildebourge de Bellême, which made him the brother-in-law of Geoffroy I de Mayenne. They had sons Guy and Gervais.[10]

Guy I de Laval was succeeded by his son, Hamon, who married Hersende and they had Guy II and Hugh. Hamon witnessed donations to Marmoutier by Fulk III d'Anjou in 1040, consented to one by his father in

---

probably in service of the castle of Ambrières and a tenant of Achard; the Manceau cartulary of Marmoutier also mentions his brother Hugues de Ambrières, and Evrard and Arrald de Ambrières; PR, 31 Henry I, 41, 108, 157; Keats-Rohan, *Domesday Descendants*, 279.

10. Broussillon, *Laval*, vol. 1, nos. 8–9, 12, 16–18, 20; Latouche, *Histoire*, 116–26: Broussillon and Angot disagreed as to whether Guy de Dénéré was the first lord of Laval; the daughters were named Hildesinde, Agnèse, and Hildeburge, although the last may have been from the second marriage; Agnèse became a nun of Ronceray in Angers.

APPENDIX I

1050, and witnessed a charter in 1064 by Duke William II, confirming a donation by Guy I de Laval, which illustrates how the lordship in northwestern Maine had shifted from Anjou to Normandy. Hamon de Laval may have accompanied King William to England, but there are no records of the Manceau family holding lands there until the reign of King Henry I. Hamon died about 1080/85 and was buried with his wife in the abbey of Marmoutier.[11]

Hamon's son, Guy II de Laval, succeeded and married first Denise de Mortain, daughter of Count Robert de Mortain, half-brother of King William. They had a daughter, Adénore, who married Raoul VII, vicomte de Maine. Guy II married second Cécile and had sons, Guy III, who succeeded, and Gervais, and daughters Agnèse, who married Hugues de Craon, and Hawise, who married Robert de Ferrers, earl of Derby. Guy II supported King William I and was a donor to Marmoutier in Tours and Ronceray in Angers. Guy II died about 1095 and was buried at Marmoutier with his first wife. Guy III was a minor in ward of his father's brother, Hugh II de Laval, who was a knight of King Henry I and tenant-in-chief of Pontefract in Yorkshire.[12] Hugh II was a fellow tenant-in-chief, neighbor and friend of Osberne de Arches, maternal ancestor of the de Hercy family by Théophanie de Arches. Hugh II's descendant married a descendant of the de Bolebec/d'Arques family.

As an adult, Guy III fought with Gauthier II de Mayenne for Fulk V of Anjou in 1118 at Sées, where the latter defeated King Henry I. However, in 1129, he and other vassals of Fulk opposed his son, Geoffroy d'Anjou, who then took his castle, but granted him pardon. Guy III and his wife Emma had two sons, Guy IV and Hamon, who went to the Holy Land, and a daughter Emma, who became abbess of Ronceray from 1163 to 1190. They supported the abbeys of Ronceray and Marmoutier, and founded the priory of Le Plessis-Millicent, built by Guy de Laval and others in 1137–39. Guy III died between 1130 and 1142.[13]

Guy IV de Laval completed the priory of Le Plessis-Millicent and founded the abbey of Clermont in Maine with St. Bernard of Clairvaux, where Guy and his wife were buried. Guy IV married Emma, daughter of Réginald de Dunstanville, first earl of Cornwall, an illegitimate son of King

11. Broussillon, vol. 1, nos. 8–9, 17, 28, 52; *CartRonceray*, ccclxii; the Falaise Roll names Hamon de Laval among the companions of William at Hastings; J. Green, *Aristocracy*, 369; Loyd, *Origins*, 53; PR 31 Henry I, 23, 27.

12. Broussillon, vol. 1, nos. 51–52, 67, 84–85, 91, 93, 111, 118; *CartRonceray*, ccclxii, ccclxviii, ccclxxx; Cécile was possibly of the family de Mayenne.

13. PR 31 Henry I, 23, 27; *CartRonceray*, ccclxxvi; Broussillon vol. 1, nos. 103, 118, 132, 140; Keats-Rohan, *Domesday Descendants*, 543 confuses Guy III and IV.

APPENDIX I

Henry I and powerful adjutant of King Henry II. Guy IV and Emma had a son, Guy V. Guy IV died about 1180/85.[14]

Guy V succeeded his father in Maine and in Yorkshire. Guy V, with Juhel II de Mayenne, Radulf de Fougères, and Hervé de Vitré, rebelled against King Henry II in 1189, supporting Prince Richard against his father. In 1202 Guy supported Arthur of Brittany against King John and had to flee to Brittany. He married Avoise, daughter of Maurice II de Craon and Isabelle de Meulan, daughter of Waleran de Meulan de Beaumont, earl of Worcestershire. They had a son, Guy VI, and three daughters, Ozanne, Emma, and Isabelle. Guy V died in 1210, his only son Guy VI a year later, leaving his daughter Emma as heir to Laval.[15]

The de Laval family intermarried with the ducal family of Mortain, with the comital family of Maine, and the royal family of England. They also intermarried with the families de Mayenne of Maine, and de Meulan/Beaumont of the Eure, and with the de Bolebec family, relatives of the de Arches, in England. They donated to the monasteries of Marmoutier in Tours, Ronceray in Angers, founded the abbeys of Clermont and La Madeleine-du-Plessis in Maine, and supported Pontefract and Nostell priories in Yorkshire. They had major holdings in Yorkshire, where they were fellow tenants-in-chief and benefactors of Nostell with Osberne de Arches, whose descendant was the mother of the de Hercy family in Nottinghamshire, and were also lords of the de Lascelles family, who were cousins of the de Hercy family.

14. RBE, 1:40, 421–23; EYC, vol. 4, no. 48; Torigni, 1:216–17; Broussillon, vol. 1, nos. 17–18, 31, 140; Keats-Rohan, *Domesday Descendants*, 543 mistakenly says Emma was daughter of Henry I.

15. *Gesta Regis Henrici Secundi*, 72; RBE, 1:77 (1190–91, Guy, Yorkshire, with William de Percy, William and Fulk Paynel, Robert de Lacy, Adam and Robert de Brus), 87 (1194–95, archbishop of York, with fee of William de Percy, William Paynel), 116 (1196–97, Guy with earl of Warwick, William Paynel, Agnes de Percy, Adam and Robert de Brus), 130 (1199–1200, Guy with countess of Warwick, William Paynel, Agnes de Percy), 163 (1201–12, with William Paynel, Adam de Brus, countess of Warwick, Agnes Percy), 421 (1166, *carta* Henry de Lacy, Guy de Laval with Simon de Lascelles, old and new fees, Herbert de Arches, Jelebert Paynel, new fees); *MA*, 3:522; Guy V was a benefactor of the abbeys of Marmoutier in Tours, and Clermont and Bellebranche in Maine; Broussillon, vol. 1, nos. 85, 118, 132, 149, 201, 233, 284, 288, 333; *RHGF*, 18:244; Ozanne died in 1205; Emma married Robert, son of Jean comte d'Alençon and Béatrice de Maine; *CartStVincent*, 1:626 (1095, Guy); Power, *Norman Frontier*, 252, n. 136, 403, 438.

Appendix II

Lords and Neighbors of the de Hercy Family in Warwickshire

DE GOURNAY

One of the most powerful noble families in Normandy was that of Gournay-en-Bray, arrondissement Dieppe, canton Gournay-en-Bray, on the Epte River, which separated Normandy from the kingdom of France. In the tenth century, Renaud was lord of Gournay. He and his wife Alberade, daughter of Gauthier de la Ferté, had two sons: Hugues I and Gauthier. Hugues I was lord of Gournay in the late tenth century. His brother, Gauthier, was lord of la Ferté and founded the priory of La Ferté-en-Bray on the order of Hugues.[1]

Hugh II de Gournay sailed from Harfleur in 1035 with Walter Giffard to help Edward the Aetheling's attempt to claim the throne of England. He fought with Count Robert of Eu for Duke William in 1053 and was a commander at Mortemer. In 1054, Duke William gave him the lands and castle of Hugues de la Ferté-en-Bray. Hugh II de Gournay fought for Duke William at Hastings and died in battle in Wales in 1074.[2]

His son, Hugh III de Gournay, fought with his father at Hastings. He married Basilie Fleitel, daughter of Gérard Fleitel and sister of Ermengarde, the wife of Walter Giffard. They had two sons: Guillaume, who died young, and Gérard, who succeeded. Hugh III was a benefactor of the abbey of Bec, where late in life he became a monk and died by 1089. His wife, Basilie, her

---

1. There is an unproven tradition that Rolf the Viking/Duke Robert I gave Gournay to one of his men named Eudes/Odo in 912; Gurnay, *Record of House of Gournay*, 1:5–6, 16, 22, 24, 26, 31; Loyd, *Origins*, 47.

2. RBA, Brompton, LeTailleur, Holinshed, Wace, 3:4818, 8455–58; "Chronique manuscrite de Normandie," *RHGF*, 11:339, 13:237; WP, 98; Delisle, *Pièces justificatives*, no. 30 (1060, witness for Duke William for Bayeux Cathedral).

APPENDIX II

niece Amfride, and Eve, wife of Guillaume Crispin, all entered the cloister at Bec when St. Anselm was abbot, and died on successive Sundays.[3]

Gérard de Gournay married Edith de Warenne, daughter of William I de Warenne and granddaughter of King William I. Gérard supported William II Rufus from 1089, and fortified his estates at Gournay, La Ferté-en-Bray, and Gaillefontaine against Curthose. He was a benefactor of the abbeys of Bec and Saint-Sauveur. Gérard and Edith went on the First Crusade and he died in Palestine. They had two daughters, Amicie and Gundreda, and a son and heir, Hugh IV. Amicie de Gournay married Richard II Talbot and was the mother of Hugh and William Talbot. She and her husband were donors to the abbey of Valmont and the priory of Sainte-Foi at Longueville. Gundreda married Nigel d'Albini.[4]

As a youth, Hugh IV de Gournay was educated at court with Prince Henry, whom he later served when he became King Henry I. In 1116 he witnessed a charter for King Henry I with Thomas and William de St John. Hugh IV rebelled against King Henry I in 1118, took the castle of Le Plessis and gave it to Hugh Talbot, his relative (*nepos*), but it was soon retaken by the king. After the death of King Henry I, Hugh IV supported King Stephen and thereby incurred the wrath of his successor, King Henry II. Hugh IV married first Béatrice de Vermandois, daughter of Hugues I Capet of France, and second Mélisende de Coucy, daughter of Thomas comte d'Amiens. By his second wife, Hugh IV had sons Gérard, who died young, and Hugh V, who succeeded him. He supported the abbeys of Saint-Sauveur and Bec in Normandy, to which he made donations for the souls of his first wife and his young son by her. With his second wife, he founded the abbey of Beaubec in 1127 and the priory of Clairruissel for nuns of Fontevraud in 1140. Hugh IV went on the Second Crusade with King Louis VII of France in 1147–49. Hugh IV had a sister, Amicie, who married Richard II Talbot. In 1172 he still held twelve knights' fees in Normandy. Hugh IV died about 1178/79.[5]

3. *Actes Henri II*, vol. 2, no. 744; *RRAN*, vol. 1, nos. 6a (1167, Hugh *signum* with king, queen, son, Gerald de Neufmarché), 69 (1073, William I grant to Marmoutier, Hugh with king), 105 (1071–77, William I, grant to St-Etienne Caen, witnessed by king, queen, Robert de Mortain, Hugh de Gournay, Vicomte Richard d'Avranches, Walter Giffard, Hugh de Grandmesnil), 125, 170–71 (1179–82, William I to Caen, Hugh *signum* with king, queen, bishops, Robert de Mortain, Hugh of Chester, Walter Giffard, Hugh de Grandmesnil), vol. 2, App. no. lxxvi; Gurnay, *Record*, 52, 61; Keats-Rohan, *Domesday People*, 263–64; Power, *Norman Frontier*, 504.

4. OV, 4:182–87, 214–15, 236–37, 5:34–35; WJ, 2:viii, 8; *Actes Henri II*, vol. 2, no. 744; EYC, vol. 9, nos. 116, 118, 123, 149–51 (Gundreda); *RRAN*, vol. 2, App. no. lxxvi (1113, grant by Hugh to Bec); *Charters Redvers*, no. 1 (1080–1107); Gurnay, *Record*, 123–24; Keats-Rohan, *Domesday Descendants*, 492.

5. OV, 6:188–95, 198–200, 278–79, 368–69, 450–51, 486–87; *RRAN*, 2:1013, 1102,

APPENDIX II

Hugh V de Gournay paid relief for his father's estates to King Henry II from 1179 to 1188. He held lands in Warwickshire, Buckinghamshire, and Norfolk. Hugh V de Gournay was one of King Richard I's commanders in the Third Crusade, fighting with Richard at Acre in 1191, after which King Richard made him governor of Acre. However, he turned against Richard during the latter's captivity. He collaborated with King Philippe-Auguste of France during King Richard's imprisonment and when Richard was released in 1194, Hugh forfeited all his lands as a traitor, including Pillerton, Warwickshire, which the king then gave to Hugh de Hercy. Since Gournay lay between Normandy and France, it was a crucial site in the wars of Kings Richard and John against France. However, after the murder of Prince Arthur by King John became known, Hugh surrendered his strategic castle at Gournay-en-Bray to the king of France in April 1203. On May 4, King John confiscated Gournay's property in England, including Pillerton. Gournay was not, however, welcomed at the French court. He remained in exile in Cambrai until the Emperor Otto facilitated his reconciliation with King John. He married Juliane de Dammartin and they had two sons, Gérard who inherited but died soon after, and Hugh VI, who then succeeded, and a daughter Mélisende. Hugh V donated to the abbey of Fécamp for the souls of his wife, Juliane, and children. At the end of his life, he became a Knight Templar in Pictavia and died in October 1214.[6] The possession of Pillerton Hersey and Kineton, Warwickshire, was in constant dispute between Hugh V de Gournay and Hugh de Hercy.

1303, 1680, App. no. lxxvi; vol. 3, no. 132; RBE, 2:628; Torigni, 1:138–39, 168–69; EYC, vol. 9, nos. 115–16, 118, 123, 149–51; Gundreda, daughter of Gérard de Gournay and wife of Nigel d'Aubigny, donated property to the hospital of St. Leonard in York, and the hospital of St. Michael the Archangel to Whitby Abbey for the soul of her son Roger; *Charters of Mowbray* 1107–91, nos. 21, 31, 33, 37, 47, 49, 98–99, 155–56, 170, 201, 218, 228, 300, 302; *Actes Henri II*, 2:532, 636, 768; arr. Dieppe; cell of Savigny, in 1147 became Cistercian; Gurnay, *Record*, 111–12, 123–24; Gurnay, *Supplement*, 737; Keats-Rohan, *Domesday Descendants*, 492–93.

6. RBE, 2:477, 537, 792; charter dated 1198, confirmed by King Richard I same year); Gurnay, *Record*, 141, 156; *Gallia christiana*, 11:29; *NeustriaPia*, 891; *Cartulary of Missenden Abbey*, 3:558–61; EYC, 9:115–16, 118, 123, 149–50; RRAN, vol. 2, App. lxxvi; *Annales monastici*, 3:42; Hugh founded the abbey of Bellosanne in 1198 and the priory of Saint-Aubin-en-Bray in 1200; Juliane was the daughter of Aubrey comte de Dammartin, seigneur de Lillebonne; Pictavia generally means of Poitou; Hugh VI paid a fine for his succession in 1216; he married twice, had a daughter Juliane, and died in 1239; *RotPat*, 57; Powicke, *Loss of Normandy*, 109, 150, 160–61, 285–86, 340–41; Power, *Norman Frontier*, 27: 1172 military service on border marches, 80: about 1170, at Le Mans son of Hugh de Gournay acknowledged receiving five marks for transaction in Buckinghamshire from a Norman monk in the presence of the seneschal from Brittany, 355–57, 429: the Gournays valued their English lands more than their Norman lands.

APPENDIX II

The de Gournay family intermarried with ducal family and with the Fleitels and Talbots of the Pays de Caux; they were related by marriage to the Giffards and de Warennes. In England the de Gournay family held land in Warwickshire which went to Hugh de Hercy, first by gift of King Richard I and later after litigation. They were major actors with the de Hercy family in Warwickshire and close relatives of the Talbot family with whom the Hercys married. They also held some land in Buckinghamshire.

BASSET

The Basset family was probably from Ouilly-le-Basset, arrondissement Caen, canton Falaise, on the Orne River, where they were tenants of the d'Oilly family. The town was later given the name Basset as an honorific. In Normandy they were, in the words of Orderic Vitalis, "*de ignobili stirpe,*" (of ignoble roots) raised up "from the dust" (*de pulvere*) by King Henry I.[7]

Ralph Basset went to England with Duke William and fought at Hastings. In 1086, Ralph Basset held one fee of Robert d'Oilly, his neighbor in Western Normandy, in Buckinghamshire. Gilbert Basset held also of d'Oilly in Oxfordshire, and William Basset held of Hugh de Beauchamp in Bedfordshire. Although Ralph Basset had been merely a minor Domesday tenant in 1086, his rise under King Henry I was spectacular, when he became an important royal justice in England, holding court in eleven shires. Such an officeholder or *minister* in the king's service could acquire great power and wealth. In 1109, Ralph and Gilbert Basset made donations to Eynsham Abbey, which were confirmed by King Henry I. In 1121, Ralph Basset donated one carucate of the land he held in Colston-Bassset, Nottinghamshire, to Eynsham. As justice, he reputedly hanged forty-four thieves in 1124 in Leicestershire. He entered Abingdon Abbey as a monk shortly before his death.[8]

7. The name Basset meant "low stature" in old French; the town is now called Pont-d'Oilly, a union of smaller towns on both sides of the Orne River; it is possible that the Bassets were related to or members of the d'Oilly family; *Basset Charters*, v; PR 31 Henry I 3, 7, 9, 14–15, 34, 36, 39, 41, 44, 48–49, 55–56, 60, 64, 68, 70, 72–74, 76–81, 86–87, 90–92, 97–99, 105–06; Round, *Ancient Charters*, no. 6; *RRAN*, vol. 2, app. cxxvii; RBE, 1:223, 329–31, 2:483–85; Gilbert's son, Robert, became a monk of Abingdon; Loyd, *Origins*, 12; Keats-Rohan, *Domesday People*, 327–28: has it backwards, origin at Montreuil, later at Ouilly.

8. RBA, Brompton, Leland, Hollinshed, Dives, Falaise (Raoul); Marworth, Bucks, Milton, Bedfordshire, with Adelaide and Ivo de Grandmesnil, Miles Crispin; OV, 2:30–31; 3:16–17 ("new man" of Henry I); RBE, 1:72, 81–82, 104, 126, 129, 171–73, 329–31; *Eynsham Cartulary*, nos. 7, 100; PR 31 Henry I, 3, 7, 14–15, 39, 73, 76, 80–81, 87, 90, 97–98; Ralph witnessed a donation charter of King Henry I to Thorney; *RRAN*, vol. 2,

APPENDIX II

His son, Richard Basset, was also a royal justice, and co-sheriff of Buckinghamshire and Huntingdonshire in 1129–30. He held the small fee in Montreuil-au-Houlme, Orne, which had been given to his father as a reward for his service. Neither Ralph nor Richard held many lands in England until King Henry I arranged the marriage of Richard to Mathilde Ridel, daughter and heir of Geoffrey Ridel and Geva d'Avranches, illegitimate daughter of Hugh d'Avranches, earl of Chester. Both Basset and Ridel were among King Henry I's new men and he treated them well. On the death of Mathilde's brothers on the *White Ship* in 1120, King Henry I granted the wardship of the Ridel estates, including the inheritance of Geva d'Avranches, and of the minor Robert Ridel to Richard Basset until Robert should be knighted and marry a niece of Richard Basset. After that Richard would receive £20 in land and four enfeoffed knights from the king as his marriage portion to Mathilde. Minority in wardship was often a time when the regent expropriated much of the family's property, although he was legally entitled to the income. The right to choose a spouse for the heir was also quite valuable. According to the Pipe Roll of 1130, Richard Basset held fees in Nottinghamshire at Colston and Wiverton, near the de Hériz family, and also in Warwickshire and Buckinghamshire. Richard Basset built a stone castle in Normandy to show off his wealth and founded a monastery at Launde, Leicestershire. King Henry I confirmed donations of Richard and Mathilde Basset of land from Colston, Nottinghamshire, to Launde.[9]

Richard Basset and Mathilde Ridel had daughters Sibyl and Mathilda, and sons Geoffrey II Ridel, who took his mother's name, Ralph II, and William Basset. Geoffrey II succeeded, but gave his lands in England to his

App. lxxxii; the royal justices gradually came to replace honourial courts), cxxvii; *MA*, 1:308, 3:86–87; *CartRameseia*, nos. 164, 177; *Rolls of Arms Henry III*, Walford's Roll, no. 92, p. 185; *BassetCharters*, xxviii–xxx; Thoroton, *Nottinghamshire*, 1:161; Hollister, *Henry I*, 358; J. Green, "Basset, Ralph," ODNB, 4:268–69; J. Green, *Aristocracy*, 9, 17, 180, 249, 266; Keats-Rohan, *Domesday People*, 209, 327–28, 467.

9. *Basset Charters*, nos. 47, 49 (1120/23, grant witnessed by Robert, Osmund and Turstin Basset); Richard was also made custodian of the revenues of Peterborough Abbey in 1125; RBE, 1:329–31; PR 31 Henry I, 5, 8–9, 34, 36, 41, 44, 48–49, 55–56, 60, 64, 68, 70, 72, 74, 77–79, 86, 91–92, 99, 105–6; *RRAN*, 2:1389, App. clxxxix, cclxi, vol. 3, nos. 43, 284; CEC, 39–40, 52, 64, 104, 129; *MA*, 1:351, 432, 3:487, 6:1, 187–89; *CartRameseia*, no. 174; in the reign of Stephen, Robert Basset, brother or cousin of Ralph, who witnessed his marriage settlement, also witnessed nine times for Earl Ranulf II of Chester, and donated land he held under the earl of Chester to the Templars; other donations to the Templars were made by Turgis of Avranches, Robert de Ferrers, and Robert II d'Oilly; Thoroton, *Nottinghamshire*, 1:161; Coss, *Lady*, 25–26: Geva was the only woman on the witness list; Waugh, *Lordship*, 210–13, 221–23; J. Green, *Aristocracy*, 180–81, 213, 267, 404, 411; Keats-Rohan, *Domesday People*, 230–231; Keats-Rohan, *Domesday Descendants*, 166.

APPENDIX II

brother Ralph II, in exchange for the lands in Normandy Ralph had inherited. Geoffrey certified that in 1135 Ralph II held of him one knight's fee in Colston, Nottinghamshire, which had come from their grandfather Ridel. From 1159 to 1162, Ralph II was sheriff of Warwickshire and Leicestershire. He died in 1163/64, leaving a son Ralph III. The youngest brother, William II, was undersheriff during his brother's term as sheriff, sheriff himself in 1163–64, and died about 1185.[10]

Thomas I Basset was sheriff of Oxfordshire under King Henry II. He married Alice de Dunstanville and they were the parents of Gilbert, Thomas II, and Alan Basset. Thomas I died in 1182. Gilbert held lands in Wallingford and Buckinghamshire, but exchanged his English lands for the Norman lands of his brother Thomas II. Gilbert married Egeline de Courtenay, daughter of Hawise d'Avranches.[11]

Thomas II Basset was given the barony of Headington, Oxfordshire, by King John in 1202. He was one of the *consiliarii inquissimi* of King John. He served as sheriff of Oxfordshire and constable of Oxford. He paid five hundred marks to hold in ward Henry de Neubourg de Beaumont, future earl of Warwick, in 1205. Since wardships were lucrative, they were often bought and sold. Wardship was imposed on orphaned minors who were given to a *prochain ami*. Wards could not inherit until they reached majority, fifteen for an estate in land, twenty-one for a military fee. Wardship was a valuable asset for the king who assigned it and for the guardian because he was entitled to take the fruits of the ward's estates and arrange his or her marriage during the minority. Thomas II Basset later had John de Hercy of Pillerton, Warwickshire, in ward. Thomas had three daughters, who were his coheirs; Thomas died in 1220. Philippa, the eldest, married his ward Henry de Beaumont, earl of Warwick. The younger brother of Thomas II,

---

10. *RDP*, 1:7; *Basset Charters*, nos. 175–76; OV, 6:16–17; *RRAN*, vol. 2, App. cclxi, clxxxix, vol. 3, nos. 43–44; *CartRameseia*, no. 177; *BeauchampChart*, no. 4; CEC, no. 40; PR 31 Henry I, 64, 70, 72, 81; RBE, 1:223, 308–9, 319, 329–31, 344, 397; HKF, 2:270; Thoroton, *Nottinghamshire*, 1:161; Keats-Rohan, *Domesday Descendants*, 164–67, 1107.

11. In 1166, Gilbert II Basset held seven fees, Thurstin Basset six fees and two parts, Osmund Basset one and a quarter fees, and Fulk Basset one fee of the d'Oilly family, all in the Honour of Wallingford, Oxfordshire; Alan Basset held five fees, including a fee in nearby Wicombe, Buckinghamshire; according to the scutage rolls of King John, Thurstin Basset still held six fees, Thomas Basset five fees, Gilbert Basset seven, Alan Basset five, William Basset one and a quarter, William de Arches, three fees, William Paynel four fees, William de Kineton a fifth part, all of Wallingford; RBE, 1:51; 69, 95, 120, 126, 136, 146, 198, 308–310, 319–20; *RRAN*, vol. 3, nos. 587, 795; *Basset Charters*, xiii–xv, xxxiii–iv, nos. 178, 182–83, 186; *RotChart*, 88–90, 106, 131, 147, 155, 157–61; *MA*, 6:1, 434, 446 (witness for King Henry II with William de Laval, William du Hommet; *CartStFrideswide*, vol. 2, nos. 786–87, 793: Joan Basset, sister of Thomas I, married Aubrey comte de Dammartin; Keats-Rohan, *Domesday Descendants*, 167.

APPENDIX II

Alan Basset, was in high favor with Kings Richard I and John, whom he accompanied to Scotland, Ireland, and at Runnymede. Both Thomas and Alan were named in Magna Carta as among the king's counselors. Alan had a daughter Aline Basset who married Richard Talbot, son of Gilbert Talbot of Linton. Alan's son, Philip, was justiciar of England under Henry III.[12]

The Bassets also had interests in Yorkshire. Robert Basset donated land to Rievaulx Abbey, which was confirmed by King Richard in 1189. A grant of land in fee to William Basset in 1170–76 was witnessed by John and Ralph Basset and Walter, his brother. William Basset held pleas in Doncaster in 1178. Confirmation of a donation by William earl of Warwick and his wife Mathilda de Percy, who had Alan de Arches in ward, to Fountains Abbey in North Yorkshire was witnessed first by Henry de Neubourg and second by Simon Basset on 28 December 1175. William's father, Reynold, and brother Peter made donations to Kirkham Abbey. Peter Basset was second witness to a confirmation of donation by William de Percy between 1170 and 1185.[13]

Ralph III Basset had a son, Ralph IV, who held a knight's fee in Colston-Basset, Nottinghamshire, and was summoned to answer a property dispute by Launde Abbey. He married Isabel, and they had a son, Ralph V, who married Margaret de Somery, daughter of Roger IV de Somery of Dudley, Worcestershire, and Nicole d'Albini. They had a son, Ralph VI, who was made Lord Basset by Parliament in 1295. He had market and fair in Colston-Basset. His daughter, Maud, married William de Hériz.[14]

Later Bassets lived in Normanton, Nottinghamshire, holding of Richard Stanhope. William Basset, who died in 1442, married Katherine, sister of Richard Stanhope. The Hercys and Stanhopes later intermarried. Thomas

---

12. RBE, 1:69, 91, 95, 109, 126, 146; Emma and Alice Dammartin held one knight's fee in Warwickshire in 1196–97, two in 1199–1200, RBE, 2:778; *Basset Charters*, xv–xvii, nos. 183, 199; *RRAN*, vol. 3, nos. 587, 795; *ROF*, 7 John, 293; CPR, Henry III, 166; CFR, Henry III, 1219–20, no. 152, Henry III, 1223–24, 8, no. 421; CCR, Henry III (1226–57), 252; *Testa de Nevill*, 1:118, 261; Basset had William III de Percy in wardship from 1200 to 1213–14, and Percy married his daughter Joan; Green, *Aristocracy*, 265; Chibnall, *Anglo-Norman England*, 182; D. Carpenter, *Minority*, 11: although Basset was not the greatest baron in Oxfordshire, knights preferred to serve him on the basis of good lordship.

13. *CartRievelle*, cxcii, 125–26, cxc, 139; RBE, 1:180; EYC, vol. 1, nos. 295, 301, 303, 634, 635, vol. 2, no. 984, 986, vol. 3, nos. 1878–79, 1887, 1896, vol. 11, nos. 38; Rievaulx, clxxiii; Robert and Alice, William and Peter witnessed a charter in 1180–89, a grant of land to the church of Norton, Yorkshire, was pledged by the donors in the hands of Peter Basset in 1169–73; Thoroton, *Nottinghamshire*, 1:162; J. Green, *Aristocracy*, 138, 180–81, 249, 404, 422.

14. *MA*, 4:107, 6:135; RBE, 1:342; CPE, 6:174; Morice, *Mémoires*, vol. 1, col. 496; Thoroton, *Nottinghamshire*, 1:161–62.

Basset, who died in 1477, married Margaret, daughter of William Mering, another family related by marriage to the Hercys. Edward Basset, who died in 1580, married Elizabeth, daughter of George Lascelles, ward and relative of Humphrey II and John Hercy.[15]

The Basset family intermarried in England with relatives of the de Hercy family and with the families d'Avranches, de Beauchamp and de Hériz of the Avranchin, de Neubourg/Beaumont of Calvados, de Lascelles of the Orne, Talbot of the Pays de Caux, and Dammartin of the Ile de France. In Nottinghamshire, they married with the families of Stanhope, Mering, and Lascelles, all of whom were related to the de Hercy family by blood or marriage. In England, they held estates in Warwickshire, Oxfordshire, Nottinghamshire, Yorkshire, Buckinghamshire, and Bedfordshire. They interacted with the de Hercy family in Warwickshire, with the de Arches in Yorkshire, the de Hériz in Nottinghamshire with whom they intermarried, and possibly also with the de Hersin in Buckinghamshire. In Oxfordshire, they held the minor John I de Hercy of Warwickshire in ward. They supported the abbey of St-Évroul in Normandy, supported Eynsham, Rievaulx, Abingdon, and Kirksham Abbeys in England, and founded the priory of Launde.

OTHER LORDS IN WARWICKSHIRE

During the reign of King Henry I, Henry de Bolebec and Picot de Lascelles, both related to the de Hercy family, held in Warwickshire of Robert Marmion. In 1161–62, landholders in Warwickshire included William de Beauchamp and the earl of Chester.

The de St. John family were often co-witnesses with the Bassets. In 1166, Thomas de St. John of the Avanchin held lands of the earl of Warwick in Warwickshire and of the bishop of Worcester in Worcestershire. The St. John family were the immediate lords of the de Hériz family in Western Normandy. William II de St. John married Olive, daughter of Count Stephen of Brittany, previously married to Henry de Fougères, and came to hold the manor of Long Bennington in Lincolnshire. He married second Godehild Paynel. William and his first wife donated to Lucerne Abbey. In 1170 he was a tutor of Henry the Young King and attended the coronation of King Richard. At the beginning of the reign of King John, William de St. John held in Warwickshire, where he was mentioned with Gilbert Basset. William de St. John was one of the witnesses of the 1225 Magna Carta of King Henry III. William was present at the consecration of the archbishop of Canterbury in 1234. His son, Robert, by his second wife, was seneschal

---

15. Thoroton, *Nottinghamshire*, 1:161–62, 2:188.

of the Aquitaine. Roger de St. John held land in Oxfordshire with Guy de Laval, Gervais Paynel, Robert Marmion, and Thomas de St-Valéry. John de St. John held in Oxfordshire and Berkshire. His widow and son withheld knight's service from the earl of Warwick for Shinfield and Swallowfield, Berkshire, towns later associated with the Hercy family in Berkshire. Robert's son John de St. John was seneschal of Gascony, a major military commander for King Edward I and a member of his Council.[16]

16. DB Picot de Lascelles held five fees in Yorkshire of Count Alan, and four fees in Lincolnshire; other Domesday landholders in Warwickshire were King William, the bishop of Bayeux, Evesham Abbey, Robert le Dispenser, Urse d'Abetot, Adelaide, wife of Hugh de Grandmesnil, and Roger de Bully; RBE, 1:18, 30, 59, 108, 109, 109–10, 138–39, 269, 301, 324–27, 2:550, 552, 652, 660–61, 702; MA, 2:6; RRAN, vol. 2, App. clxxiv, 897; RRAN, vol. 3, nos. 296, 362a, 365a, 366, 443, 632, 644, 651, 795; William de Beauchamp held in Warwickshire, in Buckinghamshire, and in Nottinghamshire of the Honour of Tickhill with Ralph Tesson and William de Hercy; in 1166 he held two fees of Gervais Paynel in Staffordshire; PR, 30 Henry I, 108; PR 31 Henry I, 3; EYC, 4:69, 89; CDF, nos. 792, 849, 850; *Early Charters*, no. 182; Dugdale, *Antiquities*, 1:614; *VCH, Warwick*, 5:133, 135, 308, 325–26; Prestwich, *Edward I*, 381–82, 385, 484–85, 495, 511; Keats-Rohan, *Domesday Descendants*, 690–91.

Appendix III

Lords and Neighbors of the de Arches Family in Yorkshire

DE LAVAL

Hugh II de Laval of Maine was a tenant-in-chief of King Henry I in Yorkshire, although not a landholder in Domesday, since King William I did not give land to knights from Maine. Hugh II de Laval, brother of Guy II de Laval of Maine, was an important knight of King Henry I, who gave him the Honour of Pontefract in Yorkshire after the exile of Robert de Lacy. Hugh had his nephew, Guy III de Laval, in ward, and thereby was also regent of Laval in Maine. Holding major lordships on both sides of the Channel was complex, but still feasible. Hugh II de Laval and Osberne de Arches were both tenants-in-chief in Yorkshire. Hugh II married Dameta, and they had a son, Guy. They were benefactors of the monasteries at Pontefract and Nostell in Yorkshire. Between 1119 and 1128 King Henry I confirmed donations by Hugh II de Laval, Robert de Lacy, and Osberne de Arches to the canons of Nostell. Hugh II died in 1129/30. Hugh's heir, Guy de Laval, held one of the knights' fees of Pontefract of Henry de Lacy, and ten knights held of him.[1]

---

1. PR 31 Henry I, 23; Broussillon, vol. 1, no. 103, p. 79–81; *CartRonceray*, no. 375; *MA*, 5:118, 121; EYC, vol. 3, nos. 1428, 1432–33, 1435, 1439; *RRAN*, vol. 2, nos. 1203, 1207, 1256, 1400, 1460, 1494, 1626; RBE, 1:40–41, 77; *Testa de Nevill*, 1:202; Guy had a son of the same name who held many fees in Yorkshire and several in Lincolnshire, and lived at least until 1212, and also a son Gilbert, who held in Northumberland; Loyd, *Origins*, 53; Hollister, *Henry I*, 282; Bates, *Normans and Empire*, 147; J. Green, *Aristocracy*, 131, 135, 369; Keats-Rohan, *Domesday People*, 275: Hasteng and other vassals of Robert de Lacy and Hugh de Laval were donors to St. Oswald's Nostell; Keats-Rohan, *Domesday Descendants*, 543, incorrectly posits Hugh II was son of Guy II and Denise de Mortain.

APPENDIX III

The de Laval family were neighbors of the de Hercé family in Maine. In England, Mathilda, daughter and co-heir of Hugh IV de Bolebec, related to the de Arches family, married a later Hugh de Laval between 1262 and 1267.[2] Thus the de Laval family, neighbors of the de Arches family in the twelfth century, intermarried with the de Bolebec family in England, making them relatives of the de Arches family by marriage in the thirteenth. The de Laval family were donors to Nostell Priory with the de Arches, de Lascelles, and de Lacy families. In addition, the de Laval family had the de Lascelles family, relatives of the de Hercy family, as tenants and the de Lascelles often witnessed documents for the de Lavals.

DE LACY

Ilbert de Lacy of Lassy, Calvados, in Western Normandy fought at Hastings, probably under Odo of Bayeux. King William gave him many manors in Yorkshire, first in 1067, and more in 1071. By 1086 Ilbert de Lacy was tenant-in-chief of 186 manors in Yorkshire, including the great Honour of Pontefract in the West Riding, which he held of the king with castle service. He built his castle on a hill, near the Great Northern Road. He also held ten manors in Nottinghamshire as tenant-in-chief, one in Wallingford, Buckinghamshire, one in Headington, Oxfordshire, and many in Lincolnshire, which he held of Bishop Odo. He subinfeuded Leeds to Ralph Paynel, his tenant in two other Yorkshire manors. In 1086-87, King William I confirmed Ilbert de Lacy's donation of Hamilton to the monks of Selby Abbey in north Yorkshire. Ilbert also donated lands to St. Mary's York. Ilbert also donated to Sainte-Trinité in Rouen when his mother entered that convent. Ilbert married Hawise, and they had two sons, Robert I and Hugh. Hugh died young and was buried in Sainte-Trinité de Rouen. Ilbert and Robert built the Augustinian priory of St. Oswald at Nostell in Yorkshire. Ilbert died about 1093 and was succeeded by his son Robert.[3]

---

2. PR 31 Henry I, 27; *IPM*, vol. 1 (Henry III), nos. 528, 689, pp. 151, 217; vol. 2 (Edward I) no. 130, p. 86.

3. Wace, 3:8471, 8527; DB Yorkshire, vol. 1, 9, vol. 2, CW 1 (with Osberne de Arches), 2-3, 23, SW Sk 4-12, SW Ba 5-7, 8 (with Osberne de Arches), 9-11, SW Sf 37, SW O 2-14, 16, SW St 1, 3-8, 10-16, SW Ag 1-8, 13, 15-16, SW M 1-10; DB Nottinghamshire, 20:1-8; his manors in Nottinghamshire were in the south, in Newark and Bingham Hundreds, and included Thoroton, Aslockton, East Stoke, Shelton, and Sibthorpe; *MA*, 3:534, 536, 547, 4:120, 5:533, 6:89; EYC, vol. 3, nos. 1414-18, 1423, 1483, 1491; *RRAN*, vol. 3, no. 817; J. Green, *Aristocracy*, 116, 131, 135, 180, 283; Keats-Rohan, *Domesday People*, 277-78.

APPENDIX III

Robert I de Lacy increased the Yorkshire lands and founded the Cluniac priory of St. John at Pontefract. The foundation charter was witnessed by William Peverel. Robert married Mathilda, and they had sons Ilbert II, Henry, and Robert. King Henry I confirmed donations to Nostell by Robert I de Lacy, Hugh de Laval, and their vassals, including two fees donated by William de Arches. In 1114 Robert I de Lacy and his son Ilbert II were exiled from England and lost Pontefract with its sixty fees. Pontefract was then given to Hugh II de Laval by King Henry I. Robert I retained his estates in Normandy and died before 1129.[4]

The Norman estates of Robert I de Lacy were held by his younger son, Henry de Lacy, in 1133. His elder son Ilbert II was restored to some of his English estates by King Stephen. He held two fees of the archbishop of York and twenty fees in Pontefract in 1166. Ilbert II married Alice de Gant, but they had no children. Ilbert II fought at the battles of the Standard in 1138 and Lincoln in 1141. He was taken prisoner at Lincoln in 1141 and died by 1143. After his death, Alice donated property to Pontefract Priory for the soul of her husband, which charter was witnessed by William Peverel. Ilbert II was succeeded by his brother Henry. Henry de Lacy confirmed the donation of land to Selby Abbey by John de Lascelles, whose son Simon was his tenant. The de Lascelles were related to the de Hercy family.[5]

The de Lacy family were lords and neighbors of the de Arches family. They held great lands in Yorkshire, and also manors in Nottinghamshire, Buckinghamshire, and Headington, Oxfordshire. They confirmed documents for the de Lascelles family. They were co-donors to Nostell with the de Laval and de Arches families. They supported the monasteries of Selby, Saint Mary's York, and Saint John's Pontefract in Yorkshire.

---

4. *MA*, 3:499–500, 548–50, 4:120–22, 5:533; *Liber Vitae Dunhelmensis* 73; *RRAN*, vol. 3, nos. 46, 58, 204, 271, 428–29, 621–22; *Ancient Charters*, 1 (1095–1100, exchange of lands between Robert de Lacy and Urse d'Abetot); *EYC*, vol. 3, nos. 1428, 1492; gift of Ralph de Lascelles, knight of Pontefract, noted only in later confirmation; Robert I de Lacy exchanged lands in Lincolnshire with Urse d'Abetot, with the approval of the bishop and the sheriff; Keats-Rohan, *Domesday Descendants*, 537–38.

5. *RBE*, 1:40–41, 53, 77, 412–13, 421–24; *RRAN*, vol. 3, nos. 46, 204, 271, 428–31, 621–22, 664, 797; *MA*, 3:207–08, 211, 225–26, 489, 5:118, 122, 130, 136, 532; Henry married Aubreye, daughter of Eustace FitzJohn, and they had a son, Robert de Lacy, who married Isabel de Warenne; *EYC*, vol. 1, no. 642, vol. 3, nos. 1492, 1544, 1567; *Chartulary of Pontefract* 1:xvii, 33; *CEC*, nos. 16–17, 69; *RHGF*, 23:135; Howlett, *Chronicles*, 3:140; *OV*, 5:128; *CPE*, 7:676; Lassy in Western Normandy was still held by Ilbert and Gilbert de Lacy in 1164; Keats-Rohan, *Domesday Descendants*, 537–38.

APPENDIX III

DE PERCY

William I de Percy and Hugh d'Avranches, both of Western Normandy, came to England with King William I in December 1067, although some sources said de Percy fought at Hastings. William was called Algernon because he wore a beard, which was unusual at the time. William held Bolton-Percy in Yorkshire; by 1069; Bolton became the residence of the high sheriffs of Yorkshire. Hugh d'Avranches gave him the lordship of Whitby in Yorkshire when he was made earl of Chester in 1070. William fought with King William against the Scots in 1072 and thereafter was made constable of York. He was Domesday tenant-in-chief of 132 lordships in Yorkshire and also of many in Lincolnshire. According to Domesday, his many manors in Yorkshire included Whitby, and many in Craven, held of Earl Hugh of Chester and the archbishop of Durham. William I married Emma de Port, from Port-en-Bessin, Calvados, arrondissement Bayeux, daughter of Hugh de Port, who fought at Hastings.[6]

In 1074/8, Reinfrid, a former soldier and knight of William I de Percy became a Benedictine monk at Evesham. Reinfrid's son, Fulk, was dapifer of Alan de Percy and steward of Osberne de Arches; Fulk's son, Robert, married Alice de St. Quentin, granddaughter of Osberne de Arches. Reinfrid approached William I de Percy to ask for his help in refounding a monastery at Whitby on the coast of north Yorkshire. William agreed as tenant, and his lord Earl Hugh of Chester donated the land, the town, and its church. With the help of Abbot Stephen, the monastery was restored and occupied by the monks. At this point, William de Percy changed his mind and tried to drive the monks away. Abbot Stephen complained to the king when both he and the king were in Normandy and obtained a royal charter. In the meantime, Alan of Richmond had given the monks land and a church which later became St. Mary's York. William de Percy's brother Serlo de Percy became a Benedictine monk and petitioned King William II Rufus to reinstate the monks at Whitby. Serlo had been a childhood friend of King William II. William de Percy reluctantly gave a charter to Serlo, now prior, to build a church at Whitby to pray for the souls of the late king and queen, for their son King William II, for Earl Hugh, and for himself, his wife

6. Wace, 3:8480; Brompton, Leland, Auchinleck; Falaise and Dives both have Guillaume de Perci; DB Yorkshire, 1:13, C 10, 3, Y 1, 3, 4, N 1, 2:30, W 2, CN 1, CE 25, 27, 29–30, CW 25, 31, 33, 35, 40, SW Sk 18, SW Ba 3–4 (with Osbern de Arches), 12, SW Sf 6, 19, 23, 25–26, 30, SW An 4 (with Osberne de Arches), 5–7, 17, SW Bu 9, 19–21, 32–33, 35–36, 39–44, SN L 1, 11, 21–22, 25, SN D 3, 5–9, 13, SN B 22, SN Bi 4–5, SE Wei 4–5, 7, SW Sn 4–6, 9–10, SE Wa 1, se p 1–2, 4, 7, SE Tu 6–7; *MA*, 1:409–10, 3:544–46; EYC, 11:123; CEC, no.5; *RRAN*, vol. 1, no. 220, vol. 3, 942; Keats-Rohan, *Domesday People*, 266–67, 478–79.

and son; the charter was witnessed by his wife and three of his sons, and by his brother Ernald de Percy. Serlo became abbot and was later succeeded as abbot by his nephew William. Over the years William I de Percy, his wife Emma, and their four sons, Alan, Walter, William, and Richard, and Osberne de Arches generously supported Whitby, where a stone abbey was built in 1100. William I de Percy fought in the First Crusade and died near Jerusalem in 1097/8. His widow later donated a house to Whitby and was buried in the monastery.[7]

William's brother Ernald de Percy was a witness to the foundation charter of Whitby and was its supporter. He also donated a church and other property to Guisborough Priory, witnessed by Robert de Brus. Ernald left sons Ernald II and Robert, and daughter Hawise, who married Ralph II de Neville. Ernald II confirmed his father's donation to Guisborough and, with Peter de Brus, witnessed a charter for Robert de Brus. Robert de Percy held three knights' fees of the de Brus family. Robert donated by quitclaim, a release of title, to St. Peter's York and confirmed the gifts of his father, grandfather and uncle to Guisborough. Robert's son William succeeded Ernald II and married Agnes, daughter of Roger de Flamville and Juetta II de Arches. William died in 1203 and was succeeded by his son Walter de Percy.[8]

Alan I de Percy, son of William I and Emma de Port, succeeded his father in 1096. He married Emma, daughter of Gilbert de Gant and Alice de Montfort-sur-Risle. They had sons William II and Walter II, and Alan died about 1130–35. Alan witnessed the charter of the foundation of Bridlington Priory by Walter de Gant and a donation charter by King Henry I to Worksop Priory in Nottinghamshire. Alan and his wife donated to Bridlington, Guisborough, and St. Peter's York. Gifts of Alan I were witnessed by Gilbert de Arches.[9]

William II de Percy of Topcliffe, Yorkshire, succeeded and held lands with his neighbors in Yorkshire: Guy de Laval, Robert and Adam de Brus, William Fossard, William Paynel, Henry de Lacy, and Ralph de Bolebec.

---

7. *MA*, 1:409–12, 417–18, 3:544–46; *EYC*, vol. 1, no. 350, vol. 2, nos. 650, 855, vol. 11, nos. 1, 2–3, 123; *CEC*, no. 5; *RRAN*, vol. 3, no. 942; *CartWhiteby*, 1–7, no. i, 31, no. xxvii, 48, no. xlv, 69, no. lxxiv; Ellis, "Biographical Notes," 302–3: Fulk witnessed the donation charter of William de Percy and in 1099 gave Whitby two carucates of land with the permission of Osberne de Arches, confirmed in 1125 by Fulk's son Robert with permission of his lord, William de Arches; Robert married Alice de St. Quentin.

8. *EYC*, vol. 2, nos. 647, 746–47, 749–51; *RBE*, 1:77; *Rolls of Arms*, Glover's Roll, no. 48, p. 124.

9. *CEC*, no. 3; *EYC*, vol. 2, no. 1207, vol. 3, 942, vol. 11, nos. 1–3, 5–6, 123; *Abstract Bridlington*, 19–20, 31; *MA*, 1:410; *RRAN*, vol. 2, app, clxxxv, vol. 3, 942; PR 31 Henry I, 20; Keats-Rohan, *Domesday Descendants*, 629–31.

APPENDIX III

In the reign of King Henry I, Gilbert de Arches and William de Hommet held of him. William II donated to Whitby, Sallay, and Fountains Abbeys; some of his gifts were witnessed by William and Gilbert de Arches. He married first Alice de Tonbridge, daughter of Richard de Bienfaite de Clare and Alice d'Avranches, and second Sibyl de Valognes, whose family was from the Cotentin. He died in 1174/75, leaving two daughters as co-heirs, Agnes, who married, illegitimate son of Duke Godefroy de Louvain and brother of Queen Adelisa, second wife of King Henry I, and died in 1203, and Mathilda, who married William earl of Warwick, son of Roger de Beaumont de Warwick and Gundreda de Warenne. Mathilde held Alan de Arches in ward. The Percy barony in Yorkshire was divided between the two husbands. Agnes held fifteen fees in Yorkshire in her own right, and more with William Paynel, Adam de Brus, Guy de Laval, her husband and her sister. Agnes had sons Sir Henry and Richard, who assumed the name Percy. About 1188, Sir Henry married Isabel de Brus, daughter of Adam II de Brus and Juetta II de Arches.[10]

The de Percy family intermarried with members of the de Arches, de Brus, de Port, d'Avranches families and with de Beaumont earls of Warwick. They had vassal relationships with the d'Avranches and de Brus families. Matilda de Percy held Alan de Arches in ward. They were co-witnesses with members of the de Arches and de Brus families. They supported Whitby Abbey and the priories of Guisborough and Bridlington.

---

10. RBE, 1:28–29, 40–41, 77, 87, 116–17, 130, 163, 165, 416, 424–26, 2:490, 588, 700; *MA*, 1:417, 5:510–15, 6:1, 93; EYC, vol. 1, nos. 331, 548–49, vol. 2, nos. 668, 1202, vol. 3, no. 1864, vol. 6, no. 48, vol. 11, nos. 9, 11, 12, 14, 16–17, 20–22, 27, 97–8, 100, 102, 104, 106, 123; CartWhiteby, 46–47, no. xliii; CEC, no. 35; *Testa de Nevill*, 1:398; they had a son, William III de Percy, who married first Joan de Briwere and had five daughters, then second, Ellen de Balliol, by whom he had Henry de Percy, who married Eleanor de Warenne; their grandson, Sir Henry Percy, married Mary Plantagenet, daughter of Henry of Lancaster and Maud de Chaworth, in 1334; their son married Margaret de Neville; their son was Sir Henry Percy, called "Hotspur"; William III inherited, subject to his grandmother Agnes's gift of half of the barony to her younger son Richard; Richard married Agnes de Neville, but died without legitimate children, so that the barony was reunited under William III; William II's brother Walter II married by 1153 Avice de Rumilly, daughter of William FitzRanulf du Bessin and widow of William Paynel; she held two knights' fees in Yorkshire, and donated to Drax Priory, witnessed by Robert de Gant and his wife Adelise Paynel; they had sons Robert and Henry, who became abbot of Whitby; Walter II de Percy was a benefactor of Whitby Abbey; Picot de Percy witnessed charters for William I and Alan de Percy; he donated to Whitby; Robert de Percy, son of Picot, held three knights' fees in Bolton Percy, Yorkshire, of William II de Percy; Robert donated to Sallay Abbey and Nostell Priory; after he died in 1175, his widow, Cecilia, became a nun at Nun Appleton; they left sons William and Picot; William donated to Nostell Priory; Keats-Rohan, *Domesday Descendants*, 629–31.

APPENDIX III

PAYNEL

Ralph I Paynel, the brother of Guillaume I Paynel of Western Normandy, fought with Duke William in the conquest. Ralph remained in England after Hastings, and was rewarded with extensive lands in Yorkshire, Lincolnshire, and Somerset. King William I gave him all the lands of Merlesweyn, sheriff of Lincolnshire under King Edward. Domesday recorded Ralph Paynel as a tenant-in-chief in Yorkshire, where he held twenty-three lordships, and also held fees of Ilbert de Lacy and Osberne de Arches. In Yorkshire, he secured four bovates of land in Moor Monkton from Osberne de Arches. He was sheriff of Yorkshire under King William II Rufus from 1087 to 1093, and was later followed in office by Osberne de Arches. He married first the sister or daughter of Ilbert de Lacy, and second Mathilda, daughter and co-heir of Richard de Sourdeval, of the Avranchin, canton Mortain, who held many manors of the count of Mortain in Yorkshire. By his first wife, he had a son, William, and by his second wife, Mathilda, he had sons Jordan, Elias, and Alexander. He held Drax in North Yorkshire and acquired Hooten Paynel, now part of the borough of Doncaster, in South Yorkshire on the border of the West Riding, through his second wife.[11]

Ralph I Paynel gave the lands of the defunct priory of Holy Trinity in York to Marmoutier in 1089 with permission of his wife Mathilda and his four sons. Marmoutier then sent monks and established a Benedictine priory in York, which Ralph supported. He donated lands to St. Mary's York and Selby Abbey in North Yorkshire. Under King Henry I, Ralph Paynel and Robert de Brus were co-witnesses to a charter in Yorkshire.[12] Ralph I Paynel died between 1118 and 1124.

His eldest son, William Paynel, succeeded his father at Drax, Yorkshire, by 1124, where he held sixteen fees under King Henry I. He founded an Augustinian priory at Drax in the 1130s and the Benedictine abbey

11. Wace, 3:8499: des Mostiers Hubert Paienals, 8512: de Saint Johan e de Brehal; Brompton: Paynel; Leland: Hubert Paignel, Panel, alias Paignel; Holinshed: Painell; Duchesne: Paynel; Dives: Raoul Painel; DB Yorkshire, vol. 1, 16, C 25, vol. 2, CN 2, CW 38 (with Osberne de Arches), SW Ba9, SW Bu 1 (with Osberne de Arches), 8–9, 27, 43, SN Ma 5, 20–22, SN B 22, SE How 10–11, SE Bt 6, SE Th 1; EYC, vol. 3, no. 1864, vol. 6, nos. 1, 2–6, 9–12, pp. 1–65 (Clay had the advantage of viewing the departmental archives of St.-Lô, which were destroyed in the American bombing of July 1944); *RRAN*, vol. 3, no. 119; *MA*, 5:609 (Ralph witness for King William II); *RHGF*, 13:237; *Testa de Nevill*, 1:248; *CPE*, 8:284, 10:319; Keats-Rohan, *Domesday People*, 342; Keats-Rohan, *Domesday Descendants* 1057.

12. EYC, vol. 2, no. 930, vol. 6, nos. 1–7, 9–10, 14; CEC, no. 5; *RRAN*, vol. 3, no. 985; *MA*, 3:501, 548–50, no. 5; *carta* King William II concerning St. Mary's York, gifts by Osberne de Arches, Ilbert de Lacy, Ralph Paynel, William Peverel, Robert de Brus and others; PR 31 Henry I, 98; RBE, 1:434; Keats-Rohan, *Domesday People*, 342.

of Hambye in Normandy about 1145. In 1141, William and his knights took Nottingham Castle from William Peverel for the empress, but lost it soon after. William married first the daughter of William, son of Wimund d'Avranches, by whom he had sons Hugh and Fulk I, and second Avice de Rumilly, daughter and co-heir of William Meschin FitzRanulf du Bessin and Cecily de Rumilly, by whom he had a daughter Alice. Through the second marriage the Paynel family acquired Garthorpe in Leicestershire. William died about 1146-47. His widow, Avice, donated to the canons of Drax for the soul of her husband. She remarried Walter de Percy. William was succeeded by his sons Hugh, Fulk I, Thomas, and John. They supported Drax and Bridlington priories in Yorkshire, and the hospital of St. John of Jerusalem. Fulk I inherited Drax and Hambye and married Lesceline de Subligny. Fulk was a constant witness to the charters of Henry II in Normandy. He held Bingham in Nottinghamshire and Garthorpe in Leicestershire. When Fulk died, King John gave land in Garthorpe or its equivalent to Hugh de Hercy of Pillerton, Warwickshire. Fulk's son, William II, inherited Bingham and Garthorpe and married Eleonor de Vitré. Fulk II inherited Drax, Hambye, Bingham, and Garthorpe on the death of his brother's infant son, and married first Cecily Tesson and second Agatha du Hommet. Fulk II was one of the barons who made a summary of the rights of Henry II and Richard I in ecclesiastical patronage for King John in 1205. He lost his lands in Normandy, but King John accorded him lands in England.[13]

By his second wife, Mathilda de Sourdeval, Ralph Paynel had sons Jordan, Alexander, and Elias. Jordan inherited Hooten Paynel, which had belonged to his mother. He married Gertrude, daughter of Nigel Fossard, but they did not have children. Jordan made a donation to Bridlington Priory in memory of his wife, which was confirmed by King Stephen. Jordan I died about 1147 and was succeeded by his younger brother, Alexander, who married Agnes, daughter of Robert Fitz Nigel Fossard. Agnes donated land in Bramham, Yorkshire, to Nostell Priory. Alexander and Agnes had sons William and Jordan II. Alexander died by 1153 and William succeeded. In 1161/62, William held in Yorkshire with William Fossard and William de Percy. His 1166 *carta* included Fulk and Jordan Paynel. In 1167/68, William held in Yorkshire with Guy de Laval, Adam and Robert de Brus, William Fossard, William de Percy, Henry de Lacy, and Ralph de Bolebec.

13. PR 31 Henry I, 23; RBE, 1:40-41; Avice married second Walter de Percy, son of Alan I de Percy, by 1153, and had sons Robert and Henry, who became abbot of Whitby; EYC, vol. 2, no. 1214, vol. 3, nos. 1768, 1864, vol. 6, nos. 13-16, 21-22, 33-34, 45-46, 62-66, 117, 133, vol. 7, nos. 32-34, p. 42 (Garthorpe held by Meschin in 1124-29 survey); RRAN, vol. 3, nos. 111, 119, 332, 581, 703; MA, 3:501, 6:1, 194-96; *Thurgarton Cartulary*, no. 574; Keats-Rohan, *Domesday Descendants*, 1057-58.

APPENDIX III

William held twenty fees in Yorkshire in 1171/72 with William Fossard, Henry de Lacy, and Robert and Adam de Brus. In 1190, he held fifteen fees in Yorkshire with William de Percy, Robert de Lacy, Guy de Laval, Robert and Adam de Brus, and Fulk Paynel, and in 1194 of the archbishop of York with the countess of Warwick and Guy de Laval. William inherited Hooton Paynell and married Frethesant. Their daughter, also named Frethesant, married first Geoffrey Luterel of Gameston and Bridgeford, Nottinghamshire, and second Henry II de Neufmarché, son of Henry de Neufmarché. Jordan II Paynel witnessed a grant in Yorkshire between 1160 and 1175. Adam Paynel, son of Jordan II Paynel, was a witness for Robert de Brus II in Yorkshire under King Henry II. Adam donated a toft to the church of Guisborough in Yorkshire between 1174 and 1195. The youngest son of Ralph Paynel, Elias, although he had received military training to be a knight, became a Benedictine monk, prior of Holy Trinity York and abbot of Selby from 1143 to 1153.[14]

The Paynel family of Western Normandy, where they were close neighbors of the de Hériz family, intermarried with the de Lacy, Sourdeval, Fossard, Subligny, Tesson, de Brus, and du Hommet families of the Avranchin, Cotentin, and Calvados. In Yorkshire they were vasssals of the de Lacy and de Arches families and neighbors of the de Laval, de Brus, de Percy, de Lacy, and de Bolebec families. They supported the abbey of Hambye in the Cotentin and the priories of Drax, Bridlington, and Guisborough in Yorkshire.

DE BRUS

The family de Brus of the Cotentin in Western Normandy was mentioned by Wace as at Hastings as part of a contingent with their Avranchin/Cotentin neighbors de Saint-Jean, de Bréhal, and du Hommet.[15] Robert I de Brus witnessed charters for Kings William II Rufus and Henry I and served King Henry I in England after the battle of Tinchebrai in 1106. King Henry I gave Robert great estates, including eighty manors in the West Riding of Yorkshire and thirteen manors around Skelton in North Yorkshire. In

---

14. EYC, vol. 2, nos. 678, 805–06, 1018, 1020, 1022, vol. 6, nos. 9–10, 18, 86, 115–16, 117, 129–30, 132–33, 144–46, RBE, 1:29, 40–41, 52–53, 77, 87, 95, 116–17, 130, 145, 163–64, 421–24, 430; *RRAN*, vol. 3, no. 119; CPE, 8:284; PR 31 Henry I, 23; 4 John 65; CFR, *Henry III*, 1217–18, 2, 72; *Testa de Nevill*, 1:248–49; in 1166, Gilbert Paynel held in Yorkshire of Henry de Lacy, with Guy de Laval, Simon de Lascelles, Herbert de Arches, and Walter de Somerville; Keats-Rohan, *Domesday Descendants*, 985, 1055–58.

15. Wace, 3:8512: named them together: *"De Saint Johan e de Brehal, Cels de Bruis e de Homez"*; also named by Leland, Falaise, and Dives; *MA*, 6:268–70; but problem of chronology since Robert died in 1141.

1140 he built a stone castle at Skelton. Robert witnessed a donation charter to Whitby between 1094 and 1100 for Hugh d'Avranches, earl of Chester, who may have given him fees at Skelton. Between 1103 and 1106, he was a witness with Ralph Paynel for a donation of William count of Mortain to Marmoutier Abbey. In 1109, he witnessed for King Henry I at a council held in Nottingham. From 1109 to 1114, he witnessed charters in Yorkshire, and one for King Henry I in Oxfordshire. Robert I married first Agnes Bainard, daughter of the sheriff of Yorkshire, and second Agnes Paynel of Carlisle, daughter and heir of Fulk and Béatrice Paynel, who were tenants of the de Brus family in Yorkshire. King William I had given the lands of Guisborough to his half-brother, Robert de Mortain, who gave them to Robert de Brus. In 1119, Robert and his wife Agnes founded and endowed Guisborough Priory with Augustinian canons in north Yorkshire where they and their son, Adam I, are buried. The first prior of Guisborough was Robert's brother, William de Brus, from 1119 to about 1145. Robert also donated to Bridlington Priory and St. Mary's York. Around 1120, Robert I de Brus and David, son of King Malcolm of Scotland, became friends and companions in arms at King Henry I's court and later accompanied the king to Normandy. David became king of Scotland in 1124 and gave Robert lordship of the border land of Annandale in Scotland. After the death of King Henry I of England, Robert de Brus and King David of Scotland supported opposite sides in the civil war that followed. At the battle of the Standard in 1138, Robert I de Brus and his elder son Adam I fought with the English, while his younger son Robert II fought with King David. Robert I de Brus died in May 1141; Agnes after 1155.[16]

Adam I de Brus, son of Robert I and his first wife Agnes, succeeded to his father's English lands as lord of Skelton in 1141/2. He supported Guisborough Priory. He married Agnes d'Aumale, daughter of Étienne comte d'Aumale, who was the son of Adelaide de Normandie, illegitimate daughter

---

16. *MA*, 3:540, 631–32, 6:1, 265–70, 903; *EYC*, vol. 2, nos. 647–48, 650, 673, 680; *ESC*, no. lii, 47, no. liv, 48–49; variously spelled Guisborough, Gisborne, Gisburne; Madden, *Collectanea*, (1837), 4:26; Bridlington charter witnessed by Ernald de Percy and Peter I de Brus; Robert I de Brus had another son, Robert II, who succeeded to Annandale in Scotland; Robert II was a donor to Guisborough and the hospital of St. Peter, York; he married Euphemie, (*nepta*) niece or relative of William comte d'Aumale and Agnes d'Aumale, wife of Adam I de Brus; they had three sons, Robert III, William, and Bernard. Robert III succeeded to Annandale and married Isabel, the illegitimate daughter of King William I of Scotland, and died in 1191; his brother, William, then succeeded to Annandale and married Christina; he paid scutage in Yorkshire in 1190/91 and died by 1214; Keats-Rohan, *Domesday Descendants*, 355, suggests Peter I was the son of Robert I.

of Duke Robert II and sister of King William I. Adam I died about 1143/5. His first son predeceased him and the second, Adam II de Brus, succeeded.[17]

Adam II de Brus, great-grandnephew of King William I, was a minor at the time of his father's death. He came of age in 1155 and succeeded as lord of Skelton. He held fifteen fees of the archbishop of York with William de Percy, William Fossard, William and Fulk Paynel, Henry and Robert de Lacy, Ralph de Bolebec, and Jocelyn de Louvain. Both Adam I and Adam II were donors to Saint Sauveur-le-Vicomte in the Cotentin. Adam II donated to Guisborough for the souls of his father and grandfather. Adam II was called a loyal supporter of King Henry II by a contemporary, although he often paid scutage to avoid military service. Adam II de Brus married Juetta II de Arches, daughter and heir of William de Arches. They had a daughter, Isabel, and a son, Peter. Juetta I de Arches gave the town of Askham to her granddaughter, Isabel de Brus. Adam II de Brus inherited seven knights' fees of de Arches, including Thorp Arch. Adam made many donations to Guisborough, witnessed by Robert and Gerard de Lascelles, and to Rievaulx, witnessed by William de Hériz, showing contact between the de Brus and the de Lascelles and de Hériz families, both Hercy relatives. Juetta II and Adam II donated the church of Thorp Arch to the archbishop of York. She donated the town of Stainton in Durham to Nun Monkton with consent of her husband and heirs, land of her father in the fee of Mowbray to the church of St. Peter in York and made grants to other churches. Adam II de Brus died 1196. As a widow, Juetta controlled the estates. Their daughter, Isabel, married Henry de Percy, son of Jocelyn of Louvain and Agnes de Percy.[18] Their son, Sir Peter II de Brus, succeeded in 1196/97 as lord of Skelton. He held eleven knights' fees in Yorkshire, was in favor with King John, and died in 1211. His son Sir Peter III continued the family tradition of supporting Guisborough. Peter III married Hawise de Lancaster; he died returning from the Holy Land in 1241. Their son, Peter IV, died without issue by 1272, ending the male line of the de Brus family in Yorkshire. Their daughter and co-heir, Agnes de Brus, married Walter II de Faucomberg, son of Piers II de Faucomberg and Margaret de Monfichet. The Faucomberg family were related to the de Arches family. Her sister and co-heir, Katherine, inherited Thorp Arch, Tybthorp, and other properties associated with

---

17. *MA*, 3:632; 6:1, 267; Agnes's sister Adelise married Ingelger de Bohun; another sister married Gérard de Picquigny; her niece, Euphemia, married Robert II de Brus; EYC, 2:651; Keats-Rohan, *Domesday Descendants*, 354–55.

18. *MA*, 6:1, 267–68; 1155/65; EYC, 2:548–549, 553, 2:655–57, 659, 664, 668; RBE, 1:40–41, 52–53, 77, 87–88, 116–17, 434–35; PR 2 Richard I, 73, 8 Richard I; *Gesta Regis Henrici Secondi* 1:51, 65–66; Blakely, *Brus Family*, 42–44, 53, 64–65, 100, 144.

the de Arches family. Adam I and II, Peter II and III, and Agnes were all buried in Guisborough Priory.[19]

Prince, later King, David I of Scotland had given the border lordship of Annandale to his companion in arms, Robert de Brus. William de Brus, son of Robert II of Annandale was succeeded by his son Robert IV of Annandale, who married Isabel of Huntingdon, daughter of King David of Scotland and Mathilde of Chester, and died in 1245. Robert IV's elder son, Robert V of Annandale, married first Isabel de Clare, daughter of Gilbert de Clare, earl of Hertford and Gloucester, and Isabel Marshal of Pembroke. Robert V married second, Christiane, widow of Thomas de Lascelles of Bolton, Cumberland, whose family was related to the Hercy family.[20]

The de Brus family intermarried with the ducal family and with the de Arches, Paynel, de Percy, de Fauconberg, and de Lascelles families, and with the royal family of Scotland. They witnessed for Kings William II and Henry I, and for the lords d'Avranches and de Mortain. They supported St. Sauveur-le-Vicomte in the Cotentin and Guisborough and Bridlington priories in Yorkshire.

DE LASCELLES

The de Lascelles were from the Orne in Western Normandy. Their ancestor came to England with William the Conqueror in 1066 and fought at Hastings. In 1086, Picot de Lascelles held five knights' fees under Count Alan of Richmond, two and a half in Yorkshire and two and a half in Lincolnshire, and castle-guard at Richmond in the months of October and November. In 1130, Picot's sons Roger I, Turgis, and John de Lascelles held land in

---

19. RBE, 1:122, 163–64, 2:490, EYC, vol. 9, no. 55; *ROF*, 2 John, 109; *MA*, 6:1, 268; CPE, 5:269; from Picardy, castellan of St. Omer, name also spelled Fauquembergues; EYC, vol. 1, nos. 538, 548–49, 553, 555; Blakely, *Brus Family*, 215–16 (grants nos. 89–94).

20. The son of Robert V de Brus and Isabel de Clare, Robert VI, married Margaret countess of Carrick, daughter of Nigel, earl of Carrick, and Margaret Stewart; their daughter Isabel Bruce married King Erik II of Norway; their son, Robert VII "The Bruce," became in 1292 earl of Carrick and in 1306 King Robert I of Scotland; King Robert defeated the English at Bannockburn in 1314; he married first Isabel de Mar and they had a daughter, Marjory, who married Walter, son of James, high steward of Scotland, and Egidia de Burgh; King Robert married second Elizabeth de Burgh; their son became King David II of Scotland; King David married Joan of England, daughter of King Edward II and Isabelle de France, but was defeated and imprisoned in England and died without issue in 1371; the throne of Scotland then passed to the house of Stewart/Stuart through Robert Stewart, the son of David's eldest sister, Marjory, and Walter, high steward of Scotland; Robert Stewart became King Robert II.

APPENDIX III

Yorkshire, and Roger also in Lincolnshire. The castle-guard return of Henry I shows Roger holding five knights' fees of the Honour of Richmond. Roger witnessed charters for Alan count of Richmond. Roger witnessed the charter in which Osberne de Arches donated to St. Mary's York. Roger supported Count Stephen of Richmond and himself donated tithes to St. Mary's York. He was succeeded by his son, Picot II, in 1146. Picot II held Escrick of the abbey of St. Mary's York. Picot II held lands in Yorkshire and in Warwickshire in 1166. He married the daughter of Roald the constable of Richmond. He died by 1179 and was succeeded by his minor sons Roger II and Robert. Roger's lands in Lincolnshire were great enough that he had a dapifer or steward, named Luke. In 1195 he was paid 62s. 4d. for maintaining himself in the king's service under the archbishop of York. In 1212, Sir Roger was addressed as knight. He supported the barons against King John and in 1217 King Henry III. In 1318, the duke of Lancaster appointed John de Lascelles constable of Conisbrough Castle, of which Baldwin de Hercy had been constable a century earlier.[21]

The de Lascelles family was connected with de Brus and de Lacy families in Yorkshire. Robert de Lascelles held one fee of de Brus and William de Lascelles two fees in 1135. Between 1145 and 1154, Gerard de Lascelles witnessed the marriage contract for the daughter of Robert de Brus, and between 1165 and 1185 charters of Adam de Brus to the monks of Byland, Guisborough, and Rievaulx Abbeys, and between 1170 and 1190 charters of Adam II de Brus. Geoffrey de Lascelles was a tenant of the Brus fee. In the late thirteenth century, Avice, daughter of Roger III de Lascelles, married Robert de Lacy. In the fourteenth century, Ralph de Lascelles, son of Ralph, married Mathilde de Lacy.[22]

21. PR 31 Henry I, 22–23, 25, 27, 30, 32, 92, 117; EYC, vol. 1, no. 527 (1106–16, Osberne de Arches to St. Mary's York, Roger witness with Robert and Adam de Brus); EYC, vol. 3, nos. 1543–46, vol. 4, nos. 9, 13–14, 18, 28, 65, 102–03, vol. 5, nos. 186, 213–14, 233, 238, 279, 283, 292–93, 352, pp.10–11, 15, 90, 182–86, vol. 6, 14, vol. 7, 126; MA, 3:501; RBE, 1:327 (1166, Picot one old fee in Warwickshire), 421–23, 427; Survey of 1,108 confirmed holdings of Picot de Lascelles in Yorkshire; La Selle (now La Selle-le Forge), Orne, arr. Argentan, canton Fiers, and Messei, arr. Argentan, canton la Ferté-Macé; CPR, 1358–61, 555–56; MSAN, 15:92: in 1165 William de Lascelles sued his uncle Ralph over inheritance of LaSelle and Messei; the name Picot can mean "pikeman"; Loyd, Origins, 55, has Loucelles; Keats-Rohan, Domesday People, 324–25; Keats-Rohan, Domesday Descendants, 535–36.

22. EYC, vol. 2, p.13; EYC, vol. 2, nos. 650, 657, 659 (1170–90, Adam II de Brus, gift to Guisborough, Gerard de Lascelles witness), 665, 714, 716, 728, 744, 773, vol. 3, no. 1428; no.1508, 1546; EYC, vol. 5, p. 326, vol. 11, no. 232; William witnessed a quitclaim in the late twelfth century, no. 234; PR 43 Henry III, 1459, 314; Charters of Mowbray, nos. 206, 207; Robert de Lascelles and Alice his wife filed a plea concerning land belonging to Alice.

APPENDIX III

The de Lascelles family held land primarily in Yorkshire, but also a few fees in Lincolnshire, Buckinghamshire, Cheshire, and Warwickshire. In 1166, Simon de Lascelles held two knights' fees of Guy de Laval in Lincolnshire and one of Henry de Lacy in Yorkshire, as did Herbert de Arches two fees. In the reign of King John, Duncan de Lascelles held four knights' fees in Buckinghamshire/Bedfordshire. In 1210-12, Roger II de Lascelles held five fees in Chester; John, son and heir of Simon, one in the Honour of Lacy and another in Lincolnshire. He had a son, William, and a daughter and co-heir Agnes, who married Miles Basset of Berkshire. Later the de Lascelles held lands in Nottinghamshire.[23]

The de Lascelles family contributed generously to monasteries in Yorkshire. In 1121-27, King Henry I confirmed the donation of lands to St. Oswald's Priory in Nostell by Robert de Lacy and Hugh de Laval and their vassals, including Robert de Lascelles, William de Arches, and Ralph de Lascelles. Roger's brother, John de Lascelles of Escrick, donated a house and land to the monks of Selby Abbey in North Yorkshire between 1141 and 1147, his donation confirmed by Henry de Lacy. He made another later donation to Selby for the soul of his brother Robert. Between 1154 and 1159, Robert de Lascelles, with permission of Mathilde his wife and Gerard his heir donated one caracute of land in Morton to Rievaulx Abbey in North Yorkshire, witnessed by his son Gerard, Fulk Paynel, Richard Talbot, and others, and confirmed between 1170 and 1176 by Geoffrey de Lascelles, with consent of his brothers Robert and William, witnessed by Gerard de Lascelles and his son Adam, Robert and William de Lascelles, and Geoffrey Ridel. Between 1170 and 1180, Robert and William de Lascelles witnessed a charter to Whitby, and between 1175 and 1189, Geoffrey witnessed a charter to the same. Between 1178 and 1181, William de Lascelles, deacon, with other canons and deacons of York, witnessed a confirmation charter to Rievaulx, and another before 1185, in which he was called *clericus*. Between 1182 and 1206, Ralph I de Lascelles made a quitclaim to Whitby witnessed by William de Lascelles. William witnessed a donation to monks of Byland Abbey in North Yorkshire between 1180 and 1200. Humphrey de Lascelles, brother of Simon, donated land and his body for burial to the monks of Bretton Priory in the West Riding and his son Richard donated to the Hospitallers of Jerusalem. Humphrey and his son Richard witnessed donations to the abbey of Fountains. In 1190-1202 Thomas de Lascelles was first witness of a charter to Fountains. In 1218-19, Thomas was accused of imprisoning his servant, seizing his chattels, and expelling his family.

---

23. RBE, 1:139, 327, 379, 421-23, 427, 2:519, 521-22, 536, 587; held Sturton and Gateford in Nottinghamshire in reign of Henry VIII.

APPENDIX III

Thomas claimed the servant had not given him his account and owed him money; Thomas was acquitted. In 1205–15, Picot III de Lascelles was the sole witness of a grant by Brian FitzAlan to William Neville. In 1294, Roger, William, and Robert de Lascelles witnessed a grant to St. Peter's Hospital in York. At the same time, a similar grant to St. Peter's was made by Alan de Percy, confirmed by William de Percy, and witnessed by Gilbert de Arches.[24]

In the reign of Henry I, Ralph de Lascelles donated one bovate in Comberworth to Nostell, showing an early connection to that town. Robert Constable of Halsham had a great-grandson William Constable of Halsham and Burton, who had a son, Simon le Constable of Burton and of Legsby, Yorkshire, who married Catherine Comberworth, daughter of Robert Comberworth of Comberworth in the late thirteenth century. They had a son Robert, who married Avice/Alice de Lascelles in 1301; Avice was the daughter and co-heir of Roger de Lascelles. Sir Ralph de Lascelles of Escrick, Yorkshire, born about 1270, married Maud Constable, daughter of Sir William Constable of Flamborough. They had sons Walter and Richard. The great-grandson of Richard Lascelles of Escrick was Raffe Lascelles who held Sturton in Nottinghamshire. Robert Fitz William le Constable was the illegitimate son of the constable of Chester; his son Robert had a son William, who married the daughter of Maud de Percy; their son Robert had a son Sir William who married Alicia, daughter of Lucy de Brus; their son, Sir Robert, had Sir Marmaduke, who had a son Robert, father of Sir Marmaduke who married Catherline Comberworth, daughter of Robert Comberworth of Somerby, Lincolnshire. About 1405, Sir Thomas de Hercy of Nottinghamshire married Catherine Comberworth, the widow of Sir Marmaduke Constable. The de Hercy and de Lascelles families considered each other cousins through their common Comberworth and Constable ancestors.[25]

---

24. EYC, vol. 1, no. 632; vol. 2, p.13, nos. 727–28, 775; 893–94, 962, vol. 3, nos. 1428, 1543–44, 1546, 1696, 1700–1702, 1704–6, 1708, 1710–12, 1729, 1747, 1840, 1860, 1872, 1878, vol. 5, nos. 375, vol. 9, 79, 131; RBE, 1:138–39, 327, 379, 422–23, 427; 2:519, 521–22, 536, 587; CChR, Henry III–Edward I, 1257–1300, 124, 231; Thomas, *Vassals*, 63.

25. East Riding Archives, DDCC/135/5/ 20 and 28, records and deeds Constable family; Sir William Fauconberg was a witness; CPR, Richard II, 1381–85, 200; CCR, Richard II, 1392–96, 95–96, there were places called Comberworth in Yorkshire and Lincolnshire; Goldberg, *Medieval England*, 253: in the fourteenth century, Robert Lascelles, a merchant in York, sued a chandler in church court for debts owed; Dugdale, *Visitation of Yorkshire*, 302; Jones, *History*, 284; *Visitation of 1480–1500*, 33, MS Ashmole 831: has Sir Ralph son of Sir John, son of Sir Richard of Escrick.

Appendix IV
Other Possible Places of Origin of the de Hériz Family

THE SECOND POSSIBLE LOCATION of the de Hériz family was in Hérils in western Calvados in the arrondissement of Bayeux, canton Trévières. Charters from the cathedral of Nôtre Dame in Bayeux establish that the town of Hérils was called Hériz at least in the years 1135–1142, 1147, and 1166.[1]

Hérils came under the lordship of Robert de Neubourg, younger son of Henry de Beaumont de Neubourg, earl of Warwick. Robert de Neubourg administered his father's lands in Normandy. When Earl Henry died in 1119, his eldest son, Roger, inherited the earldom of Warwick and Robert inherited lands in Calvados and the castles of Neubourg in the Eure and Annebecq in the Orne. He was a donor to the abbeys of Bec and Préaux. Robert supported Geoffroy Plantagenet of Anjou from 1136 and was seneschal and justiciar of Normandy from 1154 to 1159 under King Henry II.[2]

At some point between 1135 and 1142, the men of Hérils confirmed that the lands held by Goscelin, *succentor* (subcantor) of the cathedral of Bayeux, in Hérils and the church of Hérils, had been given in alms to

---

1. Hérils was later absorbed into Maisons and no longer exists; also called Herith in 1146–47; CEC, nos. 35, 59, 66, 183, 204; after the death of Richard d'Avranches, earl of Chester, in 1120, Trévières was held by his successor, Earl Ranulf I of Chester and the Bessin, who was succeeded by Earl Hugh; charters of earls Ranulf I and II were witnessed by William de Percy and Robert de Trévières; Keats-Rohan, *Domesday People*, 376, postulates that Hérils was the seat of Robert de Hériz.

2. OV, 6:188–91, 200–01; in 1138 the king had him intervene in a quarrel of his brother Earl Roger of Warwick; CPE, 12/2 360, n.g.; Fulk II Paynel married Agathe du Hommet and had sons Fulk III, who married the dame de Bréhal, William, who married Pernelle Tesson, and John, and a daughter, Lucie, who married André II de Vitré; these marriages link the families de Subligny and Paynel of the Avranchin with the du Hommet family of the Cotentin and Calvados; the first marriage of Agathe du Hommet had been to Guillaume de Fougères in Brittany, by whom she had a daughter Clémence, who married first Alain de Dinan and second Earl Ranulf III of Chester; Crouch, *Image*, 33, 38, 53, 77, 206.

Goscelin. In 1146, Robert de Neubourg declared that he made the donation of the church of Hérils, a tenth of the town, the land of Goscelin, and also half of the church of Somervieu to the cathedral of Bayeux. In these documents, Hérils was generally called Hériz and less often Hérith. The donation by de Neubourg was confirmed by Geoffroy duke of Normandy in 1147. The lord of Hérils also held Somervieu, arrondissement Bayeux, a place where the bishops of Bayeux had a castle. Somervieu was later spelled Somerville.[3]

There is little evidence of a de Hériz family at Hérils or Somervieu in the eleventh or twelfth centuries, except the spelling of the place name as Hériz in the mid-twelfth century. There is circumstantial evidence of possible connections between a de Hériz family and the du Hommet and de Neubourg families.

The Le Héricy family held land at Fierville-en-Bessin, arrondissment Caen, southwest of Caen in Calvados. There are two inscriptions in Fierville-en-Bessin associating the site with the Le Héricy family, spelled in one Le Hérissy, and Le Héricie in the other. The first, on a tomb in the church, reads "*Cy gist noble dame Isabeau de Couvert, en son vivant dame d'Estreham-le-Perroux, femme de noble homme Le Hérissy, escuyier, seigneur de Fierville, morte l'an 1511.*" The other inscription is found on a clock: "*Le Héricie, seigneur de Fierville. MDXXII.*"[4]

Fierville-en-Bessin in Calvados was in the diocese of Bayeux, but the patron of its parish church was the abbot of Fontenay. In the eleventh century, Herluin de Fierville, a vassal of Radulf de Tesson, had contributed with his lord to the foundation of Fontenay Abbey. The charter concerned episcopal rights over the parishes of Fontenay, Fierville, and others. The charter was signed by Radulf Tesson and Herluin de Fierville, and by King William I and Queen Mathilde of England. In the mid-twelfth century, Jourdain de la Roche-Tesson, lord of Grippon and Subligny near La Rochelle, was also baron of the canton of Trévières in Calvados, in which the towns of Hérils and Étréham, the latter held by the Le Héricy family of Fierville-en-Bessin, were located.[5]

Richard Le Héricy, knight of Fierville, was documented in 1110 and 1180, although this may have been two different men with the same name.

---

3. *Bayeux Livre Noir*, lxvi, lxxxiv, 12, 127–29, 253–54, 291; *RRAN*, vol. 3, no. 59; *MSAN*, 25:175; Torigni, 2:338–39; Power, "Aristocratic *Acta*," 273: he was "eldest son of the ducal constable," she was the "daughter of the ducal seneschal"; William I du Hommet of the Cotentin had married Lucie, daughter of Robert de Neubourg; the donation was also confirmed by William du Hommet, constable of Normandy, in 1166, and was witnessed by Richard du Hommet.

4. Fierville, "Monographie," in *MSAN*, 25:155–98, inscriptions: 174.

5. Fierville, 175.

APPENDIX IV

Radulf Le Héricy, knight, in 1152 married Guillemette de Roncherolles of Eastern Normandy, whose dowry included several rents in Calvados. He was later a benefactor of the Cistercian abbey of Barbery, arrondissement Caen, canton Bretteville, which was a daughter cell of Savigny. Barbery was also supported by Radulf Tesson, who was lord of both Bretteville and Fierville. Radulf or Richard Le Héricy's son, Richard II, was documented in 1210. His son Guillaume I Le Héricy, knight, married Emma before 1269, and was the father of Gilles Le Héricy, knight and lord of Fierville-en-Bessin where the family is documented through 1730. Guillaume, brother of Gilles, also a knight, held at Pierrepont, also spelled Pompierre, arrondissement Caen, canton Falaise, and his descendants at Pierrepont and Vieux also held in Calvados. This might correlate with a possible connection between the de Hériz and de Pierrepont families in Normandy as well as in Nottinghamshire. The descendants of Gilles also held Préaux, Creullet at Creully, Vaussieux, and Marcelet en Saint-Manvieu, all in the arrondissement of Caen, and Étréham, arrodissement Bayeux, canton Trévières.[6]

Another town named Fierville was in the Cotentin: Fierville-le-Dézert, arrondissement Saint-Lô, canton Pont-Hébert, which was a hamlet consisting of a quarter of a *fief d'haubert* held of the lord du Hommet, who held it of the duke. In 1080, Geoffrey de Fierville witnessed the charter of King William I confirming the foundation of the abbey of Sainte-Trinité de Lessay, arrondissment Coutances, canton Lessay. This charter was signed by the king, the queen, their three sons, and much of the royal court, including Bishop Odo of Bayeux, Lanfranc, Saint Anselm, Robert de Beaumont, Hugh de Grandmesnil, Guillaume du Hommet, Mathilde his wife, and, near the end of the list, Geoffroy de Fierville (Gaufridus de Feravilla). This indicates that Geoffroy associated with many of the highest persons in the court of King William I. Later, Henri de Fierville witnessed a charter confirming a donation to the abbey of Savigny in the Avranchin for Richard du Hommet. Another witness was Geoffroy de Subligny, indicating a possible connection to the de Hériz family of La Rochelle. About 1200, Radulf de

---

6. LeMarois, "Famille Le Héricy"; Vaussieux now Vaux-sur-Seulles, in 2014 owned by the Comte Alfred d'Héricy; archives of the Le Héricy family preserved at the Château Fayel in the Oise mention the branches at Marcelet, Étréham, and Vaussieux in Calvados; Étréham was the site of a large Merovingian necropolis; Sarah Hériz, born about 1285 in England, married Simon de Pierrepont (son of William); Thoroton, *Nottinghamshire*, 1:176, 179–80: Robert Pierrepont, knight, married Sara, sister of John de Hériz, knight; in 1431 Jean Le Héricy, knight and lord of Fierville and Creullet, married Guillemette de Creullet, daughter of Guillemette de Beauchamp; in 1599 Auguste Le Héricy of Pontpierre married Anne de Morel d'Aubigny; in 1639, Anne Le Héricy de Creullet married Robert de Pierrepont of Baudreville, arr. Coutances, in the Cotentin; de la Chenaye, *Dictionnaire de la Noblesse*, 10:42–43, 584–86.

APPENDIX IV

Fierville confirmed his own donation to Savigny of holdings in the parish of Villers, now Villières-Fossard, arrondissement Saint-Lô, canton Pont-Hébert. Villers was the home of the de Villers family, who held lands in Nottinghamshire and were patrons of Thurgarton Priory near the de Hériz manor of Gonalston in Nottinghamshires, and of the Fossard family, which intermarried with the Paynels and made donations with Osberne de Arches in Yorkshire.[7] In 1184, Thomas de Périers of the Cotentin donated patronage of the church of Saint-Martin in Tribehou, arrondissment Saint-Lô, and other holdings to Lucerne Abbey. In 1217, Lucerne gave some of these holdings to the church of Saint-Thomas de Mesnil-Vité, in exchange for Radulf de Fierville donating six quarters of froment and properties in Tribehou to Lucerne. In 1229, Guillaume du Hommet, constable of Normandy, confirmed the donation by Radulf de Fierville to Saint-Lô of the chapel of Saint-Thomas-du-Mesnil-Vité, with revenues from Esglande and Villers-Fossard. Radulf II de Fierville, succeeded by 1245 and donated property from the parish of Fierville-en-Bessin in Calvados to the abbey of Fontenay.[8] These events connect the Fierville family in the Cotentin both to the Avranchin and Lucerne Abbey and to the Fierville family in Calvados, which was called Le Héricy.

Connections between families may be traced through heraldry if the arms were unusual. However, heraldry was not used by lower level knights in France until about 1200. The *hérisson*, or hedgehog, was rare in medieval heraldry. The family name in French heraldry was spelled: Le Héricy, les Héricy, le Héricey, d'Hérissi (Fierville), de Hérissy (Marcelet, Étréham), and le Héricée. The arms of the Le Héricy family at Fierville in Calvados were *d'argent, a trois hérissons d'or*, a silver shield with three gold hedgehogs. The arms of Gilles de Héricy were *d'argent a trois hérissons de gueules*, a silver shield with three hedgehogs in red. This family also later held Étréham, Creully, Préaux, Marcelet, and Pontpierre with similar arms (*gueules*). In the northern Cotentin, the village Saint-Martin-d'Audouville also bore the same arms of three hedgehogs. Radulf de Saint-Cyr of the Cotentin donated

---

7. Fierville, 158–60, 163, 181–82, 188; le Hommet d'Artenay, arr. Saint-Lô, canton Pont-Hébert; Torigni, 1:322: Hériz named as place in Cotentin; *Gallia christiana*, 1, xi, *Instrumenta*, col. 228; at about the same time, Geoffroy de Fierville was one of five witnesses to the donation of tithes of the church of Angoville to Lessay Abbey by Gilbert de Broc who had become a monk there; there were two places called Broc in the Cotentin: one near Valognes, the other near Audouville-le-Hubert; *Thurgarton Cartulary*, clvii–clxii, nos. 177–79; the de Villers also held of Stephen de Mortain, and of Henry de Lacy in Yorkshire; *CartLuzerne*, 21; Keats-Rohan, *Domesday Descendants*, 770–71.

8. Fierville, 160–61, 184–86; *CartLuzerne*, 17, 38, 50–52, 223, 225: Charter of Radulf de Fierville, confirmation by bishop of Coutances, both 1217; Esglande, canton Pont-Hébert.

APPENDIX IV

the lands of his tenant, Radulf le Hérice, to Montebourg Abbey. Saint-Martin d'Audouville, Saint-Cyr, and Montebourg were all in the canton of Valognes in the Montebourg group of communes.[9] In the de Héricy arms there were two hedgehogs in the top row and one below. However, most other uses of hedgehogs in heraldry had only one. The three hedgehogs were in the arms of the de Hériz family in England, as seen in a window and monument in the church at Stapleford, and the windows and tomb effigies in the church at Gonalston, Nottinghamshire, both de Hériz manors.

Some have speculated that the arms of the Hériz of La Rochelle were different: *d'argent, a la bande d'azur, chargée de trois molettes d'éperon d'or*. But these were almost identical to the arms of their lords, the family of Saint-Jean-le-Thomas, *d'argent plain au chef de gueles chargée de deux molettes d'éperon du champ* and those of Lucerne Abbey, *d'argent au chef de gueles chargé de deux molettes d'éperon d'argent*. There is no independent evidence of the arms of the de Hériz family at La Rochelle and they were vassals of Saint-Jean and immediate neighbors of and major donors to Lucerne Abbey. Moreover, heraldry only came into use in Normandy at a later time.[10]

The four loci of the de Hériz and Le Héricy families in Western Normandy, La Rochelle in the Avranchin, Saint-Lô in the Cotentin, and Hérils and Fierville in Calvados, were quite probably interconnected. The same

---

9. *DGH*, 2:288, 5:327; Fierville: squire, *d'argent a trois hérissons de sable*; Étréham: knight, *d'argent a trois hérissons gules*; there was a Jacques d'Hérisson who carried arms with three hedgehogs and commanded the artillery of King Henri IV (reigned 1589–1610); portrayed on a *jeton*, private coin, dated 1598 (Loire-Atlantique); Grandmaison, *Dictionnaire Héraldique*, 464, notes *d'argent trois hérissons de sable* for Hérisson in Brittany and Héricy in Normandy; there were Les Héricy in Bazeilles in the Ardenne, Hargriniere in Brittany and in Maine, with three hedgehogs; towns also bore the arms of three hedgehogs: Saint-Martin-d'Audouville in the Manche, Mortefontaine in the l'Oise, or one hedgehog: Hérisson in the Allier, Coudekerque-Branche in the Nord, arr. Dunkerque, La Petite Raon in the Vosges, Sainte-Marie-sur-Mer in the Loire Atlantique; people named Hérisson possessed lands in Brittany, especially in the Ille-et-Vilaine, near the border with Maine, including the Hérisson family from Ville-Hellouin, Bretagne, whose arms were *d'argent a trois hérissons de sable*; there was also a Hérissiere in Brittany, in St. Herblain near Nantes, held by the de Vitré family of Ille-et-Vilaine, arr. Rennes; Andre de Vitré married Agnèse, daughter of Robert count de Mortain, who had claim to the succession of Robert de Gorron; Power, *Norman Frontier*, 502; Prestwich, *Armies*, 222: heraldry began in England in the time of King Henry I with banners, which have not survived; later there were seals; Clemmensen, "Early Arms," 61–88: urges caution in arguing from heraldry because there is little surviving evidence before the seals of the thirteenth century.

10. *Revue de l'Avranchin* (1934), 388; Grandmaison, *Dictionnaire Héraldique* adds *a la bordure engrelée de gueules*; Le Héricher,*Avranchin*, 68: *d'azur a trois molettes d'epéron d'argent*; Clemmensen, "Early Arms," 61–63.

lords appear frequently in Normandy and also in England: d'Avranches, du Hommet, Paynel, Peverel. The origins of most of those families in Normandy were in the Avranchin/Cotentin, with the d'Avranches, du Hommet, and Paynel families also rooted in Calvados. Only the family of La Rochelle in the Avranchin and the town of Hérils in Calvados were explicitly called Hériz. In the mid-twelfth century, Jourdain de la Roche-Tesson, lord of Grippon and Subligny near La Rochelle in the Avranchin, was also baron of the canton of Trévières in Calvados, in which the towns of Hérils and Étreham were located, substantiating a connection between the two. The evidence from heraldry supports the family of Le Héricy, but also appears in the Cotentin. The family of La Rochelle was probably too small to have had individual arms, using instead an adaptation of the arms of their lords. History supports the family of La Rochelle as the primary locus of origin of the de Hériz family in England, where the immediate vassalage of the family was to William Peverel, who with his men of the Avranchin, fought at Hastings and founded Lenton Priory in Nottinghamshire.

The name de Hériz appears among the companions of William the Conqueror in 1066. Auchinleck has Hériz; Leland has Heryce. The later French rolls of Falaise named Hugues d'Héricy and Dives has d'Héricy, which suggest Le Héricy of Fierville, but could also be Hérils or Hériz. These sources also mention the Saint John, Subligny, Paynel, Beauchamp, Tesson, and Peverel families from the Avranchin cluster. The first known de Hériz in England was Robert de Hériz, early in the reign of King Henry I, named among the vassals of William Peverel from the Avranchin.[11] Although the de Hériz family in Normandy may be connected to all four sites, it is most likely that the de Hériz family in England came from La Rochelle Normande.

Most of the early family names of the wives of de Hériz, de Hérils, and Le Héricy in Normandy are unknown, although the Le Héricy family intermarried later with the de Pierrepont and de Beauchamp families. In England the de Hériz family intermarried with the de Hercy and de Pierrepont families. In Normandy, they were vassals or tenants of the d'Avranches, de Saint-Jean families, and possibly also of the de Neubourg, du Hommet, and Tesson families. They were close neighbors of the Paynel, de Beauchamp, and Peverel families. In England, they were vassals or tenants of the Peverel family. In Normandy, they may have held lands in the Avranchin, Cotentin, and Calvados. In England they held lands in Nottinghamshire, Derbyshire,

11. RBA: Auchinleck 4339: Hériz, St. John, Paynel, Peverel; Leland: Heryce, St. John; Wace, 3:8469 (Soligny), 8512 (St. John); Le Tailleur: Soubligny; Holingshed: St. John, Somerville, Sourdeval; Dives: d'Hericy, Richard de Sourdeval; Falaise: Hugues d'Hericy, William de St. Jean, Richard de Sourdeval, le Sire de Soligny.

APPENDIX IV

Yorkshire, and in Pillerton, Warwickshire. They supported the monasteries of Lucerne in the Avranchin, possibly also Savigny and Montebourg in the Avranchin/Cotentin and Fontenay and Barbery in Calvados; in England they supported Lenton Priory in Nottinghamshire.

Appendix V

Neighbors and Lords of the de Hériz Family in Normandy

AVRANCHIN
PAYNEL

The town of La Haye-Pesnel was located on a hill by the Thar River and was named for the Paynel family. It was adjacent to Lucerne Abbey. During its history the town had three castles; two were motte and bailey castles made of wood on the hilltop. The earliest, Le Châtel, was built on an old Roman site; the second, Le Château-Ganne, was the residence of the Paynel family. After its destruction, a third castle, the Logis, was built. Hugh d'Avranches made the chapel of Saint-Jacques-de-la-Haye-Pesnel into a priory of his abbey of Saint-Sever.

The lower- to middle-level family of Paganel/Paynel/Pesnel emerged from the area of Les Moutiers-Hubert, arrondissement Lisieux, in Calvados, but the family also settled in La Haye-Pesnel, arrondissment Avranches, near the home of the de Hériz family in La Rochelle, and Hambye, arrondissement Coutances, in the Cotentin. The name is a diminutive of the Latin *pagus* and the French *paysan*, meaning "person of the land."[1]

Guillaume I and Radulf/Ralph I Paynel were sons of the lord of Moutiers-Hubert. Guillaume I Paynel succeeded as lord of Les Moutiers-Hubert and Hambye. Wace named the lord of Moutiers-Hubert fighting at Hastings. Orderic Vitalis mentioned Guillaume Paynel as an important man who died in 1087, the same year as William the Conquerer.[2] His son, Guillaume II, succeeded as lord of Les Moutiers-Hubert and Hambye.

---

1. The name is a diminutive of pagan, from Roman *pagus* and French *payson*; the rural population was Christianized later than urban, thus the origin of word "pagan"; Loyd, *Origins*, 77; Keats-Rohan, *Domesday People*, 342.

2. Wace, 3:8500; *Extrait, RHGF*, 13:237; OV, 4:112–13.

APPENDIX V

Guillaume II married the daughter of Guillaume Fitz Wimund d'Avranches. In 1145 Guillaume II founded a Benedictine abbey at Hambye, an area of hills and forests in the southern Cotentin, with permission of his four sons: Hugh I, Fulk I, Thomas, and Jean. They also had daughters Amaurie, who married Raoul de Neubourg, baron of Annebecq, and Lucie, who married André de Vitré. Hugh I succeeded to Les Moutiers-Hubert, and Fulk I to Hambye and Bréhal. Hugh I married Nicole and had sons, Pierre and Guillaume, who donated to the abbey of Saint-Étienne at Caen. In 1172, he had five knights to serve the duke, and six knights in his own service. He died as a monk in the abbey of Saint-Étienne de Caen about 1180.[3]

Fulk I Paynel married Lesceline de Subligny, lady of Grippon, daughter of Denise d'Avranches and Hasculf de Subligny; her father was cofounder of Lucerne Abbey. Fulk I Paynel was lord of Hambye, Bricquebec, Bréhal, de Gacé, Grippon, Marcey, Fontenay-le-Paisnel, and La Haye-Pesnel. Fulk I also held a fee at Briqueville in the Cotentin of Le Mont-Saint-Michel and two knights' fees in Yorkshire. Fulk I donated to the abbeys of Hambye and Drax. Fulk witnessed a confirmation by Henry II between 1178 and 1183. In 1180, Fulk I farmed lands of his wife Lesceline in the Avranchin. He died in 1183. Fulk I and Lesceline Paynel had sons William III, Fulk II, Hasculf, and John. William III Paynel was lord of Hambye in Normandy and Drax in Yorkshire. He married Eléanore de Vitré, whose brother André granted her de Vitré lands in the Bessin as her dowry, witnessed by John de Subligny. William III died in 1184 without an heir.[4]

The second son, Fulk II Paynel, became lord of Hambye, La Haye-Pesnel, Bréhal, Grippon, and Subligny in the Avranchin/Cotentin, and Drax in Yorkshire. He donated to Hambye and Drax. He married first Cécile Tesson, daughter of Jourdain and Léticie Tesson of Saint-Sauveur-le-Vicomte in the Cotentin, and second Agathe du Hommet, daughter of Richard du Hommet and Agnes de Say of Calvados. In 1204, King John took the Yorkshire lands of Fulk II, who had supported the French king against him, and gave them to his cousin, Hugh Paynel, who had supported King John and thereby lost his lands in Normandy. In 1214, King John granted permission for Fulk's

---

3. *Neustria Pia*, 821; CPE, 4:317; EYC, vol. 6, nos. 1–5, 9–10, 15–16, 86, 133; *RRAN*, vol. 3, no. 653, 985; RBE, 2:627; *MA*, 3:501, 549; the ruins of the abbey of Hambye contain the graves of Jeanne Paynel and her husband, Louis d'Estouteville, who saved Le Mont-Saint-Michel from the English in the Hundred Years War.

4. EYC, vol. 3, no. 1460, vol. 6, nos. 1, 9–10, 15–16, 21–22, 34, 45–46, 64, 117; *RRAN*, vol. 3, nos. 111, 332, 581, 653, 703; RBE, 1:77, 430; Torigni, 2:302–05, 366–69 (knights: Fulk, William, and Robert de St. Jean, Hasculf de Subligny, Jordon Taisson); Clemmensen, "Early Arms," 76: Drax and Hambye had the same coat of arms; Power, *Norman Frontier*, 14, 33, 145, 147, 240, 330; Keats-Rohan, *Domesday Descendants*, 1055–58.

APPENDIX V

son by his second wife to marry Pernelle Tesson, daughter and heir of Raoul Tesson of La Roche-Tesson.[5]

A later Fulk Paynel, knight, was lord of La Haye Pesnel and Aubigny. He and his wife Étiennette founded a hospital at La Haye-Pesnel in 1235 and a church at Hocquigny in 1236. Olivier Paynel was lord of La Haye-Pesnel in 1260 through parage and a donor to Lucerne Abbey. Jean Paynel of Marcey, arrondissement Avranches, son of Guillaume Paynel, knight, was also a supporter of Lucerne Abbey in 1276.[6]

Thus, although the Paynel family originated in Calvados, major parts of its holdings were in Hambye in the Cotentin and in La Haye-Pesnel, the central town in the Avranchin cluster of La Rochelle, Lucerne, La HayePesnel and Beauchamp, interacting with the de Hériz, de Saint-Jean, de Subligny, and de Beauchamp families. These families were involved with supporting Lucerne Abbey adjacent to La Haye-Pesnel, which was cofounded by Hasculf de Subligny, father-in-law of Fulk I Paynel.[7]

The Paynel family is significant for understanding the origins of the de Hériz family. It was interrelated by marriage with the families d'Avranches, de Subligny, de Sourdeval, Tesson, and Fossard of the Avranchin/Cotentin, Meschin/Chester, du Hommet, and de Lacy of Calvados, and de Vitré in Brittany. They founded the abbey of Hambye and supported the monasteries of Lucerne and Saint-Étienne-de-Caen in Normandy. In England they interacted with the de Hercy family in Warwickshire and Worcestershire, with the de Arches in Yorkshire and the de Hériz in Nottinghamshire.

DE BEAUCHAMP

Beauchamp, arrondissement Avranches, is a small town within the canton La Haye-Pesnel in the Avranchin.[8] In eleventh-century Normandy the de Beauchamp family was not prominent and little is known of them, except

5. *MA*, 5:204; *Ex chronico Savigniacensis*, *RHGF*, 18:351; RBE, 1:163–65, 423, 2:491; EYC, vol. 6, nos. 15–17, 21–22; *RRAN*, vol. 3, no. 332; *Actes Henri II*, 2:455–56, 549; Torigni, 1:280–81; Keats-Rohan, *Domesday Descendants*, 522, 1056: Agathe was the daughter of Richard du Hommet, although the *Chronicon Savigniacensis* called her *filia Willelmi*.

6. Desroches, *Histoire du Mont Saint-Michel*, 392, 394–95; *CartHotel-Dieu*, 8; *CartLuzerne*, 90–91 (1260, carta Olivier Paynel), 113 (1276, confirmed by John), 113–14 (confirmed by bishops in 1265, 1276 and 1284).

7. *CartLuzerne*, 96, 113–14, 166, 246.

8. Canton Bréhal; le Héricher, *Avranchin*, 5; Keats-Rohan, *Domesday People*, 260: Beauchamp, canton la Haye-Pesnel; Loyd, *Origins*, 20–21 placed it in Brouay in the canton of Tilly-sur-Seulles in Calvados.

that they did have a small castle on a promontory above the river. They lived in immediate proximity to the Paynel, de Saint-Jean, and de Hériz families. The de Beauchamp family rapidly gained great stature in England and Normandy after 1100 under King Henry I. There were two main branches of the family in England: the first in Bedfordshire and Buckinghamshire, the second in Worcestershire and later in Warwickshire.

In Normandy, Robert de Beauchamp served the English King Henry I. Under King Henry II, Hugues de Beauchamp owed knight service to the count of Mortain. In 1287, Jean-Marie de Beauchamp sold part of La Haye-Pesnel, which was under the "noble Lord" Radulf de Beauchamp. In 1300, Radulf de Beauchamp, knight, made donations to Lucerne Abbey for his own soul and those of Nicole his wife and Guillaume, his son.[9] In England they interacted with the de Hercy family in Warwickshire, Nottinghamshire, and Worcestershire, with the de Hériz in Nottinghamshire and the de Hersin in Buckinghamshire.

COTENTIN DE PERCY

William I de Percy was from Percy in the Cotentin, arrondissement Saint-Lô, canton Percy/Villedieu-les-Poeles, which was near Hambye and under the lordship of the Paynels. This de Percy family had the same arms as the English Percys and both supported Saint-Sauveur-le-Vicomte. In 1170, Gerbert de Percy held one fee and four knights in Guilberville, arrondissement Saint-Lô, near Percy, and in 1176 exchanged land with John de Subligny. Richard de Percy was named as a founding donor to Lucerne Abbey in the list of those to be remembered in gratitude by the abbey. The papal bull of Urban III, promulgated in 1186, listed the donations of Robert de Percy to Lucerne Abbey immediately before those of Robert de Hériz and his son Roger.[10] William I de Percy went to England in 1066 with Duke Wil-

9. Le Héricher, *Avranchin*, 2:5–7; *CartLuzerne*, 133, 147, 192.

10. EYC, vol. 11, pp. 11–19; *CartLuzerne*, 224, 240; *Gallia christiana. Lucerna* iii; *Neustria pia. Lucerna*, 1:vi; 22 Henry II, 141; during the reign of King Henry II, Juliane de Percy, daughter of Roger de Percy, donated lands from her dowry to Saint-Sauveur with permission of her brother Robert de Percy and his four sons; RBE, 1:44, 165–67, 216, 226, 2:640; the brothers Ernald and William I de Percy were benefactors of Saint-Pierre-sur-Dives, Calvados, arr. Lisieux; MA, 5:513; Keats-Rohan, *Domesday People*, 478: opts for Percy-en-Auge in Calvados , arr. Lisieux (which she mistakenly puts it in the Eure), on the basis of the English William and Ernald de Percy's support for Saint-Pierre-sur-Dives near Lisieux for their origin over Percy, Manche, and the fact that his wife was from Calvados, despite his close association with Hugh d'Avranches and St. Sauveur; so too Loyd, *Origins*, 77, has Percy-en-Auge although he has the correct

liam, and married Emma de Port. Their granddaughter Mathilde married William de Beaumont, earl of Warwick, and had Alan de Arches in ward. William's grandnephew married Agnes, daughter of Juetta II de Arches. Their great-grandson, Henry de Percy, married Isabel de Brus, daughter of Juetta II de Arches. The de Brus and de Arches families were related to the de Hercy family.

The Percy family intermarried in England with the de Brus family of the Cotentin, the de Port family of Calvados, and with the d'Arques and de Beaumont families of Eastern Normandy. They held lands primarily in Yorkshire. They supported the monasteries of Lucerne, Saint-Sauveur-le-Vicomte, and Saint-Pierre-sur-Dives in Western Normandy, and in England, the Benedictine abbey of Whitby, which they refounded, and Nostell, Drax, and Bridlington priories, all in Yorkshire. In England the Percy family interacted with and intermarried with the de Arches and de Brus families, Hercy relatives, in Yorkshire.

TESSON

The Tesson, also spelled Taisson, family held La Roche-Tesson, arrondissement Saint-Lô, canton Percy, in the Cotentin, where they had a château. Like the Saint-Jean family, the Tesson family held La Roche-Tesson as a fief of Le Mont-Saint-Michel. They held Grippon and Subligny in La Haye Pesnel and intermarried with the Paynel family. They also held in Cinglais, arrondissement Caen, in Calvados. They supported the abbeys of Lucerne in the Avranchin, Saint-Sauveur in the Cotentin, and Fontenay in Calvados. They provide a connection between Lucerne and La Haye Paynel in the Avranchin with the Cotentin and Calvados.

Radulf II Tesson fought with Duke William at Hastings. He was given lands in Nottinghamshire and Yorkshire. He supported Savigny and Saint-Sauveur Abbeys. He had sons Jourdain and Olivier. Jourdain Tesson succeeded his father about 1130 as lord of La Roche-Tesson. He was also baron of Trévières in Calvados, a possible seat of the de Hériz family, where he held ten knights' fees and had thirty knights in his own service. In 1173, Jourdain was one of the leaders of King Henry II's army, fighting against King Louis VII of France. Jourdain I married Léticie de Saint-Sauveur, daughter and heir of Roger II, vicomte of the Cotentin, and Cécile de Port. Jourdain and Léticie provided the land for and donated to the abbey of Saint-Sauveur-le-Vicomte. They had three sons: Radulf IV, Roger, and Jourdain II, all of

---

department; the evidence is stronger for Percy in the Cotentin; Keats-Rohan, *Domesday Descendants*, 630.

APPENDIX V

whom donated to Saint-Sauveur, and a daughter Cécile, who married Fulk II Paynel, lord of La Haye-Pesnel, Grippon, and Subligny, son of Fulk I of Hambye and Lesceline de Subligny, widow of Olivier I Tesson. Jourdain died in 1178.[11]

Olivier I Tesson, brother of Jourdain I, married Lesceline de Subligny, dame de Grippon, daughter of Hasculph de Subligny, founder of Lucerne Abbey. After the death of Olivier, about 1140, Lesceline married Fulk I Paynel of Hambye. The son of Olivier and Lesceline, Radulf Tesson, became lord of Grippon and Subligny. Their grandson, Olivier II Tesson, married Gilberte du Hommet.[12]

Radulf IV Tesson was seneschal of Normandy in 1201. He supported Sainte-Marie de Barbery and confirmed his parents' donations to Hambye. In England, he held of the Honour of Tickhill in Yorkshire and north Nottinghamshire, with Richard Basset and William de Beauchamp, in which soon Théophanie de Arches and Malveysin de Hercy would also hold fees. Tesson also held in North Wheatley, Nottinghamshire. He married Mathilde de la Lande-Patry of the Orne, daughter of Enguérand Patry and the daughter of Richard de Creully and Mathilde de St.Clair, dame de Villers-Fossard. Creully was held in the thirteenth century by the Le Héricy family; Villers-Fossard was held by Radulf de Fierville under the du Hommet family, and was connected to the Le Héricy family of Fierville. Ranulf IV and Mathilde had three daughters. Pernelle, the eldest, married Guillaume Paynel of Hambye, son of Fulk II Paynel and his second wife, Agathe du Hommet. Radulf IV Tesson lost his lands in England in 1204 for supporting the French king against King John. After the death of Radulf IV in 1213/14, Pernelle inherited Hambye and Percy in the Cotentin. In 1236, Peter Tesson made donations to Lucerne Abbey.[13]

The Tesson family intermarried with the Paynel, de Subligny, de Saint-Sauveur, de Villers-Fossard, and du Hommet families of the Avranchin/Cotentin, and the Marmion and de Creully families of Calvados; most of these families were connected with the de Hériz family. They held land in La Haye-Pesnel, Hambye, Saint-Sauveur, and Savigny in the Avranchin/

---

11. Lerosey, *Histoire de Saint-Sauveur-le-Vicomte* 20; Delisle, *Histoire*, 34–35, 80, 99, 149, 243, 301; *RHGF*, 8:694; RBE, 1:52, 2:628; *RRAN*, vol. 3, nos. 245, 299, 324–26, 653, 810; Torigni, 1:332–33, 2:372–73; PR 31 Henry I, 9, 24, 27, 70, 95, 122; *Neustria pia*, 540; Loyd, *Origins*, 101–02; Keats-Rohan, *Domesday Descendants*, 1121–22.

12. Jehan, grandson of Olivier II and Gilberte, married Marie Paynel of Hocquigny in La Haye-Paynel; their daughter Catherine married Jehan de Villiers, baron du Hommet.

13. *Testa de Nevill*, 149, 230, 270, 286; RBE, 1:97, 162, 2:552, 803; Anisy, *Calvados* 1:iii, 140; *CartLuzerne*, 65–66; *Neustria pia*, 3:2, 540; *Recueil l'Échiquier de Normandie*, 35, n. 137.

Cotentin, and also in Trévières, Thury, and Fontenay in Calvados. In England, they held in Nottinghamshire and Yorkshire. They supported the abbeys of Lucerne, Saint-Sauveur-le-Vicomte, and Hambye in the Avranchin/Cotentin, and Fontenay and Barbery in Calvados. They are important in understanding the origins of the de Hériz family in Normandy.

DU HOMMET

The du Hommet family came from Le Hommet, arrondissement Saint-Lô, canton Pont-Hébert, in the Cotentin. Le Hommet may have been a Scandinavian settlement called Holm, meaning "moat." There is evidence of the family there from the 1020s. Wace recorded "*celz de Homez*" (plural) among Duke William's army at Hastings. The first castle was built at Le Hommet during the dukedom of Robert Curthose by the Sieur du Hommet.[14]

William du Hommet had a daughter or granddaughter and heir who married Robert, who was, according to tradition, the *nepos episcopi* (nephew, son, or grandson) of Bishop Odo of Bayeux, and thus a relative of Duke William. Robert became du Hommet, taking the surname of his wife. In 1133, Robert owed knight service to the bishop of Bayeux for three fiefs in Calvados and also held lands in Northamptonshire, Lincolnshire, and Sussex.[15]

Robert had a son, Richard I du Hommet, who worked for Eléanore of Aquitaine and was royal constable under her spouse, Henry of Anjou, duke of Normandy, future King Henry II of England. Richard witnessed 331 charters, more than any other lay witness, for Duke Henry between 1146 and 1153, and more after 1154 for him as king of England. About 1158, he witnessed King Henry's donation to Lucerne Abbey. Richard du Hommet was an important member of King Henry II's court. The king made Richard his constable, a title thence held by the du Hommet family for over a century. The constableship involved military duties and Richard led King Henry's armies in England and Normandy from 1153 to 1173. In 1172, he held three and a half knights' fees in Normandy, with eighteen knights in

---

14. *MRSN*, 1:lxxix; *Bayeux, Livre Noir*, 1:110–12 (1181–95, donation by William, confirmed by Cecily); Power, "Aristocratic *Acta*," 261–62; based on Pancarte of St. Fromond, which is problematic; Musset, "Les origines," in *BSAN*, 42 (1955–56) 475–89; Wace, 3:8513; evidence is lacking in other MSS of a presence at Hastings; Loyd, *Origins*, 52.

15. Robert *nepos Episcopi*; others who held nearby were Ranulf III le Meschin, Alan de Percy, Count Odo of Bayeux, and the count of Bretagne; Keats-Rohan, *Domesday People*, 85; Lindsay Survey fol. 16, 10; Keats-Rohan, *Domesday Descendants*, 522; Power, "Aristocratic *Acta*," 262, 264.

his own service.[16] Richard married Agnèse de Beaumont-le-Richard, arrondissment Bayeux, canton Trévières, in Calvados, daughter and coheir of Jourdain de Say, lord of Aunay in Calvados, and Lucie d'Aunay de Rumilly.[17]

In 1166, William and Richard du Hommet witnessed the charter in which Robert de Neubourg donated the church of Hérils to Bayeux. In 1170, King Henry II gave him the forest of La Luthumière in the Cotentin, which was near Brus. Later King Philippe-Auguste of France confiscated the lands of Adam de Brus and gave William du Hommet the whole lordship. Richard shared his lands by *parage* among his three sons: William, Enguérand, who died in 1181, and Jourdain, who went on crusade with King Richard I as his constable and died in the Holy Land in 1192.[18]

William du Hommet succeeded his father as constable of Normandy; his office was confirmed by King Henry II in 1180. William received the greatest share of the patrimony. William confirmed the donation of the church of Hérils to Bayeux in 1166 by Robert de Neubourg, previously witnessed by his father. In 1166, William du Hommet held one old knight's fee of the Percy fee in Yorkshire with Gilbert de Arches. As constable, William du Hommet witnessed numerous charters for King Henry II between 1155 and 1188. William married Lucie, daughter of Robert de Neubourg of Calvados, seneschal of Normandy, receiving a dowry in the Cotentin

---

16. *CartLuzerne*, 3; EYC, vol. 3, no. 1386; *Bayeux livre noir*, 1:128–29, 161; RBE, 1:202, 208, 2:630, 655–56, 673–75, 794; *Actes Henri II*, vol. 1, no. 62, vol. 2, nos. 455, 466; RRAN, vol. 3, nos. 22, 29, 44, 58, 60, 64–65, 90, 126–28, 130, 140, 180, 206, 272, 309–10, 321, 332, 438, 459, 492, 574, 582, 584, 600, 653, 810, 823, 875, 900, 902, 999; Torigny, 1:42–44, 353; *Gesta Regis Henrici Secundi*, 1:51–52, 56–58; MA, 4:261; Power, "Aristocratic Acta," 260–61, 265, 271; J. Green, *Aristocracy*, 217; Keats-Rohan, *Domesday Descendants*, 522.

17. PR 31 Henry I, 4, 84; Torigny, 2:93, 1181; charter 1181/89; MA, 4:150–51; the de Say family were originally from the Cotentin; Power, "Aristocratic Acta," 263; a Nicholas de Say was mentioned in a *carta* of Lucerne Abbey about 1200; *CartLuzerne*, 35; the du Hommet family received Rumilly in the Cotentin and Beaumont-le-Richard in Calvados and divided the inheritance of Agnèse's brothers; de Say founded an abbey at Aunay in 1131, a daughter abbey of Savigny; Keats-Rohan, *Domesday Descendants*, 680.

18. *Gallia christiana*, 11:xxiv, col. 88; *Actes Henri II*, vol. 2, no. 745; *Bayeux livre noir*, 128–29; *Archives Départmentales de Calvados*, H 667; *CartWorcester*, vol. 1, nos. 44, 50; EYC, vol. 7, no. 56; Torigni, 1:350–51; MA, 4:150–51; RRAN, vol. 3, nos. 22, 44, 58, 60, 64–65, 90, 126–28, 130, 140, 180, 206, 272, 309–10, 321, 332, 438, 459, 492, 574, 582, 584, 600, 653, 810, 823, 875, 900, 902, 999; RBE, 1:425, 2:630; Torigni, 1:248–51; *CartOseney*, vol. 4, nos. 24, 53, 64, 492; Power, "Aristocratic Acta," 263, 271–72, 280; in 1172, Richard and his son Jourdain du Hommet had thirty-one knights serving them and owed the service of six and a half knights to the duke of Normandy; in 1178, Richard entered Aunay Abbey, where he spent the last year and a half of his life as a monk; he was buried there in February 1181; Keats-Rohan, *Domesday Descendants*, 522.

APPENDIX V

and Bessin. Through this marriage William du Hommet became Robert de Neubourg's successor as lord of Hérils and Somervieu in Calvados and Saint-Audouville-la-Hubert in the Cotentin, all three places associated with the de Hériz family. In 1184, William made two charters as constable for Lucerne Abbey in the Avranchin. William made a donation to Bayeux in 1202–5, witnessed by his son Jourdain, bishop of Lisieux. William supported Kings Richard I and John until 1204. After the English lost Normandy, William remained there, but King John still confirmed his charters. Near the end of his life, William entered the abbey of Aunay where he died in 1205.[19]

William and Lucie had many children: seven sons, including Richard II, who succeeded, and Jourdain, who was appointed bishop of Lisieux by King Henry II, serving from 1202 to 1218; their daughter Agathe married first Guillaume de Fougères, and second, Fulk II Paynel, son of Fulk I Paynel of Hambye and Lesceline de Subligny, who died in 1214. From her first marriage Agathe had Clémence de Fougères, who married Ranulf III, earl of Chester, and Geoffroy de Fougères; from her second, she had Fulk III Paynel, Lucie, who married André de Vitré, and William, who married Petronilla Tesson.[20]

Richard II du Hommet married Gille, daughter of Richard de La Haye-des-Puits in the Cotentin, son of Robert, whose sister Cecilia was married to Roger de Saint-Jean. His younger brother, Bishop Jourdain du Hommet of Lisieux, founded the abbey of Mondaye, a daughter cell of the abbey of Lucerne, about 1202, with Raoul de Percy, who was lord of the place and husband of Alice de Gennes, daughter of Raoul de Gennes and Jeanne du Hommet, daughter of Enguérand du Hommet, uncle of Bishop Jourdain. Mondaye was in Calvados, arrondissement Bayeux, seven miles south of Bayeux.[21]

---

19. *Actes Henri II*, 2:549; *Bayeux livre noir*, 1:128–29, 147; EYC, vol. 3, nos. 1278, 1455; *Gallia christiana*, 11:xxvi, col. 90; RBE, 1:65, 82, 91, 99–100, 103, 124, 129, 136–37, 143, 172–73, 396, 424–25, 2:517, 534–35, 537–39, 644–45, 799, 805; Power, "Aristocratic *Acta*," 267, 269, 273, 278, 280–82; *CartLuzerne*, 16–17; *ROF*, 249; *Basset Charters*, nos. 252–53; his wife Lucie founded a home for lepers at Sainte-Cathérine-du-Dézert in the Cotentin next to Le Hommet, to which King Henry II made a donation; William I sometimes held Christmas courts at Le Hommet during the reign of Henry II; Keats-Rohan, *Domesday Descendants*, 522.

20. *Gallia christiana*, 11:xxvi, col. 90; *Actes Henri II*, vol. 2, no. 745; his other children were sons Enguérand and Thomas, and daughters Lucie and Agnèse; Power, "Aristocratic *Acta*," 268, 282; Keats-Rohan, *Domesday Descendants*, 522, apparently in error made Agathe the daughter of Richard I: death of her son *obiit Gaufridus dominus Filgeriarum, filius Willelmi et Agathae, filiae Willelmi de Humeto*.

21. *Gallia christiana*, 11:xxvi, col. 90; Gille was herself patron of Lessay and Blanchelande Abbeys. Richard II died in 1199, before his father; he had sons Guillaume

APPENDIX V

The family du Hommet is an example of a family from the Cotentin connected with two possible sites of origin of the de Hériz family: Lucerne Abbey and the families around it in the Avranchin and Hérils in Calvados. They were related by marriage to the dukes of Normandy through Odo of Bayeux and to the families d'Avranches, Paynel, de Subligny, Tesson, and de Brus of the Avranchin/Cotentin, the de Say, de Neubourg and de Beaumont-le-Richard families of Calvados, and the families de Fougères and de Vitré of Brittany. In England they held lands in Lincolnshire, Yorkshire, Buckinghamshire, Norfolk, and Sussex. They supported the abbeys of Lucerne, Bayeux, Aunay, Mondaye, and Lessay in Normandy, and Notley Abbey in Buckinghamshire. They are important primarily because of their connection with the origins of the de Heriz family in Normandy, but they also interacted with the de Arches family in Yorkshire.

DE BRUS

The de Brus family came from Bruis in the northern Cotentin, arrondissement Cherbourg, canton Valognes. The town was then called Bruis, Brus, and Brusse, derived from the Latin *brutius*, and after the fourteenth century was called Brix. Situated on a hill, it was an excellent point of defense against invaders from Roman times. The forest of Brus belonged to the dukes of Normandy and after 1204 to the king of France. Duke William II hunted there and barely escaped being assassinated there in 1046 by riding all night to Falaise.[22]

Adam de Brus founded the priory of La Luthumière at Brus in 1106, a dependency of the Benedictine abbey of Saint-Sauveur-le-Vicomte, and built the Château d'Adam at Brus.[23] Robert I de Brus, who died in 1141, had married Agnes Paynel. William II du Hommet, constable of Normandy, married Lucie de Brus. The family held lands in Brus until 1204, when King John lost Normandy. They were given a choice between their lands

---

II, who died about 1240, and Jourdain, both of whom succeeded as constables of Normandy; Thébault, "Le 'premier cartulaire'," *AN*, 61 (2011) 29–40; Power, "Aristocratic Acta," 269, 280; *Neustria Pia*, 905; Raoul de Percy, knight, donated land and the church of Saint-Martin de Mondaye to the Premonstratensian canons of Mondaye, with the permission of his wife Alice and their sons Guillaume and Raoul, in exchange for other lands; Raoul de Percy and Alice were buried in the abbey of Mondaye.

22. Douglas, *William*, 48; *AN*, vol. 14 (1964) 503.

23. Lerosey, *HistoireSaint-Sauveur*, 43–44, 235; *Gallia christiana*, xi, col. 923; *Neustria pia*, "Prioritatus"; Blakely, *Brus Family*, 5; LePatourel, *Norman Empire*, 306; Delattre, *La Manche*, 42.

in Normandy and their much greater estates in England, which was what they chose.

The de Brus family intermarried with the families of Paynel from the Avranchin, du Hommet from the Cotentin, and in England with the de Arches family of the Pays de Caux, the de Percy family of the Cotentin, and with the kings of Scotland. They held extensive lands in England, primarily in Yorkshire. They founded the priory of La Luthumière and supported Saint-Sauveur-le-Vicomte in the Cotentin, founded Guisborough Priory in Yorkshire, and supported Bridlington Priory and St. Mary's York. In England they intermarried and interacted with the de Arches family, Hercy relatives, in Yorkshire.

CALVADOS AND ORNE

The eastern part of Western Normandy is Calvados, where Duke William II was born in the town of Falaise. Calvados was also the home of the de Lacy family of Yorkshire. The families de Hériz, d'Avranches, Paynel, and du Hommet had branches both in the Avranchin/Cotentin and in Calvados. The Basset and de Grandmesnil families had roots both in Calvados and in the Orne, south of Calvados. The de Lascelles family was from the Orne, or possibly Calvados. Also in this part of Western Normandy were the capital of Duke William at Caen, the episcopal sees of Bayeux and Lisieux in Calvados, and the great abbey of St. Évroul in the Orne.

DE LASCELLES

The de Lascelles family were related by marriage to the de Hercé family in England. Their place of origin in Normandy is unclear. The two possibilities were both tiny villages in the eleventh century. The first and less likely is Loucelles in Calvados, arrondissement Bayeux. It is about twelve kilometers southeast of Bayeux and about seventeen south of Caen. There is a small church of Nôtre-Dame built in the twelfth or thirteenth century. But there are no remnants of a manor house before the end of the sixteenth century. A Gervais de Loucelles was named as a witness for Guillaume du Hommet in 1198. In later spellings of the name, however, the *o* is consistently a dominant vowel, not an article. The second possible and more likely site is La Selle-la-Forge in the Orne, arrondissement now Argentan, earlier Domfront, southwest of Falaise and north of Domfront. Little is known of the early history of this village, except that its name in earlier times was La Selle; the inhabitants were called *sellois*. The name "La Selle" makes this

APPENDIX V

the more likely place of origin. In addition, this is supported by the fact that later William de Lascelles in England sued his uncle Ralph over the inheritance of La Selle and Messei, the town adjacent to La Selle. However, nothing is known of the de Lascelles family in Normandy. One member of the family accompanied Duke William to England and fought at Hastings.[24] He was amply rewarded by the king and by 1086 Picot de Lascelles held manors in Yorkshire and Lincolnshire. In England the de Lascelles family interacted with the de Arches in Yorkshire and were relatives of the de Hercy family of Nottinghamshire.

24. PR 31 Henry I 22, 23, 25, 92; Caumont, *Statistique monumentale*, 1:255–57; the present church in La Selle is from the late nineteenth century; RBA, (Lascales), Duchesne (Lastels); there was a Picot on the Dives list; *MSAN*, 15:92; Keats-Rohan, *Domesday People*, 324–25, suggests Picot de Lascelles was possibly Breton because he held of Alan of Richmond in Yorkshire and Lincolnshire, but many others did who were not.

Appendix VI

Buckinghamshire: Wingrave and Rowsham

WINGRAVE MANOR IN BUCKINGHAMSHIRE was located on a hill, overlooking Aylesbury. Rowsham was about half way between Wingrave and Aylesbury. Wingrave consisted of a number of manors, including Rowsham, most of which were held of the Honour of Wallingford. At the time of Domesday Book in 1086, Wingrave was held by three people: King William's half-brother, Count Robert of Mortain of Western Normandy, Milo Crispin of Eastern Normandy, and Gunfrid de Chocques of the Artois, all tenants-in-chief. All three of these men had fought with William at Hastings. The manors were subdivided into fees. Wingrave was part of the de Chocques fee. Rowsham was connected to the de Chocques and de Mortain fees. Wingrave and Rowsham were later both associated with the de Hersi(n) family.[1]

Gunfrid de Chocques, a companion of William in 1066, held the fees that descended to Hugh de Hersi. Chocques was in the Artois, east of Picardy, a minor fee held of the family of Houdain, also in the Artois, arrondissement Béthune. The de Chocques fee in Wingrave consisted of eight villagers, three smallholders, one slave, five ploughlands and meadows, and had belonged to King Edward before 1066. In 1120, the Wingrave fees were divided among the de Chocques, Lens, and Béthune families, which were all from the Artois and interrelated by marriage. Gunfrid was succeeded by his son or grandson, Anselm de Chokes, the anglicized spelling of Chocques, in 1129. Anselm married Aegelina de St. Pol, whose younger sister Adelaide married Robert de Béthune. At the time of the death of King Henry I in 1135, the Wingrave fees were held by Anselm, who was later succeeded

---

1. DB Buckinghamshire, 12:9 (Count de Mortain), 23:20–22 (Milo Crispin), 50:1 (Gunfrid de Chocques); Wallingford was an important large pre- and post-conquest royal town, southwest of Aylesbury, in Berkshire (now in Oxfordshire); FA, 1:78; VCH, Buckingham, vol. 3, "Wingrave" 272.

by his son Robert. The 1166 *carta* of Robert de Chokes mentions Henry de Pinkeny as one of his vassals holding in Wingrave at that time. The de Pinkeny family came from Picquigny in Picardy which lies between Eastern Normandy and the Artois.[2]

A plea written in 1199 by Robert de Hersi concerned one and a half knights' fees and appurtenances held in Wingrave and Rowsham in the Vale of Aylesbury, by his father, Hugh de Hersi, during the reign of King Henry I and at the time of his death in December 1135. Hugh's son, Robert de Hersi, held the fees in Wingrave in 1195 under King Richard I and had paid scutage for these fees under King Richard. Robert sued Robert de Pinkeny on 8 November 1199 in the court of assizes over one and a half knights' fees with appurtenances in Wingrave and Rowsham. Pinkeny appeared in his own defense and trial was set for eight days after the feast of St. Hillary on January 13, when four knights would appoint twelve jurors. On 23 April 1200, Robert de Hersin and Robert de Pinkeny argued their case over Wingrave and Rowsham. Robert de Hersin lost the case because, after the death of King Richard, he was declared to be with the new king's enemies, those who had previously supported King Richard I against his brother and successor John.[3]

In these documents, Robert was called de Hersin. There is a town named Hersin-Coupigny, arrondissement Béthune, in the Artois, west of Béthune and northwest of Lens. It is probable that the family named here was from Hersin rather than Hercé, since the other families holding the Chokes fees in Wingrave in 1086 were from this area of the Artois. However, in 1086, the other fees in Wingrave were held by Normans and by the reign of Henry I, the surrounding area was held by the de Bolebec, Giffard, and de Beauchamp families of Normandy and by the de Pinkeny family of Picardy. Achard d'Ambrieres and the Gorron family, neighbors of the

---

2. The name was also spelled de Chokes and Cioches; DB: in 1086 Gunfrid held forty-two fees, mostly in Northamptonshire and Lincolnshire; Robert also held in Northamptonshire in 1160–62, RBE, 1:26, 50, 63, 81, 129, 172, 317–18, 334, 2:598: in 1211–12; the Honour of Chokes was centered in Northamptonshire, 700, 727–28; HKF, 1:20–28, 39–41, 45–46, 297–98; later it went to Béthune, who forfeited it, and then to Gorham of Gorron; *MA*, 6:1018; Torigni, 1:100–101; PR 31 Henry I, 64, 66, 81, 84; FA 1:78; *RCR*, 2:103, 190; *VCH*, Buckingham, "Wingrave," 272; Keats-Rohan, *Domesday People*, 206, 239–41, 462; Keats-Rohan, *Domesday Descendants*, 324, 396–97, 636.

3. PR 2 John (1199), N.S. X, 108, 3 John (1201), N.S. XIV, 165, 4 John (1202), N.S. XV, 23, 5 John (1203), N.S. XVI, 90; *RCR*, II, 103, 190 (8 November 1199, 23 April 1200); in the first document, the name is spelled de Hersi, but in the second document, it is spelled de Hersan and Hersin; *CRR*, 1:38, 62–63; PR 7 Richard I, N.S. VI, 204, 8 Richard I, N.S. VII, 156, 9 Richard I, N.S. VIII, 201, 10 Richard I, N.S. IX, 11: recorded a decision in Robert's favor in 1195, 1196, 1197 and 1198, and repeated in PR 2 John, N.S. XII, 257 (1200); *VCH*, Buckingham, 3:272; Rowsham was then called Rollesham.

de Hercé family in Maine, as well as d'Avranches and de St. John, lords of the de Hériz family in Western Normandy, and de Bolebec, relative of the de Arches family of Eastern Normandy, and also the Talbots, all held in Buckinghamshire at this time.

LORDS IN BUCKINGHAMSHIRE

The towns around Wingrave were in Cottesloe Hundred. In the north, Wing was held by the count of Mortain in 1086 and until 1104, and by Hugh Talbot in the twelfth century. The Hercys were later related to the Talbots. Nearby Linslade and Soulby were held by Hugh de Beauchamp of Western Normandy. King William II Rufus addressed Hugh de Beauchamp as lord of the barons of Buckinghamshire. In the east were Crafton, held by the count of Mortain and the bishop of Lisieux, and Mentmore, held by Earl Hugh d'Avranches of Chester, all from Western Normandy. In the west were Whitchurch, held by Hugh de Bolebec, a relative of the de Arches family which intermarried with the de Hercys, and his relative Walter Giffard of Eastern Normandy, Hardwick, held by the count of Mortain and Milo Crispin of Eastern Normandy, and Aston Abbotts, held by the church of St. Albans, which was connected to the de Gorron family of Maine. Thomas and William de St. John witnessed a charter for the king to St. Albans with Hugh de Gournay in 1116. According to the list of knights' fees made by King Henry II in 1166, the greatest landholders in Buckinghamshire were Walter Giffard, who had as tenants Hugh de Bolebec and Richard Talbot, Walter de Bolebec, brother and guardian of the heir of Hugh, and Gilbert de Pinkeny, with his sons Robert, Henry, and Gilbert. In 1172, the count of Mortain, the earl of Chester, William d'Avranches, Hugh de Beauchamp, Achard d'Ambrieres, and Richard Talbot held in Buckinghamshire, continued to hold lands in Normandy and administered cross-Channel estates. Hugh de Gournay, who was in dispute with Hugh de Hercy in Warwickshire, also held lands in Buckinghamshire during the reign of King Richard, with William de Rochelle, possibly a member of the de Hériz family, and Baldwin de Béthune.[4]

---

4. DB Buckinghamshire, 12.7 (Wing, count of Mortain), B4,13 (Earl Hugh d'Avranches), 23 (Milo Crispin), B7, 14.1-2, 16, 26 (Hugh de Bolebec), 14.1-49 (Walter Giffard), 25.1-3; *RRAN*, 1:334, 370, 3:20: the church of Wing had been given to an abbey in Angers, 870; RBE, 1:312, 316-18, 2:537, 563, 700, 792.

APPENDIX VI

DE GORRON

Wingrave church was given to the abbey of St. Albans. The de Gorron family, immediate neighbors and possibly lords of the de Hercé family in Maine, held one and a half fees in Wingrave and Rowsham of the Honour of Chokes and held the fees of St. Albans. Geoffrey de Gorron was abbot of St. Albans from 1119 until his death in 1146, and Robert was abbot from 1151 until 1166. In the reign of King John, Henry de Gorron (Gorham) of Maine held Flore and Cransley in Northamptonshire in the Honour of Chokes. Robert de Pinkeny held of him. The fees may have been granted to Henry de Gorron after Robert de Pinkeny forfeited them for supporting France.[5]

DE PICQUIGNY

Picquigny was in Picardy, arrondissement Amiens, not far from Saint-Valéry-sur-Somme, with which family the Picquigny family intermarried. Ansculf and Gilo de Picquigny, sons of Guérmond, vidame d'Amiens, came to England in 1066 and fought at Hastings. In England, the name was anglicized to Pinkeny. Ansculf, his son William and his brother Gilo were given numerous manors in England by King William I. In Buckinghamshire in 1086, Ansculf de Pinkeny held thirteen and a half hides in Aylesbury of William FitzAnsculf de Chocques. Ansculf de Picquigny was sheriff of Buckinghamshire and died by 1086. He was succeeded in his lands by his son William FitzAnsculf, who was also tenant-in-chief in Worcestershire. William was succeeded by his daughter and heir, Beatrice, who married Fulk Paynel, giving him Dudley in Worcestershire. Nearby in the south, Ellesborough, in Aylesbury Hundred, was held by William Fitz Ansculf de Picquigny.[6]

Ansculf's brother, Gilo, held Weedon Pinkeny as tenant-in-chief, where he built a castle. Gilo founded the priory of Weedon Pinkeny, which his descendants supported. About this time, the barony of Pinkeny owed fifteen knights to the guard of Windsor Castle. Gilo was succeeded in 1130 by

---

5. RBE, 1:359–60, 2:558; *Gesta Abbatum Sancti Albani*, 1:73, 95, 100; HKF, 2:20–29, 36, 44–49; Matthew of Paris, *ChronMag*, 2:187; *VCH*, Hertford, vol. 4, "St. Albans Abbey," 374–78; Keats-Rohan, *Domesday Descendants*, 482.

6. DB Buckinghamshire: Wingrave: 12.9 (count of Mortain), 23.20 (Milo Crispin), 50.1 (Gunfrid de Chocques), 12.7 (Wing), 18, 23, 25.1–2, 6.1, 12.8, 8.2, 13.1, 14.16 (Whitchurch), 11, 12, 23–24, 17.2 (Ellesborough); MA, 5:11, 204, 6:2, 1018; RBE, 1:71, 90, 144, 172, 174, 317–18, 334; PR 30 Henry I, 75; Guermond II de Picquigny married the daughter of Renaud de St. Valéry; Loyd, *Origins*, 78; Keats-Rohan, *Domesday People*, 206, 484; Keats-Rohan, *Domesday Descendants*, 635, 1055.

APPENDIX VI

his son Ralph, who died in 1158. Ralph's son, Gilbert, held eleven knights' fees in 1166 and land worth 15s. in 1171–72; the latter entry also mentioned Gilbert de Bolebec 20s., Simon de Beauchamp £45, the Honour of Wallingford per Thomas Basset, £100, 5s., and the Honour of Giffard £56. Gilbert de Pinkeny was sheriff of Berkshire from 1157 to 1160. Gilbert's son and successor, Henry I de Pinkeny, great-grandson of Gilo, in 1166 held five fees of his father including one and a half fees in Wingrave of the Honour of Chokes. Many of the de Chokes fees passed to the Honour of Weedon Pinkeny. Henry had many fees in Northamptonshire and Buckinghamshire for which he paid scutage to avoid military service. During the reign of King Richard I, in 1190–91, Henry I de Pinkeny held thirteen and a half knights' fees worth £ 6, 16s., and his son Robert de Pinkeny one and a half knights' fees in Buckinghamshire, worth 15s., holding with Walter and Herbert de Bolebec, Milo and Hugh de Beauchamp, Gervase de Paynel, and Henry de Neufmarché. In 1194–95, Henry de Pinkeny held the same, with Simon de Beauchamp, Herbert de Bolebec, Gervais Paynel, Henry de Neufmarché, and Gilbert Basset. In 1196–97, Henry de Pinkeny held thirteen and a half fees, with Herbert de Bolebec holding one, and Henry de Neufmarché one half. In the reign of King John, Henry de Pinkeny held seventeen and a half knights' fees in Buckinghamshire, as did Herbert and Walter de Bolebec, Alan Basset, Milo, Richard, Hugh, Elias, and Richard de Beauchamp, the earl of Chester, Duncan de Lascelles, Thomas de St. Valéry, Hugh de Gournay, and the Honours of Giffard and Peverel of Nottingham. Henry died in 1209 and was succeeded by his son, Robert.[7]

Although the de Hersi(n) and de Pinkeny families were on opposite sides of lawsuits in the reigns of Kings Richard and John in Buckinghamshire, there were connections between the de Pinkeny family and the Herce family in Worcestershire, and also between the de Pinkeny and the de Arches family of Yorkshire through their de Bolebec, de St. Valéry, and de Neufmarché relatives. Henry II de Pinkeny, grandson of Henry I, was second witness to a donation to Fountains Abbey in Yorkshire in 1154–72. Peter de Pinkeny witnessed a charter donation to Fountains with Thurstin and Richard de Arches between 1176 and 1184.[8]

---

7. DB Buckinghamshire, 17.2, 20, 51.1–3; RBE, 1:36–37, 52, 71, 90–91, 94, 109, 129, 136–37, 172, 294, 317–19; 2:670; PR 30 Henry I, 47, 64, 79, 99; before 1086, Ansculf de Picquigny had exchanged land in Ellesborough for half of Princes Risborough on orders of King William I; *Feet of Fines* 10 Richard I (20 November 1198), 53: Henry de Pinkeny exchanged land in Ellesborough for land in Fulmer, Buckinghamshire; *MA*, 6:2, 1018; HKF, 1:45–46; Keats-Rohan, *Domesday People*, 206; Keats-Rohan, *Domesday Descendants*, 635–38.

8. EYC, vol. 11, nos. 138, 160.

APPENDIX VI

DE BOLEBEC

According to Domesday Book, Hugh I de Bolebec held lands in Buckinghamshire which became the barony of Whitchurch. The manor of Whitchurch in the Vale of Aylesbury was held by the Bolebec family from the late eleventh century. Hugh I de Bolebec, originally from Bolebec in Eastern Normandy, went to England with Duke William. He was both a Domesday tenant-in-chief and a tenant of Walter Giffard. He held Whitchurch as a tenant of Giffard. He was a donor to the Augustinian Misssenden Abbey in Buckinghamshire, and to the Benedictine Ramsay Abbey in Cambridgeshire. He died after 1086. His sons were Walter I de Bolebec, baron of Whitchurch, who succeeded, and Herbert de Bolebec, who also held land in Buckinghamshire. Herbert married Emma and they had a son Gilbert who held a fee in Buckinghamshire in 1160–62 and was a donor to Missenden Abbey. In 1166, Gilbert de Bolebec noted that his father Herbert had held during the reign of Henry I and Hugh de Beauchamp held of him. Robert de Whitchurch, possibly related to the Bolebec family, held three virgates of land in Wingrave and Rowsham in the reign of Richard I.[9]

Baron Hugh II de Bolebec, son of Walter I, succeeded his father in 1142 as lord of Whitchurch where he built Bolebec Castle in 1147. With his parents, he made a number of donations to Ramsay Abbey between 1133 and 1137. Baron Hugh II died in 1165, leaving a son and two daughters. Walter II de Bolebec succeeded and had a daughter Isabel who was in ward to Aubrey II de Vere, whom she later married. Aubrey II de Vere was the second earl of Oxford and master chamberlain of England and Normandy from 1194 to 1214. Walter died in 1190 and Isabel died in 1206 without issue. Hugh II's two daughters, Constance and Isabel, inherited successively. Constance married Elias de Beauchamp and died without issue. Isabel married first Henry de Nonant who died in 1206, and second Robert de Vere, brother of Aubrey and third earl of Oxford, whereby she became countess of Oxford. Countess Isabel was a great patron of the Dominican Order;

---

9. DB Buckinghamshire, B7, 14.1–2, 16, 26.1–11; Hugh de Bolebec also held of Walter Giffard; *RRAN*, vol. 3, nos. 24, 944; RBE, 1:136–39, 312–13, 318–19, 2:536, 695 Gilbert married Richildis and had a son and heir Herbert II; Walter I de Bolebec was later granted Styford in Northumberland by King Henry I, for which he was obligated to provide five knights and castle-guard to Newcastle; he married first Eleanor/Helevise and they had one son, Hugh II; they donated lands to Ramsey Abbey between 1133 and 1137; he married second Sibylla and they had a son, Walter II; Walter I died in 1142 and was succeeded by Hugh II in Buckinghamshire and by Walter II in Northumberland; Loyd, *Origins*, 17; J. Green, *Aristocracy*, 45, 120; Keats-Rohan, *Domesday People*, 261; Keats-Rohan, *Domesday Descendants*, 334–35.

her husband was master chamberlain of England from 1214 to 1221, royal judge, and one of the twenty-five barons elected to enforce Magna Carta.[10]

GIFFARD

King William I gave Walter I Giffard, son of Osbern de Bolebec of Eastern Normandy, 107 knights' fees in England, of which forty-eight were in Buckinghamshire. Walter I Giffard was one of the vice-regents of England in 1067 with Hugh de Grandmesnil, Hugh de Montfort, and William de Warenne, and was a commissioner for Domesday. He was a Domesday tenant-in-chief in Buckinghamshire, where he founded Notley Abbey. He remained comte de Longueville in Eastern Normandy, where in 1070 he built a stone castle. He married Ermengarde, the daughter of Gerard Fleitel. They had several children, including Walter II Giffard, who may have fought with his father at Hastings, William Giffard, who was chancellor to King William II Rufus and was made bishop of Winchester by King Henry I, a daughter, Rohaise, who married Sir Richard de Clare, and another daughter who entered the abbey of Bec. Walter I Giffard died in 1087.[11]

Walter II Giffard succeeded his father and was made the first earl of Buckingham in 1093 by King William II Rufus, for whom he fought against Robert Curthose in Normandy. In 1097, the king gave him command of troops defending the Vexin against the king of France and made him castellan of Windsor. He was lord of Longueville, where he founded the Cluniac priory of Saint-Foy, and Bolebec in Eastern Normandy, and held fees in ten counties in England. After the death of Rufus, he supported Robert Curthose. He married Agnes de Ribemont and left a minor son, Walter III, who was raised by his mother. He died in England in July 1102, but was buried at Longueville, as was his widow later.[12]

---

10. *MA*, 5:479, 6:2, 479, 868; *RRAN*, vol. 3, nos. 4, 874, 961; *CartRamsay*, nos. xci, xcii, xcv; *CartMissenden*, vol. 3, nos. 626–27, 667; *RDP*, Rols 4, 5, 11; RBE, 1:119, 138, 312, 316–17, 437; 2:491, 536, 724; HKF, 1:62–63; Keats-Rohan, *Domesday Descendants*, 334–35.

11. DB Buckinghamshire, 14.1–49; OV, 1:14–15, 264–65, 3:252–53, 6:36–7, 224–25, 236–37; *RRAN*, vol. 1, nos. 11, 23, 123, 144, 170–71, vol. 2, 488–89, 492, 510, 524; RBE, 1:312; EYC, vol. 8, nos. 4–5; Rohaise Giffard married Richard FitzGilbert de Bienfaite de Clare, son of Gilbert de Brionne, count of Eu; Richard refounded the priory of St. Neots in Cambridgeshire/Huntingdonshire as a dependency of Bec Abbey with the help of St. Anselm, abbot of Bec and later archbishop of Canterbury; St. Neots was supported by the de Hercy family of Warwickshire; PR 5 Henry II, 40; Keats-Rohan, *Domesday People*, 363–64, 456–57; Keats-Rohan, *Domesday Descendants*, 994.

12. OV, 6:36–37; *RRAN*, 1:325, 2:911, 974, 1285, 1693; *MA*, 5:269, no.3; Keats-Rohan, *Domesday Descendants*, 995.

APPENDIX VI

Walter III Giffard, earl of Buckingham, was a loyal supporter of King Henry I, for whom he fought at Brenneville and Brémule, thereby saving Longueville. He stayed in Normandy during the reign of King Stephen. He married Ermengarde, but they had no children. They were generous supporters of Longueville Priory, and he founded a leprosarium at Vaudreville. He also donated to the abbeys of Le Tréport and Saint-Ouen, Rouen. During the reign of King Henry I, Walter Giffard had as tenants Hugh I de Bolebec twenty fees, Richard Talbot two fees, Elias Giffard two, Mathilda de Bec one, all relatives or neighbors in Normandy. After he died on 18 September 1164 without children, his English and Norman estates escheated to the king. He was buried in Notley Abbey in Buckinghamshire. His uncle, Richard de Clare, succeeded as earl of Buckingham. In 1172, the Norman Giffards had 102 knights, making them one of the strongest families in Normandy. King Richard I restored the estates to the descendants of Rohaise Giffard de Clare: Richard de Clare, earl of Hertford, and Isabel de Clare, wife of William Marshal and countess of Pembroke.[13]

William and Roger Giffard donated to Kenilworth Priory in Warwickshire, confirmed by William earl of Warwick and King Henry II about 1161-64. One of the witnesses was Giffard de la Lucerne in the Avranchin, implying a possible connection with Lucerne Abbey and with the de Hériz and Giffard families, although the name could have been a sobriquet. William Giffard was dapifer of Roger, earl of Warwick, and in 1166 held two fees of William, earl of Warwick. The heir of Andrew Giffard held one fee in Avon Dasset, Warwickshire, under the earl of Warwick. The de Hercy family also held in Avon Dasset. Richard Giffard held one fee of Walter de Mayenne in Lodestone, Yorkshire, in 1166.[14]

The Giffards were descended from the dukes of Normandy and the de Bolebec family. They held extensive lands in Buckinghamshire, and also fees in Yorkshire, Warwickshire, and seven other counties. In England they refounded the priory of St. Neots in Cambridgeshire, supported by the Hercys of Pillerton, Warwickshire, and donated to Kenilworth Priory in Warwickshire.

---

13. OV, 6:224-237; RBE, 1:312; *RRAN*, vol. 3, nos. 284, 600, 653, 734, 909; *CartMissenden*, 3:667-68, 679; *ChronAbingdon*, 2:85; WJ, 2:268-71; Keats-Rohan, *Domesday Descendants*, 994-95.

14. RBE, 1:18, 195-96, 325-27; *MA*, 6:1, 223-24, no. 7; BL Harley 3650, 6 (La Lucerne); *CartWorcester*, no. 9 (1135-41); *Beauchamp Charters*, no. 285; Keats-Rohan, *Domesday Descendants*, 994-96.

APPENDIX VI

DE BEAUCHAMP

Hugh I de Beauchamp, from Beauchamp, canton La Haye-Pesnel in the Avranchin, went to England after the conquest, although he was attested on some rolls as at Hastings. According to Domesday Book by 1086 he held lands in Buckinghamshire, Bedfordshire, and Hertfordshire. He was sheriff of Bedfordshire under Kings William I and William II, who confirmed his holdings. Hugh de Beauchamp and Ralph Paynel together witnessed a charter whereby King William II Rufus donated a market to Thorney Priory. Hugh and his wife Mathilde were donors to Ramsay Abbey. They had sons Simon I and Robert de Beauchamp.[15] Hugh I died about 1114 and was succeeded by his son, Simon I de Beauchamp.

In 1114 Simon I de Beauchamp witnessed the charter by which King Henry I granted the lands of Roger of Worcester to Walter de Beauchamp, and a donation of Walter de Bolebec to Ramsay. Simon held lands in Buckinghamshire and Bedfordshire under King Henry I. In Bedfordshire, Hugh de Beauchamp and Simon Basset held of him. Simon de Beauchamp had one daughter, who married Hugh de Beaumont, youngest son of Robert de Beaumont, earl of Leicester and count of Meulan, and Elisabeth de Vermandois. In 1138, King Stephen made Simon I de Beauchamp earl of Bedford, but he died soon after and was succeeded by Miles, son of his younger brother Robert.[16]

Robert de Beauchamp held thirty-four fees of the bishop of Bath and of the count of Mortain. Robert had two sons: Miles, who inherited first, and held lands in Buckinghamshire and Bedfordshire, and Payn, who succeeded him. The brothers fought against King Stephen, supporting the empress, for whom Miles witnessed charters. Her son, King Henry II, restored the castle and earldom of Bedford to the de Beauchamps. Miles's brother Payn married Rohaise, daughter of Aubrey de Vere, chamberlain of England, and Adelisa de Clare. Ver, arrondissement Coutances, is a town just north of Beauchamp in the Avranchin. The couple were founders of the Cistercian priory of Newenham in Bedfordshire and donors to several other priories. Their son, Simon II, succeeded in 1156 to lands in Buckinghamshire and

15. Brompton, Leland, Holinshed, Duchesne, Dives, and Falaise; DB Buckinghamshire, 25:1–3; *RRAN*, vol. 1, nos. 370, 477; *MA*, 2:602; RBE, 1:370, 373; Loyd, *Origins*, 20–21; Keats-Rohan, *Domesday People*, 260.

16. *RRAN*, vol. 2, App. lxxxix; *RRAN*, vol. 3, nos. 271, 777, 944; RBE, 2:670, 695; *CartRameseia*, nos. lv, lxix, lxxviii, xci, clxvii, clxi, clxxvi, clxxviii; OV, 6:510–11; PR 31 Henry I, 48, 62, 82, 103; *BeauchampChart*, no. 4 (1114); his eldest brother was earl of Worcestershire, middle brother earl of Leicester and Hereford; death between Easter 1136 and end of 1137; J. Green, *Aristocracy*, 297, 376; Keats-Rohan, *Domesday Descendants*, 313.

Bedfordshire with Herbert de Bolebec and Henry de Picquigny, and was sheriff of both counties from 1194 to 1197. Simon II de Beauchamp donated to Newenham and Greenfield priories. He married Isabel and had sons William and Robert. Simon II de Beauchamp died in 1207 and was succeeded by his son William.[17]

In 1157, Hugh de Beauchamp held fees in Buckinghamshire under Gilbert de Bolebec. Hugh held lands in Normandy in 1172 under the count of Mortain. He died on the third crusade after 1190. Hugh had sons Oliver, who died young, Hugh II, Miles, and Richard. Hugh II held lands in Buckinghamshire, Bedfordshire, and Derbyshire.

Most of the lords in Buckinghamshire came to England from Normandy, the Artois and Picardy with William the Conqueror. Although the immediate lords of the de Chocques fee of Wingrave were from the Artois in 1086, the majority of landholders around Wingrave were from Western Normandy: de Mortain, d'Avranches, de Beauchamp, and de St. John from the Avranchin, Basset and de Lacy from Calvados. The de Bolebec and Giffard families were from Eastern Normandy.[18] Many of these lords still held lands in Normandy.[19]

Until the reign of King Henry I, no Manceau lords held property in Buckinghamshire. Although Achard d'Ambrieres held land in Tryringham and came from Maine, he was still a Norman. The Benedictine abbey of St. Albans, located about twenty-five miles southwest of Wingrave, held in Wingrave during the reign of King Henry I. Its abbots, Geoffrey de Gorham and his nephew Robert de Gorham, were members of the de Gorron family, which, although of Breton origin, had been the immediate neighbors and lords of the de Hercé family in Maine. Henry de Gorron held in Wingrave and Rowsham in the reign of King John.

This Hersi(n) family was probably from Hersin in the Artois, but it should be kept in mind that the other neighbors around their holdings in Buckinghamshire were from Normandy and Maine as early as the reign of Henry I, and, especially during and after the reign of Henry II, were the same neighbors and lords the de Hercys had elsewhere in Worcestershire, Warwickshire, Yorkshire, and Nottinghamshire. The evidence is not sufficient

---

17. *RRAN*, 3:68, 81, 275, 582, 634; *MA*, 2:601, xii, 4:101, 5:346, 6:101, 374, 950; *BeauchampChart*, nos. 4, 6, 9; *EYC*, vol. 3, no. 1390, vol. 5, no. 389; PR, 31 Henry I, 81–82, 102, 104; RBE, 1:35, 52, 71, 90, 318–22, 352, 2:537, 636; CCR, 51 Henry III, 281; *Testa de Nevill*, 1:152;. Loyd, *Origins*, 110; Keats-Rohan, *Domesday Descendants*, 311–15.

18. DB Buckinghamshire, 4.38, E2 (Ilbert de Lacy), 19.4 (Ralph Basset), 16 (William Peverel).

19. RBE, 2:628–32, 632–35, 643–44.

APPENDIX VI

to decide whether or not the de Hersin family of Buckinghamshire were related to the Hercys of Warwickshire, although it is unlikely.

Appendix VII

John Hercy the Surveyor

KING JAMES I INHERITED a kingdom of debts. He lived extravagantly, maintaining two courts, one for himself and one for the queen, with a lavish lifestyle of masques, hunting, and drunkenness. His court expenses increased by 50 percent from 1603 to 1610. He was unable to manage Parliament to provide revenues, so he raised money by enclosing and leasing royal forests and selling royal estates, peerages, and knighthoods.

John Hercy was a royal surveyor under James I. The Privy Council ordered a survey of crown lands in 1603. The earl of Dorset was in charge and his surveyor was John Hercy. The purpose was to value copyhold lands for fee-farm, so the tenants could pay the appropriate value to hold them in fee simple, and the process would raise money for the crown. Copyhold land was held at the will of the lord according to the custom of the manor. Fee-farm land was held in fee simple at a fixed rent with no homage or service. In the beginning, the surveys were based on documents; later, surveyors were hired to actually measure the estates. In September 1603, John Hercy was paid £355, 7s. and another £40 on 13 December for surveying work. That year he appears to have been the only royal surveyor. On 24 February 1604, he received £49, 15s. 4d. for surveying manors in Berkshire, Oxfordshire, and Hampshire, which included £10 for his clerks; on 28 February £60 for surveying manors in Wiltshire and Gloucestershire, and in September for manors in Middlesex and in December for some in Surrey. In April 1605 he was paid to survey manors in Essex and the southern Midlands. Also that year, Sir Robert Johnson complained to the earl of Salisbury that he wanted to survey a certain division in the south, but that "Mr. Hersey endeavours to have that division." In March 1606 John Hercy worked in Somerset and Dorset, and in May in Gloucestershire. In July 1607 a survey of the crown custody lands was ordered and divided into five circuits. Three men named John Hercy, including the son of the first John Hercy, headed three of the

APPENDIX VII

five circuits. In 1607 he was sent to the royal manor of Theobalds with two measurers. By June 1607 he had surveyed manors in most of the counties of southeastern England. On June 29, he was ordered to return to the manors he had surveyed in eight counties to assist the commissioners in the sale of copyholds in fee-farm. The existing drafts of his surveys were annotated with tenant offers to buy their land.[1]

In February 1608, John Hercy was commissioned to negotiate the sale of fee-farms in Hampshire, Wiltshire, Somerset, Devonshire, and Dorset. On 20 March 1608, the earl of Dorset expressed thanks for the surveys done by John Hercy in Wiltshire and hope that the work would continue. On 27 June Hercy was paid for his work in 1608, when the fee-farm program was ended. This resulted in the valuations being frozen at their value in 1609, making it difficult later to increase royal revenues. On 14 March 1609, John Hercy wrote a report on the survey of the king's manor of Charing in Kent, stating that the tower was in need of major repairs and in danger of falling down, that the lessee was not bound to make repairs, and that the king might take at least part of the timber needed for the repairs from his woods in Charing. In April 1609 Hercy was paid for making copies of his surveys. In November 1609, he noted the "slowness" of copyholders to buy at the new and higher valuations. Between 1603 and 1610, he was paid £2,636, a very large sum for the time. The Hercy surveys were still in use in the 1620s.[2]

The provenance of John Hercy the surveyor is not certain, although he likely lived in Berkshire and/or London because of his proximity to the court and his area of practice. John Hercy the surveyor was steward of the manor of Knowle in Warwickshire. He may or may not be the same person, but may be related to John Hercy of Fillongley in Warwickshire. Both places are in northwest Warwickshire.[3]

---

1. *Exchequer* 403/2723, fols. 197r, 227v, 233; 403/2724, fols. 82r, 157r; 403/2725, fols. 6r, 28v, 47v, 62v, 135v, 140r, 150v, 158r, 210v; 403/2726, fols. 15r, 22v, 43v-44r, 155r, 210v; *State Papers of James I*, 14/32, fol. 158v, 160v; Hoyle, *Estates*, 220-22.

2. *Exchequer* 403/2727, fols.215v, 230r-235v; 403/2728, fols. 153r, 159r; 403/2723-2730; *State Papers of James I*, 14/49, no. 60; 14/32, 85, 16/69, fol. 16r, 21v, 47r, 71v; Hoyle, *Estates*, 223-24, 236, 240; West Sussex Record Office, Cap/1/4/9/24; *Cecil Papers*, 1608-9, March 14.

3. *Exchequer*, 403/2723, fol. 31v; see 403/2726, fol. 43v on three John Hercys; Hoyle, *Estates*, 220, n. 69; TNA, Cap/1/4/9/24 (6 May 1603); *Cal. State Papers, Interregnum, Warrants of the Protector and Council*, 12 April 1658: a John Hersey married Dorothea Lee or Lear on 16 December 1617 at Winkfield, where she was buried on 31 May 1639; on 12 April 1658, a John Hercy was granted a passport to France by the Lord Protector Cromwell and Council; Oliver Cromwell died that year and soon after the monarchy was restored.

Appendix VIII

Some Notes on the de Hercé Family in France after 1066

THE NAMES OF MEMBERS of the de Hercé family in Maine are known from the mid-twelfth century. Guillaume de Hercé was born about 1150 in the Cour-Hercé in Colombiers-du-Plessis, on the edge of the present Hercé. He was a chevalier banneret, one of the knights of Maine who carried a banner for King Philippe-Auguste of France. A knight banneret was one with sufficient wealth, stature, and vassals that he led a company of men in battle. He carried a square banner when other knights carried a pennant. Guillaume de Hercé took the cross in 1190 and went on the Third Crusade with Kings Philippe-Auguste of France and Richard I of England in 1191. The two kings met at Vézelay on 4 July 1190 and marched together to Lyon. There they separated and reconvened in Messina in September, but quarreled over Richard's failure to marry Alix, half-sister of Philippe-Auguste. They came back together in the siege of Acre in June 1191. After the victory, they quarreled over the subsequent rule of the Holy Land. Philippe-Auguste returned to France, leaving his army with Richard, who continued to fight in the Holy Land until 9 October 1192. Presumably Guillaume de Hercé would then have fought under Richard. On his return, Richard was captured and held prisoner until he was ransomed and released on 4 February 1194. King Richard then went to England where he granted land to his men, including Hugh de Hercy, to whom he gave Pillerton, Warwickshire.[1] Although the relationship is not known, Hugh could have been the son or brother of Guillaume, or he could have been a castle knight of Richard or of a magnate in England.

Guillaume de Hercé married Jacquine de Vasse and they had two children. When he died, he was succeeded by their son, Julien I de Hercé,

---

1. Hozier, *Armorial général*, 151; Courcelles, *Dictionnaire*, 3:289; Prestwich, *Armies*, 13–15; Crouch, *Image*, 86–90.

seigneur de Hercé. Their daughter, Jeanne de Hercé, married Isaac de Mauclerc de la Muzanchère. The son of Julien I, Robert I de Hercé, married his first cousin, Marie-Anne Mauclerc de la Muzanchère, the daughter of Jeanne, in 1226. They had sons, Julien II, knight and lord of Hercé, Gorron, Lévaré, La Tannière, and Vaudemusson, who lived from about 1230 to 1277, and Robert II de Hercé. Julien II lived in the Cour-Hercé, then in the parish of Colombiers-du-Plessis. He wanted a church nearer to his manor so, in about 1260, he built the church of Saint-Pierre-des-Bois in Hercé. Julien II had a daughter and heir, Jeanne de Hercé, lady of Hercé and Vaudemusson, who married in 1277 Ory de Benoist, knight and lord of Boisberault, a fief of Gorron. He renounced his right to inherit. In 1374, their daughter or granddaughter Marie de Benoist, married Jean II des Vaux of Champéon, southeast of Ambrières, who became lord of Levaré, the town adjoining Hercé on the west, and died in 1392. The des Vaux family was known from charters of Saint-Vincent-du Mans in the late eleventh and early twelfth centuries, and later from those of the abbey of Fontaine-Daniel, southwest of Mayenne, where they had a burial chapel. A stained-glass window in the church of Hercé showed the union of the two families, pairing the arms of de Hercé and des Vaux. The arms of the de Hercé family are azur with three herses of gold; a herse was a descending grill or portcullis used in castles to protect the entrance. The de Hercé family continued to possess the land, while the des Vaux family held the rents. The parish church of Saint-Pierre-des-Bois in Hercé, built by the de Hercé family, was mentioned in the cartularies of the abbeys of Fontaine-Daniel in the thirteenth and Savigny in the fourteenth centuries, both of which held rents or fiefs in Hercé. Robert II succeeded his brother and had a son Jean I, who married Scholastique Girard and had a son Jean II, who married Marguérite de Champagne. They had a son Colin who married Guillermine le Bouesne, and had a son Guillaume II, who married Brisegaude de Brecé. They had a daughter Françoise and a son Jean III, seigneur des Loges au Maine. Robin de Hercé married Péronnelle de Mayenne, great-granddaughter of Juhel II de Mayenne. Robin was an equerry serving both Briant de Montjean, arrondissment Laval, at Angers in 1380 and Robert de Ferrières, lord of Vautorte, arrondissement Mayenne, canton Ernée, at Chartres.[2]

In the sixteenth century, Olive de Hercé, daughter of Guillaume II de Hercé, married Léonard Achard, descendant of the Achards of Ambrières. Also in the sixteenth century, François, son of Jean IV de Hercé, in 1529 married Catherine de Rabinard, and had a son Jean V, lord of La

---

2. Hozier, *Armorial général*, 151; Courcelle, 289; Angot, *Dictionaire historique*, 424; Hercé, *Père, Maire*, 3, 197.

APPENDIX VIII

Haye-Peau-du-Loup, who in 1552 married Marguérite de Vanembras. They had a son César, who in 1606 married Marie Regnault de la Lavery and had a son Jean VI. In 1669, Jean VI was declared noble, retroactive to 1527. Jean VI married Jeanne Baslin and had a son Jean VII, who was a captain in a regiment of Tours in 1689. In 1678, Jean VII married Anne des Vaux. The family held the château du Plessis at Columbiers, where, in 1697, Jeanne des Vaux bequeathed all the property she legally could to her son from her second marriage, Jean VIII de Hercé. She founded a church at le Plessis d'Esseulay. The family also held La Haie-Peau-du-Loup, which in the seventeenth century had a small castle, and Vaudemusson, Brecé, and other small towns around Hercé.

Jean VIII de Hercé married Françoise des Ormes de la Panissaie, daughter of the controller of salt at Ernée. Their son, Jean-Baptiste de Hercé, knight and lord of le Plessis, married Françoise Tanquerel, daughter of the procurator general of the duchy of Mayenne. They were the parents of nineteen children, thirteen of whom survived to adulthood. They built a town house, called the Hotel de Hercé, in Mayenne on the Place de Cheverus. Jean-Baptiste died on 23 August 1767. Their children, as aristocrats and clerics, were to suffer much during the Revolution. Three sons were knights, one was both bishop and count; three others were clerics; two daughters were nuns.

The eldest son, Jean-René de Hercé, was a knight and lord of la Haie, du Plessis, and Condray. In 1757, he married Françoise Urbaine Marie Billiard de Lorière, daughter of the criminal judge of the duchy of Mayenne. Their son, Jean-Armand (1759–1841) was the principal page of King Louis XVI. Later he was named captain of dragoons of the regiment of Noailles in 1781. In 1785 he completed a genealogy of the de Hercé family, now lost, which he updated in 1831 and 1841. He fought in many battles during the Revolution on the royalist side. He was exiled to Germany, then Holland, and finally England, where he joined his uncles in Bath. He took part in the Quiberon expedition as a major of infantry, but his group landed in the Channel Islands and retreated to England after the defeat of the lead group. In London in 1797 he was made a knight of St. Louis and lieutenant-colonel of cavalry, probably by the future king Charles X. His lands, confiscated during the Revolution, were restored in 1803, but he sold them since he saw little future for the aristocracy in France. In 1814, he was elected head of a deputation from Mayenne to King Louis XVIII and in 1816 he was named commandant of the garde nationale.

The second son, Urbain-René de Hercé (1726–1795), studied at the Sorbonne for nine years, earning a licenciate in law and a doctorate in theology. In 1751, he returned to Mayenne as a priest. In August 1754, Bishop

Pierre Mauclerc de la Muzanchère of Nantes appointed him vicar general and administrator of the diocese, and later gave him the abbey Nôtre-Dame de Noyers in Tours. In 1767, he was consecrated bishop of Dol, in Brittany, at Saint-Sulpice. En route to Dol, he passed through Mayenne and gave the last rites to his dying father. He appointed his younger brother François, also a priest, as his vicar general. Urbain-René was a member of the États de Bretagne from 1783. When he was made president in 1784, the king gave him the abbey of Nôtre-Dame des Vaux. In 1788, he led a delegation from the Parlement of Bretagne to the royal court. Speaking before the king and his ministers, he criticized the finance minister and a recent royal decree, for which he was sent home by the secretary of state and forbidden to leave his diocese without permission of the king. There in 1789 he defended the Breton Parlement against the violation of their right to immunity and the imprisonment of forty deputies of the aristocracy. As bishop in March 1790, he opposed the decrees of the Assemblée Nationale against the clergy. After the fall of the Bastille, in June his office as bishop was suppressed and he retired to the château des Ormes and then to the seminary in Mayenne. On 10 July 1790, the Civil Constitution of the Clergy, making clergy employees of the state, became law. The de Hercé brothers refused to swear to the constitution. In 1791 the Directoire declared him "disobedient to the decrees of the Assembly and a perturber of public order." He and his brother François, bishop and vicar general of diocese of Dol, were arrested in March 1791 and jailed at Cordeliers, where they were held in a cell with two other priests. With the help of their nephew, they obtained passports and escaped to exile in Jersey in October 1792, where there were over three thousand exiled French priests. They were joined there by their nephew Jean-François and brother Jean-François-Simon, who fell ill and was advised to take the waters in Bath in England. So they all moved to Bath in May 1794. There was a large group of exiled French aristocrats and clergy in Bath. They returned to France with a group of exiles supported by the English, in what was called the Quiberon expedition. Urbain-René was named apostolic vicar and chaplain of the army. It was poorly planned and roundly defeated. The de Hercé brothers were arrested after debarking, were given a summary trial before a military commission, and were both martyred with eleven other priests by firing squad at Vannes on 28 July 1795. It was said that the French soldiers refused to shoot them and they were replaced by volunteers from the mob of Paris. The bodies were thrown in a common grave but recovered and reburied in the cathedral of Vannes in 1814.

The fourth brother, Jean-François-Simon de Hercé (1743–1796), knight and seigneur du Plessis, served as an officer in the royal navy for sixteen years and was made a knight of St. Louis in 1775. He married Jeanne/

APPENDIX VIII

Anne du Bois de la Basmaignée. They had seven sons and four daughters and lived in the Hotel de Hercé in Mayenne. In 1789 he served in the assembly of Maine and was elected to the États Généraux. During the Revolution he fled from France to Holland, then to Jersey and finally to Bath, where he died in 1796.[3]

Their elder son was also named Jean-François (1776–1849). He learned English and Italian in his father's house in Mayenne. He was given a tutor, P. Zerilli, a former Jesuit, after the order was suppressed in France. Under him, the young Jean-François learned Latin and Greek. As a child, his intelligence was noted by his uncle, Bishop Urbain-René, who took him under his wing. He and his tutor moved to the household of his uncles in Dol. Later his father placed him in the collège de Navarre in Paris for two years while he was serving in the États Généraux at Versailles. After the Assemblée Nationale was dissolved in September 1791, his father took him back to Mayenne, where he rejoined his uncles, exiled from Dol, and aunt Charlotte. At age seventeen, in 1792, he went to Laval to try to bring food to his uncles and tutor in prison and helped them get passports. He went with them as far as St. Malo but was not allowed on their ship. So he left in a fishing boat in a storm for Jersey and joined his uncles there, then continued on with his uncles and father to Bath. Later he took part in the Quiberon expedition but did not debark and survived. He took care of his dying father, and spent six years in England after his death, working as a teacher. He returned to France at the request of his mother and married an aristocrat, Marie de la Haie de Bellegarde, on 11 September 1811. The wedding was performed by his brother Julien-César, shortly before his own death. Jean-François became mayor of St-Ouen-des-Vallon, the town of his wife. In February 1814, he was appointed mayor of Laval by imperial decree of Napoleon I. In 1817, King Louis XVIII appointed him deputy, which made it necessary to spend much time in Paris. In 1825 his wife died and their only child, Marie Lucie, married Guillaume d'Ozouville. Jean-François then entered the seminary at age fifty-four, studying under Lamennais. Jean-François was ordained a priest in 1830. He was made pastor of Sainte-Trinité, the future cathedral of Laval. He turned down offers to become bishop of Saint-Brieuc, Orléans, and Vannes; but in 1835, he finally accepted to be coadjutor bishop of Nantes, where he put his skills in languages to work ministering to the many foreigners in the busy port. In May 1838 he became the beloved bishop of Nantes where he reformed and reorganized the diocese, opening new churches and schools, and finishing the building of the cathedral, which had been severely damaged during the Revolution. His younger brother,

---

3. Hercé, *Père, Maire*, 4–5, 225.

APPENDIX VIII

Louis (1778–1842), was mayor of Mayenne from 1816 to 1830, where there is a square named after him. Louis was also a royalist deputy in 1824.[4]

The eldest sister, Charlotte, studied at the elite royal academy for girls founded at Saint-Cyr by Madame de Maintenon. She served as aid and bookkeeper for her brother when he was bishop of Dol. Jeanne-Françoise and Marie-Joseph became sisters of the Hospitalières of Ernée and were imprisoned during the Revolution. The fourth sister, Louise-Elisabeth, married. Two other brothers, René Urbain of the royal artillery and René-César of the royal navy were killed in battle. Other brothers Louis-Joachim served in the coast guard and then took the habit of a Feuillant, a reformed Cistercian monk; Jean-Baptiste entered the seminary of Angers and became vicar general and archdeacon for the bishop of Luçon. The youngest brother, Julien-César de Hercé (1744–1811), held an MA from Angers and a licentiate in law. He was a priest, canon regular, and vicar general of the diocese of Nantes. In 1778, the king gave him the abbey of Bellefontaine. In 1794, as a noble and a priest, he fled to England during the Terror where he joined his uncles in Bath and took part in the Quiberon expedition but survived. On 30 September 1811, he died suddenly at Chalons in the company of his nephew Jean-Armand.[5]

---

4. Courcelles, *Dictionaire*, 289; Maupoint, *Vie de Monseigneur Jean-François de Hercé*; Hercé, *Père, Maire*, 3–176; he learned German, Hebrew, Arabic, Farsi, Syriac, and other languages; Durand, *Diocese de Nantes*, 196–98

5. Hercé, *Père, Maire*, 4, 224–25.

Maps

Maine

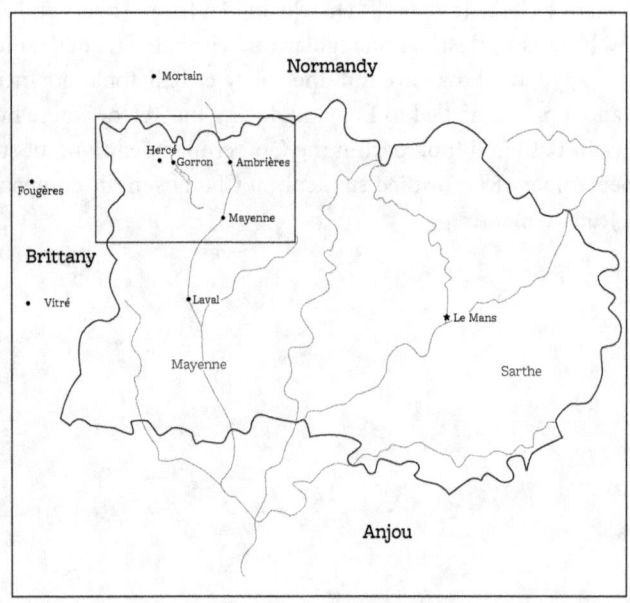

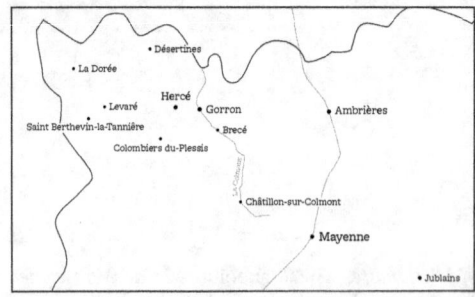

MAPS

Eastern Normandy

MAPS

Western Normandy

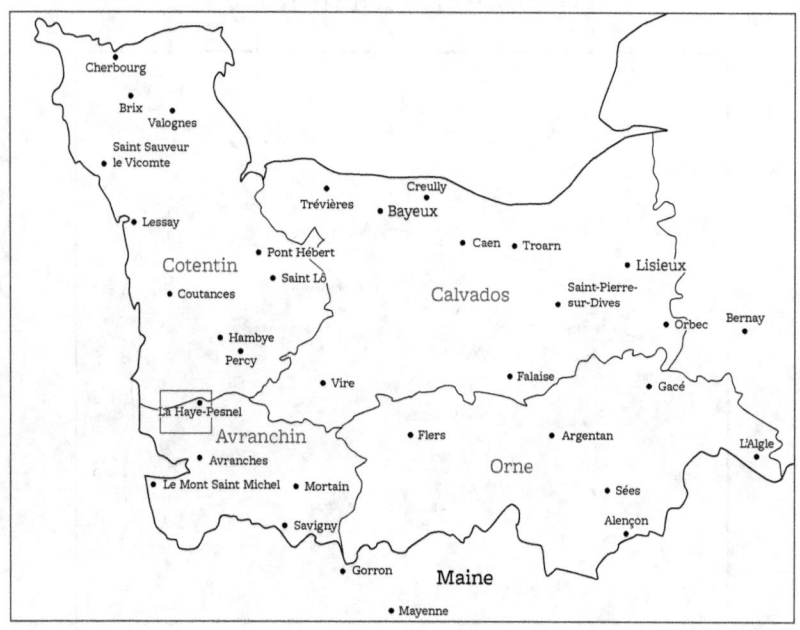

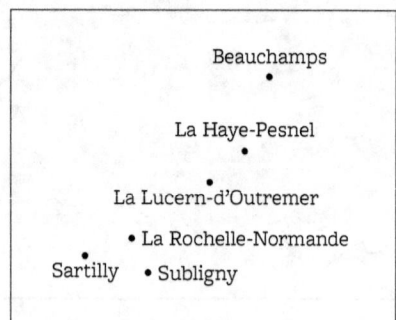

Warwickshire

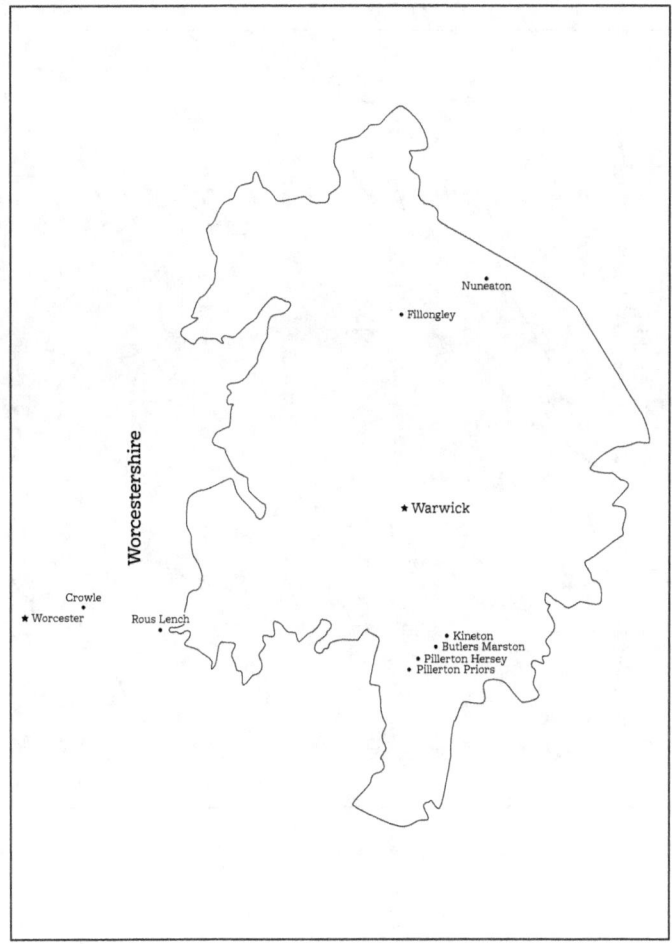

MAPS

North Nottinghamshire

MAPS

Berkshire

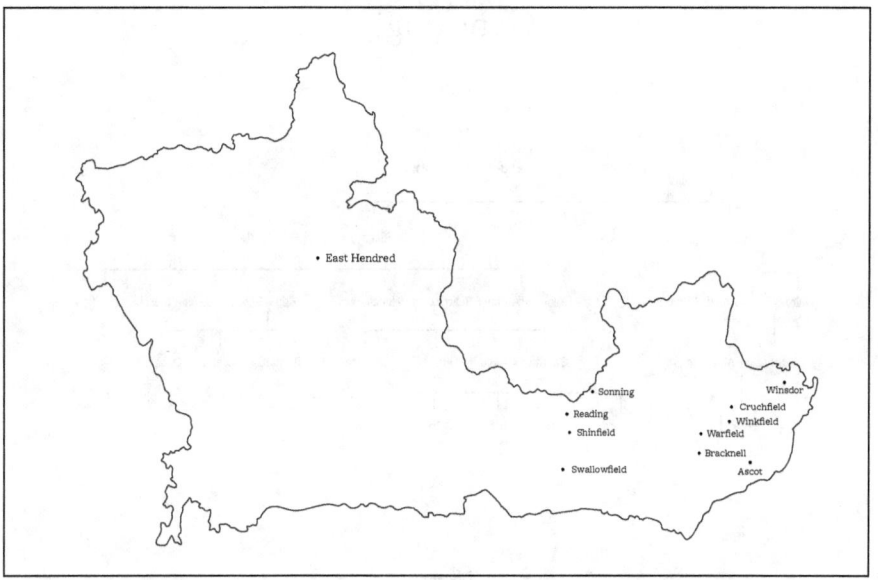

Genealogies

D'Auffay

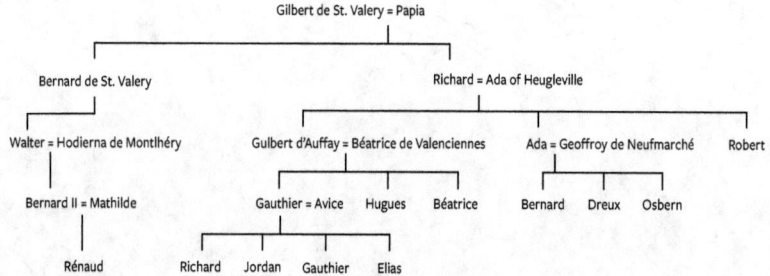

D'Arques

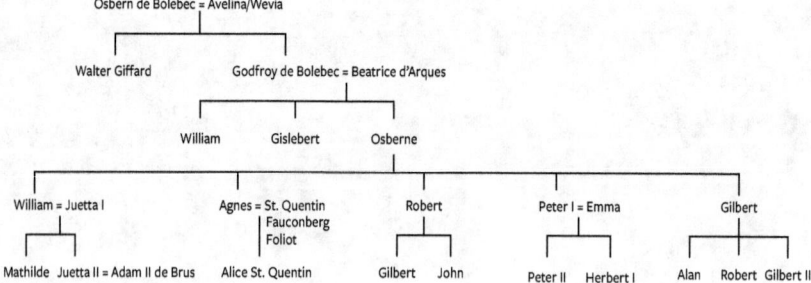

Hercy

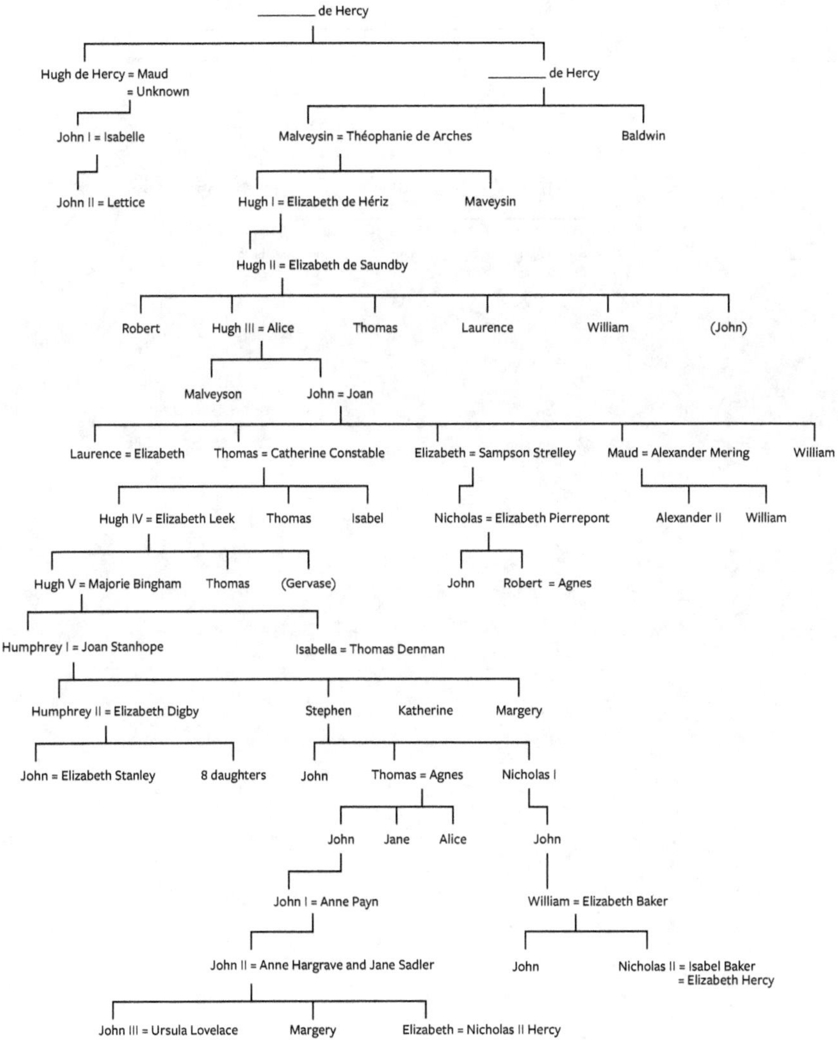

_______ de Hercy
Hugh de Hercy = Maud
= Unknown
_______ de Hercy
John I = Isabelle
Malveysin = Théophanie de Arches
Baldwin
John II = Lettice
Hugh I = Elizabeth de Hériz
Maveysin
Hugh II = Elizabeth de Saundby
Robert
Hugh III = Alice
Thomas
Laurence
William
(John)
Malveyson
John = Joan
Laurence = Elizabeth
Thomas = Catherine Constable
Elizabeth = Sampson Strelley
Maud = Alexander Mering
William
Hugh IV = Elizabeth Leek
Thomas
Isabel
Nicholas = Elizabeth Pierrepont
Alexander II
William
Hugh V = Majorie Bingham
Thomas
(Gervase)
John
Robert = Agnes
Humphrey I = Joan Stanhope
Isabella = Thomas Denman
Humphrey II = Elizabeth Digby
Stephen
Katherine
Margery
John = Elizabeth Stanley
8 daughters
John
Thomas = Agnes
Nicholas I
John
Jane
Alice
John
John I = Anne Payn
William = Elizabeth Baker
John II = Anne Hargrave and Jane Sadler
John
Nicholas II = Isabel Baker
= Elizabeth Hercy
John III = Ursula Lovelace
Margery
Elizabeth = Nicholas II Hercy

GENEALOGIES

Hériz

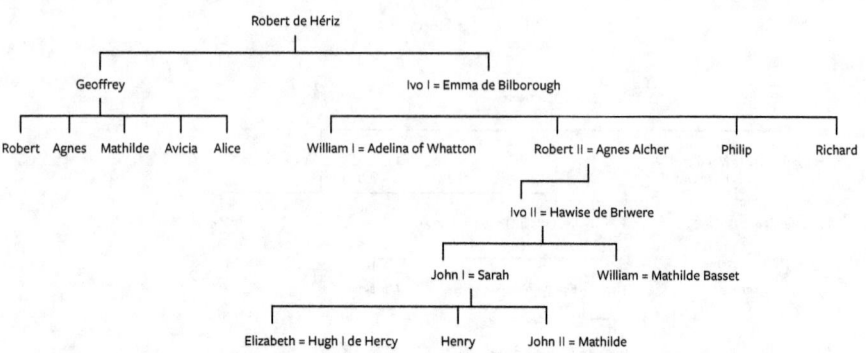

Illustrations

La Cour Hercé.

ILLUSTRATIONS

Châteaux and River of Mayenne.

St. Mary the Virgin Church, Pillerton Hersey, Warwickshire.

ILLUSTRATIONS

Tickhill Castle Gate, Tickhill, Yorkshire.

Church of St. Helen, Grove, Nottinghamshire.

ILLUSTRATIONS

Incised grave slabs of Hugh IV Hercy and Elizabeth Leek Hercy, Church of St. Helen, Grove. Photograph courtesy of Geoff Buxton and the Southwell and Nottingham Church History Project.

Grove Hall, ca. 1900. Tudor House on right.
Transactions of Thoroton Society 24 (1920).

ILLUSTRATIONS

Hériz tomb effigies, Church of St. Laurence, Gonalston, Nottinghamshire.

Hériz arms in window, Church of St. Laurence, Gonalston.

ILLUSTRATIONS

Tomb effigy of Sir William de Saundby, Church of St. Martin,
Saundby, Nottinghamshire.

Tomb effigies of Sir Sampson and Elizabeth Hercy de Strelley,
All Saints Church, Strelley, Nottinghamshire.

ILLUSTRATIONS

Effigy of Elizabeth Hercy de Strelley, All Saints Church, Strelley, Nottinghamshire.

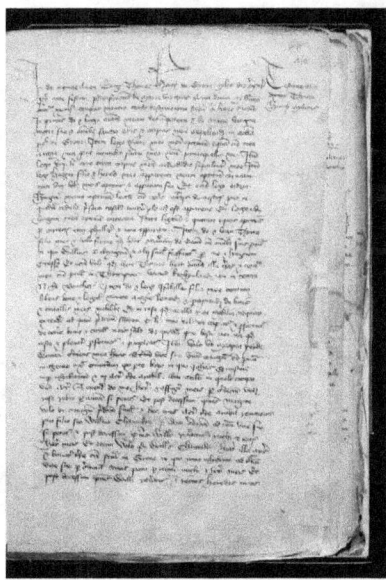

Will of Sir Thomas de Hercy, 1425. York Diocesan Archive: Archbishops' registers. Borthwick Institute for Archives, University of York. Abp. Reg. Vacancy Register 5A. Image reproduced by permission of Borthwick Institute for Archives, University of York.

Crown and Rose, Westminster Abbey.

West Retford Hall, Retford, Nottinghamshire.

ILLUSTRATIONS

King Edward VI School, Retford, Nottinghamshire.

Church of St. Mary, Winkfield, Berkshire.

ILLUSTRATIONS

Cruchfield Manor, Cruchfield, Berkshire.

Bibliography

PRIMARY SOURCES

Abstracts of Probate Acts in the Prerogative Court of Canterbury. London, 1906.
Actes Henri II: Recueil des actes de Henri II: roi d'Angleterre et duc de Normandie. Paris: Imprimerie Nationale, 1909.
Alumni Cantabrigenses. Part 1. Cambridge: Cambridge University Press, 1922.
Alumni Oxonienses. The Members of the University of Oxford 1500–1714. Oxford: Parker, 1891.
Anglo-Saxon Chronicle. Translated by Dorothy Whitelock et al. New Brunswick, NJ: Rutgers University Press, 1961.
Annales Cestrienses. London: Record Society, 1887.
Annales Monastici. Translated by Henry Luard. London: Longman, 1864–69.
The "Annals" of Flodoard of Reims: 919–66. Translated by Steven Fanning and Bernard Bachrach. Toronto: Broadview, 2004.
Annals of Nottinghamshire. London: Simpkin, 1852.
Basset Charters c. 1120–1250. Publications of the Pipe Roll Society, LXXXVIII, N.S. L. London: Ruddock, 1995.
The Battle Abbey Roll. Translated by the Duchess of Cleveland. 3 vols. London: Murray, 1889.
Bayeux Livre Noir: Antiquus cartularius ecclesiae Baiocensis (livre noir). Vol. 1. Paris: Picard, 1902.
The Beauchamp Cartulary Charters 1100–1268. Translated by Emma Mason. London: Pipe Roll Society, 1980.
Bracton, Henry de. *Bracton's Notebook*. Edited by William F. Maitland. London: 1887.
Bridlington Charter: Abstracts of the Charters and Other Documents Contained in the Chartulary Priory of Bridlington in the East Riding of the County of York. Leeds: Whitehead, 1912.
Calendarium Inquisitionem Post Mortem sive Escaetarum. London: PRO, 1806–1955.
Calendar of the Charter Rolls Preserved in the Public Record Office. London: HMSO, 1903–27.
Calendar of the Close Rolls Preserved in the Public Record Office. London: HMSO, 1892–1963.
Calendar of Documents Preserved in France 918–1206. London: HMSO, 1899.
Calendar of Documents Relating to Scotland. Edinburgh: General Register House, 1884.

BIBLIOGRAPHY

Calendar of Entries in the Papal Registers Relating to Great Britain and Ireland. London: HMSO, 1897.
Calendar of Letter-Books Preserved among the Archives of the Corporation of the City of London. Letter-Book G. London: Francis, 1905.
Calendar of Nottinghamshire Coroners' Inquests 1486–1558. Nottingham: Thoroton Society Record Series, no. 25, 1969.
Calendar of Plea and Memoranda Roles Preserved among the Archives of the Corporation of the City of London. Cambridge: Cambridge University Press, 1926–61.
Calendar of State Papers Domestic: Interregnum. London: University of London, 1885.
Calendar of State Papers, Domestic Series of the Reigns of Edward VI, Mary, Elizabeth 1547–1580. London: Longman, 1856.
Calendar of the Fine Rolls Preserved in the Public Record Office. London: HMSO, 1911–1962.
Calendar of the Liberate Rolls preserved in the Public Record Office. London: HMSO, 1916–64.
Calendar of the Patent Rolls Preserved in the Public Record Office. London: HMSO, 1891–1916.
A Calendar of the Shrewsbury and Talbot Papers in Lambeth Palace Library and the College of Arms. 2 vols. Derbyshire Archaeological Society Record Series, 1966–1971.
Calendar of the State Papers Relating to Scotland and Mary, Queen of Scots 1557–1603. Edinburgh: General Register House, 1905.
Calverley Charters: The Calverley Charters Presented to the British Museum. Vol. 6. Leeds: Whitehead, 1904.
Cartulaire de l'abbaye cistercienne de Fontaine-Daniel. Mayenne: Poirier-Reale, 1896.
Cartulaire de l'Abbaye de Sainte-Trinité du Mont de Rouen. Paris: Crapelet, 1840.
Cartulaire de l'Abbaye de Saint-Michel du Tréport. Paris: Firmin-Didot, 1880.
Cartulaire de l'Abbaye de Saint-Vincent au Mans. Le Mans: St-Denis, 1886–1913.
Cartulaire de l'Abbaye du Ronceray d'Angers. Paris: Picard, 1900.
Cartulaire de l'Hotel-Dieu de La Haye-Pesnel. 1687. Bibliothèque municipale d'Avranches, MS 219, Avranches, France.
Cartulaire de Saint-Michel de l'Abbayette, prieuré de l'Abbaye du Mont-Saint-Michel. Paris: 1894.
Cartulaire Manceau de Marmoutier. Laval: 1911.
Cartularium abbathiae de Rievelle. Durham: 1889.
Cartularium abbathiae de Whitby, Ordinis S. Benedicti. Durham: Surtees Society, 1879.
Cartularium monasterii de Rameseia. 3 vols. London: Longman, 1884–93.
Cartularium prioratus de Gyseburne. London: Surtees Society, 1889–91.
The Cartulary of Blyth Priory. Translated by R. T. Timson. London: HMSO, 1973.
The Cartulary of Missenden Abbey. Pt. 3. London: HMSO, 1962.
The Cartulary of St. Leonard's Hospital, York. Translated by David X. Carpenter. York and Suffolk: YAS and Boydell, 2015.
Cartulary of Oseney Abbey. Oxford Historical Society, vols. 89–91, 97–98, 101. Oxford: Clarendon, 1929–36.
The Cartulary of the Monastery of St. Frideswide at Oxford. Oxford: Clarendon, 1895–96.
The Cartulary of Worcester Cathedral Priory (Register I). London: Ruddock, 1968.

BIBLIOGRAPHY

The Charters of the Anglo-Norman Earls of Chester, c. 1071–1237. Translated by Geoffrey Barraclough. The Record Society of Lancashire and Cheshire, vol. 126. Gloucester: Sutton, 1988.

Charters of the Honour of Mowbray 1107–1191. Translated by D. E. Greenway. London: Oxford University Press, 1972.

Charters of the Redvers Family and the Earldom of Devon, 1090–1217. Translated by Robert Bearman. Devon and Cornwall Record Society, N.S. vol. 37. Woodbridge, Suffolk: Boydell,1994.

The Chartulary of St. John of Pontefract. YAS Record Series 25 (1899), 30 (1902).

Cherry, Henry Curtis. *Antiquarum et insignium familiarum in comitatu Bercheriensi prosapiae.* 1851. Special Collections. University of Reading.

Chesnay-Desbois, F.-A. de la. *Dictionnaire de la Noblesse.* 3rd ed. Vol. 10. Paris: Schlesinger, 1866.

———. *Dictionnaire généalogique, héraldique, historique et chronologique.* 3 vols. Paris: 1757.

The Chronicle of Florence of Worcester. London: Bohn, 1854.

Chronicles of the Reigns of Stephen, Henry II and Richard I. London: Longman, 1886.

The Chronography of Robert of Torigni. 2 vols. Translated by Thomas Bisson. Oxford: Clarendon, 2020.

Clergy of the Church of England Database. http://theclergydatabase.org.uk.

Cokayne, G. E. *The Complete Peerage of England, Scotland, Ireland, Great Britain and the United Kingdom.* 2nd ed. 13 vols. London: St. Catherine's, 1910–98.

Curia Regis Rolls of the Reigns of Richard I and John. 7 vols. London: PRO, 1922–35.

Descriptive Catalogue of Ancient Deeds in the Public Record Office. 6 vols. London: HMSO, 1890–1915.

Domesday Book. Translated by John Morris. 34 vols. Chichester: Phillimore, 1975–1986.

Domo Capitulari Westmonasteriensi Asservatorum Abbrevatio. London: Record Commission, 1811.

Douglas, D. C., and G. W. Greenaway, eds. *English Historical Documents 1042–1189.* Vol. 2. London: Eyre & Spottiswood, 1953.

Dubosc, M., ed. *Cartulaire de la Luzerne.* 1878. Archives Départmentales de la Manche. Saint-Lô, France.

Dugdale, William, ed. *Visitation of Yorkshire.* Exeter: Pollard, 1900.

Early Charters of the Cathedral Church of St. Paul, London. London: Royal Historical Society, 1938.

Early Scottish Charters Prior to 1153. Glasgow: MacLehose, 1905.

Episcopal Registers, Diocese of Worcester. Worcester Historical Society. Oxford: Parker, 1898.

Excerpta e Rotulis Finium in Turri Londonensi asservatis. London: Public Record Commission, 1835.

Eynsham Cartulary. Oxford: Oxford Historical Society, 1907.

Farrer, William, ed. *Honours and Knights' Fees.* 3 vols. London: Longmans, Green, 1923–25.

Farrer, William, and C. Clay, eds. *Early Yorkshire Charters.* 14 vols. Vols. 1–2. Edinburgh: Ballantine, 1914–16. Vols. 3–12. Yorkshire: Yorkshire Record Society, 1935–65.

The Four Visitations of Berkshire. London: Harleian Society, 1907–08.

Gallia christiana. 16 vols. Paris: 1715–1865.

BIBLIOGRAPHY

Gascon Rolls. Translated by Yves Renouard. London: HMSO, 1964. http://www.gasconrolls.org.
Gesta Abbatum Monasterii Sancti Albani. Vol. 1. London: Longmans, 1867.
Gesta Regis Henrici Secundi Benedicti Abbatis. London: Longmans, 1867.
Gesta Stephani. Translated by K. R. Potter and R. H. C. Davis. Oxford: Oxford Medieval Texts, 1976.
Glanvill. *The Treatise on the Laws and Customs of the Realm of England.* Translated by G. D. G. Hall. London: Nelson, 1965.
The Great Roll of the Pipe for the Forty-Third Year of the Reign of King Henry III: Michaelmas 1259. Exchequer Pipe Office, Pipe Rolls, 372:103. London: The National Archives Public Record Office, 2012.
The Great Roll of the Pipe for the Reigns of Kings Richard I and John. N.S. I–XX. London: PRO, 1925–64.
The Great Roll of the Pipe for the Thirty-First Year of the Reign of King Henry I. Michaelmas 1130. Publications of the Pipe Roll Society, XCV, N.S. lvii. Translated by Judith A. Green. London: Pipe Roll Society, 2012.
The Great Roll of the Pipe for the Twenty-Sixth Year of the Reign of King Henry III, edited by Henry Lewis Cannon. London: Oxford University Press, 1918.
Heraldic Visitation of the Northern Counties in 1530. London: Whittaker, 1863.
Historia Ecclesie Abbendonensis: The History of the Church of Abingdon. Translated by John Hudson. 2 vols. Oxford: Clarendon, 2002–07.
The History of Parliament: The House of Commons. Special Collections Library, University of Nottingham. The History of Parliament Trust. Stroud: Sutton, 1936–92.
History of Parliament Online. History of Parliament Trust. http://www.historyofparliamentonline.org.
Hozier, Louis de. *Armorial général des registres de la noblesse de France.* Vol. 3. Paris: Didot, 1867.
Inquisitions and Assessments Relating to Feudal Aids with Other Analogous Documents Preserved in the Public Record Office 1284–1431. 6 vols. London: HMSO, 1899–1920.
The "Lands of the Normans" in England (1204–1244). Digital Humanities Institute. Sheffield: University of Sheffield, 2007. https://www.dhi.ac.uk/normans/search.html.
Lay Subsidy Roll for the County of Worcester, Circ. 1280. Oxford: Parker, 1893.
Lenton Priory Estate Accounts 1296 to 1298. Thoroton Society Record Series, 19 (1959).
Letters and Papers, Foreign and Domestic of the Reign of Henry VIII. 22 vols. London: HMSO, 1862–1910.
Liber Rubeus de Scaccario. 3 vols. London: 1896.
List of Early Chancery Proceedings Preserved in the Public Record Office. Vol. 8. New York: Kraus, 1963. First published 1901–36 by HMSO (London).
Lists of the Clergy of North Nottinghamshire, edited by K. S. S. Train. Thoroton Society Record Series, vol 20. Nottingham, England: Thoroton Society, 1961.
London Marriage Licenses 1521–1869. London: Quaritch, 1887.
The Lost Cartulary of Bolton Priory. Translated by Katrina Legg. Woodbridge, Suffolk: Boydell, 2009.
Magni Rotuli Scaccarii Normanniae sub Regibus Angliae. Translated by Thomas Stapleton. 2 vols. London: Society of Antiquaries of London, 1840–44.

BIBLIOGRAPHY

Manuscripts of the Duke of Rutland: The Manuscripts of His Grace the Duke of Rutland Preserved at Belvoir Castle. Vol. 1. Historical Manuscripts Commission, Twelfth Report, Appendix, pt. 4. London: HMSO, 1888. https://archive.org/details/hists52199677/page/n3/mode/2up.
The Marriage, Baptismal, and Burial Registers of the Collegiate Church or Abbey of Westminster. Edited by Joseph Lemuel Chester. London: 1876.
Matthew of Paris. *Chronica Majora.* Translated by H. R. Luard. New York: Cambridge University Press, 2012.
Medieval Soldier Database. http://www.medievalsoldier.org
Mémoires de la Société des Antiquaires de Normandie. Caen. 1824–79.
Mémoires de la Société d'Histoire et de l'Archéologie de Bretagne. Société de Bretagne. 1920–2011.
Monasticon Anglicanum. 6 vols. 1817–30. Reprint, London: 1846.
Neustria Pia. Translated by A. du Monstier. Rouen: 1663.
Nottinghamshire: Extracts from the County Records of the Eighteenth Century. Nottingham: Forman, 1947.
Nottinghamshire Household Inventories. Thoroton Society Record Series, 22. Nottingham: Thoroton Society, 1963.
Orderic Vitalis. *The Ecclesiastical History of Orderic Vitalis.* Translated by Marjorie Chibnall. 6 vols. Oxford: Clarendon, 1969–80.
Parliamentary Writs and Writs of Military Summons. Translated by Francis Palgrave. 2 vols. London: Eyre & Strahan, 1827–34.
Parliament Rolls of Medieval England, 1275–1504. Translated by Chris Given-Wilson. 16 vols. Woodbridge: Boydell, 2012.
Pedes finium Eboracensis, regnante Johanne. Durham: Surtees Society, 1897.
Proceedings and Ordinances of the Privy Council of England. 7 vols. London: Eyre & Spottiswoode, 1834–37.
Recueil des actes de Charles III le Simple, roi de France. Paris: 1949.
Recueil des actes des ducs de Normandie de 911 à 1066. Caen: 1961.
Recueil des chartes de l'abbaye de Cluny. 6 vols. Paris: 1876–93.
Recueil des Historiens des Gaules et de la France. 24 vols. Paris: Palmé, 1869–1904.
Recueil de jugements de l'Échiqieur de Normandie. Paris: Impériale, 1864.
The Red Book of Worcester. 2 vols. London: Worcester Historical Society, 1937.
Regesta Regum Anglo-Normannorum. Vol. 1, translated by H. W. C. Davis. Vol. 2 translated by C. Johnson and H. A. Cronne. Vols. 3 and 4 translated by H. A. Cronne and R. H. C. Davis. Oxford: Clarendon, 1913–69.
Register of the Diocese of Worcester during the Vacancy of the See (September 1307–December 1308). Worcester Historical Society. Oxford: Parker, 1897.
Register of the University of Oxford. 3 vols. Oxford: Clarendon, 1885.
Register of William Greenfield, Lord Archbishop of York, 1306–1315. Publications of the Surtees Society, vols. 152–53. Durham: Surtees Society, 1931–40.
Register of William Wickwane, Lord Archbishop of York 1279–85. Publications of the Surtees Society, vol. 114. Durham: Surtees Society, 1907.
Reports on the Manuscripts of Lord Middleton preserved at Wollaton Hamm, Nottinghamshire. Historical Manuscripts Commission. London: HMSO, 1911.
A Roll of Arms of the Reign of Edward the Second. London: Pickering, 1829.
Rolls of Arms Henry III. Translated by Hugh London. Woodbridge, Suffolk: Boydell, 2009.

BIBLIOGRAPHY

Rolls of Parliament. Vols. 1 and 6. London: 1832.
Rotuli Chartarum in Turri Londonensi asservati. 2 vols. London: Record Commission, 1837.
Rotuli Curiae Regis. 2 vols. London: Eyre & Spottiswoode, 1835.
Rotuli de Dominabus et Pueris et Puellis de Donatione Regis in XII Comitatibus 3 Henry II (1185). London: Pipe Roll Society, 1913.
Rotuli de Liberate ac de Misis et Praestitis. London: Record Commission, 1844.
Rotuli de oblatis et finibus in turri Londonensi asservati. London: Record Commission, 1844.
Rotuli hundredorum temp Hen.III and Edw. I. 2 vols. London: King George III, 1812–1818.
Rotuli Litterarum Clausarum in Turri Londonensi asservati. London: Record Commission, 1833–44.
Rotuli Litterarum Patentium in Turri Londonensi asservati. London: Record Commission, 1835.
Rotuli Parliamentorum. Vol. 2. London, 1767. Internet Archive. https://archive.org/details/bim_eighteenth-century_rotuli-parliamentorum-u_great-britain-parliamen_1767_2.
Rotuli scaccarii regum scotorum. Edinburgh: General Register House, 1878–1908.
Round, J. H. *Ancient Charters, Royal and Private*. London: Pipe Roll Society, 1888.
Royal and Other Historical Letters of the Reign of Henry III. London: Longmans, 1862–66.
The Royal Visitation of 1559: Act Book for the Northern Province. Gateshead, Northumberland: Surtees Society, 1975.
Rufford Charters. 3 vols. Thoroton Society Record Series. Nottingham, England: Thoroton Society, 1972–80.
Shaw, William. *The Knights of England*. Vol. 2. London: Sharratt & Hughes, 1906.
"The Siege of Caerlaverock." Translated by C. W. Scott-Giles. Baldock, Hertfordshire: The Heraldry Society, 1960.
Southwell and Nottingham Church History Project. http://southwellchurches.nottingham.ac.uk.
Talbot Papers. Edited by James H. Coyne. Ottawa: Royal Society of Canada, 1909.
Testa de Nevill: Liber Feodorum. The Book of Fees. 2 vols. London: HMSO, 1920.
Testamenta Eboracensia. 6 vols. London: Nichols, 1836–1902.
The Thurgarton Cartulary. Stamford, Lincolnshire: Watkins, 1994.
Victoria History of the Counties of England. 230 vols. London: 1899–present. https://www.history.ac.uk/research/victoria-county-history/county-histories-progress.
The Visitations of the County of Nottingham in the Years 1569 and 1614. London: Harleian Society, 1871.
Visitations of the North. Durham: Surtees Society, 1912.
The Visitations of the County of Oxford. London: Taylor, 1871.
Wace. *The History of the Norman People. Wace's Roman de Rou*. Translated by Glyn S. Burgess. Woodbridge, Suffolk: Boydell, 2004.
William of Jumièges. *Gesta Normannorum Ducum*. Translated by Elisabeth M. C. van Houts. 2 vols. Oxford: Clarendon, 1992–95.
William of Malmesbury. *Gesta Regum Anglorum*. Translated by R. A. B. Mynors. Oxford: Clarendon, 1998.

William of Poitiers. *Gesta Guillelmi*. Translated by R. H. C. Davis and Marjorie Chibnall. Oxford: Clarendon, 1998.

Yeatman, John Pym. *Extracts from the Pipe Rolls for the Counties of Nottingham and Derby*. London: Bemrose, 1886.

SECONDARY SOURCES

Angot, Alphonse. *Dictionnaire historique, topographique et biliographique de la Mayenne*. 4 vols. Laval: Goupil, 1900–02.

Armitage-Smith, Sydney. *John of Gaunt*. New York: Barnes & Noble, 1964.

Bailey, Mark. *The English Manor c. 1200–c. 1500*. Manchester: Manchester University Press, 2002.

Baker, J. H. *An Introduction to English Legal History*. 4th ed. Oxford: Oxford University Press, 2002.

Barton, Richard E. *Lordship in the County of Maine c. 890–1160*. Woodbridge, Suffolk: Boydell, 2004.

Bates, David. *Normandy before 1066*. London: Longman, 1982.

———. *The Normans and Empire*. Oxford: Oxford University Press, 2013.

Bates, David, and Anne Curry. *England and Normandy in the Middle Ages*. London: Bloomsbury, 1994.

Bennett, Judith. *Ale, Beer, and Brewsters in England*. Oxford: Oxford University Press, 1996.

———. *Women in the Medieval English Countryside*. Oxford: Oxford University Press, 1987.

Bennett, Judith, and Ruth Karras, eds. *The Oxford Handbook of Women and Gender in Medieval Europe*. Oxford: Oxford University Press, 2013.

Bennett, Judith, et al., eds. *Sisters and Workers in the Middle Ages*. Chicago: University of Chicago Press, 1989.

Bisson, Thomas. *Cultures of Power*. Philadelphia: University of Pennsylvania Press, 1995.

Bitel, Lisa, and Felice Lifschitz, eds. *Gender and Christianity in Medieval Europe*. Philadelphia: University of Pennsylvania Press, 2008.

Blakely, Ruth M. *The Brus Family in England and Scotland, 1100–1295*. Woodbridge, Suffolk: Boydell, 2005.

Blamires, Alcuin. *The Case for Women in Medieval Culture*. Oxford: Clarendon, 1997.

Bogg, Edmund. *Lower Warfeland, the Old City of York and the Ainsty*. York: Sampson, 1904.

Borman, Tracy. *Thomas Cromwell*. London: Hodder, 2014.

Bouchard, Constance Brittain. *Strong of Body, Brave and Noble*. Ithaca, NY: Cornell University Press, 1998.

Bradley, E. T. *Life of the Lady Arabella Stuart*. 2 vols. London: Bentley, 1889.

Brand, Paul. *The Origins of the English Legal Profession*. Oxford: Blackwell, 1992.

Broussillon, Bernard. *La Maison de Laval, 1020–1605*. Paris: Picard, 1895.

Brown, Cornelius. *A History of Nottinghamshire*. London: Stock, 1896.

———. *Lives of Nottinghamshire Worthies and of Celebrated and Remarkable Men of the County*. London: Sotheran, 1882.

Brown, R. Allen. *Castles, Conquest and Charters: Collected Papers*. Woodbridge, Suffolk: Boydell, 1989.
———. *The Normans and the Norman Conquest*. Woodbridge, Suffolk: Boydell, 1994.
Burgess, Walter. *The Pastor of the Pilgrims*. New York: Harcourt Brace, 1920.
Burke, John Bernard. *A Genealogical and Heraldic History of the Commoners of Great Britain and Ireland*. London: Colburn, 1838.
———. *A Genealogical and Heraldic History of the Extinct and Dormant Baronetcies of England, Ireland, and Scotland*. London: Smith, 1844.
———. *A Visitation of the Seats and Arms on the Noblemen and Gentlemen of Great Britain*. 2 vols. London: Hurst & Blackette, 1853.
Butler, Sara M. *Divorce in Medieval England: From One to Two Persons in Law*. London: Routledge, 2013.
———. *The Language of Abuse: Marital Violence in Later Medieval England*. Leiden: Brill, 2007.
Cantor, Leonard. *The Changing English Countryside 1400–1700*. London: Routledge, 1987.
Carpenter, Christine. *Locality and Polity*. Cambridge: Cambridge University Press, 1992.
Carpenter, David. *Henry III*. New Haven: Yale University Press, 2020.
———. *The Minority of Henry III*. Berkeley: University of California Press, 1990.
———. *The Struggle for Mastery*. London: Penguin, 2003.
Caumont, Arcisse de. *Statistique monumentale du Calvados*. Vol. 1. Herouville-Saint-Calir: Athenes, 1867.
Chadwick, William. *King John of England*. London: Smith, 1865.
Chase, Martin, and Maryanne Kowaleski, eds. *Reading and Writing in Medieval England*. Woodbridge, Suffolk: Boydell, 2019.
Chester, Joseph. *Allegations for Marriage Licences Issued by the Bishop of London 1611–1828*. London: Harleian Society, 1828.
Chibnall, Marjorie. *Anglo-Norman England*. Oxford: Blackwell, 1986.
Child, Francis. *English and Scottish Popular Ballads*. Boston: Houghton Mifflin, 1904.
Clay, John. *Familiae Minorum Gentium*. London: Harleian Society, 1894–96.
Clemmensen, Steen. "Early Arms: As Attributed, Adopted or Documented." *Coat of Arms* 232 (2016) 61–88. https://www.theheraldrysociety.com/wp-content/uploads/2019/10/CoA-232-Clemmensen-paper-2.pdf.
Collins, Arthur. *The Baronetage of England*. 3 vols. London: Wotton, 1741.
———. *The Peerage of England*. Edited by Egerton Brydges. 9 vols. London: Rivington, 1812.
Cooper, Elizabeth. *The Life and Letters of Lady Arabella Stuart*. 2 vols. London: Hurst, 1866.
Coss, Peter. *The Knight in Medieval England 1000–1400*. Dover, NH: Sutton, 1993.
———. *The Lady in Medieval England 1000–1500*. Stroud, Gloucestershire: Sutton, 1998.
———. *Lordship, Knighthood and Locality*. Cambridge: Cambridge University Press, 1991.
———. *The Origins of the English Gentry*. Cambridge: Cambridge University Press, 2003.
Courcelles, Jean-Baptiste de. *Dictionnaire universel de la noblesse de France*. Vol. 3. Paris: 1820–22.

Cox, Thomas. *Magna Britannia Antiqua and Nova, Nottinghamshire-Somersetshire.* London: Ward & Chandler, 1787.
Crouch, David. *The English Aristocracy.* New Haven: Yale University Press, 2011.
———. *The Image of Aristocracy in Britain, 1000–1300.* London: Routledge, 1992.
Crouch, David, and Jeroen Deploige. *Knighthood and Society in the High Middle Ages.* Leuven: Leuven University Press, 2020.
Delattre, Daniel. *La Manche.* Granvilliers: Delattre, 2002.
Daly, Mary. *The Church and the Second Sex.* New York: Harper, 1975.
d'Anisy, Léchaudé. *Extraits des chartes et d'autres actes Normandes et Anglo-Normande qui se trouvent dans les archives du Calvados.* Vol. 1. Caen: Mancel, 1834–35.
Delisle, L. *Histoire du château et des sires de Saint-Sauveur-le-Vicomte, suivi de pièces justificatives.* Valognes: Martin, 1867.
Denholm-Young, N. *The Country Gentry in the Fourteenth Century.* Oxford: Clarendon, 1969.
Desroches, J.-J. *Histoire du Mont Saint-Michel et de l'ancien diocèse d'Avranches.* Caen: Mancel,1838.
Deville, Achille. *Histoire du Château d'Arques.* Rouen: Periaux, 1839.
Douglas, David C. *The Norman Achievement 1050–1100.* Berkeley: University of California Press, 1969.
———. *The Norman Fate.* Berkeley: University of California Press, 1976.
———. *William the Conqueror.* Berkeley: University of California Press, 1964.
Drouet, Louis. *Recherches historique sur les vingt communes du canton de Saint-Pierre-Église.* Cherbourg: Saint-Joseph 1893.
Duby, Georges. *The Chivalrous Society.* Berkeley: University of California Press, 1980.
———. *Love and Marriage in the Middle Ages.* Chicago: University of Chicago Press, 1994.
———. *Rural Economy and Country Life in the Medieval West.* Columbia: University of South Carolina Press, 1962.
Dugdale, Sir William. *The Antiquities of Warwickshire Illustrated.* 2 vols. London: Osborn & Longman, 1730.
———. *The Baronage of England.* 2 vols. London: Newcomb, 1675–76.
Durant, Yves. *Le Diocèse de Nantes.* Paris: Beauchesne, 1985.
Ellis, A. S. "Biographical Notes on the Yorkshire Tenants Named in Domesday Book." *YAJ* 4 (1877) 114–37, 215–48.
Ellis, John M. "The Origin of the Morteynes." *Foundations* 1 (2003) 117–21.
Erdeswicke, Sampson. *Survey of Staffordshire.* London: Mears, 1720.
Erler, Mary, and Maryanne Kowaleski, eds. *Gendering the Master Narrative.* Ithaca, NY: Cornell University Press, 2003.
———. *Women and Power in the Middle Ages.* Athens: University of Georgia Press, 1988.
Fellows, George. *Arms, Armour and Alabaster, Round Nottingham.* Nottingham: Saxton, 1907.
Fierville, Charles. "Monographie." In *MSAN*, 25:155–98.
Fischer, David Hackett. *Albion's Seed.* Oxford: Oxford University Press, 1989.
Fleming, Robin. *Domesday Book and the Law.* Cambridge: Cambridge University Press, 1998.
Fletcher, Christopher. *Richard II.* Oxford: Oxford University Press, 2008.
Foxe, J. *Acts and Monuments.* 4th ed. London: Religious Tract Society, 1877.

Fuller, Thomas. *History of the Worthies of England*. London: Tegg, 1840.
Gillingham, John. *The Angevin Empire*. 2nd ed. New York: Oxford University Press, 2001.
———. *Richard I*. New Haven: Yale University Press, 1999.
Given-Wilson, Chris. *Henry VI*. New Haven: Yale University Press, 2016.
Goldberg, P. J. P. *Medieval England*. New York: Oxford University Press, 2004.
———. *Women in England c. 1275-1525*. Manchester: Manchester University Press, 1995.
———. *Women, Work, and Life Cycle in a Medieval Economy*. Oxford: Clarendon, 1992.
Goldsmith, James Lowth. *Lordship in France, 500-1500*. New York: Lang, 2003.
Goldy, Charlotte, and Amy Livingstone, eds. *Writing Medieval Women's Lives*. New York: Palgrave MacMillan, 2012.
Goodman, Anthony. *John of Gaunt*. New York: St. Martin's, 1992.
Gough, Henry. *Scotland in 1298*. London: Gardner, 1888.
Grandmaison, Charles. *Dictionnaire Héraldique*. Paris: Migne, 1852.
Grant, Raymond. *The Royal Forests of England*. Wolfeboro Falls, NH: Sutton, 1991.
Green, Herbert. "Lenton Priory." *Transactions of the Thoroton Society* 40 (1936). http://www.nottshistory.org.uk/articles/tts/tts1936/lenton/lenton13.htm.
Green, Judith. *The Aristocracy of Norman England*. Cambridge: Cambridge University Press, 1997.
———. *Henry I*. Cambridge: Cambridge University Press, 2006.
Greenhill, F. A. *Incised Effigial Slabs*. 2 vols. London: Faber, 1976.
Gristwood, Sarah. *Arbella: England's Lost Queen*. Boston: Houghton Mifflin, 2003.
Grounds, Arthur D. *A History of King Edward VI Grammar School, Retford*. Retford, Nottinghamshire: Martin, 1970.
Guilding, John M. ed. *Reading Records: Diary of the Corporation*. 4 vols. London: Parker, 1892-96.
Guilhiermoz, Paul. *Essai sur l'origine de la noblesse en France au moyen age*. Paris: Picard, 1902.
Gunn, Steven. *Early Tudor Government*. New York: St. Martin's, 1995.
———. *Henry VII's New Men and the Making of Tudor England*. Oxford: Oxford University Press, 2016.
Gurnay, Daniel. *The Record of the House of Gournay*. London: Nichols, 1848.
———. *Supplement to the Record of the House of Gournay*. King's Lynn, England: Thew, 1858.
Guyard de La Fosse, J.-B. *Histoire des seigneurs de Mayenne*. Paris: Res Universis, 1992.
Hanawalt, Barbara. *The Wealth of Wives*. Oxford: Oxford University Press, 2007.
Hercé, Jean-François de. *Père, Maire de Laval, Evêque de Nantes*. St-Ouen-des-Vallon: d'Ozouville, 1985.
Hersey, Francis Coney. *Record of the Hersey Family*. Boston, 1895.
Hersey, Stephen E. *The Hersey Family: Tracing the Descendants of William Hersey of Hingham, Massachusetts, 1635-1994*. Self-published, 1994.
Hollister, C. Warren. *Henry I*. New Haven: Yale University Press, 2001.
———. *Monarchy, Magnates and Institutions in the Anglo-Norman World*. London: Hambledon, 1986.
Horrox, Rosemary, and W. Mark Ormrod. *A Social History of England, 1200-1500*. Cambridge: Cambridge University Press, 2006.

BIBLIOGRAPHY

Howlett, Richard. *Chronicles of the Reigns of Stephen, Henry II and Richard I*. 4 vols. London: Longman, 1884–89.
Hoyle, R. W. *The Estates of the English Crown, 1558–1640*. Cambridge: Cambridge University Press, 1992.
———. *The Pilgrimage of Grace and the Politics of the 1530s*. Oxford: Oxford University Press, 2001.
Hozier, Louis Pierre de. *Armorial général des registres de la noblesse de France*. Paris: Dentu, 1867.
Hutchinson, Robert. *Thomas Cromwell*. New York: St. Martin's, 2007.
Inderwick, F. A. *Side-Lights on the Stuarts*. London: Samson Low, 1891.
Jacks, Leonard. *The Great Houses of Nottinghamshire and the County Families*. Nottingham: Bradshaw, 1881.
Jewell, Helen. *Women in Dark Age and Early Medieval Europe c. 500–1200*. New York: Palgrave Macmillan, 2007.
———. *Women in Late Medieval and Reformation Europe 1200–1550*. New York: Palgrave Macmillan, 2007.
———. *Women in Medieval England*. Manchester: University of Manchester Press, 1996.
Johnson, Elizabeth. *She Who Is*. New York: Crossroad, 1993.
Jones, Norman. *The English Reformation*. Oxford: Blackwell, 2002.
Keats-Rohan, Katherine S. B. *Domesday Descendants*. Woodbridge, Suffolk: Boydell, 2002.
———. *Domesday People*. Woodbridge, Suffolk: Boydell, 1999.
———. "Le role des Bretons dans la politique de la colonisation normande d'Angleterre." *MSHAB* 74, 1996: 181–215.
Keats-Rohan, Katherine S. B., and David E. Thornton. *Domesday Names*. Woodbridge, Suffolk: Boydell, 1997.
Keen, Maurice. *English Society in the Later Middle Ages 1348–1500*. London: Penguin, 1990.
———. *Origins of the English Gentleman*. Stroud, Gloucestershire: Tempus, 2002.
Kelly, John. *The Great Mortality*. New York: HarperCollins, 2005.
Kerry, Charles. *The History and Antiquities of the Hundred of Bray*. London: 1861.
Kirschner, Julius, and Suzanne Wemple, eds. *Women of the Medieval World*. Oxford: Blackwell, 1985.
Latouche, Robert. *Histoire du comté de Maine pendant le xe et le xie siècle*. Paris: Champion, 1910.
Lawrance, Henry. "Military Effigies in Nottinghamshire before the Black Death." *Transactions of the Thoroton Society* 28 (1924) 114–37.
Lawson, A. E. *Black's Guide to Nottinghamshire*. Edinburgh: Black, 1876.
Lefuse, M. *The Life and Times of Arabella Stuart*. London: Mills & Boon, 1913.
Le Héricher, Eduard. *Avranchin monumental et historique*. 2 vols. Avranches: Tostain, 1846.
Le Magnen, Sylvette, ed. *La Tapisserie de Bayeux*. Bayeux: Orep, 2015.
LeMarois. "Famille Le Héricy (Normandie)." https://www.lemarois.com/jlm/data/j29alehericy.html.
Lemesle, Bruno. *La société aristocratique dans le Haut-Maine (Xie–XIIe siecles)*. Rennes: Presses Universitaires de Rennes, 1999.
Le Parquier, E. *Cahiers de Doléances du Bailliage d'Arques*. Vol. 2. Lille: Robbe, 1922.

LePatourel, John. *The Norman Empire*. Oxford: Oxford University Press, 1976.
Lerosey, A. *Histoire de l'abbaye bénédictine de Saint-Sauveur-le-Vicomte*. Abbeville: Paillart, 1894.
Leyser, Henrietta. *Medieval Women*. New York: St. Martin's, 1995.
Lincoln, George. *The History of the Town of Hingham*. Reprint. Boston: New England History, 1987.
Lipscomb, George. *The History and Antiquities of the County of Buckinghamshire*. London: Hobis, 1847.
Lodge, Edmund. *Illustrations of British History, Biography, and Manners*. Vol. 3. London: Chidley, 1838.
Lord, Evelyn. *Knights Templar in Britain*. London: Routledge, 2002.
Loring, Louise. *Descendants of William Hersey of Hingham, Massachusetts*. Portland, OR: n.p., 1981.
Lovell, Mary S. *Bess of Hardwick*. New York: Norton, 2005.
Loyd, Lewis C. *The Origins of Some Anglo-Norman Families: Volume 103 of Publications of the Harleian Society*. Leeds: Genealogical Publishing Company, 1951.
MacCulloch, Diarmaid. *Thomas Cromwell*. New York: Viking, 2018.
Madden, Frederic, ed. *Collectanea Topographica et Genealogica*. Vols. 4 and 6. London: Nichols, 1834–43.
Magny, Claude de. *Premier registre du livre d'or de la noblesse de France*. Paris: 1844–61.
Magny, Edouard de. *Nobiliaire de Normandie*. 2 vols. Paris: 1862–64.
"Maison Mauvoisin." http://www.racineshistoire.free.fr (site discontinued).
Malden, Henry E. *Magna Carta Commemoration Essays*. Aberdeen: Royal Historical Society, 1927.
Manning, Roger. *Hunters and Poachers*. Oxford: Clarendon, 1993.
Marcombe, David. *English Small Town Life: Retford 1520–1642*. Oxford: Alden, 1993.
Marshall, Peter. *Reformation England 1480–1642*. London: Arnold, 2003.
Marshall, Peter, and Alex Ryrie, eds. *The Beginnings of English Protestantism*. Cambridge: Cambridge University Press, 2002.
Massingberd, W. O. *History of the Parish of Ormsby-cum-Ketsby*. Lincoln: Williamson, 1893.
Mather, Cotton. *Magnalia Christi Americana*. Hartford: Andrus, 1853.
Matusiak, John. *Henry V*. London: Routledge, 2013.
Maupoint, Armand René. *Vie de Monseigneur Jean-François de Hercé*. Paris: Bray, 1864.
McIlwain, Charles Howard. *The High Court of Parliament and Its Supremacy*. New Haven: Yale University Press, 1910.
Mellors, Robert. *Men of Nottingham and Nottinghamshire*. Nottingham: Bell, 1924.
Mertes, Kate. *The English Noble Household 1250–1600*. Oxford: Blackwell, 1988.
Mons, Rodolphe de. *Identification des notables de l'Avranchin et du Cotentin cités dans le livre noir de l'Abbaye de la Lucerne: (1143–1309)*. Vol. 83. Saint-Lo: Société d'archéologie et d'histoire de la Manche, 1992.
Morehouse, Henry James. *The History and Topography of the Parish of Kirkburton and the Graveship of Holme*. Huddersfield: Roebuch, 1861.
Morice, H. *Mémoires pour servir de preuves à l'histoire ecclesiastique et civile de Bretagne*. Paris: 1744.
Morris, William A. *The Medieval English Sheriff to 1300*. Manchester: Manchester University Press, 1927.

Musson, Anthony, and W. Mark Ormrod. *The Evolution of English Justice*. London: Macmillan, 1999.
Nichols, John. *The Progresses, Progressions, and Magnificent Festivities of King James the First*. London: Society of Antiquaries, 1828.
Ormrod, W. Mark. *Edward III*. New Haven: Yale University Press, 2011.
———. *The Reign of Edward III*. New Haven: Yale University Press, 1990.
Palmer, Robert. *The County Courts of Medieval England 1150–1350*. Princeton: Princeton University Press, 1982.
Payling, Simon. "Inheritance and Local Politics in the Later Middle Ages: The Case of Ralph, Lord Cromwell, and the Heriz Inheritance." *NMS* 30 (1986) 69–96.
———. "Law and Arbitration in Nottinghamshire 1399–1461." In *People, Politics and Community in the Later Middle Ages*, edited by Joel Rosenthal and Colin Richard, 140–60. New York: St. Martin's, 1987.
———. *Political Society in Lancastrian England: The Greater Gentry of Nottinghamshire*. Oxford: Clarendon, 1991.
Phillips, Seymour. *Edward II*. New Haven: Yale, 2010.
Pichot, Daniel. *Le Bas-Maine du Xe au XIIIe siecle*. Laval: Société d'Archéologie de l'Histoire de la Mayenne, 1995.
Piercy, John Shadrach. *The History of Retford*. Retford: Hodson, 1828.
Planché, J. R. *The Conquerer and His Companions*. 2 vols. London: Tinsley Brothers, 1874.
Pliny the Elder. *Natural History*. Vol. 2. Translated by H. Rickham. Cambridge: Harvard University Press, 1961.
Pollard, Alfred F. *Thomas Cranmer and the English Reformation*. London: Putnam, 1904.
Pollock, Frederick, and F. W. Maitland. *The History of English Law*. 2 vols. Cambridge: Cambridge University Press, 1895.
Porter, H. C. *Puritanism in Tudor England*. London: Macmillan, 1970.
Power, Daniel. "Aristocratic *Acta* in Normandy and England, c. 1150–c. 1250: The Charters and Letters of the du Hommet Constables of Normandy." In *Anglo-Norman Studies 35: Proceedings of the Battle Conference 2012*, edited by David Bates, 259–86. Cambridge: Boydell & Brewer, 2013.
———. *The Norman Frontier in the Twelfth and Early Thirteenth Centuries*. Cambridge: Cambridge University Press, 2004.
Powicke, F. Maurice. *The Loss of Normandy*. Manchester: Manchester University Press, 1913.
———. *Medieval England*. Oxford: Oxford University Press, 1931.
———. *Military Obligations in Medieval England*. Oxford: Clarendon, 1962.
———. *The Reformation in England*. London: Oxford University Press, 1941.
———. *The Thirteenth Century*. Oxford: Clarendon, 1953.
Prestwich, Michael. *Armies and Warfare in the Middle Ages*. New Haven: Yale University Press, 1996.
———. *Edward I*. New Haven: Yale University Press, 1996.
———. *English Politics in the Thirteenth Century*. New York: St. Martin's, 1990.
———. *The Three Edwards. War and State in England 1272–1377*. New York: St. Martin's, 1980.
Robertson, Mary Louise. "Thomas Cromwell's Servants." PhD diss., UCLA, 1975.

BIBLIOGRAPHY

Rosenthal, Joel, and Colin Richard. *People, Politics and Community in the Later Middle Ages*. New York: St. Martin's, 1987.
Round, John Horace. *Ancient Charters*. 2 vols. London: Wyman, 1888.
———. "Barons and Knights in the Great Charter." In *Magna Carta Commemoration Essays*, edited by Henry Malden, 46–77. London: Royal Historical Society, 1917.
———. *Feudal England*. London: Swan Sonnenschein, 1895.
Russell, Peter D. "Politics and Society in Nottinghamshire, 1327–1360." PhD diss., University of Nottingham, 2007.
Saint-Allais, Nicholas V. de. *Nobiliaire universel de France*. 20 vols. Paris: Bachelin, 1872–78.
Saul, Nigel. *Death, Art, and Memory in Medieval England*. Oxford: Oxford University Press, 2001.
———. *English Church Monuments in the Middle Ages*. Oxford: Oxford University Press, 2011.
———. *Knights and Esquires*. Oxford: Clarendon, 1981.
Scarisbrick, J. J. *The Reformation and the English People*. Oxford: Blackwell, 1984.
Schüssler Fiorenza, Elisabeth. *In Memory of Her*. New York: Crossroad, 1983.
Shaw, Stebbing. *The History and Antiquities of Staffordshire*. Vol. 2. London: Nichols, 1798–1801.
Shopkow, Leah. *The Saint and the Count*. Toronto: University of Toronto Press, 2021.
Shrewsbury, J. F. D. *History of the Bubonic Plague in the British Isles*. Cambridge: Cambridge University Press, 1970.
Smith, David M. *Studies in Clergy and Ministry in Medieval England*. York: Borthwick Institute, 1991.
Stapleton, A. *History of the Lordship of King's Clipstone*. Mansfield, England: Linney, 1980.
Stenton, Frank. *The First Century of English Feudalism 1066–1166*. 2nd ed. Oxford: Clarendon, 1961.
Stone, Lawrence. *The Crisis of the Aristocracy 1558–1641*. Oxford: Clarendon, 1965.
Strickland, Matthew. *Anglo-Norman Warfare*. Woodbridge, Suffolk: Boydell, 1992.
Thébault, Marion. "Le 'premier cartulaire' de l'abbaye de Mondaye." *Annales de Normandie* 61:1 (2011) 25–47.
Thomas, Hugh M. *The English and the Normans*. Oxford: Oxford University Press, 2003.
———. *Vassals, Heiresses, Crusaders, and Thugs. The Gentry of Angevin Yorkshire, 1154–1216*. Philadelphia: University of Pennsylvania Press, 1993.
Thoroton, R. *The Antiquities of Nottinghamshire*. Edited by J. Thoresby. 3 vols. London, 1797.
Trible, Phyllis. *God and the Rhetoric of Sexuality*. Philadelphia: Fortress, 1978.
Vincent, Nicholas. *Records, Administration and Aristocratic Society in the Anglo-Norman Realm*. Woodbridge, Suffolk: Boydell, 2009.
Walker, David. *The Normans in Britain*. Oxford: Blackwell, 1995.
Walker, Simon. *The Lancastrian Affinity 1361–1399*. Oxford: Clarendon, 1990.
Wall, Alison. *Power and Protest in England 1525–1640*. New York: Oxford University Press, 2000.
Walmsley, John, ed. *Widows, Heirs, and Heiresses in the Late Twelfth Century*. Tempe: Arizona Center for Medieval and Renaissance Studies, 2006.

Ward, Jennifer, ed. *Women of the English Nobility and Gentry 1066–1600*. Manchester: Manchester University Press, 1995.
Waugh, Scott. *England in the Reign of Edward III*. Cambridge: Cambridge University Press, 1991.
———. *The Lordship of England: Royal Wardships and Marriages in English Society and Politics*. Princeton: Princeton University Press, 1988.
West, William. *A History, Topography and Directory of Warwickshire*. Birmingham: Wrightson, 1830.
Wheater, William. *Temple Newsam*. Leeds: Goodall, 1889.
White, Robert. *Nottinghamshire, Worksop, "the Dukery" and Sherwood Forest*. London: Simpkin, 1873.
White, William. *History, Gazetteer, and Directory of Nottinghamshire*. Sheffield: White, 1832.
Whiting, Robert. *The Blind Devotion of the People*. Cambridge: Cambridge University Press, 1989.
———. *Local Responses to the English Reformation*. New York: St. Martin's, 1998.
Wilkinson, Louise J. *Women in Thirteenth-Century Lincolnshire*. Woodbridge, Suffolk: Boydell, 2007.
Wilkinson, R. F. *Notes on the History of the Parish of Ordsall*. Retford: Lang, 1940.
Williams, Marty, and Anne Echols. *Between Pit and Pedestal: Women in the Middle Ages*. Princeton: Wiener, 1994.
Wilmshurst, Edwin. *The History of the Olde Hall of the Manor of West Retford, Notts*. Retford: Hodson & Hardman, 1908.
Wilson, Derek. *England in the Age of Thomas More*. New York: HarperCollins, 1978.
———. *In the Lion's Court*. New York: St. Martin's, 2001.
———. *The Queen and the Heretic*. Oxford: Lion Hudson, 2018.
———. *A Tudor Tapestry. Men, Women and Society in Reformation England*. London: Heinemann, 1972.
Wolffe, Bertram P. *Henry VI*. New Haven: Yale University Press, 2001.
Wood, A. C. *A History of Nottinghamshire*. Nottingham: Thoroton Society, 1947.
Yeatman, John Pym. *Some Observations Upon the Law of Ancient Demesne*. Sheffield: Leader, 1884.
Yeatman, John Pym, et al. *Feudal History of Derbyshire*. 3 vols. London: Bemrose & Sons, 1886.
Young, Charles. *The Making of the Neville Family in England 1166–1400*. Woodbridge: Boydell, 1996.
———. *The Royal Forests in Medieval England*. Philadelphia: University of Pennsylvania Press, 2007.

Index of Persons

Abetot, Urse d', 69–7, 73–74, 298, 301
Ambrières, Achard d'., 30–31, 285–86, 334–35, 342
Arches, Agnes, 67, 95, 101
   Alan de, 80, 94, 100–01, 104, 296, 304, 325
   Gerbert de, 102–03, 113, 115
   Gilbert I de (Yorkshire), 98, 100
   Gilbert II de (Yorkshire), 104
   Gilbert I de (Nottianghamshire), 108
   Gilbert II de (Nottinghamshire), 94, 103–04
   Herbert I de, 102
   Herbert II de, 103
   Juetta I de, 98–99, 309
   Juetta II de, 104, 303, 309, 325
   Osberne de, 42, 76, 94–98, 103–04, 288–89, 299–300, 302–03, 305, 311, 317, 320
   Peter I de, 102–03
   Robert de, 99–100, 102–03
Arques, William d', 42–43
Auffay, Gulbert d', 12, 37–40, 53, 61, 76, 95–97
Avranches, Hugh d', 24, 49, 94–95, 294, 302, 308, 321, 324, 335
Aylesbury, Anne Denman Darrel, 236
   Thomas, 236

Bassett, Thomas II, 295–96
Beauchamp, William de, 70–73, 84, 100, 169, 297–98, 326
Bolebec, Osbern de, 42–44, 339

Brus, Adam II de, 98, 304, 309, 311–14
Bully, Roger de, 69, 94–95, 97, 103, 105–06, 112, 125, 138, 179, 298

Darrel, Anne Denman, 235–36
   Barbara Denman, 235–36
   Edward , 235–37
   William, 235–36
Denman, Francis, 235–36
   Nicholas, 189, 205, 211, 219, 233, 237, 263
   William, 155, 222, 224, 234–35

Eu, Alice de Bully d', 105, 107, 110–11

Gorron, Geoffrey de, 284, 336
   Henry de , 284, 336, 342
   Rivallon de, 33, 283
   Robert de, 284, 318
Gournay, Hugh IV de, 169, 291
   Hugh V de, 81–82, 292–94

Herce, 69, 73–75
Hercé, Charlotte, 352–53
   Guillaume I de, 30, 35, 347
   Guillaume II de, 286, 347
   Jeanne de, 347
   Jean-Baptiste de, 348
   Jean-François de, 350
   Jean-François-Simon de, 349
   Jean-René de, 348
   Julien de, 346–47
   Julien-César de, 351
   Olive de, 286, 347

INDEX OF PERSONS

(Hercé continued)
    Robert I de, 347
    Robert II de, 347
    Robin de, 35–36, 374
    Urbain-René de, 348–49
Hercy, Alice de, 142, 148
    Alice Knight de, 181, 184, 188
    Anne Hargrave, 247–49, 252
    Baldwin de, 108–10, 114, 116, 210–11, 311
    Catherine Comberworth Constable de, 152, 156–58, 191–92, 313
    Elizabeth de Hériz, 116, 119, 123–24, 126–27
    Elizabeth de Saundby de, 127, 129 141
    Elizabeth Digby, 188–89, 194
    Elizabeth Stanley, 195–96, 217, 224, 230–31
    Elizabeth Talbot Leek, 113, 130, 167, 169, 175–77, 203, 218, 238, 264, 364
    Hugh de (Warwickshire), 30, 75, 81–85, 90–94, 104
    Hugh I de (Nottinghamshire), 45, 116, 124, 126–27, 129, 149
    Hugh II de, 124, 127, 129–30, 134–36, 139, 141
    Hugh III de, 142, 145–46, 148, 150–52
    Hugh IV, 130, 158, 164–68, 170–71, 173–74, 177, 180, 203, 218, 264, 364
    Hugh V, 177–80, 234, 241
    Humphrey I, 181–88, 192, 264–65
    Humphrey II, 187–89, 192–95, 241–42
    Isabelle de, 85, 87
    Jane Sadler, 247, 250–51
    Joan de, 144, 148, 239
    Joan Stanhope, 145, 181–83, 187–88, 242, 264
    John I (Warwickshire) de, 84–88, 126, 297
    John II (Warwickshire) de, 88–91
    John de (Nottinghamshire), 144, 146, 148, 150–52
    John (Nottinghamshire), 193–212, 214–24, 228–31, 233, 235, 237, 239–40, 265–66, 268
    John II (Berkshire), 246–51
    John III (Berkshire), 250–52
    John IV (Berkshire), 253
    John (solicitor), 250, 269–79
    John (surveyor) , 344–45
    Lettice de, 88
    Malveysin de , 30, 43, 75, 83, 85, 89–90, 92–95, 104–05, 108–11, 113–15, 280, 326
    Marjorie de Bingham, 171, 177, 179–80
    Mary Aungier, 253
    Maud de, 82
    Stephen, 187–88, 194, 241–44
    Théophanie de Arches de, 37, 43, 94, 104, 111, 113, 115–16, 139–40, 288, 326
    Thomas de, 152–57, 159–62, 164, 167–68, 171, 191, 203, 281, 313, 367
    Thomas (Berkshire), 242–44, 246
    Ursula Lovelace, 250, 252–53
Hériz, , Adelina of Whatton de, 121
    Agnes Alcher de, 122–23
    Alicia de, 120
    Avicia de, 120
    Emma de Bilborough de, 120
    Geoffrey I de, 117, 120
    Hawise de Briwere de, 123, 126
    Henry de, 124, 127
    Ivo I de, 119–20, 122–23
    Ivo II de, 123, 126
    John I de, 123, 125–26
    John II de, 122–24, 131, 316
    Robert I de, 117, 119
    Robert II de, 122
    Sarah de, 123–24
    William I de, 121
Hersey, Anne Kenton, 254–55
    Anne Payn , 246–47
    Elizabeth Croade, 256–57
    John I , 242–43, 246
    Margaret Garves, 256
    Nathaniel, 254–55
    William, 256–57,

INDEX OF PERSONS

Hersi(n), 2, 31, 285, 287, 297, 333–34, 337, 342–43, 345–46
Hotham, Mary Hercy, 219, 239–40
Hyde, Anne, 236–37, 247, 279
   Edward , 236–38, 260
   Frances Aylesbury, 236

Lacy, Ilbert de, 74, 94–97, 102, 300–01, 305, 342
Lascelles, Bryan, 224, 229, 267
   George, 193, 206–08, 210–12, 217, 219–20, 224, 267, 274, 297
   Hercye, 217, 267
   John, 193, 202, 205, 208–10, 214–17, 231
   Mary, 193–94, 214
   Richard, 154, 186, 189, 192–93, 313
Laval, Hugh II de, 94, 98, 104, 288, 299, 301

Mackworth, Ellen Hercy, 238
Markham, Alice Hercy Hatfield. 237–38
   John IV, 186, 198, 200, 202, 204–08, 211, 214, 237
Mayenne, Geoffrey de, 19, 29, 32–33
Mering, Alexander, 50, 161, 204
   John, 150, 202–03, 215, 219, 239
   Katherine Hercy, 239
   Maud Hercy, 150, 239
   William, 150, 161, 171, 184, 186, 190, 192, 200, 203, 205, 237, 239, 297

Neufmarché, Geoffroy de , 10, 12, 37, 39–41, 74, 78, 95–96
Neville, Barbara Hercy , 113, 231
   Francis, 232
   George, 113, 221, 231
   Hercye, 232–33
   Robert, 184–87, 194, 200–01, 204

Peverel, William, 46, 48, 50, 71–72, 119–22, 125, 149, 301, 305–06, 319, 342

Saint-Jean, 27, 45–48, 50–53, 125
Saint-Valéry, 12, 14, 27, 37–39, 41, 93, 95–96, 104
Strelley, Elizabeth Hercy de, 149, 184, 366–67
   Sampson de, 103–04, 121, 123, 149, 168, 366
Stuart, Lady Arbella, 268–73, 276–79, 281

Talbot, Elizabeth Hardwick Cavendish, 264–69, 272, 274–77
   George, 180, 211, 264–66
   Gilbert, 72, 154, 180, 266, 268–69, 272, 274–77
   John (Leicestershire), 168–70
   Mary, 268, 271, 277–79

Whalley, Barbara Hatfield, 238
   Elizabeth Hatfield, 238
   Thomas, 238
   William, 238

Index of Places

Ambrières, 12, 21, 29–36
Arques, 9, 12–13, 27, 36–37, 39, 41–43, 45, 49, 96, 108, 206, 289, 328
Auffay, 37, 39–41, 49, 53, 96–98
Avanches, 8, 16–17, 22, 27, 45–51, 71, 79, 286, 310, 321, 323

Conisbrough, 109–10, 114, 210–11
Crowle, 73–74
Cruchfield, 232, 243, 247–54, 370

East Hendred, 242–48, 252–53

Fountains, 99–102, 104–05, 150, 296, 304, 312, 337

Gonalston, 45, 120–26, 317–18, 365
Gorron, 21, 29, 31–36, 51, 283–85, 347
Grove, 45, 93–94, 103–04, 106, 111–17, 123–24, 126–32, 136–37, 139–46, 148–49, 151–53, 155–56, 163–67, 171, 173–89, 193–96, 201, 207, 210–12, 215, 217–18, 222, 230–34, 238–39, 241, 248, 252, 264–66, 277, 280, 363–64
Guisborough, 98, 303–04, 307–11, 331

Hercé, 2, 21, 29–31, 33, 141, 264, 280, 283, 285–86, 334, 346–48, 361

Kineton, 75–77, 80, 82–83, 88–89, 91–92

La Haye Pesnel, 46–47, 50, 71, 321–26, 341

La Rochelle, 46–48, 51–52, 71, 119, 315–16, 318–19, 321, 323
Laval, 18, 21–22, 31, 287, 289, 299, 347, 350
Lucerne, 27, 46–48, 50, 52, 123, 286–87, 297, 317–18, 320–30, 340

Mayenne, 18, 21–22, 27–36, 283–87, 347–49, 351, 362

Ordsall, 111, 114–16, 128, 130–31, 139, 141, 144, 146, 148, 151, 155, 164, 171, 177–78, 180, 183, 186–87, 193–94, 200–01, 204–05, 207, 212, 218, 222–24, 231–32, 234–35, 237, 239

Pillerton Hersey, 72, 75, 77–78, 80, 83, 88–90, 111, 292, 362
Pillerton Priors, 77–79

Reading, 242–44, 246–47, 250, 252, 254–57, 262, 271, 281
Rous Lench, 73–75
Rowsham, 333–34, 336, 338, 342, 345

Saint-Valéry sur Somme, 14, 37, 53, 336, 339
Saundby, 129–30, 141, 155, 168, 175–77, 183, 186, 193, 218, 240, 366
Sonning, 243, 245–54, 257
Stapleford, 76, 119–20, 125, 141, 318, 321
Strelley, 149–50, 172, 184, 208, 366–67

INDEX OF PLACES

Thorp Arch, 96–98
Tickhill, 49, 82, 95, 103–11, 113–17,
    121–23, 129–30, 136–37, 139,
    141–42, 152–53, 177, 182, 186,
    194, 200–01, 210–11, 298, 326, 364
Treswell, 146–47, 193, 200–01, 211,
    218, 233

Weston, 97, 103–04, 115–16, 128, 130,
    141, 145–46, 148, 151–53, 166,
    171, 185–86, 189, 198, 231, 239,
    241
Whitby, 50, 79, 97, 105, 292, 302–04,
    306, 308, 312, 325
Widmerpole, 121–25
Wingrave, 285, 333–38, 342
Winkfield, 242–43, 246–53, 345, 369

www.ingramcontent.com/pod-product-compliance
Lightning Source LLC
Chambersburg PA
CBHW071237300426
44116CB00008B/1073